Integrating Landscape Ecology into Natural Resource Management

The rapidly increasing global population has dramatically increased the demands for natural resources and has caused significant changes in quantity and quality of natural resources. To achieve sustainable resource management, it is essential to obtain insightful guidance from emerging disciplines such as landscape ecology. This text addresses the links between landscape ecology and natural resource management. These links are discussed in the context of various landscape types, a diverse set of resources, and a wide range of management issues. A large number of landscape ecology concepts, principles, and methods are introduced. Critical reviews of past management practices and a large number of case studies are presented. This text provides many guidelines for managing natural resources from a landscape perspective and offers useful suggestions for landscape ecologists to carry out research relevant to natural resource management. In addition, it will be an ideal supplementary text for graduate and undergraduate ecology courses.

JIANGUO LIU is an Associate Professor at Michigan State University where he teaches and researches in the areas of landscape ecology and biodiversity conservation. He has published extensively in scientific journals such as *Science* and has edited two other ecology books. In recognition of his contributions to research, outreach, and teaching, he has been given a number of awards including a CAREER award from the National Science Foundation, a Lilly Teaching Fellowship, and an Aldo Leopold Leadership Fellowship from the Ecological Society of America.

WILLIAM W. TAYLOR is Chairperson and Professor of the Department of Fisheries and Wildlife at Michigan State University. He is an internationally recognized expert in fisheries ecology, population dynamics, and Great Lakes fisheries management. He has received numerous accolades for his teaching, research, and outreach efforts, including his tenure as President of the American Fisheries Society. He has authored numerous articles and has edited a book on fisheries policy and management.

Cambridge Studies in Landscape Ecology

Cambridge Studies in Landscape Ecology presents synthetic and comprehensive examinations of topics that reflect the breadth of the discipline of landscape ecology. Landscape ecology deals with the development and changes in the spatial structure of landscapes and their ecological consequences. Because humans are so tightly tied to landscapes, the science explicitly includes human actions as both causes and consequences of landscape patterns. The focus is on spatial relationships at a variety of scales, in both natural and highly modified landscapes, on the factors that create landscape patterns, and on the influences of landscape structure on the functioning of ecological systems and their management. Some books in the series develop theoretical or methodological approaches to studying landscapes, while others deal more directly with the effects of landscape spatial patterns on population dynamics, community structure, or ecosystem processes. Still others examine the interplay between landscapes and human societies and cultures.

The series is aimed at advanced undergraduates, graduate students, researchers and teachers, resource and land-use managers, and practitioners in other biophysical and social sciences that deal with landscapes.

The series is published in collaboration with the International Association for Landscape Ecology (IALE), which has Chapters in over 50 countries. IALE aims to develop landscape ecology as the scientific basis for the analysis, planning, and management of landscapes throughout the world. The organization advances international cooperation and interdisciplinary synthesis through scientific, scholarly, educational, and communication activities. Information on IALE is available at http://www.crle.uoguelph.ca/iale/

EDITED BY

JIANGUO LIU
MICHIGAN STATE UNIVERSITY

WILLIAM W. TAYLOR
MICHIGAN STATE UNIVERSITY

Integrating Landscape Ecology into Natural Resource Management

CAMBRIDGE
UNIVERSITY PRESS

PUBLISHED BY THE PRESS SYNDICATE OF THE UNIVERSITY OF CAMBRIDGE
The Pitt Building, Trumpington Street, Cambridge, United Kingdom

CAMBRIDGE UNIVERSITY PRESS
The Edinburgh Building, Cambridge CB2 2RU, UK
40 West 20th Street, New York, NY 10011-4211, USA
477 Williamstown Road, Port Melbourne, VIC 3207, Australia
Ruiz de Alarcón 13, 28014 Madrid, Spain
Dock House, The Waterfront, Cape Town 8001, South Africa

http://www.cambridge.org

First published 2002

Printed in the United Kingdom at the University Press, Cambridge

Typeface Lexicon (*The Enschedé Font Foundry*) 10/14 pt *System* QuarkXPress™ [SE]

A catalogue record for this book is available from the British Library

Library of Congress Cataloguing in Publication data

Integrating landscape ecology into natural resource management / edited by Jianguo Lui and William W. Taylor.
p. cm.
Includes bibliographical references (p.).
ISBN 0 521 78015 2 – ISBN 0 521 78433 6 (pb.)
1. Landscape ecology. 2. Natural resources. I. Liu, Jianguo, 1963– II. Taylor, William W.

QH541.15.L35 I56 2002
333.7 – dc21 2001052879

ISBN 0 521 78015 2 hardback
ISBN 0 521 78433 6 paperback

Contents

Contributors

Heidi Asbjornsen
Agricultural University of Norway
Department of Forest Sciences
P.O. Box 5044
Ås, Norway

Tom L. Ashwood
Environmental Sciences Division
Oak Ridge National Laboratory
Oak Ridge, TN 37831 USA

Darren J. Bender
Ottawa-Carleton Institute of Biology
Carleton University
1125 Colonel By Drive
Ottawa, ON K1S 5B6 Canada

Pete Bettinger
Forest Resources Department
College of Forestry
Oregon State University
Corvallis, OR 97331 USA

Julie M. Brennan
Ottawa-Carleton Institute of Biology
Carleton University
1125 Colonel By Drive
Ottawa, ON K1S 5B6 Canada

John M. Briggs
Department of Plant Biology
Arizona State University
Tempe, AZ 85287 USA

Brent L. Brock
Division of Biology
Kansas State University
Manhattan, KS 66506 USA

Kelly M. Burnett
USDA Forest Service
Pacific Northwest Research Station
3200 SW Jefferson Way
Corvallis, OR 97331 USA

Thomas A. Contreras
Ottawa-Carleton Institute of Biology
Carleton University
1125 Colonel By Drive
Ottawa, ON K1S 5B6 Canada

Robert C. Corry
School of Natural Resources and Environment
University of Michigan
430 East University Avenue
Ann Arbor, MI 48109 USA

Thomas R. Crow
USDA Forest Service
1831 East Highway 169
Grand Rapids, MN 55744 USA

Virginia H. Dale
Environmental Sciences Division
Oak Ridge National Laboratory
Oak Ridge, TN 37831 USA

Michael Dove
School of Forestry and Environmental Studies
301 Prospect St.
Yale University
New Haven, CT 06511 USA

John B. Dunning Jr.
Department of Forestry and Natural Resources
Purdue University
West Lafayette, IN 47905 USA

Lenore Fahrig
Ottawa-Carleton Institute of Biology
Carleton University
1125 Colonel By Drive
Ottawa, ON K1S 5B6 Canada

C. Paola Ferreri
School of Forest Resources
207 Ferguson Building
Pennsylvania State University
University Park, PA 16802 USA

Richard T.T. Forman
Graduate School of Design
Harvard University
Cambridge, MA 02138 USA

Desmond T. Fortes
Institute for Environmental Studies
University of Wisconsin
Madison, WI 53706 USA

Steven Garman
Forest Science Department
College of Forestry
Oregon State University
Corvallis, OR 97331 USA

Gordon Grant
USDA Forest Service
Pacific Northwest Research Station
3200 SW Jefferson Way
Corvallis, OR 97331 USA

Morgan Grove
USDA Forest Service
Northeastern Forest Research Station
705 Spear St.
South Burlington, VT 05403 USA

Nick M. Haddad
Department of Zoology
Box 7617
North Carolina State University
Raleigh, NC 27695 USA

Daniel B. Hayes
Department of Fisheries and Wildlife
Michigan State University
13 Natural Resources Building
East Lansing, MI 48824 USA

Richard J. Hobbs
School of Environmental Science
Murdoch University
Murdoch, WA 6150 Australia

Greg A. Hoch
Division of Biology
Kansas State University
Manhattan, KS 66506 USA

K. Norman Johnson
Forest Resources Department
College of Forestry
Oregon State University
Corvallis, OR 97331 USA

Daniel C. Josephson
Department of Natural Resources
Cornell University
Ithaca, NY 14853 USA

Robert Lambeck
CSIRO Wildlife and Ecology
Private Bag
PO Wembley, WA 6014 Australia

Bruce C. Larson
College of Forest Resources
University of Washington
Seattle, WA 98185 USA

Christopher A. Lepczyk
Department of Fisheries and Wildlife
Michigan State University
13 Natural Resources Bulding
East Lansing, MI 48824 USA

Jianguo Liu
Department of Fisheries and Widlife
Michigan State University
13 Natural Resources Building
East Lansing, MI 48824 USA

Kristine D. Lynch
Department of Fisheries and Wildlife
Michigan State University
13 Natural Resources Building
East Lansing, MI 48824 USA

Keely B. Maxwell
School of Forestry and Environmental Studies
370 Prospect St.
Yale University
New Haven, CT 06511 USA

William C. McComb
Department of Forestry and Wildlife Management
University of Massachusetts
Amherst, MA 01003 USA

Edward Mills
Department of Natural Resources
Cornell Biological Field Station
Cornell University
Ithaca, NY 14853 USA

Joan Iverson Nassauer
School of Natural Resources and Environment
University of Michigan
430 East University Avenue
Ann Arbor, MI 48109 USA

Kurt R. Newman
Department of Fisheries and Wildlife
Michigan State University
13 Natural Resources Building
East Lansing, MI 48824 USA

Barry R. Noon
Department of Fishery and Wildlife
Colorado State University
Fort Collins, CO 80523 USA

Eugene P. Odum
Institute of Ecology
University of Georgia
Athens, GA 30602 USA

Janet L. Ohmann
USDA Forest Service
Pacific Northwest Research Station
3200 SW Jefferson Way
Corvallis, OR 97331 USA

Dale Rabe
Wildlife Division
Michigan Department of Natural Resources
Lansing, MI 48909 USA

Charles F. Rabeni
Missouri Cooperative Fish and Wildlife Research Unit
University of Missouri
302 Anheuser–Busch Natural Resources
Columbia, MO 65211 USA

Gordon H. Reeves
USDA Forest Service
Pacific Northwest Research Station
3200 SW Jefferson Way
Corvallis, OR 97331 USA

Edward F. Roseman
Platte River State Fish Hatchery
15201 US 31 Highway
Beulah, MI 49617 USA

Daniel T. Rutledge
Landcare Research New Zealand Limited
Gate 10, Silverdale Road
Private Bag 3127
Hamilton, North Island, New Zealand

Leo Schibli
Society for Studies on the Biotic Resources of Oaxaca
211 Porfirio Diaz
Col. Centro
Oaxaca City, Mexico

Rebecca Schneider
Department of Natural Resources
Cornell University
Ithaca, NY 14853 USA

Ragnhildur Sigurðardóttir
School of Forestry and Environmental Studies
370 Prospect St.
Yale University
New Haven, CT 06511 USA

Thomas D. Sisk
Center for Environmental Sciences and Education
PO Box 5694
Northern Arizona University
Flagstaff, AZ 86001 USA

Patricia A. Soranno
Department of Fisheries and Wildlife
Michigan State University
13 Natural Resources Building
East Lansing, MI 48824 USA

Scott P. Sowa
Missouri Cooperative Fish and Wildlife Research Unit
University of Missouri
302 Anheuser–Busch Natural Resources
Columbia, MO 65211 USA

Thomas A. Spies
USDA Forest Service
Pacific Northwest Research Station
3200 SW Jefferson Way
Corvallis, OR 97331 USA

William W. Taylor
Department of Fisheries and Wildlife
Michigan State University
13 Natural Resources Building
East Lansing, MI 48824 USA

Monica G. Turner
Department of Zoology
University of Wisconsin–Madison
Madison, WI 53706 USA

Dean L. Urban
Nicholas School of the Environment
Duke University
Durham, NC 27708 USA

Beatrice Van Horne
Department of Biology
Colorado State University
Fort Collins, CO 80523 USA

Daniel J. Vogt
College of Forest Resources
University of Washington
Seattle, WA 98185 USA

Kristiina A. Vogt
College of Forest Resources
University of Washington
Seattle, WA 98185 USA

John A. Wiens
The Nature Conservancy
4245 North Fairfax Drive
Arlington, VA 22203 USA

Foreword

As the scale of environmental problems expands, ecology, the basic science of the environment, must then meet the challenge and expand the scale of research and management recommendations. Fortunately, during the past 50 years or so, ecology has emerged from its roots in biology to become a standalone discipline that integrates organisms, the abiotic environment, and human affairs. Thus, we see the emphasis moving from the species level to the ecosystem level on up to the landscape level that deals with complex systems such as large watersheds. Size does matter; big is different from little, because new properties emerge with an increase in scale.

An increase in problems with pests is a good example of the need to consider the bigger picture, rather than just continue trying to deal with pest species one at a time. A large agricultural landscape with conservation tillage, a diversity of crops, and lots of natural vegetation buffer strips separating crop fields has much less trouble with insect pests than a continuous monocultural landscape.

Most important of all, preservation of the life-support environment can only be accomplished on a large scale. For instance, protection of water quality and stream corridors cannot be achieved through local zoning but requires political and management action at the state, regional, national, and ultimately, the global levels.

Landscape ecology is a rapidly growing interdisciplinary field. Its concepts, theories, and methods are uniquely relevant in addressing large-scale issues in natural resource management (e.g., biodiversity conservation, land-use planning). The contributors of this book effectively show how natural resource management can benefit from landscape ecology, and how landscape ecology can be advanced by tackling challenging problems in natural resource management. The diversity of articles and topics in this book is impressive, as is the common theme of cross-disciplinary approaches. This book also provides valuable information that can be used for expanding the scope of environmental education beginning in grade school, increasing the general public's understanding of the need for better land-use planning, and thereby sending a clear message to policy-makers. Thus, this book lays a nice foundation for truly integrating theory and practice at the landscape level and beyond.

Eugene P. Odum

Preface

Traditionally, natural resources have been often managed using information collected from small scales, resulting in variable and limited success. To improve these results, many scientists and natural resource managers have recognized the need to adopt a large-scale approach to natural resource management, using the concepts, principles, and methods of landscape ecology. At the same time, many landscape ecologists have also realized that further development of landscape ecology will benefit from better connections with resource management issues. However, as is often the case between academic and non-academic worlds, landscape ecologists and natural resource managers historically have not communicated well. Landscape ecologists often do research without regard to the needs for natural resource management, and managers often do not know how to apply landscape ecology to managing natural resources.

To facilitate the communication between landscape ecologists and natural resource managers, we hosted the 13th annual conference of the US Regional Association of the International Association for Landscape Ecology (US-IALE) on the campus of Michigan State University in 1998. The conference's theme was "Applications of landscape ecology in natural resource management." Clearly, this theme of linking landscape ecology with natural resource management reflected the desire of many others, as more than 500 landscape ecologists and natural resource managers from around the world participated in the conference (the largest number ever to attend a US-IALE annual meeting). The conference was a huge success, but we were urged by many attendees to produce a book expanding upon the ideas presented at the conference, reaching a larger audience, and promoting further communication and collaboration between the landscape ecology and natural resource management communities.

Such impetus and urging from the conference attendees motivated us to edit this book that addresses the gaps and linkages between landscape ecology and natural resource management.

The specific objectives of this book are to: (1) introduce fundamental concepts, principles, and methods of landscape ecology; (2) provide practical information for natural resource managers to use; and (3) offer suggestions for landscape ecologists to carry out research relevant to natural resource management. To accomplish these objectives, this book offers a critical review of past management practices, synthesizes existing information, introduces innovative ideas, presents a large number of case studies, and provides many insightful guidelines and "rules of thumb" for managing natural resources from a landscape perspective. Furthermore, we have designed this book to closely link each major component of landscape ecology to a natural resource management paradigm (i.e., "Landscape structure and multi-scale management," "Landscape function and cross-boundary management," "Landscape change and adaptive management," and "Landscape integrity and integrated management"). To highlight these links, we have chosen a wide range of landscape types (e.g., forested, agricultural, urban, grassland, and aquatic), a diverse set of resources (e.g., land, forests, wildlife, fish, plants, insects, and water), and various management issues (e.g., biodiversity conservation, land use, timber harvesting, fishing, and wildlife management).

This book has been written for a very diverse audience, including landscape ecologists, natural resource managers, conservation biologists, social scientists, non-government organizations, policy-makers, graduate students, and advanced undergraduate students. It will also be helpful as a supplemental text for many graduate and undergraduate courses, such as Landscape Ecology, Natural Resource Management, and Conservation Biology.

We were fortunate that more than 100 landscape ecologists and natural resource managers had enthusiastically participated in this book endeavor, either as contributors (59) or as reviewers (53). To ensure the highest quality possible and the appropriate coverage of perspectives from both landscape ecologists and natural resource managers, two to four experts from both academic institutions and management agencies reviewed each chapter. Thus, it is fair to say that the completion of this book is an excellent example of close collaboration between landscape ecologists and natural resource managers. We hope that this teamwork will continue, and that this book will help to cement the bond between landscape ecology and natural resource management. Ultimately, by doing so, we can better manage the world's natural resources in a sustainable manner.

Jianguo Liu
William W. Taylor

Acknowledgments

First, we would like to express our sincere appreciation to the 59 contributors of this book. This was an unprecedented endeavor for us. Usually, academics write books for their peers. Writing this book was much more challenging because the audience includes both academic and non-academic readers. It took exceptional efforts to meet the needs from both groups. The contributors' cooperation and enthusiasm are greatly appreciated.

The manuscripts for this book were reviewed by 53 experts from academic institutions, natural resource management agencies, and private organizations. The reviewers' insightful comments and constructive suggestions have made this book better, clearer, and more readable. We gratefully acknowledge the precious time and tremendous help of the following reviewers: Jack Ahern (University of Massachusetts), James T. Anderson (West Virginia University), Mack Barrington (Oregon Department of Agriculture), David P. Bernard (ESSA Technologies Ltd., Canada), Dean Beyer (Michigan Department of Natural Resources), Rene Borgella Jr. (Cornell University), Dennis Boychuk (Integra Research, Inc., Canada), Han Chen (Ontario Ministry of Natural Resources, Canada), Christopher P. Dunn (The Morton Arboretum), Michael Francis (Colorado River Indian Tribes), Grant Gerrish (University of Hawaii–Hilo), Frank Golley (University of Georgia), Deborah Green (College of William & Mary), Timothy G. Gregoire (Yale University), Jerry Griffith (University of Kansas), Michael Jones (Michigan State University), Christina Hargis (USDA Forest Service), William Hargrove (Oak Ridge National Laboratory), Jim Harrison (US Environmental Protection Agency), Gilberto Hernández Cárdenas (Universidad Metropolitana – Iztapalapa, Mexico), Barry L. Johnson (US Geological Survey), Eric Jorgensen (US Environmental Protection Agency), Richard T. Kingsford (National Park

& Wildlife Service, Australia), Joseph W. Koebel Jr. (South Florida Water Management District), Tomas M. Koontz (Ohio State University), Christopher Lepczyk (Michigan State University), Simon Levin (Princeton University), Kristine D. Lynch (Michigan State University), Guy R. McPherson (University of Arizona), Susan Miller (USDA Forest Service), David J. Mladenoff (University of Wisconsin–Madison), Franz Mora (University of Nebraska), Tony Olsen (US Environmental Protection Agency), Diane M. Pearson (Northern Territory University, Australia), Karen A. Poiani (The Nature Conservancy), Hugh Possingham (The University of Adelaide, Australia), Harold Prince (Michigan State University), Jesse M. Purvis (National Park Service), Samuel Riffell (Michigan State University), Alistar Robertson (Charles Sturt University, Australia), George Robinson (State University of New York–Albany), Vic Rudis (USDA Forest Service), Ike Schlosser (University of North Dakota), Harold L. Schramm Jr. (Mississippi State University), Lowell H. Suring (USDA Forest Service), Jack Ward Thomas (University of Montana), Michael Walters (Michigan State University), Deane Wang (University of Vermont), Lizhu Wang (Wisconsin Department of Natural Resources), David Wear (USDA Forest Service), John F. Weishampel (University of Central Florida), X. Ben Wu (Texas A&M University), and Patrick A. Zollner (USDA Forest Service). We are particularly grateful to Christopher Lepczyk for his exceptional help in the review process.

We are pleased that this book is the first in the *Cambridge Studies in Landscape Ecology* series of the International Association for Landscape Ecology (IALE). Thanks to John Wiens (former President of IALE) for initiating this series and for encouraging us to be part of this exciting initiative. It has been our great pleasure to work with the outstanding staff at Cambridge University Press, especially Shana Coates, Alan Crowden, Anna Hodson, Carol Miller, Maria Murphy, and Claire Nugent.

The funding agencies that supported the 1998 Landscape Ecology Conference of the US Regional Association of the International Association for Landscape Ecology, which resulted in this book, are greatly appreciated. These agencies include the National Science Foundation, National Aeronautics and Space Administration, US Environmental Protection Agency, US Fish and Wildlife Service, US Geological Survey, USDA Forest Service, Michigan Department of Natural Resources, College of Agriculture and Natural Resources and Office of the Vice President for Research and Graduate Study at Michigan State University. We also thank the National Institutes of Health and Provost Lou Anna Simon at Michigan State University for additional financial support.

During the process of preparing this book, we were fortunate to receive excellent assistance from Kimberly Baker, Jayson Eageler, Linda Fortin, Kim Groop, Robert Howe, Monica Kwasnik (all at Michigan State University), Catherine Chung (University of Chicago), and Susan Robertson (Wavelength, Inc., Michigan). We also want to thank Marc Linderman (Michigan State University) for his permission to use a photo that he took as the book cover and for his help with the cover design. This book was finished when one of us (Liu) took a sabbatical in the Center for Conservation Biology (CCB) at Stanford University. The hospitality of the staff at CCB, especially Carol Boggs, Gretchen Daily, Anne Ehrlich, and Paul Ehrlich, is gratefully acknowledged.

Last but not least, we are deeply indebted to our families (especially our spouses Qiuyun Wang and Evelyn Taylor) for their understanding and extraordinary support.

Jianguo Liu
William W. Taylor

PART I

Introduction and concepts

JIANGUO LIU AND WILLIAM W. TAYLOR

1

Coupling landscape ecology with natural resource management: Paradigm shifts and new approaches

1.1 Introduction

Global human population has now exceeded 6 billion people and this rapidly increasing population has significant implications for natural resources. On the one hand, demands for natural resources have dramatically increased and will continue to increase (FAO, 1997). On the other hand, natural resources have been reduced in both quantity and quality as extraction has become more intensive and extensive than ever before (Vitousek *et al.*, 1997). As a result, much of the world's biodiversity has been lost (Ehrlich, 1988; Myers, 1990; Pimm and Gittleman, 1992), and many species have become threatened and endangered (Wilson, 1988; Rutledge *et al.*, 2001). Other ecological consequences include degradation of ecosystem goods and services (Costanza *et al.*, 1997; Daily, 1997), landscape fragmentation (Harris, 1984), and unsustainable use of natural resources (World Commission on Environment and Development, 1987; Lubchenco *et al.*, 1991). Furthermore, the management of natural resources has become more constrained and complex due to the interactions among ecological, political, socioeconomic, demographic, and behavioral factors (Thrupp, 1990; Cairns and Lackey, 1992; FEMAT, 1993; Liu, 2001; McCool and Guthrie, 2001; Chapter 19, this book). In order to address these great challenges in natural resource management and to achieve sustainability of natural resources in the future (Speth, 1992; MacDonald, 1998; Rogers and Feiss, 1998; Kates *et al.*, 2001), resource managers need insightful guidance and new perspectives from emerging disciplines such as landscape ecology (Sharitz *et al.*, 1992; Swanson and Franklin, 1992; Noss, 1983; Dale *et al.*, 2000).

Landscape ecology is an interdisciplinary field that studies landscape structure, function, and change (Forman and Godron, 1986; Hobbs, 1995). Although the term was coined by the German biogeographer Carl Troll in 1939 (Turner, 1989), landscape ecology did not draw much attention outside of

Europe until the early 1980s. During the last two decades, the field of landscape ecology has been rapidly advancing (Naveh and Lieberman, 1984; Risser *et al.*, 1984; Zonneveld and Forman, 1990; Forman 1995a; Pickett and Cadenasso, 1995; Wiens and Moss, 1999). Such rapid advancement is evidenced by the formation of the International Association for Landscape Ecology (IALE) in 1982 and its regional chapters (e.g., US-IALE, Europe-IALE, China-IALE), a large number of national and international conferences, creation of the international journal *Landscape Ecology* in 1987 (Golley, 1987, 1995), the proposition of a large number of landscape ecology concepts (e.g., Urban *et al.*, 1987; Pulliam, 1988; Turner, 1989; Levin, 1992; Wiens, 1992; Hobbs, 1995), the formulation of many principles (e.g., Risser *et al.*, 1984; Forman and Godron, 1986; Forman, 1995a,b), and the development of numerous methods and techniques (e.g., Turner and Gardner, 1991; Pulliam *et al.*, 1992; Klopatek and Gardner, 1999).

Although landscape ecology provides a spatial systems perspective and has great relevance to natural resource management (Hobbs, 1995), the application of landscape ecology in natural resource management has been lagging (Forman, 1986; Aspinall and Pearson, 2000; Chapter 18, this book). Likewise, natural resource management actions have not been fully utilized for the advancement of landscape ecology, even though they provide excellent opportunities for further landscape ecology development (e.g., Chapters 13 and 18, this book). Given these needs and potential benefits, the main goal of this book is to identify links and ways of bridging the gaps between landscape ecology and natural resource management. In this chapter, we briefly introduce a number of fundamental concepts, principles, and methods in landscape ecology; discuss how natural resource management paradigms can be modified to fit into a landscape ecology perspective; and provide an overview of this book.

1.2. A brief introduction to landscape ecology: Concepts, principles, and methods

In this section, we briefly introduce some fundamental concepts, principles, and methods in landscape ecology. More details can be found in other chapters of this book and many publications cited throughout this book.

1.2.1 Landscape structure, function, change, and integrity

Although the exact definition of a landscape can vary greatly, most landscape ecologists agree that a landscape is a heterogeneous land area (e.g., Turner, 1989; Forman, 1995a) (Fig. 1.1) that is often hierarchically structured. The basic unit in a landscape is a patch, which is a relatively homogeneous area.

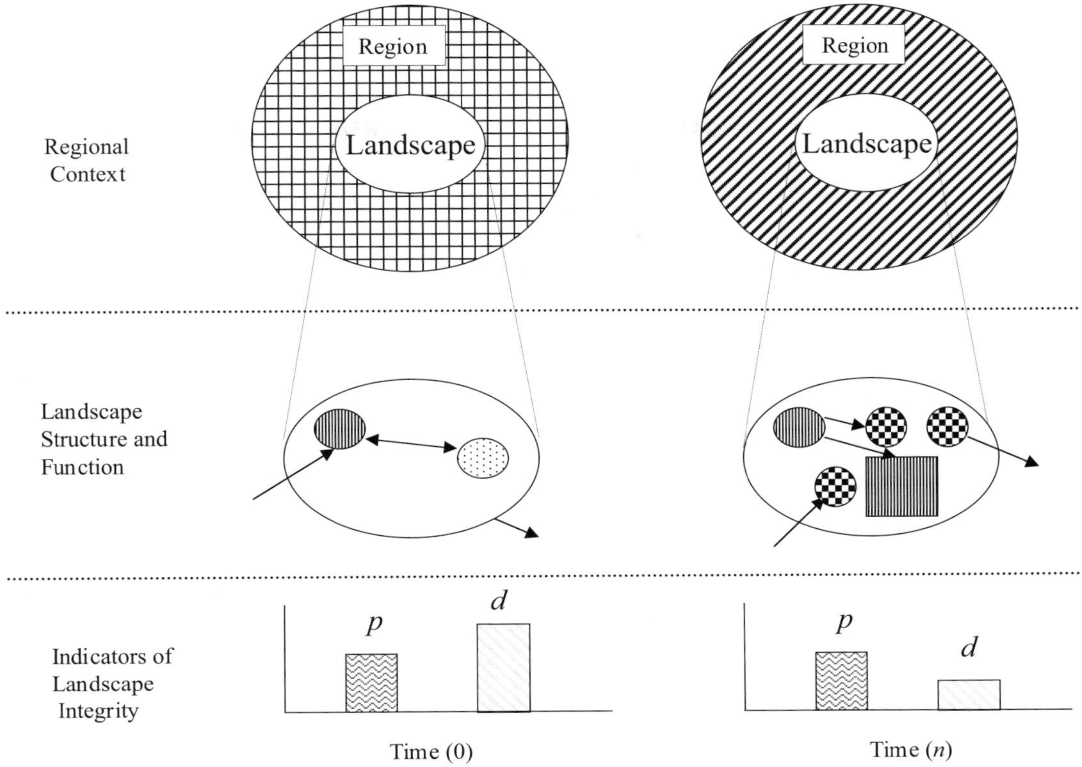

FIGURE 1.1
A diagram of regional context (top row), landscape structure and function (middle row), and landscape integrity (bottom row). Landscape changes are illustrated at two time steps: time 0 (left column) and time *n* (right column). The top row illustrates that a landscape (white ellipse) is embedded in a region (shaded ellipse). A landscape (middle row) consists of patches with different sizes and shapes. Arrows refer to landscape function (flows of energy, matter, and organisms) within and between patches and landscapes. Landscape integrity (bottom row) can be represented by different indicators such as productivity (*p*) and diversity of native species (*d*). In this example, changes in landscape structure and function as well as regional context (different shadings) cause a reduction in diversity of native species but no significant change in productivity.

The size (extent or spatial dimension) of a landscape is dependent on research and management objectives and varies with the perception of the organisms (Pearson *et al.*, 1996). Because different organisms view the same landscape differently, a landscape could range from square meters (from a small insect's perspective; Wiens and Milne, 1989) to thousands of square kilometers or larger (from humans' perspective; Forman and Godron, 1986).

Patches and landscapes are not isolated entities, but embedded in local, regional, and global contexts (Forman, 1995a; Liu and Ashton, 1999) (Fig. 1.1). A landscape is an open system with flows across landscape boundaries and interactions with other landscapes. For instance, nutrients and pollutants may follow hydrologic flows from uplands to aquatic systems (Carpenter *et al.*, 1998). Landscape functions (or processes) include matter flows, energy flows, and organism flows such as migration and dispersal among patches (Forman, 1995a) (Fig. 1.1). Through these various flows, patches and landscapes connect with and influence each other (Fig. 1.1).

Both landscape structure and landscape function change over time and across space due to natural and anthropogenic disturbances (Pickett and White, 1985; Turner *et al.*, 1997; Dale *et al.*, 1998) (Fig. 1.1). Landscapes change in a variety of ways. For instance, a contiguous large landscape may be fragmented into smaller pieces or some landscape elements may be lost (Forman, 1995a). Conversely, small landscapes or patches may coalesce into larger ones. Rates of change can be differential across a landscape (Liu *et al.*, 2001). Depending on the intensity and frequency of disturbances, some changes are very dramatic, while other changes are gradual or less obvious (Turner, 1987; Baker, 1992; Swanson *et al.*, 1998; Foster *et al.*, 1999).

While landscape structure, function, and change have been extensively studied, landscape integrity is a subject relatively unexplored. The concept of landscape integrity is different from but related to ecosystem integrity (Woodley *et al.*, 1993; De Leo and Levin, 1997), ecological integrity (Crossley, 1996; Pimentel *et al.*, 2000), and biological (or biotic) integrity (Karr, 1981; Hunter, 1999). The major difference lies in that landscape integrity is a health measurement at the landscape level (Fig. 1.1), while other integrity concepts indicate the health status of ecosystems or communities. Landscape integrity may result from complex interactions among ecosystems in the landscape and is unlikely to be a simple summation of ecosystem integrity. Landscape integrity can be measured by indicators such as productivity and diversity of native species at the landscape scale. The exact relationships between landscape integrity and landscape structure and function are unknown but are likely to be non-linear. Changes in landscape structure and function may or may not lead to significant changes in landscape integrity (Fig. 1.1). For example, modifications of some patches in a landscape may not affect its integrity due to elasticity or compensation of other patches in the landscape. Given its importance and lack of knowledge about it, we suggest that landscape integrity should be on the priority list of research by the landscape ecology community.

1.2.2 Principles

Like other disciplines, a set of principles has emerged in landscape ecology. According to Forman (1995b), a general principle integrates various sources of knowledge, addresses important questions, has a wide range of applications, has predictive ability, is established in theory, and has direct supporting evidence. Based on these criteria, Forman (1995b) lists 12 principles of landscape ecology. One of the principles states that spatial arrangement of patches is a major determinant of functional movement across the landscape. Additional principles have been proposed by others, such as Risser *et al.* (1984), Urban *et al.* (1987), Turner (1989), Ahern (1999), Ludwig (1999), and Farina (2000). These include the principle that local ecological conditions (e.g., organism abundance and species diversity) are affected by landscape context or attributes of the surrounding landscape (Dale *et al.*, 2000). For example, Pearson (1993) reported that bird species richness within a stand is largely affected by the vegetation structure in the surrounding areas. Likewise, Liu *et al.* (1999) found that food in oil palm plantations supports higher levels of wild pigs that, in turn, significantly reduce tree seedling regeneration and tree species richness in stands adjacent to the plantations.

1.2.3 Methods

Research methods in landscape ecology have progressed remarkably fast over the last two decades (e.g., Turner and Gardner, 1991; Klopatek and Gardner, 1999; Farina, 2000). These methods include approaches and tools for collection, analysis, and integration of both spatial and non-spatial data. In terms of data collection, methods like sampling (Cochran, 1977; Chapters 3 and 11, this book) and observations (Hanski, 1991; Grossman *et al.*, 1995) are routinely used in landscape ecology. Experimentation is also becoming popular (Lovejoy *et al.*, 1986; Robinson *et al.*, 1992; Wiens *et al.*, 1995; Ims, 1999), even though it is frequently faced with challenges in identifying suitable replicates (Hargrove and Pickering, 1992; Chapters 3 and 13, this book) because landscape-level experiments often must use large, yet heterogeneous areas. While sampling and experimentation usually require researchers to be physically in the field, remote sensing techniques collect information about an object without direct physical contact and have become an essential tool for obtaining large-scale spatial data in the forms of satellite imagery and aerial photography (Lillesand and Kiefer, 1994; Jensen, 1996; Chapter 16, this book). In addition, global positioning systems (GPS, satellite-based georeferencing systems) are frequently used to gather spatial data, especially for purposes of ground truthing (Liu *et al.*, 2001).

Tools for data analysis and integration include geographic information systems (GIS), spatial statistics, and modeling. Geographic information systems (Maguire *et al.*, 1991) are arguably the most important tool for storing, manipulating, analyzing, and integrating both spatial and non-spatial data. Spatial statistics or geostatistics (e.g., spatial autocorrelation, kriging, spectral analysis, trend surface analysis) are useful tools for analyzing landscape patterns (O'Neill *et al.*, 1988; Legendre and Fortin, 1989; Turner and Gardner, 1991; Li and Reynolds, 1993; Gustafson, 1998), along with specifically designed software, such as FRAGSTATS (McGarigal and Marks, 1994) and Patch Analyst (http://flash.lakeheadu.ca/~rrempel/patch/). Because landscape structure and management practices often vary across space, spatially explicit models are especially useful (Pulliam *et al.*, 1992; Liu, 1993; McKelvey *et al.*, 1993; Dunning *et al.*, 1995; Turner *et al.*, 1995). Spatially explicit models are computer-based models that account for the ecological and socioeconomic differences among different locations in landscapes and allow efficient analysis of spatial interactions (Liu *et al.*, 1994; Dunning *et al.*, 1995; Verboom and Wamelink, 1999). Combining remote sensing and GIS data, these models offer great promise to natural resource managers, because the arrangement of landscape elements differs in space and time, and the visual display makes the comparisons of management alternatives and their ecological consequences much easier (Franklin and Forman, 1987; Liu *et al.*, 1995; Turner *et al.*, 1995; Gustafson and Crow, 1996).

1.3 Shifts in paradigms of natural resource management

While traditional natural resource management has met numerous societal needs, it has also caused a host of problems (Christensen *et al.*, 1996; Kohm and Franklin, 1997), such as conflicts between management for short-term and long-term benefits, between management at small scales and large scales, and between management of different natural resources (Liu, 1995; Scott *et al.*, 1995; Dale *et al.*, 2000; McShea and Rappole, 2000). To overcome the shortcomings of traditional management, it is necessary to facilitate shifts in management paradigms using a landscape perspective. Specifically, it is essential to tie landscape structure with multi-scale management; to link landscape function with cross-boundary management; to connect landscape change with adaptive management; and to use integrated management by incorporating multi-scale, cross-boundary, and adaptive management to achieve sustainable landscape integrity (Fig. 1.2).

From single-scale management to multi-scale management

Traditional management has usually taken place at a single spatial scale. In forestry, for example, management often occurred at the stand level (Crow, 1999). Because a landscape is usually heterogeneous and ecological consequences are often scale-dependent (Toman and Ashton, 1996; Chapter 2, this book), management must be similarly carried out at multiple scales such as patch, patch group, and landscape. If no patches are the same, it may be neces-

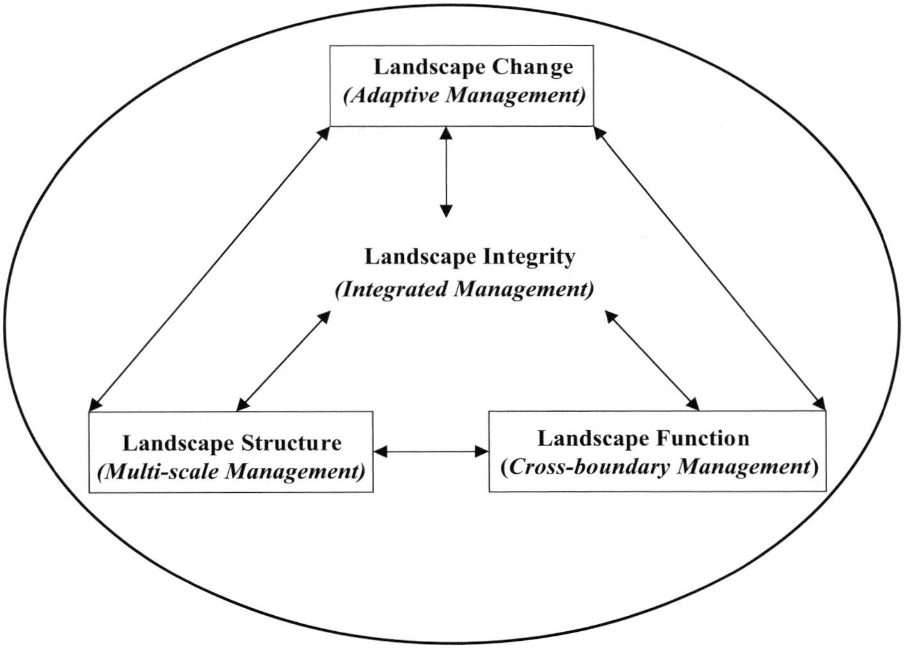

FIGURE 1.2
Relationships among the four major aspects of a landscape and the four management paradigms. Each box refers to a specific linkage between landscape ecology and natural resource management: landscape structure and multi-scale management, landscape function and cross-boundary management, and landscape change and adaptive management. Because landscape integrity and integrated management encompass all three linkages, they are represented by the entire ellipse.

sary to undertake different management activities in different patches to accommodate landscape heterogeneity. If two or more patches share the same characteristics, these patches can be grouped and be managed in the same way. For example, in an agricultural landscape with three patches (A, B, C), patch A has low soil fertility while B and C have high fertility, patches A and B have high density of pests whereas pest density in patch C is low, and all three patches have low soil moisture. In order to increase productivity and reduce costs, a multi-scale approach would be to enhance fertility (e.g., through applying organic manure) in patch A, to control pests (e.g., through integrated pest management) in patches A and B (as a patch group), and to improve water conditions (e.g., through irrigation) across the landscape (all three patches). Thus, individual patches or patch clusters need to be assessed and managed in the context of a landscape where management activities can be coordinated to achieve the overall performance of designed management plans at the landscape level.

From within-boundary management to cross-boundary management.
Conventional management was often conducted within the boundary of land ownership or within the same patch or landscape, without taking account of the interactions between the focal patch/landscape and other patches/landscapes (Reid, 1996). A cross-boundary management approach is thus needed to incorporate landscape functions (i.e., flows of energy, matter, and organisms) because landscape functions may not recognize political, management, ownership, and natural boundaries, and because management within a patch or landscape may have tremendous effects beyond the boundaries (Knight and Landres, 1998; Liu, 2001). The cross-boundary management paradigm considers the impacts of management within a focal system (patch or landscape) on other systems, as well as incorporating the impacts of management in other systems on the focal system (e.g., Chapter 7, this book). Also, it is important to study ecological and socioeconomic factors affecting landscape functions so that the functions can be enhanced or suppressed as appropriate (e.g., to create barriers for the dispersal of invasive species and to remove barriers to the movement of endangered species; Chapter 9, this book).

From static management to adaptive management
In the past, many management practices remained the same, even though significant changes had taken place on the landscape. For example, fire suppression in many regions of the US continued despite accumulation in the amount of fuel (Baker, 1994; Miller and Urban, 2000). Similarly, fishing pressures remained high despite a sharp decline in fish stocks and degradation in fish habitat (Rothschild *et al.,* 1994; Larkin, 1996). Because landscapes are constantly changing due to natural and anthropogenic disturbances (including management practices), management practices suitable for a previous condition are not always appropriate for new conditions. Thus, management strategies need to be changed accordingly. Adaptive management (Holling, 1978; Walters, 1986; Lee, 1993) has become an increasingly popular approach for addressing such dynamic and uncertain issues. The purpose of adaptive management is to accumulate knowledge and, thus, reduce uncertainty about the system. To achieve this purpose, adaptive management uses management alternatives as experiments with testable hypotheses. Furthermore, it is an iterative process that can adjust to new information, new management goals, and landscape changes over broad spatial and temporal scales.

From isolated management to integrated management
Past resource management practices often had single objectives (Scott *et al.*, 1995), which caused many unexpected negative results and varying degrees of socioeconomic and ecological conflicts (Kohm and Franklin, 1997). For

example, the goal of forest management was usually to produce as much timber as possible. However, timber harvesting had secondary effects of improving habitat for white-tailed deer by creating an abundant supply of accessible forage (Waller and Alverson, 1997). Improved habitat increased deer numbers to the point that forest regeneration in many areas had been almost completely eliminated and, thus, timber production could not be sustained (Alverson *et al.*, 1988). Additionally, overabundant deer populations caused crop damage and traffic accidents (Xie *et al.*, 2001). Furthermore, these consequences vary at multiple scales over time. This example illustrates the need for simultaneously and holistically managing deer, timber, and other natural resources in the landscape. To eliminate or minimize such conflicts and maintain high landscape integrity, it is important to take an integrated approach that incorporates multi-scale, cross-boundary, and adaptive management. It is crucial that different types of natural resource management be coordinated in both space and time. Integrated management shares many features with widely discussed ecosystem management (e.g., Grumbine, 1994; Christensen *et al.*, 1996), but integrated management also takes a landscape perspective by dynamically incorporating spatial interactions across heterogeneous landscapes to achieve sustainable landscape integrity.

1.4 Linking landscape ecology with natural resource management

The main objective of this book is to link landscape ecology with natural resource management. The linkages are discussed in six sections, comprising 20 chapters. The first section is introductory and contains this chapter, while the last section offers syntheses (Chapter 18) and perspectives (Chapters 19–20) regarding opportunities and challenges in integrating natural resource management with landscape ecology. The middle four sections (Parts II through V) link four different aspects of landscapes (structure, function, change, and integrity) with four corresponding management paradigms (multi-scale, cross-boundary, adaptive, and integrated management). Part II emphasizes multi-scale management based on landscape structure. Part III discusses the relationships between landscape function (e.g., flows of energy, matter, and species) and cross-boundary management (i.e., management across natural boundaries, ownership boundaries, political boundaries, and/or management boundaries). Part IV ties adaptive management with landscape change. Part V links landscape integrity with integrated management. We should point out that while each of Parts II–V has a particular emphasis, a certain degree of overlap is inevitable, as the four landscape aspects and the four management paradigms are interrelated. Furthermore, each of the 16 chapters in Parts II–V provides background information regarding numerous natural resource management issues; discusses relevant landscape ecology concepts, principles, or methods that are useful for addressing the management issues; presents one or more case studies (examples) that couple landscape ecology with natural resource management; and offers implications and guidelines for future landscape ecology research and natural resource management practices.

This book encompasses a variety of landscapes, including forested (Chapters 7–8, 11–14, 18, and 20), agricultural (Chapters 4, 12, 17, and 20), grassland (Chapters 2, 8, and 16), aquatic and riparian (Chapters 4–5, 7, 9, 15, 18, and 20), and urban (Chapters 6 and 12). The examples come from both publicly and privately owned lands. Public lands include federal lands (Chapters 4, 7, 10, and 13–14) and state and local government lands (Chapters 5 and 12), while private lands (Chapters 12 and 20) range from industrial and non-industrial lands (Chapter 7), farmland (Chapters 4 and 12) to residential land (Chapters 6 and 12).

A variety of natural resources are discussed in this book, including both ecosystem services and goods (Costanza *et al.*, 1997; Daily, 1997). Ecosystem goods include fish (Chapters 5, 9, and 15), crops (Chapters 4 and 17), livestock (Chapters 2, 4, and 16), and timber (Chapters 2, 7, 13–14, and 18). Ecosystem services include water (Chapters 2, 4–5, 9, and 17–18), biodiversity (Chapters 2–3, 5, 8, 10–13, and 18), non-timber resources (Chapter 18), and pollination (Chapter 4). Management issues associated with the natural resources are diverse, ranging from biodiversity conservation (Chapters 2, 4–5, 7, 12, and 17), timber harvesting (Chapters 2, 7, and 13–14), fishing (Chapters 5, 9, and 15), production yield (Chapters 2, 4, and 14–17), landscape fragmentation (Chapters 3, 12, and 14), soil erosion (Chapters 2, 4–5, and 18), pollution (Chapters 4–6, 15, and 18), urbanization (Chapters 6, 12, 15, and 18) to conflicting objectives (Chapters 2, 5, 8, and 14–15).

A large number of landscape ecology concepts have been applied to the various natural resource management issues discussed in this book. For example, the concepts of patch and scale are used in all chapters, and the term heterogeneity is used in almost every chapter. Other important concepts include spatial arrangement or configuration (Chapters 2–4, 7–8, 12, 15, and 17–18), extent and grain (Chapters 2, 4, 6–8, 10–16, and 18), landscape context or surrounding conditions (Chapters 2–6, 8–9, 11–12, 14–16, and 18–20), corridor or connectivity (Chapters 2–5, 8–11, 13, and 15–20), and source–sink habitat or metapopulation (Chapters 2–3 and 7–13). Many chapters discuss how landscape ecology principles are useful to natural resource management (Chapters 2, 5, 7, 9–10, 14, 18, and 20). For example, Wiens *et al.* (Chapter 2) state that "habitat patches close enough together to allow dispersal tend to support populations for longer periods than do patches that are far apart, and that habitat patches connected by habitat corridors or set in a landscape matrix of similar structure will foster frequent dispersal among patches" and illustrate the utilities of these principles using spotted owl population dynamics and persistence under different scenarios of landscape structure.

There are numerous landscape ecology methods developed and used in this book. These methods include sampling techniques (Chapters 3 and 11), experimentation (Chapters 2–3 and 13), observation (Chapters 3, 5, 8, 11, 13, and 16–18), and spatial statistics (Chapters 3, 5, 12, 16, and 18). In addition, various models are constructed and widely applied in predicting impacts of land use (Chapter 10), monitoring landscape changes (Chapter 11), simulating organism response to landscape structure and change (Chapters 2–3 and 13), projecting consequences of management alternatives and designs (Chapters 4, 6–7, 14, and 18), and exploring edge effects on a wide range of species (Chapter 8). Geographic information systems, remote sensing, and global positioning systems are three increasingly important spatial tools. Hoch *et al.* (Chapter 16) give a concise introduction to these tools and then apply them in grassland landscape studies. Other authors use geographic information systems and remote sensing techniques to detect and monitor landscape changes (Chapters 6, 10, and 12), to develop conservation priorities (Chapter 5), and to identify appropriate samples (Chapter 11).

Besides convincing arguments and evidence that a landscape perspective is very important in natural resource management, this book offers many specific "rules of thumb" as well as general, yet explicit, guidelines for implementing landscape ecology in the practices of natural resource management. Specific "rules of thumb" include the 50–11–40 rule and 40–20-40 rule for the management of the northern spotted owl (Chapter 2). While no management is identical in the details and the development of specific "rules of thumb" for various management actions requires detailed information, general guidelines are most useful and, thus, are provided in every chapter. For example, research and management should be conducted at multiple scales (Chapters 2–6 and 18), practices should be identified to minimize negative effects and enhance positive effects across boundaries (Chapters 7–9), modeling should be used as a cost-effective method for monitoring and predicting ecological consequences of resource management alternatives so that management actions can be adjusted accordingly (Chapters 10–13), sustained yield and productivity can be enhanced by managing natural resources in space and time (Chapters 14–17), natural and social sciences should be integrated, and the communication between academic and non-academic institutions should be enhanced (Chapters 5–6 and 18–20).

Although guidelines for landscape ecological research are often not as explicitly stated as those for natural resource management, landscape ecologists can identify research needs using the guidelines for management. Landscape ecologists can also benefit tremendously from interacting with natural resource managers who usually have rich field experience and can provide unique insights

(Chapters 13 and 18). For example, management activities can be used to design experimental treatments (Chapters 3 and 13), help landscape ecologists to maintain their landscapes of study, and assist landscape ecologists in understanding the mechanisms of landscape structure, function, change, and integrity.

Summary

There are inherent interrelationships between natural resource management and landscape ecology. On the one hand, management activities can provide unique opportunities for landscape ecology research and can change the study subjects (i.e., landscapes) (Hobbs, 1997; Liu, 2001) because management activities are disturbances that affect landscape structure, influence landscape function, drive landscape change, and alter landscape integrity. On the other hand, landscape ecology can offer useful guidance and tools for how natural resources can be better managed. For instance, landscapes can be designed and managed in a manner that spatial arrangement of patches can be altered to enhance or impede the rates of movement of species, energy, material, and disturbance.

A landscape perspective fosters multi-scale, cross-boundary, adaptive, and integrated approaches to natural resource management. This book provides numerous convincing arguments and case studies to tie landscape ecology with natural resource management. Authors of this book demonstrate that many landscape ecology concepts, principles, and methods are very useful for paradigm shifts in natural resource management. The specific "rules of thumb" and general guidelines proposed in this book are valuable to help ensure the sustainability of natural resources around the world.

Acknowledgments

We are grateful to Christopher Lepczyk for his constructive reviews of earlier drafts, which have greatly improved the chapter. We also thank Robert Howe and Linda Fortin for their helpful assistance. Financial support was provided by the National Science Foundation and National Institutes of Health.

References

Ahern, J. (1999). Integration of landscape ecology and landscape design: An evolutionary process. In *Issues in Landscape Ecology*, eds. J. A. Wiens & M. R. Moss, pp. 119–123. International Association for Landscape Ecology, Guelph, Canada.

Alverson, W. S., Waller, D. M., & Solheim, S. J. (1988). Forests too deer: Edge effects in Northern Wisconsin. *Conservation Biology*, 2: 348–358.

Aspinall, R. & Pearson, D. (2000). Integrated geographical assessment of environmental condition in water catchments: Linking landscape ecology, environmental modeling and GIS. *Journal of Environmental Management*, 59(special issue): 299–319.

Baker, W. L. (1992). The landscape ecology of large disturbances in the design and management of nature reserves. *Landscape Ecology*, 7: 181–194.

Baker, W. L. (1994). Restoration of landscape structure altered by fire suppression. *Conservation Biology*, 8: 763–769.

Cairns, M. A. & Lackey, R. T. (1992). Biodiversity and management of natural resources: The issues. *Fisheries*, 17: 6–10.

Carpenter, S. R., Caraco, N. F., Correll, D. L., Howarth, R. W., Shipley, A. N. & Smith, V. H. (1998). Nonpoint pollution of surface waters with nitrogen and phosphorus. *Ecological Applications*, 8: 559–568.

Christensen, N. L., Bartuska, A. M., Brown, J. H., Carpenter, S., D'Antonio, C., Francis, R., Franklin, J. F., MacMahon, J. A., Noss, R. F., Parsons, D. J., Peterson, C. H., Turner, M. G. & Woodmansee, R. G. (1996). The report of the Ecological Society of America committee on the scientific basis for ecosystem management. *Ecological Applications* 6: 665–691.

Cochran, W. G. (1977). *Sampling Techniques*. John Wiley, New York.

Costanza, R., dArge, R., deGroot, R., Farber, S., Grasso, M., Hannon, B., Limburg, K., Naeem, S., O'Neill, R. V., Paruelo, J., Raskin, R. G., Sutton, P. & vandenBelt, M. (1997). The value of the world's ecosystem services and natural capital. *Nature*, 387: 253–260.

Crossley, J. W. (1996). Managing ecosystems for integrity: Theoretical considerations for resource and environmental managers. *Society and Natural Resources*, 9:465–481.

Crow, T. (1999). Landscape ecology and forest management. In *Issues in Landscape Ecology*, eds. J. A. Wiens & M. R. Moss, pp. 94–96. International Association for Landscape Ecology, Guelph, Canada.

Daily, G. C. (ed.) (1997). *Nature's Services: Societal Dependence on Natural Ecosystems*. Island Press, Washington, D.C.

Dale, V. H., Lugo, A. E., MacMahon, J. A., & Pickett, S. T. A. (1998). Management implications of large, infrequent disturbances. *Ecosystems*, 1: 546–557.

Dale, V. H., Brown, S., Haeuber, R. A., Hobbs, N. T., Huntly, N., Naiman, R. J., Riebsame, W. E., Turner, M. G. & Valone, T. J. (2000). Ecological principles and guidelines for managing the use of land. *Ecological Applications*, 10: 639–670.

De Leo, G. A., & Levin, S. (1997). The multifaceted aspects of ecosystem integrity. *Conservation Ecology, 1 (1) art 3*, http://www.consecol.org/Journal/vol1/iss1/art3/

Dunning, J. B. Jr., Steward, D. J., Danielson, B. J., Noon, B. R., Root, T. L., Lamberson, R. H. & Stevens, E. E. (1995). Spatially explicit population models: Current forms and future uses. *Ecological Applications*, 5: 3–11.

Ehrlich, P. R. (1988). The loss of diversity: Causes and consequences. In *Biodiversity*, ed. E.O. Wilson, pp. 21–27. National Academy Press, Washington, D.C.

FAO [Food and Agriculture Organization] (1997). *State of the World's Forests*. United Nations Food and Agriculture Organization, Rome, Italy.

Farina, A. (2000) *Principles and Methods in Landscape Ecology*. Kluwer Academic Publishers, Boston, MA.

FEMAT [Forest Ecosystem Management Assessment Team] (1993). *Forest Ecosystem Management: An Ecological, Economic, and Social Assessment*. US Department of Agriculture Forest Service, Washington, D.C..

Forman, R. T. T. (1986). Emerging directions in landscape ecology and applications in natural resource management. In *Proceedings of the Conference on Science in the National Parks: The Plenary Sessions*, eds. R. Herrmann & T. Bostedt-Craig, pp. 59–88. US National Park Service and The George Wright Society, Fort Collins, CO.

Forman, R. T. T. (1995a). *Land Mosaics: The Ecology of Landscapes and Regions*. Cambridge University Press, Cambridge, UK.

Forman, R. T. T. (1995b). Some general principles of landscape and regional ecology. *Landscape Ecology*, 10: 133–142.

Forman, R. T. T. & Godron, M. (1986). *Landscape Ecology*. John Wiley, New York.

Foster, D. R., Fluet, M. & Boose, E. R. (1999). Human or natural disturbance: Landscape-scale dynamics of the tropical forests of Puerto Rico. *Ecological Applications*, 9: 555–572.

Franklin, J. F. & Forman, R. T. T. (1987). Creating landscape patterns by forest cutting: Ecological consequences and principles. *Landscape Ecology,* 1: 5–18.

Gardner, R. H., Milne, B. T., Turner, M. G. & O'Neill, R. V. (1987). Neutral models for the analysis of broad-scale landscape pattern. *Landscape Ecology*, 1: 19–28.

Golley, F. B. (1987). Introducing landscape ecology. *Landscape Ecology*, 1: 1.

Golley, F. B. (1995). Reaching a landmark. *Landscape Ecology*, 10: 3–4.

Grossman, G. D., Hill, J. & Petty, J. T. (1995). Observations on habitat structure, population regulation, and habitat use with respect to evolutionary significant units: A landscape perspective for lotic systems. *American Fisheries Society Symposium*, 17: 381–391.

Grumbine, R. E. (1994). What is ecosystem management? *Conservation Biology,* 8: 27–38.

Gustafson, E. J. (1998). Quantifying landscape spatial pattern: What is the state of the art? *Ecosystems,* 1: 143–156.

Gustafson, E. J. & Crow, T. R. (1996) Simulating the effects of alternative forest management strategies on landscape structure. *Journal of Environmental Management*, 46: 77–96.

Hanski, I. (1991). Single-species metapopulation dynamics: Concepts, models, and observations. *Biological Journal of the Linnean Society*, 42: 17–38.

Hargrove, W. W. & Pickering, J. (1992). Pseudoreplication: A sine qua non for regional ecology. *Landscape Ecology*, 6: 251–258.

Harris, L. D. (1984). *The Fragmented Forest: Island Biogeography Theory and the Preservation of Biotic Diversity*. University of Chicago Press, Chicago, IL.

Hobbs, R. J. (1995). Landscape ecology. In *Encyclopedia of Environmental Biology,* vol. 2, ed. W. A. Nierenberg, pp. 417–428. Academic Press, San Diego, CA.

Hobbs, R. J. (1997). Future landscapes and the future of landscape ecology. *Landscape and Urban Planning* 37: 1–9.

Holling, C. S. (ed.) (1978). *Adaptive Environmental Assessment and Management.* John Wiley, New York.

Hunter, M. L., Jr. (ed.) (1999). *Maintaining Biodiversity in Forest Ecosystems*. Cambridge University Press, Cambridge, UK.

Ims, R. A. (1999). Experimental landscape ecology. In *Issues in Landscape Ecology*, eds. J. A. Wiens & M. R. Moss, pp. 45–50. International Association for Landscape Ecology, Guelph, Canada.

Jensen, J. R. (1996). *Introductory Digital Image Processing: A Remote Sensing Perspective*, 2nd ed. Prentice Hall, Englewood Cliffs, NJ.

Karr, J. R. (1981). Assessment of biotic integrity using fish communities. *Fisheries*, 6: 21–27.

Kates, R. W., Clark, W. C., Corell, R. J., Hall, M., Jaeger, C. C., Lowe, I., McCarthy, J. J., Schellnhuber, H. J., Bolin, B., Dickson, N. M., Faucheux, S., Gallopin, G. C., Grübler, A., Huntley, B., Jäger, J., Jodha, N. S., Kasperson, R. E., Mabogunje, A., Matson, P., Mooney, H., Moore, B. III, O'Riordan, T. & Svedlin, U. (2001). Sustainability science. *Science*, 292: 641–642.

Klopatek, J. M. & Gardner, R. H. (eds.) (1999). *Landscape Ecological Analysis: Issues and Applications*. Springer-Verlag, New York.

Knight, R. L. & Landres, P. B. (eds.) (1998). *Stewardship Across Boundaries*. Island Press, Washington, D.C.

Kohm, K. A. & Franklin, J. F. (eds.). (1997). *Creating a Forestry for the 21st Century: The Science of Ecosystem Management*. Island Press, Washington, D.C.

Larkin, P. A. (1996). Concepts and issues in marine ecosystem management. *Reviews in Fish Biology and Fisheries*, 6: 139–164.

Lee, K. N. (1993). *Compass and Gyroscope: Integrating Science and Politics for the Environment*. Island Press, Washington, D.C.

Legendre, P. & Fortin, M. J. (1989). Spatial pattern and ecological analysis. *Vegetatio,* 80: 107–138.

Levin, S. A. (1992). The problem of pattern and scale in ecology. *Ecology*, 73: 1943–1967.

Li, H. & Reynolds, J. F. (1993). A new contagion index to quantify spatial patterns of landscapes. *Landscape Ecology*, 8: 155–162.

Lillesand, T. M. & Kiefer, R. W. (1994). *Remote Sensing and Image Interpretation*, 3rd ed. John Wiley, New York.

Liu, J. (1993). ECOLECON: A spatially-explicit model for ECOLogical-ECONomics of species conservation in complex forest landscapes. *Ecological Modelling*, 70: 63–87.

Liu, J. (1995). Ecosystem management for sustainable development. In *Wealth, Health and Faith: Sustainability Studies*, eds. R. Wang, J. Zhao, Z. Ouyang & T. Niu, pp. 56–59. China Environmental Science Press, Beijing, China.

Liu, J. (2001). Integrating ecology with human demography, behavior, and socioeconomics: Needs and approaches. *Ecological Modelling*, 140: 1–8.

Liu, J. & Ashton, P. S. (1999). Stimulating effects of landscape context and timber harvest on tree species diversity. *Ecological Applications*, 9: 186–201.

Liu, J., Cubbage, F. & Pulliam, H. R. (1994). Ecological and economic effects of forest structure and rotation lengths: Simulation studies using ECOLECON. *Ecological Economics*, 10: 249–265.

Liu, J., Dunning, J. B. & Pulliam, H. R. (1995). Potential impacts of a forest management plan on Bachman's Sparrows (*Aimophila aestivalis*): Linking a spatially-explicit model with GIS. *Conservation Biology*, 9: 62–79.

Liu, J., Ickes, K., Ashton, P., LaFrankie, J. & Manokaran, N. (1999). Spatial and temporal impacts of adjacent areas on the dynamics of species diversity in a primary forest. In *Spatial Modeling of Forest Landscape Change: Approaches and Applications*, eds. D., Mladenoff & W. Baker, pp. 42–69. Cambridge University Press, Cambridge, UK.

Liu, J., Linderman, M., Ouyang, Z., An, L., Yang, J. & Zhang, H. (2001). Ecological degradation in protected areas: The case of Wolong Nature Reserve for giant pandas. *Science*, 292: 98–101.

Lovejoy, T. E., Bierregaard, R. O., Rylands, A. B. Jr., Malcolm, C. E., Quintela, L. H., Harper, K. S., Brown, K. S. Jr., Powell, A. H., Powell, G. V. N., Schubart, H. O. R., & Hays, M. B. (1986). Edge and other effects of iolation on Amzon forest fragments. In *Conservation Biology: The Science of Scarcity and Diversity*, ed. M. E. Soulé, pp. 257–285. Sinauer Associates, Sunderland, M. A.

Lubchenco, J., Olson, A. M., Brubaker, L. B., Carpenter, S. R., Holland, M. M., Hubbell, S. P., Levin, S. A., MacMahon, J. A., Matson, P. A., Melillo, J. M., Mooney, H. A., Peterson, C. H., Pulliam, H. R., Real, L. A., Regal, P. J. & Risser, P. G. (1991). The Sustainable Biosphere Initiative: An ecological research agenda. *Ecology*, 72: 371–412.

Ludwig, J. A. (1999). Disturbance and landscapes: The little things count. In *Issues in Landscape Ecology*, eds. J. A. Wiens & M. R. Moss, pp. 59–63. International Association for Landscape Ecology, Guelph, Canada.

MacDonald, M. (1998). *Agendas for Sustainability: Environment and Development into the Twenty-first Century*. Routledge, New York.

Maguire, D. J., Goodchild, M. F. & Rhind, D. W. (1991). *Geographical Information Systems*. Longman, New York.

McCool, S. F. & Guthrie, K. (2001). Mapping the dimensions of successful public participation in messy natural resources management situations. *Society and Natural Resources*, 14: 309–323.

McGarigal, K. & Marks, B. J. (1994). *FRAGSTATS: Spatial Pattern Analysis Program for Quantifying Landscape Structure (Version 2.0)*. Oregon State University, Corvallis, OR.

McKelvey, K., Noon, B. R. & Lamberson, R. H. (1993). Conservation planning for species occupying fragmented landscapes: The case of the Northern Spotted Owl. In *Biotic Interactions and Global Change*, eds. P. M. Kareiva, J. G. Kingsolver & R. B. Huey, pp. 424–450. Sinauer Associates, Sunderland, MA.

McShea, W. J., & Rappole, J. H. (2000). Managing the abundance and diversity of breeding bird populations through manipulation of deer populations. *Conservation Biology*, 14: 1161–1170.

Miller, C. & Urban, D. L. (2000). Modeling the effects of fire management alternatives on Sierra Nevada mixed-conifer forests. *Ecological Applications*, 10: 85–94.

Myers, N. (1990). The biodiversity challenge: Expanded hotspots analysis. *The Environmentalist*, 10: 243–256.

Naveh, Z. & Lieberman, A. (1984). *Landscape Ecology: Theory and Application*. Springer-Verlag, New York.

Noss, R. F. (1983). A regional landscape approach to maintain diversity. *BioScience*, 33: 700–706.

O'Neill, R. V., Krummel, J. R., Gardner, R. H., Sugihara, G., Jackson, B., DeAngelis, D. L., Milne, B. T., Turner, M. G., Zygmunt, B., Christensen, S. W., Dale, V. H., & Graham, R. L. (1988). Indices of landscape pattern. *Landscape Ecology*, 1: 153–162.

Pearson, S. M. (1993). The spatial extent and

relative influence of landscape-level factors on wintering bird populations. *Landscape Ecology*, 8: 3–18.

Pearson, S. M., Turner, M. G., Gardner, R. H., & O'Neill, R. V. (1996). An organism-based perspective of habitat fragmentation. In *Biodiversity in Managed Landscapes: Theory and practice*, eds. R. C. Szaro & D. W. Johnston, pp. 77–95. Oxford University Press, New York.

Pickett, S. T. A. & Cadenasso, M. L. (1995). Landscape ecology: Spatial heterogeneity in ecological systems. *Science*, 269: 331–334.

Pickett, S. T. A. & White, P. S. (eds.) (1958). *The Ecology of Natural Disturbance and Patch Dynamics*. Academic Press, New York.

Pimentel, D., Westra, L. & Noss, R. F. (eds.) (2000). *Ecological Integrity: Integrating Environment, Conservation, and Health*. Island Press, Washington, D.C.

Pimm, S. L. & Gittleman, J. L. (1992). Biological diversity: Where is it? *Science*, 255: 940.

Pulliam, H. R. (1988). Sources, sinks, and population regulation. *American Naturalist*, 132: 652–661.

Pulliam, H. R., Dunning, J. B. & Liu, J. (1992). Population dynamics in complex landscapes: A case study. *Ecological Applications*, 2: 165–177.

Reid, W. V. (1996). Beyond protected areas: Changing perceptions of ecological management objectives. In *Biodiversity in Managed Landscapes: Theory and Practice*, eds. R. C. Szaro & D. W. Johnston, pp. 442–453. Oxford University Press, New York.

Risser, P. G., Karr, J. R., & Forman, R. T. T. (1984). *Landscape Ecology: Directions and Approaches*, Special Publication No. 2, Illinois Natural History Survey, Champaign, IL.

Robinson, G. R., Holt, R. D., Gaines, M. S., Hamburg, S. P., Johnson, M. L., Fitch, H. S., & Martinko, E. A. (1992). Diverse and contrasting effects of habitat fragmentation. *Science*, 257: 524–526.

Rogers, J. J. W. & Feiss, P. G. (1998). *People and the Earth: Basic Issues in the Sustainability of Resources and Environment*. Cambridge University Press, Cambridge, UK.

Rothschild, B. J., Ault, J. S., Goulletquer, P. & Heral, M. (1994). Decline of the Chesapeake Bay Oyster population: A century of habitat destruction and overfishing. *Marine Ecology Progress Series*, 111: 29–39.

Rutledge, J., Lepcyzk, C., Xie, J. & Liu, J. 2001. Spatial and temporal dynamics of endangered species hotspots in the United States. *Conservation Biology*, 15: 475–487.

Scott, J. M., Ables, E. D., Edwards, T. C., Eng, R. L., Gavin, T. A., Harris, L. D., Haufler, J. B., Healy, W. M., Knopf, F. L., Torgerson, O., & Weeks, H. P. (1995). Conservation of biological diversity: Perspectives and the future for the wildlife profession. *Wildlife Society Bulletin*, 23: 646–657.

Sharitz, R. R., Boring, L. R. Vanlear, D. H., & Pinder, J. E. (1992). Integrating ecological concepts with natural resource management of southern forests. *Ecological Applications*, 2: 226–237.

Speth, J. G. (1992). The transition to a sustainable society. *Proceedings of the National Academy of Sciences of the United States of America*, 89: 870–872.

Swanson, F. J. & Franklin, J. F. (1992). New forestry principles from ecosystem analysis of Pacific Northwest forests. *Ecological Applications*, 2: 262–274.

Swanson, F. J., Johnson, S. L., Gregory, S. V., & Acker, S. A. (1998). Flood disturbance in a forested mountain landscape: Interactions of land use and floods. *BioScience*, 48: 681–689.

Thrupp, L. A. (1990). Environmental initiatives in Costa Rica: A political ecology perspective. *Society and Natural Resources*, 3: 243–256.

Toman, M. A. & Ashton, P. M. S. (1996). Sustainable forest ecosystems and management: A review article. *Forest Science*, 42: 366–377.

Turner, M. G. (1987). *Landscape Heterogeneity and Disturbance*. Springer-Verlag, New York.

Turner, M. G. (1989). Landscape ecology: The effect of pattern on process. *Annual Review of Ecology and Systematics*, 20: 171–197.

Turner, M. G. & Gardner, R. H. (eds.) (1991) *Quantitative Methods in Landscape Ecology*. Springer-Verlag, New York.

Turner, M. G., Arthaud, G. J., Engstrom, R. T., Hejl, S. J., Liu, J., Loeb, S. & McKelvey, K. (1995). Usefulness of spatially explicit animal models in land management. *Ecological Applications*, 5: 12–16.

Turner, M. G., Dale, V. H. & Everham, E. E. III. (1997). Fires, hurricanes, and volcanoes: Comparing large-scale disturbances. *BioScience*, 47: 758–768.

Urban, D. L., O'Neill, R. V. & Shugart, H. H. (1987). Landscape ecology. *BioScience* 37: 119–127.

Verboom, J. & Wamelink, W. (1999). Spatial modeling in landscape ecology. In *Issues in Landscape Ecology*, eds. J. A. Wiens & M. R. Moss, pp. 38–44. International Association for Landscape Ecology, Guelph, Canada.

Vitousek, P. M., Mooney, H. A., Lubchenco, J. & Melillo, J. M. (1997). Human domination of earth's ecosystems. *Science*, 277: 494–499.

Waller, D. M. & Alverson, W. S. (1997). The white-tailed deer: A keystone herbivore. *Wildlife Society Bulletin*, 25: 217–226.

Walters, C. J. (1986). *Adaptive Management of Renewable Resources*. Macmillan, New York.

Wiens, J. A. (1992). What is landscape ecology, really? *Landscape Ecology*, 7: 149–150.

Wiens, J. A. & Milne, B. T. (1989). Scaling of 'landscapes' in landscape ecology, or, landscape ecology from a beetle's perspective. *Landscape Ecology*, 3: 87–96.

Wiens, J. A. & Moss, M. R. (eds.) (1999). *Issues in Landscape Ecology*. International Association for Landscape Ecology, Guelph, Canada.

Wiens, J. A., Crist, T. O., With, K., & Milne, B. T. (1995). Fractal patterns of insect movement in microlandscape mosaics. *Ecology*, 76: 663–666.

Wilson, E. O. (ed.) (1988). *Biodiversity*. National Academy Press, Washington D.C.

Woodley, S., Kay, J. & Francis, G. (1993). *Ecological Integrity and the Management of Ecosystems*. St. Lucie Press, Delray Beach, FL.

World Commission on Environment and Development (1987). *Our Common Future*. Oxford University Press, New York.

Xie, J., Liu, J. & Doepker, R. (2001). DeerKBS: A knowledge-based system for white-tailed deer management. *Ecological Modelling*, 140: 177–192.

Zonneveld, I. S. & Forman, R. T. T. (eds.) (1990). *Changing Landscapes: An Ecological Perspective*. Springer-Verlag, New York.

PART II

Landscape structure and multi-scale management

Landscapes are often heterogeneous, hierarchically structured, and multi-scaled. Ecological responses to landscape structure are usually scale-dependent. Thus, to better manage landscapes, many important questions regarding landscape structure and scale need to be answered. For example, how can landscape structure and scale be incorporated into natural resource management? How can the study and management of landscapes be coordinated at multiple scales? How should small patches be managed in fragmented and human-dominated landscapes? Are landscape ecology concepts developed from studying terrestrial systems applicable to aquatic systems? It is generally agreed that studying and managing landscapes requires the integration of natural and social sciences, but how can the scaling issue be dealt with when integrating these sciences? These and other related questions regarding landscape structure and multi-scale management are elegantly addressed in the five chapters of Part II. The chapter by Wiens *et al.* gives a detailed discussion of the general need for the multi-scale approach to landscape ecology study and natural resource management, while the other four chapters recommend specific scales at which research and management should occur.

In Chapter 2, Wiens *et al.* stress that natural resource management takes place in a landscape context, the effects of management actions on organisms are scale-dependent, and the responses of organisms to spatial structure and configuration are often non-linear and have thresholds. After discussing several recurrent issues in natural resource management, they suggest that it is essential to understand which scales are important to the organisms and management goals and that the scale(s) of management should be modified to cover the range of these important scales. Because there are countless organisms and landscape patterns, it is not possible to consider an equally countless number of scales. Instead, for organisms that share similar features and responses to landscape heterogeneity, Wiens *et al.* believe that scaling functions could be developed to depict and predict shared relationships, thus reducing the complexity of management scales.

Brennan *et al.* (Chapter 3) argue that multi-scale studies must be appropriately designed to provide useful information for the management of wildlife populations, because an ecological response variable is affected by both patch-level and landscape-level characteristics. In multi-scale landscape studies, the unit of observation is the landscape, and it is necessary to select a number of non-overlapping landscapes that differ in structure. However, the area of a study landscape is often large, which limits the number of landscapes that can be sampled. To minimize the logistic limitation in sample sizes of landscapes, the authors suggest using a focal patch design, where the ecological response variable is measured intensively in patches located at the centers of non-overlapping landscapes, while predictor variables are measured at both the patch and landscape scales.

Landscapes often consist of large and small patches. Although large patches in protected landscapes are important for biodiversity conservation, Corry and Nassauer (Chapter 4) show that in settled landscapes, concentration of biodiversity occurs in small patches rather than in large patches. After describing the characteristics, formation mechanisms, and values of small patches, they suggest cultural factors to be considered in conserving them, increasing the connectivity of small patches, and reducing the distances between them. Further, they demonstrate how small patches in the Corn Belt of the United States might be designed and managed for biodiversity using a multi-scale approach (field, farm, and entire Corn Belt scale).

In Chapter 5, Rabeni and Sowa convincingly argue that the concepts of landscape ecology can be applied to aquatic ecosystems. They present many aquatic concepts developed from a landscape perspective, including concepts on longitudinal changes of the biota, lateral interactions, as well as integration of longitudinal, lateral, and vertical dimensions of streams. Because stream biota are influenced by factors operating at different scales and the interactions of factors between scales, the authors believe that biota should be studied and managed at stream channel, riparian zone, and watershed levels in order to be effective. As to recreational fishing, Rabeni and Sowa suggest that the management take place at reach, stream, and ecoregion scales.

Integration of natural and social sciences is essential for effective management of natural resources, but Vogt *et al.* (Chapter 6) found that previous disciplinary studies were often conducted at different spatial scales, and these incompatibilities in the scales of analysis prevented the appropriate linkage among disciplines. They propose to use scale as a critical and effective means for integrating social and natural sciences to address natural resource issues. Their Baltimore case study suggests it is essential to collect and analyze data at several scales (neighborhood, residential area, watershed, and region) at the same time when linking social and natural sciences for natural resource management.

JOHN A. WIENS, BEATRICE VAN HORNE AND BARRY R. NOON

2

Integrating landscape structure and scale into natural resource management

2.1 Introduction

Resource managers face an almost impossible task. They are confronted with multiple goals that are promoted by interest groups championing specific and often conflicting agendas. Forceful arguments are made that management should focus on maximizing yield, preserving ecosystem integrity, fostering sustainability, enhancing biodiversity, protecting populations of endangered species, or preserving natural values (Daily and Walker, 2000). Moreover, the principles of ecology that guided management for so long – equilibrium, stability, spatial homogeneity, density-dependence, carrying capacity, orderly succession, and the like – have fallen on hard times. Predictability and certainty have given way to uncertainty, and the new paradigms of ecology emphasize spatial and temporal variability, thresholds, uncertainties, and contingencies (Wiens, 1984; Westoby *et al.*, 1989; Botkin, 1990; Pickett *et al.*, 1992; Pickett and Ostfeld, 1995; Stafford Smith, 1996). It is also apparent that these dynamics and effects play out differently at different scales of time and space (Wiens, 1989; Levin, 1992; Peterson and Parker, 1998). Robust predictions are hard to come by.

Faced with all this uncertainty, what is a resource manager to do? What help can science provide? Our thesis is that, because it focuses explicitly on the spatial relationships and dynamics of landscapes, landscape ecology can provide a particularly useful framework for effective management of natural resources. After all, most problems in resource management involve land and water use. Management of wildlife populations, for example, is often accomplished by managing "habitat" (Verner *et al.*, 1986; Morrison *et al.*, 1998; Rolstad, 1999), and many of the conflicts over grazing or timber harvesting (e.g., Graetz, 1994; West, 1996; Hunter, 1999) revolve around different perspectives on land use and its consequences (Meyer and Turner, 1994; Dale,

1997). Conservation in wetlands or riparian areas requires management not only of the aquatic system, but of the the patterns and regulation of water flows elsewhere in the landscape (e.g. Barendregt *et al.*, 1995; Ward *et al.*, 1999; Kingsford, 2000).

There are at least three challenges that confront ecologically sound land-use management. First, parcels of land can be treated as discrete and isolated management entities only in the context of ownership, administration, or politics, but not with regard to ecology. The management of land requires consideration of the landscape setting that contains the parcels of interest. Second, although land management is usually carried out over a restricted range of spatial and temporal scales, natural systems are generally not so restricted in their dynamics and interrelationships, and the scales of these dynamics may not coincide with the scales of management. Effective land-use management requires that ecological studies and perspectives be integrated across a broad range of scales. Finally, developing resource-management policies with the goal of ecological sustainability ultimately requires integration of ecology with economics, land ownership, politics, and sociology – all the forces that influence decisions about land use (COS, 1999; Daily and Walker, 2000; Dale *et al.*, 2000).

Our focus in this chapter is on the first two of these challenges. Specifically, we ask: What insights or approaches does landscape ecology offer resource managers or policy-makers who wish to base their actions on scientific knowledge, given the variability and uncertainty of Nature? We address this question by first developing the central themes of landscape ecology and then using several examples to illustrate how these themes relate to specific problems in management or conservation. We then consider some recurrent issues in natural-resource management in a landscape context. Finally, we address some ways of implementing a landscape perspective in resource management and dealing with the mismatch between the scales of ecological processes and those of management.

2.2 The central themes of landscape ecology

Landscape ecology is a diverse discipline, with many perceptions about what "landscape ecology" really is (see, e.g., Bunce and Jongman, 1993; Naveh and Lieberman, 1994; Richling *et al.*, 1994; Forman, 1995; Zonneveld, 1995; Bissonette, 1997; Hobbs, 1997; Nassauer, 1997; Farina, 1998; Wiens and Moss, 1999). In our view, landscape ecology deals with the physical structure and temporal dynamics of spatial mosaics (Wiens, 1999). It is concerned with how the elements in a mosaic are located relative to one another, with the causes of such spatial patterns, and with the ways in which the spatial configuration of landscapes affects ecological processes such as predation, dispersal, or nutrient distribution.

This view makes no explicit mention of "landscape level" or "landscape scale." Some proponents of hierarchy theory have proposed that "landscape" represents a level of organization between "ecosystem" and "biome." Others restrict the use of "landscape" to broad, kilometers-wide scales. These uses of "landscape" mesh well with resource management, which is usually implemented at the broad scales of parcels defined by habitat type, land ownership, or administrative domains and which increasingly focuses on higher levels of organization than individuals or populations (Franklin, 1993; Aber *et al.*, 2000). Considerations of hierarchies and scale are certainly important in thinking about landscapes and their consequences (e.g., Kotliar and Wiens, 1990). A "landscape," however, is neither a level nor a scale, for the reasons argued forcefully by Allen (1998) and King (1997, 1999). Spatial patterning and its causes and consequences are as relevant to individuals as to ecosystems or biomes, and to small as well as large areas. This broadened view of "landscape" and landscape ecology may make the linkage to the customary scales and levels of resource management less apparent, but it may also produce greater insights into the ways in which land use affects ecological systems. We return to this problem of meshing the scales of management with the scales of ecology in section 2.5.

2.2.1 Spatial structure and configuration matter

Historically, ecologists have sought to simplify the complexity of real-world landscapes (Wiens, 1995). Thus, most conceptualizations of spatial patterning in ecology are founded on simple patch-matrix models; island-biogeography theory (MacArthur and Wilson, 1967) is but one example. The spatial configuration of real landscapes, however, can be expressed in a bewildering array of possible patterns, and there is a seemingly endless list of measures that can be derived from landscape maps or images (e.g., Forman, 1995; McGarigal and Marks, 1995; Hargis *et al.*, 1997; Frohn, 1998; Gustafson, 1998; Fortin, 1999). All of this variety can be condensed into four essential ingredients of landscape structure.

Patch quality

Elements in a landscape are recognizable because they are different from one another and from their surroundings. The differences are generally structural: features of vegetation type, canopy height, or surface topography. A resource manager may translate these differences into differences in potential economic returns. To the organisms occupying the patches, however, they translate into differences in threats and opportunities. The abundance of predators or competitors in a patch, the availability of food or nutrients, the potential mating opportunities, the level of physiological stress, and a host of other factors all combine to determine the costs and benefits associated with the patch, and because these costs and benefits vary in time, patch quality is dynamic (Wiens, 1997).

Boundaries

The elements of a landscape are bounded, either by sharp edges or by a steepened gradient in patch properties. Boundaries play a critical role in determining the movement or flows of individuals, nutrients, materials, or disturbances across a landscape (e.g., Wiens *et al.*, 1985; Holland *et al.*, 1991; Hansen and di Castri, 1992; Gosz, 1993). A boundary that is permeable to flows contributes to the linkages among the elements in a landscape; ecological dynamics are then played out over the larger landscape. A relatively impermeable boundary, on the other hand, reflects movements back into the patch and internalizes dynamics within landscape elements. The units of "habitat" that are mapped or managed to enhance wildlife populations (e.g., reserves) are often regarded as having closed boundaries, so external influences are usually ignored. If the boundaries are permeable to the organisms of interest, however, the "habitat" is really much larger than the defined units, and a study (or management action) that is restricted within a patch may fail to capture the critical ecological dynamics.

Patch context

A landscape patch is, by definition, bounded by something else. Exactly what lies adjacent to a patch may influence both what goes on within the patch and the permeability of the patch boundary. A patch of seemingly suitable habitat for a species, for example, may be unsuitable if it is bounded by landscape elements that foster predators or competitors to which the boundary is highly permeable (e.g., Andrén, 1992). Alternatively, organisms may be able to occupy a patch of "habitat" that would otherwise be unsuitable if resources are available in neighboring patches. The surroundings of a patch in a landscape are not just a featureless matrix, but constitute a variegated mosaic in which differences among neighboring landscape elements create differences in within- and between-patch dynamics.

Connectivity

The degree to which organisms, materials, or disturbances can move across a landscape is determined by its connectivity (e.g., Turner *et al.*, 1989). Conservation biologists and resource managers often equate connectivity with corridors, linear landscape elements that link patches of similar habitat together. Quite apart from the debate about whether corridors are potentially beneficial or detrimental to populations (e.g., Noss, 1987; Simberloff and Cox, 1987; Rosenberg *et al.*, 1997; Beier and Noss, 1998; Bennett, 1999), thinking of connectivity solely in terms of corridors is overly simplistic. The ability of organisms to move through a landscape is a function of the boundary permeabilities and patch contexts that characterize a given mosaic (Taylor *et al.*, 1993; Tischendorf and Fahrig, 2000) and of the mobility of the organisms themselves. Movements can be affected by many aspects of landscape structure, not just linear strips of similar habitat.

The importance of the organism

Collectively, these four features – patch quality, boundaries, patch context, and connectivity – describe the structure of landscapes in functionally relevant terms. How each of these features is determined, however, is as much a function of the organisms and processes one considers as it is of the physical landscape itself. What is a boundary to one organism may not be to another, how patch quality varies among landscape elements depends on whether one is emphasizing individual fitness or population persistence, and how connectivity affects the propagation of disturbances across a landscape may differ for fire versus flooding. Consequently, the "landscape" that we perceive, map, and manage may not always coincide with the spatial structure and configuration that most directly influence the organisms, ecosystems, or processes that are the subjects of our efforts. To understand how landscape structure affects ecological systems, it is necessary to focus on organisms, not just maps or images (Wiens, 1989; Pearson *et al.*, 1996; Haila, 1999; Mac Nally, 1999).

This focus on organisms need not inevitably lead to the hopeless management situation in which every species in every situation at every time requires a specifically tailored management plan. Ecologists are increasingly turning their attention to "functional types," groups of species that share a common set of life-history traits, morphological or behavioral attributes, or ecological functions. Considerable progress has been made in defining functional types of plants (e.g., Lavorel *et al.*, 1997; Smith *et al.*, 1997) and systems have been proposed for functional groupings of ants (Bestelmeyer and Wiens, 1996; Andersen, 1997) and stream invertebrates (Poff, 1997). We have used information on body mass, length of migratory pathway, and habitat preferences to organize shorebirds that use wetland stopover sites during their spring migration through the Great Plains of North America into five well-defined functional groups (J. A. Wiens, B. Van Horne, and A. H. Farmer, unpublished data). If several species sharing functional properties can be managed in the same way, this would simplify the challenge of species-based management, while at the same time emphasizing important ecological properties.

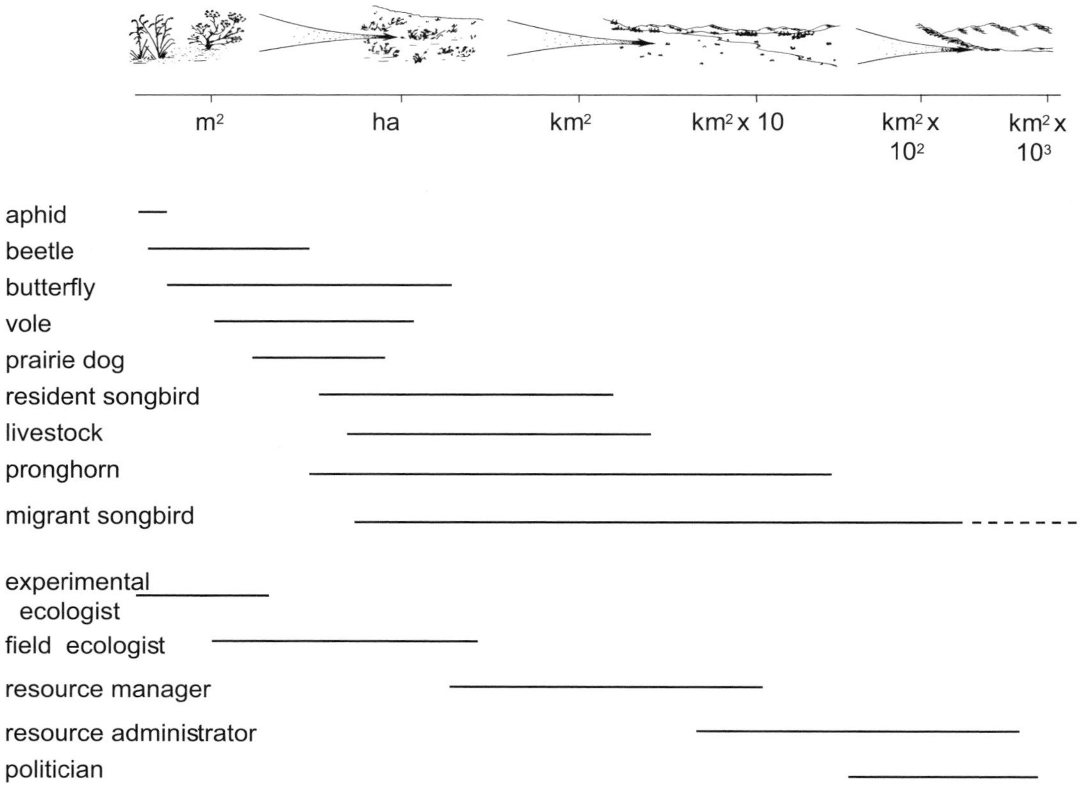

FIGURE 2.1
Diagrammatic representation of the scaling windows of various organisms occupying a western intermontane shrubsteppe landscape, and of the humans who do research or have management responsibilities for these resources at varying levels.

2.2.2 Scale matters

The prospects for developing a functional-type approach to resource management, however, depend on developing ways of dealing with scale. Organisms respond to landscape structure over a restricted range of spatial scale – a "scaling window" (Fig. 2.1). This window is bracketed by *grain*, the finest resolution with which organisms perceive spatial variation, and *extent*, the overall spatial domain that they experience over a specified time period (e.g., a year, a lifetime; Addicott *et al.,* 1987; Wiens, 1989). Other things being equal, larger organisms view the environment through a broader scaling window than do smaller organisms, and mobile organisms operate at broader scales than do more sedentary organisms. Of course, other things generally aren't equal; differences among species in physiology, food habits, foraging behavior, social organization, or dispersal abilities all contribute to the determination of scaling windows. In turn, the differences in scaling windows among organisms produce a wide array of scale-dependent patterns and dynamics in ecological systems (Wiens, 1989; Levin, 1992). Moreover, the scaling responses of organisms are often hierarchical (Kotliar and Wiens, 1990). For example, individuals may select breeding habitat at one scale and foraging locations at another, sexes may differ in the scales on which they use the environment, and populations often display hierarchical structure in their spatial dispersion patterns (Hutto, 1985; Dale, 1999).

This hierarchical structure in scaling responses is a reflection of the broader hierarchical organization of ecological systems. Proponents of hierarchy theory (e.g., Allen and Starr, 1982; O'Neill *et al.*, 1986; Allen and Hoekstra, 1992; see King, 1997) postulate that the slow dynamics seen at broad spatial scales arise from faster dynamics at finer scales and, correspondingly, that patterns and processes observable at higher hierarchical levels (communities, ecosystems) derive from the properties and behavior of individuals and species populations and their interactions. The structure and processes of systems at broad scales or higher levels, in turn, dictate the range of possible dynamics of ecological systems at finer scales or lower levels.

Of course, considerations of scale apply to time as much as to space, and temporal and spatial scaling are often closely related. Small organisms, for example, generally occupy small individual home ranges, perceive environmental structure at finer scales, and have shorter life spans than do large organisms. Several space–time "blob" diagrams that define the spatial and temporal domains of various components of systems or ecological processes have appeared in the literature (e.g., Delcourt *et al.*, 1983; Urban *et al.*, 1987; Holling *et al.*, 1996; Spies and Turner, 1999). Although such diagrams are not quantitatively precise, they do serve to draw attention to both the scale dependency of ecological phenomena and the linkages between temporal and spatial scales.

Temporal scales have relevance to resource management quite apart from their relationship to spatial scaling, however. As the temporal scale of the dynamics of an ecosystem component broadens, for example, the recovery time following disturbance becomes correspondingly long. This has two immediate consequences. First, it increases the likelihood that time lags in the responses of other components of the system to the changes produced by the disturbance will produce transient dynamics. Second, it increases the chances that something else (e.g., another disturbance) will occur before the system has recovered to its former state, perhaps compounding the effects of the initial disturbance and increasing the probability that the system will be driven to some threshold.

2.2.3 Thresholds matter

The restricted domain of response of organisms to scaling gradients (e.g., Fig. 2.1) is just one example of a much more basic feature of ecological systems: responses to environments generally exhibit strong limits and thresholds. In some respects, this is no surprise. Plant ecologists have recognized for more than a century that plant species have restricted ranges of ecological tolerance of environmental variation, and that their performance within this range usually shows some sort of peak (e.g. Curtis, 1959; Whittaker, 1975). Classical niche theory has modeled species' responses to environmental gradients as normal (Gaussian) distributions (Austin, 1999). Nonetheless, it has been commonplace (especially among animal ecologists) to regard the response of a species to environmental variation within its zone of tolerance as essentially linear. Indeed, this is the foundation of many of the functions incorporated into models of habitat suitability (HSI models) for wildlife management (Van Horne and Wiens, 1991).

Some of the thresholds that characterize species' responses to landscape structure are clearly related to scale – changing the scale on which landscape patterns are expressed may move one beyond the limits of the grain–extent scaling window of a species. Even within a limited domain of scale, however, there may be thresholds in the structural properties of landscapes and in how organisms respond to them. It is now recognized from both empirical studies and theoretical models, for example, that fragmentation of habitat within a landscape is a non-linear, threshold process (Gardner *et al.*, 1987; Andrén, 1994; With, 1999; With and King, 1999). Erosion affects landscape structure, but differences in the frequency and intensity of flooding events may produce thresholds in landform change with changes in scale (Pickup, 1991). Thresholds in demographic processes may occur when a population declines below some critical value (e.g., Lande, 1987; Lamberson *et al.*, 1994; Hanski, 1999). Nature is full of thresholds layered upon thresholds.

2.3 How do these themes relate to management?

The themes developed above now seem obvious to many ecologists, but their relevance to management issues may still appear to be somewhat distant and abstract. To illustrate how landscape ecology may relate to issues of real-world management concern, we describe three general case studies that represent a gradient of increasing complexity: northern spotted owls (*Strix occidentalis caurina*) in old-growth forests, wetland use by waterbirds, and grazing in rangelands. In the first case, the focus is on timber harvesting as the dominant land use and its consequences for a single species of interest. The management objective is to maintain viable populations of the owl and, secondarily, the old-growth forests it occupies. The management emphasis in the second example is on the maintenance of adequate wetland habitat in the face of highly variable precipitation and on mitigating the effects of wetland loss due to changing land use. The focus is on the suite of waterbird species that rely on these wetlands. In the third case, grazing by domestic livestock is the predominant disturbance. It has complex effects on both landscape structure and a multitude of organisms. Here, management is concerned primarily with sustainability of the primary land use (grazing), and concerns about the conservation of biodiversity are only slowly becoming a focus of management (Sampson and Knopf, 1996).

2.3.1 Spotted owls and the management of old-growth forests

Humans have been clearing forests since the beginnings of civilization (Perlin, 1989; Diamond, 1999), but the rate of change in distribution, structure, and composition of forests has accelerated dramatically over the past century (Perry, 1994, 1998; Williams, 1994; Hunter, 1999). This is typified by forests of the Pacific Northwest of the United States. As a result of high levels of timber harvest since the 1930s, forests have become highly fragmented and the age structure of these forests has changed from one dominated by trees >300 years old to one dominated by trees <70 years old. The natural structural heterogeneity of these forests, a consequence of historic disturbance processes such as blowdown and fire, has been replaced by an artificial pattern produced by road construction and clear-cut timber harvest.

The extent and nature of these changes are most apparent when viewed at the broad spatial scales of satellite imagery. The landscape pattern in the Pacific Northwest is now a mosaic of small patches of residual old-growth forests or (increasingly) clear-cuts surrounded by an extensive matrix of younger forest. The result is a collection of discrete patches of old forest defined by sharp edges and distinct boundaries. Changes in the spatial distribution of forest stands and the landscape context of old-forest patches have produced significant changes in ecological processes. For example, the microclimate of old-forest patches is altered when they are adjacent to younger forest, changing forest structure, composition, and successional dynamics (Chen *et al.*, 1995). Hydrological processes have also been altered: rivers and streams have become laden with silt, lost their up-slope recruitment of coarse woody debris, and experienced significant declines in anadromous fish populations (NRC, 1996). Much of the attention, however, has focused on the northern spotted owl.

Because spotted owl populations are largely restricted to late-seral forests, which now are highly fragmented and reduced in extent, populations of the owl have a spatial structure resembling a metapopulation (Levins, 1969; Hanski, 1999) – a collection of spatially distinct, local populations dependent upon colonization via dispersal from neighboring populations. An ecologically defensible conservation strategy should therefore consider the spatial context and degree of connectivity of owl populations rather than the dynamics of a few local populations. Murphy and Noon (1992) invoked several themes of landscape ecology in addressing these concerns. The importance of patch quality was evident in the principles that large habitat patches with less internal fragmentation containing large populations will tend to support a species for a longer time than will small patches or patches that are irregular in configuration. Patch context and connectivity were incorporated in the principles that habitat patches close enough together to allow dispersal tend to support populations for longer periods than do patches that are far apart, and that habitat patches connected by habitat corridors or set in a landscape matrix of similar structure will foster frequent dispersal among patches.

To examine how these principles might affect spotted owl population persistence under different scenarios, McKelvey *et al.* (1993) used a spatially explicit landscape simulation model that linked the survival and reproduction of individuals to the locations of suitable habitat in the landscape. Holding the overall amount of suitable habitat constant in the model, variations in the spatial configuration of habitat produced markedly different population projections (Fig. 2.2). Clustering of suitable habitat produced both higher and more stable population levels than did a random landscape structure (Fig. 2.2a vs. 2.2b). Moreover, a cluster with a low ratio of edge to area enhanced population stability relative to a more irregular but continuous cluster or habitat or a fragmented habitat array (Fig. 2.2b vs. 2.2c and 2.2d). Other simulations suggested that when habitat quality varies spatially, creating a mosaic of suitable habitats surrounded by marginal ("sink") habitat, population levels become less stable over time. Clearly, the spatial configuration of landscapes can affect population dynamics and the probability of long-term persistence.

In addition to considering features of landscape structure, the conservation strategy that was developed for spotted owls in the Northwest also addressed aspects of both spatial and temporal scale (Thomas *et al.*, 1990; Murphy and Noon, 1992; FEMAT, 1993; Noon and McKelvey, 1996; Lint *et al.*, 1999). Guidelines for maintaining habitat quality by managing vegetation structure and composition were developed at scales relevant to both individuals (nest tree, the nest stand, home range) and populations (local population, metapopulation). Because harvested forest requires a long recovery time to return to late-seral structure, the transient population dynamics of the owl during the period of habitat recovery also needed to be addressed. This required that all currently suitable habitat on public lands be free from timber harvest until the downward decline in the owl's population was arrested and younger forest had matured to suitable habitat.

Throughout the range of the northern spotted owl, its preferred old-growth habitat was probably naturally fragmented before the advent of widespread timber harvesting, but the accelerating loss of old-growth forest has pushed forest structure well beyond a fragmentation threshold. In addition, concerns

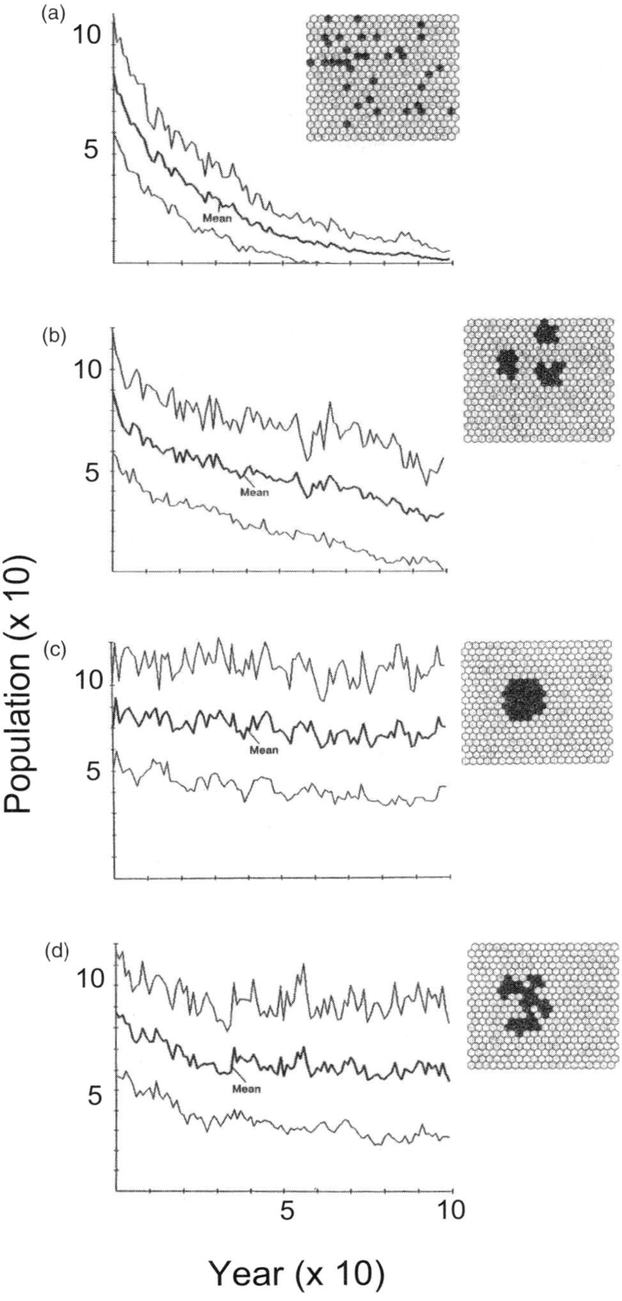

FIGURE 2.2
Graphical results of a computer simulation model of spotted owl population dynamics in relation to the spatial configuration of suitable habitat in a landscape. Each cell in the array represents one territory-sized unit, and solid cells represent suitable habitat. The amount of suitable habitat in each scenario is the same, and all population parameters are held constant. The heavy line in each graph is the mean population response, and the thin lines bracket one standard deviation from the mean. In (a), suitable habitat is randomly scattered; in (b) it is arrayed in three small blocks, whereas in (c) and (d) habitat occurs in a single large block that differs in the ratio of edge to area. Clearly, a clustering of suitable habitat yields a higher population level and lower probability of extinction than a random arrangement, and clusters that are more irregular have reduced demographic stability. After McKelvey *et al.* (1993).

have been raised that the owl is approaching a demographic threshold, particularly on the Olympic Peninsula of Washington and in the Coast Range of Oregon. The theoretical model developed by Lande (1987) showed that territorial populations, such as spotted owls, would exhibit a sharp threshold in the probability of local and regional population extinctions with increased habitat loss and fragmentation. Extension of Lande's model, parameterized according to the owl's life history and vital rates (Lande, 1988; Lamberson *et al.*, 1994), showed the northern spotted owl to be not only vulnerable but, in terms of the amount and fragmentation of forest in the Pacific Northwest, near an extinction threshold (Noon and McKelvey, 1996).

In this case, the management policy that has been developed draws heavily upon the concepts of landscape ecology. It considers the spatial configuration and arrangement of landscape elements at multiple scales and involves an evaluation of patch attributes such as size, shape, context, connectivity, spacing, and quality. The spatial scale of the conservation strategy recognizes the effects of the landscape on individual dispersal and on the linkages among local populations, and the temporal scale is sufficient to model transient population dynamics and demographic thresholds in persistence related to habitat loss and fragmentation. Spatially explicit simulation models helped to frame the consequences of alternative management strategies. And, of course, there was a tremendous amount of basic information on the natural history of the owls that underpinned these efforts. Currently, the conservation strategy for the northern spotted owl is the focal point for management of public lands in the Pacific Northwest. The responsible agencies have adopted changes in timber harvest practices and instituted efforts to accelerate the restoration of forests with late-seral characteristics (FEMAT, 1993). Given the renewal time for forest regeneration and the life history of the owl, however, it is still too early to determine if the rate of population decline will be arrested by these changes in management practices.

2.3.2 Use of wetlands by waterbirds

Wetlands face increasing threats from development, both through a direct loss of habitat through draining and land-use conversion and through diversion of the water flows that maintain them. Wetlands, and the organisms that use them, therefore have a high conservation priority (the Ramsar Convention; Davis, 1994). Their use by migratory birds, particularly waterfowl that have important recreational values, adds to their conservation significance, and many wetland areas are actively managed to enhance waterbird populations. How do the themes we developed earlier – the importance of landscape structure, scale, and thresholds – relate to these management efforts?

Two studies provide some insight on this issue. In one study, Roshier (1999, 2001) considered how waterbirds responded to variations in the availability of wetlands in the arid zone of Australia. Roughly 70% of Australia is arid, but it is not without wetlands, and waterbirds are unexpectedly abundant in this region. The distribution of wetland habitat is highly variable in space and time due to the erratic distribution of rainfall. Consequently, most wetlands retain water for a short time relative to the life span of individual birds, and many species are capable of long-distance, nomadic dispersal movements. Grey teal (*Anas gracilis*), for example, may move an average of 180 km a day and cover as much as 3200 km in straight-line distance in a few weeks (Frith, 1959). Waterbird abundance on individual wetlands or within a larger catchment may vary by as much as an order of magnitude over a three-month period (Kingsford *et al.*, 1994).

The structure of wetland landscapes in arid Australia is dynamic, as wetlands fill through flooding and then diminish and dry during droughts. Waterbirds might respond to these changes at the scale of local patches, at the broader scale of catchments or watersheds, or at a scale extending beyond individual catchments to even broader regions. Roshier used survey data from several years for a 93 000 km^2 area in northwestern New South Wales to examine these possibilities. Using wetland area as a surrogate for local patch quality, Roshier determined that neither the area of individual wetlands nor wetland area in the vicinity of a patch explained much of the variation in waterbird distribution and abundance. Moreover, the dynamics of abundance in a given wetland were statistically unrelated to the dynamics of other wetlands in the surrounding area. Changes in abundance at a catchment scale over a time period of a few months were most clearly related to changes in habitat availability in the Lake Eyre region, some 700 km away. For example, for fish-eating species, diving ducks, and grazing waterfowl, changes in wetland area in the Lake Eyre Basin accounted for 40–56% of the variation in abundance in the Paroo River catchment. Not all functional groups of waterbirds responded in the same way, however. Dabbling ducks showed an immediate decrease in abundance in the Paroo when there had been floods in the Lake Eyre Basin, which inundated wetland habitat. Abundances in the Paroo later increased as the floods receded. Food availability increases rapidly after floods, and Roshier suggested that birds move into the abundant habitat in the Lake Eyre Basin during wet periods and return to the more persistent wetlands in the Paroo River catchment during dry periods. On the other hand, the abundance of fish-eating species and diving ducks in the Paroo showed positive correlations with both increases and decreases in wetland area in the Lake Eyre Basin, suggesting that these birds might emigrate into the arid zone from more mesic regions of the continent when there had been a series of floods in the interior (cf.

Kingsford and Porter, 1999). Different groups of waterbirds apparently respond to rainfall in the Lake Eyre Basin on quite different scales of space and time, although for all the scale was broader than the Basin itself.

Wetlands are not randomly distributed across the Australian arid zone, but occur in clusters or networks defined by topography and water-flow patterns of rivers or creeks during the occasional flooding episodes. These spatial relationships contribute to the patterns of connectivity among wetlands within the regional landscape, but temporal variations in water availability lead to marked changes in wetland connectivity. Wetland availability is more restricted during dry periods than during wetter periods, and the landscape becomes more fragmented and the size of interconnected clusters of wetlands is reduced (Fig. 2.3a). The scale at which a series of wetlands becomes connected so as to form a single functional unit to a waterbird varies among species, depending on the mobility or dispersal capacity of individuals. Thus, the functionally relevant patterns of wetland connectivity in the arid zone depend not only on the geographic distribution of potentially suitable habitat and temporal variations in wetland quality (filling vs. drying) but on the dispersal capability of an organism, the stage of its annual breeding cycle, and how it perceives landscape structure. For example, heavy monsoon rains in northern Australia in March 1993 filled many wetlands, producing a continent-spanning cluster of wetlands for organisms with a dispersal distance of 200 km. The same set of wetlands would be much less interconnected for a species with a dispersal distance of only 100 km (Fig. 2.3b). Moreover, given the geographic distribution of potential wetlands, the relationship between wetland connectivity and dispersal distance is not linear, but rather is a threshold phenomenon. Small increases in dispersal capability can produce large increases in wetland connectivity (Fig. 2.4). As one might expect, the scale of dispersal distances at which such a threshold in connectivity occurs is sensitive to the abundance of wetlands in the landscape, and increases as more wetlands dry during a drought.

In North America, wetlands do not exhibit such dramatic variations in distribution and abundance, and the waterbirds that use these habitats are either residents or migrants that follow defined flyways in their seasonal migrations. Wetlands serve as vital stopovers at which birds accumulate energy stores for subsequent stages in their migration. In a second study, Farmer (Farmer and Parent, 1997; Farmer and Wiens, 1998, 1999) used a combination of field studies and dynamic modeling to assess the consequences of changes in wetland quality (indexed by calculated prey ingestion rate) and wetland distribution (proximity) for pectoral sandpipers (*Calidris melanotos*) during their migration from the Gulf Coast of Texas through the Great Plains to their breeding grounds in northern Alaska. Migrating females face the combined challenge of accumulating sufficient body fat at stopover sites to complete the migration and still have sufficient energy reserves to lay a clutch of eggs (energy limitation) while arriving at the breeding grounds in time to complete breeding before the onset of poor weather in late summer and early fall (time limitation). The modeling indicates that when wetland quality is high, a spectrum of alternative movement strategies is suitable, ranging from a series of short movements between nearby wetlands to a single direct flight from the coast to the arctic. As wetland quality decreases, the range of alternative strategies converges to a single optimum. With further reductions in wetland quality, a point is reached at which it is not possible for the birds to accumulate sufficient energy reserves in the time available to reach the breeding grounds and breed successfully, and the "optimal" strategy is to abandon migration. A threshold in patch quality has been passed.

Farmer's field studies also indicated that, as in Australia, the availability of wetland stopovers is strongly influenced by rainfall. During wet years, agricultural fields may be flooded in the spring and tilling by farmers delayed, providing abundant additional habitat to migrating shorebirds. In dry years, on the other hand, such temporary wetlands are not available and the birds must rely on more permanent wetlands, which are more widely spaced. Connectivity of wetlands within an area of tens of km^2 increases during wet years and individuals may effectively perceive multiple habitat patches as a single functional unit. This enables them to move farther from a stopover site to forage, increasing their rate of energy gain (Farmer and Parent, 1997). Farmer's simulation analyses, however, indicate that changes in wetland quality are far more important than the spacing of wetlands in a regional landscape, in terms of their effects on potential individual fitness (Farmer and Wiens, 1998, 1999; see also Weber *et al.*, 1999).

In both of these examples, the spatial distribution of elements (wetlands) in a landscape, variations in patch quality, patterns of connectivity, and the scale at which all of these are viewed have important consequences on the use of wetland habitats by waterbirds. Because the characteristics of wetlands are tied so closely to water, temporal variability is great. The patterns of distribution and connectedness of habitat patches vary with climate, and the use of particular wetlands or entire catchments by birds may be strongly influenced by conditions some distance away. The scales on which these dynamics and relationships are played out are as much a function of the behavioral and ecological traits of the organisms as they are of the landscape and environment.

How do these findings relate to wetland management? In contrast to the spotted owl example, the landscape features that clearly influence the dynamics of waterbird communities in wetlands have yet to be integrated into management policies. Indeed, most current wetland management for waterbirds is based on static views of wetlands as isolated entities. Under the Ramsar Convention, for

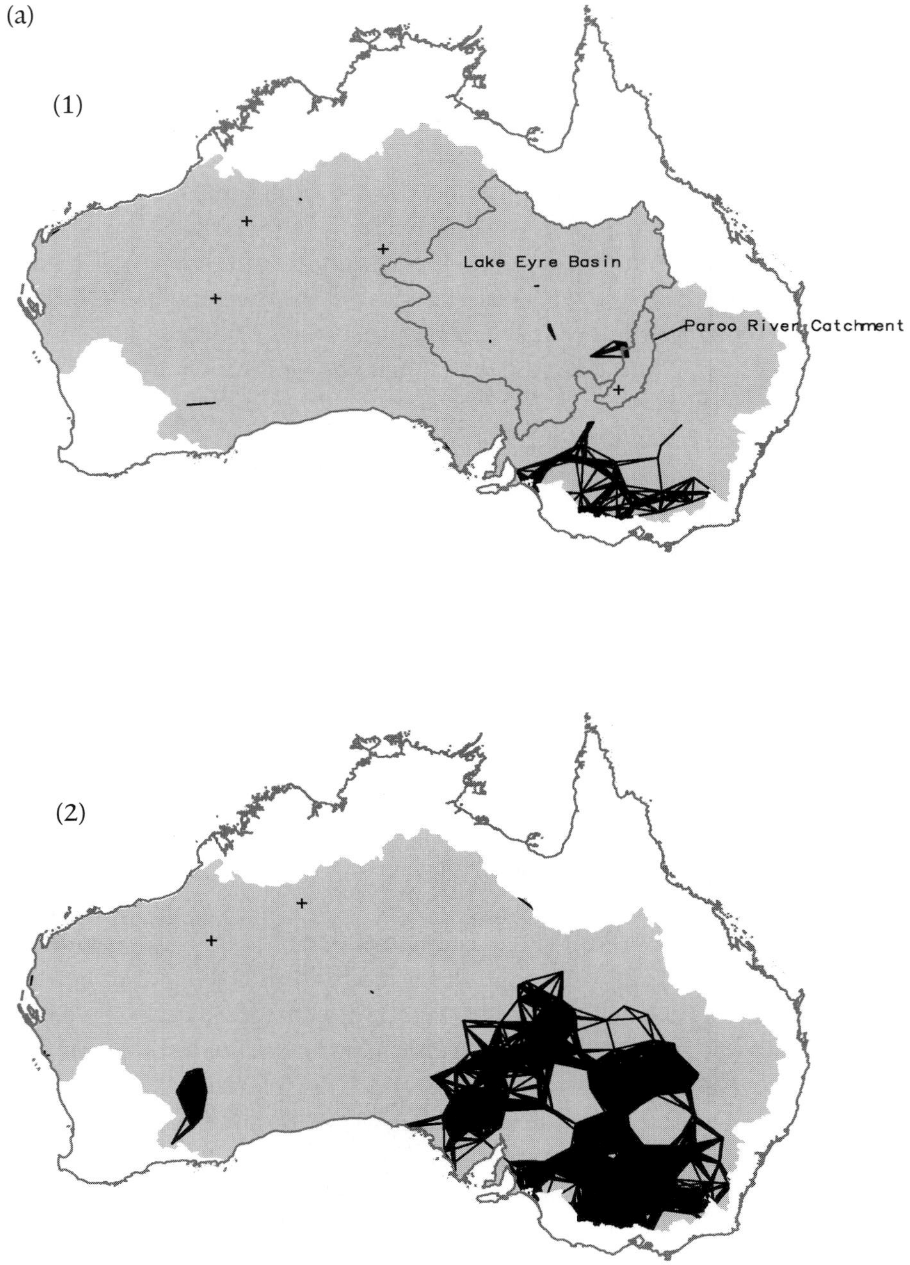

FIGURE 2.3
Patterns of connectivity among wetlands in the Australian arid zone. (a) Connectivity at a dispersal distance of 200 km in (1) March 1988 (dry period) and (2) September 1990 (wet period).

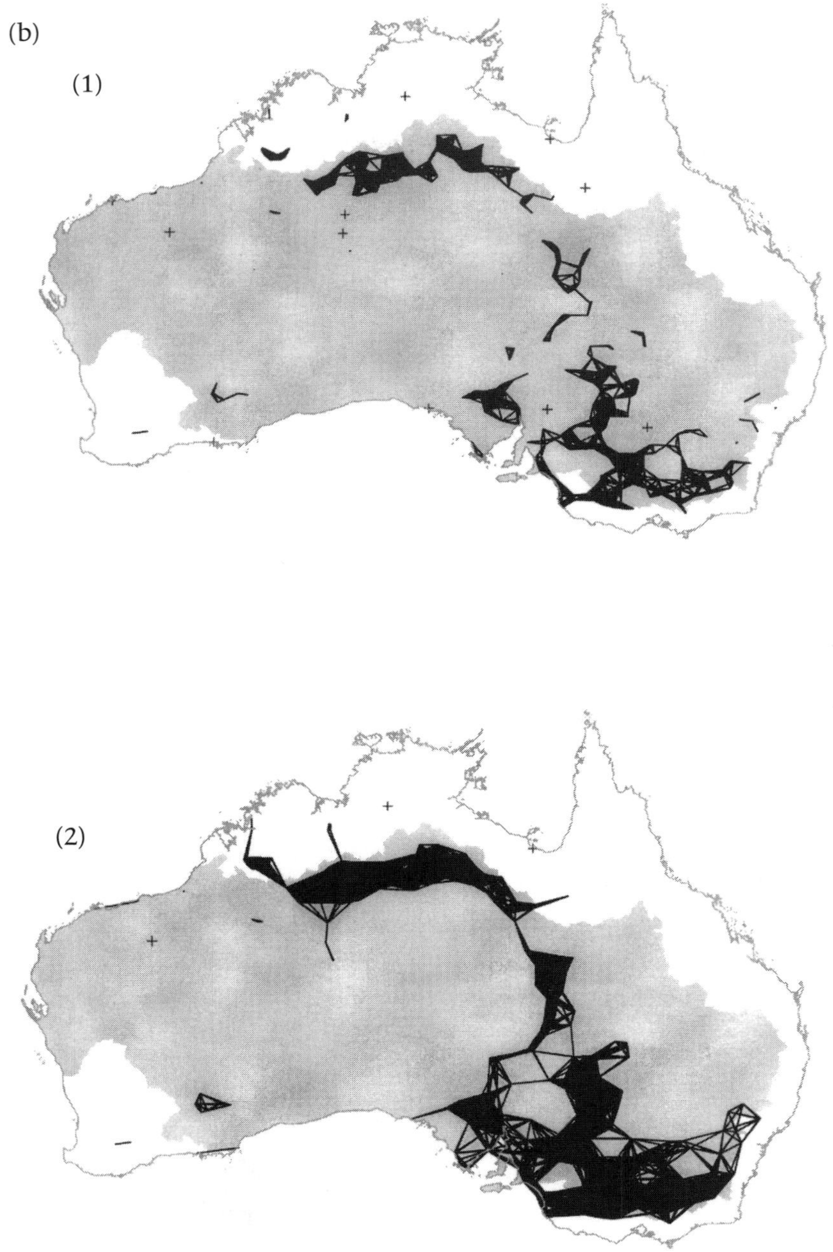

FIGURE 2.3 (*cont.*)
(b) Connectivity among wetlands after heavy monsoon rains in northern Australia in March 1993, given dispersal distances of (1) 100 km, and (2) 200 km. From Roshier (1999); see also Roshier *et al.* (2001).

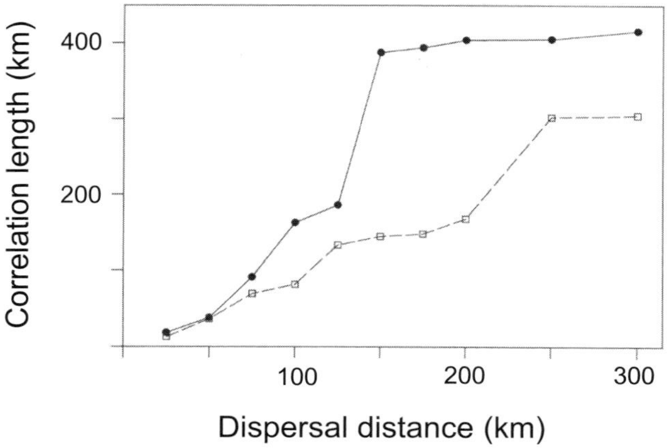

FIGURE 2.4
Relationship between wetland connectivity in the Australian arid zone (indexed by correlation length, a measure that combines the size and number of clusters of wetlands in an area with their spatial configuration; Keitt *et al.*, 1997) and individual dispersal distance for March 1987 (a relatively dry period) (•) and June 1987 (when the dry period had continued and the distribution and abundance of wetlands had declined) (□). From Roshier (1999) and Roshier *et al.* (2001).

example, the importance of internationally significant wetlands to waterbirds is based on the regularity with which a given wetland supports significant numbers of waterbirds or portions of waterbird populations (Davis, 1994), and most waterbird conservation efforts are therefore focused on areas that have high seasonal abundance (Haig *et al.*, 1998). Certainly such areas are important, but they are only part of the picture. Waterbirds may move over large areas, their abundance in a particular wetland may vary dramatically within a short period of time due to regional changes in wetland availability, and species that differ in dispersal capabilities may respond at quite different scales. Because of the broad-scale patterns of varying connectivity among wetlands, human land- or water-use practices that affect one part of the wetland web could easily impact populations over much wider areas. Decisions about resource management or the design of conservation reserves that consider only local effects are inappropriate for wide-ranging and nomadic species (Woinarski *et al.*, 1992; Roshier, 1999).

2.3.3 Grazing in arid and semi-arid rangelands

In many arid and semi-arid regions of the world, native grasslands and shrublands are extensively grazed by domestic livestock. Management of these rangelands is usually focused on maximizing livestock production and economic returns over a several-year period. Grazing often alters the structure and composition of rangeland vegetation and redistributes resources within and among vegetation patches, and the effects of these changes on the ecology and biodiversity of rangeland ecosystems vary in space, time, and scale (Friedel and James, 1995; Ash and Stafford Smith, 1996; Stafford Smith, 1996; Wallace and Dyer, 1996; Milchunas *et al.*, 1998; Bestelmeyer and Wiens, 2001). This is where landscape ecology comes in.

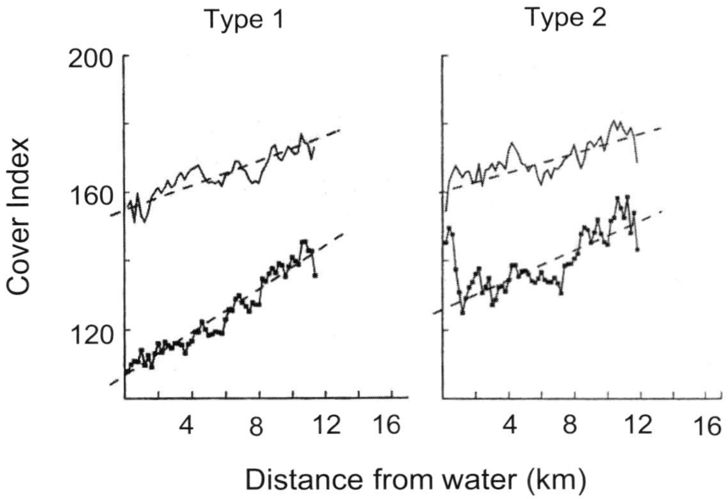

FIGURE 2.5
Mean values of a vegetation cover index derived from LANDSAT MSS imagery as a function of increasing distance from a water source in a large cattle-grazing paddock in central Australia. Landscape type 1 is attractive for grazing but has been historically degraded and suffers moderate to severe erosion, whereas landscape type 2 is less attractive for grazing and less prone to erosional degradation, and it contains more trees (mulga, *Acacia aneura*) and shrubs, especially near the water source. The change in cover-index values between 1983 (—) and 1985 (■) largely represents the loss of cover of ephemeral and perennial herbage from an exceptionally wet period to a dry period. From Pickup and Bastin (1997).

Patch quality to livestock, for example, varies with palatability and nutritional value of vegetation (Senft *et al.*, 1987), and water availability varies spatially as well. Grazing management often involves providing water at fixed sources (e.g., bores, tanks), where livestock concentrate their grazing. Consequently, the density of animals and the magnitude of grazing impacts vary inversely with distance from water (Stafford Smith and Pickup, 1990; Bestelmeyer and Wiens, 1996; James *et al.*, 1999; Nash *et al.*, 1999). The uneven distribution of grazing can create spatial patterns in the landscape that have cascading effects on the distribution and abundance of other organisms (Bestelmeyer and Wiens, 1996; James *et al.*, 1999). The reduction in vegetation coverage near the water source (e.g., Fig. 2.5) may alter the distribution of rainfall runoff and change patterns of soil erosion (Bastin *et al.*, 1993; Friedel and James, 1995; Ludwig *et al.*, 1997). In dry seasons or years, individuals may forage more widely and degradation of vegetation near the water source may be more severe than in wet periods (Fig. 2.5; Pickup and Bastin, 1997; Illius and O'Connor, 1999; James *et al.*, 1999). These effects may vary among landscapes depending on rangeland productivity, food preferences of the livestock, or proportions of woody and non-woody vegetation (Pickup, 1994; Pickup and Bastin, 1997).

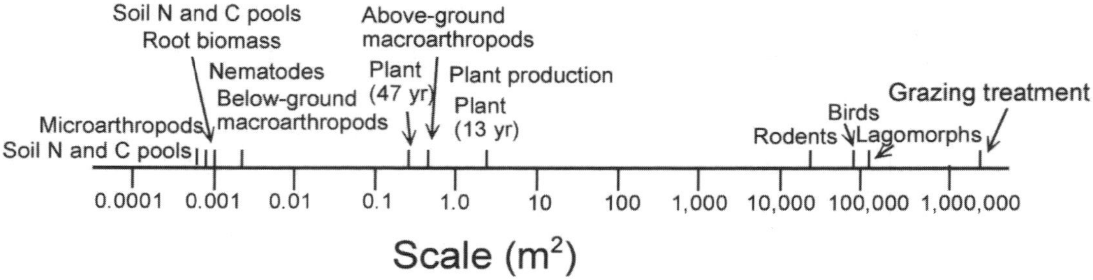

FIGURE 2.6
The scales at which different organisms or ecosystem properties have been studied to determine their responses to grazing-intensity treatments at the Shortgrass Steppe LTER (Long-Term Ecological Research) site in northeastern Colorado. From Table 1 in Milchunas *et al.* (1998).

These spatially dependent grazing patterns may have effects that extend beyond the vegetation–herbivore interaction. In the Argentine Chaco, for example, ant diversity was greater in both intensely grazed areas close to water sources and in lightly grazed areas farther away than in areas subjected to intermediate grazing pressures, largely because of changes in the occurrence of dominant ant taxa among the areas (Bestelmeyer and Wiens, 1996). In other areas, however, ant communities are affected less by grazing intensity than by soil features (Bestelmeyer and Wiens, 2001). In the shortgrass steppe of Colorado, some taxa, such as macroarthropods and birds, changed in abundance and species composition in response to differences in grazing intensity, whereas other groups (e.g., rodents, microarthropods, nematodes) changed little (Milchunas *et al.*, 1998). Although it is difficult to generalize about the effects of grazing on different taxa, it is clear that variations in patch quality, the structure of landscapes, and the spatial pattern of land-use practices (e.g., drilling of bores, construction of fencelines, placement of feed) determine the distribution of grazing and its impacts on biodiversity (Friedel and James, 1995; Brown and Ash, 1996; Stafford Smith, 1996; James *et al.*, 1999).

Grazing effects are also sensitive to the scales on which grazing levels are designated, grazing effects are measured, and landscape heterogeneity is expressed. Stocking rates of livestock and grazing impacts are usually assessed at the scale of entire paddocks. For example, Milchunas *et al.* (1998) based their evaluation of the effects of livestock grazing on shortgrass steppe rangelands largely on comparisons among 130-ha paddocks subjected to different stocking rates, but measurements of the responses to grazing by different components of the system were made at quite different scales (Fig. 2.6). Their conclusion that many components of this ecosystem are generally insensitive to grazing may be correct, but it rests on the assumptions that grazing pressures are evenly distributed over the paddock as a whole and that any scale-dependencies in the responses of system components will be neutralized by the uniformity of the grazing treatment. It is clear, however, that grazing is not evenly distributed in the large paddocks or open ranges that are used as management units in low-productivity arid and semi-arid rangelands (Coughenour, 1991; Pickup and Stafford Smith, 1993). Differences in the fine-scale distribution of grazing can affect system characteristics at the broad scale of entire paddocks or landscapes (Brown and Ash, 1996). The customary scale of grazing management (a paddock of tens to thousands of ha) therefore may not coincide with the scales of grazing activities, grazing impacts, or the responses of various components of the ecosystem. Consequently, different parts of the landscape contained within a single management unit may have quite different dynamics (Friedel, 1994). Management that assumes uniform grazing over entire paddocks or that fails to consider scaling effects, or that measures grazing impacts at inappropriate or incompatible scales, may reach conclusions that ultimately compromise the stability and persistence of grazing systems (Coughenour, 1991).

Then there is the matter of thresholds. The changes in system properties that accompany changes in grazing intensity are often nonlinear. In the Argentine Chaco, for example, the level of vegetation degradation due to grazing changes abruptly at roughly 1 km from a water source (Bestelmeyer and Wiens, 1996). Both goats and cattle graze these systems, but the goats range only 1 km from water during their daily movements, whereas the cattle move much farther. The spatial threshold in degradation is due to shift from multi-species to single-species grazing with increasing distance from water. In other situations, changes in grazing intensity can produce broad-scale, threshold changes in vegetation composition that are essentially irreversible (Noy-Meir, 1975; Friedel, 1991; Laycock, 1991; Ludwig and Tongway, 1995; Schwinning and Parsons, 1999). Thus, heavy grazing in the Sahel of Africa (Sinclair and Fryxell, 1985; Rietkerk *et al.*, 1996), the desert grasslands of the southwestern United States (Schlesinger *et al.*, 1990), and central Australian rangelands (Ludwig *et al.*, 1997, 2000) has led to sudden, "catastrophic" vegetation shifts and soil degradation (van de Koppel *et al.*, 1997). Intense grazing removes vegetation, causing greater precipitation runoff and increasing soil erosion. Scarce resources are transported downslope to lower-lying areas or are intercepted by patches of vegetation, increasing the spatial heterogeneity of soil water and nutrient resources and reducing the net availability of these resources in the system as a whole. In the Australian rangelands, such "runoff–runon" dynamics concentrate soil resources in the vegetated patches (Ludwig *et al.*, 2000), increasing plant production and promoting the growth of trees. At a threshold level of greater grazing pressure, however, the integrity of the vegetated patches may be destroyed. Runoff and erosion increase, the system may lose much of its nutrient capital, and rangeland productivity is reduced. In the desert grasslands of New Mexico, the areas in which nutrients have accumulated may be invaded by shrubs and nutrient cycling becomes increasingly restricted to the zone beneath the shrubs (Schlesinger *et al.*, 1990; Friedel, 1994). In both cases, a small incremental change in grazing intensity can move the system across a threshold into a different state. In arid and semi-arid systems, the feedbacks between plants and soil may be especially important in setting such thresholds, and the likelihood of a system passing a threshold and suffering a potentially irreversible change may depend on soil type and the form of plant-growth limitation (water vs. nutrients; Rietkerk *et al.*, 1997; van de Koppel *et al.*, 1997).

Such threshold dynamics lie at the heart of a paradigm shift that has occurred in rangeland grazing management over the past decade or two. Rather than viewing rangelands as equilibrium systems in which stocking rates can be optimized in relation to carrying capacity, managers now recognize the temporally variable, non-equilibrium nature of these systems and the need to adjust stocking rates opportunistically (Ellis and Swift, 1988; Westoby *et al.*, 1989; Stafford Smith and Pickup, 1993; Ash and Stafford Smith, 1996; Stafford Smith, 1996). The "state-and-transition" framework (Westoby *et al.*, 1989; Walker, 1993; Bellamy and Brown, 1994), for example, recognizes that rangeland ecosystems can exist in several alternative, relatively stable, states, with events such as rainfall or heavy grazing triggering sudden transitions between states. This framework has proven to be very useful in guiding opportunistic grazing management (Grice and MacLeod, 1994), but it considers only variation in time, not in space (Walker, 1993; Brown, 1994; Ludwig and Tongway, 1997). A comparable shift in thinking is required with respect to spatial variation.

Several elements of this shift seem clear. First, grazed lands should no longer be viewed as spatially homogeneous management units in which grazing is uniformly distributed. Instead, the interplay between spatial patterns of grazing activity and the structural configuration of landscapes should be explicitly recognized. Second, because the scale of management units may not capture important ecological processes, a multi-scale perspective is needed to assess the impacts of grazing (or other factors) on ecosystems (e.g., Gibson *et al.*, 1993). Third, because simple land-use decisions such as the provisioning of watering points can have far-reaching effects, the spatial aspects of land use become important. Fourth, because properties of rangeland landscapes may exhibit strong threshold dynamics in response to grazing, it is necessary to consider how the stocking rates that produce these thresholds vary with environmental conditions or landscape types. Finally, sustainable management of rangelands for both conservation values and economic returns will need to consider livestock grazing as a form of disturbance and manage it accordingly. Strategies should be developed that maintain spatial heterogeneity at multiple scales so that most species will be able to find some part of the landscape that permits their persistence (Milchunas *et al.*, 1998; James *et al.*, 1999).

Many rangeland managers and pastoralists have appreciated these points for years. In some cases they have been incorporated into management practices, at least implicitly. Both landscape ecologists and resource managers need to consider how these points, and the broader principles of landscape ecology, can be made a more central feature of rangeland management. One particularly effective way to accomplish this integration may be through the use of computer models that link the dynamics of livestock, stocking rates, range condition, climate, and economics together in ways that are actually helpful to managers and, ultimately, pastoralists (see, e.g., Ash and Stafford Smith, 1996; Johnston *et al.*, 1996a, b; Atkins *et al.*, 1999; www.rangeways.org.au).

2.3.4 Synthesis

Overall, these case studies illustrate how the basic themes of landscape ecology can affect how the nature and dynamics of ecological systems are viewed, and thus how they can be managed. Landscape structure and configuration produce both heterogeneities and complex spatial interactions in ecological systems at all hierarchical levels, from individual organisms to ecosystems. The processes that produce ecological structure and dynamics vary not only in space, but with scale as well. Moreover, the form of scale-dependency and the effects of landscape structure and configuration on ecological systems often display distinct thresholds. The rules of the ecological game change, but it is difficult to predict when or where such changes will occur. Simulation models can predict specific threshold points given precise rules for organism movement and dispersal (e.g., With and Crist, 1995). However, it is often these fundamental details of life history and behavior of organisms that limit our ability to forecast thresholds before they are crossed. Because thresholds are likely to be organism-specific, the challenge becomes even more daunting when one considers the task of multi-species management.

Despite this complexity, some preliminary guidance is possible. In stochastic systems, thresholds are best thought of as regions rather than discrete points (Lamberson *et al.*, 1992; Case, 2000). That is, functions characterizing the behavior of dynamic processes (e.g., a species persistence likelihood) do not show discrete shifts at a given value of some independent variable (e.g., amount of suitable habitat). Rather, there is a region in which the rate of change is accelerated relative to points distant from that threshold. This fact suggests that close monitoring of key ecological processes or species may be able to detect accelerated rates of change and allow intervention before irreversible change has occurred.

2.4 Issues in resource management

The case studies described above indicate that, to varying degrees, there is an increasing awareness of the importance of a landscape perspective in resource management. Indeed, many areas of resource management have undergone shifts in perspectives in recent years (Haynes *et al.*, 1996; Boyce and Hanley, 1997). These changes can, for convenience, be cast as a series of issues contrasting "old" versus "new" approaches. If landscape ecology is to contribute to ecologically informed resource management, it must have something to say on these issues.

2.4.1 Management units vs. mosaics

Traditionally, resource management focused on specified units (e.g., "plots," "habitats," "stands," "treatments," "allotments," "paddocks," "reserves") to the exclusion of the surroundings of those units. Such units were treated as if they were internally homogeneous and closed to external influences, and management operationally presumed that all of the critical components and processes needed to maintain the system or meet the management objectives were contained within the units. The relatively broad scale of these management units (tens of ha to tens of km^2; Fig. 2.1) was taken to assure that these conditions were met.

Managers and management agencies have recently begun to shift toward "mosaic management," in which spatial heterogeneity and the effects of external factors are explicitly considered (Franklin and Forman, 1987; Haynes *et al.*, 1996; Reid, 1996; COS, 1999; Crow, 1999). The focus on "habitat" as a unitary property in wildlife management, for example, has given way to an approach that recognizes that wildlife populations may depend on a variety of different elements of a landscape which must be evaluated at different spatial scales (e.g., Johnson, 1980; Lint *et al.*, 1999; Rolstad, 1999). With this comes the recognition that the way these elements are arrayed in space – the structure and configuration of the landscape – may have important consequences. For example, the final conservation strategy for the northern spotted owl is best portrayed as a map that explicitly shows the size, shape, location, and number of late-seral forest patches that collectively constitute the reserve design (Noon and McKelvey, 1996).

2.4.2 Species vs. ecosystems

Until recently, most management efforts dealing with wildlife or conservation were directed toward particular species that were of interest because of their recreational value (e.g., white-tailed deer [*Odocioleus virginianus*], ruffed grouse [*Bonasa umbellus*]), their status as predators or pests (e.g., coyotes [*Canis latrans*], prairie dogs [*Cynomys ludovicianus*]), or their rare or endangered population status (e.g., spotted owls, black-footed ferrets [*Mustella nigripes*]). With a renewed emphasis on the value of biodiversity, managers have increasingly recognized that a species-by-species approach is often not practical, and emphasis has shifted toward broader management targets. "Ecosystem management" has become not only a legislated objective, but a new buzzword in the lexicon of ecologists (see Christensen *et al.*, 1996 and the associated responses; Boyce and Hanley, 1997). "Ecosystems," however, are ultimately defined by basic processes such as energy flow and mineral cycling, and their boundaries are therefore not readily visible. In practice, the operational focus of ecosystem management is frequently "habitat," usually defined by the dominant vegetation type. There is clearly a risk that, in expanding from a species to an ecosystem emphasis, the traditional approach to management units that ignores landscape structure, temporal and spatial scale, and environmental and demographic thresholds will be perpetuated (cf. Simberloff, 1998).

Of course, the dichotomy of species vs. ecosystem management is ultimately false. Even if the management focus is on a particular species, that species is not divorced from the web of processes that operate at the ecosystem level, nor can ecosystem processes be separated from the functional properties of the species that produce them. Effective management must consider these interconnections. Nonetheless, the hope persists that the emphasis on species might be retained without having to consider the impossibly large number of species that contribute to biodiversity. This has led to the suggestion that some focal species, variously termed "indicator species," "keystone species," "ecological engineers," "umbrella species," or "link species" (Lambeck, 1997; Simberloff, 1998; COS, 1999), might serve as surrogates for a much broader suite of functionally similar species, or as indicators of the overall integrity or "health" of the larger ecological system. In most instances, the suggested focal species operate over relatively broad scales. The rationale is that, by preserving their habitats, "the ecosystem" will somehow be preserved and the elements of biodiversity that operate on finer scales will be sheltered. Usually such focal species are charismatic vertebrates. For example, Noon and Bingham (in press) have argued that, because of its large area requirements, its use of many late-seral forest types, and its diverse habitat needs, the spotted owl can act as an umbrella for many other species associated with late-seral forest in the Pacific

Northwest. If this is so, then meeting the habitat requirements of the owl may address the needs of other species with smaller area requirements and more specific habitat preferences (Berger, 1997).

Quite apart from the problem that the selection of an appropriate focal species depends on which functions or system properties are emphasized, the selection of focal species usually ignores the fact that by far the bulk of the species in any ecosystem are small invertebrates that respond to landscape structure at fine scales (Ponder and Lunney, 1999). It is not certain that managing "habitat" for wide-ranging species at broad spatial scales will adequately capture the factors and processes that determine the distribution and abundance of the many species that operate at much finer scales. By adopting a broad-scale perspective, critical thresholds in the environmental responses of such species may be overlooked. Rather than defining focal species in terms of their broad scales of operation, their presumed functional roles in ecosystem dynamics, or their charisma, it may make more sense to search for species that respond to landscape structure and change on similar scales as other species (Wiens, 2001).

2.4.3 Yield vs. sustainability

For some time, the primary goal of resource management was maximizing yield, and the effectiveness of management was gauged in terms of overall production, extraction efficiency, or economic return from some natural product. Harvest levels of wildlife or forest resources or stocking rates on grazed lands were set by some determination of how much pressure the resource could bear, generally over a relatively short time period. Determinations of renewal rates were central to this approach and notions such as "carrying capacity" suggested that site factors and intrinsic characteristics of the resource combined to determine a fixed yield. The primary tools in wildlife management, for example, were based on mathematical models of population dynamics (e.g., Getz and Haight, 1989; Clark, 1990) that emphasized age structure, recruitment rates, and mortality. Forest management traditionally relied on the concept of maximum sustainable yield. Such models generally assumed that temporal and spatial variation were unimportant, and that scale did not matter (Clark, 1990).

Over the past decade, both the temporal and spatial perspectives of management have changed, and "ecological sustainability" has become the new management goal. Broadly stated, the goal is to preserve species diversity and productivity by maintaining the composition, structure, and processes characteristic of an area or ecosystem (COS, 1999). The notion of "sustainability" is scale-dependent: what is sustainable at a local scale may not be at a regional scale. Moreover, what it is that should be sustained inevitably entails value judgments, whether based on science or other criteria (Lélé and Norgaard, 1996). In the end, "sustainability" is "one of those commonly used words which convey a sense of meaning but which evade a consistent quantitative definition" (Pickup and Stafford Smith, 1993).

The shift in management thinking toward sustainability carries with it the recognition that systems vary through time and extraction rates must be adjusted accordingly. How such variability is incorporated into management, however, may differ among systems. Where the coupling between environmental conditions and resource dynamics is relatively tight, such adjustments may be straightforward. For example, for a long time bag limits for waterfowl hunters in migratory flyways in the United States and Canada have been set on an annual basis in relation to climatic and wetland conditions in migratory and breeding areas, with considerable success (but see Johnson and Williams, 1999). Where environmental conditions are more severe and less predictable, or where time lags in responses to environmental changes are long (e.g., in low-productivity, arid rangelands), tuning extraction rates to variation in the system may not be feasible. In these situations, conservative set harvest rates may be the most realistic. Long-term sustainability of resources demands that the natural variability of a system be considered over long time frames.

Achieving sustainability also shifts attention to the spatial linkages that influence the production and stability of a resource. Sustainable management of forests, for example, aims at the maintenance of a certain composition and structure of forest stands over broad areas (Seymour and Hunter, 1999). Such management can be severely compromised by natural events such as blowdown or wildfire. The sensitivity of a forest stand to blowdown or the likelihood that a wildfire will spread, however, are influenced by the structure and configuration of the surrounding landscape mosaic, at multiple scales (Sato and Iwasa, 1993; Turner *et al.*, 1997a; Foster *et al.*, 1998; Lertzman and Fall, 1999). The example of grazing systems discussed above also shows that the functional and spatial linkages of resources and the environment may be sensitive to thresholds that, once passed, move the system into a different state. Temporal variability, spatial variability, and threshold dynamics all impose formidable constraints on managing for ecological sustainability.

2.4.4 Equilibrium vs. natural variation and disturbance

The approaches to management that developed during the 1960s to1980s relied on the assumption that resources could be managed with reference to a fixed equilibrium or target state, such as carrying capacity. Indeed, management often included suppression of natural variations such as forest fires or outbreaks of defoliating insects, enhancing the equilibrium perspective. During the 1970s, however, the ecological paradigm of equilibrium began to crumble (Wu and Loucks, 1995), and now most ecologists (and an increasing number of resource managers) recognize that natural systems are variable and that disturbance is an important natural process that should be incorporated into rather than excluded from management policies. Indeed, "new management" attempts to mimic the disturbance processes that characterize natural ecosystems. This requires an understanding of the historical range of variability (HRV) of an ecosystem (Haila, 1995; Cissel *et al.*, 1999; Landres *et al.*, 1999; Lertzman and Fall, 1999; Seymour and Hunter, 1999; Spies and Turner, 1999). The concept of HRV relates to the frequency distribution of environmental conditions, including disturbances of various sorts, that have characterized a resource or ecosystem over some period of past history (COS, 1999). The underlying premise is that the habitat conditions most likely to conserve native species or foster natural resources are those under which they evolved. Management that maintains the ecosystem within this HRV, then, should create the conditions for sustainability. It is often difficult, however, to separate the effects of natural variability from human impacts (Dayton *et al.*, 1998). Some of the concerns about anthropogenic effects on the environment center on whether human actions have pushed a system beyond the HRV, and thus beyond a threshold of sustainability.

Common sense, observations, and hierarchy theory all suggest that as the scale on which a system is viewed is expanded, the dynamics will generally occur more slowly. As a consequence, landscapes at broad scales may give the appearance of equilibrium, at least over the conventional time frames of management. This might lead one to believe that the assumptions of equilibrium-based theory are met and recent concerns about variability are unjustified. This conclusion would be wrong on two counts. First, there is mounting evidence that infrequent but large disturbances have profound and lasting impacts on ecological systems at many scales (Turner *et al.*, 1997a; Dale *et al.*, 1998). For example, in central Australia, rainfall events beyond our modern comprehension have occurred within the last 700–2000 years, and the resulting floods radically rearranged the landscape (Pickup, 1991). Much depends on how the "historic" in HRV is defined. Second, the relative stability of a landscape at broad scales may obscure the substantial variation that occurs at finer scales in both time and space, but it is at these finer scales that many of the organisms of interest actually respond to environmental conditions.

Management of ecosystems within an HRV perspective may also serve to increase the compatibility of human activities with management objectives. So long as human land (or water) use does not modify the structure or composition of landscapes too much, the ecosystem may remain within the domain of natural variability and the important ecological processes that contribute to sustainability may be maintained. This is the rationale behind ecologically sensitive approaches to timber harvesting or rangeland grazing. At some point, however, human land use may disturb the system beyond the boundaries of the HRV; at this threshold, the adaptational limits of the component species may be exceeded and the degradation of the system (from a management perspective) may become permanent. This is obvious, for example, when timber harvest or excessive grazing on steep slopes leads to loss of soil and a permanent reduction in the potential of that part of the landscape to produce resources of interest or to contribute to the conservation of natural biodiversity. Sometimes, however, it may be difficult to determine when a degradation threshold has been passed. In the Argentine Chaco, for example, extreme overgrazing close to water sources has removed so much of the vegetation that the intensely grazed zones show clearly on satellite images. Nonetheless, these portions of the landscape harbor ant species not found elsewhere and contribute to meso-scale ant community diversity (Bestelmeyer and Wiens, 1996). While it may sometimes be necessary to exclude human activities from managed areas to achieve conservation goals, in other situations it may be more effective to manage a broader landscape mosaic that includes both natural areas and human land uses.

2.4.5 Ecological integrity and ecological scales

All of the elements of resource-management philosophy that have emerged over the past decade or two – the emphasis on mosaics rather than management units, on ecosystems rather than species, on sustainability rather than yield, on variability rather than equilibrium – are combined under the banner of "ecological integrity." Increasingly, maintenance of ecological integrity is championed as the most comprehensive and ecologically sound goal of management (Haynes *et al.*, 1996; COS, 1999). A system has ecological integrity when it can maintain its structure and function, total diversity, functional organization, and critical processes (Norton, 1992). These conditions are presumed to make the ecosystem resistant to stresses imposed by changes in environmental conditions and capable of rapid recovery – it is sustainable. When the ecological integrity of an ecosystem is compromised, it becomes more susceptible to thresholds of anthropogenic environmental change.

The concept of ecological integrity is complex. It includes ecological processes at all levels of ecological organization and acknowledges the dynamic nature of ecological systems and natural processes, including disturbance. Nonetheless, several operational measures of ecological integrity have been proposed, most focused on aquatic ecosystems (e.g., De Leo and Levin, 1997). At fine scales, assessments of ecological integrity emphasize the structural and compositional aspects of ecological systems related to individual species and their dynamics. At broader scales, the focus is on processes such as primary productivity, nutrient cycling, and hydrological regimes, and less attention is given to the composition and structure of the systems from which these processes emerge (COS, 1999).

The differences among the criteria used to measure ecological integrity at different scales indicate one of the weaknesses of the concept. The focus depends on the scale, yet landscape ecology tells us clearly that patterns and processes at multiple scales may all be important in ecosystem functioning (e.g., Fig. 2.1). The use of measures of integrity focused on any particular scale (or level of ecological organization) therefore may not include important relationships among elements occurring at other scales – integrity at one scale does not assure integrity at other scales. The spatial heterogeneity of landscapes also complicates matters. If indeed the linkages and interactions among the elements in a landscape mosaic can have important effects on individual movements, population dynamics, species distributions and abundances, community structure, or disturbance spread, then "integrity" must be applied to the landscape mosaic as a whole.

Aldo Leopold once observed that "to keep every cog and wheel is the first precaution of intelligent tinkering" (Leopold, 1953: 147). It is not altogether clear that ecological systems *do* require all the pieces (i.e., species) in order to function within normal bounds and retain their integrity (Walker, 1992; Dayton *et al.*, 1998). Often, however, the focus of management or conservation is on particular pieces (e.g., an endangered species or resource of substantial economic value). The focus of "ecological integrity" then becomes ambiguous. A priority for landscape ecologists and resource managers is to develop measures of ecological integrity that recognize the effects of scale and heterogeneity, deal with both the species composition and functional properties of ecosystems, and apply to entire landscapes (Reid, 1996).

2.5 Implications and guidelines for multi-scale landscape management

One could easily conclude from this chapter that the primary contribution of landscape ecology to resource management so far has been to make life much more difficult for the manager. The central themes of landscape ecology – that spatial structure and configuration matter, scale matters, and thresholds matter – create complexities and uncertainties. Although there may be situations in which effective management may be accomplished without dealing with these complexities, we suspect that they are few. Ecologically sensitive management requires that the complexities of real landscapes and their dynamics be considered *before* concluding that they can be ignored in a particular management situation.

Managers, however, are rarely in a position to dwell on the esoterica of scientific studies or the abstractions of ecological theory. They have neither the time nor the knowledge to conduct the experiments that might reveal exactly how landscape structure or scale might affect the outcomes of a particular management practice. They would like ecologists to tell them exactly what needs to be done, so that they can at least try to do it. Ideally, they would like to have a set of "rules of thumb," such as "If landscape heterogeneity is increased by *x*%, biodiversity will increase by *y*%," or "Maintaining the coverage of suitable habitat in a landscape above *z*% will prevent the habitat from becoming fragmented for organisms that are smaller than 10 g." For example, alternatives for managing northern spotted owl habitat in the Pacific Northwest have been cast as "rules" that specify particular management practices. The "50–11–40 rule," which applies to forests outside of specified habitat conservation areas, states that in each quarter township (~23 km^2) 50% of the forest must be maintained in stands where the trunk diameter at breast height is ≥11 in (28 cm) and the forest canopy is closed over at least 40% of the area (Thomas *et al.*, 1990). The "40–20–40 rule", which applies to much of the remaining forest in the region, requires maintenance of 40% canopy closure over 40% of each watershed, with the bottoms of tree crowns averaging at least 20 ft (6 m) above the forest floor. Although they are not spatially explicit, these "rules" recognize the importance of general features of landscape structure at specified scales, and they were developed to provide habitat that would maintain owls above a population-viability threshold. The "rules" were also developed after many years of intensive study of the owls and the forests, innumerable committee deliberations, and thousands of pages of government reports. They have contributed to the management practices and constraints on allowable land uses that have been implemented on public lands in the Pacific Northwest (FEMAT, 1993). Although it is still too early to assess the adequacy of these conservation measures for owl persistence, a recent meta-analysis of owl survival based on long-term monitoring data indicated that annual survival probabilities of adult females no longer exhibited a negative trend (Franklin *et al.*, 1999), in contrast to the findings of a 1993 meta-analysis (Burnham *et al.*, 1996). Based on demographic parameters across studies, however, the population of territorial females has shown a 3.9% annual rate of decline through 1998. Thus, there is still considerable uncertainty regarding the long-term viability of the northern spotted owl.

The spotted owl case is an anomaly, however. Rarely do we have such detailed knowledge on which to base management options. Instead, management must often be implemented with the barest of information. Given the attendant uncertainties, the development of specific "rules" or prescriptions for management action is therefore both unrealistic and unwise. Instead, a series of explicit but general guidelines may be most useful (cf. Schroeder *et al.*, 1998; Schroeder and Askerooth, 1999). Such guidelines should generally follow the approach defined by Christensen (1997), Rogers (1997), Talbot (1997), Walters (1997), and others: establish management goals, identify management options, assess management performance, and adjust the management approach. To be effective in a world full of heterogeneities, scale-dependency, and thresholds, however, such guidelines must also include an explicit consideration of the landscape ecology themes that we have developed in this chapter (see Frank and Wissel, 1998).

Our suggested guidelines (Table 2.1) are self-explanatory. Obviously, one must begin by specifying the resource of interest and the management objectives. Before going any farther, however, it is essential to consider which scales are likely to be important, both to achieve the management objectives and to acknowledge the scaling properties of the biological system. Unless this is done, an otherwise excellent management plan may be doomed to fail because it is inappropriately scaled. The problem, of course, is that management units are normally much larger than the scales on which the greater share of the earth's biodiversity operates and on which relevant spatial variation in landscape features is expressed. Indeed, the incongruence of the scales of management with the temporal and spatial scales of ecological processes "presents perhaps the most daunting challenge to ecosystem management" (Christensen, 1997; see also Pringle, 1997; Chapter 18, this book). Because the scales of the elements of ecological systems are intrinsic to the system, one can't impose a management scale on Nature and expect Nature to make the necessary adjustments. Rather, the scale(s) of management should be adjusted to encompass the range of scales that are relevant to *both* the organisms and the management goals.

This challenge isn't entirely hopeless. The myriad of organisms and landscape patterns found in Nature does not necessarily imply that an equally large myriad of scales must be considered. Organisms that are similar in such features as body mass, physiology, life-history attributes, and ecological functions may operate over similar ranges of scale and respond to the spatial and temporal variations in the environment in similar ways, and it may be possible to derive "scaling functions" that capture and predict these shared relationships (Ludwig *et al.*, 2000; Wiens, 2001). Such scaling functions could help managers decide the domain of scale that would be needed to address a particular problem in a particular type of landscape. Rather than explicitly managing over a broad spectrum of scales, it may be possible to stratify management. For

Table 2.1. *A generalized check-list of steps to be followed in incorporating an awareness of the themes of landscape ecology into the development of practices for the management of natural resources.*

1. Determine the biological resource of interest (e.g., population, species, species group, community, ecosystem, biodiversity).
2. Specify explicit, operationally defined management goals and objectives (e.g., a particular harvest rate, ecological sustainability, population viability, biodiversity conservation).
3. Determine the relevant spatial and temporal scale(s) (grain and extent) to fit the management goals and objectives *and* to recognize the ecological properties of the resource of interest.
4. Stipulate which processes and disturbances are likely to be important at the specified scale(s), and assess their rates or frequency of occurrence.
5. Evaluate and measure landscape structure and configuration.
    A. Identify patches and assess their relative quality.
    B. Characterize patch boundaries (e.g., sharpness, edge:area ratios, permeability to movements).
    C. Characterize the landscape context of the patches using both structural properties (e.g., patch context) and functional properties (e.g., movement rates of organisms, dispersal distances, disturbance spread).
    D. Evaluate landscape connectivity, both structurally (e.g., corridors, fragmentation) and functionally (e.g., movement rates and habitat selection in elements of the mosaic).
6. Evaluate the likelihood and potential consequences of threshold dynamics.
    A. Landscape structure (e.g., fragmentation or connectivity thresholds).
    B. Ecosystem state (e.g., state-and-transition dynamics).
    C. Demographic thresholds.
7. Assess the likelihood and potential consequences of changing land use due to such factors as global climate change, changing economies, or changing societal values.
8. Use information from steps 3–7 to identify management options under current and potential future scenarios.
9. Implement management action(s) on landscape mosaics.
10. Assess whether management practices are meeting the goals and objectives identified in step 2, or whether the management approach should be adjusted or the goals or objectives changed (i.e., adaptive environmental management). This evaluation involves returning to step 2 and re-evaluating each step in the sequence.

example, management of landscape structure at scales of 10–1000 m^2, of ha to km^2, and of 10s-1000s of km^2 might all be part of a nested, stratified management design to maintain the biodiversity of suites of organisms that respond to environmental variation at these scales.

Models may also play an important role in incorporating landscape configuration, thresholds, and scale into management. Turner *et al.* (1997b), for example, used a spatially explicit model to explore the effects of altering or maintaining landscape heterogeneity at different spatial scales on the potential overwinter survival of ungulates in Yellowstone National Park. Many of the projections of the consequences of alternative management practices on spotted owl populations also relied heavily on spatially explicit models (e.g., Fig. 2.2). The technological capacity to model multi-scale environmental relations in detailed spatial arrays is expanding dramatically, so the value of spatially explicit models in exploring the effects of varied landscape configurations is likely to increase. This expanding technology, however, carries with it the risk of substituting complexity in computer models for the complexity of Nature. This may not help to resolve management issues, although the complex models may prove very useful in indicating how much of the complexity of Nature is likely to be important in a given management situation.

Not all models need be spatially explicit to be useful in management. A critical part of management is identifying management options and their consequences, and different sorts of models may help in this arena. Possingham (1997), for example, has outlined how Markov decision theory can be used to assess alternative management strategies for metapopulations in a patchy landscape, and Fordham *et al.* (1997) proposed using integrated scenario modeling to examine the consequences of different management actions. Farmer (Farmer and Parent, 1997; Farmer and Wiens, 1998, 1999) used dynamic optimization models to evaluate the effects of changes in wetland quality and distribution on migratory shorebirds. Broad-based programs that seek to integrate the perspectives of stakeholders, managers, and ecologists into a unified process of evaluating and testing management alternatives, such as the decision support system applied to Kruger National Park in South Africa (Rogers, 1997) or the RANGEWAYS system in Australia (www.rangeways.org.au), are built upon predictive models that include landscape properties. Modeling is also a key component of several of the steps of the adaptive environmental assessment and modeling process (Walters, 1986, 1997).

All of these approaches – modeling, developing scaling functions, proposing management guidelines – can contribute to ecologically sensitive management. Ultimately, however, implementing resource management that is founded on principles of landscape ecology requires effective communication. This isn't easy. The goals, procedures, priorities, and language of ecology differ from those of management, and each has a different perspective on the level of uncertainty about conclusions or practices that is acceptable (Bradshaw and Borchers, 2000). It takes commitment, understanding, and skill to bridge the gap and establish linkages. But everything we have said, and all of the other contributions to this book, indicate quite clearly that the effort must be made.

2.6 Summary

Landscape ecology deals with how the elements in a spatial mosaic are located relative to one another, with how these patterns come about, and with how the spatial configuration and dynamics of landscapes affect ecological patterns and processes. Because of its focus on spatial phenomena, landscape ecology provides an important foundation for the management of natural resources. Land management, after all, occurs in a landscape context, and biological systems respond to these actions over multiple scales.

Landscape ecology is characterized by three general themes: the spatial structure and configuration of landscapes have important consequences, scale matters, and thresholds in the responses of organisms to spatial pattern, or in the physical processes driving those patterns, are ubiquitous. To illustrate these themes, we develop three case studies. Northern spotted owls illustrate a situation in which the dominant land use, timber harvesting, produces dramatic alterations in landscape composition and structure that have profound effects on a single species of extraordinary interest. The use of wetland habitats by wetland birds, on the other hand, involves a different form of landscape change that affects an entire suite of organisms, not all of which respond in similar ways. Finally, grazing on semi-arid rangelands has a clear management focus of maximizing sustainable yield, but the consequences of grazing on rangeland ecosystems and biodiversity show strong spatial effects and important threshold dynamics.

We build on these case studies to consider several ongoing issues in resource management: whether to manage habitat as units or as mosaics; whether to focus on species or ecosystems; whether to emphasize short-term yield or long-term sustainability; whether to view natural systems as being equilibrial or governed by natural variability and disturbance; and how to view the integrity of ecological systems in the context of the scale-dependence that characterizes everything about these systems. Collectively, these issues and case studies show both the importance and the complexity of incorporating a landscape perspective into resource management.

It is all well and good to argue the importance of a landscape perspective in natural resource management, but ultimately managers are concerned with how all of this should be implemented in practice. While recognizing that every management situation is different from every other one in its details, we nonetheless propose that some general guidelines may be useful in ensuring that the potential influences of landscape structure, scale, and thresholds will be considered when evaluating specific management problems. Unless there are strong reasons for thinking otherwise, effective management of natural resources must begin with the assumption that spatial and temporal variation are critically important, and their effects differ at different scales.

Acknowledgments

Our thinking about the intersection of landscape ecology with management has developed through interactions with many colleagues and students over the years, and all have left their marks. An initial draft of this chapter benefited from comments from Mike Coughenour, Margaret Friedel, Greg Hayward, Richard Kingsford, Tasha Kotliar, David Roshier, Rick Schroeder, Jack Ward Thomas, and two anonymous reviewers. We especially appreciate the willingness of David Roshier to allow us to use figures from his PhD dissertation and to modify those figures for this chapter. The research of JAW and BVH on ecological scaling is supported by the United States Environmental Protection Agency (R 826764–01–0).

References

Aber, J., Christensen, N., Fernandez, I., Franklin, J., Hidinger, L., Hunter, M., MacMahon, J., Mladenoff, D., Pastor, J., Perry, D., Slangen, R.,& van Miegroet, H. (2000). *Applying Ecological Principles to Management of the U.S. National Forests*. Ecological Society of America, Washington, D.C.

Addicott, J. F., Aho, J. M., Antolin, M. R., Padilla, D. K., Richardson, J. S., & Soluk, D. A. (1987). Ecological neighborhoods: scaling environmental patterns. *Oikos, 49*: 340–346.

Allen, T. F. H. (1998). The landscape "level" is dead: Persuading the family to take it off the respirator. In *Ecological Scale: Theory and Applications*, eds. D. L. Peterson & V. T. Parker, pp. 35–54. Columbia University Press, New York.

Allen, T. F. H. & Hoekstra, T. W. (1992). *Toward a Unified Ecology*. Columbia University Press, New York.

Allen, T. F. H. & Starr, T. B. (1982). *Hierarchy: Perspectives for Ecological Complexity*. University of Chicago Press, Chicago, IL.

Andersen, A. N. (1997). Functional groups and patterns of organization in North American ant communities: A comparison with Australia. *Journal of Biogeography,* 24: 433–460.

Andrén, H. (1992). Corvid density and nest predation in relation to forest fragmentation: A landscape perspective. *Ecology,* 73: 794–804.

Andrén, H. (1994). Effects of habitat fragmentation in birds and mammals in landscapes with different proportions of suitable habitat: A review. *Oikos,* 71: 355–366.

Ash, A. J. & Stafford Smith, D. M. (1996). Evaluating stocking rate impacts in rangelands: Animals don't practice what we preach. *Rangeland Journal,* 18: 216–243.

Atkins, D., Hunt, L. P., Holm, A. M., Burnside, D. G. & Fitzgerald, D. R. (1999). Land-use values in the goldfields of Western Australia and their use in regional resource use planning. Paper presented at the VIth International Rangeland Congress, Townsville, Australia.

Austin, M. P. (1999). A silent clash of paradigms: some inconsistencies in community ecology. *Oikos, 86*: 170–178.

Barendregt, A., Wassen, M. J. & Schot, P. P. (1995). Hydrological systems beyond a nature reserve, the major problem in wetland conservation of Naardermeer (the Netherlands). *Biological Conservation,* 72: 393–405.

Bastin, G. N., Pickup, G., Chewings, V. H. &

Pearce, G. (1993). Land degradation assessment in central Australia using a grazing gradient method. *Rangeland Journal*, 15: 190–216.

Beier, P. & Noss, R. F. (1998). Do habitat corridors provide connectivity? *Conservation Biology*, 12: 1241–1252.

Bellamy, J. A. & Brown, J. R. (1994). State and transition models for rangelands. 7. Building a state and transition model for management and research on rangelands. *Tropical Grasslands*, 28: 247–255.

Bennett, A. F. (1999). *Linkages in the Landscape: The Role of Corridors and Connectivity in Wildlife Conservation*. IUCN, Gland, Switzerland.

Berger, J. (1997). Population constraints associated with the use of black rhinos as an umbrella species for desert herbivores. *Conservation Biology*, 11: 69–78.

Bestelmeyer, B. T. & Wiens, J. A. (1996). The effects of land use on the structure of ground-foraging ant communities in the Argentine Chaco. *Ecological Applications*, 6: 1225–1240.

Bestelmeyer, B. T. & Wiens, J. A. (2001). Ant biodiversity in semiarid landscape mosaics: the consequences of grazing vs. natural heterogeneity. *Ecological Applications*, 11: 1123–1140.

Bissonette, J. A. (ed.). (1997). *Wildlife and Landscape Ecology: Effects of Pattern and Scale*. Springer-Verlag, New York.

Botkin, D. B. (1990). *Discordant Harmonies: A New Ecology for the Twenty-First Century*. Oxford University Press, New York.

Boyce, M. S. & Hanley, A. (eds.). (1997). *Ecosystem Management: Applications for Sustainable Forest and Wildlife Resources*. Yale University Press, New Haven, CT.

Bradshaw, G. A. & Borchers, J. G. (2000). Uncertainty as information: Narrowing the science-policy gap. *Conservation Ecology*, 4 (1) art 7, www.http://consecol.org/vol4/iss1/art7

Brown, J. R. (1994). State and transition models for rangelands. 2. Ecology as a basis for rangeland management: Performance criteria for testing models. *Tropical Grasslands*, 28: 206–213.

Brown, J. R. & Ash, A. J. (1996). Pastures for prosperity. 4. Managing resources: Moving from sustainable yield to sustainability in tropical rangelands. *Tropical Grasslands*, 30: 47–57.

Bunce, R. G. H. & Jongman, R. H. G. (1993). An introduction to landscape ecology. In *Landscape Ecology and Agroecosystems*, eds. R. G. H. Bunce, L. Ryszkowski, & M. G. Paoletti, pp. 3–10. Lewis Publishers, Boca Raton, FL.

Burnham, K. P., Anderson, D. R. & White, G. C. (1996). Meta-analysis of vital rates of the northern spotted owl. *Studies in Avian Biology*, 17: 92–101.

Case, T. J. (2000). *An Illustrated Guide to Theoretical Ecology*. Oxford University Press, New York.

Chen, J., Franklin, J. F. & Spies, T. A. (1995). Growing season microclimatic gradients extending into old-growth Douglas-fir forests from clearcut edges. *Ecological Applications*, 5: 74–86.

Christensen, N. L. Jr. (1997). Managing for heterogeneity and complexity on dynamic landscapes. In *The Ecological Basis of Conservation. Heterogeneity, Ecosystems, and Biodiversity*, eds. S. T. A. Pickett, R. S. Ostfeld, M. Shachak & G. E. Likens, pp. 167–186. Chapman & Hall, New York.

Christensen, N. L., Bartuska, A. M., Brown, J. H., Carpenter, S., D'Antonio, C., Francis, R., Franklin, J. F., MacMahon, J. A., Noss, R. F., Parsons, D. J., Peterson, C. H., Turner, M. G. & Woodmansee, R. G. (1996). The report of the Ecological Society of America Committee on the Scientific Basis for Ecosystem Management. *Ecological Applications*, 6: 665–691.

Cissel, J. H., Swanson, F. J. & Weisberg, P. J. (1999). Landscape management using historical fire regimes: Blue River, Oregon. *Ecological Applications*, 9: 1217–1231.

Clark, C. W. (1990). *Mathematical Bioeconomics*. New York, John Wiley, New York.

COS [Committee of Scientists] (1999). *Sustaining the People's Lands: Recommendations for Stewardship of the National Forests and Grasslands into the Next Century*. US Department of Agriculture, Washington, D.C.

Coughenour, M. B. (1991). Spatial components of plant–herbivore interactions in pastoral, ranching, and native ungulate ecosystems. *Journal of Range Management*, 44: 530–542.

Crow, T. R. (1999). Landscape ecology and forest management. In *Issues in Landscape Ecology*, eds. J. A. Wiens & M. R. Moss, pp. 94–96. International Association for Landscape Ecology, Guelph, Canada.

Curtis, J. T. (1959). *The Vegetation of Wisconsin: An Ordination of Plant Communities*. University of Wisconsin Press, Madison, WI.

Daily, G. C. & Walker, B. H. (2000). Seeking the great transition. *Nature*, 403: 243–245.

Dale, M. R. T. (1999). *Spatial Pattern Analysis in Plant Ecology*. Cambridge University Press, Cambridge.

Dale, V. H. (1997). The relationship between land-use change and climate change. *Ecological Applications*, 7: 753–769.

Dale, V. H., Lugo, A. E., MacMahon, J. A. & Pickett, S. T. A. (1998). Ecosystem management in the context of large, infrequent disturbances. *Ecosystems*, 1: 546–557.

Dale, V. H., Brown, S., Haeuber, R., Hobbs, N. T., Huntly, N., Naiman, R. J., Riebsame, W. E., Turner, M. G. & Valone, T. (2000). Ecological principles and guidelines for managing the use of land. *Ecological Applications*, 10: 639–670.

Davis, T. J. (1994). *The Ramsar Convention Manual: A Guide to the Convention of Wetlands of International Importance especially as Waterfowl Habitat*. Ramsar Convention Bureau. Gland, Switzerland.

Dayton, P. K., Tegner, M. J., Edwards, P. B. & Riser, K. L. (1998). Sliding baselines, ghosts, and reduced expectations in kelp forest communities. *Ecological Applications*, 8: 309–322.

De Leo, G. A. & Levin, S. (1997). The multifaceted aspects of ecosystem integrity. *Conservation Ecology, 1 (1) art 3*, http://www.consecol.org/Journal/vol1/iss1/art3

Delcourt, H. R., Delcourt, P. A. & Webb, T. (1983). Dynamic plant ecology: the spectrum of vegetational change in space and time. *Quaternary Science Review*, 1: 153–175.

Diamond, J. (1999). *Guns, Germs, and Steel: The Fates of Human Societies*. W.W. Norton, New York.

Ellis, J. E. & Swift, D. M. (1988). Stability of African pastoral ecosystems: Alternative paradigms and implications for development. *Journal of Range Management*, 41: 450–459.

Farina, A. (1998). *Principles and Methods in Landscape Ecology*. Chapman & Hall, London.

Farmer, A. H. & Parent, A. H. (1997). Effects of the landscape on shorebird movements at spring migration stopovers. *Condor*, 99: 698–707.

Farmer, A. H. & Wiens, J. A. (1998). Optimal migration schedules depend on the landscape and the physical environment: a dynamic programming view. *Journal of Avian Biology*, 29: 405–415.

Farmer, A. H. & Wiens, J. A. (1999). Models and reality: Time–energy trade-offs in pectoral sandpiper (*Calidris melanotos*) migration. *Ecology*, 80: 2566–2580.

FEMAT [Forest Ecosystem Management Assessment Team] (1993). *Forest Ecosystem Management: An Ecological, Economic, and Social Assessment*. US Department of Agriculture and US Department of Interior, Portland, OR.

Fordham, D. P., Hood, L. M. & Malafant, K. W. J. (1997). Complexity in landscapes and resource planning: packaging science for decision makers. In *Frontiers in Ecology: Building the Links*, eds. N. Klomp & I. Lunt, pp. 277–285. Elsevier, Oxford, U.K.

Forman, R. T. T. (1995). *Land Mosaics: The Ecology of Landscapes and Regions*. Cambridge University Press, Cambridge, UK.

Fortin, M.-J. (1999). Spatial statistics in landscape ecology. In *Landscape Ecological Analysis: Issues and Applications*, eds. J. M. Klopatek & R. H. Gardner, pp. 253–279. Springer-Verlag, New York.

Foster, D. R., Knight, D. H. & Franklin, J. F. (1998). Landscape patterns and legacies resulting from large, infrequent forest disturbances. *Ecosystems*, 1: 497–510.

Frank, K. & Wissel, C. (1998). Spatial aspects of metapopulation survival: From model results to rules of thumb for landscape management. *Landscape Ecology*, 13: 363–379.

Franklin, A. B., Burnham, K. P., White, G. C., Anthony, R. G., Forsman, E. D., Schwarz, C., Nichols, J. D. & Hines, J. (1999). *Range-Wide Status and Trends in Northern Spotted Owl Populations*. Colorado Cooperative Fish and Wildlife Research Unit, US Geographical Survey, Biological Resources Division, Colorado State University, Fort Collins, CO.

Franklin, J. F. (1993). Preserving biodiversity: species, ecosystems, or landscapes? *Ecological Applications*, 3: 202–205.

Franklin, J. F. & Forman, R. T. T. (1987). Creating landscape patterns by forest cutting: Ecological consequences and principles. *Landscape Ecology,* 1: 5–18.

Friedel, M. H. (1991). Range condition assessment and the concept of thresholds: a viewpoint. *Journal of Range Management,* 44: 422–426.

Friedel, M. H. (1994). How spatial and temporal scale affect the perception of change in rangelands. *Rangeland Journal,* 16: 16–25.

Friedel, M. H. & James, C. D. (1995). How does grazing of native pastures affect their biodiversity? In *Conserving Biodiversity: Threats and Solutions,* eds. R. A. Bradstock, T. D. Auld, D. A. Keith, R. T. Kingsford, D. Lunney, & D. P. Sivertsen, pp. 249–259. Surrey Beatty, Chipping Norton, NSW.

Frith, H. J. (1959). The ecology of wild ducks in inland New South Wales. 2. Movements. *CSIRO Wildlife Research,* 4: 108–130.

Frohn, R. C. (1998). *Remote Sensing for Landscape Ecology*. Lewis Publishers, Boca Raton, FL.

Gardner, R. H., Milne, B. T., Turner, M. G. & O'Neill, R. V. (1987). Neutral models for the analysis of broad-scale landscape pattern. *Landscape Ecology,* 1: 19–28.

Getz, W. M. & Haight, R. G. (1989). *Population Harvesting*. Princeton University Press, Princeton, NJ.

Gibson, D. J., Seastedt, T. R. & Briggs, J. M. (1993). Management practices in tallgrass prairie: Large- and small-scale experimental effects on species composition. *Journal of Applied Ecology,* 30: 247–255.

Gosz, J. R. (1993). Ecotone hierarchies. *Ecological Applications,* 3: 369–376.

Graetz, D. (1994). Grasslands. In *Changes in Land Use and Land Cover: A Global Perspective,* eds. W. B. Meyer & B. L. Turner II, pp. 125–147. Cambridge University Press, Cambridge, UK.

Grice, A. C. & MacLeod, N. D. (1994). State and transition models for rangelands. 6. State and transition models as aids to communication between scientists and land managers. *Tropical Grasslands,* 28: 241–246.

Gustafson, E. J. (1998). Quantifying landscape spatial pattern: What is the state of the art? *Ecosystems,* 1: 143–156.

Haig, S. M., Mehlman, D. W. & Oring, L. W. (1998). Avian movements and wetland connectivity in landscape conservation. *Conservation Biology,* 12: 749–758.

Haila, Y. (1995). Natural dynamics as a model for management: Is the analogue practicable? In *Northern Wilderness Areas: Ecology, Sustainability, Values,* eds. A.-L. Sippola, P. Alaraudanjoki, B. Forbes, & V. Hallikainen, vol. 7, pp. 9–26. Arctic Centre Publications, Rovaniemi, Finland.

Haila, Y. (1999). Islands and fragments. In *Maintaining Biodiversity in Forest Ecosystems,* eds. M. L. Hunter, Jr., pp. 234–264. Cambridge University Press, Cambridge, UK.

Hansen, A. J. & di Castri, F. (eds.) (1992). *Landscape Boundaries: Consequences for Biotic Diversity and Ecological Flows*. Springer-Verlag, New York.

Hanski, I. (1999). *Metapopulation Ecology*. Oxford University Press, New York.

Hargis, C. D., Bissonette, J. A. & David, J. L. (1997). Understanding measures of landscape pattern. In *Wildlife and Landscape Ecology: Effects of Pattern and Scale,* ed. J. A. Bissonette, pp. 231–261. Springer-Verlag, New York.

Haynes, R. W., Graham, R. T. & Quigley, T. M. (1996). *A Framework for Ecosystem Management in the Interior Columbia Basin including Portions of the Klamath and Great Basins,* General Technical Report no. PNW-GTR-374. US Department of Agriculture, Forest Service, Pacific Northwest Research Station, Portland, OR.

Hobbs, R. (1997). Future landscapes and the future of landscape ecology. *Landscape and Urban Planning,* 37: 1–9.

Holland, M. M., Risser, P. G. & Naiman, R. J. (eds.). (1991). *Ecotones: The Role of Landscape Boundaries in the Management and Restoration of Changing Environments*. Chapman & Hall, New York.

Holling, C. S., Peterson, G., Marples, P., Sendzimir, J., Redford, K., Gunderson, L. & Lambert, D. (1996). Self-organization in ecosystems: lumpy geometries, periodicities and morphologies. In *Global Change and Terrestrial Ecosystems,* eds. B. Walker & W. Steffen, pp. 346–384. Cambridge University Press, Cambridge, UK.

Hunter, M. L., Jr. (1999). *Maintaining Biodiversity in Forest Ecosystems*. Cambridge University Press, Cambridge, UK.

Hutto, R. L. (1985). Habitat selection by

nonbreeding, migratory land birds. In *Habitat Selection in Birds*, ed. M. L. Cody, pp. 455–476. Academic Press, New York.

Illius, A. W. & O'Connor, T. G. (1999). On the relevance of nonequilibrium concepts to arid and semiarid grazing systems. *Ecological Applications*, 9: 798–813.

James, C. D., Landsberg, J. & Morton, S. R. (1999). Provision of watering points in the Australian arid zone: A review of effects on biota. *Journal of Arid Environments*, 41: 87–121.

Johnson, D. H. (1980). The comparison of usage and availability measurements for evaluating resource preference. *Ecology*, 61: 65–71.

Johnson, F. & Williams, K. (1999). Protocol and practice in the adaptive management of waterfowl harvests. *Conservation Ecology*, *3*(1) art 8, http://www.consecol.org/vol3/iss1/art8

Johnston, P. W., McKeon, G. M. & Day, K. A. (1996a). Objective 'safe' grazing capacities for south-west Queensland Australia: Development of a model for individual properties. *Rangeland Journal*, 18: 244–258.

Johnston, P. W., Tannock, P. R. & Beale, I. F. (1996b). Objective 'safe' grazing capacities for south-west Queensland Australia: Model application and evaluation. *Rangeland Journal*, 18: 259–269.

Keitt, T. H., Urban, D. L. & Milne, B. T. (1997). Detecting critical scales in fragmented landscapes. *Conservation Ecology*, *1* (1) art 4, http://www.consecol.org/vol1/iss1/art 4

King, A. W. (1997). Hierarchy theory: A guide to system structure for wildlife biologists. In *Wildlife and Landscape Ecology: Effects of Pattern and Scale*, ed. J. A. Bissonette, pp. 185–212. Springer-Verlag, New York.

King, A. W. (1999). Hierarchy theory and the landscape . . . level? Or: words do matter. In *Issues in Landscape Ecology*, eds. J. A. Wiens & M. R. Moss, pp. 6–9. International Association for Landscape Ecology, Guelph, Canada.

Kingsford, R. T. (2000). Ecological impacts of dams, water diversions and river management on floodplain wetlands in Australia. *Austral Ecology*, *25*: 109–127.

Kingsford, R. T. & Porter, J. L. (1999). Wetlands and waterbirds of the Paroo and Warrego rivers. In *A Free-Flowing River: The Ecology of the Paroo River*, ed. R. T. Kingsford, pp. 23–50. National Parks and Wildlife Service, Sydney, NSW.

Kingsford, R. T., Bedward, M. & Porter, J. L. (1994). *Waterbirds and wetlands in Northwestern New South Wales*, Occasional Paper no. 19. National Parks and Wildlife Service, Sydney, NSW.

Kotliar, N. B. & Wiens, J. A. (1990). Multiple scales of patchiness and patch structure: A hierarchical framework for the study of heterogeneity. *Oikos*, 59: 253–260.

Lambeck, R. J. (1997). Focal species: A multi-species umbrella for nature conservation. *Conservation Biology*, 11: 849–857.

Lamberson, R. H., McKelvey, R., Noon, B. R. & Voss, C. (1992). A dynamic analysis of northern spotted owl viability in a fragmented forested landscape. *Conservation Biology*, 6: 505–512.

Lamberson, R. H., McKelvey, R., Noon, B. R. & Voss, C. (1994). The effects of varying dispersal capabilities on the population dynamics of the northern spotted owl. *Conservation Biology*, 8: 185–195.

Lande, R. (1987). Extinction thresholds in demographic models of territorial populations. *American Naturalist*, 130: 624–635.

Lande, R. (1988). Demographic models of the northern spotted owl. *Oecologia*, 75: 601–607.

Landres, P. B., Morgan, P. & Swanson, F. J. (1999). Overview of the use of natural variability concepts in managing ecological systems. *Ecological Applications*, 9: 1179–1188.

Lavorel, S., McIntyre, S., Landsberg, J. & Forbes, T. D. A. (1997). Plant functional classifications: from general groups to specific groups based on responses to disturbance. *Trends in Ecology and Evolution*, 12: 474–478.

Laycock, W. A. (1991). Stable states and thresholds of range condition on North American rangelands: A viewpoint. *Journal of Range Management*, 44: 427–433.

Leopold, A. (1953). *Round River: From the Journals of Aldo Leopold*. Oxford University Press, New York.

Lertzman, K. & Fall, J. (1999). From forest stands to landscapes: Spatial scales and the roles of disturbances. In *Ecological Scale: Theory and Applications*, eds. D. L. Peterson & V. T. Parker, pp. 339–367. Columbia University Press, New York.

Levin, S. A. (1992). The problem of pattern and scale in ecology. *Ecology*, 73: 1943–1967.

Levins, R. (1969). Some demographic and genetic consequences of environmental heterogeneity for biological control. *Bulletin of the Entomological Society of America,* 15: 237–240.

Lélé, S. & Norgaard, R. B. (1996). Sustainability and the scientist's burden. *Conservation Biology,* 10: 354–365.

Lint, J., Noon, B., Anthony, R., Forsman, E., Raphael, M., Collopy, M. & Starkey, E. (1999). *Northern Spotted Owl Effectiveness Monitoring Plan for the Northwest Forest Plan*, General Technical Report no. PNW-GTR-440. US Department of Agriculture Forest Service, Portland, OR.

Ludwig, J. A. & Tongway, D. J. (1995). Spatial organization of landscape and its function in semi-arid woodlands, Australia. *Landscape Ecology,* 10: 51–63.

Ludwig, J. A. & Tongway, D. J. (1997). A landscape approach to rangeland ecology. In *Landscape Ecology: Function and Management. Principles from Australia's Rangelands*, eds. J. Ludwig, D. Tongway, D. Freudenberger, J. Noble & K. Hodgkinson, pp. 1–12. CSIRO Publishing, Collingwood, VIC.

Ludwig, J., Tongway, D., Freudenberger, D., Noble, J. & Hodgkinson, K. (eds.) (1997). *Landscape Ecology: Function and Management: Principles from Australia's Rangelands*. CSIRO Publishing, Collingwood, VIC.

Ludwig, J. A., Wiens, J. A. & Tongway, D. J. (2000). A scaling rule for landscape patches and how it applies to conserving soil resources in savannas. *Ecosystems,* 3: 84–97.

MacArthur, R. H. & Wilson, E. O. (1967). *The Theory of Island Biogeography*. Princeton University Press, Princeton, NJ.

Mac Nally, R. (1999). Dealing with scale in ecology. In *Issues in Landscape Ecology*, eds. J. A. Wiens & M. R. Moss, pp. 10–17. International Association for Landscape Ecology, Guelph, Canada.

McGarigal, K. & Marks, B. (1995). *FRAGSTATS: Spatial Analysis Program for Quantifying Landscape Structure*, General Technical Report no. PNW-GTR-351. U.S. Department of Agriculture Forest Service, Portland, OR.

McKelvey, K., Noon, B. R. & Lamberson, R. H. (1993). Conservation planning for species occupying fragmented landscapes: The case of the Northern Spotted Owl. In *Biotic Interactions and Global Change*, eds. P. M. Kareiva, J. G. Kingsolver, & R. B. Huey, pp. 424–450. Sinauer Associates, Sunderland, MA.

Meyer, W. B. & Turner, B. L., II (Eds.) (1994). *Changes in Land Use and Land Cover: A Global Perspective*. Cambridge University Press, Cambridge, UK.

Milchunas, D. G., Lauenroth, W. K. & Burke, I. C. (1998). Livestock grazing: animal and plant biodiversity of shortgrass steppe and the relationship to ecosystem function. *Oikos,* 83: 65–74.

Morrison, M. L., Marcot, B. G. & Mannan, R. W. (1998). *Wildlife–Habitat Relationships: Concepts and Applications*, 2nd ed. University of Wisconsin Press, Madison, WI.

Murphy, D. D. & Noon, B. R. (1992). Integrating scientific methods with habitat conservation planning: Reserve design for the northern spotted owl. *Ecological Applications,* 2: 3–17.

Nash, M. S., Whitford, W. G., de Soyza, A. G., Van Zee, J. W. & Havstad, K. M. (1999). Livestock activity and Chihuahuan Desert annual-plant communities: Boundary analysis of disturbance gradients. *Ecological Applications,* 9: 814–823.

Nassauer, J. I. (ed.). (1997). *Placing Nature: Culture and Landscape Ecology*. Island Press, Washington, D.C.

Naveh, Z. & Lieberman, A. (1994). *Landscape Ecology: Theory and Application*, 2nd edn. Springer-Verlag, New York.

Noon, B. R. & McKelvey, K. S. (1996). A common framework for conservation planning: Linking individual and metapopulation models. In *Metapopulations and Wildlife Conservation*, ed. D. R. McCullough, pp. 139–165. Island Press, Washington, D.C.

Norton, B. G. (1992). A new paradigm for environmental management. In *Ecosystem Health: New Goals for Environmental Management*, eds. R. Costanza, B. G. Norton, & B. D. Haskell, pp. 23–41. Island Press, Washington, D.C.

Noss, R. F. (1987). Corridors in real landscapes: A reply to Simberloff and Cox. *Conservation Biology,* 1: 159–164.

Noy-Meir, I. (1975). Stability of grazing systems: An application of predator–prey graphs. *Journal of Ecology,* 63: 459–481.

NRC [National Research Council]. (1996).

Upstream: Salmon and Society in the Pacific Northwest. National Academy Press, Washington, D.C.

O'Neill, R. V., DeAngelis, D. L., Waide, J. B. & Allen, T. F. H. (1986). *A Hierarchical Concept of Ecosystems*. Princeton University Press, Princeton, N.J.

Pearson, S. M., Turner, M. G., Gardner, R. H. & O'Neill, R. V. (1996). An organism-based perspective of habitat fragmentation. In *Biodiversity in Managed Landscapes: Theory and Practice*, eds. R. C. Szaro & D. W. Johnston, pp. 77–95. Oxford University Press, New York.

Perlin, J. A. (1989). *Forest Journey: The Role of Wood in the Development of Civilization*. W.W. Norton, New York.

Perry, D. A. (1994). *Forest Ecosystems*. Johns Hopkins University Press, Baltimore, MD.

Perry, D. A. (1998). The scientific basis of forestry. *Annual Review of Ecology and Systematics,* 29: 435–466.

Peterson, D. L. & Parker, V. T. (eds.) (1998). *Ecological Scale: Theory and Applications*. Columbia University Press, New York.

Pickett, S. T. A. & Ostfeld, R. S. (1995). The shifting paradigm in ecology. In *A New Century for Natural Resources Management*, eds. R. L. Knight & S. F. Bates, pp. 261–279. Island Press, Washington, D.C.

Pickett, S. T. A., Parker, V. T. & Fiedler, P. (1992). The new paradigm in ecology: Implications for conservation biology above the species level. In *Conservation Biology: The Theory and Practice of Nature Conservation, Preservation, and Management*, eds. P. Fiedler & S. Jain, pp. 65–88. Chapman & Hall, New York.

Pickup, G. (1991). Event frequency and landscape stability on the floodplain systems of arid central Australia. *Quaternary Science Reviews,* 10: 463–473.

Pickup, G. (1994). Modelling patterns of defoliation by grazing animals in rangelands. *Journal of Applied Ecology,* 31: 231–246.

Pickup, G. & Bastin, G. N. (1997). Spatial distribution of cattle in arid rangelands as detected by patterns of change in vegetation cover. *Journal of Applied Ecology,* 34: 657–667.

Pickup, G. & Stafford Smith, D. M. (1993). Problems, prospects and procedures for assessing sustainability of pastoral land management in arid Australia. *Journal of Biogeography,* 20: 471–487.

Poff, N. L. (1997). Landscape filters and species traits: Towards mechanistic understanding and prediction in stream ecology. *Journal of the North American Benthological Society,* 16: 391–409.

Ponder, W. & Lunney, D. (eds.) (1999). *The Other 99%: The Conservation and Biodiversity of Invertebrates*. The Royal Zoological Society of New South Wales, Mosman, NSW.

Possingham, H. P. (1997). State-dependent decision analysis for conservation biology. In *The Ecological Basis of Conservation: Heterogeneity, Ecosystems, and Biodiversity*, eds. S. T. A. Pickett, R. S. Ostfeld, M. Shachak, & G. E. Likens, pp. 298–304. Springer-Verlag, New York.

Pringle, C. M. (1997). Expanding scientific research programs to address conservation challenges in freshwater ecosystems. In *The Ecological Basis of Conservation: Heterogeneity, Ecosystems, and Biodiversity*, eds. S. T. A. Pickett, R. S. Ostfeld, M. Shachak, & G. E. Likens, pp. 305–319. Chapman & Hall, New York.

Reid, W. V. (1996). Beyond protected areas: Changing perceptions of ecological management objectives. In *Biodiversity in Managed Landscapes: Theory and Practice*, eds. R. C. Szaro & D. W. Johnston, pp. 442–453. Oxford University Press, New York.

Richling, A., Malinowska, E. & Lechnio, J. (eds.) (1994). *Landscape Research and its Applications in Environmental Management*. Faculty of Geography and Regional Studies, Warsaw University, Warsaw.

Rietkerk, M., Keltner, P., Stroosnijder, L. & Prins, H. H. T. (1996). Sahelian rangeland development: A catastrophe? *Journal of Range Management,* 49: 512–519.

Rietkerk, M., van den Bosch, F. & van de Koppel, J. (1997). Site-specific properties and irreversible vegetation changes in semi-arid grazing systems. *Oikos,* 80: 241–252.

Rogers, K. H. (1997). Operationalizing ecology under a new paradigm: An African perspective. In *The Ecological Basis of Conservation. Heterogeneity, Ecosystems, and Biodiversity*, eds. S. T. A. Pickett, R. S. Ostfeld, M. Shachak, & G. E. Likens, pp. 60–77. Chapman & Hall, New York.

Rolstad, J. (1999). Landscape ecology and wildlife management. In *Issues in Landscape*

Ecology, eds. J. A. Wiens & M. R. Moss, pp. 88–93. International Association for Landscape Ecology, Guelph, Canada.

Rosenberg, D. K., Noon, B. R. & Meslow, E. C. (1997). Biological corridors: Form, function, and efficacy. *BioScience*, 47: 677–687.

Roshier, D. A. (1999). Variation in wetland availability and the responses of waterbirds in arid Australia. PhD thesis, Charles Sturt University, Wagga Wagga, NSW.

Roshier, D. A., Robertson, A. I., Kingsford, R. T. & Green, D. G. (2001). Continental-scale interactions with temporary resources may explain the paradox of large populations of desert waterbirds in Australia. *Landscape Ecology*, 16: 547–556.

Sampson, F. B. & Knopf, F. L. (eds.) (1996). *Prairie Conservation*. Island Press, Washington, DC.

Sato, K. & Iwasa, Y. (1993). Modeling of wave regeneration in subalpine *Abies* forests: Population dynamics with spatial structure. *Ecology*, 74: 1538–1550.

Schlesinger, W. H., Reynolds, J. F., Cunningham, G. L., Huenneke, L. F., Jarrell, W. M., Virginia, R. A. & Whitford, W. G. (1990). Biological feedbacks in global desertification. *Science*, 247: 1043–1048.

Schroeder, R. L. & Askerooth, K. (1999). *A Habitat-Based Approach to Management of Tallgrass Prairies at the Tewaukon National Wildlife Refuge*, Information and Technology Report USGS/BRD/ITR – 2000–0001). US Department of the Interior and US Geological Survey, Washington, D.C.

Schroeder, R. L., King, W. J. & Cornely, J. E. (1998). *Selecting Habitat Management Strategies on Refuges* Information and Technology Report no. USGS/BRD/ITR – 1998–003. US Department of the Interior and US Geological Survey, Washington, D.C.

Schwinning, S. & Parsons, A. J. (1999). The stability of grazing systems revisited: spatial models and the role of heterogeneity. *Functional Ecology*, 13: 737–747.

Senft, R. L., Coughenour, M. B., Bailey, D. W., Rittenhouse, L. R., Sala, O. E. & Swift, D. M. (1987). Large herbivore foraging and ecological hierarchies. *BioScience*, 37: 789–799.

Seymour, R. S. & Hunter, M. L. Jr. (1999). Principles of ecological forestry. In *Maintaining Biodiversity in Forest Ecosystems*, ed. M. L. Hunter, Jr., pp. 22–61. Cambridge University Press, Cambridge, UK.

Simberloff, D. (1998). Flagships, umbrellas and keystones: Is single-species management passé in the landscape era? *Biological Conservation*, 83: 247–257.

Simberloff, D. & Cox, J. (1987). Consequences and costs of conservation corridors. *Conservation Biology*, 1: 63–71.

Sinclair, A. R. E. & Fryxell, J. M. (1985). The Sahel of Africa: Ecology of a disaster. *Canadian Journal of Zoology*, 63: 987–994.

Smith, T. M., Shugart, H. H. & Woodward, F. I. (eds.). (1997). *Plant Functional Types: Their Relevance to Ecosystem Properties and Global Change*. Cambridge University Press, Cambridge, UK

Spies, T. A. & Turner, M. G. (1999). Dynamic forest mosaics. In *Maintaining Biodiversity in Forest Ecosystems*, ed. M. L. Hunter, Jr., pp. 95–160. Cambridge University Press, Cambridge, UK.

Stafford Smith, D. M. (1996). Management of rangelands: Paradigms and their limits. In *The Ecology and Management of Grazing Systems*, eds. J. Hodgson & A. Illius, pp. 325–357. CAB International, Wallingford, UK.

Stafford Smith, D. M. & Pickup, G. (1990). Pattern and production in arid lands. *Proceedings of the Ecological Society of Australia*, 16: 195–200.

Stafford Smith, D. M. & Pickup, G. (1993). Out of Africa, looking in: Understanding vegetation change. In *Range Ecology at Disequilibrium: New Models of Natural Variability and Pastoral Adaptation in African Savannas*, eds. R. H. Behnke, Jr., I. Scoones, & C. Kerven, pp. 196–226. Overseas Development Institute, London.

Talbot, L. M. (1997). The linkages between ecology and conservation policy. In *The Ecological Basis of Conservation. Heterogeneity, Ecosystems, and Biodiversity*, eds. S. T. A. Pickett, T. S. Ostfeld, M. Shachak, & G. E. Likens, pp. 368–378. Chapman & Hall, New York.

Taylor, P. D., Fahrig, L., Henein, K. & Merriam, G. (1993). Connectivity is a vital element of landscape structure. *Oikos*, 68: 571–573.

Thomas, J. W., Forsman, E. D., Lint, J. B., Meslow, E. C., Noon, B. R. & Verner, J. (1990). *A Conservation Strategy for the Northern Spotted Owl: Report of the Interagency Scientific*

Committee. US Department of Agriculture Forest Service, US Department of Interior Bureau of Land Management, Fish and Wildlife Service, and National Park Service, Washington, D.C.

Tischendorf, L. & Fahrig, L. (2000). On the usage and measurement of landscape connectivity. *Oikos,* 90: 7–19.

Turner, M. G., Gardner, R. H., Dale, V. H. & O'Neill, R. V. (1989). Predicting the spread of disturbance across heterogeneous landscapes. *Oikos,* 55: 121–129.

Turner, M. G., Dale, V. H. & Everham, E. H. III (1997a). Fires, hurricanes, and volcanoes: comparing large disturbances. *BioScience,* 47: 758–768.

Turner, M. G., Pearson, S. M., Romme, W. H. & Wallace, L. L. (1997b). Landscape heterogeneity and ungulate dynamics: What spatial scales are important? In *Wildlife and Landscape Ecology. Effects of Pattern and Scale*, ed. J. A. Bissonette, pp. 331–348. Springer-Verlag, New York.

Urban, D. L., O'Neill, R. V. & Shugart, H. H. Jr. (1987). Landscape ecology. *BioScience,* 37: 119–127.

van de Koppel, J., Rietkerk, M. & Weissing, F. J. (1997). Catastrophic vegetation shifts and soil degradation in terrestrial grazing systems. *Trends in Ecology and Evolution,* 12: 352–356.

Van Horne, B. & Wiens, J. A. (1991). *Forest Bird Habitat Suitability Models and the Development of General Habitat Models*, Fish and Wildlife Research 8. US Department of the Interior, Fish and Wildlife Service, Washington, D.C.

Verner, J., Morrison, M. L. & Ralph, C. J. (eds.). (1986). *Wildlife 2000: Modeling Habitat Relationships of Terrestrial Vertebrates*. University of Wisconsin Press, Madison, WI.

Walker, B. H. (1992). Biodiversity and ecological redundancy. *Conservation Biology,* 6: 18–23.

Walker, B. H. (1993). Rangeland ecology: understanding and managing change. *Ambio,* 22: 80–87.

Wallace, L. L. & Dyer, M. I. (1996). Grazing effects on grassland ecosystems. In *Ecosystem Disturbance and Wildlife Conservation in Western Grasslands: A Symposium Proceedings*, ed. D. M. Finch, General Technical Report no. RM-GTR-285, pp. 13–19. US Department of Agriculture Forest Service, Rocky Mountain Forest and Range Experiment Station. Fort Collins, CO.

Walters, C. J. (1986). *Adaptive Management of Renewable Resources*. Macmillan, New York.

Walters, C. J. (1997). Adaptive policy design: Thinking at large spatial scales. In *Wildlife and Landscape Ecology: Effects of Pattern and Scale*, ed. J. A. Bissonette, pp. 386–394. Springer-Verlag, New York.

Ward, J. V., Malard, F. & Tockner, K. (1999). Landscape ecology integrates pattern and process in river corridors. In *Issues in Landscape Ecology*, eds. J. A. Wiens & M. R. Moss, pp. 97–102. International Association for Landscape Ecology, Guelph, Canada.

Weber, T. P., Houston, A. I. & Ens, B. J. (1999). Consequences of habitat loss at migratory stopover sites: A theoretical investigation. *Journal of Avian Biology,* 30: 416–426.

West, N. E. (1996). Strategies for maintenance and repair of biotic community diversity on rangelands. In *Biodiversity in Managed Landscapes*, eds. R. C. Szaro & D. W. Johnston, pp. 326–346. Oxford University Press, New York.

Westoby, M., Walker, B. H. & Noy-Meir, I. (1989). Opportunistic management for rangelands not at equilibrium. *Journal of Range Management,* 42: 266–274.

Whittaker, R. H. (1975). *Communities and Ecosystems*. Macmillan, New York.

Wiens, J. A. (1984). On understanding a non-equilibrium world: Myth and reality in community patterns and processes. In *Ecological Communities: Conceptual Issues and the Evidence*, eds. D. R. Strong, Jr., D. Simberloff, L. G. Abele, & A. B. Thistle, pp. 439–457. Princeton University Press, Princeton, NJ.

Wiens, J. A. (1989). Spatial scaling in ecology. *Functional Ecology,* 3: 383–397.

Wiens, J. A. (1995). Landscape mosaics and ecological theory. In *Mosaic Landscapes and Ecological Processes,* eds. L. Hansson, L. Fahrig, & G. Merriam, pp. 1–26. Chapman & Hall, London.

Wiens, J. A. (1997). The emerging role of patchiness in conservation biology. In *The Ecological Basis of Conservation*, eds. S. T. A. Pickett, R. S. Ostfeld, S. M. & G. E. Likens, pp. 93–107. Chapman & Hall, New York.

Wiens, J. A. (1999). The science and practice of landscape ecology. In *Landscape Ecological*

Analysis: Issues and Applications, eds. J. M. Klopatek & R. H. Gardner, pp. 371–383. Springer-Verlag, New York.

Wiens, J. A. (2001). Understanding the problem of scale in experimental ecology. In *Scaling Relationships in Experimental Ecology*, eds. R. H. Gardner, M. Kemp, V. Kennedy, & J. Petersen, pp. 61–88. Columbia University Press, New York.

Wiens, J. A. & Moss, M. R. (eds.) (1999). *Issues in Landscape Ecology*. International Association for Landscape Ecology, Guelph, Canada.

Wiens, J. A., Crawford, C. S. & Gosz, J. R. (1985). Boundary dynamics: A conceptual framework for studying landscape ecosystems. *Oikos*, 45: 421–427.

Williams, M. (1994). Forests and tree cover. In *Changes in Land Use and Land Cover: A Global Perspective*, eds. W. B. Meyer and B. L. Turner II, pp. 97–124. Cambridge University Press, Cambridge, UK.

With, K. A. (1999). Is landscape connectivity necessary and sufficient for wildlife management? In *Forest Fragmentation: Wildlife and Management Implications*, eds. J. A. Rochelle, L. A. Lehmann, & J. Wisniewski, pp. 97–115. Brill.

With, K. A. & Crist, T. O. (1995). Critical thresholds in species' responses to landscape structure. *Ecology*, 76: 2446–2459.

With, K. A. & King, A. W. (1999). Dispersal success on fractal landscapes: A consequence of lacunarity thresholds. *Landscape Ecology*, 14: 73–82.

Woinarski, J. C. Z., Whitehead, P. J., Bowman, D. M. J. S. & Russell-Smith, J. (1992). Conservation of mobile species in a variable environment: The problem of reserve design in the Northern Territory, Australia. *Global Ecology and Biogeography Letters*, 2: 1–10.

Wu, J. & Loucks, O. L. (1995). From balance of nature to hierarchical patch dynamics: a paradigm shift in ecology. *Quarterly Review of Biology*, 70: 439–466.

Zonneveld, I. S. (1995). *Land Ecology*. SPB Academic Publishing, Amsterdam.

JULIE M. BRENNAN, DARREN J. BENDER, THOMAS A. CONTRERAS, AND LENORE FAHRIG

3

Focal patch landscape studies for wildlife management: Optimizing sampling effort across scales

3.1 Introduction

With ever-increasing loss and degradation of wildlife habitat, wildlife management decisions depend on a solid understanding of the influence of both patch characteristics and landscape structure on populations. Appropriately designed multi-scale ecological studies are becoming more and more important in determining how current and future land-use management decisions will affect the survival of natural populations. Effective management plans for populations and regions depend on clear and interpretable results from properly designed studies.

Historically, researchers designed studies to examine the effects of patch-scale characteristics on population dynamics. A patch is defined as a discrete area of contiguous and homogeneous habitat. Patch-based ecological studies address the relationship between the inherent characteristics of the individual patches (e.g., patch size, patch quality, patch isolation) and some ecological pattern (e.g., distribution and abundance of organisms) or process (e.g., dispersal, disturbance regimes, predation, or competition) (e.g., reviews by Andrén, 1994 and Bender *et al.*, 1998).

Recently, researchers have begun to recognize the importance of considering the effect of the landscape context of the patch. A landscape-scale ecological study addresses one or more of (1) the effect of landscape structure on the distribution and/or abundance of organisms, (2) the effect of landscape structure on an ecological process(es) (e.g., animal movement), or (3) the effect of ecological process(es) (e.g., fire), or organisms (e.g., beavers; see Johnston, 1995), on landscape structure. Landscape structure implies spatial heterogeneity, which is described in terms of landscape composition and configuration. Landscape composition is the amount of the different landscape elements (e.g., habitat types, road cover) in the landscape. Landscape configuration describes the spatial arrangements of these elements. Without examining the influence of the landscape context in which patches and populations are embedded, it is impossible to assess how changes in the properties of a landscape will affect populations. Studies that examine effects at several spatial scales have suggested the importance of considering landscape factors as well as local or patch factors for successful wildlife management planning (Jokimaki and Huhta, 1996; Findlay and Houlahan, 1997; Sisk *et al.*, 1997; Saab, 1999; Pope *et al.*, 2000).

However, the very nature of landscapes, i.e., their potential complexity and size, can make the definition of landscapes and the design of landscape-scale studies difficult (Allen, 1998; Goodwin and Fahrig, 1998). If landscapes are defined inappropriately and/or the designs of studies are improper, unsuccessful management recommendations may follow from these studies. The purpose of this chapter is to provide guidelines for the design of sampling strategies for landscape-scale studies. These guidelines will assist managers in critically evaluating the studies on which they base their management decisions. We first discuss how to define landscape size relevant to the pattern or process being studied or question being asked. We then address the decision-making process required when designing a multi-scale landscape study and selecting landscapes best suited for answering a particular question. Finally, we provide information on the tools currently available for measuring and analyzing differences in spatial pattern and other landscape properties between sample landscapes, and address some of the data considerations unique to a landscape-scale ecological study.

3.2 How big is a landscape?

In landscape ecology, ecological patterns and processes are defined and studied within the context of a landscape. It is therefore important to define both the functional and physical size of a landscape for a particular study. The size of landscape determines how a researcher or resource manager will interpret observations and assess the impact of spatial pattern on populations.

Landscapes are often defined as a geographical region that has a particular heterogeneity of cover types (Forman and Godron, 1986; Wiens, 1992). However, this definition is based on a human perception of heterogeneity (Allen, 1998; Goodwin and Fahrig, 1998). Since ecological patterns and processes occur over a wide range of scales, the size of a landscape should in fact be tied to the scale of the pattern or process under study. For example, a single hectare of forest may represent a heterogeneous landscape for a species of ant, whereas a fire ecology study conducted in a 1000-ha continuously forested area should not be considered a landscape-scale study if the area is homogeneous with respect to the process(es) studied. Landscapes are therefore "relative" entities, with the scale and heterogeneity of a landscape being determined by the scale and heterogeneity relevant to the question being asked and the ecological process under consideration (Wiens, 1989; Fahrig and Grez, 1996; King, 1997; Allen, 1998; Goodwin and Fahrig, 1998).

We suggest two criteria for defining the scale of landscapes: (1) what is the hypothesis concerning the relationship between landscape structure and the ecological response of interest? and (2) what are the relevant processes and at what spatial scale do they occur? For example, Henein *et al.* (1998) used empirical data and simulation models to study how the life-history characteristics of two forest species, Eastern chipmunk (*Tamias striatus*) and white-footed mouse (*Peromyscus leucopus*), affect their responses to differences in landscape connectedness. Henein *et al.* (1998) found that chipmunk movements through a landscape were restricted by the amount and configuration of both forest patches and wooded fencerows. White-footed mice, on the other hand, were found to be habitat generalists. Their movements are much less dependent on the amount and configuration of forest patches or wooded fencerows and they range much more widely. From a design perspective, this affects the size of sample landscapes required to assess differences in mouse and chipmunk population responses to landscape structure. The scale of landscape appropriate for assessing effects of landscape pattern on chipmunk populations is smaller than the scale required for white-footed mice in the same region. Therefore, the interaction of ecological processes with landscape heterogeneity will determine the scale of a study. In the above example, a lack of knowledge of dispersal or movement distances could result in inappropriate sampling designs and interpretation of results.

Recognizing that a particular landscape scale is appropriate does not always mean that landscapes of that size and type are available, particularly if a large number of sample landscapes is required. It may then be necessary to adjust sampling design to compensate for these problems (see section 3.4). Also, while it is difficult enough to determine the appropriate landscape scale for a single species, in many instances management of natural systems requires consideration of more than one species simultaneously. In these cases, functional groupings of species by habitat use and movement scale may be useful in determining appropriate landscape size (see Noble and Gitay, 1996). Most multi-species studies actually use a single definition of landscape scale (e.g., Findlay and Houlahan, 1997; Jonsen and Fahrig, 1997; Holland and Fahrig, 2000; A. J. McAllister, H. G. Merriam, and L. Fahrig, unpublished data). Since different species respond to habitat structure at different scales, the choice of landscape scale is somewhat arbitrary. When the appropriate size of the landscape is not obvious (or perhaps even when it is), analyses should be conducted using several landscape sizes (e.g., Findlay and Houlahan, 1997; Pedlar *et al.*, 1997; Pope *et al.*, 2000; Langlois *et al.*, 2001), spanning the known or suspected range of appropriate scales for all the species in the study. The number and sizes of these landscapes will be discussed further in sections 3.4 and 3.6 (case study).

3.3 Importance of measuring multiple landscapes

Landscape ecologists often study the effects of landscape structure on the abundance or distribution of organisms. A landscape-scale study is therefore one that examines the effect of landscape context on an ecological response (dependent) variable. It answers the question: Does the structure of the landscape in which this observation is imbedded affect the observation's value? This question can be answered only by comparing the response variable across several landscapes with different structures. This comparison imposes a particular design on a landscape-scale study, where each data point represents a single landscape. The entire study comprises several non-overlapping landscapes having different structures and the appropriate size of each landscape is determined as described in the previous section. In the statistical analyses, measures of landscape structure are the predictor (independent) variables and measures of abundance and/or distribution are the response variables.

The use of non-overlapping landscapes is important for two main reasons. First, the researcher's ability to uncover effects of landscape structure on ecological response variable(s) depends on the sample landscapes covering a range of different structures. Since overlapping landscapes have similar structures, the range of variation in the predictor variables would be low, and the ability to detect relationships between landscape structure and ecological response(s) would also be low. Second, the use of non-overlapping landscapes reduces problems associated with lack of statistical independence of data points. Lack of independence results in inflated measures of statistical significance in parametric statistical tests.

Such a broad-scale sampling design, using individual landscapes as data points, may seem impractical. However, this constraint is lessening with increasing availability of remotely sensed data, allowing much easier measurement of landscape structural variables. Measurement of the ecological response variable across many landscapes usually presents a greater challenge, and we propose as a practical solution the "focal patch study," in section 3.4. Recent studies of effects of landscape structure on diversity, density, and/or distribution of organisms are listed in Table 3.1.

Table 3.1. *Examples of landscape-scale empirical studies*

Response variable	Number and size of landscapes	Landscape structure variables	Multiple landscape scales?	Major finding	Reference
Wetland species richness	30, 2-km radius	Road density, forest cover in landscapes	Yes	Species richness decreased with increasing road density and decreasing forest cover	Findlay and Houlahan (1997)
Species richness of specialist vs. generalist insects in alfalfa fields	26, 1-km radius	Habitat diversity in landscapes	No	Positive relationship between landscape diversity and insect diversity	Jonsen and Fahrig (1997)
Family richness of herbivorous insects in alfalfa fields	59, 1-km radius	Length of woody field border within landscapes	No	Positive effect of amount of woody border in the landscape on family richness	Holland and Fahrig (2000)
Bird species diversity, richness, evenness	29, 30–86 ha	Agricultural intensity in landscape	No	Negative relationships between agricultural intensity and bird species diversity, richness, and evenness	A. J. McAllister *et al.* (unpublished data)
Density of bird species	30, 250–300 ha	Amounts and configurations of habitat types	No	Most species showed strong density relationships with landscape composition (amounts of different forest types)	McGarigal and McComb (1995)
Relative density of raccoons (*Procyon lotor*)	57, 1-km radius	Amount of forest in landscape	No	Raccoon density highest at intermediate forest amount	Pedlar *et al.* (1997)

Relative density of leopard frogs (*Rana pipiens*) in ponds	34, 1.5-km radius	Amount of forage habitat and number of occupied breeding sites in landscape	Yes	Leopard frog density increased with amount of forage habitat and the number of occupied breeding sites in the landscape	Pope *et al.* (2000)
Presence/absence of forest breeding birds	94, 10 × 10 km	Amount and fragmentation of forest cover	No	Amount of forest cover had a much stronger effect than forest fragmentation on bird distribution	Trzcinski *et al.* (1999)
Presence/absence of hanta virus antibodies in deermice (*Peromyscus maniculatus*)	101, 4-km radius	Amount and fragmentation of deermouse habitat in landscapes	Yes	Significant quadratic (U-shaped) effect of habitat amount and a (smaller) significant positive effect of landscape fragmentation on distribution of the virus	Langlois *et al.* (2001)

Table 3.2. *Summary of multi-scale landscape study approaches based on the cost of measuring the response and predictor variables*

		Predictor variable cost	
		Low	High
Response variable cost	Low	**Ideal** – more well-studied patches – higher landscape sample size (see Fig. 3.1a)	**Multi-patch landscape study** – more well-studied patches – lower landscape sample size (see Fig. 3.1c)
	High	**Focal patch landscape study** – fewer well-studied patches – higher landscape sample size (see Fig. 3.1b)	**Not feasible**

3.4 Trade-offs in landscape study design

In the previous two sections we outlined the importance of conducting empirical studies at the appropriate landscape scale in many landscapes. Where the process of interest occurs at a small spatial scale, studies designed with these criteria in mind should be feasible. However, there can be logistic limitations, such as time, funding, travel, or number of personnel, to conducting multi-scale studies over a large area. For a given sampling effort, larger landscapes cannot be sampled as intensively as smaller ones. Furthermore, if a manipulative approach is required rather than an observational one, application of the "treatment" may not be feasible at a broad spatial scale, and creating the treatment condition may be impossible if it requires removing threatened habitat. For this reason, manipulative studies are difficult to conduct across many large landscapes; it is usually more feasible to conduct the study at a smaller spatial scale. Careful consideration must then be given to identifying an appropriate compromise among spatial scale, sampling intensity, replication, and degree of experimental manipulation to achieve the most reliable results as a basis for appropriate management decisions.

The appropriate trade-off between number of landscapes and within-landscape sampling intensity will depend on whether the cost of obtaining data is higher for the response variable(s) or predictor variable(s) (Table 3.2 and Fig. 3.1). When remotely sensed information can be readily obtained, variables describing landscape structure are usually more easily measured than those describing organism abundance/distribution. In this case statistical power is maximized by maximizing the number of landscapes sampled and minimizing the intensity of sampling within each landscape. When remotely sensed data are unavailable, the effort required to quantify the structure of each landscape is high, and the number of landscapes sampled will have to be smaller (Table 3.2.). In this case, statistical power can be improved with more intense sampling of the response variable within each landscape, thus reducing the error associated with the response variable.

Another factor to consider is how many scales to include in a study design. Data are collected at both the patch and the landscape scale as defined in section 3.2. However, there is always at least some uncertainty about the appropriate scale for a study because there is never perfect a priori information (e.g., animal movement ranges) from which to determine the appropriate scales. Assessing the influence of landscape structure on the response variable (Fig. 3.2) at several scales can allow one to determine the scale at which the landscape has the strongest influence. Where possible, we suggest the range of scales should cover from about an order of magnitude smaller to an order of magnitude larger than the scale thought a priori to be most appropriate for the process or species. For example, Findlay and Houlahan (1997) determined that wetland species richness was strongly correlated with forest cover and road density up to 1000 to 2000 m away. This distance was an order of magnitude higher than the existing 120 m buffer to protect wetland diversity established in government policy. In cases where landscape-scale measurements can be taken easily, this range can be broken into a large number of sampling scales, thus increasing the accuracy with which the most relevant scale can be determined.

The trade-off between number and size of landscapes and sampling intensity is evident from a comparison of two studies of the effects of landscape forest cover and fragmentation on forest breeding birds. McGarigal and McComb (1995) studied the abundance of breeding birds in 30 landscapes of 250–300 ha each, whereas Trzcinski *et al.* (1999) studied the presence/absence of forest breeding birds in 94 landscapes of 100 km^2 each. The smaller number and size (250–300 ha) of landscapes studied by McGarigal and McComb (1995) permitted them to conduct intensive sampling at each location (32–38 samples points for each landscape = 1046 sampling points) for each of 15 species of birds. In contrast, Trzcinski *et al.* (1999) were limited to using presence/absence *Breeding Bird Atlas* data resulting in a much less intensively studied response variable.

The trade-off between experimental manipulation and landscape size is illustrated in a study by Wiens *et al.* (1997). The authors created "mini-landscapes" that were mosaics of grassy patches and bare ground. Each landscape was 25 m^2, and five different landscape structures (treatments) were studied. The response variable was the movement behavior of tenebrionid beetles across the landscapes. Ten beetles in each of the five treatment areas

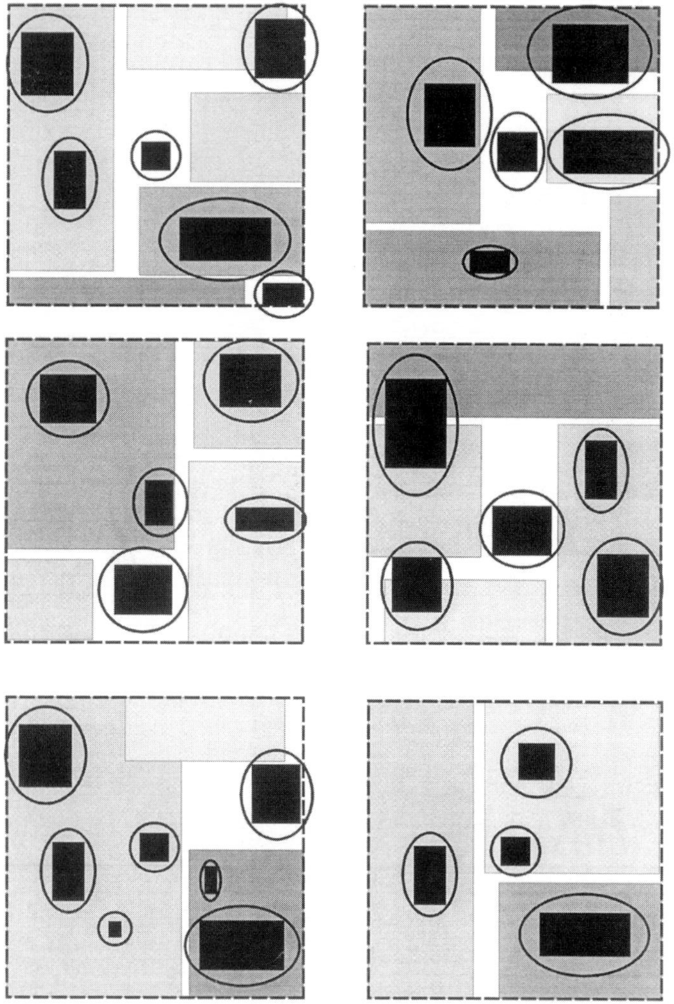

a

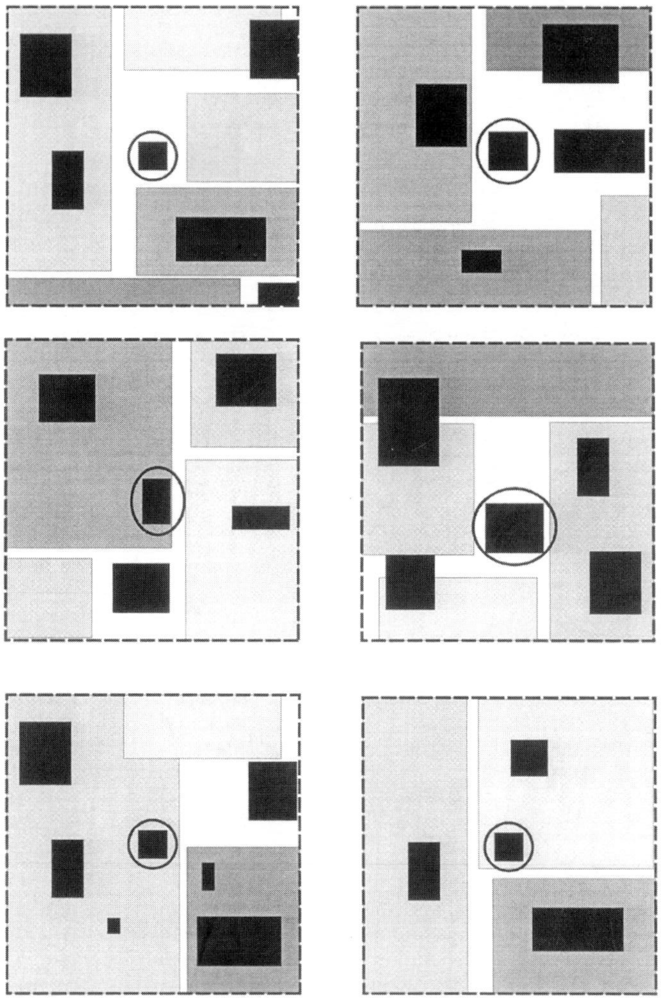

b

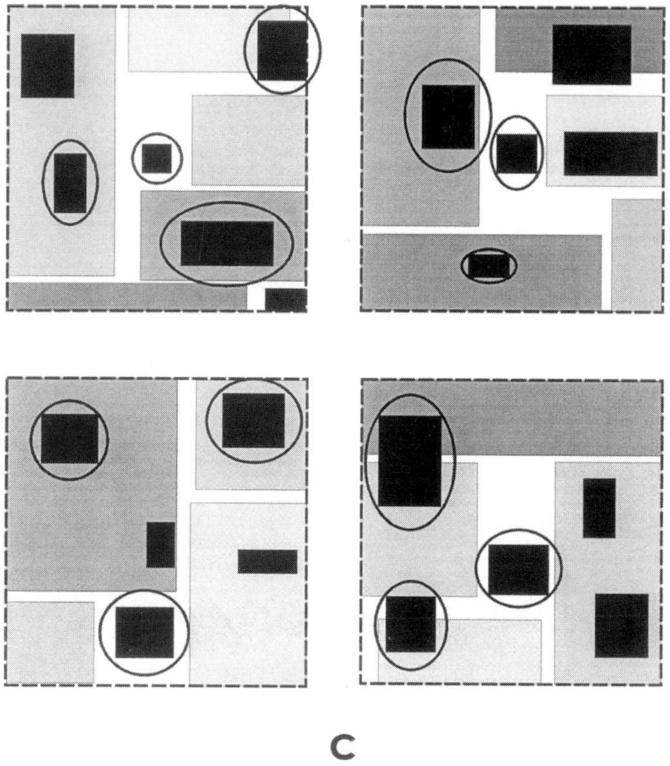

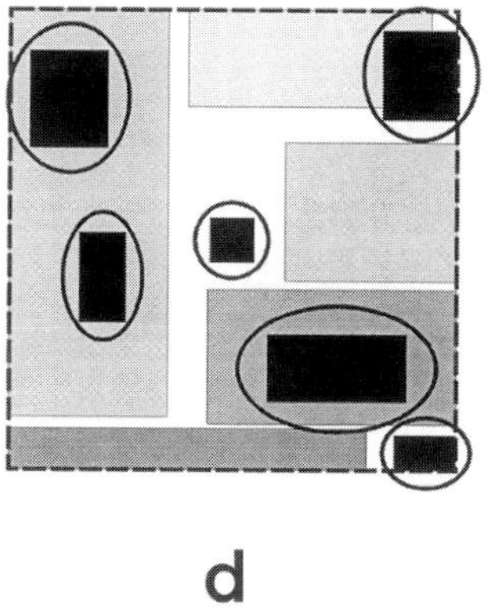

FIGURE 3.1
Sampling strategy to illustrate sampling effort across scales. Black areas represent habitat patches. Circles indicate sampled patches. The remaining areas (white and shades of grey) represent different habitats in the matrix. Dashed lines represent landscape boundaries. (a) Ideal sampling strategy where multiple patches and multiple landscapes are sampled. (b) Sampling strategy where landscape sample size is maximized. Fewer patches are sampled but sampling is more intense. This approach is more suitable when landscape structural variables can be remotely sensed (or are otherwise less costly to obtain). This is the focal patch design. (c) Sampling strategy where fewer landscapes are measured, but each landscape is measured more intensely in more patches. This is a multi-patch landscape study and is more suitable when landscape structural variables are more costly to obtain. (d) Patch-scale study design. This design does not constitute a landscape-scale study.

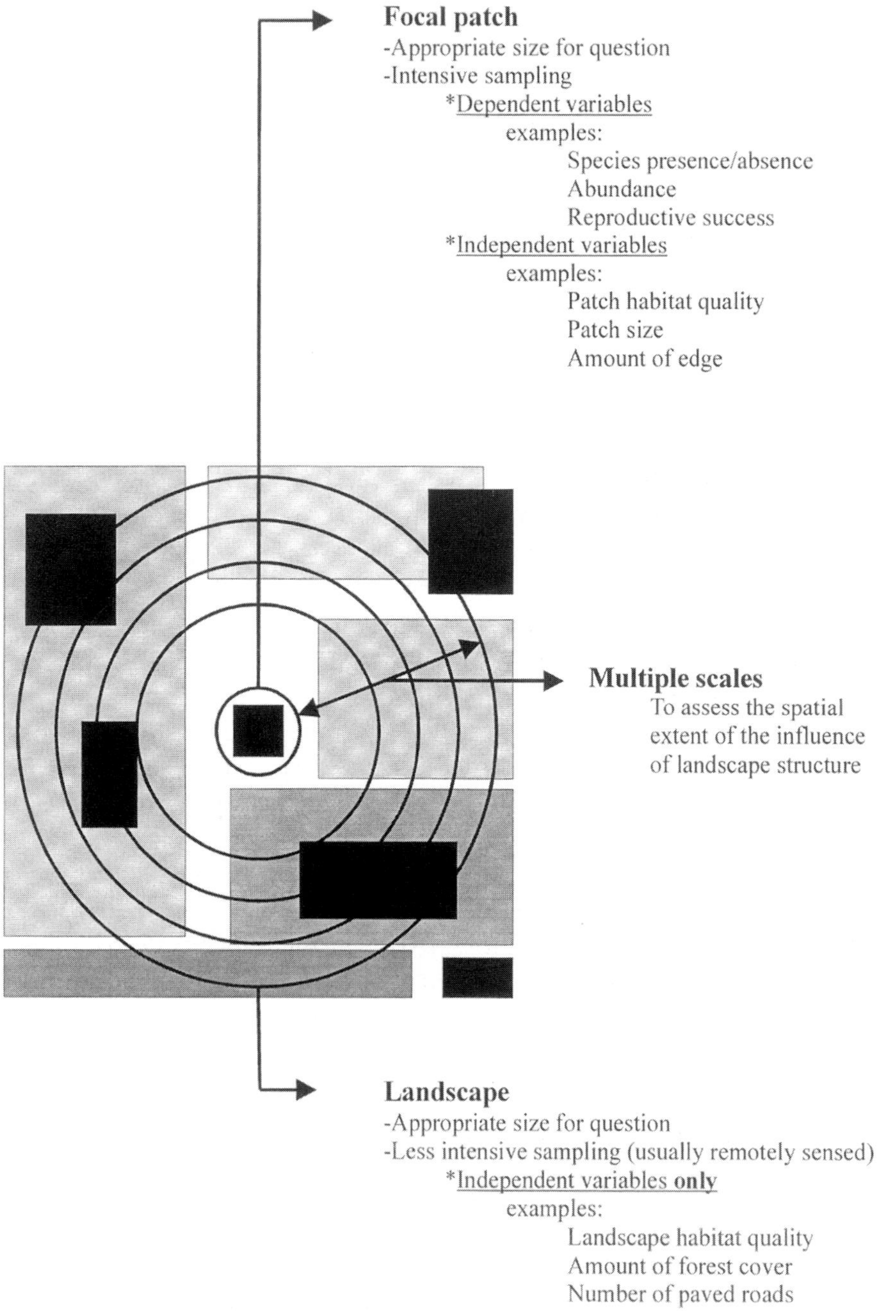

FIGURE 3.2
Focal patch landscape scale study sampling design.

were followed and their locations recorded for 100 time steps. Because of the short-distance movements of the beetle, the landscape size was large enough to observe the process of interest (section 3.2). The study is thus at an appropriate scale for the question, has reasonable sampling intensity and number of landscapes, and controls for the effects of extraneous variables by the experimental design. The limitation of this type of study is that it is difficult to extrapolate the results to larger scales (e.g., long-distance movements over the life-time of a beetle; larger movement distances associated with other organisms).

One possibility for ensuring large sample size and intensive sampling effort is the "focal-patch study" in which the response variable is measured intensively in several focal patches, each of which is located in the center of a landscape. The landscapes are non-overlapping (section 3.5.2) and predictors are measured at both the patch and whole landscape scales (Fig. 3.2). Focusing sampling efforts of the response variable on focal patches allows for intensive data collection on the species of interest that can then be related to the characteristics of the surrounding landscape. The focus on a central patch for detailed measurement of population response reduces the trade-off between sampling intensity and replication (e.g., Pope *et al.*, 2000).

Furthermore, because it is not always possible, or appropriate, to apply a "treatment" to a landscape, we suggest a quasi-experimental approach to landscape sampling designs (this approach is not limited to focal-patch studies). Landscapes are not manipulated but are chosen using strict, non-random selection criteria to ensure a wide range of values of the predictor variables and to avoid correlations among predictor variables, thus increasing the power of statistical inferences. For example, Trzcinski *et al.* (1999) selected landscapes such that the independent effects of the amount and fragmentation of forest cover on bird distribution could be estimated. We suggest that the combined approach of focal patches and strict selection criteria may be the most appropriate design for obtaining reliable information from landscape ecological studies to be used as the basis for management decisions.

3.5 Overview of analysis tools and data considerations

In a multi-scale landscape study design, the researcher uses hybrid-analysis schemes that examine both patch-scale and landscape-scale analysis. For example, in the focal-patch design we advocate in this chapter, spatial information from patch-scale analysis (e.g., patch size and shape) is combined with landscape-scale attributes (e.g., total amount of breeding habitat in landscape, density of barriers to movement such as roads). This approach is termed multi-scale analysis because it integrates local (patch-scale) information with landscape-scale information. We briefly address the approach to take in analyzing multi-scale landscape patterns and provide some of the data considerations unique to a landscape-scale ecological study. For a more comprehensive discussion on landscape-scale analysis methods, the reader should consult Klopatek and Gardner (1999) or Turner and Gardner (1991).

3.5.1 Landscape pattern analysis

Landscape pattern analyses can take many forms, but generally they are performed at two scales. One approach is to look within individual landscapes to see how attributes of patches are related to ecological properties within the patches. This approach has been popularized by metapopulation theory (Hanski and Gilpin, 1991) which emphasizes patch occupancy and patch characteristics, such as patch number, size, and isolation, to predict regional population dynamics and persistence. Because this approach explicitly examines patches within a landscape(s), this constitutes a patch-scale analysis. Another approach is the landscape-scale analysis which explicitly studies properties that emerge only at the landscape scale (e.g., landscape connectivity, percentage habitat cover, road density).

Two sets of methods are available for landscape pattern analysis. The first is geostatistical methods, which are applied to data that consist only of mapped points. We focus more on the second method, which is more common in landscape ecology: pattern-based analysis. This method is applied to patch-based or raster maps. A complete review of techniques from both types of methods is beyond the scope of this chapter. For a more in-depth discussion of these techniques, we recommend reviews by Legendre and Fortin (1989), Turner *et al.* (1991), Legendre (1993), and Gustafson (1998).

Geostatistical methods

Geostatistical methods assume that some properties of a landscape (e.g., rainfall) vary continuously over space, and that one can estimate this variation by sampling it at many (usually irregularly spaced) locations (Burrough, 1995). An example of a useful geostatistical technique is trend surface analysis (Gittins, 1968). Trend surface analysis techniques are used to extrapolate from the sample points to the broad-scale spatial pattern, using two-dimensional non-linear regression techniques. They can be used either (1) among landscapes, to categorize each landscape with respect to some variable, prior to hypothesis testing, or (2) within landscapes, to characterize statistically the trend in a variable so that its effects can be removed statistically (detrended) prior to hypothesis testing with another landscape variable (Cormack and Ord, 1979; Legendre and Fortin, 1989).

Pattern-based methods

Pattern-based methods are used to quantify the composition and configuration of landscapes. They include patch-based, landscape-based, and transect-based measures. One should bear in mind that these approaches are not always interchangeable. For example, some landscape properties can be derived from knowledge about the landscape's constituent patches (see below) but the reverse is not true and, therefore, patch-scale pattern analysis is not equivalent to landscape-scale pattern analysis. Nevertheless, the patch paradigm is popular in ecology (e.g., metapopulation theory; Hanski and Gilpin, 1991; see also review by Andrén, 1994). In addition to patch size and isolation, various measures of patch shape, such as edge:interior ratios or patch fractal dimension, are often measured as predictors of ecological variables (e.g., Lindenmayer *et al.*, 1999). Isolation measures, such as nearest-neighbor scores and dispersion indices, are generally calculated from point-based data. However, all the measures can be calculated from patch-based or raster-based maps and can be performed on binary and categorical data, so they are generally applicable. The main deficiency with all pattern-based measures, particularly patch-based measures, is that there is little consensus as to which properties are most significant for ecological analysis in general (e.g., see Andrén, 1994; Bender *et al.*, 1998; Hargis *et al.*, 1998). Also, many of the indices provide similar information, resulting in redundancy when one performs analyses using multiple measures (Ritters *et al.*, 1995; Hargis *et al.*, 1998; see also section "Data Reduction" below).

Comparison of pattern across landscapes requires landscape-based methods for pattern analysis. Common landscape-based properties are the amount of habitat in the landscape and landscape connectivity. Landscape connectivity is an operational term rather than a quantifiable measure, but several landscape-based indices have been reported as indices of connectivity (see Schumaker, 1996; Tischendorf and Fahrig, 2000a). Landscape contagion (O'Neill *et al.*, 1988), fractal dimension (Palmer, 1988; Milne, 1991) and lacunarity (Plotnick *et al.*, 1993) are all indices related to the connectedness or aggregation of one type of landscape element (e.g., breeding habitat for a particular species) for raster-based maps. Other commonly used landscape-based measures use aggregate properties of all the patches within a landscape (e.g., mean patch area, total amount of edge). Some progress has been made in establishing general relationships among landscape-based measures through simulation modeling that examines the behavior of different landscape-based measures in different types of landscapes (see Gustafson and Parker, 1992; Ritters *et al.*, 1995; Schumaker, 1996; Hargis *et al.*, 1998; Tischendorf and Fahrig, 2000b). Empirical support for this work, though, is still lacking.

Transect-based measures differ from the patch and landscape-based measures in that location is expressed in one-dimensional (1D) space. Transects can be used to estimate landscape pattern (e.g., pattern of forest canopy gaps) by sampling only a small portion of the landscape, assuming that the pattern across the transect(s) is representative of the landscape. Transect-based data can be preferable to mapping entire regions when the spatial pattern under observation is fairly regular across the landscape. Also, some analysis techniques are calculated more easily using 1D data than 2D data. For example, spectral analysis methods such as Fourier analysis, which can determine the characteristic scales of a repeated pattern like the pattern of clumping of grasses, can be performed easily on transect data (Turner *et al.*, 1991).

3.5.2 Statistical considerations associated with landscape-scale data

Landscape studies are subject to the same limitations that must be overcome in any study. Any study should seek to maximize replication and interspersion of observations while also minimizing sampling error (Hurlbert, 1984). However, at least three additional considerations unique to landscape studies must also be addressed. First, spatial autocorrelation among data often arises in landscape studies, and this poses a problem when applying some of the common statistical hypothesis tests, which assume independence of data points. Second, the presence of broad-scale spatial trends in the data may mask finer-scale patterns that may be of greater interest. Third, because many factors that affect variables of interest are spatially dependent, there may be spatially correlated common causes that exist in landscape data. This makes identifying important determinants of the phenomenon under investigation (e.g., the distribution and abundance of a species) more challenging because non-causal factors are difficult to separate from causal ones. Each of these potential pitfalls is discussed below with suggestions to minimize their influence.

Spatial autocorrelation

Spatial autocorrelation is a concern for landscape data, and it should be tested for whenever one is concerned that proximate sites (or worse yet, overlapping landscapes) consistently behave more similarly than distant sites with respect to some variable (e.g., vegetation type). The most common techniques for statistical hypothesis testing are those statistics lumped together under the term general linear models (GLM), which include familiar procedures such as multiple regression and ANOVA (Neter *et al.*, 1990). Uncorrected spatial autocorrelation among study sites (landscapes or focal patches) can artificially inflate the significance of GLM tests, potentially leading the researcher to unreliable conclusions (for reviews see Legendre and Fortin, 1989; Legendre, 1993).

If spatially autocorrelated data must be used, one must resort to alternative means for hypothesis testing. Legendre and Fortin (1989) and Legendre (1993) advocate the use of techniques such as the partial Mantel test for hypothesis testing when faced with autocorrelated data. However, these methods have not been quickly adopted by ecologists, probably because they are computationally intensive and not entirely straightforward to interpret. Another potential solution is the use of distribution-free statistical procedures, such as randomization and bootstrapping tests (e.g., Manly, 1997). These methods also have not been readily adopted by ecologists, presumably because the randomization routines necessary for calculating the statistics must often be customized on a case-by-case basis, necessitating that the user be familiar with at least a rudimentary level of programming or scripting.

Broad-scale spatial trends

When there are broad-scale trends in the data but the autocorrelation of the response variable is small, one can statistically remove unwanted trends from the data and proceed with the standard GLM statistics. For example, if there are latitudinal and/or longitudinal trends in the data, one can correct for these effects statistically using trend-surface analysis (e.g., Venier and Fahrig, 1998). One creates a polynomial regression model where the response variable is the variable of interest (e.g., species abundance) and the predictor variables are latitude and longitude, expressed in units such as decimal degrees. Performing subsequent statistical analyses on the residuals of the polynomial regression (rather than on the original response variable) eliminates the effect of the spatial trend. A similar method can also be performed using ANCOVA if the unwanted trend varies in only one direction. Randomized blocked-ANOVA (Neter *et al.*, 1990) designs are also useful if there is a natural clustering or grouping of sites, but one must be careful that variables of interest are not similarly grouped. If the predictor variables of interest are not sufficiently interspersed throughout the landscape, then blocking may remove any apparent relationship between the response and predictor variables of interest.

A promising method for dealing with spatially correlated data is generalized additive models (GAM) (Hastie and Tibshirani, 1990; Hastie, 1992). GAM statistics are an extension of GLM techniques, but make fewer assumptions regarding the data, and are capable of modeling non-linear relationships. Preisler *et al.* (1997) propose a method based on a GAM that (1) estimates the spatial effects in the data, and (2) statistically controls for these effects while simultaneously examining the effects of other predictor variables. The authors claim that this method offers good explanatory power using predictor variables of interest, even when there are other unmeasured variables that also vary spatially. The method is also appealing because it can be performed using the standard output of existing statistical packages, and there is a broad choice of designs (e.g., ANOVA, regression, ANCOVA, etc.).

Spatially-correlated common causes

Another problem that is common in landscape studies occurs when apparent relations among the data are due to spatially correlated factors with a common cause. For example, imagine that a researcher was interested in sampling frog populations in areas with differing amounts of forest cover to assess the relationship between forest cover and frog abundance. One may select multiple landscapes for investigation, choosing sites that display a wide range of amounts of forest cover. However, also imagine that continuous forest cover only occurs in areas where the soil is poorly drained, and areas with little forest cover tend to occur in well-drained soils that have been cleared mostly for agricultural purposes. Once the samples have been analyzed, it would be difficult to interpret any observed relationships between forest cover and frog abundance because of the effects of soil drainage (and therefore, presence of natural wetlands) and human land use. It may be that forest cover is correlated with frog abundance, but there is no direct relationship between the two variables (i.e., forest cover has no causal effect on frog populations). Instead, the relationship arises because frog abundance and forest cover have common causes (human impacts due to difference in drainage) that produce a spatial correlation.

Although such confounding effects are not unique to landscape data, there is certainly a strong likelihood that they will be encountered in landscape studies because so many environmental and human factors are spatially dependent. Statistical techniques such as path analysis (Li, 1975) and structural equation modeling (Maruyama, 1998) have been developed to analyze and interpret causal relations among many variables. However, it is often easier to eliminate confounding effects in the design stage by carefully selecting landscapes so that confounding factors are not correlated. Non-random selection of landscapes can also help to eliminate problems with spatially autocorrelated data at the source, and certainly can minimize broad-scale spatial trends when landscapes with varying degrees of some attribute are carefully interspersed. Although this advice (non-random sampling) seems to violate statistical dogma, we feel that the benefits of carefully selected landscapes far outweigh the potential introduction of bias that might occur when sample landscapes are selected in a non-random, quasi-experimental fashion.

Data reduction

Finally, one is often faced with a barrage of potential landscape pattern indices with no a priori conception of which variables will be most useful and which will be redundant. Although it is possible to construct statistical models that test all possible predictor variables, this is undesirable because (1) more predictor variables results in lower statistical power, (2) there is an increased chance of spurious statistical relationships, and (3) the computations necessary for finding the exact parameter solutions may take a long time or may not be possible at all. Thus, some form of variable reduction may be desirable.

Gustafson and Parker (1992), Schumaker (1996), and Hargis *et al.* (1998) demonstrate where redundancies are likely among landscape metrics, and provide guidance as to what metrics should be used. An alternative solution is to combine the landscape structure variables in some form of factor analysis, such as principal components analysis (PCA), and use the first few PCA axes as predictor variables in subsequent statistical analyses in place of the original larger set of intercorrelated variables (e.g., Saab, 1999). This both reduces the number of predictor variables and ensures that the predictor variables are uncorrelated. This method has been used by McGarigal and McComb (1995) and Trzcinski *et al.* (1999) to derive measures of habitat fragmentation that are independent of habitat amount in the landscape.

3.6 Case study: Effects of landscape structure on the abundance of the northern leopard frog

Pope *et al.* (2000) examined the effects of landscape structure on the abundance of northern leopard frogs (*Rana pipiens*) in the region surrounding Ottawa, Canada. The authors studied 34 circular landscapes, each with a radius of 1.5 km (or 3 km in diameter). Within each landscape they (and 34 volunteers) assessed the abundance of northern leopard frogs over four census periods. They also surveyed all other potential breeding sites within these landscapes for a total of 107 sampling sites. The authors demonstrated that the relative abundance of *R. pipiens* in a landscape was influenced by the amount of summer foraging habitat (grassy field or meadows), the amount of breeding habitat (adjacent ponds), and the water pH and amount of spawning habitat in the focal ponds.

Focal patch design

Thirty-four non-overlapping landscapes were selected in which the response variable, relative abundance of the northern leopard frog, was measured intensely at one focal pond in each landscape. The landscapes were selected using the criteria described in the following section. The predictor variables were measured at both the patch (pond characteristics) and the landscape scale (amount of breeding and summer habitat based on remotely sensed information).

Strict selection criteria

This study was not an experimental one where "treatments" were applied. Instead, it used a quasi-experimental approach where the ponds were chosen to minimize correlations between the predictor landscape-scale variables. The landscapes were selected to minimize the correlations between the amount of summer foraging habitat and the density of potential breeding areas in the landscapes, taking advantage of existing difference in landscape structure. In practical terms, this means the authors selected ponds that had one of the following four categories of landscape structure: summer foraging habitat near/breeding area near, summer foraging habitat near/breeding area far, summer foraging habitat far/breeding area near, and summer foraging habitat far/breeding area far.

Landscape size

A circular landscape with a 1.5-km radius from the focal pond was selected because it represented the shortest distance in which there was at least one site (pond, stream, or large drainage ditch) from which dispersers might move. Northern leopard frogs typically move 1 to 2 km between habitats within a year, so the size of the landscape reflected this movement distance. Given the size of the area sampled, the intensity of sampling conducted at each landscape, and the number of survey sites, a landscape sample size of 34 was the largest possible.

Multi-scales – the patch, the landscape and sizes in between

The variables in this study were assessed at both the patch scale (the pond) as well as at the 1.5-km radius landscapes scale, a size determined by the movement habits of the northern leopard frog. The 1.5-km radius landscape was also the largest possible, given the requirement of non-overlapping landscapes and that all breeding sites within each landscape had to be surveyed for leopard frogs. The landscape structure variables were also quantified at several smaller landscape scales to determine the scale at which the effect of landscape structure is strongest.

Patch-scale variables The pond's habitat was assessed in detail to determine pond quality (patch scale predictor variables). The authors examined pond perimeter length, amount of spawning habitat, and water pH.

Landscape-scale variables The amount of all possible types of summer habitat was assessed in the surrounding landscape using remotely sensed data that were later ground truthed. The number of all possible breeding sites was also determined within 1.5 km of the pond based on remotely sensed data; the number of sites with calling males was based on the surveys.

Multiple-scale variables The amount of all possible types of summer habitat was also assessed within four smaller landscapes sizes of 0.25, 0.5, 0.75, and 1 km from the focal pond, based on the remotely sensed information.

Multi-scale analysis methods The authors conducted a multi-scale analysis that simultaneously included variables from all scales in the study. They used a stepwise Poisson regression analysis of the landscape and patch variables on their estimates of core pond leopard frog relative abundance. They found a significant effect of two of the patch variables (water pH and the amount of spawning habitat) and two of the landscape structure variables (amount of summer habitat within 1 km of the pond and number of breeding sites with calling males within 1.5 km) on the relative abundance of the northern leopard frog. There was a potential challenge in interpreting the results of the analysis because of the presence of strong correlations among the landscape structure variables across the five scales. The authors addressed this by calculating the landscape variables in non-overlapping rings and re-analyzing the data. They found qualitatively similar results, suggesting that the multi-scale analysis can be used to determine the strongest scale of influence of landscape structural variables.

Management implications

This case study illustrates the importance of managing populations at both the local scale and the appropriate landscape scale. Leopard frog population survival depends on both pond characteristics and landscape structure up to 1.5 km away from the pond. Adequate amounts of both breeding habitat and summer forage habitat must be maintained in the landscape. Maintaining good breeding habitat is intuitively critical to maintaining frog populations, but in the absence of good summer foraging habitat in the landscape, leopard frogs may not survive to maturity. Considering only the number and arrangement of breeding ponds would have led to erroneous conclusions about the potential persistence of leopard frog populations.

3.7 Implications and guidelines for conducting multi-scale landscape studies for wildlife management

In conclusion, we recommend the following four guidelines for conducting landscape-scale studies: (1) determine the appropriate landscape scale, (2) use multiple landscapes, at multiple scales if possible, (3) consider both patch- and landscape-scale factors, and (4) consider design trade-offs of intensity of sampling vs. adequate sample size.

To determine the appropriate scale the researcher or manager must first formulate a hypothesis, with response and predictor variables clearly defined. The response variable determines the species of interest and the measures required (e.g., presence/absence, abundance, species richness). This in turn determines the intensity of sampling required for the response variable. The hypothesized relationship between the predictor variables and the response variable determines the appropriate landscape size. For example, if the hypothesis relates landscape structure to an individual-level response (e.g., foraging success), then the appropriate landscape size depends on short-term (e.g., daily) movement distances. If the hypothesis relates landscape structure to population abundance, then the appropriate landscape scale depends on the scale of inter-population dispersal events.

In most landscape ecological studies the objective is to relate landscape structure to an ecological response. Therefore, many landscapes with different structures are needed. When the application of an experimental "treatment" is inappropriate (as it often is), sample landscapes should be chosen using strict a priori selection criteria to minimize correlations among predictor variables, and to ensure wide variation in the landscape structure (predictor) variables.

Studies have shown that failing to consider the effects of both patch and landscape characteristics may lead to unsuccessful management decisions. Findlay and Houlahan (1997) examined the effect of landscape structure on species richness in 30 wetlands (Table 3.1). They determined that an increase in road density and a decrease in forest cover surrounding each wetland had a negative effect on species richness. They also determined that larger wetlands were positively related to species diversity. One of the results suggested that increasing the amount of road surface by 2m/ha within 1 km of the wetland, or decreasing forest cover by about 20% within 2 km, had a similar effect on species richness as reducing the size of the wetland by 50%. This illustrates the point that the context of a patch is important. Management policies that only considered wetland quality might have failed because the landscape context was not addressed.

In studies where large landscapes are required, trade-offs between sampling intensity and sample size (number of landscapes) will be particularly severe. The number of sample landscapes should be maximized in spite of these limitations. We suggest that the focal-patch approach with strict landscape selection criteria is the best compromise when landscape structure variables can be measured relatively easily. The focal-patch design reduces the trade-off between sampling intensity and replication. It also increases the power of statistical tests through the use of strict criteria to select landscapes, thus reducing the required sample size.

3.8 Summary

A multi-scale landscape study must be designed properly to provide appropriate information for management of natural populations. Multi-scale studies address the effects of both patch characteristics (e.g., patch size or quality) and landscape structural characteristics (composition, configuration) on an ecological response variable. The size of the landscape must be determined based on knowledge of the organism and the research question. In a multi-scale landscape study, the unit of observation is the landscape. Therefore, several non-overlapping landscapes should be selected that differ in structure. Because of the size of study landscapes, however, logistical limitations may reduce landscape sample size. To counter these limitations we suggest the use of the focal patch design, where the ecological response variable is measured intensely at patches located at the centers of non-overlapping landscapes.

Acknowledgments

We thank members of the Landscape Ecology Laboratory at Carleton University and members of the Institute of Ecosystem Studies (Millbrook, New York) Discussion Group, especially Kringen Henein, Jeff Holland, Melissa Vance, Charles Canham, Richard Ostfeld, David Strayer, and Clive Jones, for suggestions and lively discussion of this manuscript. This work was supported by a Natural Sciences and Engineering Research Council of Canada (NSERC) grant to L. Fahrig, a NSERC scholarship to D. Bender, and both NSERC and FCAR scholarships to J. Brennan.

References

Allen, T. F. H. (1998). The landscape level is dead: Persuading the family to take it off the respirator. In *Ecological Scale*, eds. D. L. Peterson & V. T. Parker, pp. 35–54. Columbia University Press, New York.

Andrén, H. (1994). Effects of habitat fragmentation on birds and mammals in landscapes with different proportions of suitable habitat: A review. *Oikos*, 71: 355–366.

Bender, D. J., Contreras, T. A. & Fahrig, L. (1998). Habitat loss and population decline: a meta-analysis of the patch size effect. *Ecology*, 79: 517–533.

Burrough, P. (1995). Spatial aspects of ecological data. In *Data Analysis in Community and Landscape Ecology*, eds. R. Jongman, C. ter Braak & O. van Tongeren, pp. 213–251. Cambridge University Press, Cambridge, UK.

Cormack, R. M. & Ord, J. K. (eds.) (1979). *Spatial and Temporal Analysis in Ecology*. International Cooperative Publishing House, Fairland, MD.

Fahrig, L. & Grez, A. A. (1996). Population spatial structure, human-caused landscape changes and species survival. *Revista Chilena de Historia Natural*, 69: 5–13.

Findlay, C. S. & Houlahan, J. (1997). Anthropogenic correlates of species richness in southeastern Ontario wetlands. *Conservation Biology*, 11: 1000–1009.

Forman, R. T. T. & Godron, M. (1986). *Landscape Ecology*. John Wiley, New York.

Gittins, R. (1968). Trend-surface analysis of ecological data. *Journal of Ecology*, 56: 845–859.

Goodwin, B. J. & Fahrig, L. (1998). Spatial scaling and animal population dynamics. In *Ecological Scale*, eds. D. L. Peterson & V. T. Parker, pp. 193–206. Columbia University Press, New York.

Gustafson, E. J. (1998). Quantifying spatial pattern: What is state of the art? *Ecosystems*, 1: 143–156.

Gustafson, E. J. & Parker, G. R. (1992).

Relationship between landcover proportion and indices of landscape spatial pattern. *Landscape Ecology*, 7: 101–110.

Hanski, I. & Gilpin, M. (1991). Single-species metapopulation dynamics: Concepts, models and observations. *Biological Journal of the Linnean Society*, 42: 17–38.

Hargis, C., Bissonette, J. & David, J. (1998). The behavior of landscape metrics commonly used in the study of habitat fragmentation. *Landscape Ecology*, 13: 167–186.

Hastie, T. (1992). Generalized additive models. In *Statistical Models in S*, eds. J. Chambers & T. Hastie, pp. 249–307. Wadsworth, Pacific Grove, CA.

Hastie T. & Tibshirani, R. (1990). *Generalized Additive Models*. Chapman & Hall, London.

Henein, K., Wegner, J. & Merriam, H. G. (1998). Population effects of landscape model manipulation on two behaviourally different woodland small mammals. *Oikos*, 81: 168–186.

Holland, J. & Fahrig, L. (2000). Effect of woody borders on insect density and diversity in crop fields: A landscape-scale analysis. *Agriculture, Ecosystems and Environment*, 78: 115–122.

Hurlbert, S. H. (1984). Pseudoreplication and the design of ecological field experiments. *Ecological Monographs*, 54: 187–211.

Johnston, C. A. (1995). Effects of animals on landscape pattern. In *Mosaic Landscapes and Ecological Processes*, eds. L. Hansson, L. Fahrig & G. Merriam, pp. 57–80. Chapman & Hall, London.

Jokimaki, J. & Huhta, E. (1996). Effects of landscape matrix and habitat structure of a bird community in northern Finland: a multi-scale approach. *Ornis Fennica*, 73: 97–113.

Jonsen, I. D. & Fahrig, L. (1997). Response of generalist and specialist insect herbivores to landscape spatial structure. *Landscape Ecology*, 12: 185–197.

King, A. W. (1997). Hierarchy theory: A guide to system structure for wildlife biologists. In *Wildlife and Landscape Ecology: Effects of Pattern and Scale*, ed. J. A. Bissonette, pp. 185–212. Springer-Verlag, New York.

Klopatek, J. M. & Gardner, R. H. (eds.) (1999). *Landscape Ecological Analysis: Issues and Applications*. Springer-Verlag, New York.

Langlois, J. P., Fahrig, L., Merriam, H. G. & Artsob, H. (2001). Landscape structure influences continental distribution of hantavirus in deer mice. *Ecology*, 16: 255–266.

Legendre, P. (1993). Spatial autocorrelation: Trouble or new paradigm? *Ecology*, 74: 1659–1673.

Legendre, P. & Fortin, M.-J. (1989). Spatial pattern and ecological analysis. *Vegetatio*, 80: 107–138.

Li, C. C. (1975). *Path Analysis: A Primer*. Boxwood Press, Pacific Grove, CA.

Lindenmayer, D. B., Cunningham, R. B. & Pope, M. L. (1999). A large-scale "experiment" to examine the effects of landscape context and habitat fragmentation on mammals. *Biological Conservation*, 88: 387–403.

Manly, B. F. J. (1997). *Randomization and Monte Carlo Methods in Biology*, 2nd edn. Chapman & Hall, London.

Maruyama, G. M. (1998). *Basics of Structural Equation Modelling*. Sage, Thousand Oaks, CA.

McGarigal, K. & McComb, W. C. (1995). Relationships between landscape structure and breeding birds in the Oregon Coast Range. *Ecological Monographs*, 65: 235–260.

Milne, B. T. (1991). Lessons from applying fractal models to landscape patterns. In *Quantitative Methods in Landscape Ecology*, eds. M. G. Turner & R. H. Gardner, pp. 199–235. Springer-Verlag, New York.

Neter, J., Wasserman, W. & Kutner, M. (1990). *Applied Linear Statistical Models*, 3rd edn. Irwin, Homewood, CA.

Noble, I. R. & Gitay, H. (1996). A functional classification for predicting the dynamics of landscapes. *Journal of Vegetation Science*, 7: 329–336.

O'Neill, R. V., Krummel, J. R., Gardner, R. H., Sugihara, G., Jackson, B., DeAngelis, D. L., Milne, B. T., Turner, M. G., Zygmunt, B., Christensen, S. W., Dale, V. H. & Graham, R. L. (1988). Indices of landscape pattern. *Landscape Ecology*, 1: 153–162.

Palmer, M. W. (1988). Fractal geometry: A tool for describing spatial patterns of plant communities. *Vegetatio*, 75: 91–102.

Pedlar, J. H., Fahrig, L. & Merriam, H. G. (1997). Raccoon habitat use at two spatial scales. *Journal of Wildlife Management*, 61: 102–112.

Plotnick, R. E., Gardner, R. H. & O'Neill, R. V. (1993). Lacunarity indices as measures of landscape texture. *Landscape Ecology*, 8: 201–211.

Pope, S. E., Fahrig, L. & Merriam, H. G. (2000). Landscape complementation and metapopulation effects on leopard frog populations. *Ecology*, 81: 2489–2508.

Preisler, H., Rappaport, N. & Wood, D. (1997). Regression methods for spatially correlated data: An example using beetle attacks in a seed orchard. *Forest Science*, 43: 71–77.

Ritters, K. H., O'Neill, R. V., Hunsaker, C. T., Wickham, J. D., Yankee, D. H., Timmins, S. P., Jones, K. B. & Jackson, B. L. (1995). A factor analysis of landscape pattern and structure measures. *Landscape Ecology*, 10: 23–39.

Saab, V. (1999). Importance of spatial scale to habitat use by breeding birds in riparian forests: A hierarchical analysis. *Ecological Applications*, 9: 135–151.

Schumaker, N. H. (1996). Using landscape indices to predict habitat connectivity. *Ecology*, 77: 1210–1225.

Sisk, T. D., Haddad, N. M. & Ehrlich, P. (1997). Bird assemblages in patchy woodlands: Modeling the effects of edge and matrix habitats. *Ecological Applications*, 7: 1170–1180.

Tischendorf, L. & Fahrig, L. (2000a). On the usage and measurement of landscape connectivity. *Oikos*, 90: 7–19.

Tischendorf, L. & Fahrig, L. (2000b). How should we measure landscape connectivity? *Landscape Ecology*, 15: 633–641.

Trzcinski, M. K., Fahrig, L. & Merriam, H. G. (1999). Independent effects of forest cover and fragmentation on the distribution of forest breeding birds. *Ecological Applications*, 9: 586–593.

Turner, M. G. & Gardner, R. H. (eds.) (1991). *Quantitative Methods in Landscape Ecology*. Springer-Verlag, New York.

Turner, S., O'Neill, R. V., Conley, W., Conley, M. R. & Humphries, H. (1991). Pattern and scale: Statistics for landscape ecology. In *Quantitative Methods in Landscape Ecology*, eds. M. G. Turner & R. H. Gardner, pp. 17–49. Springer-Verlag, New York.

Venier, L. A. & Fahrig, L. (1998). Intra-specific abundance–distribution relationships. *Oikos*, 82: 483–490.

Wiens, J. A. (1989). Spatial scaling in ecology. *Functional Ecology*, 3: 385–397.

Wiens, J. A. (1992). What is landscape ecology, really? *Landscape Ecology*, 7: 149–150.

Wiens, J. A., Schooley, R. L. & Weeks, R. D. Jr. (1997). Patchy landscapes and animal movements: Do beetles percolate? *Oikos*, 78: 257–264.

4

Managing for small-patch patterns in human-dominated landscapes: Cultural factors and Corn Belt agriculture

4.1 Introduction

Habitat fragmentation is the nearly inevitable result of contemporary land use. Beyond the biodiversity shadow cast by reserves and habitat protection plans, settlement patterns continue to extirpate remaining habitats. This reality should lead landscape ecologists and natural resource managers to vigorously investigate small patches of habitat. While accumulating knowledge of landscape structure and function leaves no doubt about the critical importance of large indigenous habitat patches, knowledge of the ecological function of small patches is comparatively meager. Yet opportunities for preserving or creating small patches characterize human land use. Informed by landscape ecology, conservation biology, ecosystem management, and restoration ecology, humans have only recently begun to preserve and reconnect the pieces of what were once large, continuous ecosystems. The undeniable trend of contemporary settlement patterns suggests that the small shall inherit the earth. How these small patches can serve ecological functions is a pragmatic question for landscape ecology.

A bird's-eye view of settled landscapes today presents a striking image of the impact of humans on the natural world. The landscape pattern observed is profoundly influenced by culture, created according to political systems, economic uses, aesthetic preferences, and social conventions (Nassauer, 1995). Culture, defined as "the sum total of ways of living built up by a group of human beings and transmitted from one generation to another" (Random House, 1987), not only influences landscape patterns, it can also suggest new landscapes designed to promote ecological function (Nassauer, 1995). New landscape patterns designed without consideration of the appearance of cultural values on the land are not culturally sustainable (Nassauer, 1992, 1997). Cultural values, perceived and expressed in contemporary land uses, should influence new, normative landscape patterns. This chapter examines the relationship between cultural factors and small patch patterns in contemporary Corn Belt agricultural landscapes, and it suggests implications for new agricultural landscape patterns that could be designed to promote ecological function.

Settled landscapes are composed primarily of large, human-constructed patches, often controlled for economic production or aesthetic effect, and exhibiting low biodiversity. Paving, buildings, mown turf, horticultural species, and crop monocultures characterize these large patch types. For example, crop monocultures of corn and soybeans in the Midwest can extend across a square mile. Shopping centers, central business districts, and stadium sites are large patches that typify urban areas. Settlement fragments formerly large patches of native biodiversity, and results in the loss of habitat and the creation of more small patches. Within the context of settlement, these small patches may exhibit their own, more modest potential for habitat. We explore how cultural values and traditions limit but also suggest possibilities for small patch patterns that maintain or improve biodiversity amid the larger patches of human land use.

The classification of landscape patches as "small" or "large" depends on the habitat type and scale of management interest. A small patch in a forest may be different from a small patch on a farm, and a small patch on a farm in New England may be different from a small patch on a farm in the Midwest. Descriptive patch size – large or small – refers to the scale of management in these different landscapes. According to one definition, small patches interject landscape heterogeneity on a scale of a few hundred square meters (Ludwig, 1999). Schwartz and van Mantgem (1997) characterize small patches in the Corn Belt of the Midwest as areas less than 10 hectares in size. In our examination of Corn Belt agricultural landscapes, small patches range from several square meters to 10 hectares, and include the elongated shapes of narrow strips common to roadsides and field boundaries. Small patch types can be labeled to indicate their origins or imply their functions (Forman and Godron, 1986). Biodiversity patches are resource-rich habitats with more species than their surroundings (Ludwig, 1999) and are called habitat patches in this chapter.

Small habitat patches in human-dominated landscapes change how ecological systems function. Small patches provide habitat for edge species and species that are dispersing, decrease erosion and fetch, and increase species density (Forman, 1995). The spatial pattern of small patches within a landscape is important to their ecological effect. Small patches change material transport by altering wind flows (Ryszkowski and Kedziora, 1987; Hobbs, 1993). They affect the accumulation of precipitation; areas adjacent to small woody patches experience altered moisture regimes and soil moisture and temperature (Ryszkowski and Kedziora, 1987; Ryszkowski *et al.*, 1999). Small patches of perennial vegetation influence local carbon and oxygen cycles (Lal *et al.*, 1999), and small woody patches remove nutrients and hold nitrogen, phosphorus, and potassium in agricultural landscapes (Peterjohn and Correll, 1984; Edwards and Owens, 1991; Cooper *et al.*, 1995; Ryszkowski *et al.*, 1999). They provide a source of soil invertebrates, pollen, and seeds to the adjacent landscape (Forman, 1995) and insects beneficial to adjacent crops (Nentwig, 1989; Thomas *et al.*, 1991; Colunga-Garcia *et al.*, 1997; Dyer and Landis, 1997; Landis *et al.*, 2000). In the Western Australia wheatbelt, small fragments of indigenous vegetation barely maintain the ecological processes that were once provided by intact indigenous land covers (Hobbs, 1993). As habitat, small patches can also have negative consequences – such as increased predation and parasitism and increased environmental fluctuation – for some area-sensitive populations (Herkert, 1994; Forman, 1995).

Though small patches cannot provide the same ecological functions as large habitat patches, their present and potential contribution to the function of human-dominated landscapes calls for further inquiry. Reserve and protected area design have focused on the importance of large patches (Noss and Cooperrider, 1994). While Forman's (1995) *aggregate-with-outliers* principle of land planning and management recommends a pattern of a few large patches with several small patches for habitat and biodiversity functions, the significance of small patches remains under-recognized. Beneficial locations for large patches are known (Forman, 1995, lists these criteria: context, whole landscape, key locations, targeted ecological characteristics, and targeted spatial attributes), but normative criteria for locating small habitat patches is uncertain.

In this chapter we investigate some cultural factors that affect small patch patterns in one human-dominated landscape type, Corn Belt agriculture. We identify small patch patterns that express cultural values and traditions, and we review the landscape ecological effects of those patterns. Finally, we illustrate possible landscape patterns that could enhance ecological functions and are consistent with cultural values and traditions.

4.2 Cultural factors that affect small patch patterns

Since landscape patterns are informed and limited by culture, understanding culture allows us to better investigate and change landscape patterns. Humans construct and manage landscapes based upon their perceptions – what they see, know, and feel. New landscape patterns are expressions of culture (Nassauer, 1995).

Settled landscapes are shaped by many cultural factors, including:

- land division, settlement patterns, and ownership traditions (including land, trade, resource, and tax policy; land ownership rights, and environmental law);
- applied science and technology values and traditions (including productivity and progressiveness); and
- stewardship values (including conservation and health), and aesthetic values.

The particular spatial characteristics of these "ways of living" change with time and vary from one culture to another. What makes the values and traditions powerful in shaping landscape patterns is that they motivate human behavior, often without articulation or deliberation. Cultural factors are the unseen foundation for human actions that shape landscapes. We do things the way we know how to do them. For example, eighteenth-century French settlers in North America, who valued river access for fur trading, divided land into long lots each of which had access to the river (Quebec, Canada; Michigan, Illinois and Louisiana, USA; Hart, 1968, 1975, 1998). In contrast, eighteenth-century settlers in New England, USA, divided land by a metes-and-bounds system that incorporated visible landmark features like trees, rocks, and rivers as boundaries. Each system created a different landscape pattern that dramatically affects these same landscapes today.

The value farmers place on increased production and on being progressive also leads to land management decisions that produce more food, but may not always be more profitable (Cochrane and Runge, 1992). In the past 50 years, cultural values of increased production and progressive agriculture have been associated with bigger equipment, bigger fields, and bigger farms in the Corn Belt of the United States (Hart, 1968; Nassauer and Westmacott, 1987). Given this trend, small habitat patches are eliminated to allow large equipment to maneuver efficiently. As different policy incentives and agricultural techniques emerge, the landscape patterns associated with cultural values of increased production and progressiveness could change.

While management decisions related to land division and ownership, or applied science and technology are often related to economics, farmers make stewardship and aesthetic decisions even when economic returns from these decisions will not yield short term profits (Nassauer, 1988, 1989). Rather the resulting appearance of the landscape, which shows that the farmer takes pride in the farm or shows that the farmer is a good steward, is the more important consideration. Particular stewardship practices and landscape patterns change with time and new knowledge, while the cultural value of stewardship remains.

The same cultural factors that influence existing landscape structure can be used to suggest more ecologically beneficial patterns. If cultural factors are strategically employed in natural resources policy, planning, and management, resulting landscapes can include small habitat patches that fit cultural expectations while they enhance Corn Belt ecological functions. These new landscape patterns not only will be ecologically beneficial, they will be culturally sustainable (Nassauer, 1997), maintained by people because their value is immediately apparent.

4.3 Example: Small patches in the Midwest Corn Belt

4.3.1 Description of the Midwest Corn Belt

The Corn Belt is a 12-state region in the Midwest of the United States (Fig. 4.1) of low relief that was covered mostly by tallgrass prairie prior to settlement by Europeans. The pioneer settlement waves of the early 1800s, along with the steel plowshare, nearly eliminated the prairie (Schennum, 1986; Hurt, 1991; Hudson, 1992; Hart, 1998). By the late 1800s the dominant land use of the Midwest was agriculture and the dominant crop grown on the farms between Chicago and central Nebraska was corn (Hudson, 1992). Often called the "heartland" of America, the Corn Belt is the epitome of American rural culture – family farms, small towns, and people considered hard-working, principled, and wholesome (Sayre, 1999). In 1960, typical Iowa farms produced chickens, eggs, pork or beef, milk, corn, oats, and hay; every farm had a pasture and garden (Hart, 1998), and the landscape displayed a variety of patch types. Today, typical Iowa farms produce corn and soybeans only; chickens, eggs, pork, beef, and milk are produced in specialized facilities in a decreasing number of locations. Consequently, contemporary Corn Belt landscapes are dominated by large, homogeneous patches of crop monocultures. Perennial land cover, herbaceous or woody, is increasingly rare: less than 0.1% of native tallgrass prairie communities remain in Illinois (Schwartz and van Mantgem, 1997).

Despite extensive modifications for row-crop production across the Corn Belt, small habitat patches remain – woodlots, farmsteads, roadsides, railroad rights-of-way, field boundaries, erosive or wet areas, some forms of grazing agriculture, and stream corridors. Wisconsin woodlots average 5.6 hectares in area (Dunn *et al.*, 1990, 1993). Half of the farmer-owned woodlots in Illinois are less than 8 hectares in area (Young *et al.*, 1985). On erodible land, Conservation Reserve Program fields with perennial grass cover average 8.1 hectares in Ohio (Swanson *et al.*, 1999). Remnant ecosystems in Illinois are very small: of 253 high-quality prairie remnants, 83% are less than 4 hectares, and 30% are less than 0.4 hectares (Robertson *et al.*, 1997); 93% of Illinois' wetland complexes

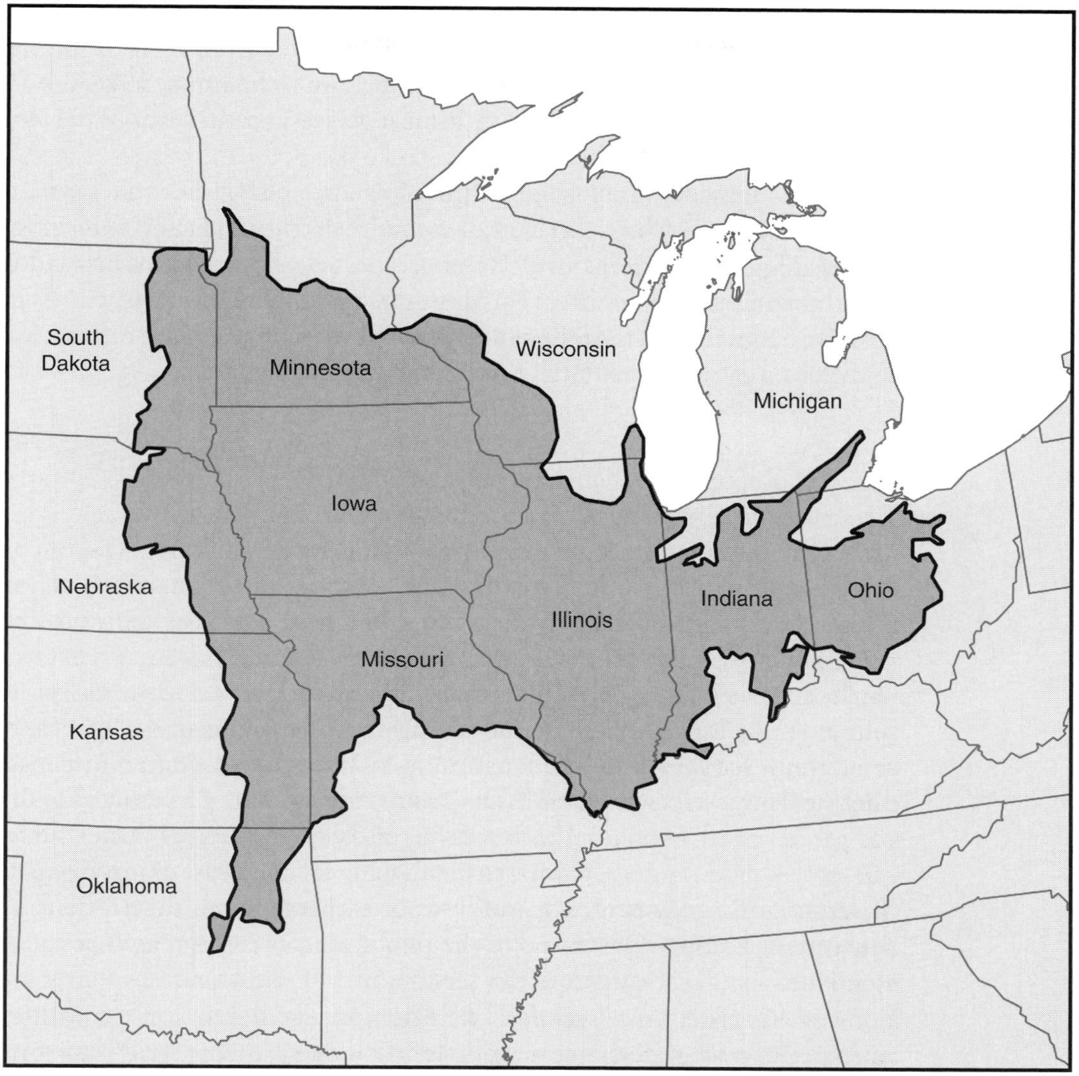

FIGURE 4.1
The Corn Belt (central feed grains land resource region) of the USA. (Source: US Department of Agriculture Natural Resources Conservation Service, Resource Assessment Division. Map Identification Number 3966. September 28, 1998).

are less than 4 hectares and nearly 2/3 are less than 0.4 hectares (Havera *et al.*, 1997). Wetlands restored in Iowa under the North American Waterfowl Management Plan have averaged 2 hectares in area (Bishop *et al.*, 1998). A comprehensive survey of Iowa found over 1000 potential prairie remnants, most of which occur as small patches (Schennum, 1986). Eighty-one percent of the ungrazed, unmowed, native prairie remnants in Story County, Iowa, are small patches (about 1.2 hectares) on railroad rights-of-way (Braband, 1986). The cultural tradition of harvesting "wild" hay (prairie vegetation) is one of the key reasons that small prairie patches remain in Iowa (Schennum, 1986; Smith, 1998; Sayre, 1999). In the Corn Belt, the most pervasive contributions to biodiversity come from small patches.

In the context of Corn Belt agriculture, small patches are essential repositories of biodiversity. They exist as a consequence of cultural factors interacting with ecological characteristics of the landscape. Below, we describe how cultural values and traditions affect existing small-patch landscape structure and ecological function. In the following section, we describe how these values and traditions could affect potential new landscape patterns.

4.3.2 The effect of culture on small patch characteristics in the Corn Belt

Land division, settlement patterns, and ownership traditions

Land division, settlement patterns, and land ownership patterns can be described as traditions, customary ways of living. Each represents a way of doing things that seems self-evident, but that actually is one of many possible cultural expressions on the land. Each influences the size and location of small patches. Many forms of land division could have delineated the Midwest for settlement by Europeans in the nineteenth-century (Johnson, 1976). Yet the square-mile sections (note: the square mile is a cultural tradition, equivalent to 2.59 km^2) imposed by the 1785 Public Land Ordinance are perpetuated to this day in the roads that bound each section, in the description of farm land for sale, and in mile-long (1.61 km) farm fields delineated for ease of management by large farm equipment. For purposes of ownership and description, the square-mile sections (640 acres) of the public land survey are further subdivided into smaller squares (quarter sections of 160 acres, quarter-quarter sections of 40 acres). This Euclidean tradition, invented and applied without reference to ecological characteristics (Johnson, 1957; Meine, 1997), accounts for the highly regular rectilinear geometry of Midwest agricultural landscapes.

In the Corn Belt's grid of land division, small habitat patches are likely to occur at field and ownership boundaries, along streams, or on highly erodible, less productive, or hydric soils. Small woodland, wetland, or prairie patches can be points of convergence of many different field types or they can be engulfed by a single field (Schennum, 1986), so that each becomes an isolated island of biodiversity within the crop. Functional responses like species flow are affected by these patch type adjacencies (Forman and Godron, 1986; Forman, 1995).

In the Corn Belt, small patches that reflect natural constraints on cultivation are managed differently on land division boundaries. Constraints like streams, steep topography, droughtiness, or hydric soils are more likely to be managed as small patches if they occur on the edge of a field. In the center of a field or farm, for instance, drainage may be a high priority to manage a wet area, but if that same area occurs along an ownership or field boundary, drainage may be a low priority. Natural constraints may be virtually ignored or overcome with technology where they do not fall on a land division boundary. Such technological management limits landscape ecological networks that depend on small patch connections, for example the seasonal flows among prairie pothole wetlands of the Midwest (Galatowitsch and van der Valk, 1994). Incompletely drained hydric soils that retain some of their previous, seasonally connected wetland pattern are apparent in Story County, Iowa, where surface water accumulates in the pattern of former prairie pothole wetlands (Fig. 4.2, color plate).

As Corn Belt fields get larger, their boundaries frequently correspond with square-mile section lines bounded by roads. Homogeneous row-crop fields can extend from one section road to another. Iowa farms have increased from a 1964 average size of 88 hectares to a 1997 average of 137 hectares – over ½ of a square-mile section, not including extensive rented land (US Department of Agriculture National Agricultural Statistics Service, 1999). Roadsides remain areas of relatively high habitat diversity if they are managed to maintain biodiversity functions for mammals (Braband, 1986; Merriam and Lanoue, 1990; Wegner and Merriam, 1990; Kirsch, 1997), birds (Braband, 1986; Best *et al.*, 1995; Sutter *et al.*, 2000), and beneficial insects (Marino and Landis, 1996; Orr and Pleasants, 1996). In the landscape matrix of large fields, roadsides also can reduce soil loss and filter pollution from chemical fertilizers and pesticides.

Policy and market-based economic incentives for cultivation have encouraged removal of small patches that do not correspond to field or ownership boundaries. Small patches of woody or perennial herbaceous vegetation that were used for shelter or grazing within traditional mixed livestock/grain farming typically are eliminated in grain production. Farms have become more specialized, reducing the overall heterogeneity of any given square-mile section. Changes in Iowa agriculture (Table 4.1) from mixed livestock and crop operations to exclusive grain cropping with separate, intensive concentrations of livestock feeding have increased cultivation pressures on formerly heterogeneous landscapes, resulting in the loss of small patches – pastures, barnyards, fencerows and field boundaries, and livestock shelterbelts (Hart, 1998). Between 1939 and 1990, for example, an Iowa watershed had a 50% decrease in the number of farm fields and a corresponding increase in field area (Waide and Hatfield, 1995).

The farmstead, where people live on the land that they farm, includes small areas of greater habitat value relative to Corn Belt croplands. Farmsteads – small areas of canopy trees and woody and herbaceous plants that can augment the habitat value of cropland – are dotted across the more homogeneous agricultural landscape at an interval roughly corresponding to farm size. In the

Table 4.1. *Iowa farm diversity changes between 1964 and 1997*

Production description	1964	1997	Amount of change from 1964
Total number of farms	154 162	90 792	−41%
Number of farms producing hogs	106 184	17 243	−84%
Number of hogs produced	13 700 000	14 700 000	+7%
Number of farms producing beef	65 402	27 452	−58%
Number of beef cows	1 247 101	1 029 172	−17%
Number of farms producing eggs	73 804	1 892	−97%
Number of laying hens	19 500 000	24 900 000	+28%
Number of farms producing milk	59 673	4 208	−93%
Number of milk cows	735 647	222 142	−70%
Area in hay production (ha)	1 296 000	638 000	−51%
Area in corn production (ha)	3 892 000	4 692 000	+21%
Area in soybean production (ha)	1 689 000	4 025 000	+138%

Source: US Department of Agriculture National Agricultural Statistics Service (1999).

dry lands of Nebraska, farms are larger (state average is 358 ha) and farmsteads are more sparse than in the higher moisture landscape of central Iowa (state average farm size is 137 ha). In all of the Corn Belt, farms were bigger and farmsteads were less dense in 1997 than they were in 1964, where the number of farms in Iowa has decreased 41% (Table 4.1).

Applied science and technology

Agricultural field equipment, a critical component of agricultural applied science and technology, is a cultural phenomenon. The equipment that farmers choose is a reflection of their values. The value that Midwestern farmers place upon being progressive and increasing production is demonstrated in their persistent interest in new forms of equipment, from the four-row corn planter typical of the 1950s to the 24-row planter seen today. Not all forms of progressive agriculture have been related to increased production. The moldboard plow typical in the 1970s has been widely replaced by the chisel plow used for conservation tillage in the 1990s. Now, precision agriculture field equipment has begun to augment large-scale farm equipment to implement finer-scale inputs of nutrients, pesticides, and seeds according to soil and crop variability. Progressiveness may come to be tempered by farmers' valuing profits more than overall levels of production. However, for the past 50 years, US agricultural policy has provided incentives for farmers to value overall production levels (Cochrane and Runge, 1992).

The agricultural technology farmers choose and the way they apply it affect small-patch patterns within the larger landscape pattern of land division, settlement patterns, and ownership traditions. Small habitat patches that do not fit emerging agricultural techniques are removed, but new techniques may introduce small patch opportunities. For example, farmers who plant newly available, genetically modified Bt (*Bacillus thuringiensis*) corn are required, as an insect resistance management strategy, to also plant small patches of non-Bt corn as a refuge for European corn borer (*Ostrinia nubilalis*; Pioneer Hi-Bred Limited, 1999). The very recent innovation of precision agriculture is leading to changes in agricultural techniques that could bring small patches back into the cultivated landscape by changing planting, crop protection, and harvest patterns with better information and more responsive field equipment.

Bigger equipment, fewer and smaller patches Field equipment size has profoundly influenced small patches in this century, in a continuous trend to bigger machines and larger fields. This larger agricultural field equipment requires more coarse rectilinear tillage patterns. Field equipment width has increased (Quick and Buchele, 1978; Hurt, 1991), with a resulting increase in field size (Hart, 1968) and a loss of small habitat patches (wet areas, field boundaries, small woods, remnant prairies, farm lanes, or other interstices). Small habitat patches are removed if they interfere with crop tillage, planting, protection, and harvesting operations. Ecological functions of remaining small habitat patches are affected by adjacent crop disturbance (Braband, 1986; Freemark and Boutin, 1995; Boutin and Jobin, 1998).

When small patches are removed to support increasingly large farm equipment, the distance between remaining small habitat patches increases, diminishing landscape diversity, and decreasing the ability of species to disperse to suitable habitats through the farm landscape (Bunce and Howard, 1990; Opdam, 1990; Mankin and Warner, 1997). Distance between wooded patches in Wisconsin mixed farming increased from an average of 150 meters in 1882 to 400 meters in 1978 (Dunn *et al.*, 1990, 1993). Grassland birds find suitable habitats in Conservation Reserve Program grass patches that are 10 hectares or more, or are smaller but adjacent to other grasslands (Swanson *et al.*, 1999).

Agricultural drainage has been employed to accommodate farm equipment access (especially as machinery increases in size and weight) and facilitate longer cropping seasons. Subsurface drainage facilitates nutrient losses: nitrates lost from row-crops by subsurface drainage flow are 35 times higher than losses from Conservation Reserve fields (Randall *et al.*, 1997). Subsurface drainage fragments landscape structure by isolating and shrinking small wet patches (Spaling, 1995), changes watershed boundaries, concentrates nutrients and chemical residues, and increases rates of water and contaminant flows (Spaling and Smit, 1995).

With increased equipment size, more land is disturbed with each wider field pass. Farm equipment demands large homogeneous landscape patches for efficient mobility. Tillage, planting, crop protection, and harvesting equipment all differ in width and responsiveness because the physical size and maneuverability of each piece of specialized equipment vary. A narrow planter may be able to respond to a wet area by not planting crop seed (i.e., by maneuvering around or suspending seed flow), but the same area may be unavoidable to wider equipment during crop protection or harvest operations.

Large-scale agricultural equipment makes small habitat patch persistence difficult, but it can create opportunities for small patches along boundaries. As equipment increases in size and cultivation intensifies, small patches such as wetlands or farmsteads may disappear. But inaccessibility to large field equipment has allowed some indigenous prairie patches to remain in Iowa farm landscapes (Schennum, 1986). Field corners where cultivation, planting, spraying, and harvesting may be difficult or time-consuming with large equipment can become small habitat patches if farmers' aesthetic values do not lead them to mow or eliminate weeds along these edges.

Precision agriculture, more small patches? Precision agriculture is an emerging technology that has been called "farming by the foot [of measure]" (Batchelor *et al.*, 1997). Precision agriculture involves four sub-systems: soil and crop sensing to determine characteristics and yields; locational sensing (global positioning systems); field data mapping (geographic information systems); and precise, variable application mechanisms with automatic control ("smart" farm equipment; Stafford, 1996). The greatest potential agronomic benefit of precision farming is increased profitability and the decrease of unnecessary or excessive crop inputs (Wallace, 1994; Fountas, 1998). Progressive farmers are only beginning to adopt precision agriculture (Fountas, 1998), but like conservation tillage or genetically modified crops, precision agriculture could pervasively affect small-patch patterns in the Corn Belt.

Precision agriculture's variable farm equipment could change landscape patterns both by removing some existing small patches and by creating opportunities for new small patches. Larger farm equipment and costly new technologies will be used, and farmers may seek to remove small patches that interfere with mobility. But new equipment with variable application mechanisms will respond flexibly to soil and crop information and identify areas that could become small habitat patches.

If profitability increases with the use of precision agriculture techniques, it may be another force that drives out smaller producers, those who cannot afford the scale of farm equipment and technology necessary (van Schilfgaarde, 1999). This would further reinforce the current trend toward larger fields and farms. The technology and decision-support systems of precision agriculture could be used to estimate the profitability of fields and of areas (e.g., soil types) that are not currently row-cropped. This could mean a conversion of non-crop cover to annual row-crops where profitability is likely. On the other hand, it could mean the conversion of cropland to non-crop cover where profitability is negative or erratic.

Much of the effect of precision agriculture is uncertain until widespread adoption and successful management produces a record of results. However, precision agriculture technology could support ecological ways of thinking about small patches in agroecosystems by encouraging the conservation and establishment of small habitat patches in areas where profitability is questionable. New types of small patches could result, increasing heterogeneity and the number of small patches throughout the crop field. Some of the increased heterogeneity could result from managing crop variability with differential inputs or by creating new land covers among crops. More precise applications of crop inputs could decrease non-point source pollution. Decreased unintended drift of agrichemicals will reduce pollution of non-target ecosystems (Paice *et al.*, 1996, 1998). Precision agriculture could improve profitability while it decreases unintended ecological effects.

New small habitat patches could be established if precision agriculture is used to suspend all crop inputs (seed, fertilizer, pesticide) in small, unprofitable areas (e.g., an extremely eroded knoll or very wet soils) and replace them with an alternative cover of perennial vegetation (Corry and Nassauer, 1998). The vegetative composition could vary, but would likely need to be herbaceous to reduce interference with field operations. Small patches of forage (grasses and legumes) could be purposeful to a livestock producer, or perennial polycultures (Soule and Piper, 1992) may provide additional economic diversity to grain producers. Federal (USA) agricultural policy could encourage farmers to enhance biodiversity by planting herbaceous native prairie species on small patches identified by precision agriculture, just as federal agricultural policy targeted parcel selection and biodiversity goals for Conservation Reserve parcels under the Federal Agriculture Improvement and Reform Act of 1996 (P.L. 104–127). Finding herbaceous compositions that can co-exist with common row-crops improves the potential of precision agriculture to result in new small habitat patch patterns.

Stewardship values and landscape aesthetic values

Stewardship values and landscape aesthetic values are different from land division and ownership traditions, and different from applied science and technology, in that they seldom are rationalized as purely economic choices. Instead, farmers manage land for good stewardship or to display certain aesthetic characteristics, like neatness, knowing that their values or the values of their community underpin their decisions. Corn Belt farmers value soil and water conservation practices that they know represent good stewardship. Fields and farmsteads that look neat and weed-free are valued because they demonstrate that the farmer is taking good care of them (Nassauer, 1979, 1988, 1989; Nassauer and Westmacott, 1987). Because farmers employ stewardship and aesthetic values knowing that their management choices are not for short-term profit, these values may be particularly powerful in enhancing small-patch patterns. For example, one Iowa farmer whom we interviewed in 1998 told us that while it made sense to him to use 24-row planting equipment across the 650 hectares of corn and soybeans that he farmed, he had planted a prairie restoration on 4 less profitable hectares simply because he enjoyed the way it looked.

While stewardship values tend to encourage small patches of best management practices such as Conservation Reserve Program fields, grassed waterways, or riparian buffer strips, which are relatively diverse habitat in the context of Corn Belt agriculture, the neatness aesthetic tends to discourage diverse habitat. A neat agricultural landscape is likely to be one in which patches of mixed herbaceous perennials along roadsides, railways, field boundaries, or untilled corners are replaced with row-crops or regularly mown turf monocultures. A fence-line may be removed, or a curving field boundary that skirts a riparian woodland may be simplified into a rectilinear shape to gain a few square meters for cultivation but also to demonstrate the work ethic of the farmer. Pride of ownership may yield agricultural landscapes that have been tidied well beyond the point of economic return.

Elsewhere, Nassauer has discussed policy and design solutions to this apparent contradiction between the aesthetic of care and habitat diversity in agricultural landscapes (Nassauer and Westmacott, 1987; Nassauer, 1988, 1989). She demonstrates that when recognizable characteristics of care are incorporated in the most visible areas, the good care employed in introducing habitat diversity to the larger agricultural landscape is made recognizable to people by visual cues. These recognizable characteristics include: highly selected areas of mowing along trail or road edges; distinct, bold patterns (like strip cropping); incorporation of vividly flowering forbs; labeling of ecological function with explanatory signs. Neatness can be used sparingly (Nassauer, 1997). Small patches can be sustained in the Corn Belt agricultural landscape to improve ecological functions (e.g., sediment removal and habitat) if they display recognizable landscape characteristics that convey farmers' good care or are immediately recognizable as good stewardship.

4.4 Recommendations to effect landscape change and apply multi-scale management

Small-patch patterns are affected by the cultural factors of land division, settlement patterns, and ownership, applied science and technology, and landscape aesthetics and stewardship. These factors create opportunities to introduce and maintain small habitat patches on multiple scales: within fields, within farms, and across the Corn Belt by technology or policy. To increase the ecological function of small patches in Corn Belt agricultural landscapes, we offer the following recommendations to policy-makers, planners, managers, conservationists, and farmers:

4.4.1 Field scale

Enhance habitat by designing the shape and plant composition of small patches to show immediately recognizable good care

Virtually all small patches are more likely to be sustained over time if they exhibit recognizable good care. Policy incentives, conservation plans, and farm management can make habitat patches immediately apparent as good stewardship (e.g., with strip patterns, flowering vegetation, and recognizably neat edges). Best management practices could be designed to enhance biodiversity while achieving stewardship, increasing the cultural value of small patches in the agricultural landscape. Figure 4.3 (color plate) shows a simulated, prospective stripcropping pattern of corn, soybeans, and native prairie vegetation (Nassauer *et al.*, 2002) that is designed to simultaneously achieve biodiversity and yield benefits (Cruse, 1990; Ghaffarzadeh, 1997; Exner *et al.*, 1999). This attractive pattern of alternating row-crops and prairie cover is likely to provide good habitat (Stallman and Best, 1996a,b; M. Clark and B. Danielson, unpublished data) while it enhances the flows of native flora and fauna and decreases the losses of nutrients and sediments across the cultivated landscape (Gilley *et al.*, 1997). Corn Belt farmers value the recognizable stewardship of this soil-conserving stripcropping pattern (J. I. Nassauer and R. Corry, unpublished data). The same principles used in designing this pattern can be used in designing other small patch types, like roadsides and farmsteads.

Enhance the habitat value of small uncultivated patches within the agricultural landscape: farmsteads, pastures, Conservation Reserve parcels.

While Corn Belt farms continue to become larger and more homogeneously characterized by row-crop production, small patches of different land uses remain. Several of these (e.g., farmsteads, pastures and Conservation Reserve parcels) can be designed and managed to enhance biodiversity – either across the entire land use or in small areas within that land use. For example, if the design and management of the farmstead include gardens of native species, rather than mown turf, the habitat value of nearby small patches is extended. Farmsteads display neatness through mown turf, clutter-free yards, and well-maintained buildings and fences. Farmers typically apply the aesthetic of care to uncultivated land uses. In pastures, care is displayed by removal of dead wood and maintenance of an even, weed-free forage. Early in the Conservation Reserve Program, some farmers were reluctant to enroll in the program because the habitat created on the Program looked weedy and unkempt (Nassauer, 1989). If neatness is used sparingly and other recognizable signs of good care are employed as well, small habitat patches can be encouraged as part of farmsteads, pastures, and other uncultivated land uses in agricultural landscapes.

4.4.2 Farm scale

Enhance habitat on land division boundaries: Roadsides, easements, and field boundaries

These boundaries are places where small habitat patches are likely to occur, even in a landscape of very large fields. Their function as habitat can be reinforced by their plant composition and management. By selecting plants from native ecosystems and changing disturbance practices to enhance native biodiversity, management can improve the ecological function of small patches that conform to land division and ownership boundaries.

Boundaries offer an opportunity to create a network of native, perennial vegetation habitat linkages across farms and throughout the cultivated landscape. Figure 4.4 (color plate) illustrates how a roadside network could improve native biodiversity with prairie plant species and altered mowing and pesticide application practices that create habitat for ground-nesting birds (Best *et al.*, 1995; Waide and Hatfield, 1995), reduce crop pest habitat (Pleasants and Bitzer, 1999), and enhance crop pest–predator habitat (Orr and Pleasants, 1996; Landis *et al.*, 2000). When native vegetation includes colorful, flowering plant species, the boundaries become noticeably attractive while providing a nectar source important to pollinators (Orr and Pleasants, 1996; Steffan-Dewenter and Tscharntke, 1999).

Design field shapes to conform to the dimensions and capabilities of field equipment and to intentionally enhance the patch size, connectivity, and biodiversity of small patches that are difficult to access with field equipment

Farm landscapes are highly machined. The limited maneuverability of large field equipment creates abruptly machined boundaries and opportunities for small patches where planters or combines cannot gain access. New small patches should take advantage of machinery access difficulties. Management can maintain geometric boundaries and fit new small patches to common management patterns (e.g., corners, field borders, fencerows). More importantly, conservation planners and farm consultants could design field shapes to aggregate small patches resulting from equipment access limitations. For example, field shapes that include broad turning radii adjacent to roadside ditches, or that create turning semicircles where adjacent fields intersect, could result in larger small patches that could be managed for their herbaceous biodiversity and still allow large equipment to pass over them at some times of the year.

Figure 4.5 (color plate) shows a remnant patch (10.1 ha) of wet tallgrass prairie in Story County, Iowa. This part of the landscape was not converted to cropland perhaps because of the difficulty or expense of providing drainage. While the heterogeneous pattern of wet and dry patches within the remnant patch indicates a diversity of shapes, the overall shape conforms to the needs of farm equipment. The remnant occurs along field divisions, in the center of the section, in a place where its interference with farm equipment is minimized. Most noticeable are the straight boundaries around the patch, where edges are maintained by machinery.

Oblique landscape elements, such as railways and powerline corridors, offer opportunities to conserve or create small habitat patches in acute corners. Where the grid system of land division meets with oblique features, machinery inaccessibility is an opportunity to establish small habitat patches, and is one reason why many small remnant patches still exist in the Corn Belt (Braband, 1986; Schennum, 1986).

4.4.3 Corn Belt scale

Encourage new technology, like precision agriculture, to be applied in ways that enhance small-patch biodiversity

Precision agriculture is being adopted by progressive farmers with large grain operations, and will undoubtedly influence landscape change in the Corn Belt. Precision agriculture's data will lead to more fine-grained knowledge of soil variability, and responsive ("smart") farm equipment will vary inputs to manage for highest profitability. Soil conditions that limit profitable production of corn or soybeans suggest possible small-patch locations. If profitability of small within-field areas is negative – such as might be the case in chronically wet, droughty, or eroded soils – agricultural policy incentives could encourage the planting of alternative cover types for biodiversity. Variable-rate farm equipment could be used to create a more diverse pattern of small patches (Corry and Nassauer, 1998). If farmers are encouraged through technical assistance and agricultural policy to plant alternative covers that improve biodiversity, "smart" farm equipment makes it easier to incorporate small habitat patches while maintaining seed, fertilizer, and pesticide delivery to target areas.

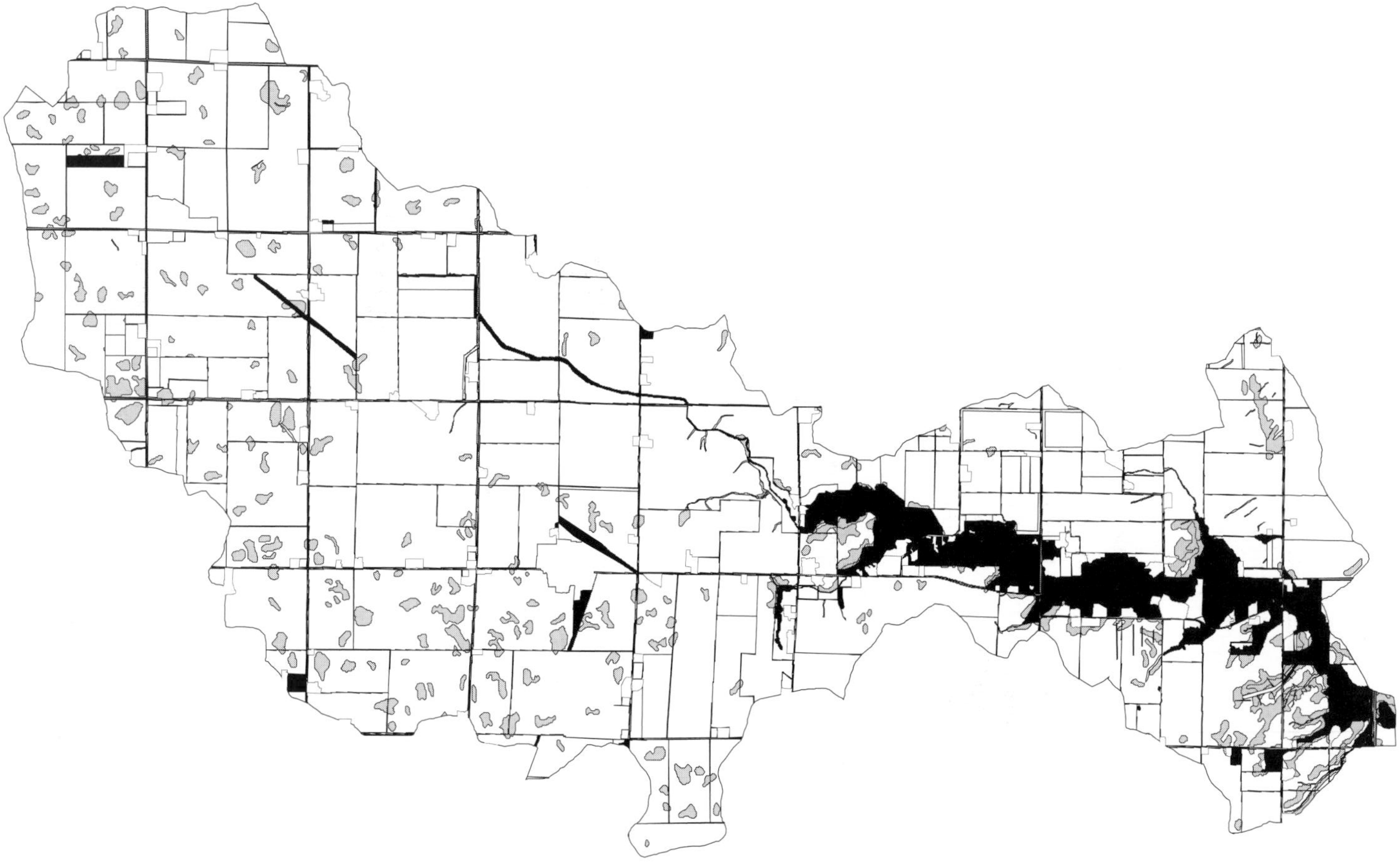

FIGURE 4.6
Corn Belt landscape scenario watershed map (Walnut Creek, Story County, Iowa) showing precision agriculture small patches (gray) perforating the landscape with biodiversity (black polygons represent perennial woody and herbaceous cover).

Such agricultural policy would be similar to criteria for selecting Conservation Reserve Program fields that were relatively erodible. Small patches of herbaceous perennial habitat dotted across cultivated fields could extend the habitat functions of larger Conservation Reserve parcels or other habitat reserves. The resulting landscape pattern would be consistent with Forman's *aggregate-with-outliers* land planning and management principle (Forman, 1995).

The small patches that might result from applying precision agriculture are approximated in a map interpreting soils data of the Walnut Creek watershed, Iowa (Fig. 4.6). The effect of such actions across a watershed is striking, as new small patches could appear in several fields and begin to create a landscape-scale pattern of biodiversity.

4.5 Summary

Small patches are the most common repositories of biodiversity in the Corn Belt. We have shown how small-patch characteristics resulting from the cultural factors of land division, ownership, and settlement pattern traditions; applied science and technology values and traditions; and aesthetic and stewardship values can be examined for their ecological implications and designed to enhance their ecological effects. Complementing large indigenous vegetation patches that function as core habitats, small habitat patches may improve ecosystem functions in settled landscapes. We have demonstrated some of the ways that small patches might be designed and managed in the Corn Belt.

Cultural factors should be considered in the development of management strategies to improve biodiversity in at least three ways. First, managers should seek opportunities to increase the number of small habitat patches by conserving them where they now exist, by establishing new patches, and by enhancing the biodiversity of small patches, while recognizably displaying cultural values for the appearance of each land-use type. Second, connectivity of small patches should be increased by using cultural boundaries to create a network of native biodiversity. Third, management should use applied science and technology to decrease interpatch distance between small habitat patches by increasing the number and connectivity of small patches.

All of these management strategies should consider the opportunities and constraints afforded by cultural factors because landscape patterns designed without consideration of cultural factors are not sustainable (Nassauer, 1997). Policy incentives and technical advice for creating and managing small habitat patch patterns could help create new landscape structures for the Corn Belt and other cultivated landscapes and ultimately improve the ecological functions of everyday places.

Acknowledgments

This research has been funded in part by NSF-EPA Project no. R8253335–01–0 and a Natural Systems Agriculture Fellowship from The Land Institute. We appreciate reviews conducted by Jianguo Liu, M. Elsbeth McPhee, and three anonymous peers.

References

Batchelor, B., Whigham, K., DeWitt, J., Heitt, T. & Roth-Eastman, K. (1997). *Introduction to Precision Agriculture*. Report no. Pm-1703. Iowa State University, Ames, IA.

Best, L. B., Freemark, K. E., Dinsmore, J. J. & Camp, M. (1995). A review and synthesis of habitat use by breeding birds in agricultural landscapes of Iowa. *American Midland Naturalist*, 134: 1–29.

Bishop, R. A., Joens, J. & Zohrer, J. (1998). Iowa's wetlands, present and future with a focus on prairie potholes. *Journal of the Iowa Academy of Sciences*, 105: 89–93.

Boutin, C. & Jobin, B. (1998). Intensity of agricultural practices and effects on adjacent habitats. *Ecological Applications*, 8: 544–557.

Braband, L. (1986). Railroad grasslands as bird and mammal habitats in central Iowa. In *The Prairie: Past, Present, and Future: Proceedings of the 9th North American Prairie Conference*, July 29–August 1, 1984, Moorhead, Minnesota, eds. G. K. Clambey & R. H. Pemble, pp. 86–90. Tri-College University Center for Environmental Studies, Fargo, ND.

Bunce, R. G. H. & Howard, D. C. (eds.) (1990). *Species Dispersal in Agricultural Habitats*. Pinter Publishers, Irvington, NY.

Cochrane, W. W. & Runge, C. F. (1992). *Reforming Farm Policy: Toward a National Agenda*. Iowa State University Press, Ames, IA.

Colunga-Garcia, M., Gage, S. H. & Landis, D. A. (1997). Response of an assemblage of Coccinellidae (Coleoptera) to a diverse agricultural landscape. *Environmental Entomology*, 26: 797–804.

Cooper, A. B., Smith, C. M. & Smith, M. J. (1995). Effects of riparian set-aside on soil characteristics in an agricultural landscape: Implications for nutrient transport and retention. *Agriculture, Ecosystems and Environment*, 55: 61–67.

Corry, R. C. & Nassauer, J. I. (1998). Using precision agriculture to enhance landscape structure in a Corn Belt agricultural watershed. In *Proceedings of the 4th International Conference on Precision Agriculture*, eds. P. C. Robert, R. H. Rust & W. E. Larson, pp. 547–557. Agronomy Society of America, Crop Science Society of America, Soil Science Society of America, St. Paul, MN.

Cruse, R. M. (1990). Strip intercropping. In *Farming Systems for Iowa: Seeking Alternatives*, ed. D. Keeney, pp. 39–41. Leopold Center for Sustainable Agriculture, Ames, IA.

Dunn, C. P., Sharpe, D. M., Guntenspergen, G. R., Stearns, F. & Yang, Z. (1990). Methods for analyzing temporal changes in landscape pattern. In *Quantitative Methods in Landscape Ecology*, eds. M. G. Turner & R. H. Gardner, pp. 173–198. Springer-Verlag, New York.

Dunn, C. P., Stearns, F., Guntenspergen, G. R. & Sharpe, D. M. (1993). Ecological benefits of the Conservation Reserve Program. *Conservation Biology*, 7: 132–139.

Dyer, L. E. & Landis, D. A. (1997). Influence of noncrop habitats on the distribution of *Eriborus terebrans* (Hymenoptera: Ichneumonidae) in cornfields. *Environmental Entomology*, 26: 924–932.

Edwards, W. M. & Owens, L. B. (1991). Large storm effects on total soil erosion. *Journal of Soil and Water Conservation*, 46: 75–78.

Exner, D. N., Davidson, D. G., Ghaffarzadeh, M. & Cruse, R. M. (1999). Yields and returns from strip intercropping on six Iowa farms. *American Journal of Alternative Agriculture*, 14: 69–77.

Forman, R. T. T. (1995). *Land Mosaics*. Cambridge University Press, Cambridge, UK.

Forman, R. T. T. & Godron, M. (1986). *Landscape Ecology*. John Wiley, Toronto, Canada.

Fountas, S. (1998). Market research on the views and perceptions of farmers about the role of crop management within precision farming. MSc thesis, Silsoe College, Cranfield University, Bedford, UK.

Freemark, K. & Boutin, C. (1995). Impacts of agricultural herbicide use on terrestrial wildlife in temperate landscapes: A review with special reference to North America. *Agriculture, Ecosystems and Environment*, 52: 67–91.

Galatowitsch, S. M. & van der Valk, A. G. (1994). *Restoring Prairie Wetlands: An Ecological Approach*. Iowa State University Press, Ames, IA.

Ghaffarzadeh, M. (1997). Economic and biological benefits of intercropping berseem clover with oat in corn–soybean–oat rotations. *Journal of Production Agriculture*, 10: 314–319.

Gilley, J. E., Kramer, L. A., Cruse, R. M. & Hull, A. (1997). Sediment movement within a strip intercropping system. *Journal of Soil and Water Conservation*, 52: 443–447.

Hart, J. F. (1968). Field patterns in Indiana. *Geographical Review*, 58: 450–471.

Hart, J. F. (1975). *The Look of the Land*. Prentice-Hall, Englewood Cliffs, NJ.

Hart, J. F. (1998). *The Rural Landscape*. Johns Hopkins University Press, Baltimore, MD.

Havera, S. P., Suloway, L. B. & Hoffman, J. E. (1997). Wetlands in the Midwest with special reference to Illinois. In *Conservation in Highly Fragmented Landscapes*, ed. M. W. Schwartz, pp. 88–104. Chapman & Hall, New York.

Herkert, J. R. (1994). The effects of habitat fragmentation on midwestern grassland bird communities. *Ecological Applications*, 4: 461–471.

Hobbs, R. J. (1993). Effects of landscape fragmentation on ecosystem processes in the western Australian Wheatbelt. *Biological Conservation*, 64: 193–201.

Hudson, J. C. (1992). *Crossing the Heartland: Chicago to Denver*. Rutgers University Press, New Brunswick, NJ.

Hurt, R. D. (1991). Agricultural technology in the twentieth century. *Journal of the West*, 30: 2–100.

Johnson, H. B. (1957). Rational and ecological aspects of the quarter section: An example from Minnesota. *Geographical Review*, 47: 330–348.

Johnson, H. B. (1976). *Order upon the Land: The US Rectangular Land Survey and the Upper Mississippi Country*. Oxford University Press, New York.

Kirsch, E. M. (1997). Small mammal community composition in cornfields, roadside ditches, and prairies in eastern Nebraska. *Natural Areas Journal*, 17: 204–211.

Lal, R., Follett, R. F., Kimble, J. & Cole, C. V. (1999). Managing US cropland to sequester carbon in soil. *Journal of Soil and Water Conservation*, 54: 374–381.

Landis, D. A., Wratten, S. D. & Gurr, G. M. (2000). Habitat management to conserve natural enemies of arthropod pests in agriculture. *Annual Review of Entomology*, 45: 175–201.

Ludwig, J. A. (1999). Disturbance and landscapes: The little things count. In *Issues in Landscape Ecology*, eds. J. A. Wiens & M. R. Moss, pp. 59–63. International Association for Landscape Ecology, Guelph, Canada.

Mankin, P. C. & Warner, R. E. (1997). Mammals of Illinois and the Midwest: Ecological and conservation issues for human-dominated landscapes. In *Conservation in Highly Fragmented Landscapes*, ed. M. W. Schwartz, pp. 135–153. Chapman & Hall, New York.

Marino, P. C. & Landis, D. A. (1996). Effect of landscape structure on parasitoid diversity and parasitism in agroecosystems. *Ecological Applications*, 6: 276–284.

Meine, C. (1997). Inherit the grid. In *Placing Nature: Culture and Landscape Ecology*, ed. J. I. Nassauer, pp. 45–62. Island Press, Washington, D.C.

Merriam, G. & Lanoue, A. (1990). Corridor use by small mammals: Field measurement for three experimental types of *Peromyscus leucopus*. *Landscape Ecology*, 4: 123–132.

Nassauer, J. I. (1979). *Managing for naturalness in wildland and agricultural landscapes*. Report no. PSW-35. US Department of Agriculture Pacific Southwest Forest and Range Experiment Station, Berkeley, CA.

Nassauer, J. I. (1988). *Landscape Care: Perceptions of Local People in Landscape Ecology and Sustainable Development*, Landscape and Land Use Planning no. 8. American Society of Landscape Architects, Washington, D. C.

Nassauer, J. I. (1989). Agricultural policy and aesthetic objectives. *Journal of Soil and Water Conservation*, 44: 384–387.

Nassauer, J. I. (1992). The appearance of ecological systems as a matter of policy. *Landscape Ecology*, 6: 239–250.

Nassauer, J. I. (1995). Culture and changing landscape structure. *Landscape Ecology*, 10: 229–237.

Nassauer, J. I. (1997). The culture of nature. Cultural sustainability: Aligning aesthetics and ecology. In *Placing Nature: Culture and Landscape Ecology*, ed. J. I. Nassauer, pp. 65–83. Island Press, Washington, D.C.

Nassauer, J. I., Corry, R. C. & Cruse, R. M. (2002). Alternative future landscapes scenarios: A means to consider agricultural policy. *Journal of Soil and Water Conservation*, 57:2.

Nassauer, J. I. & Westmacott, R. (1987). Progressiveness among farmers as a factor in heterogeneity of farmed landscapes. In *Landscape Heterogeneity and Disturbance*, ed. M. G. Turner, pp. 199–210. Springer-Verlag, New York.

Nentwig, W. (1989). Augmentation of beneficial arthropods by strip management 2. Successional strips in a winter wheat field. *Journal of Plant Diseases and Protection*, 1: 89–99.

Noss, R. F. & Cooperrider, A. (1994). *Saving Nature's Legacy*. Island Press, Washington, D. C.

Opdam, P. (1990). Dispersal in fragmented populations: The key to survival. In *Species Dispersal in Agricultural Habitats*, eds. R. G. H. Bunce & D. C. Howard, pp. 3–17. Belhaven Press, New York.

Orr, D. B. & Pleasants, J. M. (1996). The potential of native prairie plant species to enhance the effectiveness of the *Ostrinia nubilalis* parasitoid *Macrocentrus grandii*. *Journal of the Kansas Entomological Society*, 69: 133–143.

Paice, M. E. R., Miller, P. C. H. & Day, W. (1996). Control requirements for spatially selective herbicide sprayers. *Computers and Electronics in Agriculture*, 14: 163–177.

Paice, M. E. R., Day, W., Rew, L. J. & Howard, A. (1998). A stochastic simulation model for evaluating the concept of patch spraying. *Weed Research*, 38: 373–388.

Peterjohn, W. T. & Correll, D. L. (1984). Nutrient dynamics in an agricultural watershed: Observations on the role of a riparian forest. *Ecology*, 65: 1466–1475.

Pioneer Hi-Bred Limited (1999). *1999/2000 Crop Notes*. Pioneer Hi-Bred Limited, Chatham, Canada.

Pleasants, J. M. & Bitzer, R. J. (1999). Aggregation sites for adult European corn borers (Lepidoptera : Crambidae): A comparison of prairie and non-native vegetation. *Environmental Entomology*, 28: 608–617.

Quick, G. & Buchele, W. (1978). *The Grain Harvesters*. American Society of Agricultural Engineers, St. Joseph, MI.

Randall, G. W., Huggins, D. R., Russelle, M. P., Fuchs, D. J., Nelson, W. W. & Anderson, J. L. (1997). Nitrate losses through subsurface tile drainage in Conservation Reserve Program, alfalfa, and row crop systems. *Journal of Environmental Quality*, 26: 1240–1247.

Random House (1987). *The Random House Dictionary of the English Language*. Random House, New York.

Robertson, K. R., Anderson, R. C. & Schwartz, M. W. (1997). The tallgrass prairie mosaic. In *Conservation in Highly Fragmented Landscapes*, ed. M. W. Schwartz, pp. 154–188. Chapman & Hall, New York.

Ryszkowski, L. & Kedziora, A. (1987). Impact of agricultural landscape structure on energy flow and water cycling. *Landscape Ecology*, 1: 85–94.

Ryszkowski, L., Bartoszewicz, A. & Kedziora, A. (1999). Management of matter fluxes by biogeochemical barriers at the agricultural landscape level. *Landscape Ecology*, 14: 479–492.

Sayre, R. F. (1999). *Recovering the Prairie*. University of Wisconsin Press, Madison, WI.

Schennum, W. E. (1986). A comprehensive survey for prairie remnants in Iowa: Methods and preliminary results. In *The Prairie: Past, Present, and Future: Proceedings of the 9th North American Prairie Conference*, July 29–August 1, 1984, Moorhead, Minnesota, eds. G. K. Clambey & R. H. Pemble, pp. 163–168. Tri-College University Center for Environmental Studies, Fargo, ND.

Schwartz, M. W. & van Mantgem, P. J. (1997). The value of small preserves in chronically fragmented landscapes. In *Conservation in Highly Fragmented Landscapes*, ed. M. W. Schwartz, pp. 379–394. Chapman & Hall, New York.

Smith, D. D. (1998). Iowa prairie: Original extent and loss, preservation and recovery attempts. *Journal of the Iowa Academy of Science*, 105: 94–108.

Soule, J. D. & Piper, J. K. (1992). *Farming in*

Nature's Image: An Ecological Approach to Agriculture. Island Press, Washington, D.C.

Spaling, H. (1995). Analyzing cumulative environmental effects of agricultural land drainage in southern Ontario, Canada. *Agriculture Ecosystems and Environment*, 53: 279–292.

Spaling, H. & Smit, B. (1995). A conceptual model of cumulative environmental effects of agricultural land drainage. *Agriculture, Ecosystems and Environment*, 53: 99–108.

Stafford, J. V. (1996). Introduction: Spatially variable field operations. *Computers and Electronics in Agriculture*, 14: 99–100.

Stallman, H. R. & Best, L. B. (1996a). Bird use of an experimental strip intercropping system in northeast Iowa. *Journal of Wildlife Management*, 60: 354–362.

Stallman, H. R. & Best, L. B. (1996b). Small-mammal use of an experimental strip intercropping system in northeastern Iowa. *American Midland Naturalist*, 135: 266–273.

Steffan-Dewenter, I. & Tscharntke, T. (1999). Effects of habitat isolation on pollinator communities and seed set. *Oecologia*, 121: 432–440.

Sutter, G. C., Davis, S. K. & Duncan, D. C. (2000). Grassland songbird abundance along roads and trails in southern Saskatchewan. *Journal of Field Ornithology*, 71: 110–116.

Swanson, D. A., Scott, D. P. & Risley, D. L. (1999). Wildlife benefits of the Conservation Reserve Program in Ohio. *Journal of Soil and Water Conservation*, 54: 390–394.

Thomas, M. B., Wratten, S. D. & Sotherton, N. W. (1991). Creation of island habitats in farmland to manipulate populations of beneficial arthropods: Predator densities and emigration. *Journal of Applied Ecology*, 28: 906–917.

US Department of Agriculture National Agricultural Statistics Service (1999). *1997 Census of Agriculture: Iowa State and County Data*. Report no. AC97–A-15. US Department of Agriculture, Washington, D.C.

van Schilfgaarde, J. (1999). Is precision agriculture sustainable? *American Journal of Alternative Agriculture*, 14: 43–46.

Waide, J. B. & Hatfield, J. L. (1995). *Preliminary MASTER Assessment of the Impacts of Alternative Agricultural Management Practices on Ecological and Water Resource Attributes of Walnut Creek Watershed, Iowa*. Report no. 07IMG1718: 68–CO-0050. FTN Associates, Limited, Little Rock, AR.

Wallace, A. (1994). High-precision agriculture is an excellent tool for conservation of natural resources. *Communications in Soil Science and Plant Analysis*, 25: 45–49.

Wegner, J. & Merriam, G. (1990). Use of spatial elements in a farmland mosaic by a woodland rodent. *Biological Conservation*, 54: 263–276.

Young, R. A., Reichenbach, M. & Perkuhn, F. (1985). PNIF management: A social-psychological study of owners in Illinois. *Northern Journal of Applied Forestry*, 2: 91–94.

CHARLES F. RABENI AND SCOTT P. SOWA

5

A landscape approach to managing the biota of streams

5.1 Introduction

Although landscape ecology is generally considered a terrestrial discipline, ecologists working on streams and rivers have long been interested in the spatial relations and geographical distribution of aquatic organisms and their habitats. In fact, if a landscape is defined as a spatially heterogeneous area, and landscape ecology as the study of its structure, function, and change (Turner, 1989), then landscape ecology has the potential to be an important force in the appropriate management of streams and rivers. The application of landscape ecology to riverine management is particularly well suited to three classes of activities: conservation of biodiversity, fisheries management, and restoration/rehabilitation of biological integrity.

In this chapter we review relevant stream-ecology concepts that encompass a landscape perspective and link these concepts to current management practices. We argue, with examples, that scale-dependent processes that are valuable to society underlie biotic patterns in streams. We show how recent evidence links certain land-use activities with altered stream condition, and attempt to present the underlying mechanisms responsible. To show the integration of landscape principles with practical management, we present examples related to stream restoration, recreational fishing, and a case study of an ongoing project to prioritize the conservation of aquatic biodiversity on a regional basis.

5.2 Landscape elements of stream ecology

Several categories of concepts have been developed to explain how streams function in the context of the landscape (Ward, 1989; Lorenz *et al.*, 1997): concepts that focus on longitudinal changes of the biota; concepts emphasizing lateral interactions; concepts that integrate longitudinal, lateral, and vertical dimensions of streams; and concepts emphasizing spatial hierarchies and temporal changes.

5.2.1 Spatial relations

The *biological zonation concept* examined the distribution of stream fauna from headwaters to river mouth and was related to broad-scale influences of flow and temperature for fishes (Huet, 1954) and invertebrates (Illies and Botosaneanu, 1963). This concept detailed how species distributions changed along a gradient, but was not much concerned with interactions outside the wetted channel. Other concepts have related continuums of stream processes to particular landscape influences.

The *river continuum concept* (RCC) (Vannote *et al.*, 1980) described both functional and structural aspects along entire rivers: specifically that the resident fauna evolved in response to changes in the physical environment. The abiotic environment presents a gradient of physical and geomorphic conditions throughout a river system that controls energy relationships and the corresponding biota. In headwaters, primary production is limited by shading, and inputs from riparian vegetation provide the major carbon inputs. The invertebrate community is dominated by shredders that break down coarse particulate organic matter. In midreaches, where shading is less prevalent, within-stream primary production by attached algae is the dominant energy source. Taking advantage of this energy source are invertebrates capable of scraping algae from exposed surfaces. Environmental heterogeneity is high, resulting in high species diversity. Farther downstream, in what are referred to as big rivers, greater depths and turbidity reduce primary production, and major energy sources are inputs of detritus from upstream, tributaries, and the floodplain. Collector invertebrates, those subsisting on fine particulate organic matter, tend to dominate. The river continuum concept linked invertebrate associations to available organic resources that reflect the influence of the landscape through which the river flows.

The spatial organization of nutrients within the context of the RCC was examined by the *nutrient spiraling concept* (Newbold *et al.*, 1981) to explain the use of nutrients as they move downstream. Spiraling length refers to the distance along the river traveled by a nutrient element during a cycle between abiotic and biotic components. Spiraling efficiency, the length of the spiral, depends upon flow conditions and biotic and abiotic retention mechanisms. The *stream hydraulics concept* (Statzner and Higler, 1986) argues that the longitudinal zonation of stream fauna is a result of distinct changes in stream hydraulics determined by geomorphological and hydrological conditions on the river rather than gradual gradients of abiotic factors.

While many concepts involved influences and biotic changes occurring longitudinally along a stream, or lateral influences adjacent to the stream, others have proposed a more catchment-oriented view to understanding processes in lotic systems. *Integrated catchment concepts,* which recognized how stream biota were influenced by general features of the landscape, were developed by Ross (1963) using caddisflies as a model and by Hynes (1975) who synthesized current thinking about how geology and vegetation influence water quality and thus the productivity of streams. More recently there have been classification schemes (e.g., Frissell *et al.*, 1986) using a hierarchical theory framework for streams that emphasized the relation of a stream to its catchment across a wide range of spatial and temporal scales.

5.2.2 Temporal relations

Long-standing management strategies for rivers and streams that emphasize the stabilization of habitats, reduction of flow variations, and general taming of running waters have been challenged and criticized by emerging ideas that a dynamic stream subject to periodic unpredictable disturbances is a stream with naturally high biodiversity and productivity. Increasingly, scientists are understanding important temporal aspects of running water systems that overlay spatial considerations. The intuitive notion that altering flows of rivers and streams will detrimentally impact resident biota was formalized with The *natural flow paradigm* (Poff *et al.*, 1997). That synthesis examined how region and scale-specific flow regimes, specifically the magnitude, frequency, duration, timing, and rate of change of flows, regulate ecological processes and are of central importance in sustaining ecological integrity.

The *flood pulse concept* (Junk *et al.*, 1989) more fully integrated lateral and temporal aspects of the river continuum concept by explaining the importance of an intact channel floodplain system to the overall functioning of large rivers. It examined the physical and ecological linkages between the main channel and its floodplain as a holistic unit. Annual flooding brings carbon and other nutrients, sediment, and biota onto the floodplain, which determines the overall fertility of the floodplain. Systems undergoing periodic flooding show high habitat diversity, but with varying stability and persistence. This encourages high biotic diversities. Many river organisms have life-cycle events timed to the annual flood and use it extensively for spawning, as a food base, and as a refuge. Large rivers with intact natural floodplains provide the additional societal benefits of reducing flood effects; stimulating fish production; and providing additional filtration of nutrients, toxins, and sediments by floodplain vegetation.

Disturbance is a central organizing principle of landscape ecology and understanding its application to lotic ecosystems has the potential to contribute substantially to effective management. Reice *et al.* (1990) concluded from an extensive review of disturbance studies in streams that the resident biota often conform to Huston's dynamic equilibrium model (1979). This concept states that if the recurrence interval of a disturbance is shorter than the time necessary for biotic interactions of competition or predation to eliminate other species, the poorer competitors persist in the system and diversity is high. Thus, the natural state of a stream community, as measured by community structure or as biodiversity, can be viewed as being in perpetual recovery from a catastrophe.

As is known for terrestrial situations, the response of stream biota to a disturbance is not uniform throughout the system but will depend upon the number, size, and arrangement of habitats, or *patches*. A patch is a homogeneous spatial unit defined on the basis of topography, substrate, habitat type, or any other parameter of interest, the size of which is appropriate to the organism or question at hand. A patch can be of any size and examples in streams are a single stone, a riffle, a riffle–run–pool complex, or an entire headwaters section. A framework for the application of patch dynamics to problems in lotic ecology was provided by Pringle *et al.* (1988) who viewed streams as mosaics of patches. The mosaic of patches, their sizes, densities, relations to one another, and durations, all affect lotic system function. Patch characteristics influence taxonomic diversity and abundance, and the simplification of patch characteristics usually results in simplification of associated biota. Not only do patch mosaics increase habitat diversity, they are differentially susceptible to various levels of disturbance, so the patch mosaic influences, to a great extent, the overall response of the biota to disturbances of different magnitudes, frequencies, and durations. Such a hierarchical framework of both river and patch dynamics concepts at the catchment scale allows the prediction of patterns of ecological variables in the river basin (Lorenz *et al.*, 1997).

Most stream ecology concepts reviewed here are based, to some extent, on landscape ecology principles. They derive much of their explanatory power by acknowledging the spatial or temporal heterogeneity of a stream system, dividing that stream system into smaller, more homogeneous areas, e.g., upstream–downstream, channel–floodplain, and then explaining how the structure and function of these small units interact to determine the overall structure and function of the larger area. We will next explore the extent of how these concepts are being transferred into useful management tools.

5.3 Issues of scale in riverine management

"Watershed management" and "ecosystem management" are common phrases found in management plans and strategic planning documents of most natural resource agencies. Programs dealing with streams presently emphasize a broader scale or landscape perspective, but rarely consider the integration of landscape ecology principles. However, viewing a stream in its geographic context is an important step for aquatic managers who have generally lacked the perspective of space and time long held by geomorphologists and other physical scientists (Swanson *et al.*, 1988).

5.3.1 The importance of scale

Understanding and predicting for management purposes requires elucidating the mechanisms underlying observed patterns, and it is important to recognize that these mechanisms often operate at different scales than those on which the patterns are observed (Levin, 1992). Management of stream biota is usually carried out as management of habitat (primarily physical structure and water quality, but also flow and food), and understanding the temporal and spatial relations of organisms to their habitats is vital. The habitat for a stream-dwelling organism may be defined as the local physicochemical and biological features of the site that constitute the environment throughout its life cycle. Of importance to a manager is that, although organisms respond to local conditions, some of these conditions originate far from the stream. Some locally expressed elements of the habitat – such as water temperature, nutrients, dissolved oxygen, sediment composition, and flow regime – are reflections of broader-scale catchment influences (Fig. 5.1). These watershed-level influences may determine the overall livability of a stream and its capacity for production and biodiversity. The US National Academy of Sciences report on the restoration of aquatic ecosystems stressed that the recognition of watershed-level factors as agents of change within stream systems is the critical first step toward conservation and restoration of the processes that create and maintain habitats of native stream biota (National Research Council, 1992).

Because it is likely that stream biota are influenced by factors operating at different scales and the interaction of factors between scales, sorting out the causative variables is of paramount concern to managers. A scientist studying site-specific phenomena of a stream views the world from a different perspective than a scientist using remote sensing to examine landscape-level features of that same stream. It should not be surprising given these different perspectives that different conclusions concerning the structure and functioning of any one system occur. The most common approach to examining environmental influences on stream biota has been non-mechanistic and correlative. Wiley *et al.* (1997) showed how contradictory findings are possible when examining factors controlling stream communities from different spatial scales in Michigan trout streams. Landscape-level analyses determined that a biotic community was

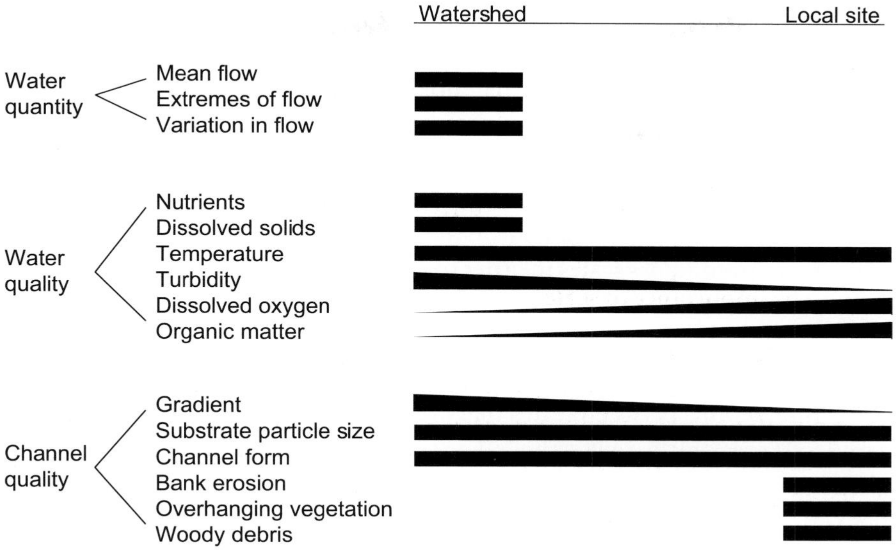

FIGURE 5.1
Influences on stream biota delineated into factors operating primarily at the local site level, requiring local management, and those originating at the watershed level, requiring watershed-scale management. Adapted from Rabeni (1995).

responsive to large-scale patterns of geology and hydrology. Site-based studies, however, showed local physical and biotic control. This study is also significant because it provides a model, based on the decomposition of variances from ANOVA, for integrating processes operating at different scales, and emphasizes that quantifying the importance of factors operating at different scales requires not only sampling at different spatial scales, but also repeated site-based sampling over time.

Managers of streams must recognize that the well-being of the fauna depends upon conditions in the stream channel, riparian zone, and watershed, and that larger spatial scales often relate to longer timeframes. Because influences are hierarchical in nature, where larger broad-scale factors influence smaller-scale factors, but not vice versa (Wiens, 1989), management must occur at the proper scale to be effective. This is easier said than done because while much is known about small-scale processes that influence biota, little is understood of the important influences of large-scale processes. Poff (1997) presented a potentially useful concept on how environmental constraints imposed at different scales – termed "habitat filters" – may determine local community composition. Species must have appropriate functional attributes (species traits) to pass through the nested filters that can be associated with many hierarchical levels, including the watershed, reach, or channel unit. This is a biologically based approach that could offer more understanding than the more common correlative approaches to predicting causes of species distributions.

Hierarchies of space or time may not match hierarchies of processes and factors affecting populations. For example, physical and biological factors believed to be important to the production of Atlantic salmon (*Salmo salar*) were arranged in a process hierarchy that was shown not to be particularly well correlated with a hierarchy of scale (Armstrong *et al.*, 1998) – thus emphasizing the need to integrate across scales in order to understand biotic conditions.

5.3.2 Scale effects: Interaction of land and stream

Interactions between scales that are of interest to management can occur at multiple areas within watersheds. For example, a common practice to improve salmonid spawning habitat has been to add gravel to silted-in riffles. Most of these efforts fail after a short period because the cause is a change in sediment loading caused by the alteration of channel structure. An illustration at a watershed scale of the consequences of ignoring basic scale issues is the fish-habitat restoration efforts at Fish Creek, on the Mt. Hood National Forest, in Oregon (Reeves *et al.*, 1997). This watershed was subjected to several decades of intense road building and logging. Salvage logging occurred in the riparian zone prior to the mid-1980s and an intensive debris-clearing operation was carried out in the channel in 1964. Beginning around 1981 the US Forest Service embarked on an ambitious program to restore in-channel habitat for salmon and trout. During the period from 1986 to 1988 more than 500 log and boulder structures were anchored together with cable and epoxy and located along the stream bank. A major rain and associated flood in 1996 caused extensive landslides that delivered substantial sediment to the stream. Almost half of over 200 landslides that were inventoried were caused by timber harvest, while a third were caused by roads. The flood dislodged and destroyed over half of the habitat restoration structures. Most structures were carried entirely out of the basin. In retrospect, it is apparent that land managers failed to link the effects of past land management activities with processes governing the stream. Efforts should have been made to address catchment up-slope conditions before initiating in-channel projects.

5.3.3 Scale issues in recreational fisheries management

Fisheries management can be considerably enhanced by a multi-scale perspective which we illustrate with results of studies of the relations of a fish population to stream conditions in the Jacks Fork River, Missouri, at three spatial scales: the ecoregion, the stream system, and the stream reach (Rabeni and Sowa, 1996) (Fig. 5.2). The question of interest was related to recreational

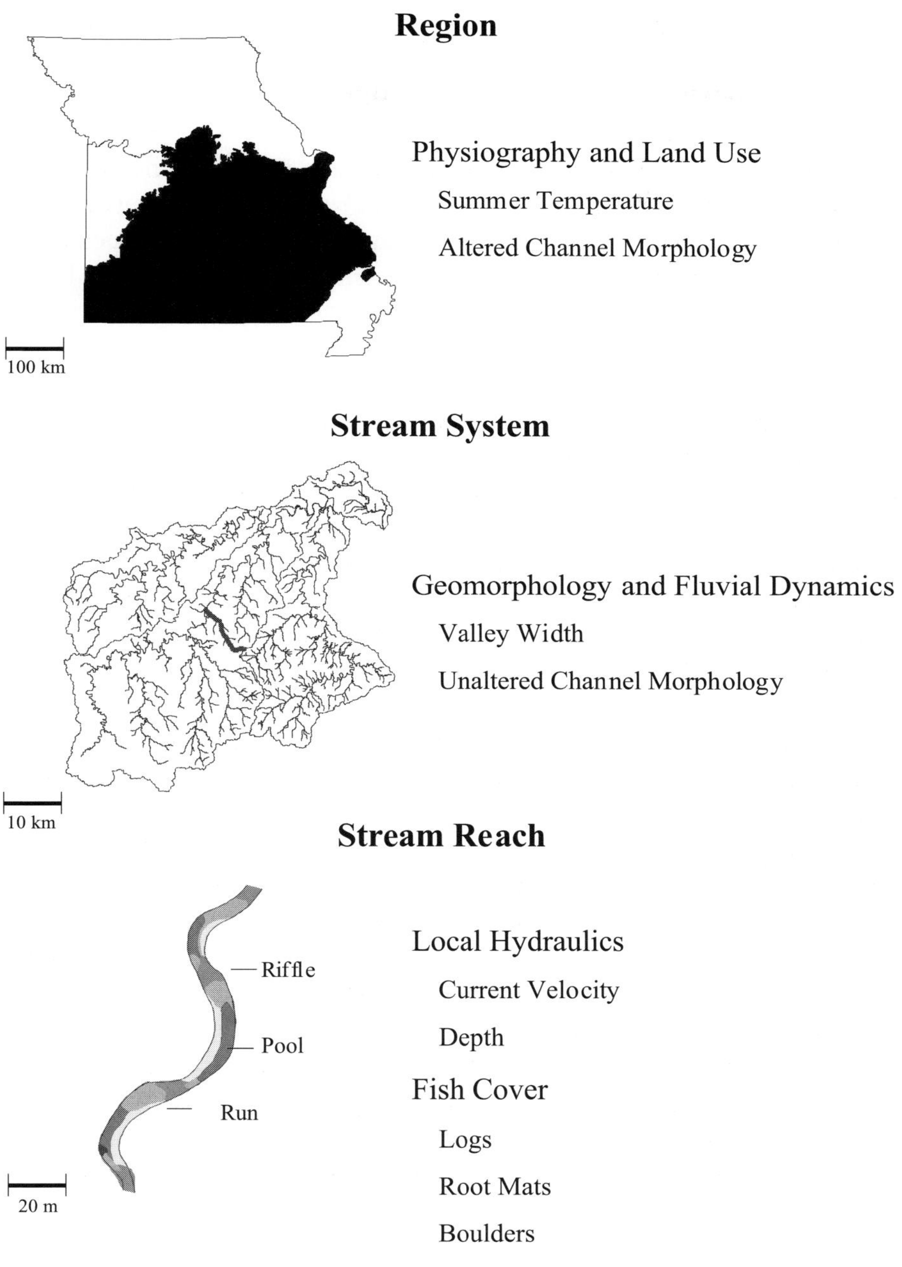

FIGURE 5.2
Factors affecting population characteristics of smallmouth bass at three spatial scales.

fishing: What were the manageable factors to improve fishing opportunities for smallmouth bass (*Micropterus dolomieu*) in Missouri streams? This necessitated determining the most important factors influencing smallmouth bass distribution and abundance.

First, we assessed reach-scale habitat influences. Habitat use of smallmouth bass during warm-water periods was evaluated by underwater observation and radio telemetry, where fish were found to be associated with some type of cover: logs, rootwads, or boulders. With the onset of winter there was a shift in habitat use from strong associations with downed trees, logs, and rootwads to a much greater association with boulders. Water depth and current velocities were important as elements of intraspecific segregation where larger fish occupied slower and deeper habitats. Fish in all seasons avoided shallow water and existed almost exclusively in current velocities below 0.2 m/s. Our conclusions, derived from study at the reach scale, were that fish use of habitat was related to, and probably influenced by, local depths, water velocities, substrate composition, and fish cover characteristics.

At the stream-system scale, we evaluated habitat use by modeling relations of fish population characteristics to various habitat elements (Fig. 5.2). Our multiple regression models showed little or no significant associations of either density or biomass of smallmouth bass with any aspect of depth, velocity, substrate, or woody structure. Variables explaining the most variation in smallmouth bass population characteristics were the amount of boulders and the amount of undercut bank.

The fluvial–geomorphic forces shaping a particular reach of the Jacks Fork River differ within the catchment. In upstream areas the stream is constrained by limestone formations and water flows in narrow valleys with adjacent bedrock bluffs and channel sinuosity is low. Along bedrock bluffs, cobbles and boulders dominate the stream bed material. Between bluffs, fine alluvium supports dense and well-rooted riparian vegetation that has been undercut by the forces of high water. Downstream the valley widens considerably and sinuosity increases. Bedrock bluffs and undercut banks become a smaller proportion of the stream's length and the channel is increasingly bordered by alluvial materials. Populations of smallmouth bass are greatest in upstream reaches and there is a strong, significant inverse relation between valley width and fish abundance. Thus, valley width appears to be a good indicator of the overall potential of a reach to support a smallmouth bass population. This stream-scale analysis demonstrates how the potential to support smallmouth bass in a particular stretch of stream may be predicted by habitat variables controlled by fluvial–geomorphic processes.

Finally, to assess the regional-scale influences, we performed a more encompassing analysis of smallmouth bass abundance in a number of streams throughout the Ozark Border region. Multiple regression models relating habitat conditions to fish population density and biomass indicated that fewer and smaller fish were found in streams that had higher summer temperatures (due to reduced shading) and high pool-to-riffle area ratios. These significant variables related to the broad-scale features of the physiographic setting. We concluded that these variables were important because contemporary temperature regimes have increased relative to historical conditions, and natural pool–riffle morphology has changed to more uniform run–pool conditions because of land-use activities related to agriculture in the region.

Cover characteristics were not related to the abundance of fish across streams, which contradicts conclusions made from studies at smaller spatial scales. However, when each stream of the regional study was partitioned in half, the portion of stream with the most cover usually possessed the greatest biomass and density of fish. This again supports the premise of the existence of a hierarchical influence of scale effects in aquatic systems, where the broader-scale influences set limits for smaller-scale determinants. The sum of information gained from hierarchical investigations will help determine where the most efficient management efforts should be placed. In our example, it is evident that attempts at improving the smallmouth fishery will require more than just local habitat manipulations. Efforts must focus on restoring more natural thermal regimes and channel morphology, which will require widespread land-use changes and riparian restorations.

5.3.4 Social and political considerations of managing at multiple scales

Most stream management continues to deal with such matters as point-source pollution, local physical fish-habitat repairs, the obvious effect of a disturbance such as a road crossing, construction, or the stocking of a recreational fish species. These small projects are relatively easy to attack and results of actions are often immediate and therefore satisfying. Local activities often garner strong political and agency support. Management at the landscape level is much more complex, both scientifically and politically. Management strategies requiring control of a substantial percentage of a catchment and which are not likely to show results for several decades frequently have little political support, regardless of how soundly grounded in science the strategies might be.

Management approaches encompassing at least broad-scale spatial perspectives are becoming more common, although acknowledgments of, or interest in, interactions across scales are rare. So-called "Big Picture" programs are found within many US federal natural resource agencies. Examples include the Environmental Protection Agency's Regional EMAP program, each region of which encompasses several states; the US Geological Survey's (USGS)/NAWQA (National Water Quality Assessment) program which is national but selective in scope; many ecosystem-based research initiates (e.g., Yellowstone, Everglades) by the Biological Resources Division of the USGS; and the Ecosystem Teams initiatives from each of the regional offices of the US Fish and Wildlife Service. Programs within a single agency are apt to show the greatest success because there tends to be a single goal or at least a set of common goals. However, using a broad-scale perspective usually means involving more interest groups or "stakeholders." Williams *et al.* (1997) report on 13 case studies where coalitions of government agencies – federal, state, regional, and local – along with diverse non-government agencies have implemented comprehensive watershed-level restorations. While some were meeting restoration objectives, the authors admit they had a difficult time finding many successful examples of true watershed restoration – ones that incorporated watershed-level ecological principles. Most so-called watershed restorations were narrowly focused, without clear objectives, too short term, and with little or no means of evaluation.

Even the most well-planned and funded programs are hindered by naturally competing political interests. A case in point is the large-scale experimental disturbance floods carried out on the Colorado River. As Schmidt *et al.* (1998) explain, restoration of something the size and complexity of a major river will involve different goals which will differentially affect the status of individual resources. Trade-offs are required because no strategy will improve the status of every riverine resource. Compromises often leave adherents of a particular position unsatisfied and less likely to be strong proponents of further projects.

Another obstacle to practical broad-scale management is the presence of political boundaries that do not capture the extent of the needed management area. For example, Allan *et al.* (1997) examined the Raisin River basin in Michigan and found scale-dependent influences on stream health. Local conditions determined habitat structure and vegetation cover, whereas land use and land cover at considerable distances from the stream influenced important processes such as nutrient input, sediment delivery, and aspects of flow. However, Allan *et al.* (1997) concluded that implementation of a comprehensive management plan for this river would be nearly impossible due to the jurisdictional complexity of governmental responsibility. Eighteen federal, state, regional, and local entities were involved in regulatory and planning activities which was entirely too many for effective coordination. In Michigan, local-level governments wield the most authority, but their geographically limited authority precludes appropriate efforts to manage entire river basins.

An extreme example of jurisdictional complexity is found in attempts to properly manage fish species of the Mississippi River and its tributaries. Fish species that move between management jurisdictions create complex resource-management problems related to development of regulations, licensing, enforcement, and management strategies. In the Mississippi River basin some fishes have limited distributions but may be differentially managed by states on either side of the river, while many species (i.e., catfish species, sturgeon species, and paddlefish) may move hundreds of kilometers during their lifetimes which would involve multiple management jurisdictions. Recently 26 state conservation departments having fisheries management jurisdiction in the Mississippi River basin (the Mississippi, Missouri, Tennessee, Ohio, Arkansas, and Red rivers and their tributaries) have banded together to form the Mississippi Interstate Cooperative Resource Agreement (MICRA) to share resources, facilities, and funding for implementation of strategic plans to address management needs of interjurisdictional fisheries. MICRA's mission includes improving the communication and coordination among responsible management entities on a basin-wide basis. While it is too early to report on the overall efficacy of the organization, it is heartening to observe that the agencies involved recognize that biological concerns transcend state boundaries and that effective management requires basin-wide perspective.

5.4 Linking landscape ecology concepts to management

While stream ecological theory has formed a good basis for the application of landscape principles, advances in the aquatic arena lag substantially behind those of terrestrial interests. Two views are emerging on how best to apply landscape ecology principles to the management of streams and rivers. One centers on determining the influence of watershed (terrestrial) factors on stream biota, and emphasizes the lateral dimension. The second view is primarily longitudinal and is concerned with factors within and immediately adjacent to the channel. Each view incorporates important landscape perspectives dealing with multiple spatial scales. While the two approaches are sometimes integrated, it may be useful, for management purposes, to view the application of landscape ecology principles to riverine management as two separate but complementary approaches. One or the other view will take precedence, depending upon the management objectives.

5.4.1 Terrestrial patches

Managing stream systems effectively will require understanding how the spatial extent, arrangement, and heterogeneity of surrounding terrestrial landscape patches influence the structure, function, and quality of stream resources. This has not yet been accomplished. But because of the development of remote sensing and GIS (geographic information systems) technologies, scientists are quantifying associations between watershed-level attributes and the resident biota of streams in that watershed. Information is fast accumulating on three important management questions:

(1) How much of a particular land use (i.e., extent) is necessary to impact stream biota?
(2) What is the relative influence of near-channel activities versus those further removed in the watershed in structuring quality habitat and biotic communities?
(3) What is the time-scale for restoration of stream biota?

Land use

Watershed-level factors that influence functional interactions at the stream–land ecotone, and among physical habitat attributes and refugia, are often ultimately linked to the quantity, timing, and quality of rainfall runoff and sediment supply, factors strongly linked to land-use alterations. However, responses by biota to land-use changes within a watershed are not instantaneous, and are often difficult to predict. While it is relatively easy to document alterations in physical habitat of streams, it is more difficult to determine whether such changes are biologically relevant. Oftentimes the effects of land-use changes are overshadowed by natural variation. Richards *et al.* (1996) related the status of benthic invertebrate communities from 58 catchments in central Michigan as being highly influenced by surficial geology's control over channel morphology and hydrologic patterns. Although land-use alterations were substantial, their effects were masked by geology.

A consequence of land-use change especially in urban and agricultural areas has been alteration of the water table and runoff patterns. Many landscapes in formerly glaciated regions or on floodplains of large rivers were historically wetter, where headwater and bottomland marshes and wetlands were more common (Larimore and Bayley, 1996). An altered hydrologic regime has substantial effects on riverine fauna. For example, many fish assemblages were historically adapted to the regular, slow springtime rises in discharge for spawning and other life activities, and were able to complete the year with moderate, but adequate flows (Poff *et al.*, 1997). Many intensive land-use activities have reduced the water storage capacity of the soil, and drastically lowered water levels. Species must now cope with much greater flows during limited periods of the year and lesser flows the rest of the time. Land use that is different from the historical, and which is substantial, may have influence on stream biota. These relations are just beginning to be quantified. The health of fish assemblages in some Wisconsin streams, as measured by a fish index of biotic integrity, was negatively correlated with the amount of upstream urban development and the amount of agricultural land (Wang *et al.*, 1997). Fish-assemblage health was positively related to the amount of upstream forest in the watershed. There appeared to be threshold levels for the amounts of a particular land use before the fish assemblage was influenced. A decline in the condition of the fish assemblage was noted when 20% or more of the watershed was urbanized. Impacts attributed to agriculture were noted when more than 50% of the watershed was used for this purpose.

Influence of riparian buffers

The long-held view that the biological integrity of streams could be managed solely by attention to the riparian buffer is being challenged, and the relative importance of stream buffers in the context of overall watershed land uses in determining stream biotic health is beginning to be explored. The few comparative studies available indicate two important points: That attention to buffer strips alone may not be sufficient to protect aquatic life, and that the scale of the study may influence the strength of the predictive variables. In a study of Michigan watersheds with differing land uses, Lammert and Allan (1999) quantified both streamside and whole-watershed conditions. They concluded that biological integrity was best associated with near-stream land use and habitats and not at all to regional land use. However, in a related study encompassing a greater variety of regional land uses, Roth *et al.* (1996) concluded that these catchment-scale factors were more important than streamside vegetation as a determinant of fish assemblage structure. Richards *et al.* (1996) expanded on these findings to show how the interacting influences on stream biota between land use and streamside vegetation is mediated by the prevailing conditions of catchment size and surficial geology. Clearly, the physical conditions of the watershed, anthropogenic alterations to the landscape, and the quality and quantity of the riparian vegetation are all important in influencing the biological communities of streams.

Time

Landscape influences on riverine biota operate on a variety of time-scales. Differing flow conditions throughout a watershed, differing transport of sediment through drainage basins, and downstream movement of sediment to and from floodplain storage can result in disturbances that propagate slowly through drainage networks in unpredictable ways, in what geomorphologists euphemistically refer to as a "complex response" (Schumm, 1977). Moreover, in larger drainage basins, many different land-use changes and natural climatic variations may take place simultaneously. Thus, it is probable that present biotic conditions are a result of often unknown past events, and as a correlate, restoration activities will take an unknown, but likely long, time to show a response from the biota.

It is encouraging that in some instances where land-use activities have improved over time there has been a concomitant improvement in stream conditions. For example, beginning in about 1940 there were substantial changes in basin-wide agricultural practices in southwestern Wisconsin. Steep-sloping pastures were abandoned and they reverted to forest. Contour and deep plowing were initiated on a wide scale. These changes increased rainfall infiltration and decreased overland flow. Long-term flow records on streams showed a corresponding decrease in peak flows and increased and more sustained base flows (Gebert and Krug, 1996). This study indicates the potential benefits accorded to aquatic biota from best management practices (BMPs) on agricultural watersheds, if our time frame is long enough. However, time frames for complete restoration of stream biota within a watershed are likely to be discouragingly long. For example, Harding *et al.* (1998) showed the best indicator of present-day invertebrate and fish diversity in a set of North Carolina streams was land-use practices of the 1950s rather than any present-day condition. Past land-use activity, particularly agriculture, may result in long-term modifications of the biota regardless of reforestation of riparian areas.

These examples describing associations among the biota and particular landscape features are an important first step in watershed management of stream biota. However, management prescriptions having some generality require elucidating the mechanisms behind the associations. The relevance of landscape ecology to riverine management will be greatly enhanced when relations between some biological measure of stream quality and the spatial arrangement or heterogeneity of landcover patches throughout a watershed are better understood. We suspect that important factors influencing biological integrity, such as runoff and soil erosion, are dependent upon where a given land use exists on the landscape, e.g., ridge top vs. sides slope vs. valley bottom, and its relation to other landscape patches, e.g., riparian buffers or grass filter strips. Examining such complex spatial relations will likely be a major emphasis of stream scientists over the next decade, especially as more geospatial data become readily available and exposure to GIS and remote sensing technologies increases.

5.4.2 Stream-channel patches

While quantifying relations between land use in the watershed and the biota of streams will advance our understanding of how large-scale watershed factors affect the stream habitat, there is also a need to focus landscape principles on the stream and its immediate channel, and to examine how the spatial arrangement and heterogeneity of stream patches influence the structure, function, and quality of stream resources. Stream ecologists are paying increasing attention to this subject (an excellent example is the symposium on "Heterogeneity in Streams" published in Volume 16(1) of the *Journal of the North American Benthological Society*). We previously defined a patch as a relatively homogeneous spatial unit whose size is appropriate to the organism or question at hand. Unfortunately, most attention by aquatic biologists is at spatial scales smaller than those commonly examined by landscape ecologists (e.g., patches >1000 m^2) and that are most amenable to management. Patches in a stream that we believe to be particularly useful to management, given with typical longitudinal size ranges, are the hydraulic habitat unit such as a riffle or pool (1–100 m), a reach which is a length of stream between tributary junctions (100–1000 m), and the segment which encompasses several reaches, e.g., headwaters and midreaches (1000–10 000 m).

There are compelling theoretical and practical reasons to examine streams in terms of distinct units or patches of a variety of sizes. We agree with Pringle *et al.* (1988) that viewing stream systems within a catchment as a mosaic of patches provides a fresh perspective for stream-related research and management. Such a perspective can actually complement some of the dominant paradigms in stream ecology which emphasize the upstream–downstream linearity of lotic ecosystems by providing the necessary reductionist tool for evaluating such concepts. For example, Townsend (1996) argues that the river continuum concept is even more useful when viewed as a patch-dynamic system because it emphasizes the nature of an open system and the linkages needed to process organic matter from upstream to downstream.

The utility of viewing the stream as a mosaic of patches may be illustrated by two recent studies. Researchers in Illinois found discontinuities in the generally accepted concept that fish species richness steadily increases from upstream to downstream or from small to large streams (Osborne and Wiley, 1992). Significantly higher numbers of fish species were found in main channel tributaries than in headwater tributaries, probably resulting from their proximity to the main channel which acts as a refuge during drought periods and also a colonizing source after periods of drought. These results emphasized that the position of a stream in the drainage network was as important as stream size in determining fish species richness.

Large-scale spatial habitat (i.e., patch) relations are important because many stream organisms respond to or require particular microhabitat conditions of current velocity, substrate type, or depth at one spatial scale, while also responding to combinations of the same variables, termed habitat types – e.g., riffles, runs, and pools – at a larger scale. In a Minnesota stream, the composition of the fish community depended upon the large-scale spatial relation between the stream channel and the location of in-channel beaver ponds (Schlosser, 1995). The ponds acted as reproductive "sources" for fishes on the landscape while the stream channel acted as reproductive "sinks." Stream flows influenced the permeability of the boundary between habitats and influenced the ability of fish to disperse over fairly long distances.

Viewing the channel and riparian corridors of all streams in a catchment as a mosaic of patches may provide a more efficient management approach than viewing the resource as a continuum of physical, chemical, and biological processes. Effective management requires an accurate inventory of resources (Fajen, 1981). Before an inventory is generated, there must be a classification system, because an inventory without classification is simply an unorganized list (Lotspeich and Platts, 1982). Classifying stream resources into distinct patches and mapping their specific location enables resource professionals to compile a variety of inventory statistics on the distribution and abundance of each patch type. Thus, the patch approach that delineates discrete units is amenable to a variety of spatial analyses while still retaining their ecological importance. Viewing all streams in a catchment as a mosaic of patches can also enhance communication among resource professionals. Humans naturally think and communicate in terms of classes (Gauch, 1982), and cognitive scientists have long understood that humans learn and communicate through a process of categorization (Barsalou, 1992).

Advances in landscape ecology have been possible, in part, because of a common understanding of what constitutes a landscape element or patch. Vegetation, land use, and landform are the three most prevalent landscape features used to delineate ecologically meaningful patches in the terrestrial setting. Comparable aquatic analogs need to be identified and correctly mapped, then stream ecologists will have the means to examine spatially explicit questions dealing with how species distribution, abundance, composition, diversity, and persistence relate to landscape elements such as patch size, juxtaposition of patches, isolation or fragmentation of patches, heterogeneity of patches, and patch dynamics.

Aerial photography, satellite imagery, digital elevation models, and various US Geological Survey maps are widely available and provide data to the terrestrial landscape ecologist suitable for delineating, mapping, and spatially analyzing vegetation, land use, or landform patches (Risser *et al.*, 1984). In contrast, these same information sources do not typically provide stream ecologists with the data necessary to define ecological units or patches relevant to the abiotic and biotic processes operating in stream environments. Some of the most important environmental factors (e.g., current velocity) cannot be visualized at all and can only be mapped through field investigations. As a result, stream resource professionals who almost unconsciously view an individual stream reach as a matrix of patches (e.g., riffles, pools, and runs) have a difficult time of viewing entire watersheds as a matrix of stream types or entire regions as a matrix of watershed types. The only practical way such a view of stream environments can be generated is within a GIS.

5.5 Assessing biodiversity conservation needs

A comprehensive conservation assessment methodology for aquatic environments is sorely needed as a tool to combat loss of biodiversity. The potential extinction rate for North American freshwater fauna is five times higher than that for terrestrial fauna (Ricciardi and Rasmussen, 1999). The Nature Conservancy estimates that in the United States 68% of all freshwater mussel species, 51% of crayfish species, 40% of amphibian species, and 39% of freshwater fish species are either vulnerable, imperiled, critically imperiled, or presumed extinct (Master *et al.*, 1998). In addition, the status of only 4% of federally listed aquatic species with official recovery plans has improved (Williams and Neves, 1992).

Attempts to stem the loss of biodiversity throughout the world have usually proceeded on a species-by-species and threat-by-threat basis (Scott *et al.*, 1993). This approach has been shown to be inefficient, expensive, and likely to lead to economic conflict (Pitelka, 1981; Hutto *et al.*, 1987; Scott *et al.*, 1987; Noss, 1991). Existing programs designed to prevent extinction of endangered and threatened species do not usually address the larger problems of fragmentation, habitat loss, and disruption of ecological processes (Noss *et al.*, 1995). What is needed is a "coarse-filter" approach to biodiversity conservation which assesses conservation needs at higher levels of biological organization, proactively identifies opportunities for conservation, and complements the reactive "fine-filter," single-species, approach exemplified by the US Endangered Species Act (Hutto *et al.*, 1987; Scott *et al.*, 1987).

5.5.1 Developing conservation priorities at multiple spatial scales

Gap analysis uses GIS for identifying the degree to which native species and natural communities are represented in our present-day mix of conservation lands (Scott *et al.*, 1987). The National Gap Analysis Program (GAP), sponsored and coordinated by the Biological Resources Division of the US Geological Survey, develops geospatial data and conducts conservation assessments for terrestrial environments. The Missouri Aquatic Gap Analysis Project was initiated in 1997 as the first statewide project for the aquatic component of GAP. This project has developed a broadly applicable assessment methodology that identifies and prioritizes biodiversity conservation needs for riverine environments (Sowa, 1999). It is based on a classification system that characterizes biodiversity by focusing on ecological and evolutionary processes responsible for the formation and distribution of native aquatic assemblages, and includes physical attributes. Spatially explicit GIS data layers of riverine ecosystems at multiple scales with corresponding assessment statistics allow users to evaluate the relative *distinctiveness* and *conservation status* of each ecosystem and have a sound basis for establishing conservation priorities. The project is briefly explained here with emphasis on the utility of the resulting information and its relation to landscape ecology.

The Missouri Aquatic Gap Analysis Project uses a hierarchical classification framework based on those developed by The Nature Conservancy (Higgins *et al.*, 1999) and the US Forest Service (Maxwell *et al.*, 1995), as well as elements of Frissell *et al.* (1986), Pflieger (1989), and Seelbach *et al.* (1997) to describe riverine ecosystems according to natural physical and biological factors that exert primary control over the ecological and evolutionary processes operating at, and the patterns observed at, each spatial scale (Angermeier and Schlosser, 1995) (Table 5.1). Digital maps (1:100 000) were developed for three levels in the hierarchy: Ecological Drainage Units (EDU), Aquatic Ecological Systems (AES), and valley segment types (Fig. 5.3a–c, color plate; Table 5.1). Units delineated in each map were attributed with the upper levels of the hierarchy of which they are part and all of the fish, mussel, crayfish, and snail species known to occur within the unit. The *biological potential* for each valley segment is then predicted by matching taxa habitat affinities, developed from the literature, to every valley segment type likely to provide suitable habitat.

The relative *biological distinctiveness* and relative *conservation status* of all AESs within an EDU are determined (Abell *et al.*, 2000) (Fig. 5.3b, d, color plate). Metrics associated with several factors are used to calculate both indices for each (Fig. 5.3d, color plate). The biological distinctiveness and conservation status indices are assigned into more general categories and integrated to generate an overall *conservation priority* for each AES similar to Abell *et al.* (2000) (Fig. 5.3b, d, color plate).

The conservation priorities of each AES are transferred to the corresponding valley segments, where some additional criteria refine and establish the final priorities unique to particular valley segments (Fig. 5.3c, d, color plate). The result of this assessment methodology is a fully attributed map with an ecologically meaningful set of priorities at a scale that planners and managers can understand and use to guide their conservation efforts (Fig. 5.3d, color plate).

Conservation priorities are not an end in themselves but the beginning of a difficult decision-making process to determine what conservation actions are necessary to effectively conserve aquatic biodiversity. For riverine environments our objective should be to identify the minimum set of stream segments in the proper *spatial arrangement* to ensure the maintenance of the ecological integrity of each EDU (Sowa, 1999). Efforts to identify this minimum set of stream segments must be guided by the principles of landscape ecology and conservation biology. We must encourage stream ecologists to utilize the tools and data generated from Aquatic GAP projects to elucidate how such principles specifically apply to stream ecosystems.

The principles of landscape ecology that have been incorporated into the Missouri Aquatic Gap Analysis Project make it more ecologically realistic. For example, in the first six levels of classification hierarchy, two of the primary classification criteria are homogeneity of pattern (both biological and physical) and connectivity or isolation of units. At the valley segment scale, principles of landscape ecology are used to define boundaries between valley segment types. For example, each stream segment is initially classified into one of four patch sizes (i.e., headwater, creek, small river, large river). Boundaries of valley segments are further refined according to the proximity of patches (e.g., a headwater flowing into another headwater versus a headwater flowing into a large river) and juxtaposition (i.e., mid-valley stream segment versus adjacent to the valley wall).

The digital format of the data is easily incorporated into a portable and updateable decision-support system that can be used in the office or the field. A digital data source documenting critical stream segments, watersheds, and riparian corridors could be used by a variety of resource professionals. Examples include assisting managers with permit review processes of Sections 401 and 404 of the Clean Water Act; identifying specific locations for implementing federal and state landowner incentive programs such as riparian set-aside programs; and identifying locations of new state parks, national wildlife refuges, or expanding existing reserves. Fisheries managers could use the species distribution data, valley-segment data, and conservation status data to help establish or refine recreational fishing regulations. In addition, since the valley-segment data layer accounts for natural variation among stream segments it can be used for developing sound experimental designs for stream research or biomonitoring. Using this data layer will substantially increase the probability that any observed differences among sites are due to treatment effects or anthropogenic factors. Finally, as an educational tool for the public, the system would assist in visualizing and simplifying complex ecological concepts, watershed processes, and the status and trends in stream resource health.

Digital maps developed from Aquatic GAP projects will provide researchers with digital tools and data for elucidating relations between spatial pattern and ecological processes at multiple scales. For example, researchers can use the data to examine if the spatial heterogeneity and arrangement of habitat units within valley segment types influence species composition, abundance, or

Table 5.1. *Hierarchical framework*[a] *with defining physical and biological features used for classifying and mapping riverine ecosystems in the Missouri Aquatic Gap Pilot Project.*

Ecological Unit	Description	Defining physical features	Defining biological features
Zones	Six major zoogeographic zones of the world.	Continental boundaries Global climate	Family level patterns Endemism
Subzones	Subcontinental zoogeographic strata with relatively unique aquatic assemblages created in large part by plate tectonics and mountain building.	Major river networks and basin boundaries Regional climate	Family level patterns Endemism
Regions	Subzone zoogeographic strata created in large part by drainage network patterns that determine dispersal routes and isolation mechanisms.	Major river networks and basin boundaries Regional climate	Family and species level patterns Endemism
Sub-regions	Region stratification units. Large areas of similar climate and physiography that correspond to broad vegetation regions.	Regional climate Physiography General physiognomy of vegetation	Family and species level patterns Endemism
Ecological drainage units	Sub-region stratification units. Aggregates of watersheds within a distinct physiographic setting that share relatively unique aquatic assemblages.	Drainage boundaries Physiography	Family and species level patterns Endemism Genetics
Aquatic ecological systems	Hydrologic subunits of ecological drainage units with similar physiographic settings, basin morphometry and position within the larger drainage (e.g., located in the headwaters versus near the drainage outlet).	Drainage boundaries Position within ecological drainage unit Physiography Local climate Basin morphometry	Species level patterns Endemism Genetics Diagnostic species of foraging, reproductive, and habitat-use guilds

Valley segment type	Valley segment types stratify stream networks of aquatic ecological systems into major functional components that define broad similarities in fluvial processes, sediment transport, riparian interactions, and thermal regime.	Temperature Stream size Permanence of flow Position within drainage network Valley geomorphology	Species level patterns Diagnostic species of foraging, reproductive, and habitat-use guilds
Habitat unit type	Distinct hydrogeomorphic subunits of valley segment types (e.g., riffle, pool, run).	Depth Velocity Substrate Position within the channel Physical forming features	Species level patterns Diagnostic species of foraging, reproductive, and habitat-use guilds

Notes:

[a] Hierarchy is adapted after the classification hierarchies of Frissell *et al.* (1986), Pflieger (1989), and primarily Maxwell *et al.* (1995), Seelbach *et al.* (1997), and Higgins *et al.* (1999).

resilience to disturbance. These same questions could just as easily be addressed at any other level in the hierarchy.

When these digital tools and data become more widely available, as more states begin to implement Aquatic GAP projects, stream ecologists will become more prominent in the field of landscape ecology and in the development and refinement of landscape ecology principles. This level of involvement will be critical to conserving aquatic biodiversity and making full use of the data and information generated from an Aquatic GAP project.

5.6 Guidelines for riverine management

To best use what is known about how landscape ecology can benefit riverine management, we offer the following "rules of thumb" and suggestions, some of which can be immediately applied and some which require further research.

(1) Adopt a landscape perspective. Spatial scale has to become a primary focus of the planning and operational aspects of management. Applying landscape ecology concepts is not just examining a larger geographical area, but it is a necessary first step. Because broad geographical concerns are likely associated with long time frames, a different perspective on time is also required. Natural processes disrupting stream biota, and natural restorative processes, both operate in time frames far different from management agency budget cycles, graduate studies, or even entire careers.

(2) Apply landscape principles. Develop standard analogs to terrestrial landscape concepts of vegetation, land use, and landform. Apply what is known about how terrestrial land uses affect biota. Develop a better understanding of the role of riparian buffer strips as mitigators of particular land uses. Apply the most basic tenet of landscape ecology by concentrating on the spatial structure of entire heterogeneous mosaics, determine the biota–patch relations within the mosaics and the interactions among patches over time.

(3) Develop digital layers and technology specific to the aquatic realm. The technology available to organize and quantify spatial data on the terrestrial landscape is well in place (Johnson and Gage, 1997). Tools to apply landscape principles to aquatic systems are somewhat different and involve not necessarily retrofitting those used by terrestrial biologists, but developing those that will give the ability to map underwater environments and "observe" biota. Doppler and side-scanning radars, miniaturization of radio and sonic transmitters for tracking, bathometric

mapping integrated with geographic positioning systems (GPS) and GIS all show promise in allowing a better understanding of biota and their habitats. However, the scarcity of GIS layers of natural resources and human uses is limiting to progress and it is necessary to promote the development of high-resolution data to characterize aquatic resources.

The lack of standards for how data are collected, stored, coded, georeferenced, and analyzed seriously hinders the sharing of information among professionals. Standards should not be viewed as a constraint to progress but as a necessity for conservation.

(4) Learn to deal effectively with competing interests. The technology will no doubt provide the necessary tools to properly analyze the natural world. The ability to interpret these data for meaningful ecological outcomes is a current challenge eagerly embraced by scientists. The most problematic step in managing riverine systems is effectively operating in the human dimensions arena. It is likely that a high percentage of biologically sound plans and projects that encompass a broad-scale view are either never initiated or never brought to completion because of the increased complexity when projects cross agency lines, political boundaries, or competing interests. Translating new knowledge into practical management strategies will be easy in theory, but will involve coordination with numerous interest groups at unprecedented levels.

5.7 Summary

Managing the biota of riverine ecosystems – be it for watershed restoration, conserving biodiversity, or for improving recreational fishing – requires above all a holistic understanding of ecological processes underlying biological attributes of importance. The well-being of fauna depends upon conditions in the stream channel, riparian zone, and watershed. Because influences are hierarchical in nature, where larger broad-scale factors influence smaller-scale factors, management must occur at the proper scale to be effective. Only the landscape perspective allows the potential for understanding the full integration of processes operating throughout a river system.

Managing stream habitat is usually the focus of programs charged with managing stream biota, but habitat is influenced by factors operating at different scales and the interaction of factors between scales, so sorting out the causative variables is of paramount concern to managers. While much is known about small-scale processes that influence stream biota, little is understood about the influences of large-scale processes. In Missouri, it was necessary to take a multi-scale research approach in order to reveal factors limiting smallmouth bass populations in the state and the spatial scale at which fisheries management efforts should be focused. As evidenced by this and other studies discussed in the chapter, fisheries management can be considerably enhanced by such multi-scale perspectives.

Landscape ecology principles have traditionally been woven into the fabric of stream ecological theory. Concepts that focus on longitudinal changes of biota, concepts emphasizing lateral interactions and catchment-level processes, as well as spatial and temporal scale, are all part of modern stream ecological theory. Much of the explanatory power of these concepts is derived by acknowledging the spatial or temporal heterogeneity of a stream system, by breaking stream systems into relatively homogeneous areas – e.g., upstream–downstream, channel–floodplain – and explaining how the structure and function of these homogeneous units interact to determine overall structure and function of larger areas. Still, the lack of stream-related research publications in journals that focus on landscape ecology is evidence that many stream ecologists have not yet recognized either the importance of landscape ecology to the conservation of lotic ecosystems or their ability to scientifically advance such concepts.

Advances in landscape ecology have been possible, in part, because of a common understanding of what constitutes a landscape element or patch. To answer some of the most basic questions of interest to landscape ecologists, a similar common understanding must be developed among stream ecologists. Stream ecologists must develop analogs to separating forests from grasslands (e.g., streams and lakes), separating forest types (e.g., stream types), fragmentation factors (e.g., channelization), and barriers to dispersal (e.g., reservoirs). Once these analogs have been defined, and more importantly, mapped, stream ecologists will more readily examine spatially explicit questions that relate species distribution, abundance, composition, diversity, and persistence to patch size, juxtaposition of patches, isolation or fragmentation of patches, heterogeneity of patches, or patch dynamics. Only by answering such questions as they pertain specifically to lotic environments will the more difficult task of integrating principles of landscape ecology into the management of stream ecosystems begin.

The relevance of landscape ecology to riverine management will be greatly enhanced when relations between the biological measures of stream quality and the spatial arrangement or heterogeneity of landcover patches throughout a watershed, and the spatial arrangement and heterogeneity of stream-channel patches throughout drainage networks (at multiple spatial scales), are better elucidated. Such a patch-dynamics perspective can assist in integrating some of the dominant paradigms in stream ecology into management programs by providing the necessary reductionist tool for evaluating such concepts, by delineating units amenable to generating inventory statistics, and by enhancing communication among resource professionals, since humans naturally think and communicate in terms of classes or categories. Examining such complex spatial relations in this manner will likely be a major emphasis of stream ecologists over the next decade, especially as more geospatial data become available and as more stream ecologists become exposed to remote sensing, GIS, and spatial statistics.

Incorporating principles of landscape ecology and conservation biology into riverine management over large geographic areas will be critical to stemming the loss of freshwater biodiversity. The Missouri Aquatic GAP Analysis Project has developed a broadly applicable assessment methodology that identifies and prioritizes biodiversity conservation needs for riverine environments at multiple spatial scales. It is based on a classification system that characterizes biodiversity by focusing on ecological and evolutionary processes responsible for the formation and distribution of native aquatic assemblages and includes physical attributes. Spatially explicit GIS data layers of riverine ecosystems at multiple scales with corresponding assessment statistics allow users to evaluate the relative distinctiveness and conservation status of each ecosystem and to have a sound basis for establishing conservation priorities.

Acknowledgments

This is a contribution from the Missouri Cooperative Fish and Wildlife Research Unit (US Geological Survey, Missouri Department of Conservation, University of Missouri, and Wildlife Management Institute cooperating). We appreciate the assistance of D. Galat, K. Doisy, S. Clark, G. Annis, M. Morey, G. Sorensen, and D. Diamond.

References

Abell, R. A., Olson, D. M., Dinerstein, E., Hurley, P. T., Diggs, J. T., Eichbaum, W., Walters, S., Wettengel, W., Allnutt, T., Loucks, C. J. & Hedao, P. (2000). *Freshwater Ecoregions of North America: A Conservation Assessment*. World Wildlife Fund–United States, Island Press, Washington, D.C.

Allan, J. D., Erickson, D. L. & Fay, J. (1997). The influence of catchment land use on stream integrity across multiple spatial scales. *Freshwater Biology*, 37: 149–161.

Angermeier, P. L. & Schlosser, I. J. (1995). Conserving aquatic biodiversity: Beyond species and populations. *American Fisheries Society Symposium*, 17: 402–414.

Armstrong, J. D., Grant, J. W. A., Forsgren, H. L., Fausch, K. D., DeGraaf, R. M., Fleming, I. A., Prowse, T. D. & Schlosser, I. J. (1998). The application of science to the management of Atlantic salmon (*Salmo salar*): Integration across scales. *Canadian Journal of Fisheries and Aquatic Sciences*, 55(Suppl. 1): 303–311.

Barsalou, L. W. (1992). *Cognitive Psychology: An Overview for Cognitive Scientists*. Lawrence Erlbaum Associates, Hillsdale, NJ.

Fajen, O. F. (1981). Warmwater stream management with emphasis on bass streams in Missouri. In *Warmwater Streams Symposium*, ed. L. A. Krumholz, pp. 252–265. American Fisheries Society, Bethesda, MD.

Frissell, C. A., Liss, W. J., Warren, C. E. & Hurley, M. D. (1986). A hierarchical framework for stream habitat classification: Viewing streams in a watershed context. *Environmental Management*, 10: 199–214.

Gauch, H. G. (1982). *Multivariate Analysis in Community Ecology*. Cambridge University Press, Cambridge, UK.

Gebert, W. A. & Krug, W. R. (1996). Streamflow trends in Wisconsin's driftless area. *Water Resources Bulletin*, 32: 733–744.

Harding, J. S., Benfield, E. F., Bolstad, P. V., Helfman, G. S. & Jones, E. B. D. III (1998). Stream biodiversity: The ghost of land use past. *Proceedings of the National Academy of Sciences of the United States of America*, 95: 14 843–14 847.

Higgins, J., Lammert, M. & Bryer, M. (1999). *The Nature Conservancy's Aquatic Community Classification Framework*. The Nature Conservancy, Arlington, VA.

Huet, M. (1954). Biologie, profils en long et en travers des eaux courantes. *Bulletin Français de Pisciculture*, 175: 41–53.

Huston, M. (1979). A general hypothesis of species diversity. *American Naturalist*, 113: 81–101.

Hutto, R. L., Reel, S.& Landres, P. B. (1987). A critical evaluation of the species approach to biological conservation. *Endangered Species Update*, 4(12): 1–4.

Hynes, H. B. N. (1975). The stream and its valley. *Verhandlungen Internationale Vereinigung für Theoretische und Angewandte Limnologie*, 19: 1–15.

Illies, J. & Botosaneanu, L. (1963). Problèmes et méthodes de la classification et de la zonation écologiques des eaux courantes, considérées surtout du point de vue faunistique. *Mitteilungen Internationale Vereinigung Limnologie*, 12: 1–57.

Johnson, L. B. & Gage, S. H. (1997). Landscape approaches to the analysis of aquatic ecosystems. *Freshwater Biology*, 37: 113–132.

Junk, J. W., Bayley, P. B. & Sparks, R. E. (1989). The flood pulse concept in river–floodplain systems. In *Proceedings of the International Large River Symposium, Canadian Journal of Fisheries and Aquatic Sciences* Special Publication no. 106, ed. D. P. Dodge, pp. 110–127.

Lammert, M. & Allan, J. D. (1999). Assessing biotic integrity of streams: Effects of scale in measuring the influence of landuse/cover and habitat structure on fish and macroinvertebrates. *Environmental Management*, 23: 257–270.

Larimore, R. W. & Bayley, P. B. (1996). *The Fishes of Champaign County, Illinois, during a Century of Alterations of a Prairie Ecosystem*. Illinois Natural History Survey Bulletin no. 35, Champaign, IL.

Levin, S. A. (1992). The problem of pattern and scale in ecology. *Ecology*, 73: 1943–1967.

Lorenz, C. M., Van Dijk, G. M., Van Hattum, A. G. M. & Cofino, W. P. (1997). Concepts in river ecology: Implications for indicator development. *Regulated Rivers: Research and Management*, 13: 501–516.

Lotspeich, F. B. & Platts, W. S. (1982). An integrated land–aquatic classification system. *North American Journal of Fisheries Management*, 2: 138–149.

Master, L. L., Flack, S. R. & Stein, B. A., (eds.) (1998). *Rivers of Life: Critical Watersheds for Protecting Freshwater Diversity*. The Nature Conservancy, Arlington, VA.

Maxwell, J. R., Edwards, C. J., Jensen, M. E., Paustian, S. J., Parrott, H. & Hill, D. M. (1995). *A Hierarchical Framework of Aquatic Ecological Units in North America (Nearctic Zone)*. North Central Forest Experiment Station General Technical Report no. NC-176. US Forest Service, St. Paul, MN.

National Research Council (1992). *Restoration of Aquatic Ecosystems*. National Academy of Sciences, Washington, D.C.

Newbold, J. D., Elwood, J. W., O'Neill, R. V. & Van Winkle, W. (1981). Nutrient spiralling in streams: The concept and its field measurement. *Canadian Journal of Fisheries and Aquatic Sciences*, 38: 860–863.

Noss, R. F. (1991). From endangered species to biodiversity. In *Balancing on the Brink of Extinction: The Endangered Species Act and Lessons for the Future*, ed. K. A. Kohm, pp. 49–61. Island Press, Washington, D.C.

Noss, R. F., LaRoe, E. T. III & Scott, J. M. (1995). Endangered Ecosystems of the United States: A Preliminary Assessment of Loss and Degradation. USGS–Biological Resources Division Biological Report no. 28. US Department of the Interior, Washington, D.C.

Osborne, L. L. & Wiley, M. J. (1992). Influence of tributary spatial position on the structure of warmwater fish communities. *Canadian Journal of Fisheries and Aquatic Sciences*, 49(4): 671–681.

Pflieger, W. L. (1989). Aquatic Community Classification System for Missouri, Aquatic Series no. 19, *Missouri Department of Conservation*. Jefferson City, MO.

Pitelka, F. A. (1981). The condor case: An uphill struggle in a downhill crush. *Auk*, 98: 634–635.

Poff, N. L. (1997). Landscape filters and species traits: Towards mechanistic understanding and prediction in stream ecology. *Journal of the North American Benthological Society*, 16: 391–409.

Poff, N. L., Allen, J. D., Bain, M. B., Karr, J. R., Prestegaard, K. L., Richter, B. D., Sparks, R. E. & Stromberg, J. C. (1997). The natural flow regime: A paradigm for river conservation and restoration. *BioScience*, 47: 769–784.

Pringle, C. M., Naiman, R. J., Bretschko, G., Karr, J. R., Oswood, M. W., Webster, J. R., Welcomme, R. L. & Winterbourn, M. J. (1988). Patch dynamics in lotic systems: The stream as a mosaic. *Journal of the North American Benthological Society*, 7: 503–524.

Rabeni, C. F. (1995). Warmwater streams. In *Inland Fisheries Management in North America*, eds. C. C. Kohler & W. A. Hubert, pp. 427–444. American Fisheries Society, Bethesda, MD.

Rabeni, C. F. & Sowa, S. P. (1996). Integrating biological realism into habitat restoration and conservation strategies for small streams. *Canadian Journal of Fisheries and Aquatic Sciences*, 53(Suppl. 1): 252–259.

Reeves, G. H., Hohler, D. B., Hansen, B. E., Everest, F. H., Sedell, J. R., Hickman, T. L. & Shivley, D. (1997). Fish habitat restoration in the Pacific Northwest: Fish Creek of Oregon. In *Watershed Restoration: Principles and Practices*, eds. J. E. Williams, C. A. Wood & M. P. Dombeck, pp. 335–359. American Fisheries Society, Bethesda, MD.

Reice, S. R., Wissmar, R. C. & Naiman, R. J. (1990). Disturbance regimes, resilience, and recovery of animal communities and habitats in lotic ecosystems. *Environmental Management*, 14: 647–659.

Ricciardi, A. & Rasmussen, J. B. (1999). Extinction rates of North American freshwater fauna. *Conservation Biology*, 13: 1220–1222.

Richards, C., Johnson, L. B. & Host, G. E. (1996). Landscape-scale influences on stream habitats and biota. *Canadian Journal of Fisheries and Aquatic Sciences*, 53 (Suppl. 1): 295–311.

Risser, P. G., Karr, J. R. & Forman, R. T. T. (1984). *Landscape Ecology: Directions and Approaches*, a workshop held at Allerton Park, Piatt County, Illinois, April 1983. Illinois Natural History Survey Special Publication no. 2, Champaign, IL.

Ross, H. H. (1963). Stream communities and terrestrial biomes. *Archiwum Hydrobiologia*, 59: 235–242.

Roth, N. E., Allan, J. D. & Erickson, D. L. (1996). Landscape influences on stream biotic integrity assessed at multiple spatial scales. *Landscape Ecology*, 11: 141–156.

Schlosser, I. J. (1995). Dispersal, boundary processes, and trophic-level interactions in streams and adjacent beaver ponds. *Ecology*, 76: 908–925.

Schmidt, J. C., Webb, R. H., Valdez, R. A., Marzolf, G. R. & Stevens, L. E. (1998). Science and values in river restoration in the Grand Canyon: There is no restoration or rehabilitation strategy that will improve the status of every riverine resource. *BioScience*, 48: 735–747.

Schumm, S. A. (1977). *The Fluvial System*. John Wiley, New York.

Scott, J. M., Csuti, B., Jacobi, J. D. & Estes, J. E. (1987). Species richness: A geographic approach to protecting future biological diversity. *BioScience*, 37: 782–788.

Scott, J. M., Davis, F., Csuti, B., Noss, R., Butterfield, B., Groves, C., Anderson, J., Caicco, S., D'Erchia, F., Edwards, T. C., Ulliman, J. & Wright, R. G. (1993). Gap analysis: A geographical approach to protection of biological diversity. *Wildlife Monographs*, 123: 1–41.

Seelbach, P. S., Wiley, M. J., Kotanchik, J. C. & Baker, M. E. (1997). A Landscape-Based Ecological Classification System for River Valley Segments in Lower Michigan (MI-VSEC version 1.0), Research Report no. 2036. State of Michigan Department of Natural Resources Fisheries Division Lansing, MI.

Sowa, S. P. (1999). *Implementing the Aquatic Component of GAP Analysis in Riverine Environments*. Missouri Resource Assessment Partnership, Columbia, MO.

Statzner, B. & Higler, B. (1986). Stream hydraulics as a major determinant of benthic invertebrate zonation patterns. *Freshwater Biology*, 16: 127–139.

Swanson, F. J., Kratz, T. K., Caine, N. & Woodmansee, R. G. (1988). Landform effects on ecosystem patterns and processes. *BioScience*, 38: 92–98.

Townsend, C. R. (1996). Concepts in river ecology: Pattern and process in the catchment hierarchy. *Archiv fur Hydrobiologie* (Suppl.), 113: 3–21.

Turner, M. G. (1989). Landscape ecology: The effect of pattern on process. *Annual Review of Ecology and Systematics*, 20: 171–197.

Vannote, R. L., Minshall, G. W., Cummins, K. W., Sedell, J. R. & Cushing, C. E. (1980). The river continuum concept. *Canadian Journal of Fisheries and Aquatic Sciences*, 37: 130–137.

Wang, L., Lyons, J., Kanehl, P. & Gatti, R. (1997). Influences of watershed land use on habitat quality and biotic integrity in Wisconsin streams. *Fisheries*, 22: 6–12.

Ward, J. V. (1989). The four-dimensional nature of lotic systems. *Journal of the North American Benthological Society*, 8: 2–8.

Wiens, J. A. (1989). Spatial scaling in ecology. *Functional Ecology*, 3: 385–397.

Wiley, M. J., Kohler, S. L. & Seelbach, P. W. (1997). Reconciling landscape and local views of aquatic communities: Lessons from Michigan trout streams. *Freshwater Biology*, 37: 133–148.

Williams, J. E. & Neves, R. J. (1992). Introducing the elements of biological diversity in the aquatic environment. *Transactions of the North American Wildlife and Natural Resources Conference*, 57: 345–354.

Williams, J. E., Wood, C. A. & Dombeck, M. P. (eds.) (1997). *Watershed Restoration: Principles and Practices*. American Fisheries Society, Bethesda, MD.

KRISTIINA A. VOGT, MORGAN GROVE, HEIDI ASBJORNSEN,
KEELY B. MAXWELL, DANIEL J. VOGT, RAGNHILDUR SIGURÐARDÓTTIR,
BRUCE C. LARSON, LEO SCHIBLI, AND MICHAEL DOVE

6

Linking ecological and social scales for natural resource management

6.1 Introduction

Natural resource management has moved from a single disciplinary and one resource management approach to an interdisciplinary and ecosystem-based approach. Many conceptual models are being developed to understand and implement ecosystem management and forest certification initiatives that require an integration of data from both the social and natural systems (Vogt *et al.*, 1997, 1999a,b). These changed approaches to natural resource management arose from a perception that variables critical in controlling the health and functioning of an ecosystem could only be determined by integrating information from both the social and the natural sciences (Vogt *et al.*, 1997). However, it has been difficult to take many of the theoretical discussions and the frameworks or conceptual models that they have produced and to operationalize or put them into practice on the ground.

Despite these discussions and the recognition of their importance, social and natural science data have been ineffectively incorporated into the management and trade-off assessments of natural resources (Berry and Vogt, 1999). We hypothesize that some of this has occurred because of the distinct spatial scales being used by different disciplines which have not allowed for integration of information to occur at a causal level. The complexity and uncertainty of data needed to understand ecosystems by both social and natural scientists have also made it difficult for managers to recognize when the wrong indicators are being monitored or whether a system could degrade due to management (Larson *et al.*, 1999; Vogt *et al.*, 1999c). The need to link data causally from both disciplines as part of ecosystem management has given greater impetus to develop practical tools that would allow this integration to be accomplished. However, today much of that integration has been mainly occurring at the level of conceptualization and development of frameworks of analysis.

Table 6.1. *The smallest to large-scale levels of analysis existing in the social and natural sciences*

Natural sciences	Social sciences
Biotic individual approach	*Biotic individual approach*
1. Genes	1. Individual
2. Protoplasm	2. Household
3. Cells	3. Kin, clan, caste
4. Tissues	4. Neighborhood
5. Organs	5. Village or city
6. Organ systems	6. Watershed
7. Individual (e.g., producers, consumers, carnivores, omnivores, decomposers – fungi, bacteria, etc.)	7. County 8. State 9. Region
8. Family	10. Society
9. Population	11. Country
10. Community	
Functional ecosystem approach	*Functional ecosystem approach*
1. Inorganic or organic substrate	1. Social order
2. Patch or microsite	identity (age, gender, class, caste, clan)
3. Stand or plot	hierarchy (wealth, power, status, knowledge, territory)
4. Vegetative type	
5. Ecosystem type	2. Social order and cycles
6. Soil type	(a) physiological
7. Watershed	(b) individual
8. Landscape	(c) social norms or rules for behavior
9. Region	(d) institutional
10. Biome	3. Social institutions
11. Globe	health, justice, faith, commerce, education, leisure, government, sustenance
	institutional cycles
	4. Cultural resources (organizations, beliefs, myths)
	5. Socioeconomic resources (information, population, labor, capital)
	6. Environmental cycles
	energy, land, water, materials, nutrients, flora, fauna
	environmental cycles (natural disturbances)

Note:
The scale of analysis increases from a smaller to a larger scale with increasing category numbers – the smallest scale starts with category number 1. Only within the functional ecosystem approach in the social sciences does each category potentially not have the ability to contain scales ranging from the smallest to the largest.

Sources: Odum (1959); Burch (1988); Grove (1996); Machlis *et al.* (1997); Vogt *et al.* (1997).

The focus of this chapter will be to discuss one issue, the spatial scales of analyses, that we feel is a significant constraint reducing the ability of managers to conduct holistic analyses of their resources. The spatial scales commonly used in assessments are defined by the boundaries of the management unit (see Table 6.1 for the typical scales used by researchers). To satisfactorily achieve holistic management of natural resources, implicit consideration of spatial scale and identification of what scales are appropriate need to become an integral part of the suite of tools used by a manager. The primary objective of this chapter is to further advance the dialogue on scale issues and to discuss more explicitly how consideration of scale would allow for more effective management. Several points will be considered that have constrained integration in natural resource management. First, each discipline tends to utilize its own spatial scales of analyses which are generally different from other disciplines. Second, there is a tendency within each discipline to identify the most sensitive spatial scale of analysis for each natural resource problem as determined by the dominant scales of analyses particular to that discipline. Finally, there is a tendency of the scale of analysis in the social sciences not to match the scale used in the natural sciences. If these assumptions are correct, they suggest a need for managers to identify relevant scales of analyses for each management unit that should vary based on the spatial characteristics of the management unit and the matrix landscape within which it is imbedded. This would require the manager to select a scale based on causal or mechanistic relationships that are sensitive at the selected scale and may even suggest the need to examine several scales simultaneously.

This chapter will not summarize much of the previous scientific discussion that has occurred on scale but will emphasize how managers should use spatial scale when integrating social and natural science sides of management. A case study of the Baltimore Ecosystem will be used to highlight some of the points being made with respect to scale and to demonstrate how scale can be used to resolve natural resource problems at different scales of analysis.

6.2 Spatial scales relevant for natural resource managers

Any discussion of spatial scale issues in the social and natural sciences should begin with an examination of how scale has been incorporated into research and an understanding of why particular scales were selected. This discussion will begin to inform a manager of the appropriate scales to consider when linking social and natural science information and whether it is realistic to assume that this integration should occur at the same spatial scale. The dominant and sensitive spatial scales relevant in the different subdisciplines in ecology, conservation, and the social sciences will be analyzed in the next section. This will be followed by a discussion of scaling and scale issues that must be considered when integrating social and natural science data to achieve ecosystem management.

6.2.1 Dominant scale uses assessed from publications in the social and natural sciences

It is informative to review the literature and determine what similarities and differences exist in the typical scales of analyses used by the dominant disciplines germane to natural resource management. We documented the spatial scale of analysis used by researchers who published in two ecological journals (i.e., *Conservation Biology*, *Ecology*) and two social science journals (i.e., *Human Ecology*, *Society and Natural Resources*). Journals were selected for inclusion in this analysis that published interdisciplinary papers, but were written primarily for audiences in the natural or social sciences, since the purpose of this exercise is to inform ecosystem managers. The results of this survey are given in Table 6.2 for the year 1996.

A surprisingly high number of articles published in the social and natural sciences do not even give the spatial scale of their study (the exception is *Human Ecology*). For example, spatial scale was not mentioned in 60.7% of the articles published in *Conservation Biology*, 38.2% of the articles in *Ecology*, and 66.6% of the articles in *Society and Natural Resources* (Table 6.2). In articles where scale was not reported, scale was not considered relevant in half of the studies and was not "place-based" for the other half. *Human Ecology* had a higher percentage of the articles having clearly defined spatial scale – only 14.4% of the articles did not specify a scale. The tendency for studies not to give the scale at which their research is being conducted suggests a perception that the spatial scale is not a critical factor for understanding the system. Since many studies did not mention scale nor define their spatial scale of analysis, it suggests that researchers have (1) alternative conceptualizations of what scale is and how to define it, and (2) different perceptions of the importance of locating their analysis unit (e.g., village ecosystem) within the landscape.

Summarization of the scale data by groupings for the four journals also shows a lack of a common spatial scale of analysis among them (Table 6.2). In general, this small survey of a few journals suggests that most social science studies were conducted at larger scales than what was commonly used in the natural sciences.

Conservation Biology was characterized by having no one scale being the dominant unit of analysis – the smallest scale (<0.01 ha) was equally represented (7.1%) as was the largest scale (>10 000) (5.7%) (Table 6.2). This reflects the tendency of this discipline to undertake plot studies to understand smaller

Table 6.2. *Scale of analysis used by studies published in four journals* (Conservation Biology, Ecology, Human Ecology, and Society and Natural Resources) *for a one-year period in 1996*

	Number of times cited in 1996 (% of total citations in each spatial scale category by journal)			
Spatial scale (ha)	Conservation Biology	Ecology	Human Ecology	Society and Natural Resources
<0.01	10 (7.1%)	95 (39.9%)	0 (0%)	1 (2.1%)
>0.01 to <0.1	6 (4.3%)	6 (2.5%)	0 (0%)	0 (0%)
>0.1 to <1	6 (4.3%)	14 (5.9%)	0 (0%)	1 (2.1%)
>1 to <10	4 (2.9%)	13 (5.5%)	10 (37.0%)	2 (4.2%)
>10 to <100	6 (4.3%)	7 (2.9%)	2 (7.4%)	0 (0%)
>100 to <10 000	7 (5.0%)	4 (1.7%)	6 (22.2%)	5 (10.4%)
>10 000 to <100 000	8 (5.7%)	1 (0.1%)	4 (14.8%)	5 (10.4%)
>100 000	8 (5.7%)	7 (2.9%)	1 (3.7%)	2 (4.2%)
Not given[a]	40 (28.6%)	55 (23.1%)	2 (7.4%)	16 (33.3%)
Scale not relevant[b]	45 (32.1%)	36 (15.1%)	2 (7.4%)	16 (33.3%)
Total number articles	136	219	23	38

Notes:

[a] Many of these articles may have given scales in terms of household, village, national park, etc., but did not give an explicit mention of the areal measurement unit.

[b] Articles not spatially based (e.g., models, conceptual theory oriented articles, measurements taken from "populations" without saying where).

animals or bounded activities as well as landscape studies to understand the territory necessary for survival of a species. The results from *Conservation Biology* markedly contrasted with the *Ecology* journal. *Ecology* showed a dominance of the smallest scale of analysis (<0.01 ha, e.g., 10 m × 10 m plot) with 40% of the total studies being conducted at this scale. The *Ecology* journal publishes many articles by population and community ecologists who tend to conduct their research on small plot sizes.

Human Ecology did not record any studies that had research plot sizes less than 1 hectare in size (Table 6.2). In 1996, *Human Ecology* had 37% of the articles having study plot areas that were greater than 1 but less than 10 hectares in size (e.g., 100 m × 100 m to 316.2 m × 316.2 m). Most of the studies in this journal were at the household or village level. The scales in the two social science journals, if mentioned, were given in terms of socially determined areas, e.g., village, province, rather than landscape or ecosystem differentiations. *Human Ecology* also showed that 22.2% of the studies used study areas 100 to 10 000 ha in size and 14.8% used study area sizes of 10 000 to 100 000 ha. Similarly, *Society and Natural Resources* had over 20% of the articles reporting their research areas to vary between 100 and 100 000 ha in size. At least during 1996, *Society and Natural Resources* published no studies that were conducted at the second smallest size grouping (0.01 to 0.1 ha) and in a middle-level spatial area (10 to 100 ha).

6.2.2 Scale delineation rationale in the sciences contributing to natural resource management

Many of the scales selected for use by different disciplines are based on the selection of those scales that are the most sensitive to answering the question being pursued by each researcher in their field of specialty. For example, the smaller scale of analysis selected by an ecophysiologist is the only scale at which a physiological process in particular tissues of a plant can be detected mechanistically. Clarification of study area sizes selected by scientists implementing ecosystem management or conservation follows below.

The past tendency by ecologists to study systems using a biotic or functional approach (Vogt *et al.*, 1997) have reinforced a few spatial scales of analysis (see Table 6.1). Early in ecology, the biotic approach was the dominant tool being used to study ecological systems (Clements, 1916; Whittaker, 1953; Billings, 1985; Ashton, 1992). In the 1980s, the importance of the ecosystem and functional approaches was finally recognized (Vogt *et al.*, 1997). Since ecosystem ecologists generally used larger spatial scales than the biotic approach, the scale of system analysis increased with the adoption of the ecosystem approach. Researchers using the biotic approach focus on individual interactions with nature. Those using a functional approach are ecosystem based and frequently the individual is not a relevant unit of analysis and therefore not ever explicitly considered. Natural scientists using the biotic approach focus on smaller scales of analysis compared to those who use a functional research focus where the spatial scales of analysis are larger (Table 6.1).

In ecosystem ecology, the spatial scale is identified by the boundaries of ecosystems where the function of the system changes. However, determining the exact boundaries of an ecosystem is a subjective process because the scale at which the system is being observed influences this decision (Giampietro, 1994). By definition, the boundaries of the ecosystem should be demarcated where there is a significant change in the rate at which energy or materials move between two systems (Allen and Hoekstra, 1992). In practice, it is impractical to study the entire ecosystem so representative areas are identified within that larger ecosystem for study. Ecosystem ecologists have used two dominant spatial scales of analysis within this larger system – the stand or plot, and the watershed. The stand typically varies from 0.05 to 1.0 ha in size and is a small fraction of the total ecosystem under study. Site selection becomes crucial at the stand scale since the heterogeneity of the system may mask the processes being studied. When selecting replicate stands, ecosystem ecologists spend a considerable amount of time locating plots that are similar to one another and representative of the ecosystem but distant enough to decrease chances of pseudo-replication. Plot-size choices often reflected the assumption that the processes and patterns examined are indifferent to scale (Wiens, 1989). The other scale used by ecosystem ecologists is the watershed where there is no subjectivity in site selection because the scale is clearly defined by the boundaries of the watershed. Watersheds selected for scientific study (vs. all watersheds) are typically <100 ha in size (Bormann and Likens, 1979; Hornbeck and Swank, 1992). Traditionally, the watershed was defined as a topographically specific area where all the precipitation falling into that area drained into one stream. Since a watershed-scale approach does integrate the heterogeneity that can be found within its bounded space, some researchers use the word watershed as an equivalent term to a landscape.

More recently, landscape ecologists have also focused on the landscape as a spatial unit of measure. Landscape ecology looks at broad spatial scales and attempts to understand the development and dynamics of spatial heterogeneity, interactions and exchange across heterogeneous landscapes, and the influences of spatial heterogeneity on processes (Turner, 1989; Forman, 1995). The landscape scale contrasts the watershed approach because it explicitly incorporates the heterogeneity in the system. It also does not limit studies to an area necessarily linked by flows of water, nutrients, and other materials.

Conservation Biology has focused on the species of interest and defined the scale of analysis by the habitat requirements for that species so that no fixed spatial scale is common (see Table 6.2). Out of all of the subdisciplines in ecology, conservation biology has most explicitly dealt with spatial relationships since the early 1960s when the relationships between the amount of habitat area and number of species were converted to mathematical relationships (Preston, 1962). MacArthur and Wilson further developed these relationships between species and habitat area in 1963 when they published their *island biogeography theory* (MacArthur and Wilson, 1963). These ideas are still an important element of conservation biology although the patterns predicted by the island biogeography theory are not always supported by subsequent studies (Smith, 1990). Species–area relationships focused conservation biologists into explicitly examining the spatial scale of their management area as defined by the species of conservation priority. For example, the scale of interest can vary significantly since the habitat area for a salamander is a stand while for a bear it is a landscape. This lack of a specific spatial scale of analysis compared to other disciplines was quite apparent from the data summarized in Table 6.2.

In the social sciences, the spatial scale of analyses frequently varies from the small to the large scale within one study. The small scale typically consists of household surveys while the large scale assesses the condition and changes in the natural resource-base across a village or other defined area utilized by the people in question. Conway (1986) included a hierarchy of information needs in both the social (e.g., the family to kin group and tribe) and natural systems (e.g., village to mini-watersheds and to the valley). Freudenberger (1997) also used the larger scale of the landscape (e.g., remote sensing to identify locations with significant land-use changes) to identify locations of her more in-depth small-scale studies at the household level. The focus in Table 6.2 on the larger scales of analyses in the two social science journals reflects the inclusion of the natural system to identify the largest scale of assessment. Many social scientists conduct research at the household or community/village level as these are seen to be the most fundamental units of productivity and social order (Moran, 1984; Siralt *et al.*, 1994). Traditional data-gathering techniques in the social sciences are geared towards these two scales (Molnar, 1989). Broader political and economic issues have only recently been included as important factors influencing smaller-scale decision-making, and social and natural systems (Moran, 1984; Fox, 1992).

Other social science studies require information to be collected at several different scales. In order to conduct impact assessment for their human ecosystem model, Machlis *et al.* (1994) recommended analyses that would include the family unit, the community, country, region, nation, and eventually the globe. The study by Grove and Hohmann (1992) was a landscape study that used social data collected at the household, community, regional, state, and national levels.

The use of similar scales and theoretical frameworks by social and natural sciences can be found in the literature. Use of similar scales was *not* the result of social and natural scientists working in interdisciplinary teams or reading each other's literature. These frameworks evolved from each discipline attempting to deal with their own problems. Excellent examples showing the development of similar conceptual frameworks by social and natural scientists is the research on urban expansion (Burgess, 1925; Park *et al.*, 1925) and the design of biosphere reserves. Burgess (1925) did not consider the environment as part of his theory on urban expansion but emphasized the relations between humans and the artificial construct of a city. That study defined specific activities occurring within concentric circles that radiated out from the center of the city. The center of the city was dominated by the business sectors and radiated out to the urban parts of the city. The key unit of analysis for Burgess (1925) was the city. The concept of the human community articulated by Burgess (1925) is similar to the reserve design adopted by the Man and the Biosphere (MAB) program.

The MAB reserve concept does not use the city analog but instead focuses on the interactions of humans with the surrounding environment (typically forests). The MAB reserve concept consists of a core area in the center of a reserve that is not to be utilized by humans, but should remain as habitat for native animals and plants. The next concentric circle located adjacent to the core area is defined as areas where humans can harvest products from the forest but this utilization should not visibly change the character of the forest. The last outer circle is the zone of intensive human activity (e.g., villages, agricultural fields) and has few, if any, of the characteristics of the core area. Both the city model and the biosphere reserve model define zones of human activity using the concentric circle concept. This separation of activities by spatial scale is very artificial and in practice does not typically occur (e.g., human activities are difficult to exclude from the MAB reserve core areas).

6.2.3 Scaling issues

Scaling is an important research topic because most of our past data collection has occurred at smaller scales and not at the larger scale where natural resource decisions and policy need to be formulated (Levin, 1992). Scaling issues are further compounded by the fact that different scales (given in Table 6.2) are also not discrete or disjointed in time and space (Magnusen, 1990) so that temporally distinct activities can feed back to affect a different scale relative to where the activity was originally generated. Several factors have contributed to making it difficult for managers to translate information collected at smaller scales to make practical decisions at larger scales. Three of these factors will be briefly discussed here: (1) changing amount and type of data with scale, (2) preference by scientists to study smaller scales because of the ease of experimentation and use of controls for the experimental system (see section 6.2.1), and (3) the loss of predictive ability (i.e., causal relationships) when transferring information between scales.

In the 1980s, much attention began to be placed on producing tools to scale data from the small to the larger scales of the landscape and the globe in the natural sciences. Developing scaling tools was important to allow the significant volumes of data already collected by physiologists as well as community and ecosystem ecologists to be used (Running and Coughlan, 1988; Running and Nemani, 1988; Ehleringer and Field, 1993; Running and Hunt, 1993). At the same time, model development in the social sciences began to integrate information from different scales (Burch, 1988; Fox, 1992; Cortner *et al.*, 1996). This need for linking data between small and large scales was an impetus for the development of hierarchy theory.

Already in the 1980s, hydrologists realized the problems resulting from modeling watershed dynamics as uniform. This realization stimulated research to link hydrologic models with geographic imformation systems (GIS) to spatially analyze a watershed to incorporate its heterogeneity (Beasley *et al.*, 1982; Young *et al.*, 1989; Arnold *et al.*, 1990; Fraser, 1999). Hydrologists have also accepted the importance of the spatial resolution of input variables in determining the results of their modeling efforts (Fraser, 1999). This conclusion resulted from the use of non-linear equations in models so that "their statistical properties (mean and variance) for a given area will change if input data are aggregated to a coarser resolution" (Fraser, 1999). Dubayah *et al.* (1997) demonstrated this phenomenon when they obtained different results from input variables aggregated at a 1-km compared to a 10-km resolution. This last example again demonstrates the importance of identifying the most sensitive scale of analysis for each natural resource problem.

Scientists generally accept the statement that the type and amount of data needed to assay the resistance and resilience characteristics of an ecosystem are sensitive to scale of analysis. As a generality, the smallest scale has the largest data requirements to explain how that ecosystem functions (Gosz, 1993). Other variables and, in most cases, fewer variables are needed to predict ecosystem characteristics as one progresses up to larger scales. Each scale also has different stresses that are important in regulating processes at that scale (Turner *et al.*, 1995). Therefore, there is an inability to automatically sum up the parts of a system at one scale and then examine that system from a larger scale. In addition, each scale itself may have many linked scales (e.g., forested landscape to a drainage basin or watershed to a forest stand or ecosystem to gaps within the forest and individual trees). Therefore when analyzing landscapes at different scales, it is important to recognize that each organism defines and perceives patches differently within that landscape (Wiens, 1989; Levin, 1992; Milne, 1992; Turner *et al.*, 1995).

The difficulties of transferring data between scales have generated much of the discussion related to hierarchy theory (O'Neill *et al.*, 1986, 1989). Unfortunately, the tools or good examples demonstrating the implementation of hierarchy theory have been slow to develop (Turner *et al.*, 1995). Some of this difficulty is a result of the non-linear transformations of process and relationships that occur when making transitions among scales (Walters and Holling, 1990). The existence of "chaos" or the loss of predictive capability between different scales of analysis creates problems for global-scale policy analyses when utilizing information generated at smaller scales (Stern *et al.*, 1992; Nilsson and Schopfhauser, 1995; Lele and Norgaard, 1996). Depending upon what data from the lower scale are used may skew the results synthesized at the higher scale. This is especially relevant when the scaled-up data results are associated with data from a lower scale that has a large degree of variation.

Global warming and carbon sequestration in forests (Schroeder, 1992; Brown *et al.*, 1993; Houghton, 1996) also illustrate problems arising from aggregating incomplete data collected at lower scales to address a problem at a larger scale. We suggest that some global warming debates are being analyzed at the wrong scale because the final scale of analysis is not sensitive to the variables initially used to drive the analyses. This lack of sensitivity at the global scale results from inadequate data summarization and how existing data are being scaled to the globe. When scaling data, any errors in the synthesis of the data will strongly affect the conclusions that are reached. For example, most of the global warming studies cited above did not adjust their data analyses to account for the selectivity of data from a few study sites. They also did not adjust their analyses to compensate for missing information. Vegetative community classifications and aboveground biomass data have been used as the main data to scale-up plot specific data to address global warming issues. However, belowground vegetative biomass and soil organic matter can sequester carbon at levels two to three times higher than the aboveground biomass (see Lugo and Brown, 1993; Vogt *et al.*, 1996). Therefore, the synthesis and scaling of ecological information to produce the global value should be highly suspect. These analyses result in an assumption that particular management practices will be useful for counteracting global warming when in fact averaging and lack of data on several ecosystem components means that the suggestions may not be supported by data. Instead of assuming the need to scale-up to answer global environmental questions, it may be more important to identify which scale is most sensitive in reflecting the processes relevant for policymakers and for which credible data can be produced.

Tools and approaches to scale information from the smaller to the larger scale are evolving and mathematical models are an integral part of these analyses. For example, ecophysiologists have used process-based models for addressing scaling issues from leaf to canopy levels and from stand to ecosystem levels (Ehleringer and Field, 1993). These models have used either a bottom-up or a top-down approach (e.g., Reynolds *et al.*, 1993; Running and Hunt, 1993). Bottom-up modeling, scaling from smaller to higher scales, involves extending calculations from an easily measured and reasonably well understood unit to processes at a more encompassing scale. The most familiar bottom-up models have taken knowledge at leaf or sub-leaf scales, combined these with environmental information, and derived descriptions of how a stand functions under a range of circumstances (Jarvis, 1993). A major problem with the bottom-up models is the complexity of information needed, especially in heterogeneous systems. Bottom-up models can thus be too complicated to be of general use in scaling to higher levels. Furthermore, the output from bottom-up models is open-ended, which makes the models more sensitive to input errors (Jarvis, 1993). In contrast, top-down approaches have been constrained totally through an experimentally determined relationship with a crucial driving variable. The empirical relationships that have been derived prevent the extreme predictions that may result from the bottom-up models. Top-down models have, however, less mechanistic insight and are thus limited in their application to scaling information up to another level. Dawson and Chapin (1993), Reynolds *et al.* (1993), and others have argued that these two modeling approaches are interdependent and should be used concurrently for addressing scaling issues. In order to simplify the task of scaling without losing predictive power, Dawson and Chapin (1993) also suggested that the plants within a community should be grouped together according to their form–function relationships.

6.2.4 Ecological and social systems and their integration

The disciplinary focus of scientists and the use of specific scales by discipline have resulted in the development of constraints to integrating ecological and social systems (see Tables 6.1, 6.2). A historical precedence exists for natural scientists to consider spatial scales in their study system that was not as prevalent in the social sciences. It is only recently that social scientists have been explicitly making their data scale dependent. Although natural scientists considered scale explicitly, their use of a few scales by discipline (see section 6.2.1) have also created problems for integrating ecological and social scales. For example, the current integration of ecological and social scales is being conducted at larger scales than the study system was originally studied, necessitating the development of new scaling tools that are still evolving (section 6.2.3). The following section will present a brief introduction on how researchers have linked social and natural systems and how each perceives spatial scale.

The types of data collected by social and natural scientists have contributed to difficulties in integrating information from different disciplines. The quantitative type of data collected by many natural scientists has been easier for policy-makers to utilize compared to the more qualitative data collected in the social sciences (Rifkin, 1996). Frequently, social science data was ignored in past policy-making decisions because of the difficulty of using qualitative data. The predominant use of economics as a natural resource assessment tool is based on its ability to give quantitative results. Since natural scientists appear to give more credibility to quantitative data, this has made it difficult for both the social and natural scientists to interact and integrate their studies. The rise of the Rapid Rural Appraisal and the more broadly focused Participatory Rural Appraisal (Chambers, 1994) approaches have partly been an effort by social scientists to decrease the need to conduct cumbersome surveys to obtain quantitative results that are easily transmittable and utilizable in policy-making. These approaches allow meaningful results to be obtained, since there is an ability to quantify multiple activities and patterns even if they cannot be analyzed statistically. Rifkin (1996) suggested that the value of the Rapid Rural Appraisal approach for social scientists has been to provide a framework for data collection and analysis that is spatially explicit.

Several decades ago, social scientists recognized the interactions and constraints placed by the ecological system on the social system (Hawley, 1950; Duncan, 1961; Young, 1974; Rambo, 1983; Rosa and Machlis, 1983; Vayda, 1983; Hawley, 1986; Burch, 1988; Grove and Burch, 1997). However, although they recognized the importance of these linkages, they did not explicitly address or produce a model to deal with the spatial relationships between humans and natural resources (Machlis *et al.*, 1997). This means that the social sciences did not deal with the issues of scale and hierarchy theory in any way comparable to the high attention given to these topics by the natural sciences. Although the social sciences have not explicitly dealt with the issue of scale and hierarchy theory (Fox, 1992), scale probably drives the conflicts perceived to exist between the different disciplines in the social sciences. For example, the arguments and differences existing between psychologists (Lynch, 1960; Sommer, 1969), sociologists (Firey, 1945; Schnore, 1958; Bailey and Mulcahy, 1972; Young, 1974, 1992; Field and Burch, 1988; Catton, 1992, 1994), geographers (Agnew and Duncan, 1989), and political scientists (Masters, 1989) may be attributed more to the use of different scales and criteria (Allen and Hoekstra, 1992) than questions of who is right or wrong. For instance, psychologists and sociologists argue about whether individual behavior creates social structures or whether social structures determine individual behavior. Rather than seeing this as a mutually exclusive dichotomy, it may be more appropriate to conceive of such a question as a matter of scale and to ask about the relative relationship between individual behavior and social structure for a given question. With this approach, research questions are more resolvable by actually promoting discussions between scientists.

Natural scientists historically did not incorporate people into their analysis of a natural system but focused on finding ecosystems to study that were "virgin" (e.g., minimal human influence) and that could be isolated from the social system (Vogt *et al.*, 1997). The philosophy was that there was a need to understand the natural system first and that most human activities could be treated more as harvesting or removal of products from that system. The approach taken by most natural scientists was to link human communities with the natural resources by measuring the impact of a particular human activity (e.g., chemical pollution) on a defined natural resource area (Bormann and Likens, 1979). This approach maintains the idea that ecological systems are mostly constrained by the natural system and that the social system is a minor constraint to its functioning. Only recently has the importance of the social system as a driver of natural resource conditions been articulated (Stern *et al.*, 1992). Other natural scientists have moved beyond these strictly ecological approaches to assessing the health of natural resources by attempting to see what concepts can be derived from comparing natural systems to human health (Rapport *et al.*, 1985; Levin, 1989; O'Laughlin *et al.*, 1994). However, these ecosystem health assessments have been mainly driven by satisfying the human desired values/products from a natural system and not from understanding the constraints of the ecological system (Vogt *et al.*, 1999c). The importance of human legacies, other than chemicals or land-use patterns, in controlling or constraining ecosystem function has been only recently addressed by natural scientists (Vogt *et al.*, 1999b).

Already in 1994, Miller suggested that part of the data analysis problems encountered between integrating social and natural sciences can be traced to how each discipline measures and records spatial data. For example, it is not unusual to collect georeference data in the natural sciences. In contrast, the social sciences had not previously considered georeferenced data important to collect (Fox, 1992). In fact, many of the important driving variables studied by social scientists (e.g., cultural, political, institutional, and economic conditions) do not appear to be driven by spatial scale processes (Miller, 1994). This suggests that social scientists did not explicitly consider space itself as a factor that affected the resistance and resilience characteristics of human ecosystems (see Table 6.1). However, each social science variable listed in Table 6.1 has an implicit scale inherent to itself even when no scale is implied. For example, each institutional structure has a zone of authority that it influences which can be spatially expressed. This zone of influence becomes the spatial scale at which the impacts of an institution should be examined. In fact, social scientists have typically defined spatial scales to include the political boundaries that constrain the activities occurring in the area being studied. However, in most cases the political boundaries do not track the ecological boundaries as identified by ecologists so that the scales of analysis are distinctly different (Lee *et al.*, 1990; Miller, 1994) (Table 6.2). In fact, boundaries generated by social variables have not been typically analyzed by natural scientists. Natural scientists have been historically more interested in understanding the processes and functions occurring at the scales of vegetative communities or soil types (see Vogt *et al.*, 1996).

Increasingly, social scientists are beginning to realize the need for the adoption of a hierarchical or multi-scale approach to their research. This approach has been adopted for use in several interdisciplinary research projects where natural scientists are adapting and integrating approaches from various disciplines to understand a specific phenomenon (Pickett *et al.*, 1989; Grimm *et al.*, 2000). Watershed-scale research (e.g., hydrological studies) has been especially amenable to linking social and ecological data in human-dominated landscapes (see section 6.3.). Hydrologists had already developed the tools needed to combine GIS technology with modeling to examine how abiotic attributes of different areas within a watershed contribute variable amounts of water and nutrients to stream flow (Hewlett and Nutter, 1969; Dunne and Leopold, 1978; Black, 1991). Recently, these techniques have been successfully used to link the biotic attributes of a watershed with their social attributes (e.g., indirect effects from land-use change and forest/vegetation management and direct effects from inputs of fertilizers, pesticides, and toxins). By spatially linking social and ecological information within a watershed and determining how these related to different types of allocation mechanisms, the differential flows and cycles of critical resources within the watershed could be understood (Burch and DeLuca, 1984; Zonneveld, 1989; Parker and Burch, 1992; Grove and Burch, 1997).

6.3 A multi-scale approach to social ecological research: The case of the Baltimore Ecosystem Study

The Baltimore Ecosystem Study (BES) is one of 21 long-term ecological research sites (LTER) of the National Science Foundation. The BES is distinguished from nearly all the other LTER sites because it is one of only two urban sites (the other being the Central Arizona Project, Phoenix, Arizona) where integration of information from the social and natural sciences was a primary focus for establishing these LTERs. Research scientists for these two urban sites have been recruited from both the social and biophysical sciences and have adopted integrated, multi-scale approaches from the inception of the research.

The research described here was conducted for the Gwynns Falls Watershed of the BES. The Gwynns Falls Watershed (76° 30′W, 39°15′N) is approximately 17,150 ha in size. This watershed lies in Baltimore City and Baltimore County, Maryland and drains directly into the Chesapeake Bay. The research briefly described here illustrates the usefulness of a multi-scale approach to link social (e.g., social stratification) and natural science variables (e.g., vegetation structure) to understand what regulates the health of this watershed.

6.3.1 Description of the research

The Baltimore Ecosystem Study LTER has adopted a multi-scale (e.g., within and between watersheds) approach to its research that considers social and natural science variables at several, broad scales of ecological analyses:

organismal, population, community, ecosystem, and landscape (Grove and Burch, 1997; Pickett *et al.*, 1997). Both biophysical and social drivers and endogenous and exogenous change can drive the system dynamics. For instance, endogenous change in a neighborhood may include changes in demographic structure, housing conditions, or vegetation, while exogenous change may include changes in financial markets, regional transportation, or climate.

This multi-scale approach focuses purposefully on different social and ecological scales. Some social scales include different levels of social organization such as individuals, families, communities, and societies. BES uses a hierarchical, multi-scale approach because it attempts to understand the strong and weak ties within and among scales in order to uncover the ways that components at different scales are related to one another. Thus, lower-level units interact to generate higher-level behaviors and higher-level units control those at lower levels. For instance, a hierarchical approach to urban ecological systems may attempt to understand the ways that the interactions among households within a neighborhood may affect the ability of a neighborhood to attract public and private investments (Grove, 1996). At another level, the competition among neighborhoods in terms of relative political power subsequently affects the quality of government services that each household receives (Grove, 1996).

Some examples of theory that that may be used in this hierarchical approach are:

- Regional variations: Urban–rural dynamics (Morrill, 1974; Cronon, 1991; Rusk, 1993) (Fig. 6.1a, color plate).
- Municipal variations: Distribution and dynamics of land-use change (Burgess, 1925; Hoyt, 1939; Harris and Ullman, 1945; Guest, 1977) (Fig. 6.1b, color plate).
- Neighborhood variations: Power relationships between neighborhoods (Shevky and Bell, 1955; Timms, 1971; Johnston, 1976; Agnew, 1987; Logan and Molotch, 1987; Harvey, 1989) (Fig. 6.1c, color plate).
- Household variations: Household behavior within communities (Fortmann, 1986; Fortmann and Bruce, 1988; Fox, 1992; Grove and Hohmann, 1992; Burch and Grove, 1993; Grove, 1996) (Fig. 6.1d, color plate).

The answer to whether one scale is more dominant or sensitive than another will vary in relationship to the research or management question. Thus, it is crucial that researchers and managers begin to conceive of their questions in terms of scale.

A particular area of interest has been to understand how social stratification of groups (i.e., power structures) affects green investments made by private firms and public agencies in neighborhoods within the watershed (Grove, 1996) (Fig. 6.1b, color plate). The theoretical foundation for this question comes from Logan and Molotch's (1987) political economy of place theory. Logan and Molotch argued that patterns and processes of social stratification between people and place have significant environmental implications. According to Logan and Molotch's theoretical framework, the key social variables affecting access to power, the allocation of private and public resources, and subsequently the biophysical characteristics of wealthy residential areas include: (1) The presence of homeowners and the absence of renters or absentee landowners, (2) residents who are either able to migrate to more desirable and healthy areas, who are effective at community organizing, or who are willing to become involved in local politics, (3) elites who have differential access to government control over public investment, pollution control, and land-use decision-making. Conversely, low income and heavily populated minority areas are disproportionately in or next to polluted areas, have residents who are unable to migrate to more desirable and healthy areas, and have fewer human resources in terms of leadership, knowledge, tactical and legal skills, and communication networks to manipulate existing power structures.

Logan and Molotch (1987) and Choldin (1984) described these sociocultural and biophysical interactions as a dynamic process. In this process, residents act individually and collectively to control and maximize the exchange and use values of their neighborhood. This results from residents restoring, maintaining, or improving their current place or migrating to a more desirable place. Some of these acts of restoring, maintaining, or improving include changing the biophysical characteristics of residential areas (e.g., planting trees, parks, lawns, and community gardens, and keeping clean streets). These restoration activities produce an environment that is both socially and biophysically heterogeneous.

Logan and Molotch's theory was applied to one of the watersheds of the BES study area. The selection of variables and indices of social stratification for the classification of social areas or neighborhoods used the theoretical parameters identified by Logan and Molotch (1987), Choldin (1984) and Bullard (1990). These variables and indices were also further adjusted to incorporate recent adjustments recommended by Johnston (1976), Murdie (1976), and Hamm (1982). These indices of residential social stratification included a socioeconomic index (income and education), a household index (homeownership), and an ethnicity (race and ethnicity) index.

A classification of vegetation structure was developed using Bormann and Likens's (1979) theory of vegetation regulation of watershed hydrology and the data requirements of various hydrologic ecosystem models. At the ground surface, areas were classified as impervious or pervious. At the canopy level, areas were classified as having or not having a vegetation canopy layer. The four classes of vegetation structure included: (1) Impervious surfaces/no canopy cover, (2) impervious surfaces/canopy cover, (3) pervious (vegetation cover) / no canopy cover, and (4) pervious (vegetation cover)/canopy cover. Statistical analyses of data were conducted for residential land uses only. In addition, the research included a temporal component (1970–90) to explore possible time lag or non-linear relationships.

6.3.2 Results of the interdisciplinary watershed analysis

The results indicated a significant relationship between two of the three indices of social stratification – socioeconomic factors and ethnicity – and vegetation structure. Further, a time lag was found between independent variables and dependent variables (1970 social data and 1990 biological data) (Fig. 6.2, color plate). In retrospect, these results were realistic considering that the primary response variable being measured – tree canopies – takes time to grow and die. This highlighted the importance of considering the rate at which response variables may change and the time frames necessary to measure that change thus demonstrating the linkage between spatial and temporal scales that needs to be considered when determining what scale is appropriate to study for a given problem.

The absence of a relationship between indices of homeownership and vegetation structure was puzzling since the literature suggested such a relationship should exist. Extensive literature from rural forestry has indicated the importance of ownership and property regimes to land cover (Coase, 1960; Hardin, 1968; Ciriacy-Wantrup and Bishop, 1975; Fortmann and Bruce, 1988; MacPherson, 1989; Raintree, 1985; Ostrom, 1990; Bromley, 1991). Further, community foresters and community organizers in Baltimore City reported the significance of ownership to their activities. Thus, alternative explanations needed to be explored.

The spatial structure of the three social stratification indices was re-examined to try to tease apart the lack of a relationship between ownership and land cover. It was apparent that there was strong spatial structure for socioeconomic status and ethnicity, but not for homeownership on a watershed or city/county basis. These results suggested the need to examine these data at a different scale – that the data were reflecting a scale phenomenon. Perhaps, the relationship between homeownership and vegetation structure was effective at an alternative scale. Based on an initial exploratory data collection, scale-dependency for this relationship was verified (McManus and Steer, 1998). The relationship between ownership and vegetation structure occurred at a neighborhood level (i.e., Fig. 6.1d, color plate: vegetation structure varied in relation to household ownership patterns within a neighborhood).

The research described for the Baltimore Ecosystem Study illustrates the significance of scale for deductive and inductive (exploratory) research, particularly for interdisciplinary research. In particular, it highlights the need for researchers to be explicit about the relationships among theory, methods, and measures within an hierarchical context and to consider specific tools and techniques to assess the spatial and temporal structure of their research question (Grove, 1999; Gustafson, 1998). The results also have significant implications for natural resource management. The results from this research have helped planners and community foresters to recognize and understand the importance of a multiple-scale approach, particularly the idea that different processes occur at different scales. For instance, strategies for targeting community forestry activities, community organizing, and local capacity building are important considerations at a citywide scale (Fig. 6.1c, color plate) while community participation is related to ownership patterns at a neighborhood scale (Fig. 6.1d, color plate). Therefore, community forestry activities need to focus on the development of private or community ownership of open access/abandoned lands at a neighborhood scale. These findings provide an example of how natural resource managers may develop more comprehensive and effective strategies by knowing what to do, where to do it, *and at what scale*.

6.4 Integration of social and natural science spatial scales for management

Adequately incorporating spatial scales into natural resource management requires a practical approach that can be easily implemented but where decisions are based on specific guidelines that will allow non-subjective identification of the scale or scales of analysis. Managers need to recognize the large contrast that exists between scientific research conducted by academia and the research needed to inform management, that the information and analytical needs are different, and that these differences need to be taken into account when planning research to be used to answer management questions. It is also important to recognize that the problem definition is itself linked to a scale. So in contemplating issues of scale for management, managers must take one step backwards and use scale as part of an analysis to ensure the right question is being answered.

Few research investigations have integrated the social and natural sciences. Even if the hurdle of deciding to include both social and natural sciences in the same investigation was removed, their integration is formidable because of the propensity of each to use different spatial scales of analysis (Table 6.2). It is important to identify what types of environmental problems can be dealt with at the same social and natural science scales and what type of problems require different scales of analysis. Answering these points will begin to allow us to use "scale" as one of the common integrating tools to link the social and natural sciences. At the same time, it is also important to understand that no one scale will automatically address all environmental issues. Fox (1992) found that determining the appropriate scale of analysis is an iterative and not a one-step process, especially when conducting interdisciplinary research. This finding also reinforces the possibility that the social and natural science scales will differ so that the best approach should be decided on a case-by-case basis. If this generalization is correct, it can be a useful tool for integrating research from the social and natural sciences.

To determine the most appropriate scale(s) to use, the first step would be to ask if the study's hypothesis dictates the scale that should be used (Fig. 6.3). If this is the case, this scale must be used regardless of the specific disciplines required to answer the question. Usually the scale will not be dictated by the hypothesis alone and must be selected using a procedure like that shown in Fig. 6.3.

Now the most important question becomes which discipline is most suitable for proving or disproving the hypothesis (Fig. 6.3). The most suitable discipline, whether from the social or natural sciences, should have the greatest impact on the quality of the conclusions. Each discipline prefers particular scales of analysis as shown in Tables 6.1 and 6.2. Traditionally the focus has been on which discipline has a better approach for evaluating the problem, but the discussion should be shifted to which particular discipline is more important for solving the particular problem. Once the evaluator determines which discipline is best suited for solving the specific environmental problem, the selected discipline will dictate the scale of analysis. It is impossible to separate the question of the most appropriate scale for the analysis from the question of the discipline having the greatest impact on the conclusion.

After choosing a discipline, other factors must be considered (Fig. 6.3). Is the primary scale of analysis used by this discipline incompatible with the scales used by the other disciplines relevant to the problem? If there is no incompatibility, then the scale selected by the appropriate discipline should also be used for all other disciplines. If there is incompatibility, one must determine if the primary scale can be modified. If it is impossible to eliminate this incompatibility, multiple scales must then be utilized.

Some natural resource problems can be studied at the scale of a substrate or small plots. For example, a piece of coarse wood, hedgerows and even soil aggregates can be meaningful ecological scales for management when conserving microbes and soil animals whose life cycles occur at micro-site scales

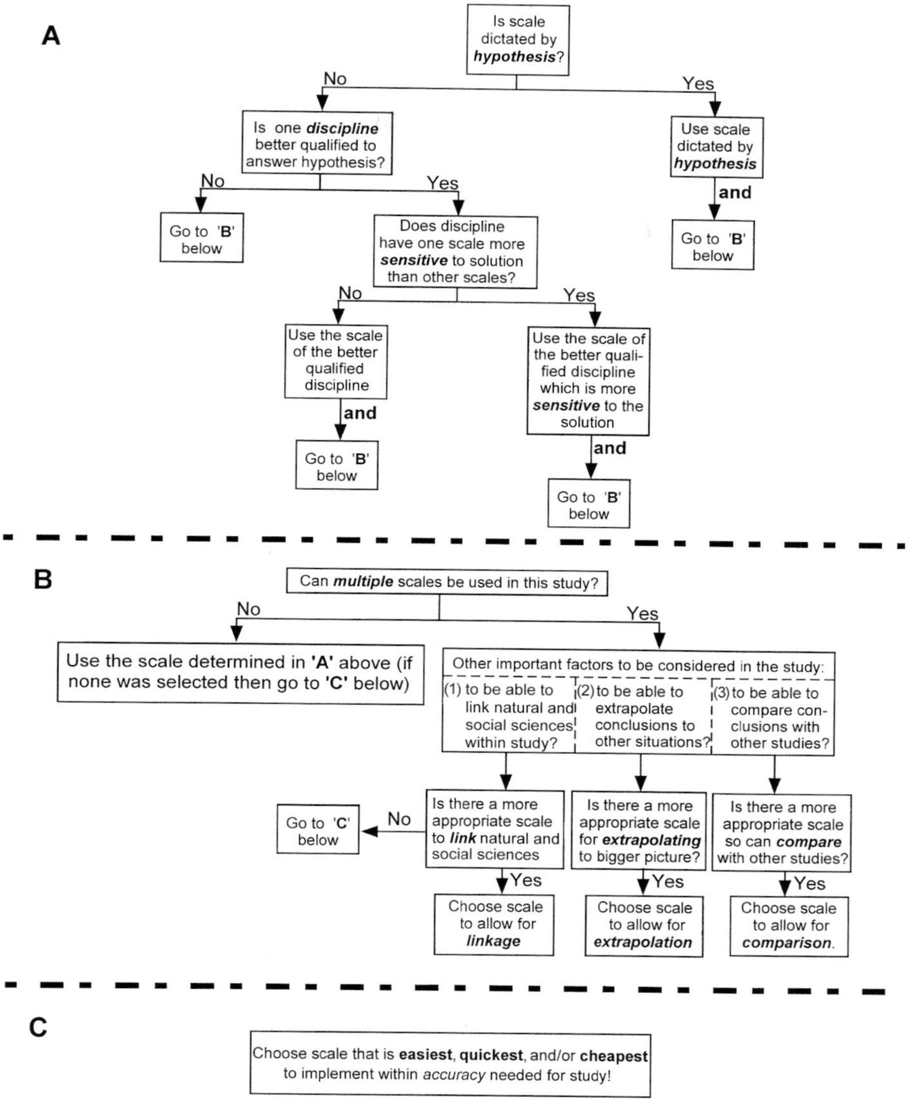

FIGURE 6.3
A conceptual model of one decision-matrix approach to determine what scale of spatial analysis is appropriate for any natural resource problem.

(Franklin, 1993). When human use has to be factored into this management, however, the small scale will not be adequate as a study scale. For example, if the microbes produce sporocarps harvested by humans, the scale of analysis will have to be a landscape. In this example, it will be important to understand the distribution of the successional stages of the vegetative communities that are the sources of spores needed to reinoculate and maintain the sporocarps in each management unit.

Managers may want to routinely consider multiple scales of analysis whenever dealing with a management problem because of the complexity of natural resource issues. Although one scale may ultimately be identified as the most sensitive scale for a particular problem, the initial approach should include multiple scales so that a manager can be confident that the appropriate scale is ultimately selected. No consistent rules have been reported in the literature that would allow a manager to link natural resource problems with their sensitive scales of analysis. For example, Farmer (1981) suggested the landscape level was too large when conducting macro-scale planning of agricultural development and the intervillage variation was more important to monitor. However, Moran (1984) suggested that hypotheses should be restricted to one level but that it is important to understand how other levels affect the process. For example, Moran (1984) recommended studying resource use in the Amazon using a nested approach involving a systematic sampling of localities, districts, and sub-regions, because information flows through each level of analysis. Spaling and Smit (1995) suggested that assessing the health of agro-ecosystems needs a watershed management plan that combines landscape analysis with examination of fields.

Managers in the past used the boundaries of the management unit as the spatial scale of analysis. However, using property boundaries to define the spatial scale can be flawed. This type of approach assumes that there is no impact of the management unit on adjacent systems. It also assumes the management unit is, or is not, influenced by the landscape within which it is imbedded. Agrosystems are a good example of the problems in defining the spatial scale by ownership boundaries (Conway, 1986). The activities occurring on the farm are not restricted to the human-defined borders. Depending on the type of agriculture being practiced, the zone needing to be analyzed may expand considerably outside the zone of the fields themselves. For example, the impacts of applying pesticides and/or fertilizers can be frequently measured outside the boundary of the farm itself and change how systems outside of the farm function (Spaling and Smit, 1995).

At times, the largest scale of analysis as defined by political or institutional boundaries may be insufficient to manage a resource when a resource cannot be contained within the defined boundaries or where there is an overlap of institutional control over a given resource. Many examples of the defined boundaries being inadequate as a management scale can be found in the literature (Clark and Minta, 1994). For example, the park boundaries for Yellowstone National Park are defined as the core area of what is needed for the conservation of the grizzly bear (*Ursus arctos*), however the administrative boundaries of the park are inadequate to conserve the grizzly bear. Likewise, property boundaries are insufficient in the Everglades National Park where the park boundaries do not match the jurisdictional boundaries that control local and regional uses within the landscape (Harwell *et al.*, 1996). Therefore, the scale of the Everglades needs to be larger than the park boundaries in order to study the drivers of ecosystem health.

There is a need to produce the tools to determine what scale is most appropriate to measure in any system. This is greatly facilitated if a formal process will allow the scales of analysis to be determined in a non-subjective manner. Past studies can be used as examples to direct us to understand what scale of analysis was considered most relevant or sensitive. They are useful to consider because they suggest the scale that was most successful in addressing a specific natural resource problem.

A decision matrix that can be used by managers to determine what scales of analysis are appropriate for them to consider is diagrammed in Fig. 6.3. A flow diagram similar to this can be used as a tool or guide to help determine the most appropriate scale(s). For the diagram to be useful, one must focus on the relationship of the disciplines to the solution and the linkage of disciplines using scales. With a tool such as this, one can more effectively manage natural resources and determine their relevant spatial scales for analysis.

The decisions being made in forest management highlight the utility of the decision matrix diagram presented in Fig. 6.3. Forest management decisions need to be addressed at different scales depending on the questions and objectives. Furthermore, the questions being asked are best addressed by certain disciplines and each of these disciplines uses different scales. For example, problems in analysis emerge if the questions being asked change. One example is intensive management of plantations. If the question concerns tree growth and timber yield, the relevant disciplines are tree physiology and biometrics and the resulting appropriate scale is a single tree or a small plot of trees. If questions arise concerning treatment effects on site productivity, the scale may be the forest stand because the appropriate disciplines are soil science and community ecology. If, however, the effects of intensive management on the total ecosystem were questioned, ecosystem ecology would be the relevant field and an area much larger than the forest stand must be studied.

In forest management, the issue of appropriate scale becomes more interesting if the question involves a social science component. If the economic value of the intensive management is questioned, then mixed scales might have to be used because timber yield studies must be used in conjunction with regional price studies. In some cases, the answer will be much more sensitive to price fluctuations than tree growth so that economics might be the dominant discipline for the analysis at the regional scale.

If natural forest dynamics are expected to occur in areas with less intensive management, it might be necessary to study landscape size areas to study the impact of these dynamics. To address questions of biodiversity, the landscape will have to include the different developmental stages relevant for maintaining that biodiversity (Oliver and Larson, 1996). The relevant disciplines might be forest stand dynamics or landscape ecology, and the scale necessary for study would depend on which discipline most sensitively reflects the problem.

This same decision matrix can be used to define the relevant scales in the social sciences as well (Fig. 6.3). Identifying social science scales is further complicated by some social variables appearing to not have an inherent scale or to have multiple scales embedded within each variable (see Table 6.1). Identifying a discipline to focus on does not necessarily facilitate scale determination in the social sciences. For example, even if the dominant discipline is constant (e.g., political science), the appropriate scale can vary. Governments at several different scales control how natural resources are managed (Machlis *et al.*, 1997) and which scale of government is most important should determine the scale of analysis even when political science has been identified as the relevant discipline. The impacts of policies are felt at different scales (Walters and Holling, 1990) – a fact that is important to keep in mind when determining the scale of investigation. The government boundary will probably not be the sensitive scale of analysis for many natural resource problems. For example, Freudenburg and Gramling (1994) suggested that the government level is not sufficient to explain poverty occurring at the smaller scales of resource-dependent communities.

6.5 Summary

Since the acceptance of the ecosystem management and sustainable development paradigms as the management philosophy of many federal agencies that manage natural resources, there has been an impetus to determine how to link social and natural systems. Yet, frameworks or models that integrate the natural and social sciences have been difficult to operationalize for natural resource management. We propose that the explicit incorporation of scale can be used as a critical and effective means for integrating different social and biophysical disciplines to address specific natural resource problems. The ecosystem management paradigm does require the explicit delineation of the spatial scales and boundaries of the management unit (Vogt *et al.*, 1997, 1999c). However, the definition of the scale of the management unit has created problems because it tries to define the scale by the natural system and as the spatial extent of the management unit (Fox, 1992). The social system has not been used by natural scientists to influence the scale-dependency of an analysis for ecosystem management. In practice, identifying the spatial scale of analysis appears to be somewhat arbitrary. Researchers in both disciplines have tended to use concrete, uniform definitions of what spatial scales are relevant for research (Table 6.2) that followed disciplinary lines.

The watershed scale has been generally accepted as the relevant scale for implementing ecosystem management (FEMAT, 1993; Montgomery, 1995). It is not clear if resource managers recognize the implications of choosing this scale of analysis for their management unit. On the surface, selecting this scale appears to simplify the decisions that have to be made by a natural resource manager because the problems of scale identification are eliminated. This approach also reflects the shift from, for example, managing forests from a product-based approach to the management of processes. Acceptance of the watershed scale as a unit of measurement sets limits on the type of questions that can be addressed because only certain measurement variables are sensitive at this scale (Conway, 1986; King, 1993).

The landscape scale appears to be one scale where the natural and social sciences can link because data collection is compatible with the existing tools utilized by both disciplines (Miller, 1994; Grove, 1996). Care must be taken to avoid the assumption that this is the only scale at which effective linking of the social and natural sciences can occur. The dominance of few scales of analyses in both the social and natural sciences (Table 6.2) will probably limit future integration of both fields if one scale is accepted as the primary scale of analysis. This scale of analysis is relevant for particular types of environmental problems but is not the universal answer for those questions where the sensitive variables exist at smaller scales.

Frameworks and tools will need to be developed to identify the sensitive scales of analysis that are disciplinary- (Table 6.2) and ecosystem-based and able to integrate information from both the social and natural sciences (such as shown in Fig. 6.3). Managers will have to recognize the limitations of aggregating information from smaller scales to elucidate patterns across larger scales more typical to natural resource management problems (Levin, 1992). Since the scales selected for data collection by each discipline are those that have been found to be the most sensitive to address their question (see section 6.1), scaling research data between scales should result in the loss of the causal relationships that were developed at that scale. Therefore, the implications of using different scales and how the scales are defined as shown in Table 6.1 are important to understand when managing natural resources.

Making scale relevant for management will require the development of causal (e.g., mechanistic) relationships between the management unit and natural and social science factors that will identify the appropriate scale(s) for each site. This will require managers to avoid using the wrong scale of analysis just because it is convenient and because data has been collected in the past at that particular scale (the idea being that the most sensitive scale may not have been identified then). It will also require managers to avoid scaling information from the small to the large scales unless there is a clear link between the information and the different scales; information may be lost with scaling so that sensitive variables may no longer be monitored.

To assist in the integration of social and natural sciences for natural resource management, researchers will need to explicitly recognize and address issues of scale differently from their traditional, disciplinary approaches. Instead of emphasizing the need for scale-dependent information that may be associated with their respective disciplines, it may be more important to determine what is the most appropriate scale(s) to address various natural resource issues. Integrating the social and natural sciences will require improving our understanding of how space is currently perceived by each discipline.

Many of the tools being currently used to study natural resource uses and the trade-off between different uses within human-dominated landscapes assume that scale should be similar for both the social and natural sciences (Montgomery, 1995; Driver *et al.*, 1996). It is important to understand that the sensitive scales of analysis may differ between the social and natural sciences. However, the existence of different scales by discipline is not a valid argument for not integrating the two fields. It is interesting to analyze whether social and natural sciences can be mechanistically linked using spatial scales even when the appropriate scales of analysis might differ for each.

This chapter has shown how the appropriate scale for studying social and ecological systems often varies depending on the scale at which the most sensitive variables are most strongly expressed and can therefore be easily measured. Currently, different disciplines have their preferred scales of analysis where they concentrate their research efforts and therefore indirectly the scales of analysis used for management. This type of approach has been more prevalent in the natural sciences since individual researchers by necessity have scales in which they are specialists. The social scientists until recently did not explicitly deal with scale even though their research did encompass several different scales of analysis. There is a need to acknowledge that different disciplines have spatial scale preferences and that these will constrain the integration of the social and natural sciences since they are not asking questions at the same scale. These incompatibilities in the scales of analysis are major detriments to successfully implementing ecosystem management, conservation planning and sustainable development.

There is also a need to recognize that focusing on one scale of analysis will not allow management to integrate those social and natural science factors constraining management activities. The Baltimore case study presented in this paper showed the importance of using several scales of analysis when attempting to link the social and natural systems in management. Once the most sensitive scale of analysis has been identified, it is important that management does not emphasize that scale alone to identify all the parameters or indicators that would sensitively reflect that scale. The Baltimore case study also demonstrated how the generation of data at one scale provided important information determining how the identified scale of interest should be assessed. It becomes crucial that information obtained at different scales and about different systems is continually exchanged and evaluated through a parallel and interactive research approach. Unfortunately, this essential step of integrating information is often not addressed until after the research is completed and the results are presented. At this point, policy-makers and managers often face difficulties in drawing coherent and unified conclusions since an understanding of how their different study systems were interrelated was not incorporated in the research process nor in the results.

Acknowledgments

For the Vogts, ideas developed in this paper occurred while conducting research supported by the National Science Foundation on the Long-Term Ecological Research Program in the Luquillo Experimental Forest, Puerto Rico, the Northeastern Forest Service Global Change Program, and a National Science Foundation grant to Yale University. For Morgan Grove, research support on the Baltimore Ecosystem Study was provided by the Burlington Laboratory (4454) and Global Change Program, Northeastern Forest Research Station, US Department of Agriculture Forest Service, the National Science Foundation (NSF Grant DEB-9714835) and Environmental Protection Agency (EPA Grant R-825792–01–0).

References

Agnew, J. A. (1987). *Place and Politics: The Geographical Mediation of State and Society.* Allen & Unwin, Boston, MA.

Agnew, J. A. & Duncan, J. S. (eds.) (1989). *The Power of Place: Bringing Together Geographical and Sociological Imaginations.* Unwin Hyman, Boston, MA.

Allen, T. F. H. & Hoekstra, T. W. (1992). *Toward a Unified Ecology.* Columbia University Press, New York.

Arnold, J. G., Williams, J. R., Nicks, A. D. & Sammons, N. B. (1990). *SWRRB: A Bain Scale Simulation Model for Soil and Water Resources Management.* Texas A&M University Press, College Station, TX.

Ashton, P. M. S. (1992). Some measurements of the microclimate within a Sri Lankan tropical rainforest. *Agricultural and Forest Meteorology*, 59: 217–235.

Bailey, K. D. & Mulcahy, P. (1972) Sociocultural

versus neoclassical ecology: A contribution to the problem of scope in sociology. *Sociological Quarterly*, 13(Winter): 37–48.

Beasley, D. B., Huggins, L. F. & Monke, J. (1982). Modeling sediment yields from agricultural watersheds. *Journal of Soil and Water Conservation*, 37: 113–116.

Berry, J. K. & Vogt, K. A. (1999). Human values integral to certification. In *Forest Certification: Roots, Issues, Challenges and Benefits*, eds. K. A. Vogt, B. C. Larson, D. J. Vogt, J. C. Gordon & A. Fanzeres, pp. 97–102, CRC Press, Boca Raton, FL.

Billings, W. D. (1985) The historical development of physiological plant ecology. In *Physiological Ecology of North American Plant Communities*, eds. B. F. Chabot & H. A. Mooney, pp. 1–15. Chapman & Hall, New York.

Black, P. E. (1991). *Watershed Hydrology*. Prentice-Hall, Inc., Englewood, NJ.

Bormann, F. H. & Likens, G. E. (1979). *Pattern and Process in a Forested Ecosystem: Disturbance, Development and the Steady State based on the Hubbard Brook Ecosystem Study*. Springer-Verlag. New York.

Bromley, D.W. (1991). *Environment and Economy: Property Rights and Public Policy*. Basil Blackwell, Cambridge, MA.

Brown, S., Hall, C. A. S., Knabe, W., Raich, J., Trexler, M. C. & Woomer, P. (1993). Tropical forests: Their past, present, and potential future role in the terrestrial carbon budget. *Water, Air, and Soil Pollution*, 70: 71–94.

Bullard, R. D. (1990). *Dumping in Dixie: Race, Class and Environmental Quality*. Westview Press, Boulder, CO.

Burch, W. R. Jr. (1988). Human ecology and environmental management. In *Ecosystem Management for Parks and Wilderness*, eds. J. K. Agee & R. J. Darryll, pp. 145–159. University of Washington Press, Seattle, WA.

Burch, W. R. Jr. & DeLuca, D. R. (1984). *Measuring the Social Impact of Natural Resource Policies*. New Mexico University Press, Albuquerque, NM.

Burch, W. R., Jr. & Grove, J. M. (1993). People, trees and participation on the urban frontier. *Unasylva*, 44(173): 19–27.

Burgess, E. W. (1925). The growth of the city: An introduction to a research project. In *The City*, eds. R. E. Park, E. W. Burgess & R. D. McKenzie, pp. 47–62, University of Chicago Press, Chicago, IL.

Catton, W. R., Jr. (1992). Separation versus unification in sociological human ecology. In *Advances in Human Ecology*, vol. 1, ed. L. Freese, pp. 65–99. JAI Press, Greenwich, NY.

Catton, W. R. Jr. (1994). Foundations of human ecology. *Sociological Perspectives*, 37: 75–95.

Chambers, R. (1994). The origins and practice of participatory rural appraisal. *World Development*, 22: 953–969.

Choldin, H. M. (1984). Subcommunities: Neighborhoods and suburbs in ecological perspective. In *Sociological Human Ecology: Contemporary Issues and Applications*, eds. M. Micklin & H. M. Choldin, pp. 237–276, Westview Press, Boulder, CO.

Ciriacy-Wantrup, S. V. & Bishop, R. C. (1975). Common property as a concept in natural resource policy. *Natural Resources Journal*, 15: 713–727.

Clark, T. W. & Minta, S. C. (1994). *Greater Yellowstone's Future: Prospects for Ecosystem Science, Management and Policy*. Homestead Publishing, Moose, WY.

Clements, F. E. (1916). *Plant Succession: An Analysis of the Development of Vegetation*, Publication no. 242. Carnegie Institution of Washington, Washington, D.C.

Coase, R. H. (1960). The problem of social cost. *Journal of Law and Economics*, 3: 1–44.

Conway, G. (1986). *Agroecosystem Analysis for Research and Development*. Winrock International Institute, Morrilton, AR.

Cortner, H., Shannon, M., Wallace, M., Burke, S. Moote, M. (1996). *Institutional Barriers and Incentives for Ecosystem Management: A Problem Analysis*. General Technical Report no. PNW-GTR-354. US Department of Agriculture, Portland, OR.

Cronon, W. (1991). *Nature's Metropolis: Chicago and the Great West*. W.W. Norton, New York.

Dawson, T. E. & Chapin, F. S. (1993). Grouping plants by their form-function characteristics as an avenue for simplification in scaling between leaves and landscapes. In *Scaling Physiological Processes, Leaves to Globe*, eds. J. R. Ehleringer & C. B. Field, pp. 313–319. Academic Press, Boca Raton, FL.

Driver, B. L., Manning, C. J. & Peterson, G. L. (1996). Toward better integration of the social and biophysical components of ecosystems management.. In *Natural Resource Management: The Human Dimension*, ed. A. W. Ewert, pp. 109–127. Westview Press, Boulder, CO.

Dubayah, R., Wood, E. F. & Lavallee, D. (1997). Multiscaling analysis in distributed modeling and remote sensing: An application using soil moisture. In *Scale in Remote Sensing and GIS*, eds. D. A. Quattrochi & M. F. Goodchild, pp. 93–112. Lewis Publishers, Boca Raton, FL.

Duncan, O. D. (1961). From social system to ecosystem. *Sociological Inquiry*, 31: 140–149.

Dunne, T. & Leopold, L. B. (1978). *Water in Environmental Planning*. W. H. Freeman, New York.

Ehleringer, J. R. & Field, C. B. (1993). *Scaling Physiological Processes: Leaf to Globe*. Academic Press, San Diego, CA.

Farmer, B. H. (1981). The 'Green Revolution' in Southeast Asia. *Geography*, 66: 202–207.

FEMAT [Forest Ecosystem Management Assessment Team]. (1993). *Forest Ecosystem Management: An Ecological, Economic and Social Assessment*, No. 1993–793–071. US Government Printing Office. Washington, D.C.

Field, D. R. & Burch W. R. Jr. (eds.) (1988). *Rural Sociology and the Environment*. Social Ecology Press, Middleton, WI.

Firey, W. (1945). Sentiment and symbolism as ecological variables. *American Sociological Review*, 10(April): 140–48.

Forman, R. T. T. (1995). *Land Mosaics: The Ecology of Landscapes and Regions*. Cambridge University Press, Cambridge, UK.

Fortmann, L. (1986). *The Role of Local Institutions in Communal Area Development in Botswana*, Research Paper no. 91. University of Wisconsin Land Tenure Center, Madison, WI.

Fortmann, L. & Bruce, J. W. (eds.) (1988). *Whose Trees? Proprietary Dimensions of Forestry*. Westview Press, Boulder, CO.

Fox, J. (1992). The problem of scale in community resource management. *Environmental Management*, 16(3): 289–297.

Franklin, J. F. (1993). Preserving biodiversity: Species, ecosystems, or landscapes. *Ecological Applications*, 3: 202–205.

Fraser, R. H. (1999). *SEDMOD: A GIS-based delivery model for diffuse source pollutants*. PhD dissertation, School of Forestry and Environmental Studies, Yale University.

Freudenberger, K. S. (1997). *Rapid rural appraisal: Participatory rural appraisal*, Notes to accompany an introductory course. Yale University, New Haven, CT.

Freudenburg, W. R. & Gramling, R. (1994). Natural resources and rural poverty: A closer look. *Society and Natural Resources*, 7: 5–22.

Giampietro, W. (1994). Using hierarchy theory to explore the concept of sustainable development. *Futures*, 26(6): 616–625.

Gosz, J. R. (1993). Ecotone hierarchies. *Ecological Applications*, 3: 369–376.

Grimm, N., Grove, J. M., Pickett, S. T. A. & Redman, C. (2000). Integrated approaches to long-term studies of urban ecological systems. *BioScience*, 50: 571–584.

Grove, J. M. (1996). *The relationship between patterns and processes of social stratification and vegetation of an urban–rural watershed*. PhD Dissertation, Yale University.

Grove, J. M. (1999). New tools for exploring theory and methods in human ecosystem and landscape research: Computer modeling, remote sensing and geographic information systems. In *Integrating Social Science and Ecosystem Management*, ed. K. Cordell, pp. 219–236. Sagamore Press, Champaign, IL.

Grove, J. M. & Burch, W. R. Jr. (1997). A social ecology approach and applications of urban ecosystem and landscape analyses: A case study of Baltimore, Maryland. *Urban Ecosystems*, 1: 259–275.

Grove, J. M. & Hohmann, M. (1992). GIS and social forestry. *Journal of Forestry*, 90: 10–15.

Guest, A. M. (1977). Residential segregation in urban areas. In *Contemporary Topics in Urban Sociology*, ed. K. P. Schwirian, pp. 269–336, General Learning Press, Morristown, NJ.

Gustafson, E. J. (1998). Quantifying landscape spatial pattern: What is the state of the art?." *Ecosystems*, 1: 143–156.

Hamm, B. (1982). Social area analysis and factorial ecology: A review of substantive findings. In *Urban Patterns: Studies in Human Ecology*, revd edn, ed. A. Theodorson, pp. 316–337. Pennsylvania State University Press, University Park, PA.

Hardin, G. (1968). The tragedy of the commons. *Science*, 162: 1243–1248.

Harris, C. D. & Ullman, E. L. (1945). The nature of cities. *Annals of the American Academy of Political and Social Science*, 242: 7–17.

Harvey, D. (1989). *The Urban Experience*. Johns Hopkins University Press, Baltimore, MD.

Harwell, M., Long, J., Bartuska, A., Gentile, J., Harwell, C., Myers, V. & Ogden, J. (1996). Ecosystem management to achieve ecological sustainability: The case of South Florida. *Environmental Management*, 20: 497–521.

Hawley, A. H. (1950). *Human Ecology: A Theory of Community Structure*. Ronald Press, New York.

Hawley, A. H. (1986). *Human Ecology: A Theoretical Essay*. University of Chicago Press, Chicago, IL.

Hewlett, J. D. & Nutter, W. L. (1969). *An Outline of Forest Hydrology*, rev. edn. University of Georgia Press, Athens, GA.

Hornbeck, J. W. & Swank, W. T. (1992). Watershed ecosystem analysis as a basis for multiple-use management of eastern forests. *Ecological Applications*, 2: 238–247.

Houghton, R. A. (1996). Converting terrestrial ecosystems from sources to sinks of carbon. *Ambio*, 25: 267–272.

Hoyt, H. (1939). *The Structure and Growth of Residential Neighborhoods in American Cities*. Federal Housing Administration, Washington, D.C.

Jarvis, P. G. (1993). Prospects for bottom-up models. In *Scaling Physiological Processes, Leaves to Globe*, eds. J. R. Ehleringer & C. B. Field, pp. 115–126. Academic Press, Boca Raton, FL.

Johnston, R. J. (1976). Residential area characteristics: Research methods for identifying urban sub-areas–social area analysis and factorial ecology. In *Spatial Perspectives on Problems and Policies*, vol. 2, eds. D. T. Herbert & R. J. Johnston, pp. 193–235. John Wiley, New York.

King, A. W. (1993). Considerations of scale and hierarchy. In *Ecological Integrity and the Management of Ecosystems*, eds. S. Woodley, J. Kay & G. Francis. St. Lucie Press, Delray Beach, FL.

Larson, B. C., Vogt, D. J., Gordon, J. C. & Fanzeres, A. (1999). Indicators for inclusion in assessments: Types, minimum number, and those derived from non-human values. In *Forest Certification: Roots, Issues, Challenges and Benefits*, eds. K. A. Vogt, B. C. Larson, D. J. Vogt, J. C. Gordon & A. Fanzeres, pp. 177–226. CRC Press, Boca Raton, FL.

Lee, R. G., Field, D. R. & Burch, W. R. Jr., (eds.) (1990). *Community and Forestry: Continuities in the Sociology of Natural Resources*. Westview Press, Boulder, CO.

Lele, S. & Norgaard, R. (1996). Sustainability and the scientist's burden. *Conservation Biology*, 10: 354–365.

Levin, S. (1989). Challenges in the development of a theory of ecosystem structure and function. *In Perspectives in Ecological Theory*, eds. J. Roughgarden, R. M. May & S. A. Levin, pp. 242–255. Princeton University Press, Princeton, NJ.

Levin, S. A. (1992). The problem of pattern and scale in ecology. *Ecology*, 73: 1943–1967.

Logan, J. R. & Molotch, H. L. (1987). *Urban Fortunes: The Political Economy of Place*. University of California Press, Los Angeles, CA.

Lugo, A. E. & Brown, S. (1993). Management of tropical soils as sinks or sources of atmospheric carbon. *Plant and Soil*, 149: 27–41.

Lynch, K. (1960). *The Image of the City*. M.I.T. Press, Boston, MA.

MacArthur, R. H. & Wilson, E. O. (1963). An equilibrium theory of insular zoogeography. *Evolution*, 17: 373–387.

Machlis, G. E., Force, J. E. & Dalton, S. E. (1994). *Monitoring Social Indicators for Ecosystem Management*, Technical Paper no. 43-0E00-4-9186. Interior Columbia River Basin Project, Portland, OR.

Machlis, G. E., Force, J. E. & Burch, W. R. Jr. (1997). The human ecosystem. 1. The human ecosystem as an organizing concept in ecosystem management. *Society and Natural Resources*, 10: 347–367.

MacPherson, C. B. ed. (1989). *Property: Mainstream and Critical Positions*. University of Toronto Press, Toronto, Canada.

Magnusen, J. (1990). Long term ecological research and the invisible present. *BioScience*, 40: 495–501.

Masters, R. D. (1989). *The Nature of Politics*. Yale University Press, New Haven, CT.

McManus, C. R. & Steer, K. N. (1998). *Towards a Unified Strategy for Open Space Management in Baltimore: Community-Managed Open Spaces*. Parks and People Foundation, Baltimore, MD.

Miller, R. B. (1994). Interactions and collaboration in global change across the social and natural sciences. *Ambio*, 23: 19–24.
Milne, B. (1992). Indications of landscape condition at many scales. In *Ecological Indicators*. vol. 2, eds. D. McKenzie, E. Hyatt & J. McDonald, pp. 883–895. Elsevier Applied Sciences, London.
Molnar, A. (1989). *Community Forestry, Rapid Appraisal*. Food and Agriculture Organization, Rome.
Montgomery, D. (1995). Input and output oriented approaches to implementing ecosystem management. *Environmental Management*, 19: 183–188.
Moran, E. (1984). The problem of analytical level shifting in Amazonian research. In *The Ecosystem Concept in Anthropology*, ed. E. Moran, pp. 265–287. Westview Press, Boulder, CO.
Morrill, R. L. (1974). *The Spatial Organization of Society*, 2nd edn. Duxbury Press, Duxbury, MA.
Murdie, R. A. (1976). Spatial form in the residential mosaic. In *Spatial Perspectives on Problems and Policies*, vol. 2, eds. D. T. Herbert & R. J. Johnston, pp. 237–272. John Wiley, New York.
Nilsson, S. & Schopfhauser, W. (1995).The carbon-sequestration potential of a global afforestation program. *Climatic Change*, 30: 267–293.
O'Laughlin, J., Livingston, R. L., Their, R., Thornton, J., Toweill, D. E. & Morelan, L. (1994). Defining and measuring forest health. In *Assessing Forest Ecosystem Health in the Inland West*, eds. R. N. Sampson & D. L. Adams, pp. 65–86. Haworth Press, New York.
O'Neill, R. V., DeAngelis, D. L., Waide, J. B. & Allen, T. F. H. (1986). *A Hierarchical Concept of Ecosystems*, vol. 23. Princeton University Press, Princeton, NJ.
O'Neill, R. V., Johnson, A. R. & King, A. W. (1989). A hierarchical framework for the analysis of scale. *Landscape Ecology*, 3: 193–205.
Odum, E. P. (1959). *Fundamentals of Ecology*, 2nd edn. W. B. Saunders, Philadelphia, PA.
Oliver, C. D. & Larson, B. C. (1996). *Forest Stand Dynamics*. McGraw-Hill, New York.
Ostrom, E. (1990). *Governing the Commons: The Evolution of Institutions for Collective Action*: Cambridge University Press, Cambridge, UK.
Park, R. E., Burgess, E.W. & McKenzie, R. D. (eds.) (1925). *The City*. University of Chicago Press, Chicago, IL.
Parker, J. K. & Burch, W. R. Jr. (1992). Toward a social ecology for agroforestry in Asia. In *Social Science Applications in Asian Agroforestry*, eds. W. R. Burch, Jr. & J. K. Parker, pp. 60–84. IBH Publishing, New Delhi, India.
Pickett, S., Kolasa, J., Armesto, J. & Collins, S. (1989). The ecological concept of disturbance: Its expression at various hierarchical levels. *Oikos*, 54: 129–136.
Pickett, S., Burch, W., Dalton, S., Foresman, T., Grove, J. & Rowntree, R. (1997). A conceptual framework for the study of human ecosystems in urban areas. *Urban Ecosystems*, 1: 185–199.
Pickett, S. T. A., Burch, W. R. Jr. & Grove, J. M. (1999). Interdisciplinary research: Maintaining the constructive impulse in a culture of criticism. *Ecosystems*, 2: 302–307.
Preston, F. W. (1962). The canonical distribution of commonness and rarity. Parts 1 and 2. *Ecology*, 43: 185–215, 410–432.
Raintree, J. B. (ed.) (1985). *Land, Trees and Tenure, Proceedings of an International Workshop on Tenure Issues in Agroforestry*, Nairobi, May 27–31. University of Wisconsin Land Tenure Center, Madison, WI.
Rambo, A. T. (1983). *Conceptual Approaches to Human Ecology*, Research Report no. 14, East–West Environment and Policy Institute, Honolulu, HI.
Rapport, D. J., Regier, H. A. & Hutchinson, T. C. (1985). Ecosystem behavior under stress. *American Naturalist*, 125: 617–640.
Reynolds, J. F., Hilbert, D. W. & Kemp, P. R. (1993). Scaling ecophysiology from plant to the ecosystem: a conceptual framework. In *Scaling Physiological Processes: Leaves to Globe, eds. J. R.* Ehleringer & C. B. Field, pp. 127–140. Academic Press, Boca Raton, FL.
Rifkin, S. B. (1996). Rapid rural appraisal: Its use and value for health planners and managers. *Public Administration*, 74: 509–526.
Rosa, E. A. & Machlis, G. E. (1983). Energetic theories of society: An evaluative review. *Sociological Inquiry*, 53: 152–178.
Running, S. W. & Coughlan, J. C. (1988). A general model for forest ecosystem processes

for regional applications. 1. Hydrologic balance, canopy gas exchange, and primary production processes. *Ecological Modelling*, 42: 125–154.

Running, S. W. & Hunt, E. R. Jr. (1993). Generalization of a forest ecosystem process model for other biomes, BIOME-BGC, and an application for global-scale models. In *Scaling Physiological Processes*, eds. J. R. Ehleringer & C. B. Field, pp. 141–158. Academic Press, San Diego, CA.

Running, S. W. & Nemani, R. R. (1988). Relating seasonal patterns of the AVHRR vegetation index to simulated photosynthesis and transpiration of forests in different climates. *Remote Sensing and the Environment*, 24: 347–367.

Rusk, D. (1993). *Cities without Suburbs*. Woodrow Wilson Center Press, Washington, D.C.

Schnore, L. F. (1958). Social morphology and human ecology. *American Journal of Sociology*, 63(May): 620–34.

Schroeder, P. (1992). Carbon storage potential of short rotation tropical tree plantations. *Forest Ecology and Management*, 50: 31–41.

Shevky, E. & Bell, W. (1955). *Social Area Analysis: Theory, Illustrative Application and Computational Procedure*. Stanford University Press, Stanford, CA.

Siralt, M., Pasodjo, S., Podger, N., Flavelle, A. & Fox, J. (1994). Mapping customary land in east Kalimantan, Indonesia: A tool for forest management. *Ambio*, 23: 411–417.

Smith, R. L. (1990). *Ecology and Field Biology*, 4th edn. Harper & Row, New York.

Sommer, R. (1969). *Personal Space: The Behavioral Basis of Design*. Prentice Hall, Englewood Cliffs, NJ.

Spaling, H. & Smit, B. (1995). Agroecosystem health and cumulative effects assessment: an application to land drainage and wetlands. *Ecosystem Health*, 1: 260–272.

Stern, P. C., Young, O. R. & Druckman, D. (1992). Human causes of global change. In *Global Environmental Change: Understanding the Human Dimensions*, eds. P. C. Stem, O. R. Young & D. Druckman, pp. 44–100. National Academy Press, Washington D.C.

Timms, D. (1971). *The Urban Mosaic: Towards a Theory of Residential Differentiation*. Cambridge University Press, Cambridge, UK.

Turner, M. G. (1989). Landscape ecology: the Effect of pattern on process. *Annual Review of Ecology and Systematics*, 20: 171–197.

Turner, M. G., Gardner, R. H. & O'Neill, R. V. (1995). Ecological dynamics at broad scales: ecosystems and landscapes. *BioScience* (Suppl.) S29–S35.

Vayda, A. P. (1983). Progressive contextualization: Methods for research in human ecology. *Human Ecology*, 11: 265–281.

Vogt, K. A., Vogt, D. J., Palmiotto, P., Boon, P., O'Hara, J. & Asbjornsen, H. (1996). Review of root dynamics in forest ecosystems grouped by climate, climatic forest type and species. *Plant and Soil*, 187: 159–219.

Vogt, K. A., Gordon, J. C., Wargo, J. P., Vogt, D. J., Asbjornsen, H., Palmiotto, P. A., Clark, H. J., O'Hara, J. L., Keeton, W. S., Patel-Weynand, T. & Witten, E. (1997). *Ecosystems: Balancing Science with Management*. Springer-Verlag, New York.

Vogt, K. A., Rod, B., Patel-Weynand, T., Fanzeres, A., Larson, B. C., Kusuma, I., Potts, C., Brownlee, A., Kretser, H. K. Heintz, J. & Hiegel, A. (1999a). Sustainability. In *Forest Certification: Roots, Issues, Challenges and Benefits*, eds. K. A. Vogt, B. C. Larson, D. J. Vogt, J. C. Gordon & A. Fanzeres, pp. 59–67. CRC Press, Boca Raton, FL.

Vogt, K. A., Berry, J. K. & Mayerson, F. A. B. (1999b). Social legacies constraining natural resource uses. In *Forest Certification: Roots, Issues, Challenges and Benefits*, eds. K. A. Vogt, B. C. Larson, D. J. Vogt, J. C. Gordon & A. Fanzeres, pp. 220–226. CRC Press, Boca Raton, FL.

Vogt, K. A., Larson, B. C., Vogt, D. J., Gordon, J. C. & Fanzeres, A. (1999c). Indicators for inclusion in assessments: Types, minimum number, and those derived from non-human values. In *Forest Certification: Roots, Issues, Challenges and Benefits*, eds. K. A. Vogt, B. C. Larson, D. J. Vogt, J. C. Gordon & A. Fanzeres, pp. 177–266. CRC Press, Boca Raton, FL.

Walters, C. J. & Holling, C. S. (1990). Large-scale management experiments and learning by doing. *Ecology*, 71: 2060–2068.

Whittaker, R. H. (1953) A consideration of climax theory: The climax as a population pattern. *Ecological Monographs*, 23: 41–78.

Wiens, J. A. (1989). Spatial scaling in ecology. *Functional Ecology*, 3: 385–397.

Young, G. L. (1974). Human ecology as an

interdisciplinary concept: A critical inquiry. *Advances in Ecological Research*, 8: 1–105.
Young, G. L. (1992). Between the atom and the void: Hierarchy in human ecology. In *Advances in Human Ecology*, vol. 1, ed. L. Freese, pp. 119–147. JAI Press, Greenwich, CT.
Young, R. A., Onstad, C. A., Bosch, D. D. & Anderson, W. P. (1989). AGNPS: A nonpoint source pollution model for evaluating agricultural watersheds. *Journal of Soil and Water Conservation*, 44: 168–172.
Zonneveld, I. S. (1989) The land unit: A fundamental concept in landscape ecology and its applications. *Landscape Ecology*, 3: 67–86.

PART III

Landscape function and cross-boundary management

As research and management expand from small scales to large scales, boundary-related issues become increasingly important, because large areas encompass various boundaries, such as natural boundaries (e.g., watershed boundaries and boundaries of a natural forest stand), ownership boundaries, political boundaries, and management boundaries. While research and management within a boundary are not easy, research and management across boundaries are even more challenging because a host of additional factors needs to be considered. First, landscape functions, such as flows of energy, matter, and organisms, cross a number of boundaries, as they may not recognize various boundaries. As a result, the effects of management activities within a boundary may extend to a larger area. Second, people (e.g., landowners, managers, and resource users) within different boundaries have different goals (e.g., social, economic, and ecological). Thus, solutions to management practices for multi-boundary landscapes depend not only on the management within individual boundaries but also on the coordination of management across boundaries as well as the integration of natural and social sciences. To address these topics, Part III includes three chapters concerned with boundaries between ownerships, between patches within a landscape, and between aquatic and terrestrial landscapes.

Spies *et al.* (Chapter 7) find that there are both significant opportunities and challenges in managing natural resources across multi-ownership landscapes, because of spatial interactions across ownership boundaries. Using the Oregon Coast Range Physiographic Province as a case study, the authors demonstrate how ownership patterns influence ecological patterns and processes, and how management activities by one owner can impact other owners. Through an interdisciplinary study, the authors show how landscape ecology can help policy-makers, managers, and the public understand the consequences of individual owner decisions across multi-ownership landscapes.

Edges are transitional areas between different patches and different landscapes, increasingly common and particularly important in fragmented and human-impacted landscapes. Although edge effects have been recognized for a long time, the "law of edge effects" did not appropriately differentiate responses among different species and at types of edges. To better understand edge effects on different species, Sisk and Haddad (Chapter 8) have developed an effective area model that incorporates areas of habitat patches, distance from patch edge, and sensitivity of focal species to the influences of the adjacent habitats. Case studies suggest that the model is a useful tool for understanding animal behavior, for predicting ecological processes, and for estimating impacts of management alternatives on distribution, abundance, and persistence of focal species and coexisting species in the landscapes.

In Chapter 9, Schneider *et al.* present a large body of evidence depicting flows of organisms, water, and matter between the land and water and among seemingly isolated water bodies. Changes in the flows of water and matter (e.g., dissolved substances, organic debris, and sediment) impact organisms both directly (e.g., by modifying conduits across the landscape) and indirectly (e.g., by modifying the availability of resources on which they depend). They suggest that some flows of organisms need to be protected or enhanced so that metapopulations can be maintained and species life histories can be completed. In other cases, water bodies need to be isolated to prevent the spread of invasive organisms.

THOMAS A. SPIES, GORDON H. REEVES, KELLY M. BURNETT,
WILLIAM C. MCCOMB, K. NORMAN JOHNSON, GORDON GRANT,
JANET L. OHMANN, STEVEN L. GARMAN, AND PETE BETTINGER

7

Assessing the ecological consequences of forest policies in a multi-ownership province in Oregon

7.1 Introduction

Advances in landscape ecology, ecosystem management, geographic information systems, and remote sensing have led us from the stand, to the landscape, and to broader scales in natural resources planning and management. As science and management have expanded to these scales, they frequently encompass multi-ownership landscapes. The management and scientific challenges posed by multi-ownership landscapes are especially complex. Species and ecosystems do not recognize legal boundaries between ownerships (Forman, 1995; Landres *et al.*, 1998), and the landscape dynamics of individual ownerships is controlled by a complex of economic, social, political, and biophysical forces. The aggregate ecological conditions of landscapes are controlled by the spatial pattern and dynamics of individual owners and ecological interactions among those ownerships. Solutions to problems of conservation policy and practices for multi-ownership landscapes do not lie in isolated owner-by-owner planning and management. Broader scale approaches are needed. Work in multi-ownership landscapes also reveals the need for increased integration among ecological and social sciences. In most contemporary landscapes, the dominant disturbance regimes are directly or indirectly controlled by human activities. In this chapter we will present a case study to demonstrate the importance of taking a multi-ownership view of landscapes and describe an approach we are developing to assess the effects of different forest management policies on ecological components of a province (i.e., subregion) in coastal Oregon.

7.2 Overview of multi-ownership landscape assessments and management

Interest in conservation planning, policy, and management in multi-ownership landscapes is increasing rapidly (Kreutzwiser and Wright, 1990;

Davis and Liu, 1991; Keiter and Boyce, 1991; O'Connell and Noss, 1992; Schonewald-Cox *et al.*, 1992; Turner *et al.*, 1996; Wear *et al.*, 1996; Maltamo *et al.*, 1997; Landres *et al.*, 1998). Several large regional assessments, most notably, the Southern California Natural Community Conservation Planning effort (Ogden, 1999) and the Northern Forest Lands Assessment (Hagenstein, 1999) have addressed multi-ownership regional issues. In one of the first published research studies focusing on dynamics of a multi-ownership landscape, Wear *et al.* (1996) found recent changes in social forces could result in a convergence of land cover types in a multi-ownership watershed in North Carolina. They found that forest cover increased over time across ownerships as timber management activities decreased on public and private lands. This study also found that overall landscape condition was most sensitive to land-use decisions on private lands rather than those on public lands. They concluded that the spatial arrangement of public and private lands will control ecosystem pattern and function at landscape scale.

Evaluation of these and other landscape and ecosystem management efforts indicates that the greatest obstacles for continued integration of landscape ecology into multi-ownership planning and management are not scientific and technological, but social. Yaffee *et al.* (1996) found that social opposition, institutional barriers, and inadequate stakeholder involvement were far greater impediments to progress at implementing ecosystem management than was scientific uncertainty. Often opposition to new approaches comes from misperceptions about the problem and its solutions, mistrust about whether land managers will do what they say they will do, or concerns about private property rights.

Different stakeholders often see differences in the state and direction of ecosystems and the feasibility of new approaches. However, it is questionable just how well we can really see the dimensions of large landscape issues (Lee, 1993). Our current capacity to visualize and understand the function of ecosystems over large areas and long time periods and to grasp the interdisciplinary linkages is typically inadequate. Although barriers may be primarily social, landscape ecology and new technologies can facilitate shared learning about multi-ownership landscapes and thereby foster the integration of landscape concepts into planning and management (McLain and Lee, 1996). Many significant ecological research problems remain to be solved, including understanding the effects of spatial pattern on ecological processes such as movement of disturbances and dispersal of organisms, developing ways to characterize species viability when population parameters are poorly known, finding the appropriate scale of information needed to evaluate landscape effects, and identifying landscape-scale ecological goals and criteria and indicators.

Policy-makers and managers are struggling with many kinds of cross-boundary landscape problems. Organisms such as the wolf (*Canis lupus*) in Yellowstone National Park and the upper Midwest (Mech, 1991; Mladenoff *et al.*, 1995), and whitetail deer (*Odocoileus virginianus*) in the eastern USA (Alverson *et al.*, 1994) move across ownerships and create problems when they prey on livestock or browse on crops on private lands or browse native herbaceous species in natural areas. Organisms such as salmon (*Oncorhynchus* spp.) in the Pacific Northwest, that spend their life cycle in different ownerships in a watershed, require conservation actions that can have economic impacts on private lands, e.g. leaving streamside buffers in agricultural lands and removing dams that supply irrigation water to farmers (Lee, 1997). Disturbances such as fires and floods may promote diversity and productivity of natural and semi-natural ecosystems but can cause economic losses and social upheaval in human-dominated ecosystems. Conversely, actions in human-dominated landscapes can affect natural ecosystems. Examples include the fires in Yellowstone and National Forests in the West (Knight, 1991), floods and debris flows in Oregon (Robison *et al.*, 1999), and water withdrawals for urban and agricultural uses which have affected the functioning of the Everglades in southern Florida (Ogden, 1999).

Solving multi-ownership management problems frequently comes down to finding ways to get different owners and agencies to modify or coordinate their individual behaviors to achieve some aggregate values for the landscape as a whole. This can be done through regulatory approaches (e.g., laws and policies), incentive-based approaches (e.g., subsidies or tax relief) and information-based approaches (i.e., appeals to voluntary change in behavior based on information about negative or positive effects of behavior) (Sample, 1994; Lee, 1997). Although these approaches may differ in their instruments, they all require some assessment of the ecological conditions of a landscape and the ecological and socioeconomic consequences of different courses of future action. Landscape ecology can make a significant contribution to solving complex natural resource problems by identifying the various ways in which ownerships interact in a landscape and using tools to help policy-makers and stakeholders visualize the ecological and socioeconomic consequences of their actions.

7.3 Case study: The Oregon Coast Range

We will use the Oregon Coast Range as a case study to illustrate: (1) the potential for landscape ownership pattern to have a strong effect on ecosystem goods and services within and across ownerships, (2) how integrated research can help visualize and project ecological consequences of different land management policies, and (3) the many challenges to conduct interdisciplinary research and management in multi-ownership landscapes.

7.3.1 Background

The Oregon Coast Range is an ecologically complex region of low, but highly dissected mountains, steep slopes, high stream densities and orographically related climatic zones. Forests are dominated by relatively few species: Douglas-fir (*Pseudotsuga menziesii*), western hemlock (*Tsuga heterophylla*), western redcedar (*Thuja plicata*), Sitka spruce (*Picea sitchensis*), red alder (*Alnus rubra*), and bigleaf maple (*Acer macrophyllum*). However, physiognomic forest diversity is high because of strong differences between the structure of conifer forests and deciduous forests, and because of the large amount of structural differentiation that occurs as forests develop from young forests to 400+-year-old forests (Spies and Franklin, 1991). Extensive logging and wildfires since the mid-1800s have created a forest matrix of young and mature conifer forests interspersed with patches of hardwoods (primarily red alder and bigleaf maple) and remnant patches of old growth (structurally diverse forests typically older than 200 years) (Spies and Franklin, 1991). Current amounts of old growth are well below levels that probably occurred historically (Ripple, 1994; Wimberly *et al.*, 2000). The steep slopes, and extensive stream networks, create strong interactions between stream habitats and up-slope forest dynamics (Reeves *et al.*, 1995). Stream habitat structure is controlled by inputs of water, sediment, and large woody debris from adjacent stream banks, slopes, and small tributaries.

Threats to native biological diversity in this province are exemplified through five species that are listed as threatened or endangered by the US Government: Northern spotted owl (*Strix occidentalis caurina*), marbled murrelet (*Brachyramphus marmoratus*), coho salmon (*Oncorhynchus kisutch*), chum salmon (*O. keta*), and the Oregon silverspot butterfly (*Speyeria zerene hippolyta*). Of these five, the first four are at risk because of loss of forest and stream habitat associated with logging, forest conversion to agriculture and other threats such as predation from humans and other species. The Oregon silverspot butterfly is listed as threatened because of loss of coastal grassland habitat from development and forest encroachment. Changes in forest structure and dynamics, most notably the decline of old-growth forests with their large live and dead trees, are thought to be the major causes of risk to the populations of the four vertebrate species listed above as well as many other plants, animals, and fungi (FEMAT, 1993). Other threats to biological diversity in the province include decline in the area and quality of oak (*Quercus garryana*) woodland habitat resulting from fire loss (conifer encroachment) and development on eastern slopes of the Coast Range (Defenders of Wildlife, 1998).

The Coast Range is also a socially diverse region with a mosaic of landowner classes that operate under policies that reflect their general goals, which range from industrial commodity production to wilderness protection (Table 7.1). Of the five major landowner classes, private non-industrial landowners have the most diverse goals but they still operate under the same forest practices rules (Oregon Department of Forestry, 1996) as the industrial owners. As with industrial owners, they may choose to exceed those protection rules or not to harvest trees as all. However, non-industrial private owners have about the same propensity to harvest as industrial owners but have a greater tendency toward partial cutting (Lettman and Campbell, 1997) than industrial owners. The province is dominated by private ownership with significant blocks of public lands (Fig. 7.1, color plate). In 1993, the Northwest Forest Plan (FEMAT, 1993) brought sweeping changes to forest management on the federal forests in this province, dramatically shifting the focus of these forests toward protection of biodiversity through the creation of an extensive network of late-successional reserves and riparian management zones. This shift resulted in an 80–90% reduction of timber harvest from federal lands in the Coast Range compared to the 1980s. In the future over 75% of the harvest in the Coast Range is expected to come from forest industry lands which operate under the regulations defined by the State of Oregon Forest Practices Act (Oregon Department of Forestry, 1996). By and large, the forest policies now in effect in the Coast Range were put in place owner-by-owner with little effort to understand their aggregate effects across ownerships. These policies are based on very different approaches to management: intensive management for commodity production on private industrial lands and some non-industrial private lands; active management for multiple objectives on state forest lands and some private industrial lands; and passive, reserve-based approaches for biodiversity protection on federal lands.

7.3.2 The Coastal Landscape Analysis and Modeling Study (CLAMS)

We are currently involved in a research program that is designed to test and evaluate the effects of policies in a multi-ownership province. The Coastal Landscape Analysis and Modeling Study (CLAMS) is a large interdisciplinary effort to evaluate aggregate effects of different forest policies on the ecological and socioeconomic conditions of the Coast Range province as a whole (T. A. Spies *et al.*, unpublished data). The mosaic of different management practices creates potential spatial interactions that can affect the aggregate ecological and social conditions of the entire province. In addition, the management outcomes within individual ownerships potentially can be altered by management activities on neighboring ownerships. These spatial effects occur in two

Table 7.1. *Forest policies, goals assumed under policies, and management strategies dealing with biological diversity in the Oregon Coast Range by major ownership categories*[a]

Ownership	Policies	Goals[a]	Strategies
US Forest Service	1. Northwest Forest Plan 2. Individual National Forest Plans	To protect or produce: 1. Late succesional/old-growth Forests 2. Threatened and Endangered species 3. Aquatic ecosystems 4. Commodities	1. Reserves 2. Matrix management[b] 3. Green-tree retention 4. Stream buffers 5. Adaptive Management Areas
Bureau of Land Management	Same as above	Same as above	Same as above but with different matrix prescriptions
State Forests of Oregon	Forest Plans	To protect or produce: 1. Healthy forests 2. Indigenous species 3. Abundant Timber 4. Threatened & Endangered species protection	1. "Structure-based" management[c] 2. Habitat Conservation Plans[d]
Private industrial	State Forest Practices Act	To maintain and protect: 1. Priority to growth and harvest of trees 2. Protection of environment and fish/wildlife	1. Limited retention of individual trees 2. Limited streamside protection for fish-bearing streams
Private non-industrial	Same as above	More diverse than above but typically some level of revenue from forest land	Minimums are same as above but with greater tendency to use partial harvesting

Notes:

[a] Goals are listed in approximate order of priorities. Goals may have more than one strategy.

[b] Matrix management involves use of special silvicultural practices in areas surrounding the reserves.

[c] Structure-based management uses silviculture rather than reserves to achieve stand structure goals. This involves long rotations (120–150 years) and green tree retention.

[d] Habitat Conservation Plans are landscape management plans for Threatened and Endangered species developed in conjunction with the US Fish and Wildlife Service.

general forms: (1) Uneven representation of biotic communities, physical environments, and disturbance regimes (both managed and natural) and (2) spatial interactions of ecological processes such as organism dispersal and disturbance which move across ownership boundaries.

In the following sections, we briefly describe our general approach and present an example of a simulation model of forest landscape conditions over 100 years. We follow this with some simple analyses and a discussion of the potential ecological consequences of the mosaic of different ownership policies. Although CLAMS is an integrated ecological and socioeconomic assessment, we limit our focus to ecological effects in this chapter. We conduct our analysis directly on patterns of land ownership classes (keeping all ownership classes including the Bureau of Land Management [BLM] and the US Forestry Service [USFS] separate), which we use as a surrogate for landscape structure until more sophisticated models of landscape dynamics and ecological responses are developed. Under this assumption we will underestimate actual edge and overestimate interior habitat. However, given the extreme differences in management activities among the major ownership classes (e.g., about 90% of the federal land in the Coast Range is in an ecological reserve or special management area of some kind where cutting of trees is intended to meet restoration goals) we feel that this simple analysis can give us insights into future landscape potential.

The goal of CLAMS is to develop and evaluate concepts and tools to understand patterns and dynamics of ecosystems at province scales and to analyze the aggregate ecological and socioeconomic consequences of forest policies for different owners (Table 7.1). Our approach is based on the assumption that by knowing landscape structure and dynamics of vegetation we can project consequences of different forest policies on ecological outputs such as biological diversity and socioeconomic outputs, such as employment and recreational opportunities (Fig. 7.2). The major steps in our approach are:

(1) Build high-resolution spatial models (grain size of 0.1 to 10 ha) of current biophysical conditions (e.g., vegetation, ownership patterns, topography, streams) across all ownerships using Landsat satellite imagery, forest inventory plots, and other geographic information systems (GIS) layers.
(2) Conduct surveys and interviews of forest landowners to determine their management intentions (e.g., rotation ages, thinning regimes, riparian management intensity) under current policies and develop spatial land use change models based on retrospective studies.
(3) Simulate expected successional changes in forest structure and composition under different management regimes using stand dynamics models.

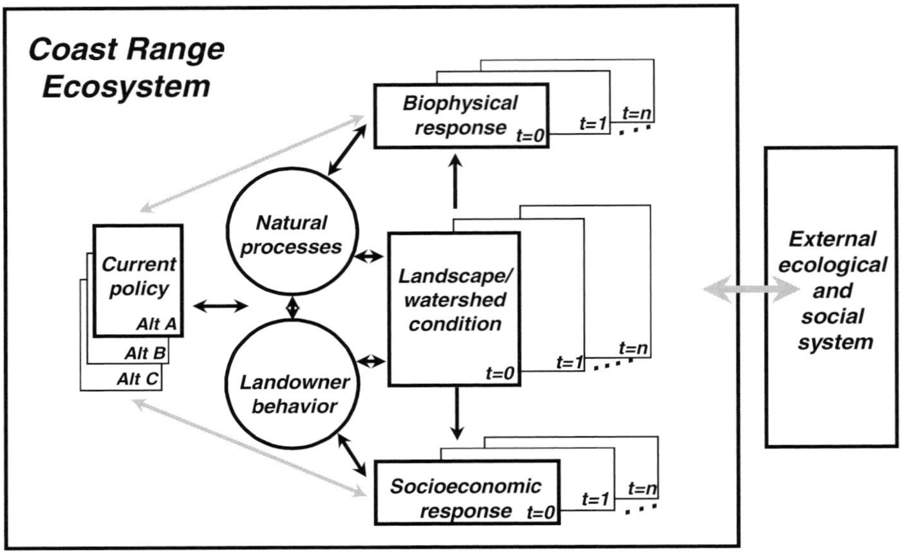

FIGURE 7.2
Coastal Landscape Analysis and Modeling Study (CLAMS) conceptual model for linking policy, ecological and social processes, landscape condition and ecological and socioeconomic outcomes to evaluate alternative forest policies.

(4) Build a landscape change simulation system based on forest management intentions and forest stand models to project future landscape structure for 100–200 years.
(5) Develop biophysical response models for habitat quality for selected terrestrial and aquatic vertebrate species, viability of selected vertebrate species, coarse-filter measures of community and landscape conditions, historical range of natural variation of forest successional stages, and landslide and debris flow potential.
(6) Develop socioeconomic response models for measures of employment and income by economic sector, timber value and production, recreational opportunities, and contingent value of biological diversity to the public.
(7) Estimate ecological and socioeconomic consequences of current forest policies using the landscape simulator and the various response models.
(8) Include outside influences such as effects of population growth on land-use change.
(9) Evaluate, test, and revise overall simulator system and sub-models.
(10) Provide policy-makers, landowners, and the public with results of spatial projections of consequences and interact with them to help inform debate and facilitate collaborative learning.

At this point in the project we are simulating only forest management-related disturbances (e.g., clear-cutting, partial cutting, thinning) and landslide and debris flow disturbances. We focus on these because they are among the most frequent in the region, potentially have large impact on measures of biological diversity, and are of great interest in policy debates. We are not simulating stochastic disturbances such as wildfire, wind, insects, and disease. Studies in the region indicate that wildfire occurs infrequently (150 to 400 years) and its spatial pattern is only weakly controlled by topography, especially for large fire events (Impara, 1997). Also, these events are likely to be even less frequent in the future because of aggressive fire suppression policies. Smaller wind and pathogen disturbances are quite frequent but they are difficult to predict and typically occur at patch sizes below our level of spatial resolution for this provincial study. We may incorporate these stochastic disturbances in future modeling efforts, either directly in the simulation model or as scenarios (e.g., effects of a large fire) for comparative analysis.

7.3.3 Projection of future landscape conditions: An example

We have developed a prototype of our landscape simulator for the Coast Range province and run it for a 100-year scenario under current policies (Table 7.1) (Fig. 7.3, color plate). Patterns of current forest condition are not uniformly distributed across ownerships. Current vegetation patterns in the province are characterized by a predominance of early and mid-sized (0–50 cm diameter at breast height [dbh] of dominants and codominants) conifer forests. Forests dominated by trees of the largest size classes (>50 cm diameter at breast height) are rare and restricted primarily to public lands. Broadleaf forests are less common than coniferous forests and tend to be concentrated in riparian areas. Old-growth forest conditions (approximately equivalent to the very large conifer class) (Fig. 7.3, color plate) are currently a small percentage of the total area and what is remaining is concentrated on BLM and USFS lands in the southwestern portion of the province. Little old growth occurs on private land, but some small remnant patches do occur and form the basis of Habitat Conservation Plans for the northern spotted owl. Conversely, open (pasturelands, meadows, agricultural lands and recent clear-cuts) and early successional stages of forest (typically forests less than 15–20 years old) occupy almost 40% of the province but are concentrated on private lands. By 50 years into the simulation of future conditions, the pattern of vegetation classes has changed dramatically. Amounts of large-dbh classes have increased, especially on federal lands, and the spatial pattern of vegetation has begun to resemble the underlying ownership pattern. Young plantations (10–30 years old) on federal lands have matured and are beginning to blend into the matrix of large conifer size classes. On private lands, intensive forest management (45–50 year rotations) keeps these landscapes cycling between early successional stages and harvest-age timber plantations. By 100 years the contrasting patterns of vegetation across ownerships are even stronger.

While total amounts of late successional forest have increased dramatically in the Coast Range in this simulation, the spatial pattern of these forests creates considerable potential edge effects and spatial pattern interactions. The simulations suggest that large watersheds of the Coast Range will develop into a mosaic of very different landscape types based on the amount and spatial pattern of forest conditions. These landscapes range from watersheds dominated by late succesional forest to watersheds dominated by early successional and mature forest plantations. Between these extremes is a wide range of mixtures of successional dominance and dispersed or blocked spatial patterns. Consequently, we hypothesize that a new landscape pattern is emerging in this province in which ownership patterns and boundaries will control patterns of biophysical processes more than in the past. The ecological and socioeconomic consequences of changing diversity and spatial pattern are the primary focus of our ongoing research efforts.

7.3.4 Spatial variation and pattern of ecosystems and ownerships

Policies and ownerships in the province are not uniformly distributed across environmental gradients and patterns of biotic communities. Different classes of ownership represent different strategies and levels of environmental protection and disturbance regimes. Consequently, in some environmental settings certain forest developmental stages and stand conditions are not well represented or could disappear. For example, in the moist coastal zone and the drier foothills ecoregions where federal ownership is 15% and 8% of the area, respectively, ecosystem conservation especially for old-growth and natural watershed processes (e.g., debris flows that deliver large woody debris to streams) is not a major management objective. However, in the interior ecoregion, federal conservation strategies cover over 30% of the area and levels of old growth may reach historical levels in this area (Wimberly *et al.*, 2000) (Fig. 7.4a). Perhaps the most important imbalance occurs in riparian areas around large lowland coastal river valleys (Fig. 7.4b). These areas were historically sites of meandering rivers with well-developed floodplains, complex aquatic habitats, and distinctive riparian forests, that were probably characterized by especially large western redcedars (*Thuja plicata*), bigleaf maples and Oregon myrtle (*Umbellularia californica*) (Robbins, 1997). They would have been highly productive habitat for many salmonid species including: Chinook (*O. tshawytscha*), coho, and chum salmon. Today nearly 70% of these lands are held by private non-industrial landowners.

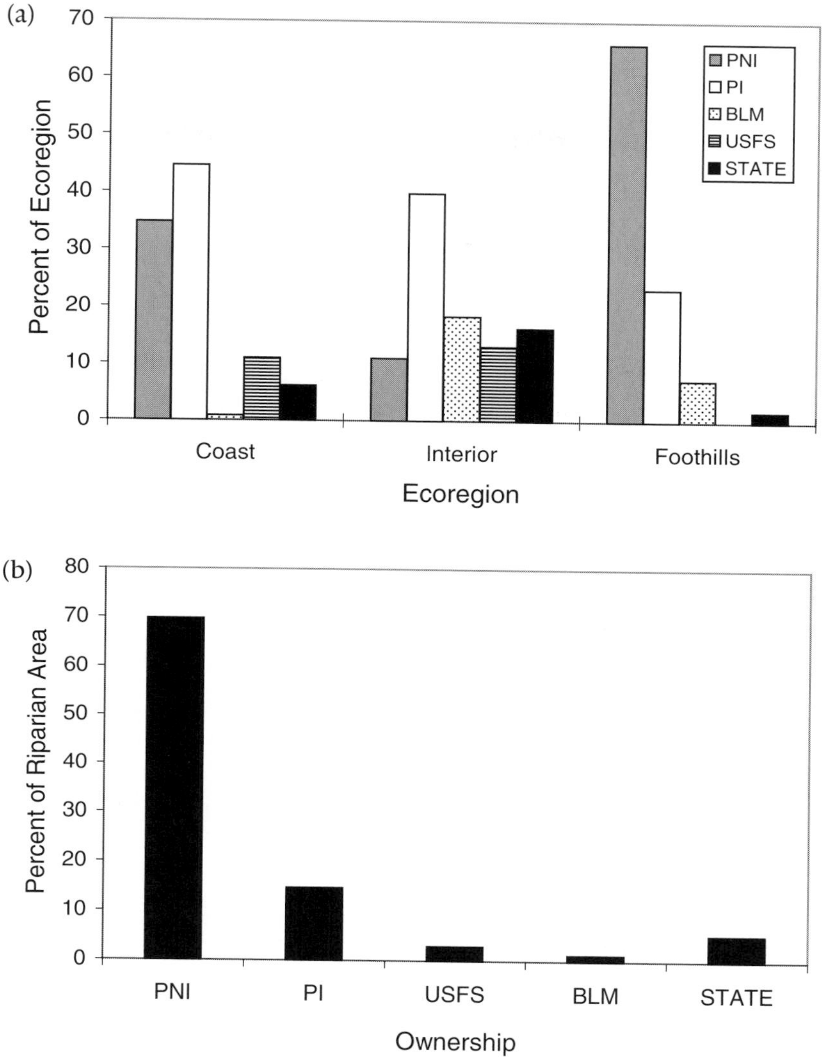

FIGURE 7.4
Frequency distribution of percentage ownership by: (a) ecoregion and (b) riparian zones along major river valleys (areas within 100 m of a river and less than 5% slope and less than 300 m elevation). PNI, private non-industrial; PI, private industrial; BLM, Bureau of Land Management; USFS, US Forestry Service.

Stream habitat here has been greatly simplified by activities related to agriculture, transportation, and urbanization that have straightened channels and removed riparian vegetation and large down wood. Consequently, the parts of the landscape that had the most diverse and productive fish habitats are among those that have been the most altered by human activity.

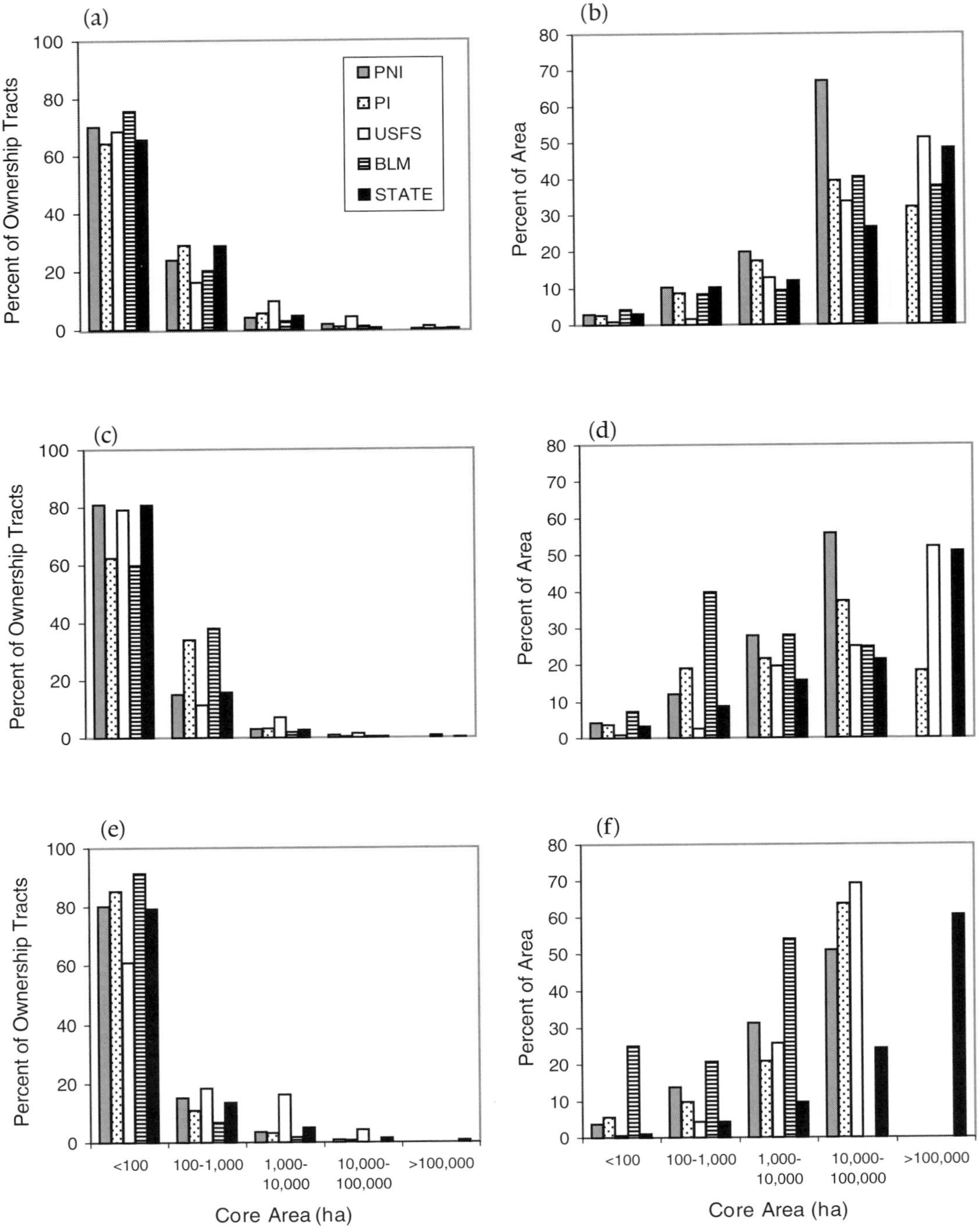

FIGURE 7.5
Size distribution of core areas for ownership classes (total area in tract and number of individual tracts) for different edge effect distances: (a, b) no edge effect; (c, d) 100 m; (e, f) 500 m. PNI, private non-industrial; PI, private industrial; BLM, Bureau of Land Management; USFS, US Forestry Service.

The individual tracts of land of ownership classes vary widely in spatial distribution and pattern. Industrial private and non-industrial private lands, which dominate in area, form the matrix which surrounds public lands. Federal lands are concentrated in the central and southwestern portions of the province. The current pattern of private and federal lands was established 70 to over 100 years ago when the now-federal lands were either recently burned-over and had low timber value or were revested to the US Government by the railroad companies following failure of federal land policies (Richardson, 1980). These revested lands now form the "checkerboard" pattern of mile-square alternating federal and private ownership that is characteristic of many BLM lands (Fig. 7.1, color plate). Large blocks of state lands occur in the north and the south. Most individual tracts of ownership classes are smaller than 100 ha (Fig. 7.5a). However, most of the area of ownership tracts occurs in large patches greater than 10 000 ha (Fig. 7.5b).

7.3.5 Spatial interactions among ownerships

A variety of landscape features and processes create potential spatial interactions among ownerships that affect the aggregate ecological conditions in the province. These spatial effects would be invisible in assessments based only on knowledge of the acreage of management actions and not their spatial distributions. The potential for neighboring ownership classes to influence conditions within a focal ownership varies by ecological process and ownership. Important landscape features and processes include edges, interior patches, roads, movement of organisms, and movement of wood and sediment. The ecological movements can be viewed as a source–sink process, a conceptual framework that helps to visualize the degree to which the ownership mosaic affects the ecological function of the province.

Edge effects

Edge effects take a variety of forms (Forman, 1995). The most important and well-documented edge effects in this region occur when tall coniferous forest stands are positioned next to shorter conifer plantations, deciduous forests or agricultural lands. In these situations edge effects can penetrate from shorter stature vegetation 50 to over 200 meters into taller stature vegetation. Edge phenomena in the region include microclimatic effects (Chen *et al.*, 1993), habitat effects (McGarigal and McComb, 1995), and disturbance, especially blowdown where tall stands are adjacent to areas of low vegetation such as clear-cuts and agricultural land (Franklin and Forman, 1987). Edge effects can also move from taller stands into shorter stands such as when tall forests shade adjacent young forests, and when ungulates forage 200–300 m into early successional stands from areas of hiding cover in tall forests (Wisdom *et al.*, 1986).

Table 7.2. *Distribution of percentage of total edge by ownership combinations and total percentage edge by ownership in the Coast Range*

	Ownership						
Ownership	PI	PNI	State	Bureau of Land Management	US Forestry Service	Miscellaneous	Total
PI	—	32.6	8.6	25.9	5.2	2.3	74.6
PNI	—	—	5.5	6.9	6.1	2.1	53.2
State	—	—	—	2.1	0.6	0.6	17.4
Bureau of Land Management	—	—	—	—	0.8	0.5	36.2
US Forestry Service	—	—	—	—	—	0.3	13.0
Miscellaneous[a]	—	—	—	—	—	—	5.8

Notes:
[a] Miscellaneous owners such as Indian tribes and counties.

The edges created by disturbances to stands are dynamic and move around the landscape depending on the rate of disturbance and the rate of regrowth of the disturbance patches. Boundaries created by ownerships also form a type of edge whose ecological effects are dependent on the degree of differences in management regimes across the ownerships. Although individual management disturbances can shift around the landscape, over time ownership boundaries can be thought of as a long-term dynamic edge whose ecological effects reflect the differences in cumulative effects of activities on either side of the boundary. Given the highly contrasting management regimes of the ownerships (see section 7.3.3), the ownership class boundaries should be a good indicator of long-term edges. The potential for edge effects derived from ownership boundaries is large – there are 24161 km of boundary edges between ownership classes, not including the edges of the province itself. Of the total boundary edge the largest percentage (65.4%) occurs among three ownership classes: private industrial, private non-industrial, and BLM (Table 7.2). Of the total of all boundary edges, 74.6% includes private industrial boundaries, 53.2% includes non-industrial private boundaries and 36.2% includes BLM boundaries. USFS boundary edges form only 13% of the total edge among ownerships in the province. Not surprisingly, edges involving the matrix of private lands constitute the vast majority of potential edge in the province (62.6%). Of course, boundary edges underestimate the total edge in the province, since edges will form between individual ownerships within a class and between forest patches within an individual ownership.

Interior area patch sizes

Some species may be favored by large patches of interior coniferous forests in the region but it is not clear if the species are responding to the total amount of habitat patches or sizes of patches/amount of edge. These include species such as the northern spotted owl (Carey *et al.*, 1992; Ripple *et al.*, 1997) and brown creeper (*Certhia americana*) (McGarigal and McComb, 1995). The stability of large forest habitat patches is probably greater than small ones because edge effects from windthrow, fires, and microclimatic change are minimal. Just as with ownership boundary edges, the size of ownership tracts serves as a rough indicator of the potential for interior patch conditions to develop across the province. These can be either large patches of early-mid successional conditions or mid to late successional conditions, depending on the ownership and their management objectives. The size distributions of potential core areas of tracts of ownerships vary by the amount of edge effect that is assumed. BLM lands show the greatest impact of potential edge effects on core area size distributions (Fig. 7.5c–f). Assuming no ownership boundary edge effects, all ownerships have the majority of their total ownership areas in tracts of at least 10 000 ha (Fig. 7.5b). When potential edge effects are taken into account, the proportion of core areas shrinks on all ownerships but changes most drastically for BLM lands, which occur primarily as small blocks in the checkerboard landscape. USFS and State of Oregon lands, on the other hand, maintain large core area ownership blocks when ownership boundary edge effects are assumed.

Roads

Roads have widespread and poorly understood impacts on many ecological processes (Forman and Alexander, 1998). Roads create edge effects for animals and people. Road densities in watersheds of the province range from less than 1 km/km^2 to over 3 km/km^2. Elk and deer avoid roads and habitat quality for elk is estimated to be reduced by half when road densities exceed 1 km/km^2 (Wisdom *et al.*, 1986). Some human recreational experiences are also lost by proximity to roads. For example, according to recreational opportunity spectra (Driver *et al.*, 1987) the primitive recreational class of experiences requires a distance of at least 2.4 km from any road. Less than 0.05% of the Coast Range would meet this criterion. Of course, roads also provide the access benefits for other types of recreation.

Movement of organisms

Movement of organisms among ownerships and landscape elements in the Coast Range occurs in two primary forms: diffuse and directional. Terrestrial animals, propagules, forest pathogens, and fire move by diffuse or non-directional movements. Fish, landslides, debris flows, floods and spread of some non-native species exhibit movements constrained by landscape features (directional movement). In some cases organisms may also move in both ways and to some extent the distinction is scale-dependent. Individual movements of animals may be directional but aggregate movement of populations may appear diffuse.

Diffuse movement by animals occurs at different scales: within home ranges, by dispersal of subadults to new areas, and by migration in and out of the province. All three types of movement occur at scales that interact with the ownership patterns of the Coast Range. Terrestrial vertebrates in the Coast Range have a spectrum of home ranges from a small fraction of a hectare for Ensatina salamander (*Ensatina eschscholtzi*) to over 5000 ha for a black bear (*Ursus americanus*). Dispersal characteristics are not known for many species, although minimum distances are assumed to be several times the diameter of a home range (Forman, 1995). Home ranges of spotted owls in the province range from an average of 1500 ha for owls in relatively unfragmented landscapes to over 2900 ha in fragmented landscapes (Carey *et al.*, 1992). For juvenile owls, median dispersal distances range from 12 to 25 km in the Coast Range (Forsman *et al.*, in press). These movement areas and distances exceed the boundaries of most blocks of ownership in the province.

Relatively little is known about dispersal of vascular plant, lichen, and fungi propagules. For many of these organisms most dispersal is very local and would be contained within ownership blocks. For example, Schrader (1998) studied the distribution of western hemlock seedlings in closed canopy forests in the Coast Range and concluded that most hemlock seeds disperse within 20 m of a potential parent tree. While lichens can disperse great distances, some such as *Lobaria oregana* effectively disperse over short distances through fragmentation of tissues when broken thalli are blown by wind from source trees to adjacent trees (B. McCune, personal communication). Consequently, this species and several other lichen species are at risk in managed landscapes because they are very slow to recolonize clear-cuts from refugia in older tree canopies (FEMAT, 1993).

Pathogens such as Swiss needle cast (*Phaeocryptopus gaumannii*), a recent serious forest management problem, have spread across several ownerships in the northern Coast Range in recent years (Campbell and Liegel, 1996). This fungal disease, which causes needles to yellow and die, drastically reduces the growth rates of Douglas-fir stands and occurs primarily on the moist ecoregion of the Coast Range. A native organism, it appears to have reached outbreak levels as a result of a combination of factors including widespread planting of Douglas-fir stands in moist climatic sub-regions and a wetter climate cycle in recent years. The infestation began in young forest plantations of non-local stock and has spread to other plantations. Initially it occurred only in younger stands but recently it appears to be spreading to stands of old trees on public lands (G. Filip, personal communication). Spore loads may have built up on younger stands to the point that the fungus is overwhelming the resistance of older native stands in other parts of the landscape.

Roads provide another mechanism for directional movement of organisms, especially non-native plant species. Distribution of invasive, non-native woody plant species such as Scotch broom (*Cytisus scoparius*) and Himalayan blackberry (*Rubus discolor*) is correlated with distance from roads and they appear to have spread through the province along major highways. Roads are also associated with the spread of *Phytophera lateralis*, a root fungus that kills Port Orford cedar (*Chamaecyparus lawsoniana*; Zobel *et al.*, 1985), a highly valuable species that occurs in the southern part of the province. The spores of the fungal disease are transported in flowing water and during the wet season can be transported on the hoofs of elk and cattle and on the tires of construction and logging machines.

Anadromous salmonids are good examples of organisms that exhibit directional movement since they migrate in and out of this province, between the Pacific Ocean and their spawning and juvenile rearing habitat. Salmonid species differ in the distance that adults swim up into a coastal stream network to spawn. Since cutthroat trout (*O. clarki*) and steelhead trout (*O. mykiss*) use smaller, steeper streams, these species generally migrate further inland. They frequently must cross non-industrial private (primarily agriculture) and private industrial forest ownerships to get to their spawning and rearing habitats, which are often concentrated, higher in watersheds on federal lands. The young spend one to two years in these streams before they move down into larger streams and rivers where they remain for up to a year before moving into the estuary and open ocean (Peterson, 1982). In contrast, chum and chinook salmon use habitats that are in the lower portions of rivers nearer the ocean where channels are usually larger and less steep, and are typically on private lands.

Movement of wood and sediment

One of the strongest spatial interactions and most important management issues in the Coast Range is the delivery of large wood and sediment from forested uplands to streams. These elements create stream channel complexity, which is important for salmonid spawning and rearing habitat. Large wood is especially important in creating channel heterogeneity in high gradient, high peak flow streams of the Coast Range. Wood gets into streams through two mechanisms: (1) the fall of streamside trees into streams, and (2) debris-flow-generating landslides. Although landslides and debris flows can reduce the quality of spawning gravels in the short term, inputs of large wood and coarse sediments to streams are important to maintaining habitat quality for species in the long term (Everest *et al.*, 1987; Reeves *et al.*, 1995).

Once a landslide occurs in these steep mountain landscapes it may become a debris flow of water, sediment, and wood moving down through stream channels. Its final resting place depends on stream gradient and stream junction angles among other factors (Benda and Cundy, 1990). Landslide-debris flows typically travel about 200–300 m with a maximum travel distance of about 2500 m (Robison *et al.*, 1999); consequently, a significant number could initiate in one ownership and be deposited in a different one.

Source–sink processes

Another way to conceptualize ecological movements in the Coast Range is as source–sink processes in which some parts of the landscape are net sources of organisms and matter and others are net sinks (Forman, 1995). In many cases these transfers will cross boundaries and some ownerships will be sources and some will be sinks, depending on the process and the intervening landscape structure.

Organisms such as deer or fungal pathogens have great potential to move out of private industrial and private non-industrial lands (source areas) and influence large areas on public lands (sinks) (Table 7.3). For example, 89% of BLM lands could be affected by organisms or processes that move 1000 m out from the margin of adjacent private industrial lands. Nearly 100% of BLM lands would fall within 5000-m movements out of private lands. Conversely, the federal lands have relatively little potential influence over private lands: only 7% and 36% of private industrial lands would be influenced by processes that move 1000 m out from the margin of USFS and BLM lands, respectively. Possible candidate organisms for these flows from private lands to federal lands include deer and elk, early successional and non-native plant species that might build up in areas of high road density and highly disturbed agricultural lands, genes from genetically altered commercial tree species and pathogens such as Swiss needle cast that could originate in relatively uniform plantations of Douglas-fir. Organisms that might move from source areas on federal lands to sink areas on private lands include the northern spotted owl and other species of late-successional forests.

Landslides and debris flows that carry large wood and sediment to streams are an example of directional source–sink phenomena that can cross ownership boundaries. Source areas for delivery of large conifer wood via landslides in coastal stream networks are steep concave headwall areas that fail periodically during high rainfall periods. These parts of the stream network are also

Table 7.3 *Estimate of percentage of sink ownerships influenced by hypothetical inputs from other organisms and processes from adjacent source ownerships for different distances of movement*

	Sink ownership				
Source ownership	Private non-industrial	Private industrial	Bureau of Land Management	US Forestry Service	State
100-m distance					
Private non-industrial	—	7	5	5	4
Private Industrial	11	—	17	5	6
Bureau of Land Management	2	6	—	1	2
US Forestry Service	2	1	1	—	0
State	2	2	1	0	—
1000-m distance					
Private non-industrial	—	46	36	47	29
Private Industrial	66	—	89	42	43
Bureau of Land Management	22	36	—	11	11
US Forestry Service	9	7	4	—	3
State	15	18	13	6	—
5000-m distance					
Private non-industrial	—	88	87	99	80
Private Industrial	96	—	100	100	93
Bureau of Land Management	60	64	—	60	37
US Forestry Service	17	18	17	—	10
State	55	60	45	48	—

places where the highest densities of large live conifers develop (Pabst and Spies, 1999) and where dead wood frequently accumulates from tree falls from steep adjoining hillslopes. It is possible, using information about topography and stream network patterns, to develop a prediction of which source will have sink areas for wood within fish-bearing stream channel segments. The degree to which source–sink processes for large wood delivery in streams interact with ownership can not be assessed without high-resolution digital elevation models (DEMs), stream network maps, and GIS models that identify potential landslide sources and debris-flow paths, and maps of forest structure. However, a simple analysis of ownership patterns of potential debris-flow source areas can be made by examining the distribution of ownership by slope class. In this analysis, areas likely to contain landslide prone sites (>30% slope) within the province are disproportionately owned by federal and state agencies (57% of steep areas vs. about 37% of all lands in the province). (This slope steepness analysis should be viewed with caution because the 30-m DEMs on which it is based will underestimate the area of steep slopes.) Conversely, topographically low areas which contain sites where debris flows would stop are disproportionately owned by private non-industrial and industrial landowners. It seems clear many sources of landslides reside on federal lands and many of the potential sinks occur on private lands. Additional important source areas of wood to streams occur in riparian areas immediately adjacent to all streams. Where large trees have been removed from these areas through harvesting, the potential source of large wood for streams will be absent.

Road networks can also be a source area for landslides that affect streams and define flow paths between uplands and stream networks. Analysis of erosion events in recent floods in the Oregon Cascades indicate that roads in midslope and ridge-top positions are net sources of sediment and debris flows while roads along valley floors tend to trap sediment and restrict the movement of debris flows before they reach streams (Wemple, 1998). Road networks may also act to expand the drainage network of a watershed, and increase the magnitude of peak flows after storm events (Jones and Grant, 1996).

7.4 Lessons learned

At this point in our effort we have learned as much about conducting integrated regional assessments as we have about the region we are studying. The lessons learned from conducting integrated assessments include both improved understanding of ecological issues at this spatial scale and the process of conducting interdisciplinary research.

7.4.1 Potential ecological effects

We have learned that recently enacted policies in the Oregon Coast Range have the potential to create novel landscape patterns of vegetation and dynamics. We hypothesize that in this emerging landscape, the complex ownership pattern, contrasting management regimes, and ecological processes create the spatial interactions that could not be predicted based on information from individual ownerships in isolation from each other. While the preceding simple analysis of the ownership patterns indicates a strong potential for aggregate effects in this province, more detailed analyses are needed to test the degree and distribution of these effects. The spatial interactions that we expect will have greatest impact on the ecological systems of this province are the following:

(1) Imbalances and gaps in seral stage distributions across environmental strata including sub-ecoregions, watersheds, and topographic positions.
(2) Gaps in distribution of habitat of relatively wide-ranging species (such as the northern spotted owl or salmonids) whose movement occurs at scales similar to that of ownership tracts and management allocations within ownerships.
(3) Decline in aquatic habitat quality in some stream reaches and watersheds where private lands occur upstream and sources of wood from debris flows are lost because of intensive forest management practices.

7.4.2 The process of building integrated provincial-scale models

The importance of problem definition and conceptual model

Without adequate problem definition and a conceptual framework, integrating landscape ecology and management issues (e.g., watershed management, old-growth forest conservation) can degenerate into separate studies that will ultimately fall short in meeting management needs. For example, in our early efforts at framing our conceptual model we discovered that we had no direct link between measures of biodiversity and socioeconomic values. Consequently, we initiated a survey of how the public valued different types and strategies of biodiversity conservation (e.g., salmon habitat protection, biodiversity reserves).

The importance of policy-makers and policy questions

Without incorporating policy-makers and specific policy questions into the research at the beginning, the potential for the research to be relevant to policy and management questions will be diminished. In dealing with multi-ownership landscapes it is extremely important to have the support of state and federal agencies. The research must also be very sensitive to private property issues and interagency institutional policies if the research is to be taken seriously and used. We have met repeatedly with representatives from forest industry to communicate our intentions, get information about their management practices, and build trust and understanding of the assessment model we are building.

The challenge of spatial information about landscapes and regions

Gathering spatial information about large landscapes and regions can be an enormous undertaking. Much of the resources for a project can be consumed in compiling spatial data bases with adequate quality to meet scientific standards and address relevant questions. In most cases, information about the accuracy of spatial information will not be available and if available, it is not always clear what level of accuracy is needed. Some spatial information such as road locations can require cooperation of private landowners.

The value of landscape projections

Spatial projections of future landscape patterns are a very powerful way to communicate landscape issues to policy-makers, managers and the public. Maps of possible future states create much interest in stakeholder groups and can foster communication and understanding. However, landscape projections should be viewed more as a simulation experiment or a type of sensitivity analysis of policy instruments than a real forecast of future conditions. Projecting the future of complex ecological and socioeconomic systems for 100 or more years requires many simplifying assumptions that should be made clear to any user.

The challenge of measuring ecological effects

Developing landscape- and regional-scale measures and models of ecological responses is a major challenge. Empirically based response models (e.g., based on logistic regression) may be useful for some areas and situations but are typically inadequate for large landscape or regional studies of multiple organisms or processes for which data do not exist. Ecologists will have to work as paleontologists do, with only a few "bones" of knowledge of an ecosystem and will have to fill in the pieces of the larger ecosystem "skeleton" without the benefit of field or experimental research. These gaps in our knowledge will be filled from theory, expert judgment, a few empirical studies, and simulation models (i.e., computer experiments). In some cases it might be possible to conduct field studies to fill in critical information needs or verify model performance, however, resources will typically not be adequate for extensive field studies over large areas.

The challenge and importance of scale

Integrated studies of large landscapes are fraught with scale problems. The spatial and temporal scales of ecological, policy, and socioeconomic processes and measures typically are not the same. The spatial scale and resolution of simulation models may not match that of data available to characterize the current or initial conditions of a landscape. For some processes, it may not be clear what scale and resolution are needed for adequate representation. Dealing with scale problems cannot be done in a single planning effort at the beginning of an assessment. Continuous attention to scale is needed to find ways to ensure that changes in one component will not create scale or resolution mismatches with other components.

Integration occurs at many levels and takes many forms

Integration is central to all aspects of landscape assessments, from developing the conceptual model to linking data bases to social interactions in a multidisciplinary team to working with different institutions. All scientists practice integration at some level, but not all scientists have the interest or time to attend to the integration needed to link landscape ecology and management in a significant way. Some scientists must pay attention to the broad-scale integration problems (ecological–social integration; institutional issues; dynamics of scientist–manager teams) if landscape ecology is to be useful in natural resources management and policy.

Conducting science in a public policy environment

Applying landscape ecology to large multi-ownership areas of the earth is not something that can be done solely within a research laboratory or an academic institution. If landscape ecology is to become relevant to natural resource issues, scientists must learn to interact with policy-makers, managers, and the public. In some cases these interactions simply may be keeping these groups informed of progress and results, in other cases the interaction can be much more involved. For example, stakeholder groups can be invited to suggest questions to address or even invited to participate in building the conceptual or computer models. These interactions can take a lot of time and be threatening to scientists and the normal process of science, but they can also help ensure the relevance and use of the results of the work. At the same time, there is a risk that segments of the public with a large stake in the outcome will attempt to manipulate the process. Consequently, engaging the public needs to be done carefully.

7.5 Implications to policy and management

Principles and empirical studies from landscape ecology indicate that policies and management actions within individual ownerships may not necessarily achieve their objectives because of effects of adjacent owners. As our simulations indicate, long-term effects of forest policies in multi-ownership landscapes can result in highly contrasting landscape patterns. The effects of this juxtaposition of habitats are not well known and require further research and monitoring. In our experience, monitoring should focus on factors such as environmental representation of ecosystems, edge effects, interior patch sizes and distributions, roads, movement of organisms, movement of energy and materials such as water, wood, and sediment, and disturbances such as fire. It appears that some organisms could occur on ownerships on which they would not otherwise be found because of the occurrence of source habitat on adjacent ownerships. These effects may be both desirable and undesirable depending on the effect and ownership. For example, spotted owls, nesting on federal lands, could use adjacent private industrial lands for foraging or dispersal of young. Thus, private lands may contribute to the overall viability of this and other species. On the other hand, actions on private lands might decrease quality of habitat on public lands and some pest organisms or disturbances that originate on one ownership may spread to adjacent ownerships. The condition of aquatic habitat within a multi-ownership basin will probably depend on the ownership patterns of key stream reaches (e.g., low gradient unconstrained streams) and woody debris source areas within a watershed. In watersheds with a diversity of owners, conservation practices will need to be based on involvement of many owners if watershed goals are to be met.

The recognition of the ecological effects of multi-ownership landscape mosaics places pressure on state and federal agencies to develop policies that take these cumulative landscape effects into account. No current policies specifically mandate multi-ownership planning and no public agencies have the broad authority over it. However, some limited multi-ownership planning activities are beginning. For example, the State of Oregon has developed a salmon recovery plan based on watershed councils that are charged to develop voluntary approaches to conserving salmon based on watershed management. This and other efforts pose a major challenge to government agencies and the public to balance competing values, mandates to protect biological diversity, and private property rights. Some policies and laws may work at cross-purposes. For example, anti-trust laws might prevent large timber companies in the Coast Range from coordinating their activities to achieve overall landscape goals.

It is difficult to identify specific practices that can mitigate negative effects within boundaries and enhance positive effects outside of boundaries. Much depends on the particular political, socioeconomic, and biophysical context of a multi-ownership landscape and of course, the goals and objectives of the particular landowners and management agencies. However, specific actions can be grouped into three major categories: (1) those that affect the underlying ownership pattern, (2) those that unilaterally change ecological conditions within a single focal ownership, and (3) those that involve changes of conditions on two or more ownerships. We will briefly describe some examples of these from the perspective of a public land agency whose goals include maintenance or restoration of natural and semi-natural ecological systems.

Land exchanges and purchases can be used to alter the fundamental pattern of ownership on a landscape. These may be done to block-up dispersed ownership units to create more core area or to obtain particular ecosystem types that are not well represented within the current ownership. Public land management agencies have been doing land exchanges for years but have typically not done so with specific landscape ecological concerns in mind.

Ecological conditions within an ownership can be modified unilaterally to buffer against outside influences. For example, forest management activities can be zoned to create a gradient of management intensity that decreases from the edge to the interior of an ownership block (Harris, 1984). It may be more possible to mitigate and slow the spread of invading species or to stop the spread of wildfire into natural areas if they are positioned near the core of public ownership blocks than if they are on the margins. Effects of grazing wild and domestic animals can be mitigated through fencing; tree windbreaks can be used to reduce erosion or facilitate invasion of desirable species (Mitchell and Wallace, 1998; Harvey, 2000). The challenge of unilateral changes (in absence of coordination among owners) will be to determine how much policies and management actions within an ownership block should be modified based on conditions or management plans on adjacent lands. Since management goals and plans and owners are likely to change over time, one strategy may be to assume a worst-case effect of outside ownerships on resources within a focal ownership. This assumption was used in conservation planning for federal forest lands in the Pacific Northwest (FEMAT, 1993). This approach might result in a relatively low-risk strategy for sensitive resources within an ownership but it might not be the optimal strategy when a diversity of owners and resource goals are considered.

Ecological conditions outside a focal ownership can be modified through negotiations among two or more landowners. These kinds of efforts often include county, regional, or state-level planning and consensus groups such as watershed councils. In many cases effective cross-boundary resource management is in its infancy, even in places such as the Greater Yellowstone Ecosystem, where these types of efforts have been going on for over ten years (Glick and Clark, 1998). However, some successes have been reported (Propst *et al.*, 1998). For example, areas of private lands can be identified to help maintain natural and semi-natural conditions outside public lands and reduce contrasts in vegetation structure at borders of public and private lands. These actions require, of course, funds to purchase lands or conservation easements or incentives for voluntary actions on private lands. Flow of energy and matter through multi-ownership landscapes can be controlled through practices such as road closures and modification of riparian vegetation to increase shade and lower stream water temperatures in downstream reaches in a watershed. In Oregon, the Oregon Department of Forestry has imposed limitations on logging on steep slopes, which may reduce risk of landslide and debris flows across a drainage network (Oregon Department of Forestry, 1996).

7.6 Summary

Multi-ownership landscapes pose significant opportunities and challenges to the integration of landscape ecology into natural resource planning and management. Basic principles of landscape ecology can be used to demonstrate the importance of taking a multi-ownership perspective. For example, evaluation of patterns of environmental variation and ownership, edge effects, and spatial interactions, including source–sink phenomena in the Oregon Coast Range Physiographic Province, demonstrates how ownership patterns control the ecological potential of whole landscapes and regions. In this landscape, some ownerships such as the Bureau of Land Management are potentially quite sensitive to effects of activities on adjacent owners because of highly fragmented pattern of patches and high edge density. Recent changes in forest policy in this province will result in a divergence of landscape conditions among ownership blocks over time and an increase in the effects of ownership pattern on aggregate ecological conditions. Analysis of the dynamics and pattern of multi-ownership landscapes requires integration among ecological and social disciplines which is a major challenge to scientists and managers. Landscape ecology can play an important role in this social process through analyses and visualization that help policy-makers, managers, and the public understand the consequences of individual owner decisions across multi-ownership landscapes. We described an interdisciplinary research effort in Oregon, the Coastal Landscape Analysis and Modeling Study (CLAMS) that is attempting to meet this need.

Acknowledgments

We would like to thank Fred Swanson and three anonymous reviewers for their helpful comments on an earlier draft. Alissa Moses conducted the GIS analyses. We would also like to acknowledge funding support from the US Department of Agriculture Forest Service, Pacific Northwest Research Station, Coastal Oregon Productivity and Enhancement (COPE) Program, Oregon State University, College of Forestry, and the Oregon Department of Forestry.

References

Alverson, W. S., Kuhlmann, W. & Waller, D. M. (1994). *Wild Forests: Conservation Biology and Public Policy*. Island Press, Washington, D.C.

Benda, L. & Cundy, T. (1990). Predicting deposition of debris flows in mountain channels. *Canadian Geotechnical Journal*, 27: 409–417.

Campbell, S. & Liegel, L. (tech. coords.) (1996). Disturbance and Forest Health in Oregon and Washington, General Technical Report PNW-381. US Department of Agriculture Forest Service Pacific Northwest Research Station, Portland, OR.

Carey, A. B., Horton, S. P. & Biswell, B. L. (1992).

Northern spotted owls: Influence of prey base and landscape character. *Ecological Monographs,* 62: 223–250.

Chen, J., Franklin, J. F. & Spies, T. A. (1993). Contrasting microclimates among clearcut, edge, and interior of old-growth Douglas-fir forests. *Agricultural and Forest Meteorology*, 63: 219–237.

Davis, L. S. & Liu, G. (1991). Integrated forest planning across multiple ownerships and decision makers. *Forest Science*, 37: 200–226.

Defenders of Wildlife (1998). *Oregon's Living Landscape: Strategies and Opportunities to Conserve Biodiversity*. Defenders of Wildlife, Washington, D.C.

Driver, B. L., Brown, P. J., Stankey, G. H. & Gregoire, T. G. (1987). The ROS planning system: evolution, basic concepts, and research needed. *Leisure Sciences*, 9: 201–212.

Everest, F. H., Beschta, R. L., Scrivener, J. C., Koski, K. V., Sedell, J. R. & Cederholm, C. J. (1987). Fine sediment and salmonid production: A paradox. In *Streamside Management: Forestry and Fishery Interactions*, eds. E. O. Salo & T. W. Cundy, pp. 98–142. Institute of Forest Resources, University of Washington, Seattle, WA.

FEMAT [Forest Ecosystem Management Assessment Team] (1993). *Forest Ecosystem Management: An Ecological, Economic, and Social Assessment*, Report of the Forest Ecosystem Management Assessment Team (FEMAT), 1993–793–071. Government Printing Office, Washington, D.C.

Forman, R. T. T. (1995). *Land Mosaics: The Ecology of Landscapes and Regions*. Cambridge University Press, Cambridge, UK.

Forman, R. T. T. & Alexander, L. E. (1998). Roads and their major ecological effects. *Annual Review of Ecology and Systematics*, 29: 207–231.

Forsman, E. D., Anthony, R. G., Reid, J. A., Loschl, P. J., Severn, S. G., Taylor, M., Biswell, B., Ellingson, A., Meslow, E. C., Miller, G. S., Swindle, K. A., Thrailkill, J. A. Wagner, F. F., & Seaman, D. E. (in press) Natal and breeding dispersal of northern spotted owls. *Wildlife Monographs*.

Franklin, J. F. & Forman, R. T. T. (1987). Creating landscape patterns by forest cutting: Ecological consequences and principles. *Landscape Ecology*, 1: 5–18.

Glick, D. A. & Clark, T. W. (1998). Overcoming boundaries: The Greater Yellowstone Ecosystem. In *Stewardship across Boundaries*, eds. R. L. Knight & P. B. Landres, pp. 237–256. Island Press, Washington, D.C.

Hagenstein, P. R. (1999). Northern forest lands assessments: Case study. In *Bioregional Assessments: Science at the Crossroads of Management and Policy*, eds. K. N. Johnson, F. J. Swanson, M. Herring & S. Greene, pp. 203–211. Island Press, Washington, D.C.

Harris, L. D. (1984). *The Fragmented Forest: Island Biogeography Theory and the Preservation of Biotic Diversity*. University of Chicago Press, Chicago, IL.

Harvey, C. A. (2000). Windbreaks enhance seed dispersal into agricultural landscape in Monteverde, Costa Rica. *Ecological Applications*, 10: 155–173.

Impara, P. C. (1997). Spatial and temporal patterns of fire in the forests of the central Oregon Coast Range. PhD dissertation, Oregon State University, Corvallis, OR.

Jones, J. A. & Grant, G. E. (1996). Peak flow responses to clearcutting and roads in small and large basins, western cascades, Oregon. *Water Resources Research*, 32: 959–974.

Keiter, R. B. & Boyce, M. S. (eds.) (1991). *The Greater Yellowstone Ecosystem: Redefining America's Wilderness Heritage*. Yale University Press, New Haven, CT.

Knight, D. H. (1991). The Yellowstone fire controversy. In *The Greater Yellowstone Ecosystem: Redefining America's Wilderness Heritage*, eds. R. B. Keiter & M. S. Boyce, pp. 87–103. Yale University Press, New Haven, CT.

Kreutzwiser, R. D. & Wright, C. S. (1990). Factors influencing integrated forest management on private industrial forest land. *Journal of Environmental Management,* 30: 31–46.

Landres, P. B., Knight, R. L., Pickett, S. T. A. & Cadenasso, M. L. (1998). Ecological effects of administrative boundaries. In *Stewardship across Boundaries,* eds. R. L. Knight & P. B. Landres. Island Press, pp. 39–64. Washington, D.C.

Lee, K. N. (1993). *Compass and Gyroscope: Integrating Science and Politics for the Environment*. Island Press, Washington, D.C.

Lee, R. G. (1997). Salmon, stewardship and human values: The challenge of integration.

In *Pacific Salmon and Their Ecosystems: Status and Future Trends*, eds. D. J. Stouder, P. A. Bisson & R. J. Naiman, pp. 639–654. Chapman & Hall, New York.

Lettman, G. & Campbell, D. (1997). *Timber Harvesting Practices on Private Forest Land in Western Oregon*. Oregon Department of Forestry, Salem, OR.

Maltamo, M., Uttera, J. & Kuusela, K. (1997). Differences in forest stand structure between forest ownership groups in central Finland. *Journal of Environmental Management*, 51: 145–167.

McGarigal, K. & McComb, W. C. (1995). Relationships between landscape structure and breeding birds in the Oregon Coast Range. *Ecological Monographs*, 65: 235–260.

McLain, R. & Lee, R. G. (1996). Adaptive management: Promises and pitfalls. *Environmental Management*, 20: 437–448.

Mech, L. D. (1991). Returning the wolf to Yellowstone. In *The Greater Yellowstone Ecosystem: Redefining America's Wilderness Heritage*, eds. R. B. Keiter & M. S. Boyce, pp. 309–322. Yale University Press, New Haven, CT.

Mitchell, J. E. & Wallace, G. (1998). Managing grazing and recreation across boundaries in the Big Cimmarron watershed. In *Stewardship across Boundaries*, eds. R. L. Knight & P. B. Landres, pp. 217–236. Island Press, Washington, D.C.

Mladenoff, D. J. T., Sickley, A., Haight, R. G. & Wydeven, A. P. (1995). A regional landscape analysis and prediction of favorable gray wolf habitat in the northern Great Lakes Region. *Conservation Biology*, 9(2): 279–294.

O'Connell, M. A. & Noss, R. F. (1992). Private land management for biodiversity conservation. *Environmental Management*, 16: 435–450.

Ogden, J. C. (1999). Everglades – South Florida assessment: Case study. In *Bioregional Assessments: Science at the Crossroads of Management and Policy*, eds. K. N. Johnson, F. J. Swanson, M. Herring & S. Greene, pp. 169–186. Island Press, Washington, D.C.

Oregon Department of Forestry (1996). Forest Practice Administrative Rules. Oregon Department of Forestry, Salem, OR. http://www.odf.state.or.us/fp/rules

Pabst, R. J. & Spies, T. A. (1999). Structure and composition of unmanaged riparian forests in the coastal mountains of Oregon. *Canadian Journal of Forest Research*, 29: 1557–1573.

Pater, D. E., Bryce, S. A., Thorson, T. D., Kagan, J., Chappell, C., Omernik, J. M., Azevedo, S. H., and Woods A. J., (1998). *Ecoregions of Western Washington and Oregon* scale 1:1 350 000. US Department of the Interior Geological Survey, Reston, VA.

Peterson, N. P. (1982). Immigration of juvenile coho salmon (*Oncorhynchus kisutch*) into riverine ponds. *Canadian Journal of Fisheries and Aquatic Sciences*, 39: 1308–1310.

Propst, L., Paleck, W. F. & Rosan, L. (1998). Partnerships across park boundaries: The Rincon Institute and Saquaro National Park. In *Stewardship across Boundaries*, eds. R. L. Knight & P. B. Landres, pp. 257–278. Island Press, Washington, D.C.

Reeves, G. H., Benda, L. E., Burnett, K. M., Bisson, P. A. & Sedell, J. R. (1995). A disturbance based ecosystem approach to maintaining and restoring freshwater habitats of evolutionarily significant units of anadromous salmonids in the Pacific Northwest. *American Fisheries Society Symposium*, 17: 334–349.

Richardson, E. (1980). *BLM's Billion-Dollar Checkerboard: Managing the O & C lands*. Forest History Society, Santa Cruz, CA.

Ripple, W. J. (1994). Historic spatial patterns of old forests of western Oregon. *Journal of Forestry*, 92: 45–49.

Ripple, W. J., Lattin, P. D., Hershey, K. T., Wagner, F. F. & Meslow, E. C. (1997). Landscape composition and pattern around northern spotted owl nest sites in southwest Oregon. *Journal of Wildlife Management*, 61: 151–158.

Robbins, W. G. (1997). *Landscapes of Promise: The Oregon Story 1800–1940*. University of Washington Press, Seattle, WA.

Robison, E. G., Mills, K., Paul, J., Dent, L. & Skaugset, A. (1999). *Storm Impacts and Landslides of 1996: Final Report*. Oregon Department of Forestry, Salem, OR.

Sample, V. A. (1994). Building partnerships for ecosystem management on mixed ownership landscapes. *Journal of Forestry*, 92(8): 41–44.

Schonewald-Cox, C., Buechner, M., Sauvajot, R. & Wilcox, B. (1992). Cross-boundary management between National Parks and surrounding lands: A review and discussion. *Environmental Management*, 16: 273–282.

Schrader, B. A. (1998). Structural development of late successional forests in the central Oregon Coast Range: Abundance, dispersal and growth of western hemlock (*Tsuga heterophylla*) regeneration. PhD dissertation, Oregon State University, Corvallis, OR.

Spies, T. A. & Franklin, J. F. (1991). The structure of natural young, mature, and old-growth Douglas-fir forests. In *Wildlife and Vegetation of Unmanaged Douglas-Fir Forests*, General Technical Report PNW-GTR-285, tech. coords. L. F. Ruggiero, K. B. Aubry, A. B. Carey & M. H. Huff, pp. 91–110. US Department of Agriculture Forest Service Pacific Northwest Research Station, Portland, OR.

Turner, M. G., Wear, D. N. & Flamm, R. O. (1996). Land ownership and land-cover changes in the southern Appalachian Highlands and the Olympic Peninsula. *Ecological Applications*, 6: 1150–1172.

Wear, D. N., Turner, M. G. & Flamm, R. O. (1996). Ecosystem management with multiple owners: Landscape dynamics in a southern Appalachian watershed. *Ecological Applications,* 6: 1173–1188.

Wemple, B. C. (1998). Investigations of runoff production and sedimentation on forest roads. PhD dissertation, Oregon State University, Corvallis, OR.

Wimberly, M. A., Spies, T. A., Long, C. J. & Whitlock, C. (2000). Simulating historical variability in the amount of old forests in the Oregon Coast Range. *Conservation Biology*, 14: 167–180.

Wisdom, M. J., Bright, L. R., Carey, C. G., Hines, W. W., Pedersen, R. J., Simthey, D. A., Thomas, J. W. & Witmer, G. W. (1986). *A Model to Evaluate Elk Habitat in Western Oregon*, Publication R6–F&WL-216. US Department of Agriculture Forest Service Pacific Northwest Region, Portland, OR.

Yaffee, S. L., Phillips, A. F., Frentz, I. C., Hardy, P. W., Maleki, S. M. & Thorpe, B. E. (1996). *Ecosystem Management in the United States: An Assessment of Current Experience*. Island Press, Washington, D.C.

Zobel, D. B., Roth, L. F. & Hawk, G. M. (1985). *Ecology, pathology, and management of Port Orford cedar* (Chamaecyparus lawsoniana), General Technical Report PNW-184. US Department of Agriculture Forest Service Pacific Northwest Forest and Range Experiment Station, Portland, OR.

8

Incorporating the effects of habitat edges into landscape models: Effective area models for cross-boundary management

8.1 Introduction

Natural resource managers are increasingly charged with meeting multiple, often conflicting goals in landscapes undergoing significant change due to shifts in land use. Conversion from native to anthropogenic habitats typically fragments the landscape, reducing the size and increasing the isolation of the resulting patches, with profound ecological impacts (see Whitcomb *et al.*, 1981; Harris, 1984; Wilcove *et al.*, 1986; Robinson *et al.*, 1995). These impacts occur both within and adjacent to the area under active management, creating new and extensive edges between habitat types. Boundaries established between management areas, for example, between timber harvest units or between reserves and adjacent agricultural fields, inevitably lead to differences in the quality of habitats on either side of the boundary, and a habitat edge results. Although edges are common components of undisturbed landscapes, the amount of edge proliferates rapidly as landscapes are fragmented (Fig. 8.1).

The creation of edges has important ecological implications at the individual, population, and ecosystem levels. Early ecologists and wildlife managers noted that community organization and species abundances are often markedly different near habitat edges (Leopold, 1933; Lay, 1938). Resource managers and conservation biologists have long attempted to translate these observations into management actions, often by attempting to maximize or minimize the amount of edge in some manner (e.g., Giles, 1971; Forman *et al.*, 1976). Despite this long history of consideration and recent advances in understanding the consequences of habitat fragmentation, the development of tools for predicting these impacts has progressed slowly. In this chapter, we offer an historical perspective on attempts to address the influence of habitat edges on wildlife and ecological processes, and we describe a spatial modeling approach that can help managers quantify these effects and incorporate species-specific data into a predictive framework for comparing the likely impacts of alternative management scenarios. We believe

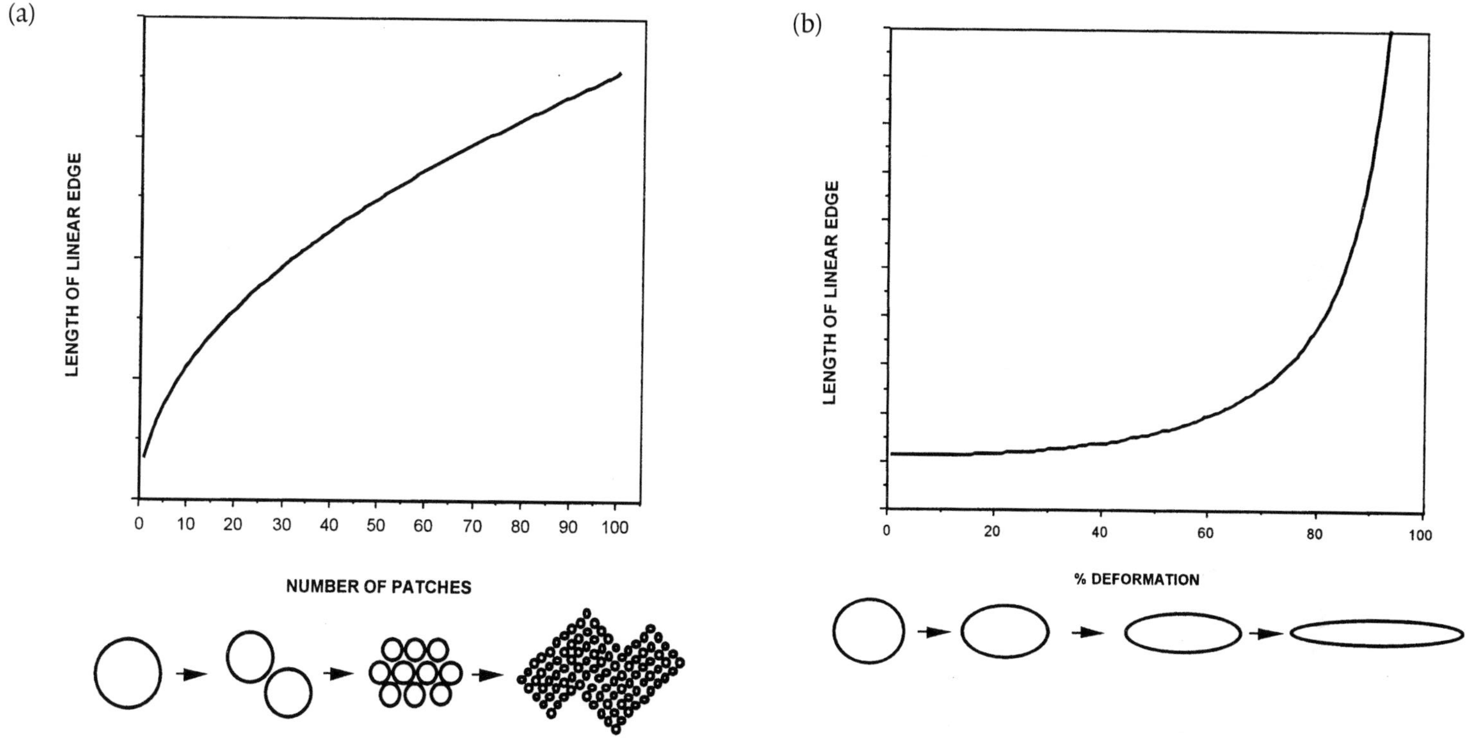

FIGURE 8.1
The proliferation of edge habitat, expressed as the increase in linear measurement of edge as (a) a constant area of 100 ha is fragmented into an increasing number of patches; and (b) as a patch of constant area is "deformed" from a circle to an increasingly narrow ellipse. The fragmentation of habitat, and the tendency of fragmentation to create long, often irregularly shaped remnants, contribute to a rapid increase in edge habitat. From Sisk and Margules, (1993).

that insightful analysis of the complex issues associated with cross-boundary management necessitates an explicit focus on habitat quality in the boundary regions.

8.2 Edge effects and cross-boundary management

When managers adopt a landscape perspective they are immediately confronted with habitat edges and their diverse and often powerful influence on biological resources. Often, management focus is on several habitat types or focal species. The adoption of a landscape perspective requires the manager to see landscapes not as collections of similar patches surrounded by "non-habitat," but as mosaics of patches of different qualities, whose shapes and spatial arrangements are important determinants of habitat quality. While cross-boundary management obviously necessitates consideration of adjacent patches, it is the consideration of edge effects that addresses the influence of adjacent habitats on the quality of habitat within a given patch. For example, cross-boundary management may require a manager to consider the implications of agricultural development outside a nature reserve on wildlife populations that move widely and often cross the administrative boundary. The proximity of the agricultural fields may have profound ecological impacts on the habitat within the nature reserve. Does agriculture supplement the food base of species residing in the reserve, or might it introduce predators or disease? How far into the reserve do these effects penetrate? These and other questions about the effects of habitat edges are an important subset of issues associated with cross-boundary management. As edges become ever more prevalent in managed landscapes, their effects become more complex, and more important to managers.

Edges impact all levels of ecological organization. Although most research has focused on how edges may influence population size or species diversity (Sisk and Battin, in press), edge influences are by no means restricted to the population and community levels. Edges may influence behavior by creating barriers to the movement of animals (Ries and Debinski, 2001; Haddad, 1999a) shifting the nature of interactions among species (Remer and Heard, 1998), or altering the distribution of key resources and microhabitats. They also may influence how ecosystems function (Laurance *et al.*, 1998) by modifying microclimatic conditions (Chen *et al.*, 1999), photosynthetic rates, and nutrient availability, among other biotic and abiotic processes (Camargo and Kapos, 1995; Murcia, 1995). Of course, the effects of habitat edges on ecological pattern and process, affecting all levels of organization from the individual to the ecosystem, are the product of a plethora of factors, and even apparently similar responses may be driven by very different mechanisms. Unfortunately, these multiple effects and the processes that drive them often have been lumped together and grossly oversimplified. Our first task is to explore the history of "edge effects" and deconstruct some unhelpful but widely held concepts. Then we will attempt to put the issue back together in a question-driven framework that will make the application of current knowledge of habitat edges more tractable in cross-boundary management.

8.2.1 Edge effects: A "catch-all" term

Edge effects have a long history in the ecological and management literature. In fact, the book that launched the modern profession of wildlife management, Aldo Leopold's *Game Management* (Leopold, 1933), popularized the term "edge effect" and provided hypotheses to explain the widely held view that edges were beneficial to wildlife. Leopold suggested that the "desirability of simultaneous access to more than one [habitat]", and "the greater richness of [edge] vegetation" supported higher abundances of many species, and higher species richness (Leopold, 1933: 130–131). These hypotheses provided the first management-oriented theory concerning the landscape-scale effects of habitat heterogeneity on animal distributions and abundances. Unfortunately, these hypotheses have been poorly tested. Instead of in-depth research regarding the causes and consequences of increasing edge habitat, these hypotheses were accepted by many as a general paradigm stating that diversity and the abundance of species would tend to increase if the amount of edge habitat present in a managed landscape were increased. The passage of "edge effects" from an idea based on limited observation and hypothesized mechanisms to a widely accepted "law of ecology" (Odum, 1958) had a far-reaching impact on land management in the United States and around the world. Many texts and habitat management guidelines discuss the advantages of creating habitat edges via land management activities, such as small forest clear-cuts or the creation of irregular boundaries around management units, in order to maximize the ratio of edge to interior habitat (Odum, 1958; Giles, 1971, 1978; Dasmann, 1981).

The hypothesis that increasing edge habitat increases species diversity and abundance may be among the most widely accepted and broadly applied guidelines in wildlife management that has not been rigorously tested or evaluated. The "law of edge effects" failed to distinguish differences in responses among species and at different types of habitat edges, and the lack of explicit predictions made it difficult to assess the impacts of edge creation. The uncritical acceptance of this "law" has had unintended consequences. For example, managing forests in a manner that maximizes forest edge tends to increase fragmentation of once-extensive forest habitats, leading to the decline of disturbance-sensitive species, such as many interior forest birds (Wilcove, 1985; Thompson, 1993; Robinson *et al.*, 1995).

8.2.2 Edge and interior species: An overused dichotomy?

In the 1970s, increasing concern about the effects of habitat fragmentation on passerine birds led to a more critical assessment of the impacts of edges on biological diversity (Terborgh, 1976; Whitcomb *et al.*, 1981; Harris, 1984). Declines in many species of neotropical migrant songbirds, and increases in cosmopolitan and feral species – some of which increased competition, predation, and parasitism in the remaining patches of forest habitat – led many ecologists to question the wisdom of managing for increased edge (Brittingham and Temple, 1983; Wilcove, 1985). In particular, studies of avian nest predators and parasites led to compelling evidence that habitat edges serve as the point of entry to interior habitats for many invasive or weedy species that have detrimental impacts on species of conservation interest (Brittingham and Temple, 1983; Wilcove *et al.*, 1986).

The increased awareness of the relationship between increasing edges and increasing nest parasitism and predation significantly altered the perceptions of managers regarding habitat edges and edge effects. Research on songbirds introduced a new dichotomy into the edge effects literature, between species thought of as "edge species", whose numbers are elevated near edges and "interior species" that fare poorly at edges and require large areas of interior habitat, well buffered from the forest edge (Whitcomb *et al.*, 1981; Brittingham and Temple, 1983). This new dichotomy improved on the old "law" by acknowledging that not all species respond similarly to habitat alterations. However, as with previous ideas about edge effects, the edge species/interior species dichotomy focused on a limited subset of the fauna and assumed a uniformity of responses within these two categories. This idea has been extended to other taxa, generating a second set of generalizations regarding edge effects. The "law of edge effects" that assumed generally beneficial impacts was replaced by the notion that edge effects are bad because they reduce the amount of habitat available to sensitive species of interior habitats.

Despite these contradictory perspectives on edge effects, or perhaps because of them, unsupported generalities about edge effects have persisted in the ecological and management literature. The resulting confusion has tended to discourage critical examination of ecological patterns and processes near habitat edges, and ecologists are just beginning to understand the underlying mechanisms (see Fagan *et al.*, 1999). Furthermore, theoretical approaches for addressing edge effects within the context of structurally complex, heterogeneous landscapes has progressed slowly (but see Turchin, 1991), as has the development of practical, predictive models useful in applied management contexts. We believe that the interaction between an increased understanding of mechanisms generating edge effects and the development of predictive tools for assessing their ecological implications will lead to a general understanding of habitat boundaries that will assist in the management of many species and their habitats in the context of complex and changing landscapes.

8.2.3 Common assumptions about edge effects

Historical paradigms concerning edge effects are characterized by overly general principles intended to expedite decision making in conservation and management. Efforts to implement rules of thumb regarding edge effects include one or more basic assumptions about the effects of edges on populations and communities. Recent research has cast doubt on most of these assumptions, as summarized below, leaving the manager with little scientific support for decision-making. While many familiar generalizations are not supported, increased appreciation of the more variable effects of habitat edges provide an improved foundation for addressing landscape heterogeneity and cross-boundary management. Some common assumptions include:

(1) *Edge effects are similar for related species.* As exemplified in early observations of increased species diversity and higher abundances of individual species at edges (e.g., Leopold, 1933; Lay, 1938; Johnston, 1947; Johnston and Odum, 1956) and in studies employing the assumed dichotomy between edge and interior species (Burgess and Sharpe, 1981), there is an underlying assumption that many species respond in a very similar manner to edges. More detailed studies of species assemblages near edges suggest that the variability inherent in edge responses is large, and that species-specific responses to edges span a continuum between the commonly employed dichotomy between edge and interior species (e.g., Noss, 1991; Sisk and Margules, 1993; Brand and George, 2001).

(2) *Edge effects extend some characteristic, fixed distance from the habitat edge into a patch.* Often, populations of all edge or interior species, or even entire avian assemblages, are assumed to respond similarly to edges, up to some fixed distance into a habitat patch (e.g., MacArthur *et al.*, 1962; Temple, 1986). A growing number of empirical studies suggest that population densities of most species change independently and idiosyncratically, and the distance of penetration of edge effects differs from species to species (Noss, 1991; Sisk, 1992). Several studies have suggested that, while the edge/interior dichotomy may be a helpful concept for distinguishing responses in some cases, knowledge of species-specific edge responses (see below) is necessary for understanding and predicting the effects of edges created through landscape management and manipulation (Laurance and Yensen, 1991; Noss, 1991; Sisk and Margules, 1993).

(3) *For a given species, edge effects are consistent, regardless of the type of edge.* The idea here is that species are intrinsically edge species or interior species, and that a particular response to edges, in general, is characteristic of the species. Thus, previous studies have assumed that a species identified as an “edge species” at the intersection between forest and grassland will

also be an edge species at the intersection of, for example, forest and shrubland. In fact, species vary in their responses to edges, depending on the type of edge. Sisk *et al.* (1997) showed that of 24 breeding birds of oak woodlands, over half showed significantly different responses to edges with chaparral vs. grassland.

(4) *Species respond similarly to the same type of edge in different locations.* If understanding edge effects is to provide any insight into habitat management, one must assume that there is some consistency in a species' response to similar edges between the same two habitat types. To date, few studies have examined this question directly, and virtually all replicated designs that have measured animal distributions across transects orthogonal to edges have shown high variance in species abundances. Perhaps the best evidence that edge responses are generally consistent, and therefore predictable, comes from modeling studies that use measured responses to infer conditions at novel edges, and then test predictions with real data (Temple, 1986; Laurance, 1991; Sisk *et al.*, 1997). These results suggest that responses show some consistency at similar edges, and that consideration of edge effects can improve on estimates of animal abundance that are based on habitat area alone (Temple and Cary, 1988; Sisk *et al.*, 1997).

8.2.4 Mechanisms that cause edge effects

Perhaps due to the rapid creation of edge habitats in fragmented landscapes, the number of studies of the influence of edges has proliferated in recent years. In a recent review of edge studies, Sisk and Battin (in press) found more than 200 papers on birds alone. However, there has been a lack of conceptual unification in studies of edge effects, causing confusion in ecology and management. In particular, many different mechanisms may lead to seemingly similar edge effects. In a recent synthesis, Fagan *et al.* (1999) identified four ways in which edges influence species interactions and cause edge effects:

(1) *Edges influence movement.* Edges may be a barrier to dispersal for animals (Stamps *et al.*, 1987; Ries and Debinski, 2001; Haddad, 1999b). Edges may create barriers, preventing dispersal through complex landscapes and isolating animals. Conversely, Sisk and Zook (1996) have shown that migrating birds can accumulate at edges, as forest birds moving through largely deforested landscapes seek the nearest forest habitat for cover and foraging. By definition, this nearest habitat is at the forest edge. Such "passive accumulation" of mobile animals may generate increased density near edges. These examples illustrate that, while animal density may be an appropriate measure of habitat use, it may be a misleading indicator of habitat quality (Van Horne, 1983).

(2) *Edges influence mortality.* Particularly for habitat interior species, edges may

lead to higher mortality in plants and animals. Higher mortality may occur in three different ways. First, edges create greater opportunity for loss of dispersers into unsuitable habitat. For example, plants with wind-dispersed seeds that are near the edge will lose more of their propagules into unsuitable habitat. Second, edges alter microclimate, including temperature, light, and moisture (Chen *et al.*, 1993; Young and Mitchell, 1994; Camargo and Kapos, 1995). In doing so, edges may impact competitive interactions between species (Remer and Heard 1998; Fagan *et al.*, 1999). Third, edges provide points of entry for predators and parasites, such as the brown-headed cowbird (*Molothrus ater*) (Wilcove *et al.*, 1986; Murcia, 1995), that may affect co-occurring species (see below).

(3) *Edges provide feeding or reproductive subsidies*. From the edge, species may be able to obtain a greater quantity and quality of food resources from each of the habitats that create the edge, leading to positive effects on population sizes (MacArthur *et al.*, 1962; Fagan *et al.*, 1999).

(4) *Edges define the boundary between two separate habitats, creating new opportunities for species to mix and interact*. By their very nature, edges influence species interactions because they often bring into proximity species that would not normally be present in the same habitat. Species that are brought together at the edge may include predators and prey, new competitors, and mutualists, generating novel interactions and creating new species assemblages.

The mechanisms that cause edge effects impact all levels of ecological organization, from individual organisms to the organization of ecosystems. Very few studies have examined the mechanistic basis for the plethora of edge effects reported in the literature (Sisk and Battin, in press), and it is unlikely that an integrated understanding of edge effects is possible without significant advances in this area. However, empirically based studies, such as those cited above, combined with recent work proposing tractable theoretical approaches (Matlack, 1993; Fagan *et al.*, 1999) provide avenues for incorporating improved understanding of the mechanisms that cause edge effects into efforts to predict their influence on interspecific interactions and, ultimately, community organization and ecosystem function. These and other efforts to draw on the considerable body of empirical data to test and refine mechanistic hypotheses and predictive approaches have been propelled by a subtle but influential shift in the way that both researchers and managers view edge effects.

8.3 Addressing edge effects through effective area models

Most approaches for predicting the impacts of habitat edges have focused on patterns in animal abundance near edges (Lay, 1938; Johnston, 1947; Kroodsma, 1982). Typically, counts of organisms, often collected within

100 m of an edge, were compared with counts from interior habitats, and observed differences were attributed to "the edge effect." In effect, the edge was viewed as a unique, homogeneous habitat type, one that should be considered in a similar manner to forest, grassland, savanna, and other primary habitats.

Over the past 20 years, as ecologists and managers focused increasingly on habitat fragmentation, conceptual approaches in community ecology and resource management moved toward a landscape-scale approach (Forman and Godron, 1981, 1988; Wiens *et al.*, 1985). This change of perspective influenced concepts of edges in subtle but profound ways. Rather than viewing edges as unique habitats, ecologists began to treat them as landscape features that mediated fundamental ecological processes, such as microclimatic conditions, resource availability, and interspecific interactions. This revised concept of edge effects emphasizes the influence of adjoining habitats on each other. Edge conditions determine the type and intensity of influences and can be seen as directional or semipermeable filters that alter conditions within a given habitat area, up to some characteristic distance from the habitat edge itself (Wiens *et al.*, 1985). Unfortunately, the objective of researchers – generally focusing on the identification of patterns in nature and the discovery of the forces creating those patterns, often does not overlap with the needs of managers, who often are more interested in the predicted outcomes of alternative habitat management options (Table 8.1).

Temple (1986) was perhaps the first to apply the revised concept of edge in a predictive framework. His early core-area model drew on empirical data concerning the penetration of nest predators into Midwestern forest fragments to assess the impacts of changing land use on "fragmentation-sensitive" species. Thus, evidence suggesting that nest parasitism occurred within about 100 m of the forest edge led to predictions that only habitat more than 100 m from the edge was suitable for interior bird species. Application of this model (Temple and Cary, 1988) proved insightful within the context of their study, but assumptions about the distance of penetration of edge effects (100 m), the unsuitability of habitat up to that depth of penetration, and the uniformity of responses of all focal species limited the usefulness of core-area models in management situations.

Laurance and Yensen (1991) relaxed some of the assumptions of the core-area approach, adding realism by allowing variation in edge responses, including the distance of penetration. They examined the implications of different edge response on patches of differing shapes, but they retained an underlying assumption that the edge effect was fixed for a particular species or environmental parameter at various types of edges, and they assumed that all edge responses were unimodal. The focus remained on "interior species" that were negatively associated with habitat edges.

Expansion of the core-area approach to include any combination of habitats, and any species or environmental parameter of interest, is the objective of

Table 8.1. *Contrasting objectives: Differing needs of researchers and resource managers when confronted with the complexity of edge effects in heterogeneous landscapes. These generalizations reflect the authors' synthesis of the differing foci of the research and management literature concerning edge effects*

Management needs	Research tendency	"Effective area models"
Goals may be related to particular species, but all species must be considered in management planning	Provide highly detailed information on particular focal species *or* focus on species diversity and other abstract measures of community organization	Response variables may include population size, relative abundance, species richness, productivity, or any variable whose value can be expressed as an *edge response function*
Consider all edge types influencing the patches of habitat for focal species	Constrain study to one edge type	Incorporate all edge types for which an edge response function can be derived
Consider variable depth of penetration, depending on species and edge type	Assume a single depth of penetration for a given effect	Incorporate a variable depth of penetration for all edge effects, based on empirical data
Capability to predict the consequences of alternative management activities on poorly studied species and habitats	Little ability to extrapolate beyond study site and focal species	Extend the specific knowledge to novel landscapes and hypothetical management activities, under explicitly identified simplifying assumptions
Ability to select the best alternative from among a finite set of feasible management actions	Focus on hypothesis testing and increased understanding	Provide managers with an empirically driven tool for examining likely outcomes of alternative management activities

effective area modeling approaches (Sisk and Margules, 1993; Sisk *et al.*, 1997) discussed in this chapter. Like the core-area approach, the effective area model assumes that the amount of suitable habitat, from the perspective of any species in a landscape, is generally different than the collective area of the patches of its habitat(s). In contrast to the concept of "core area," the *effective* area may be larger (for edge exploiters) or smaller (for edge avoiders). In addition, because managers are interested in entire landscapes, and because adjacent habitats may influence the suitability of all habitat types, not only remnant patches of the "natural" type, the effective area approach weighs the quality of all habitat patches in the landscape. This approach expands beyond the sometimes-arbitrary focus on what are perceived as interior and fragmentation-sensitive species, and incorporates the spatial complexity of real landscapes, where the number, size, shape, and spatial arrangements of habitat patches may influence habitat quality (Forman and Godron, 1981; O'Neill *et al.*, 1988; Ripple *et al.*, 1991).

The effective area model (EAM) (Sisk, 1992; Sisk *et al.*, 1997) uses quantitative measures of species-specific edge effects to weight habitat quality within a particular patch, based on distance from the edge. (Interested readers can contact the lead author for a copy of the Effective Area Model, which operates as an extension to the ArcView© GIS application [Environmental Systems Research Institute, Inc., Redlands, CA].) It then calculates an "effective habitat area" for each patch of similar habitat within the landscape or management area. The effective habitat area may differ from species to species, depending on the degree to which proximity to edges enhances or degrades the quality of habitat for that species. The idea that a given patch of habitat may be perceived and utilized in very different ways by distinct species suggests the need to consider variability in edge responses when evaluating landscape composition and structure in a management context. Consideration of the responses of multiple species to different edge conditions allows the conservation scientist to estimate the effective area of habitat available to each species, based on its characteristic responses to conditions near edges.

The EAM uses two types of input data – the edge response of each species (or of another environmental parameter of interest) and detailed landscape maps identifying habitat patches and their location in the landscape – to generate predictions of the distributions of organisms, resources, or environmental conditions in heterogeneous landscapes.

8.3.1 Edge responses

The edge response quantifies the species-specific influence of habitat edges. It can be conceptualized as the population density (or as the value of any other environmental variable) at increasing distances from the habitat edge (Fig. 8.2). Measuring edge responses typically involves sampling the variable of

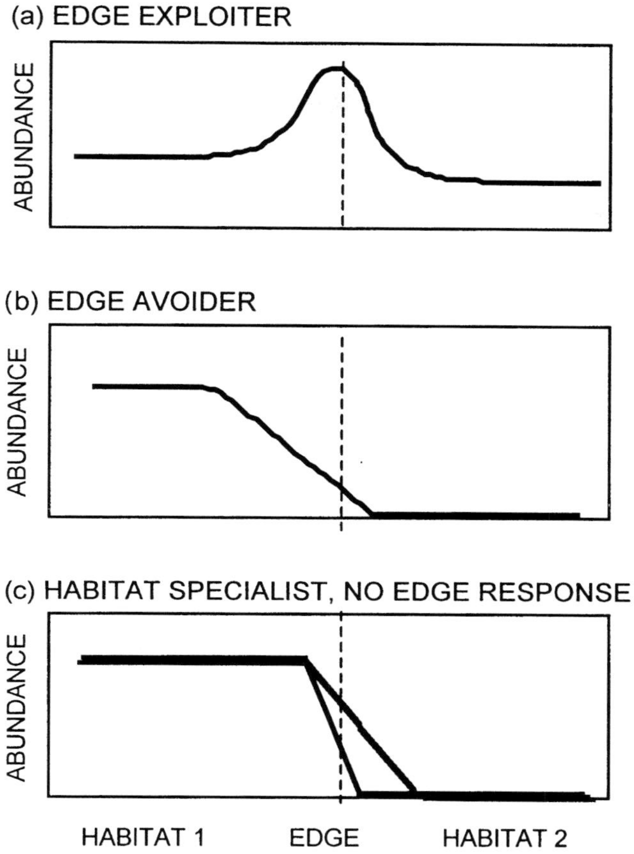

FIGURE 8.2
Hypothetical density responses for organisms occurring near abrupt edges (dashed vertical lines) between different habitat types. The three hypothetical responses illustrated above depict three classes of response in any environmental parameter of interest (in this example, animal abundance). The edge response may peak at or near the edge (a), it may decrease as one approaches the edge, even within seemingly homogeneous habitat (b), or there may be no discernible edge response, as in (c), where the parameter has distinct values in the adjoining habitat and the edge is merely the point of transition, introducing no novel effects. Adapted from Sisk *et al.* (1997).

interest along transects running orthogonal to the habitat edge. This approach captures the effects of different underlying mechanisms, including both within-patch factors (such as floristic, structural, and microclimatic attributes,) and external factors, such as the modifying influence of the surrounding matrix habitats. For some variables, including density responses for common vertebrates, edge responses may be derived from the literature. For most others, characterization of edge responses may require field research. Even in these cases, however, treating edge responses as a surrogate for detailed behavioral, demographic, and environmental parameters provides an efficient approach for quantifying sensitivity to the influences of adjoining habitats.

Several studies have determined edge responses for birds by estimating population density along a habitat gradient extending from the interior of one habitat, across the edge, and extending into the interior of the adjacent habitat (e.g., Noss, 1991; Sisk and Margules, 1993) (Fig. 8.3a–d). Edge responses of physical characteristics influencing habitat quality can be derived from high-resolution microclimatic data (Ranney *et al.*, 1981; Laurance, 1991; Chen *et al.*, 1993; Malcolm, 1994). The availability of relatively inexpensive electronic

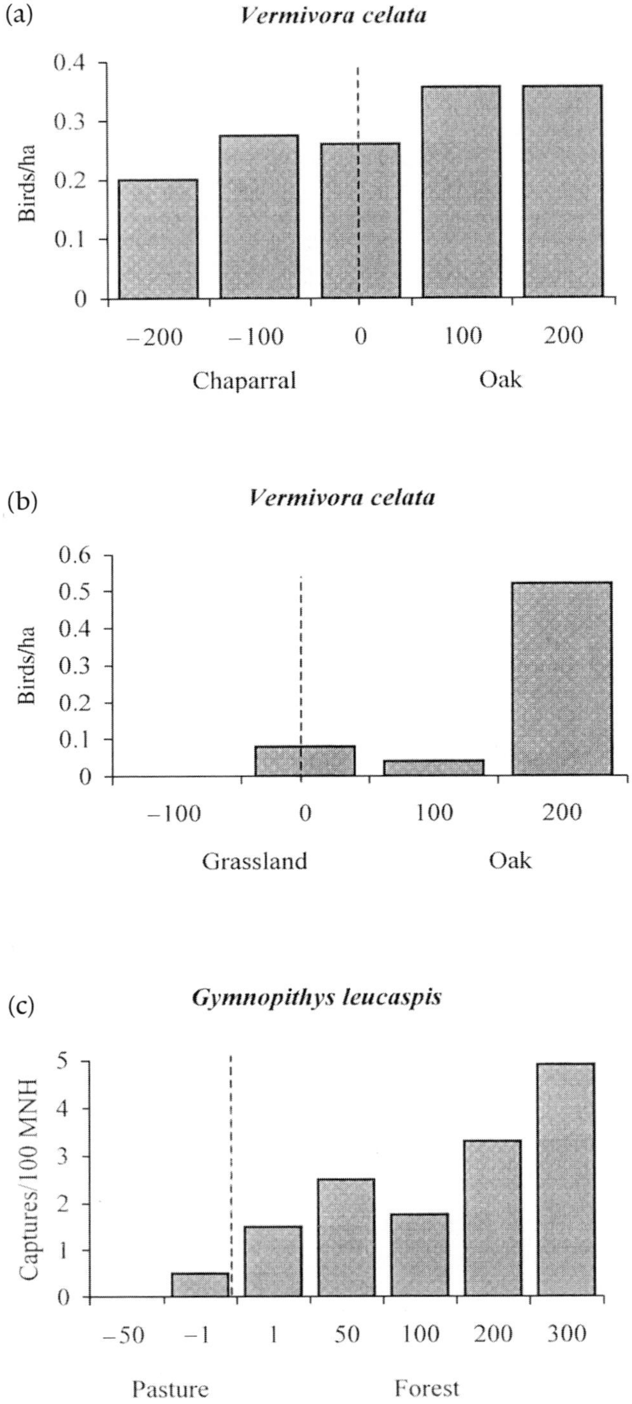
(a)
Vermivora celata
Birds/ha
0.4
0.3
0.2
0.1
0
−200
−100
0
100
200
Chaparral
Oak
(b)
Vermivora celata
Birds/ha
0.6
0.5
0.4
0.3
0.2
0.1
0
−100
0
100
200
Grassland
Oak
(c)
Gymnopithys leucaspis
Captures/100 MNH
5
4
3
2
1
0
−50
−1
1
50
100
200
300
Pasture
Forest

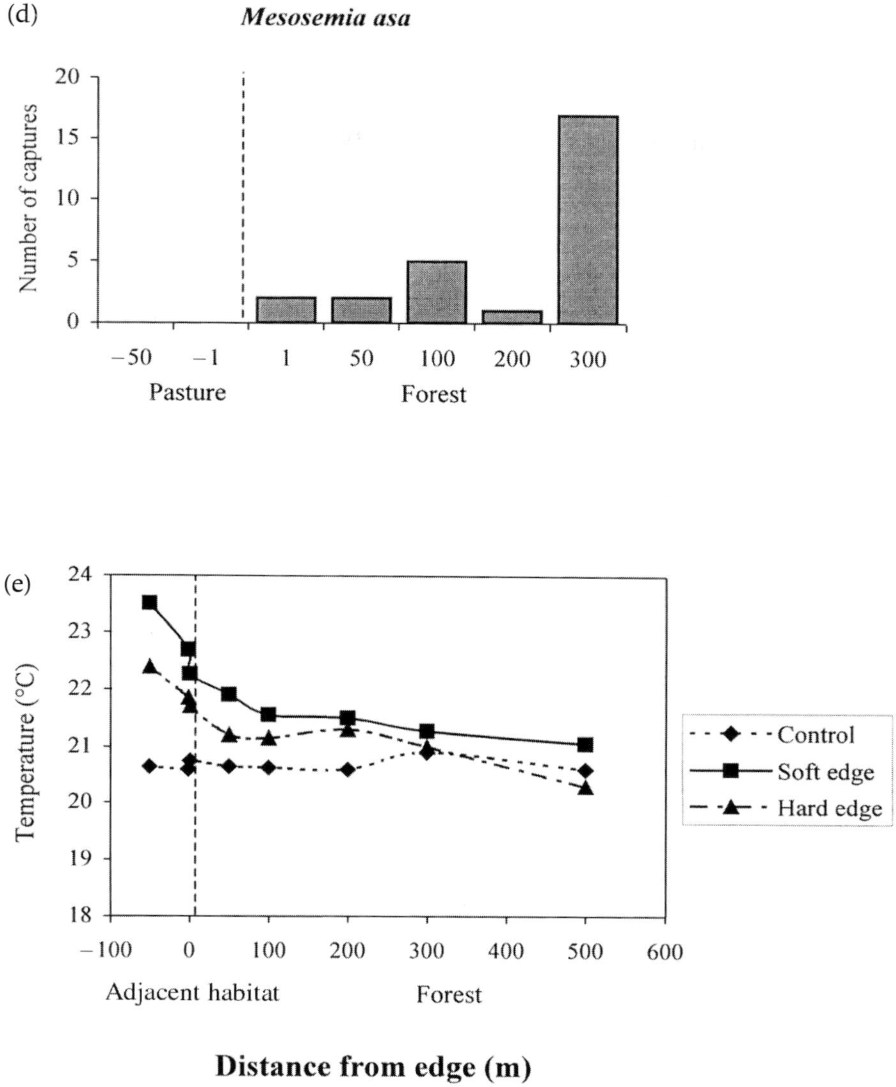

FIGURE 8.3
Empirical responses of selected animal species and microclimatic variables to habitat edges. (a) Density of orange-crowned warbler (*Vermivora celata*), a neotropical migrant bird, at oak/chaparral edges in coastal California; (b) density of orange-crowned warbler at oak/grassland edges; (c) abundance of bicolored antbird (*Gymnopithys leucaspis*), a tropical forest understory bird, expressed as the number of captures per 100 mist net hours; (d) abundance of the tropical forest butterfly *Mesosemia asa*, expressed as the number of captures per trap day; (e) temperature near "hard" edges between montane tropical forest and pasture in Costa Rica, near "soft" edges between the same forest and selectively logged forest, and in control sites located in undisturbed forest more than 5 km from the nearest pasture and sampled according to the same protocol. Dashed line indicates location of edge. All data from Sisk (1992).

sensors and automated dataloggers permits detailed monitoring of microclimatic conditions at sampling stations spanning the edge gradient, and the characterization of edge responses for parameters such as ambient temperature, relative humidity, and solar radiation (Young and Mitchell, 1994; Camargo and Kapos, 1995; Chen *et al.*, 1995) (Fig. 8.3e). When incorporated into an EAM, these microclimatic responses permit landscape-scale predictions about underlying physical characteristics that influence habitat quality.

Interestingly, the edge response of a particular species or environmental variable may vary considerably at edges between different habitat types (Sisk, 1992). For example, a woodland bird that is an edge exploiter at a boundary with shrubland (Fig. 8.3a) may be edge-avoiding at a grassland edge (Fig. 8.3b). This variability suggests that characterization of edge responses may be an ongoing and time-consuming task. Many factors, including age, sex, and social status (for some animals), seasonality and climatic conditions, might influence edge responses. In the worst-case scenario, this variability could make implementation of the EAM intractable, due to demands for empirical data. In practice, however, management decisions are usually driven by specific concerns that focus on particular types of organisms (e.g., breeding adults) and/or environmental conditions (e.g., effects of fire during the breeding season). Thus, while variability in edge responses may be great, management contexts usually constrain the potential variability to a level that can be addressed in modest empirical studies. While gathering edge response data on density, behavior, and/or environmental condition may be time consuming, it is far less demanding than the collection of the full range of demographic and dispersal data required to parameterize metapopulation models and other spatially explicit approaches that are seeing increasing use in management contexts (e.g., Dunning *et al.*, 1995; Noon and McKelvey, 1996; Wahlberg *et al.*, 1996).

8.3.2 Habitat maps

The second class of input data for the EAM is detailed habitat maps of real or hypothetical landscapes. Size, shape, and location of patches of different habitat types must be delineated for the model area. Typically, landscape-scale information can be obtained from aerial photographs and satellite images, and floristic composition may be derived from the application of appropriate classification algorithms, in conjunction with adequate field data (Turner and Gardner, 1991; Avery and Berlin, 1992; Wilkie and Finn, 1996). For many species, classification of vegetation based on floristic composition is an inadequate descriptor of habitat quality. For example, many forest birds are highly sensitive to the vegetation structure (e.g., Willson, 1974; James and Wamer, 1982). In such cases, additional data may be required, either from other remotely sensed sources (e.g., Imhoff and Sisk, 1997) or from detailed field data. Current approaches to detailed habitat mapping typically incorporate multiple data sources in a geographic information system (GIS). The increasing availability of GIS to scientists and resource managers offers a powerful organizational and analytical tool for mapping habitats and a convenient and powerful environment for applying effective area models.

While the details of habitat classification and mapping are beyond the scope of this chapter, it is important to note that use of the effective area approach assumes that complex landscapes can be mapped with sufficient detail and accuracy to capture habitat quality for the species of concern. This entails selection of appropriate map extent and scale, both of which may vary among species and environmental variables. Obviously, habitat maps developed for butterflies may be inappropriate for making predictions about amphibian densities. In practice, these distinctions can be addressed effectively and efficiently by varying the number of habitat classes and the discriminatory parameters for identifying them, and by scaling the classification algorithm to the species of interest (see Wiens, 1989; Withers and Meentemeyer, 1999).

These two classes of input data, edge responses and habitat maps, share several characteristics that make them amenable to management models:

- They are characters that tend to show consistent patterns. Edge responses are generated by the host of factors that guide habitat selection in specific situations, so they are likely to be conserved over time and space, where conditions are similar. Landscape composition and structure are discrete properties that characterize the diversity of habitat conditions encountered by all organisms.
- They tend to be discrete and definable. Edge responses and habitat characteristics, while often dynamic over ecological time-scales, can be characterized unambiguously at a given point in time that is relevant to management objectives.
- They are quantifiable. Edge responses, be they patterns in abundance, reproductive output, or environmental conditions, can be sampled effectively along transects running orthogonal to the habitat edge. Complex landscape mosaics can be mapped efficiently using appropriate combinations of remotely sensed data and field measurements.

8.3.3 Generating patch-specific predictions for landscape-scale analysis

The EAM projects edge responses onto habitat maps, generating patch-specific predictions of species abundances or environmental parameters based on within-patch variation in habitat quality induced by edge effects. Figure 8.4 illustrates how patch-specific predictions of population size are generated,

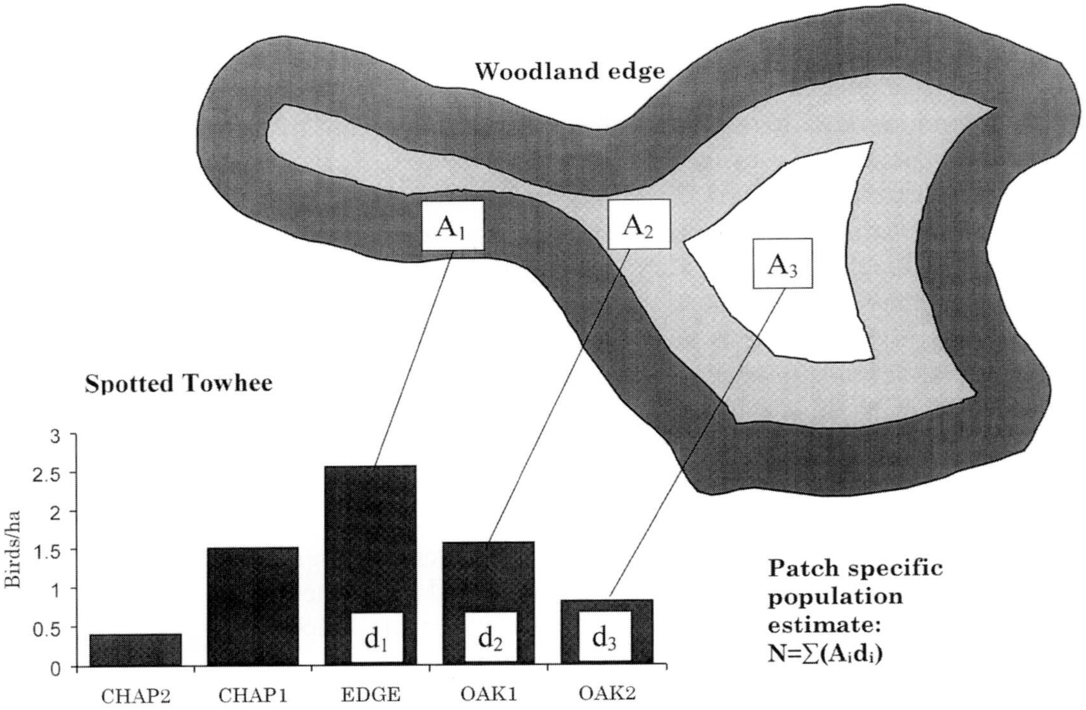

FIGURE 8.4
A schematic depiction of the effective area model. Empirical data on the response of a species (in this example the spotted towhee, *Pipilo erythrophthalmus*) or environmental parameter of interest, across a habitat gradient orthogonal to the edge, are projected onto digital habitat maps. Sub-regions for various patches are defined according to their distance from the edge, and the area of each sub-region (A_i) is multiplied by the corresponding density (d_i) from the species' edge response curve. The summation gives the expected population size in the patch. The EAM computes similar estimates for all patches in the modeled landscape. By applying the edge response to maps of alternative future conditions, the expected effects of alternative management scenarios can be compared. Adapted from Sisk *et al.* (1997).

based on empirical data describing a species' response to the habitat edge. In the illustrated case, the spotted towhee (*Pipilo erythrophthalmus*), an edge-exploiting species, is present at significantly higher density near the edge between oak woodland and chaparral habitats than in interior oak habitat 150 m or more from the edge. Estimated density near the habitat edge is projected into the band of habitat within 50 m of the edge by simply multiplying the density estimate by the area of habitat in the edge band. Similar calculations are carried out for the remaining bands, and estimates for all sub-regions of the patch are summed to produce an overall patch-specific estimate of abundance. For the 220-ha patch illustrated in Fig. 8.4, the EAM predicts approximately

470 individuals, with 70% of those expected to occur in edge habitat that constitutes only 58% of the patch area ($A_1 = 128$ ha). Similar calculations for all patches of all habitats in the landscape, and for all species of management interest, can produce estimated patterns of abundance for entire species assemblages in complex landscapes (Sisk *et al.*, 1997).

The ease of manipulating GIS-based habitat maps offers the opportunity for exploring the expected outcomes of alternative habitat management options by altering the habitat map to reflect proposed management activities, then inputting these maps into an EAM. While this relatively simple approach cannot predict population persistence and is unlikely to generate precise estimates of population size, it does provide a tool for comparing predicted outcomes for complex landscapes managed under different strategies. This "game-playing" approach allows managers to assess and rank the expected impacts of management alternatives on a wide range of parameters, from distributional and demographic trends to microclimate and resource availability – any parameter that the manager has the methodology, time, and resources to characterize along the edge gradient.

8.4 Case studies and future applications

Most work on edge effects has focused on animal abundance and community organization. More recently, effects on behavior and ecosystem processes have received increased attention. Below, we trace two case studies where the effective area model has been applied successfully, providing insights into management-relevant issues pertaining to population size and community organization. We then discuss approaches to ecosystem processes and behavior where edge effects have influenced cross-boundary management and edge-based modeling approaches have been applied, albeit in a preliminary manner. In all four cases we discuss opportunities for applying effective area models to extend these case studies into the practical realm of cross-boundary management. In a similar manner, much of the recent and ongoing research on edge effects may lend itself to applications in natural resource management.

8.4.1 Edge effects on population size

The edge effect concept has been used most frequently to characterize responses of animal densities to habitat edges. The EAM provides a rigorous approach to assess how the creation of edges, through habitat fragmentation or restoration, will influence population sizes in patchy landscapes. Traditionally, population studies have characterized species as edge or interior species, without consideration of species-specific responses to habitat boundaries.

Using this approach, core-area models have been used to determine the effects of fragmentation on population abundances (Temple, 1986; Laurance and Yensen, 1991). One recent review has successfully used such general classifications to demonstrate that, with increasing fragmentation, edge species tend to increase in population size, and interior species tend to decrease in population size (Bender *et al.*, 1998). However, an effective area approach is likely to improve predictions of population responses to fragmentation.

Haddad and Baum (1999) showed how an effective area model could be used to determine the effects of edges on population abundances. They compared the effects of edges in similar habitat patches, each 128 × 128 m (1.64 ha). The patches were open areas of habitat created by harvesting pine. The open areas were suitable habitats for several butterfly species, while the surrounding pine forest matrix did not contain several important host and nectar plant resources and, thus, was not suitable habitat for some butterfly species. The patches differed in that some were connected to nearby patches by corridors, while others were isolated. A total of 19 patches were connected to other patches, and 8 patches were completely isolated from other patches.

To estimate the densities of three butterfly species, Haddad and Baum (1999) surveyed each of the 27 patches an average of 54 times during 1996. Each patch was surveyed by dividing it into 8 transects, each separated by 16 m. Transects were walked in 6 min, excluding time spent recording data. To record the spatial location of individual butterflies, patches were subdivided into 8 × 8 m cells.

The effects of corridors and edges on butterfly densities were analyzed using Poisson regression, an appropriate approach for count data. Variables in statistical models included patch type (connected or unconnected), distance from the habitat edge (in 8 m increments corresponding to a grid system within each patch), and the densities of host and nectar plants. Two open-habitat species (*Junonia coenia* and *Euptoieta claudia*) had higher densities in connected patches, and at greater distances from habitat boundaries (Fig. 8.5a, b). A third habitat generalist species (*Papilio troilus*) did not show differences in densities in connected and unconnected patches (Fig. 8.5c). Although *P. troilus* densities increased significantly with increasing distances from the forest edge, this was due to its low density at the habitat boundary and its high density at the center of the patch. Its density at intermediate distances was constant.

Corridors are predicted to increase animal densities because they permit more rapid recolonization of habitat patches after local extinction. However, corridors change the shape and context of habitat patches within a complex landscape, and several alternative hypotheses may also explain increased butterfly densities. One hypothesis that could explain differences in densities in connected and unconnected patches is that corridors modify edge effects

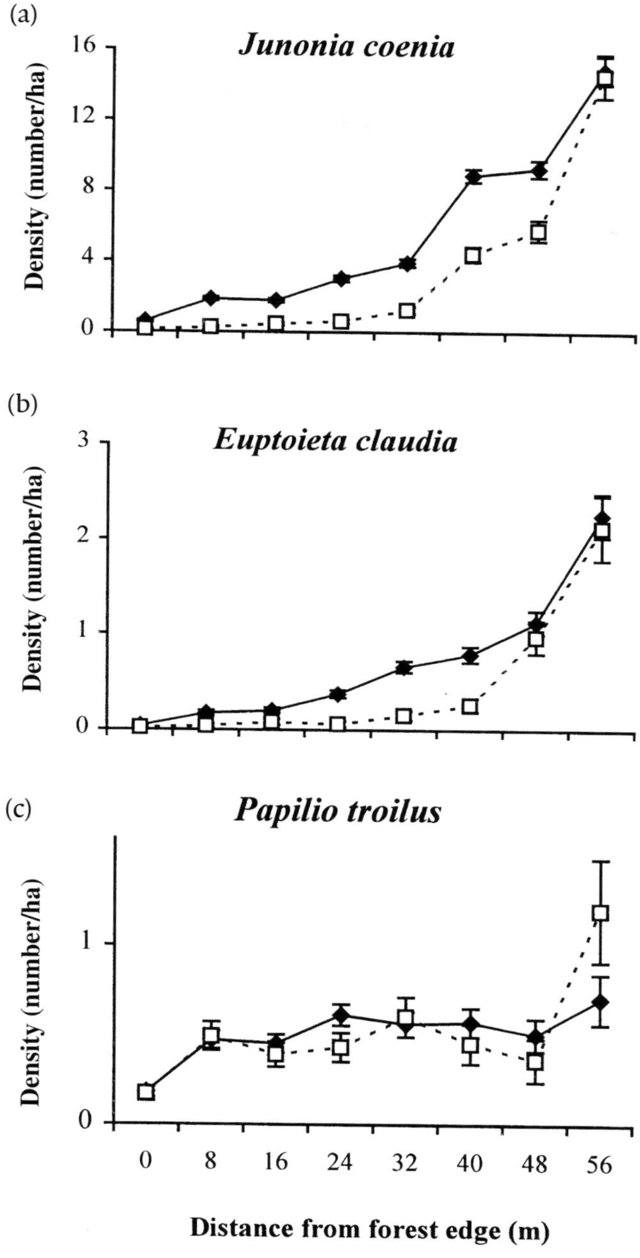

FIGURE 8.5
Densities of three butterfly species at increasing distance from the edge of managed pine forest into open patches. Patches were of equal size and shape, except that some patches were connected by corridors (–♦–) and others were not (---❑---). Two species, *Junonia coenia* and *Euptoieta claudia*, were open-habitat specialists; *Papilio troilus* was a habitat generalist. Modified from Haddad and Baum (1999).

within patches, and thus the effective habitat area within connected patches. Using the effective area model, Haddad and Baum (1999) separated the portions of corridor effects on butterfly densities that could be attributed to the effects of edges. They did this by applying estimates of densities in unconnected patches to areas in connected patches at equal distances from the edge. By using the effective area model and integrating densities over the entire patches, they could then predict butterfly densities in connected patches. They found that effects of corridors in modifying edge habitat accounted for an increase of 18–19% in butterfly densities. However, actual densities increased by 105–122%. Thus, edges explained some, but not all, of the effects of corridors on butterfly densities.

Another potential application of the effective area model could improve predictions about the effects of patch area on population sizes of insect pests. This well-developed literature has ascribed higher pest population sizes in larger patches to smaller edge:area ratios. Because the proportion of edge tends to decrease as patch size increases, the rate of emigration from larger patches should be lower, leading to larger population sizes (Kareiva, 1985; Turchin, 1986; Bach, 1988; Hill *et al.*, 1996). However, the emigration hypothesis does not seem to explain the relationship between patch size and population density in all cases (Haddad and Baum, 1999), and the relationship clearly varies in ways that can be predicted from species-specific edge responses (Bender *et al.*, 1998). Here again, the EAM may be used to provide insight into the mechanisms driving the relationship between patch area and population density.

8.4.2 Edge effects on community organization and biodiversity

As discussed above, early theories of edge effects assumed that edges promoted species diversity, as well as increased abundance of selected species. Recent research has demonstrated that community responses to edges are more complex. While edges often alter community composition, they do not necessarily have positive effects on species diversity (Wilcove *et al.*, 1986; Murcia, 1995; Sisk and Battin, in press). Several studies have demonstrated how effective area approaches can be used to predict community organization in patchy landscapes. Sisk *et al.* (1997) estimated edge responses for the breeding birds of oak, chaparral, and grassland habitats in central, coastal California. On 40 occasions in 1989–91, they surveyed birds along eight 500-m transects running orthogonal to edges between large tracts of these habitats, generating density estimates for each species that were used to characterize responses at different edge types. These data were used in an EAM to predict characteristics of bird communities in smaller oak woodland patches in two landscapes, one where the patches were surrounded by chaparral and another where patches were surrounded by grassland. Computation of predicted abundances followed the procedures described above and illustrated in Fig. 8.4. For each species, the number of individuals expected in each patch in a given landscape was summed, and species were ranked according to their predicted abundance. Sisk *et al.* (1997) demonstrated that the effective area model differentiated between similar patches of oak woodland surrounded by different matrix habitats when predicting the relative abundance of bird species. Predicted abundances for edge-sensitive species for patches surrounded by chaparral differed significantly from predictions for similarly sized patches surround by grassland, and these disparities were driven by the differing responses of many species to the two edge types. Field tests of the predictions showed that the EAM was significantly better at predicting the relative abundance than was a null model that ignored edge responses and generated predictions based on patch area, assuming homogeneous within-patch habitat quality. In this case, knowledge of species-specific edge responses was required to capture fundamental differences between bird assemblages in oak woodland patches surrounded by different habitats

Generation of landscape-scale analyses based on EAM predictions for multiple patches offers an opportunity for comparing the effects of different landscape configurations. Hypothetical landscapes that would emerge from alternative habitat management plans can be compared, and the consequences of environmental change could be tracked through time, as the landscape mosaic shifts due to natural and anthropogenic disturbance and succession. For example, Sisk and Margules (1993) used the EAM to compare the expected results of hypothetical efforts to restore avian habitat in central California. The effects of four alternative restoration plans on three bird species were compared. Results of the exercise suggested that large areas would need to be restored before significant increases in the nesting density of edge-avoiding birds were realized, while more modest efforts would tend to reduce densities of edge exploiters. We have used a similar approach to explore the value of habitat corridors of differing widths for selected species, assuming that corridors must contain suitable habitat for the focal species if they are to effectively connect large, otherwise isolated habitat patches. Fig. 8.6 illustrates the application of the EAM in evaluating the usefulness of corridors of differing widths for two tropical butterfly species. In this example, a corridor width of 50 m would provide ideal habitat for the edge-exploiting *Dione moneta*; however, a width of 250 m or more would be needed to provide high-quality habitat for the edge-avoiding *Mesosemia asa*. While common sense tells us that narrow corridors will favor edge-exploiting species and wider corridors will be needed for edge avoiders, the EAM provides a means of addressing the issue of how wide a

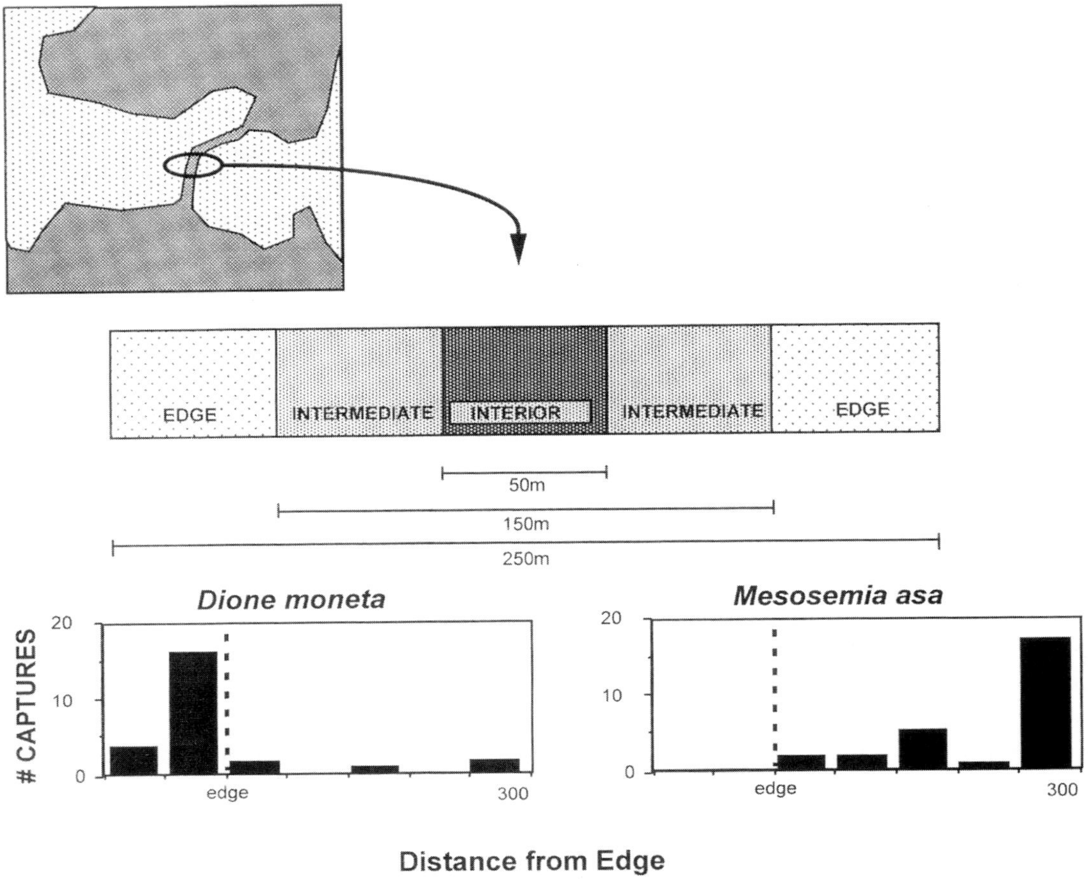

FIGURE 8.6
Application of the effective area model in assessing the effects of corridor width on habitat quality for two neotropical butterflies. Data from southern Costa Rica (H. Sparrow, unpublished data) suggest that for corridors to provide interior forest habitat for the edge-avoiding *Mesosemia asa*, a width of 250 m or more might be required. The edge-exploiting *Dione moneta*, however, would be expected to thrive in corridors as narrow as 50 m or less. The EAM provides a tool for assessing the value of habitat corridors for a wide range of species, based on their responses to habitat edges.

habitat corridor should be for a particular species, and for assessing the relative value of existing or planned corridors for a wide range of species whose sensitivity to edges may vary dramatically. For species that are able to move through corridors that do not provide suitable habitat for extended residence ("movement corridors"), behavioral models may be linked with the EAM to evaluate the edge effects on corridor effectiveness (see below).

8.4.3 Edge effects on ecosystem functioning

Few studies have addressed the effects of edges on ecosystem processes. Edges are likely to influence the physical transport of nutrients and other resources, the local light environment, photosynthetic rates, and many other variables and processes. Recent studies have begun to assess the complex effects of edges on microclimatic conditions and physical processes that influence the distribution, abundance, and productivity of plants and animals (Camargo and Kapos, 1995; Chen *et al.*, 1995; Williams-Linera *et al.*, 1998). These studies provide a tractable approach for linking edge effects on resources to their influence on ecosystems.

Laurance *et al.* (1997, 1998) have provided a powerful example of how edge effects can have catastrophic effects on ecosystems. In a landscape-scale experiment in tropical forest, they showed that forest fragmentation could lead to a collapse of biomass in the resulting small patches. They reported that fragmentation increased rates of damage, mortality, and turnover of trees in forest fragments, affecting community composition and structure. The effects on tree communities were evident at 60–100 m from the forest edge, with some evidence of effects penetrating up to 300 m. While there was little change in forest productivity at distances greater than 100 m from the edge, habitat near the edge lost an average of 3.5 tonnes biomass/ha/yr. They assert that the mechanism causing biomass decline is wind disturbance near the edge.

Using a non-spatial core-area model that draws upon empirical edge responses and an index for the shape complexity of a given patch (Laurance, 1991), Laurance and colleagues (1998) demonstrated that edges are likely to have dramatic effects on forest community structure in fragments that fall below 400 ha in area. In areas where specific reserve designs are being contemplated, their ecosystem edge response data might be used in an effective area model, given appropriate habitat maps, to assess expected biomass loss under alternative reserve designs, accounting for the number, shape, and configuration of forest patches to be retained in the landscape.

8.4.4 Edge permeability and animal behaviors: Promising applications of the EAM

Animal behaviors provide a direct, mechanistic link to population distributions, and an effective area approach may provide a useful tool for predicting the landscape-level effects of habitat fragmentation on population dynamics. For behaviors to be successfully incorporated into an effective area approach, two types of behavioral information are needed: (1) an estimate of edge permeability, or the degree to which edges form barriers to movement, and (2) the distance at which edges influence behavior.

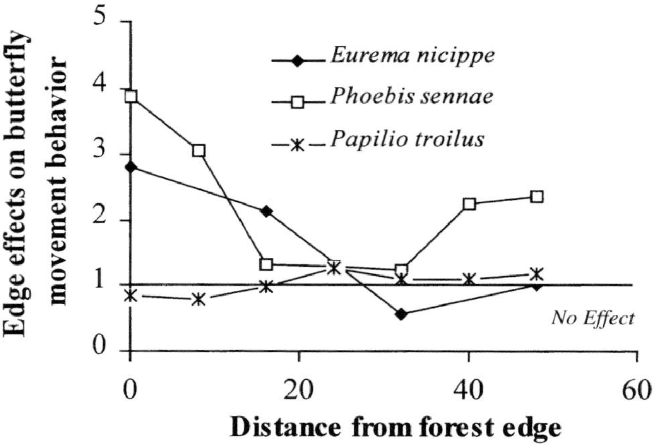

FIGURE 8.7
Effects of edges on movement behavior at increasing distances from the edge between pine forests and open patches. The *y*-axis is an index of edge permeability. A value of 1 indicates no effect of edges on movement behavior, while values higher than 1 denote an influence of edges on movement, with higher numbers indicating decreasing permeability (values less than 1 indicate a higher than random propensity to cross the edge). Two species, *Eurema nicippe* and *Phoebis sennae*, were open-habitat specialists. The third species, *Papilio troilus*, was a habitat generalist that was unaffected by edges. Modified from Haddad (1999b).

The permeability of edges influences the ability of animals or resources to cross into other habitats. To dispersing animals, edges may fall on a continuum between totally transparent and totally impenetrable. Importantly, the same edge may vary in permeability for different animal species. Haddad (1999a) showed that forest boundaries were less permeable to open-habitat specialist butterflies, but transparent to a generalist butterfly species (Fig. 8.7). In addition, edges between different habitats may vary in their permeability to any particular species. Ries and Debinski (2001) studied behaviors of butterflies at boundaries between prairie and various matrix habitats. Only one boundary, between prairie and forest, was a strong barrier to the dispersal of the monarch, *Danaus plexippus*. Boundaries with pasture, cropland, or non-prairie grassland did not have a strong influence on *D. plexippus* movement. However, all boundaries, even between structurally similar habitats such as prairie and non-prairie grassland, were barriers to movement by a prairie specialist butterfly, the regal fritillary (*Speyeria idalia*). Boundaries may influence animal behaviors or resource distributions, even at some distance from the actual edge. Haddad (1999b) showed that edges might create barriers that influence butterfly movement at up to 16 m from the edge (Fig. 8.7; see also Ries and Debinski, 2001). It is because animal behaviors may vary with distance from the edge that the effective area approach provides new and useful insights into the consequences of habitat fragmentation for animal behaviors and population densities.

Data on edge permeability and on the distance at which edges influence animal behavior could be incorporated into effective area models to predict population responses to habitat fragmentation in two stages. First, a model could be developed to simulate movement paths and population redistribution. Behavioral data could be incorporated into simulations of a correlated random walk (such an approach has been described by Haddad [1999b]) or some other simple movement model that can be used to predict population redistribution. To more realistically model the effects of habitat boundaries on movement behaviors, boundaries could influence edge permeability and turning behavior at empirically estimated distances from habitat edges. After running the model and allowing the population to redistribute itself, the effective area model could be employed, as described above, to estimate population sizes within habitat fragments. The advantage of this approach is that it allows population densities to be predicted from the mechanisms of animal behavior in complex, fragmented landscapes. In a related approach in relatively simple landscapes, Turchin (1991) incorporated behaviors at edges into analytical models that predicted population sizes.

Understanding the strength and magnitude of edge effects on behaviors may have particularly strong implications for the effectiveness of movement corridors. Corridors will most effectively promote movement of species for which boundaries are impermeable (Haddad, 1999b). In addition, the most effective width for a movement corridor is likely to be a function of the distance at which edges influence behaviors or population sizes (Figs. 8.5, 8.7). Empirical (Andraesson *et al.*, 1996) and theoretical (Tischendorf and Wissel, 1997; Haddad, 1999a) studies have shown that corridor effects on movement rates initially increase as corridor width increases, but then level off. The distance at which corridor effects on movement level off is likely to correspond to the distance at which edges influence behaviors (Haddad, 1999b). Again, the effective area approach may provide useful new insights into the effectiveness of corridors at increasing movement rates in fragmented landscapes.

8.5 Lessons and challenges

The approaches to modeling edge effects presented in this chapter are not a panacea for habitat managers faced with cross-boundary issues. They do, however, provide an approach and some examples of how our growing body of information about specific edge effects might be incorporated into a common framework that can help inform management decisions. At the same time, our examination of case studies has identified significant limitations of current approaches to effective area modeling. In the following section we present some of the key lessons learned in our attempts to develop spatial modeling approaches that incorporate edge effects, and we identify several problem areas that we believe offer exciting opportunities for future research.

8.5.1 Lessons

Lesson 1 Edges influence ecological processes at different levels of ecological organization in fragmented landscapes, from populations, communities, and ecosystems, to animal behavior. While we may be able to predict effects at a given level, interactions among levels may increase the complexity of responses. In a thought-provoking review, Fagan *et al.* (1999) identified four classes of edge effects on species interactions: Effects on behaviors, on mortality, on feeding or reproductive subsidies, and on the creation of unique habitats. Because edges bring together new assemblages of species, they affect ecological interactions near management boundaries, and edge responses may be affected. Consideration of multiple species, especially those thought to influence the focal species, will better inform cross-boundary management.

Lesson 2 Using diversity indices to quantify edge effects is seldom good enough; more important are shifts in species composition and relative abundance caused by edges. Early edge studies quantified the effects of edges on species diversity and found, in general, higher levels of diversity at the edge. In hindsight, the emphasis on the number of species was misplaced. Edges have enormous effects on which species are present and how abundant they are. Since the species found at edges are often invasive species that may have detrimental effects on edge-avoiding species of management concern, the ability to assess the effects of edge on specific species is of greater relevance to managers.

Lesson 3 Models based on simple classifications of edge and interior species are less robust than those employing species-specific edge responses. Because of simplifying assumptions about the distance that edge effects penetrate, and about the generality of edge effects across taxa, these approaches are less useful for predicting population or community responses to fragmentation. Understanding the landscape-level importance of habitat edges requires an understanding of species-specific responses to particular edge types. However, this requirement introduces a potentially crippling need for detailed empirical data (see below).

Lesson 4 Effective area models, drawing on empirical data on edge responses and digital habitat maps, permit spatially explicit predictions of how landscape pattern impacts behavior, population size, community organization, and ecosystem function. The approach also allows managers to compare the predicted outcomes from alternative management actions, perhaps the most useful aspect of the EAM in cross-boundary management.

8.5.2 Challenges

Challenge 1 Methods for efficiently obtaining sufficient data for appropriate use of the EAM. Demands for input data may be daunting, especially when multiple species are modeled in heterogeneous landscapes. What are the most efficient methods for estimating edge responses with sufficient precision to generate helpful predictions? How consistent are edge responses from place to place? Reviews of the literature, combined with incisive new field studies, should identify more efficient approaches for characterizing edge responses.

Challenge 2 Predicting edge responses from life-history, behavioral, or taxonomic data. Many different mechanisms lead to edge effects, and each of those mechanisms influences many different species. Neither ecologists nor managers will be able to measure the edge responses of every species at each type of edge in a landscape. Thus, general rules are needed to allow the prediction of edge responses for many poorly studied species. Species' edge responses are likely to be related to aspects of life history, demography, and/or behavior. Identification of the relationships between these factors and observed edge responses may allow managers to associate species and edge responses without extensive collection of new field data. This would greatly simplify the application of the effective area model to landscapes that have not been the focus of previous research efforts.

Challenge 3 Identifying the mechanisms that cause edge effects. Since the edge concept was recognized in the 1930s, hundreds of studies of edge effects have been conducted. Only recently have reviews begun to synthesize these studies to identify mechanisms that cause edge effects (Fagan *et al.*, 1999; Sisk and Battin, in press), and the impact of edges on populations and communities (Bender *et al.*, 1998). Future work must identify under what circumstances, and for which species, the various mechanisms causing edge effects are likely to be important.

Challenge 4 Application of effective area modeling requires detailed habitat maps. Current efforts often utilize vegetation maps and infer habitat quality from floristic composition. Other factors, including vegetation structure, slope, and exposure, among many others, may also influence habitat quality in subtle ways. Finding cost-efficient methods for developing habitat maps that capture variability among patches and classify habitat types appropriately is an important challenge, not only for this modeling approach, but for all efforts to develop spatially explicit models that support natural resource management.

Challenge 5 Extending the effective area model to predict the landscape level responses of animal and plant distributions, community composition, and ecosystems functioning to landscape change. Most studies have focused on population size or abundance, or on the interactions between species, especially predators and their prey. A major challenge of edge studies is to scale up from species-specific responses to predict effects on community assembly and ecosystem functioning.

8.6 Summary

Wherever management boundaries are established, differences in type and quality of habitats is likely to occur. Habitat edges are increasingly common components of all landscapes, but they are particularly important in managed and highly impacted landscapes, where human activities add to landscape heterogeneity and dramatically increase the amount of edge. The term "edge effects" has a long history in ecology and wildlife management, but it remains an enigmatic concept that too often is used to explain away a wide range of complex patterns and trends in animal behavior, distribution, and abundance.

Approaches for dealing with the often-pervasive influences of habitat edges in resource management have advanced in recent years, and tools for quantitative assessment of edge effects have been tested on diverse animal taxa in a wide range of terrestrial habitats. The effective area model builds on earlier non-spatial models to provide a flexible environment for exploring the implications of different types of edge effects on a wide range of species. By weighting different areas of habitat patches, based on their distance from the patch edge and the sensitivity of the focal species to the influences of the adjoining habitats, wildlife managers can estimate the expected impacts of alternative management decisions on species of particular interest, as well as on the co-occurring species that might influence their distribution, abundance, and persistence in the focal landscape. Early trials indicate that the EAM is an improvement over landscape models that deal with patch area alone, ignoring edge effects.

Potential applications of the EAM concept are many, ranging from considering the implications of animal behavior on population size to predicting changes in ecosystem processes following habitat fragmentation. Case studies suggest that a better understanding of the mechanisms underlying edge responses, along with more efficient approaches for identifying the nature of these responses in poorly studied species and novel landscapes, will greatly extend the applicability of effective area models in management contexts.

Acknowledgments

We thank our many colleagues in Guatemala, especially Claudio Méndez, Enio Cano, Victor Orellana, and Gustavo Orellana; in Costa Rica, especially Luis Diego Gómez, Roig Mora, Phil DeVries, Helen Sparrow, and Jim Zook; and in the USA, especially James Battin, Robert Cheney, Gretchen Daily, Paul Ehrlich, Cecilia Meyer, Barry Noon, and Leslie Ries. We also thank three anonymous reviewers whose comments greatly improved the chapter. This work was supported by the Strategic Environmental Research and Development Program (SERDP project CS-1100), the U.S.D.A. Forest Service, Savannah River, the MacArthur Foundation, and the Center for Conservation Biology, Stanford University.

References

Andraesson, H. P., Halle, S. & Ims, R. A. (1996). Optimal width of movement corridors for root voles: Not too narrow and not too wide. *Journal of Applied Ecology*, 33: 63–70.

Avery, T. E. & Berlin, G. L. (1992). *Fundamentals of Remote Sensing and Airphoto Interpretation*, 5th edn. Prentice Hall, Upper Saddle River, NJ.

Bach, C. E. (1988). Effects of host plant patch size on herbivore densities: Patterns. *Ecology*, 69: 1090–1102.

Bender, D. J., Contreras, T. A. & Fahrig, L. (1998). Habitat loss and population decline: A meta-analysis of the patch size effect. *Ecology*, 79: 517–533.

Brand, L. A. & George, T. L. (2001). Response of birds to edges in redwood forest fragments. *Auk*, 118: 678–686.

Brittingham, M. C. & Temple, S. A. (1983). Have cowbirds caused forest songbirds to decline? *BioScience*, 33: 31–35.

Burgess, R. L. & Sharpe, D. M. (eds.) (1981). *Forest Island Dynamics in Man-Dominated Landscapes*. Springer-Verlag, New York.

Camargo, J. L. C. & Kapos, V. (1995). Complex edge effects on soil moisture and microclimate in central Amazonian forest. *Journal of Tropical Ecology*, 11: 205–221.

Chen, J., Franklin, J. F. & Spies, T. A. (1993). Contrasting microclimates among clearcut, edge, and interior of old-growth Douglas-fir forest. *Agricultural and Forest Meteorology*, 63: 219–237.

Chen, J., Franklin, J. E. & Spies, T. A. (1995). Growing-season microclimatic gradients from clearcut edges into old-growth Douglas-fir forests. *Ecological Applications*, 5: 74–86.

Chen, J., Saunders, S. C., Crow, T. R., Naiman, R. H., Brosofske, D. D., Mroz, G. D., Brokshire, B. L. & Franklin, J. F. (1999). Microclimate in forest ecosystem and landscape ecology. *BioScience*, 49: 288–297.

Dasmann, R. (1981). *Wildlife Biology*. John Wiley, New York.

Dunning, J. B., Jr., Stewart, D. J., Danielson, B. J., Noon, B. R., Root, T. L., Lamberson, R. H. & Stevens, E. E. (1995). Spatially explicit population models: Current forms and future uses. *Ecological Applications*, 5: 3–11.

Fagan, W. F., Cantrell, R. S. & Cosner, C. (1999). How habitat edges change species interactions. *American Naturalist*, 153: 165–182.

Forman, R. T. T. & Godron, M. (1981). Patches and structural components for a landscape ecology. *BioScience*, 31: 733–740.

Forman, R. T. T. & Godron, M. (1988). *Landscape Ecology*. John Wiley, New York.

Forman, R. T. T., Galli, A. E. & Leck, C. F. (1976). Forest size and avian diversity in New Jersey woodlots with some land use implications. *Oecologia*, 26: 1–8.

Giles, R. H. (ed.) (1971). *Wildlife Management Techniques*. The Wildlife Society, Washington, D.C.

Giles, R. H. (1978). *Wildlife Management*. W. H. Freeman, San Francisco, CA.

Haddad, N. M. (1999a). Corridor and distance effects on interpatch movements: A landscape experiment with butterflies. *Ecological Applications*, 9: 612–622.

Haddad, N. M. (1999b). Corridor use predicted from behaviors at habitat boundaries. *American Naturalist*, 153: 215–227.

Haddad, N. M. & Baum, K. A. (1999). An experimental test of corridor effects on butterfly densities. *Ecological Applications*, 9: 623–633.

Harris, L. D. (1984). *The Fragmented Forest*. University of Chicago Press, Chicago, IL.

Hill, J. K., Thomas, C. D., & Lewis, O. T. (1996). Effects of habitat patch size and isolation on dispersal of *Hesperia comma* butterflies: Implications for metapopulation structure. *Journal of Animal Ecology*, 65: 725–735.

Imhoff, M. L. & Sisk, T. D. (1997). Remotely sensed indicators of habitat heterogeneity and effects on biological diversity. *Remote Sensing of the Environment*, 60: 217–227.

James, F. C. & Wamer, N. O. (1982). Relationships between temperate forest bird communities and vegetation structure. *Ecology*, 63: 159–171.

Johnston, D. W. & Odum, E. P. (1956). Breeding bird populations in relation to plant succession on the piedmont of Georgia. *Ecology*, 37: 50–62.

Johnston, V. R. (1947). Breeding birds of the forest edge in Illinois. *Condor*, 49: 45–52.

Kareiva, P. (1985). Finding and losing host plants by *Phyllotreta*: Patch size and surrounding habitat. *Ecology*, 66: 1809–1816.

Kroodsma, R. L. (1982). Edge effect on breeding forest birds along a powerline corridor. *Journal of Applied Ecology*, 19: 361–370.

Laurance, W. F. (1991). Edge effects in tropical forest fragments: Application of a model for the design of nature reserves. *Biological Conservation*, 57: 205–219.

Laurance, W. F. & Yensen, E. (1991). Predicting the impacts of edge effects in fragmented habitats. *Biological Conservation*, 55: 77–97.

Laurance, W. F., Laurance, S. G., Ferreira, L. V., Rankin-De Merona, J. M., Gascon, C. & Lovejoy, T. E. (1997). Biomass collapse in Amazonian forest fragments. *Science* 278: 1117–1118.

Laurance, W. F., Ferreira, L. V., Rankin-De Merona, J. M. & Laurance, S. G. (1998). Rain forest fragmentation and the dynamics of Amazonian tree communities. *Ecology*, 79: 2032–2040.

Lay, D. W. (1938). How valuable are woodland clearings to birdlife? *Wilson Bulletin*, 50: 254–256.

Leopold, A. (1933). *Game Management*. John Wiley, New York.

MacArthur, R. H., MacArthur, J. W. & Preer, J. (1962). On bird species diversity. *American Naturalist*, 46: 167–174.

Malcolm, J. R. (1994). Edge effects in central Amazonian forest fragments. *Ecology*, 75: 2438–2445.

Matlack, G. R. (1993). Microenvironment variation within and among forest edge sites in the eastern United States. *Biological Conservation*, 66: 185–194.

Murcia, C. (1995). Edge effects in fragmented forests: Implications for conservation. *Trends in Ecology and Evolution*, 10: 58–62.

Noon, B. R. & McKelvey, K. S. (1996). Management of the spotted owl: A case history in conservation biology. *Annual Reviews in Ecology and Systematics*, 27: 135–162.

Noss, R. F. (1991). Effects of edge and internal patchiness on avian habitat use in an old-growth Florida hammock. *Natural Areas Journal*, 11: 34–47.

Odum, E. P. (1958). *Fundamentals of Ecology*, 3rd edn. W. B. Saunders, Philadelphia, PA.

O'Neill, R. V., Krummel, J. R., Gardner, R. H., Sugihara, G., Jackson, B., DeAngelis, D. L., Milne, B. T., Turner, M. G., Zygmunt, B., Christensen, S. W., Dale, V. H. & Graham, R. L. (1988). Indices of landscape pattern. *Landscape Ecology*, 1: 153–162.

Ranney, J. W., Bruner, M. C. & Levinson, J. B. (1981). The importance of edge in the structure and dynamics of forest islands. In *Forest Island Dynamics in Man-Dominated Landscapes*, eds. R. L. Burgess & D. M. Sharpe, pp. 67–96. Springer-Verlag, New York.

Remer, L. C. & Heard, S. G. (1998). Local movement and edge effects on competition and coexistance in ephemeral-patch models. *American Naturalist*, 152: 896–904.

Ries, L. & Debinski, D. M. (2001). Butterfly responses to habitat edges in the highly fragmented prairies of Central Iowa. *Journal of Animal Ecology*, 70: 840–852.

Ripple, W. J., Bradshaw, G. A. & Spies, T. A. (1991). Measuring forest landscape patterns in the Cascade Range of Oregon, USA. *Biological Conservation*, 57: 73–88.

Robinson, S. K., Thompson, F. R. III, Donovon, T. M., Whitehead, D. R. & Faaborg, J. (1995).

Regional forest fragmentation and the nesting success of migratory birds. *Science*, 267: 1987–1990.
Sisk, T. D. (1992). Distributions of birds and butterflies in heterogeneous landscapes. PhD dissertation, Stanford University, Stanford, CA.
Sisk, T. D. & Battin, J. (in press) Understanding the influence of habitat edges on avian ecology: Geographic patterns and insights for western landscapes. *Studies in Avian Biology*.
Sisk, T. D. & Margules, C. R. (1993). Habitat edges and restoration: Methods for quantifying edge effects and predicting the results of restoration efforts. In *Nature Conservation* vol. 3, *Reconstruction of Fragmented Ecosystems*, eds. D. A. Saunders, R. J. Hobbs & P. R. Ehrlich, pp. 57–69. Surrey Beatty, Chipping Norton, NSW.
Sisk, T. D. & Zook, J. (1996). La influencia de la composición del paisaje en la distribución de *Catharus ustulatus* en migración por Costa Rica. *Vida Silvestre Neotropical*, 5: 120–125.
Sisk, T. D., Haddad, N. M. & Ehrlich, P. R. (1997). Bird assemblages in patchy woodlands: modeling the effects of edge and matrix habitats. *Ecological Applications*, 7: 1170–1180.
Stamps, J. A., Buechner, M. & Krishnan, V. V. (1987). The effects of edge permeability and habitat geometry on emigration from patches of habitat. *American Naturalist*, 129: 533–552.
Temple, S. A. (1986). Predicting impacts of habitat fragmentation on forest birds: A comparison of two models. In *Wildlife 2000: Modeling Habitat Relationships of Terrestrial Vertebrates*, eds. J. Verner, M. L. Morrison & C. J. Ralph, pp. 301–304. University of Wisconsin Press, Madison, WI.
Temple, S. A. & Cary, J. R. (1988). Modeling dynamics of habitat-interior bird populations in fragmented landscapes. *Conservation Biology*, 2: 340–347.
Terborgh, J. (1976). Island biogeography and conservation: Strategy and limitations. *Science*, 193: 1029–1030.
Thompson, F. R., III (1993). Simulated responses of a forest-interior bird population to forest management options in central hardwood forests of the United States. *Conservation Biology*, 7: 325–333.
Tischendorf, L. & Wissel, C. (1997). Corridors as conduits for small animals: Attainable distances depending on movement pattern, boundary reaction, and corridor width. *Oikos*, 79: 603–611.
Turchin, P. B. (1986). Modelling the effect of host patch size on Mexican bean beetle emigration. *Ecology*, 67: 124–132.
Turchin, P. B. (1991). Translating foraging movements in heterogeneous environments in the spatial distribution of foragers. *Ecology*, 72: 1253–1266.
Turner, M. G. & R. H. Gardner (eds.) (1991). *Quantitative Methods in Landscape Ecology*. Springer-Verlag, New York.
Van Horne, B. (1983). Density as a misleading indicator of habitat quality. *Journal of Wildlife Management*, 7: 893–901.
Wahlberg, N., Moilanen, A. & Hanski, I. (1996). Predicting the occurrence of endangered species in fragmented landscapes. *Science*, 273: 1536–1538.
Whitcomb, R. F., Robbins, C. S., Lynch, J. F., Whitcomb, B. L., Klimkiewicz, M. K. & Bystrak, D. (1981). Effects of forest fragmentation on avifauna of the eastern deciduous forest. In *Forest Island Dynamics in Man-Dominated Landscapes*, eds. R. L. Burgess & B. M. Sharpe, pp. 125–206. Springer-Verlag, New York.
Wiens, J. A. (1989). Spatial scaling in ecology. *Functional Ecology*, 3: 385–397.
Wiens, J. A., Crawford, C. S., & Gosz, J. R. (1985). Boundary dynamics: A conceptual framework for studying landscape ecosystems. *Oikos*, 45: 421–427.
Wilcove, D. S. (1985). Nest predation in forest tracts and the decline of migratory songbirds. *Ecology*, 66: 1211–1214.
Wilcove, D. S., McLellan, C. J. & Dobson, A. P. (1986). Habitat fragmentation in the temperate zone. In *Conservation Biology: The Science of Scarcity and Diversity*, ed. M. E. Soulé, pp. 237–256. Sinauer Associates, Sunderland, MA.
Wilkie, D. S. & Finn, J. T. (1996). *Remote Sensing Imagery for Natural Resources Monitoring*. Columbia University Press, New York.
Williams-Linera, G., DomRiguez-Gasted, V. & Garca-Zurita, M. E. (1998).

Microenvironment and floristics of different edges in fragmented tropical rainforest. *Conservation Biology*, 12: 1091–1102.

Willson, M. F. (1974). Avian community organization and habitat structure. *Ecology*, 55: 1017–1029.

Withers, M. A. & Meentemeyer, V. (1999). Concepts of scale in landscape ecology. In *Landscape Ecology Analysis: Issues and applications*, eds. J. M. Klobatek & R. H. Gardner, pp. 205–252. Springer-Verlag, New York.

Young, A. & Mitchell, N. (1994). Microclimate and vegetation edge effects in a fragmented podocarp–broadleaf forest in New Zealand. *Biological Conservation*, 67: 63–72.

REBECCA L. SCHNEIDER, EDWARD L. MILLS AND DANIEL C. JOSEPHSON

9

Aquatic–terrestrial linkages and implications for landscape management

9.1 Introduction

Historically, ponds and lakes were viewed as isolated systems, separate from their surrounding landscapes. Although a stream was recognized as a network interweaving the countryside, its border with the surrounding land was often overlooked. The interface between aquatic and terrestrial habitats was viewed as the strongest of boundaries. Indeed, the visible integrity of ponds and lakes was used as the primary justification for early definitions of "ecosystems" as largely self-contained (Odum, 1971). Several decades later, the relationship between aquatic and terrestrial landscape elements is viewed quite differently. The terrestrial habitat is integrally connected to lotic and lentic systems and provides resources that are essential to their health. The aquatic–terrestrial interface itself is recognized as a porous filter that allows a flow of organisms, water, and matter in both directions. This interface is often a special habitat with its own unique flora and fauna that contribute significantly to the functioning of the surrounding landscape.

The management of the linked aquatic–terrestrial landscape incorporates two primary topics in landscape ecology (Forman, 1995). The first topic centers on the flow of organisms across the aquatic–terrestrial boundary and among different aquatic habitat patches throughout the landscape. The second topic addresses the physical flow of water and matter as a key process linking land and water systems. Flowing water transports substances by both aboveground and belowground pathways across the interface and significantly affects the quality and health of the downstream, receiving system. Sustainability and successful management of wildlife, fisheries, and other natural resources are dependent on the integration of these subject areas.

In this chapter, we summarize our current understanding of land and water as highly interconnected landscape elements and the intervening aquatic–terrestrial interface as a permeable membrane. We also provide recommendations for an integrated management approach to protect land–water ecosystems at the landscape scale.

9.2 Overview of cross-boundary interactions

9.2.1 Organism movements

The early focus on wildlife in a landscape context emphasized individual species and the size of their home ranges. Biologists quickly realized that wildlife species rarely rely on just one habitat or ecosystem type. Instead, different species incorporate a complex selection of habitats in their life histories and move amongst these in response to different factors. Life stage is one factor that can necessitate a movement among landscape components. Increasing age and size generally are associated with a shift in an organism's requirements concerning food resources, space, reproduction, and protection from predators. These ontogenetic niche shifts (Werner and Gilliam, 1984) result in a flow of organisms from one habitat to another. Superimposed on these genetic and physiologic constraints are seasonal and interannual changes in the environment which impact the availability of the required resources and also can cause a flow of organisms across the landscape. Sustainable management of wildlife species requires protection of the entire spectrum of habitat patches that are needed throughout their life cycles, as well as the intervening corridors that connect the patches.

A considerable number of organisms, including birds, amphibians, reptiles, and invertebrates, require both aquatic and terrestrial habitats to successfully complete their life-history stages. This results in a significant flow of organisms across the aquatic–terrestrial boundary and among the different landscape elements. A key feature common to many wildlife species is the temporal nature of their movements. Movement is rarely continuous; instead, large numbers of organisms often move from land to water, or in reverse, in relatively short, specific time periods. An impressive demonstration of such heightened activity occurs each spring, when thousands of frogs and salamanders move into a given pond during just a few rainy nights in preparation for breeding (Pechmann and Semlitsch, 1986).

Organism flow across the landscape can occur at different spatial scales and encompass habitat patches located at increasing distances away from the water's edge. The destination habitats can be divided into: uplands, wetlands, and disconnected aquatic habitat patches.

Movements between aquatic and upland habitats

The most striking examples of organisms exhibiting cross-boundary movement are those that include both aquatic and terrestrial habitats in their life cycles. Obvious examples are the diverse communities of herons and other wading birds who forage daily in ponds and marshes, but also need the nearby pine trees of the forest edge or grasslands for roosting and nesting. Less apparent are amphibians and reptiles of ponds, streams, and lakes. Amphibians such as adult salamanders and frogs are a major contributor to biomass of northeastern forests (Burton and Likens, 1975) and to both biomass and species diversity of ponds in the Southeast of the United States (Semlitsch and Bodie, 1998). They consume incredible quantities of zooplankton (Taylor *et al.*, 1988) and their eggs and young are, in turn, key food items for birds, fish, raccoons, and other predators. Amazingly, these so-called "aquatic organisms" can move hundreds of meters from the nearest source of water into the surrounding upland habitats (Semlitsch, 1998).

Amphibians and some reptiles incorporate both aquatic and adjacent upland habitats into their life cycles at different times. Most aquatic turtles and water snakes spend much of their adult life in water. However, they must return to land to lay eggs. Their eggs have a solid but flexible outer shell that allows a flow of gases into and out of the eggs. Female turtles dig their nests in sand or gravel well above the water line in order to ensure that their eggs are oxygenated and well drained throughout incubation. In a study by Burke and Gibbons (1995) of one southeastern pond, 90% of the mud turtles (*Kinosternon subrubrum*), Florida cooters (*Pseudemys floridana*), and slider turtles (*Trachemys scripta*) were found to move more than 70 m into the uplands from the pond edge for nesting and hibernation. A buffer of approximately 275 m would be necessary to encompass 100% of the turtles' seasonal habitat requirements.

Aquatic–terrestrial habitat use is reversed for many salamanders and frogs in the eastern United States. In early spring, adult salamanders lay their eggs in water, attached to plant stems or free-floating in the water. Upon hatching, the juveniles are adapted for an aquatic lifestyle with tails and sometimes gills. The juveniles remain in the pond for four to six months feeding on zooplankton, algae, and aquatic invertebrates (Scott, 1990). Upon metamorphosis to adults, many species leave water and migrate to the surrounding uplands. There they live several centimeters underground, beneath leaf litter and in underground tunnels for three months up to three years, before returning for a few short weeks to breed in nearby ponds and marshes. A review of salamander migration patterns from the eastern United States indicated that, on average, salamanders are found 125 ± 73 m from the water's edge with some salamanders located as far as 625 m from the edge of wetlands (Semlitsch, 1998).

Movements between aquatic and wetland habitats

Many aquatic organisms depend on nearby wetland resources to satisfy certain life-stage requirements. Aquatic insects feed on the abundant living and decaying plant matter in wetlands (Smock, 1994). Plant stems and roots provide food, nest material, and cover for marsh birds and waterfowl. Fish use the dense forest of submerged stems in shoreline marshes for food and protective nursery habitats (Kwak, 1988). However, wetlands are one of the most dynamic components of the landscape. Their size and precise boundaries expand and contract with time depending on the amount of flooding that occurs from the adjacent stream or lake (Junk *et al.*, 1989).

The St. Lawrence River is a major North American river which drains the Laurentian Great Lakes. Studies by Farrell (2001) on this river provide an excellent illustration of how aquatic organisms shift their use of the landscape to take advantage of wetland resources. Northern pike (*Esox lucius*) and muskellunge (*E. masquinongy*) are important piscivores in the St. Lawrence River. Historically, northern pike have shifted their habitat preference from the main stem river to the flooded habitats of tributaries and marsh wetland areas for spawning in early spring. In contrast, muskellunge typically spawn later in spring in permanently submersed shallow-water areas of the river (Scott and Crossman, 1973; Farrell *et al.*, 1996), but also are known to use seasonally flooded habitats (Dombeck *et al.*, 1986). Both species use littoral areas and coastal wetlands prior to emigration to the main river.

Over the past several decades, shoreline development has severely reduced wetland habitat in Lake Ontario and the St. Lawrence River (Geis and Kee, 1977; Whillans, 1982). In addition to habitat loss, water-level fluctuations have been compressed relative to their historical range in the St. Lawrence River since completion of the St. Lawrence Seaway and power project in 1959. In effect, the Seaway reduced annual water-level fluctuations in order to maximize year-round hydroelectric power generation. Consequently, the duration of springtime floods was reduced, and seasonally flooded habitats were not always accessible to spawning fish like northern pike.

The indirect impact of such water-level management was the development of dense stands of plant communities dominated by cattail, *Typha* spp. (Geis and Kee, 1977) which is poor habitat for spawning northern pike (Franklin and Smith, 1963). Coincident with the spring disconnect between the main stem of the river and adjacent wetland habitat has been a dramatic decline in northern pike abundance (McCullough and Klindt, 1997) and reproductive success (Farrell, 2001). A recent study by Farrell (2001) has shown that most northern pike are now forced to shift their preferred, early spring spawning habitat in the flooded, warmer marshes to colder deep littoral habitats of the river in late spring, with the result that reproductive success is severely impacted. Muskellunge, on the other hand, spawn late spring to early summer when vegetation density increases in the nearshore area. Even though northern pike deposit 20 to 80 times more eggs than muskellunge, pike survival is significantly lower than that of muskellunge. Muskellunge appear to have been unaffected by the more stable water levels, and presumably have benefited from reductions in their principal competitor, the northern pike. Clearly, the northern pike–muskellunge scenario exemplifies how the linkage between the floodplain and the main stem of the river can have very significant impacts on biological communities.

Movement among aquatic habitat patches

There is growing recognition that the long-term sustainability of many aquatic-based wildlife species depends on having more than one pond or lake present in a terrestrial landscape. There can actually be an assemblage of local populations, or a metapopulation, which inhabits a network of ponds or lakes and is linked by dispersal. This complex of aquatic patches allows the metapopulation to expand and shrink over time, provides a reservoir for population overflow during good years, and provides refuges during low resources or high predation. These metapopulations change in their use of the landscape as food resources, climate conditions, predators or other factors in their environment encourage population growth or mortality within any given patch. Most studies on metapopulation dynamics are model-based. However limited field studies with turtles (Morreale et al., 1984; Scribner et al., 1986), frogs (Driscoll, 1998), and other amphibians (Gibbs, 1993) indicate the organisms' reliance on multiple habitat patches for their long-term existence. Their use of a patch complex is very different, however, as freshwater turtles may move from 2 to 5 km among lakes, while certain frog species move only tens of meters.

Interestingly, a key aspect of aquatic interpatch movements concerns the breakdown of terrestrial barriers among formerly isolated aquatic systems. Under natural conditions, watershed boundaries provide strong isolation for one river channel network and its resident organisms from even closely neighboring systems. Historically this isolation provided opportunities for the development of different community assemblages and endemic species. With increasing rapidity, humans have destroyed the protective isolation of watershed boundaries by deliberately or unintentionally transporting native and exotic organisms overland from one system to another. Fish, invertebrates, and plants are transported either involuntarily, in bait buckets and attached to boat hulls and propellers, or deliberately when fish introductions have been viewed as a boon to recreational fishing. These overland linkages have had severe impacts on the community composition and diversity of our aquatic systems (Mills *et al*, 1993).

Barriers among isolated water systems have also been broken down through the extensive development of canals. North America's Great Lakes' basin provides an excellent example of how canals dissolved natural barriers, connected

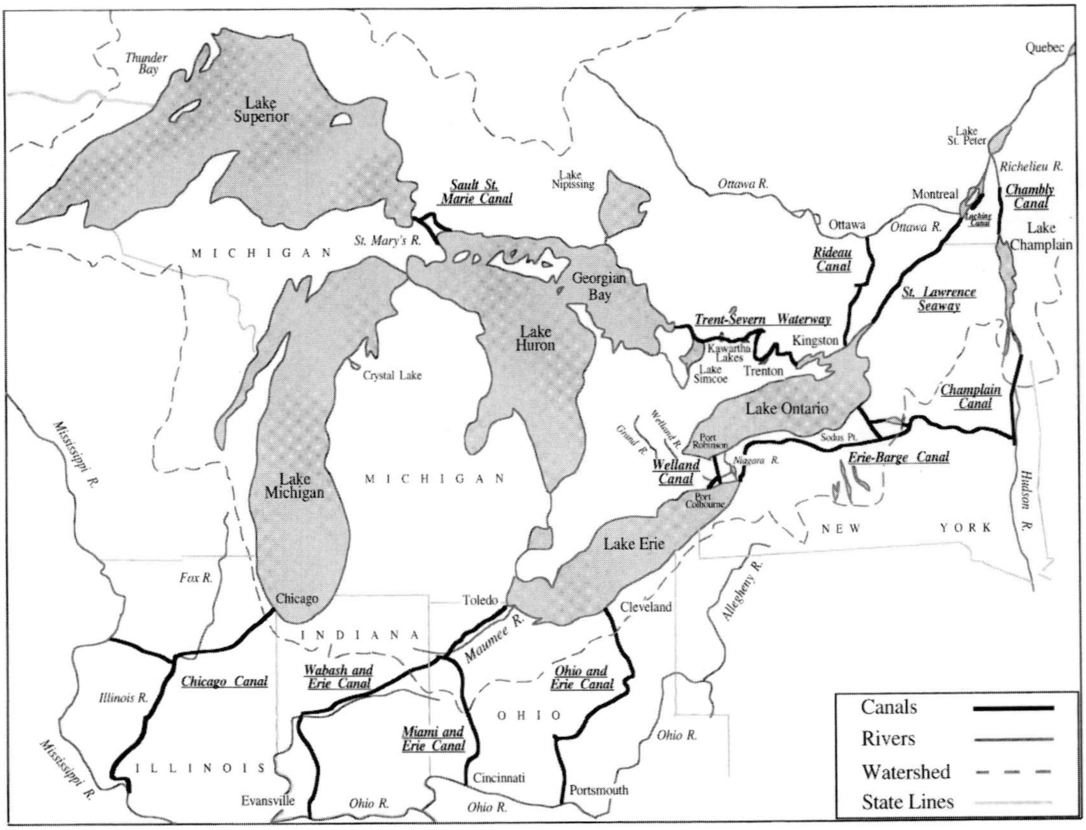

FIGURE 9.1
Map of the major canal systems showing their connections among the Great Lakes, Hudson River, St. Lawrence Seaway, Atlantic Ocean, and Mississippi River in the northeastern United States. From Mills *et al.* (1999).

adjacent watersheds, and allowed invasive species to disperse into new waters. Nearly a dozen major canals are dispersed throughout the Great Lakes landscape (Fig. 9.1) and link Great Lakes waters to the Atlantic Ocean and the Gulf of Mexico via the Mississippi drainage. At present, 146 invasive species have been melded into the Great Lakes waterscape and many wetland plants, invertebrates, fish, and algae have used interlinking canals to gain access to new habitats (Hall and Mills, 2000).

Canals have extended the Great Lakes' exposure to organisms from the entire globe. Foreign ocean-going ships containing ballast are known to bring waters with organisms from throughout the world through the St. Lawrence Seaway (Locke *et al.*, 1993). In fact, nearly one-third of the exotic species currently in the Great Lakes have been established in the last 40 years and this surge corresponds with the opening of the St. Lawrence Seaway in 1959. Canals have been the primary vector for such Great Lakes exotic species as the sea lamprey (*Petromyzon marinus*) and the alewife (*Alosa pseudoharengus*) but in many situations, the canals have been a secondary pathway (Mills *et al.*, 1999). One of the most recent and well-known examples has been the introduction of the zebra mussel (*Dreissena polymorpha*) (Mills *et al.*, 1993). The mussel most likely arrived in North America's Great Lakes in ballast water of transoceanic ships (primary vector) from Europe and used canals and other waterways to spread quickly throughout the continent.

9.2.2 Hydro-physical links between terrestrial and aquatic systems

The second focus area of this chapter concerns the diversity and magnitude of physical linkages that integrate aquatic and terrestrial landscape elements. These linkages include the two-way, aboveground flows of water and matter and the less visible, belowground movement of water and its dissolved constituents. An understanding of these linkages emphasizes the truly diffuse nature of the land–water boundary and the integral connectedness between the terrestrial and aquatic environments.

Above-ground flows of water and matter

Overbank flooding was highlighted earlier for its direct importance to organisms. Floodwaters also transport dissolved substances (including ions, nutrients, and gases), mineral-based, sedimentary particles and organic debris, ranging in size from leaf litter to tree-sized logs. Increased floodplain fertility has long been recognized as a product of the nutrients imported during flood events (Junk *et al.*, 1989). However, the other flood cargoes play equally critical roles in the structure and functioning of the recipient systems.

The saline waters of infrequent oceanic flood events are responsible for maintaining the extensive dune swale communities and high saltmarshes along the eastern Atlantic coastline of the United States (Schneider, 1984). The inundation of sea water may occur only once every one to five years, when extreme storm events superimposed on astronomically high tides transport sea water hundreds of meters inland. The floodwaters remain on the surface for a few hours, then drain rapidly into the subsurface groundwater, which becomes salty for years to come. The plants are variously adapted to saline stress and species are distributed in response to the long-lasting groundwater salinity gradients. Although overwash flooding reoccurs infrequently, the plant communities as a whole are resilient to their dynamic landscape.

Along with floodwaters, considerable quantities of sediment particles are eroded and transported between land and water when water velocities become sufficiently strong. Storm-driven waves along the coast rework beach dunes to form extensive sandy deltas or shorelines. Flood-enhanced streams alternately erode or rebuild streamside habitats on a regular basis (Gregory *et al.*, 1991). As a result of this constant flow of sediment, the land–water interface can be a highly dynamic and disturbance-maintained substrate. Both streamside and seashore plant communities are uniquely adapted to cope with such dynamic conditions. Dune grass (*Ammophila breviligulata*), willow trees (*Salix* spp.), and sycamore trees (*Platanus occidentalis*) are representative of many waterside plants which exhibit rapid rates of root growth, an ability to sprout from their stems and trunks when buried deep under sediment, and vegetative propagation from roots, stems, and other structures if torn apart by waves or erosion. Because of their tolerance to these conditions, waterside plants contribute feedback by slowing down floodwaters, trapping suspended sediments, and stabilizing shoreline sediment against erosion.

Movement of organic debris from land to water is of particular importance in riverine ecosystems (Bisson *et al.*, 1987). In the extensive networks of headwater creeks, overhanging foliage shades the water and reduces sunlight necessary for photosynthesis (Murphy and Meehan, 1991). Falling leaves are the main food source for aquatic invertebrates which are, in turn, fed upon by numerous species of fish. Leaf litter therefore forms the basis of an allochthonous food web. However, there is a strong influence of landscape position on this process (Cummins, 1974). In headwaters, most leaves enter directly into the water from the overhanging, land-based trees and shrubs. Downstream the larger, wider streams have sufficient sunlight to support in-stream photosynthesis by algae and submersed macrophytes, so leaf input is less important. However, periodic floods transport downed branches and logs, as well as leaf litter, from adjacent streamsides into the creeks and downstream into the wider rivers. The woody debris is important throughout the river channel network as the basis for debris dams, providing in-stream structure and habitat, and as a trap for sediments transported from further upstream.

Groundwater flows from upland to aquatic systems

Water also flows from land to water by invisible, shallow and deep groundwater routes. The aquatic–terrestrial interface is a critical landscape feature, acting as a gateway by which groundwater leaves the terrestrial system and enters the aquatic system. The fringing environment along the interface is the last filter available before groundwater discharges into a stream or lake. Streamsides, as well as wetlands and lakeshore marshes, comprise the interface fringe and deserve special attention.

Streamsides, or riparian zones, have been extensively studied in the past three decades. More than 400 papers have documented their ability to act as filters of groundwater, as well as surface water runoff (see reviews in Haycock *et al.*, 1997). There is good agreement on the general processes by which healthy streamside buffers work to filter and improve water quality. Aboveground, plant leaves and stems intercept and slow down floodwaters that overflow stream banks during storms. Suspended sediment falls out of the slowed waters and is trapped among the plant stems. Plant stems also trap sediment transported by overland runoff. This trapping is a primary mechanism for removing phosphorus since it is largely bound to sediment. Belowground, a dense network of fine root hairs interacts with organic matter, microbes, and sediment. Plant uptake removes both phosphorus and nitrogen dissolved in subsurface flow. Organic matter in the soil adsorbs onto trace metals and other contaminants. Finally, microbes transform and remove some contaminants. Microbial denitrification is a major mechanism for removing nitrogen before it enters the stream.

Considerable discussion has evolved around the optimum streamside buffer width to obtain various filtering functions. When this research is synthesized, it appears that, in general, a buffer width of only 2 to 10 meters is needed to remove sediment-bound phosphorus from overland runoff (Cooper and Gilliam, 1987). Wider buffers of 20 to 30 m are needed for consistent removal of 90% or more of the nitrate transported in groundwater (Vought *et al.*, 1994). However, there are numerous factors controlling this buffer width and filter effectiveness for all nutrients is diminished as the slope increases, when the groundwater table is considerably lower than the rhizosphere (Groffman *et al.*, 1992), and when infrequent, high-intensity storm events overwhelm the buffer capacity. This last factor was amply demonstrated in a North Carolina field study where one storm accounted for more than 60% of total sediment input to a streamside buffer from an agricultural field over the two-year study period (Daniels and Gilliam, 1996).

Despite numerous studies on individual streamsides, much less is known about filtering of streamsides relative to their position within a larger stream channel network. Consequently, it is difficult to make recommendations to resource managers who have limited funds and resources available for streamside protection. A synthesis of the literature suggests that there may be differences in the function of streamside filtering across the landscape. Streamsides associated with headwater streams tend to be narrow, steeply sloping and low in soil organic matter. Nitrogen filtration in headwater streams appears to be limited since the subsurface water moves rapidly through these riparian habitats and has little time for contact with substrates where filtering can occur (Hill, 1990, 1996). In contrast, third-order and larger streamsides are wider, less steep, and also contain more organic matter – so contact time is greater and filtration capacity may be greater. Stream channel networks predominantly consist of smaller headwater streams, whereas third-order and larger streams represent a small percentage of the total stream channel network (Gordon *et al.*, 1992). We speculate that, under low flow conditions, the extensive headwater streamsides may play a critical role in filtering the subsurface flow draining their respective basins. During large storm events, when discharge is increased, the filtering function most likely shifts downstream to the floodplains of the larger river system.

Interactions between organism and hydro-physical flows

Not surprisingly, the flows of organisms, water and matter are sometimes interconnected. Organisms have adapted their life histories to take advantage of the different resources resulting from the flow of water and matter. Floodwaters in streams and lakes provide a bridge to increased space, food, and refugia in adjacent wetlands. For adult fish, the water is the corridor for active migration. Alternatively, for adult invertebrates and the propagules of many fish and plants, the flowing water also provides a vector for passive transport.

So important are the temporarily available resources associated with flooding that some organisms time their reproduction to coincide with such events. Horseshoe crabs (*Limulus polyphemus*) mate and lay eggs at the spring high tide (Brockmann and Penn, 1992). Riparian trees release seeds coincident with a late fall rise in river level (Schneider and Sharitz, 1988). Some fish even use an increase in stream discharge as the specific cue that initiates egg hatching (Naesje *et al.*, 1995). Managers need to recognize and protect these links between organism reproduction and flooding in order for management efforts to be successful.

9.3 Case study: Adirondack fisheries and management at the landscape scale

The Adirondack region of New York State provides an excellent example of how ecological factors acting at the landscape scale are controlling the sustainability of lake fish communities. Management decisions both past and present, particularly regarding the introduction of exotics, are playing an important role in the long-term composition and productivity of these fisheries (Keller, 1979; Pfeiffer, 1979).

The upland Adirondack region of northern New York State encompasses an area of nearly 2.4 million hectares, with approximately 4000 lakes and ponds and thousands of kilometers of rivers and streams. The boundary is roughly approximated by the 305 m elevation contour where impassable waterfalls to the region occur. At the maximum extent of the Wisconsin glaciation in 19 000 BP, the entire region was covered by ice. As the glacier receded, the region was recolonized by movements of fishes originating from the Boreal, Atlantian, and Mississippian groups. The original upland Adirondack fish community consisted of only 23 species, from the Boreal (16 species) and Mississippian (7 species) groups (George, 1980). The original lowland Adirondack fish community consisted of an additional 58 species, from the Atlantian (20 species) and Mississippian (38 species) groups (George, 1980).

The Boreal group of cold-adapted fishes was the most successful in recolonizing the upland Adirondacks and included brook trout (*Salvelinus fontinalis*) which is, arguably, the most important sport fish of the region. As late as the 1880s, brook trout were widely distributed and abundant throughout the Adirondacks. Mather (1886) noted that brook trout occurred in most Adirondack waters and were absent from very few lakes. The simple indigenous fish communities of the uplands were protected from exotic fish species invasion by the many impassable falls (Pfeiffer, 1979).

The early 1800s ushered in 200 years of unprecedented alteration of the landscape and biota of the upland Adirondack region, with particularly negative impacts on the native upland fish community (George, 1980). Logging operations from 1800 through the mid-1950s altered the landscape through changes in plant communities, siltation of streams, and scouring of river channels by log runs. Dams, starting in the early 1800s, were constructed for flood control and downstream flow enhancement for sawmills, recreation, and other commercial uses. These operations lead to altered flow regimes and water levels and impediments to historic corridors for migrating native fishes (Pfeiffer, 1979).

Subsequent to World War II, residential development of the upland Adirondack region greatly accelerated, due to increased accessibility to the region by automobiles and planes (George, 1980). Permanent and seasonal dwellings and extensive road construction further impacted the aquatic environment due to cultural eutrophication and riparian development. An increase in industrialization was also associated with the extreme acidic precipitation of the 1960s and 1970s which caused a serious problem with lake water acidification and loss of fish and other aquatic organisms (Schofield, 1976).

Arguably, the greatest impact to the upland native fisheries of the Adirondacks resulted from widespread introductions of lowland and exotic fish species. Some fish invaded via artificial canals and other interwaterway connections. Many fish introductions in the upland Adirondack region were intended to create sport fisheries for non-native fishes, including salmonids, esocids, centrarchids, and percids (Flick and Webster, 1993; Schofield and Driscoll, 1987). Other fish introductions were intended to establish a forage fish base for large predatory fish and included alewife, smelt (*Osmerus mordax*), and golden shiner (*Notemigonus crysoleucas*). These sport fishing management actions, initiated in the late 1880s, intensified over the next 50 years, and were a primary focus for New York's Fish and Game Department (Pfeiffer, 1979).

Smallmouth bass (*Micropterus dolomieui*) was the first non-native species to expand its range into the upland Adirondack region via the Black River Canal (George, 1980) and through intentional introductions (Mather, 1886) in the mid-1800s. Mather (1886) further noted that these fish were "only in waters where they were planted or to those to which they have strayed." The bass "strayed" into other waters via interconnected waterways that served as corridors for movement and expansion of this exotic species in the Adirondacks. In a similar manner, other exotic fish species would expand their ranges into the uplands through direct introductions and movement between connected waterways.

By the 1930s, the pace of non-indigenous fish species introductions increased and profound changes in the Adirondack fish community resulted (George, 1980). Yellow perch (*Perca flavescens*), northern pike (*Esox lucius*), and chain pickerel (*E. niger*) were intentionally introduced to water bodies and expanded their ranges into other waters via aquatic corridors. These species, along with bass, were efficient competitors and predators on native species and contributed to precipitous declines in the native brook trout and other fish populations.

The predation and competition effects of introduced fish species in the Adirondacks have had widespread negative implications for native fish communities. Although introductions of exotic species have not resulted in extinction of any native species, these introductions have caused the reduction in abundance and distribution of many species and the loss of unique strains of fishes. Of particular note is the endangered status of the round whitefish (*Prosopium cylindraceum*) and the reduction of brook trout range and loss of many heritage strains (Keller, 1979).

Exotic fish introductions and habitat degradation have fragmented the Adirondack aquatic environment to the point that native fishes can no longer sustain wild populations in much of their original range. These impacts are particularly important for brook trout which normally spawn each fall and will emigrate from unsuitable lakes in search of appropriate habitat (Josephson and Youngs, 1996). These annual migrations were probably critical to the earlier wide distribution of the species. With stream corridor barriers, lake habitat degradation, and predation and competition from exotic fish in many lakes, there are very few networks of appropriate brook trout habitat left which can support the brook trout's needs for migration and habitat diversity. Original, remnant populations of heritage brook trout remain only in small headwater ponds and streams. Present-day populations of brook trout (90% of fishable populations) are maintained largely through a fall fingerling stocking program in isolated, headwater lakes (Keller, 1979).

The Adirondack Park was included in the New York Forest Preserve in 1885 "to be forever kept as wild forest lands." However past activities pursued by private interests and public agencies clearly indicate that the Adirondack region was viewed as a wealth of resources to exploit. More recently there has been an increasing awareness of the ecological processes occurring within the upland Adirondacks. This awareness, combined with the creation of the Adirondack Park Agency Act in 1971, has resulted in a shift in management priorities and some successes in improving environmental conditions. The primary goal of this act was to maintain and sustain the Adirondack Park ecosystem so that it functions as much as possible by natural processes without human interference.

Management of aquatic ecosystems in the Adirondacks is currently addressed through two different approaches: (1) maintaining water quality through enforcement of stringent regulations, and (2) fish management that focuses on individual water bodies. Much progress has been made in restoring water quality and protecting aquatic habitats in the Adirondack region, largely through land acquisition. Water quality has been improved on many lakes through zoning restrictions and guidelines for upgrading of septic systems, protecting wetlands, encouraging shoreline buffers to reduce effects of residential buildings, and limiting lakeshore/riparian development. The enactment of the Clean Air Act and its Amendments (1990) has led to improvements in airborne pollutants nationwide and decreased the trend towards acidification of many Adirondack lakes. Overall, the condition of aquatic habitat throughout the Adirondacks has considerably improved.

Efforts to restore the native fish communities are less successful, largely due to the negative, persistent, and possibly irreversible impacts of non-native fishes. Many lakes and rivers now have naturalized populations of exotic fish species. Most of the management focus is also concentrated on individual water bodies and largely for brook trout in isolated headwater lakes. The New York Department of Environmental Conservation recognizes the exotic species issue and currently regulates the introduction of fishes into Adirondack waters and requires stocking permits to reduce the unwanted introduction of fishes to remaining intact lakes. New agency initiatives will attempt to reclaim selected headwater lakes by eliminating introduced fish species and restocking with native species and strains of fish.

However, there is still a general lack of recognition of the important role that movements through aquatic corridors can play, both for reproduction of native species, such as brook trout, and for invasion of exotic species. More effective management for all fisheries will require a watershed-level approach that accounts for movements by fish between connected waterways and maintaining heterogeneity of habitats. It is important to strengthen this recognition on the part of management agencies. Reducing further introductions and fully appreciating the ramifications of interconnected waterways as corridors for fish movement is critical to ensure that future management efforts are successful.

9.4 Implications and guidelines for cross-boundary management

The interconnections between terrestrial and aquatic ecosystems must be understood, and the aquatic–terrestrial interface recognized as a porous membrane, not as a barrier to flow, in order for sustainable landscape management to occur. Strategies to protect the different flows of organisms, water, and matter described in this chapter can be summarized under four main topics that are relevant to the landscape-scale management of wildlife and water resources. These topics include: recognition of the importance of the natural hydrologic regime of aquatic systems; identification of certain features as critical landscape elements; recognizing the increased vulnerability of aquatic organisms during their terrestrial life stages; and maintaining isolation of aquatic systems to prevent invasion by exotic organisms. Each of these issues is considered in view of its implications for management and then translated into a set of guidelines for resource managers.

9.4.1 Maintenance of the natural hydrologic regime

The first main management issue concerns the alterations made by man to the hydrologic regime of many aquatic systems (Poff *et al.*, 1997). Changes in natural flow regimes, and specifically reducing the frequency and magnitude of high-water events, eliminate water connections between aquatic systems and their adjoining lands, with adverse effects on the organisms that depend on this flow (Galat *et al.*, 1998). The scenario described for the St. Lawrence River is not unique. Rather it is representative of the impacted flow regime of rivers throughout the United States and other parts of the world where natural high-flow events have been eliminated by dam operations and by diversions for irrigation, drinking water, or snow-making (Schneider *et al.*, 1989; Gleick, 1998). Certain federal and state efforts are under way to restore the hydrologic regimes of rivers. For the first time since the major dam-building efforts began in the 1940s, dams are being seriously evaluated for relicensing or even removal in order to restore the natural hydrologic regime of their associated rivers (Gleick, 1998). However, more efforts need to focus on regulating the amounts and timing of water withdrawals where water is diverted for snow-making, irrigation, or other uses.

The concern about altered hydrologic regimes also applies to lakes and ponds. It is estimated that 500 000 km^2 of land worldwide have been inundated by reservoirs (Gleick, 1998) and currently have some form of water level manipulation. For example, in the northeastern United States, water-levels of lakes and reservoirs are typically drawn down in October or November to reduce ice damage to shorelines and to store the anticipated spring snowmelt. However, winter drawdowns are also considered an effective tool for removal of aquatic weed species as the exposure freezes the shoreline sediment, destroying seed banks of wetland plants and killing their overwintering rhizomes (Bates and Smith, 1994). Albeit unintentionally, chronic winter drawdowns have most likely reduced wetlands along many lakeshores. Improved water-level management in lakes and reservoirs needs to mirror the natural hydrologic regime as much as possible.

The importance of maintaining a natural hydrologic regime also applies to managing the land–ocean interface. Artificial stabilization of barrier dunes inhibits sea-water flooding and allows non-adapted, freshwater communities, including human developments, to replace the natural plant communities behind the barrier. Armoring shorelines with bulkheads similarly artificially stabilizes coastal creek channels, an otherwise dynamic interface. However, these types of artificial barriers are generally insufficient over the long term and flooding eventually occurs. In reality, artificially established communities can not be sustained. Wherever possible, appropriate management should avoid attempts to stabilize the land–water interface and instead provide sufficient undeveloped habitat for natural dynamic processes to occur.

9.4.2 Protection of critical landscape elements

We demonstrated that many so-called "aquatic" organisms interact regularly with large portions of the adjacent upland habitat in their life cycles. However, these critical landscape habitats are currently inadequately protected. For example, federal and state regulations require upland buffers adjacent to legally identified wetlands in order to ensure wetland protection. Although a promising start, the generally accepted, minimum buffer width of 30.8 m, as adopted by New York State Department of Environmental Conservation Article 24 and by other states, is too narrow to encompass the terrestrial requirements of many organisms the law is designed to protect. For example, Semlitsch (1998) suggests that a more appropriate buffer zone would extend 164 m from the wetland edge in order to adequately protect all amphibian life stages.

Federal United States regulations also do not have any requirements for buffers adjacent to a broad array of streamsides and shorelines of lakes and ponds that are not legally recognized as wetlands. For example, neatly grown lawn and agricultural crops are often observed growing right up to the edge of a lake or stream. Current streamside protection and restoration efforts by state agencies also tend to focus on larger floodplains and ignore the smaller headwaters, even though the smaller creeks may account for the majority of the stream channel network. Given the importance of headwater creeks as sources of organic debris and stream cooling, these small streamsides deserve better management and protection. Over the past decade, landscape-scale management efforts have begun to focus on protecting streamside habitats. For example, a multi-state partnership was first signed in 1983 by Virginia, Maryland, Pennsylvania, the District of Columbia, the Chesapeake Bay Commission, and the US Environmental Protection Agency to protect and restore the Chesapeake Bay in the eastern United States. This agreement included a goal to restore 2000 miles of streamsides within the Chesapeake Bay watershed which has nearly been accomplished.

Critical landscape elements may also consist of multiple aquatic patches. Sustaining some wildlife metapopulations requires the protection of more than one aquatic patch. In a real world situation of limited funds and resources, the immediate question becomes "How many patches and which ones should be preserved?" Much of the limited knowledge comes from modeling studies that highlight the importance of the dispersal traits of the targeted species and the size and dynamics of the individual local populations. Presently, however, there are no consistent criteria by which to choose which patches are most important. Simulation models suggest that it is critical to protect the patches that have the largest populations and are centrally located for sustainability (Wahlberg *et al.*, 1996); saving smaller, more isolated patches appears to have less impact. However, Semlitsch and Bodie (1998) present a counter-perspective that protecting numerous small wetlands is more important for maintenance of certain aquatic populations because these smaller wetlands provide unique benefits, such as protection from fish predation.

Preservation of multiple aquatic patches also assumes that there is movement by metapopulations among the ponds via connecting terrestrial corridors. Protecting the quality and safety of the upland corridors is a second key factor in the success of metapopulations (Henein and Merriam, 1990). Maintaining good corridor condition is probably more relevant to organisms that walk on the ground surface than for those which fly above it. In general, corridors should be naturally vegetated to maximize protection from excessive heat, cold, or desiccation, and to provide resources for food and protection (Bennett *et al.*, 1994).

9.4.3 Decreasing vulnerability of wildlife

There are also significant management implications concerning the vulnerability of wildlife species that move from aquatic to terrestrial habitats. Punctuated or seasonal movements are brief, and sometimes nocturnal, so that these movements are generally unobserved by humans. Being short in duration, such phenomena are often misinterpreted by humans as insignificant when the opposite is actually true. Highly concentrated movements can result in greater vulnerability to human intervention and predation because large segments of the population are concentrated in time and space. For example, hundreds of spring-migrating frogs can be killed by cars in a single night (Fahrig *et al.*, 1995). Animal predators also hone in on the concentrated food resources with devastating impacts. Such predation is a major problem for sea turtle hatchlings. Although nests are located only a scant tens of meters from the ocean's waves, mortality can be high as the newly emerged sea turtles are picked off the sand by raccoons, gulls, crabs, and other predators (Ratnaswamy and Warren, 1998).

Overall predation also has increased for many ground-breeding organisms, including amphibians and reptiles, during their terrestrial life stages (Langham, 1992; McChesney and Tershy, 1998). Cats and dogs, as well as other terrestrial predators, are often deterred by aquatic conditions, but may harass or kill nesting adults and dig up subterranean animals and nests. With the continued expansion of humans into rural habitats, these domestic predators, as well as raccoons, skunks, and others, have become ubiquitous and abundant and their control is a key issue for management.

Currently, resource managers have limited options for reducing the vulnerability of wildlife to terrestrial predators. Various strategies that have been used include: physical barriers that fence predators out, cleaning up trash dumps that supplement diets of raccoons and other predators, creating extremely wide vegetated buffers that deter predator transit, and implementing pet control ordinances or incentives for pet owners to reduce the freedom of pets to roam.

9.4.4 Maintaining isolation of aquatic communities

The final topic within this chapter deals with the importance of controlling the overland movement of invasive species from one aquatic system to another. Historically isolated, native aquatic organisms are often at risk resulting from predation and competition by invasive species. These invaders can have devastating impacts on species composition and ecosystem function. There have been few successful attempts to restore such impacted communities to their original status due to the loss of unique gene pools, the difficulty of completely removing the invaders, and/or the permanent shift in nutrient status, substrate, or other basic feature of the aquatic system. Therefore, control to prevent future invasions and negative impacts has to be a top management priority.

Managers of both terrestrial and aquatic landscapes need to be aware of the risks that invasive species pose on these ecosystems. Proposed efforts to construct interwaterway connections, for example, need to be carefully evaluated before they are implemented. While some deliberate introductions, such as for sport fishing, result in significant positive benefits and opportunities, potential negative impacts need to be carefully weighed as well. Finally, education to help stakeholders of the landscape understand and appreciate the importance of native species is key to successful management of non-indigenous organisms.

9.4.5 Eight rules of thumb for managing aquatic–terrestrial linkages

In recent years, there has been a new focus on the watershed as the proper spatial unit for management for water resources. This approach represents a vast improvement over previous decisions that were determined by political boundaries. Watershed management efforts are proving extremely successful in improving and managing water quality throughout the United States. However, the watershed boundary may be irrelevant for wildlife and aquatic species that move freely from one water body to the next, regardless of intervening landscape barriers. Thus, policies strictly focused on improving water quality within a watershed may not be adequate to protect native species. Instead, an integrated approach is needed that takes into account the flow of organisms, water, and matter described here. Within an integrated setting, we consider a set of eight rules of thumb for successful cross-boundary management.

(1) Maintain, or restore as closely as possible, the natural hydrologic regime of the targeted water bodies. If it is necessary to divert water, eliminate only the very highest flows.
(2) Recognize the dynamic nature of many transition zones. Do not armor or stabilize them. Instead, provide extra space to allow flexibility in the movement of the water's edge. Encourage only native plant and animal species adapted to the natural dynamics.
(3) Protect an upland vegetated buffer area adjacent to all water bodies, including lakes, ponds, streamsides, and seashores. Wherever possible, maintain a vegetated buffer width of 150 m or greater.
(4) When designing preserves, consider all available aquatic habitat patches for their importance in sustaining aquatic wildlife species. Encompass as many patches as possible in the preserve, including a combination of large centrally located and smaller, more distant patches.
(5) Protect overland connecting corridors among water bodies, in their natural soil, microclimate, and vegetative condition.
(6) Protect the quality of groundwater before it enters streams and lakes by reducing inputs of sewage wastes, agricultural fertilizers and pesticides, livestock wastes, and other contaminants being applied in the upland recharge areas.

(7) Protect the integrity of the biological character of upland habitats by controlling and reducing the number of domestic predators.
(8) Reduce opportunities for invasive organisms to expand their range into new landscapes.

9.5 Summary

Over the past several decades, research documenting the integral connections between land and water has proliferated. In this chapter we have provided an overview of the considerable evidence showing that there are significant flows of organisms, water, and matter between the land and water and among seemingly isolated water bodies. Many amphibians, reptiles, birds, and other so-called aquatic animals are not constrained by the land–water interface. Rather they incorporate large portions of the surrounding "land"scape into their life histories for laying eggs, overwintering, and adult life stages, and as corridors to other aquatic systems. These temporary terrestrial habitats need to be protected. There are also considerable movements of organisms among isolated water bodies. In certain interactions, this flow of organisms needs to be protected so that metapopulations can be maintained. In other cases, water bodies need to be kept isolated to prevent the spread of invasive organisms. Traditional wildlife management practices have ignored the importance of these landscape linkages. There are also significant, sometimes two-way, flows between terrestrial and aquatic systems, of water, dissolved substances, organic debris, and sediment which are critical for each environment to be maintained. Reducing the flows of water and matter has impacted organisms both directly, by removing conduits across the landscape, and indirectly, by reducing the availability of resources on which they depend. It is critical that all these landscape concepts be made accessible to the natural resource managers who can directly apply them. Heightened awareness of landscape ecological principles is essential for all components of society, and education is the key to better management of the landscape and sustainable protection of our natural resources.

References

Bates, A. L. & Smith, C. S. (1994). Submersed plant invasions and decline in the southeastern United States. *Lake and Reservoir Management*, 10: 53–55.

Bennett, A. F., Henein, K. and Merriam, G. (1994). Corridor use and the elements of corridor quality: Chipmunks and fencerows in a farmland mosaic. *Biological Conservation*, 68: 155–165.

Bisson, P. A., Bilby, R. E., Bryant, M. D., Dolloff, C. A., Grette, G. B.,House, R. A., Murphy, M. L., Koski, K. V., Sedell, J. R. (1987). Large woody debris in forested streams in the Pacific Northwest: Past, present and future. In: *Streamside Management: Forestry and Fisheries Interactions*, eds. E. O. Salo & T. W. Cundy, pp. 143–190 University of Washington, Seattle, WA.

Brockmann, H. J. & Penn. D. (1992). Male mating tactics in the horseshoe crab, *Limulus polyphemus*. *Animal Behavior,* 44: 653–665.

Burke, V. J. & Gibbons, J. W. (1995). Terrestrial buffer zones and wetland conservation: A case study of freshwater turtles in a Carolina bay. *Conservation Biology* 9: 1365–1369.

Burton, T. M. & Likens, G. E. (1975). Salamander populations and biomass in the Hubbard Brook Experimental Forest, New Hampshire. *Copeia* 1975: 541–546.

Cooper, J. R. & Gilliam, J. W. (1987). Phosphorus redistribution from cultivated fields into riparian areas. *Soil Science Society of America Journal*, 51: 1600–1604.

Cummins, K. W. (1974). Stream ecosystem structure and function. *BioScience,* 24: 631–641.

Daniels, R. B. & Gilliam, J. W. (1996). Sediment and chemical load reduction by grass and riparian filters. *Soil Science Society of America Journal*, 60: 246–251.

Dombeck, M. P., Menzel, B. W. & Hinz, P. N. (1986). Natural reproduction in midwestern lakes. *American Fisheries Society Special Publication*, 15: 122–134.

Driscoll, D. A. (1998). Genetic structure, metapopulation processes and evolution influence the conservation strategies for two endangered frog species. *Biological Conservation,* 83: 43–54.

Fahrig, L., Pedlar, J. H., Pope, E. S., Taylor, P. D. and Wegner, J. F. (1995). Effect of road traffic on amphibian density. *Biological Conservation*, 73:177–182.

Farrell, J. M. (2001). Reproductive success of sympatric northern pike and muskellunge in an upper St. Lawrence River Bay. *Transactions of the American Fisheries Society*, 130(5): 796–808.

Farrell, J. M., Werner, R. G. LaPan, S. R. & Claypoole, K. A. (1996). Egg distribution and spawning habitat of northern pike and muskellunge in a St. Lawrence River marsh, New York. *Transactions of the American Fisheries Society*, 125: 127–131.

Flick, W. A. & Webster, D. A. (1993). Standing crops of brook trout in Adirondack waters before and after removal of non-trout species. *North American Journal of Fisheries Management*, 12: 783–796.

Forman, R. T. T. (1995). *Land Mosaics: The Ecology of Landscapes and Regions*. Cambridge University Press, Cambridge, UK.

Franklin, D. R. & Smith, L. L. (1963). Early life history of the northern pike, *Esox lucius* L. with special reference to the factors influencing the numerical strength of year classes. *Transactions of the American Fisheries Society,* 92: 91–110.

Galat, D. L. and 16 additional authors (1998). Flooding to restore connectivity of regulated, large-river wetlands. *BioScience,* 48: 721–733.

Geis, J. W. & Kee, J. L. (1977). *Coastal Wetlands along Lake Ontario and the St. Lawrence River in Jefferson County*, New York. State University of New York College of Environmental Science and Forestry, Syracuse, NY.

George, C. J. (1980). *The Fishes of the Adirondack Park*. Lake Monograph Program, New York State Department of Environmental Conservation, Albany, NY.

Gibbs, J. P. (1993). Importance of small wetlands for the persistence of local populations of wetland-associated animals. *Wetlands,* 13: 25–31.

Gleick, P. H. (1998). *The World's Water 1998–1999*. Island Press, Washington, D.C.

Gordon, N. D., McMahon, T. A. & Finlayson, B. L. (1992). *Stream Hydrology*. John Wiley, New York.

Gregory, S. V., Swanson, F. J., McKee W. A. & Cummins, K. W. (1991). An ecosystem perspective on riparian zones. *BioScience*, 41: 540–551.

Groffman, P. M., Gold, A. J. & Simmons, R. C. (1992). Denitrification in grass and forest vegetated filter strips. *Journal of Environmental Quality*, 20: 671–674.

Hall, S. R. & Mills, E. L. (2000). Exotic species in large lakes of the world. *Aquatic Ecosystem Health and Management*, 3: 105–135.

Haycock, N. E., Burt, T. P., Goulding K. W. T. & Pinay, G. (eds.) (1997). *Buffer Zones: Their Processes and Potential in Water Protection*. Proceedings of the International Conference on Buffer Zones, Sept 1996, Harpenden, Hertfordshire, UK. Quest Environmental, Inc.

Henein, K. & Merriam, G. (1990). The elements of connectivity where corridor quality is variable. *Landscape Ecology,* 4: 157–170.

Hill, A. R. (1990). Groundwater flow paths in relation to nitrogen chemistry in the near-stream zone. *Hydrobiology,* 206: 39–52.
Hill, A. R. (1996). Nitrate removal in stream riparian zones. *Journal of Environmental Quality,* 25: 743–755.
Josephson, D. C. & Youngs, W. D. (1996). Association between emigration and age structure in populations of brook trout (*Salvelinus fontinalis*) in Adirondack lakes. *Canadian Journal of Fisheries and Aquatic Sciences*, 53: 534–541.
Junk, W. J., Bayley, P. B. & Sparks, R. E. (1989). The flood pulse concept in river floodplain systems. *Special Publication of the Canadian Journal of Fisheries and Aquatic Sciences,* 106: 110–127.
Keller, W. T. (1979). Management of Wild and Hybrid Strain Brook Trout in New York Lakes, Ponds, and Coastal Streams. Bureau of Fisheries, New York State Department of Environmental Conservation, Albany, NY.
Kwak, T. J. (1988). Lateral movement and use of floodplain habitat by fishes of the Kankakee River, Illinois. *American Midland Naturalist,* 120: 241–249.
Langham, N. P. (1992). Feral cats (*Felis catus* L.) on New Zealand farmland. 2. Seasonal activity. *Wildlife Research*, 19: 707–720.
Locke, A., Reid, D. M., van Leeuwen, H. C. Sprules, W. G. & Carlton, J. T. (1993). Ballast water exchange as a means of controlling dispersal of freshwater organisms. *Canadian Journal of Fisheries and Aquatic Science*, 50: 2086–2093.
McChesney, J. & Tershy, R. B. (1998). History and status of introduced mammals and impacts to breeding seabirds on the California Channel and Northwestern Baja California Islands. *Colonial Waterbirds*, 21: 335–347.
McCullough, R. D. and Klindt, R. M. (1997). Thousand Islands warmwater fish stock assessment. In: *1997 Annual Report of the Bureau of Fisheries*, Lake Ontario and St. Lawrence River Unit to the Great Lakes Fisheries Commission, Lake Ontario Committee Section, pp. 1–3. Great Lakes Fisheries Commission, Ann Arbor, MI.
Mather, F. (1886). *Memoranda relating to Adirondack Fishes, with Descriptions of New Species, from Researches Made in 1882,* Adirondack Survey 12th Report. State of New York, Albany, NY.
Mills, E. L., Leach, J. H. Carlton, J. T. & Secor, C. L. (1993). Exotic species in the Great Lakes: A history of biotic crises and anthropogenic introductions. *Journal of Great Lakes Research*, 19; 1–54.
Mills, E. L., Chrisman, J. R. & Holeck. K. T. (1999). The role of canals in the spread of nonindigenous species in North America. In *Non-Indigenous Organisms in North America: Their Biology and Impact*, eds. R. Claudi & J. Leach, pp. 345–377. CRC Press, Boca Raton, FL.
Morreale, S., Gibbons, J. & Congdon, J. (1984). Significance of activity and movement in the yellow-bellied slider turtle. *Canadian Journal of Zoology*, 62: 1038–1042.
Murphy, M. L. & Meehan, W. R. (1991). Stream ecosystems. *American Fisheries Society Special Publication*, 19: 17–46.
Naesje, T., Jonsson, B. & Skurdal, J. (1995). Spring flood: A primary cue for hatching of river spawning Coregoniaea. *Canadian Journal of Fisheries and Aquatic Sciences*, 52: 2190–2196.
Odum, E. P. (1971). *Fundamentals of Ecology*. W. B. Saunders, Philadelphia, PA.
Pechmann, J. H. K. & Semlitsch, R. D. (1986). Diel activity patterns in the breeding migrations of winter breeding anurans. *Canadian Journal of Zoology*, 64: 1116–1120.
Pfeiffer, M. H. (1979). *A Comprehensive Plan for Fish Resource Management within the Adirondack Zone*. New York State Department of Environmental Conservation, Albany, NY.
Poff, N. L., Allan, J. D. Bain, M. B. Karr, J. R. Prestegaard, K. L. Richter, B. D. Sparks, R. E. & Stromberg, J. C. (1997). The natural flow regime. *BioScience*, 47: 769–784.
Ratnaswamy, M. J. & Warren, R. J. (1998). Removing raccoons to protect sea turtle nests: Are there implications for ecosystem management? *Wildlife Society Bulletin*, 26: 846–850.
Schneider, R. L. (1984). The relationship of infrequent oceanic flooding to groundwater salinity, topography and coastal vegetation. MSc. dissertation, University of Virginia, Charlottesville, VA.
Schneider, R. L. & Sharitz, R. R. (1988). Hydrochory and regeneration of a bald cypress-water tupelo swamp forest. *Ecology*, 69: 1055–1063.

Schneider, R. L., Martin, N. E. & Sharitz, R. R. (1989). Impact of dam operations on hydrology and associated floodplain forests of southeastern rivers. In *Freshwater Wetlands and Wildlife*, eds. R. R. Sharitz & J.W. Gibbons, pp. 1113–1122. U.S. Department of Energy, Office of Health and Environmental Research, Springfield, VA.

Schofield, C. L. (1976). Acid precipitation: Effects on fish. *Ambio*, 5: 228–230.

Schofield, C. L., & Driscoll, C. T. (1987). Fish species distribution in relation to water quality gradients in the North Branch of the Moose River basin. *Biogeochemistry*, 3: 63–95.

Scott, D. E. (1990). The effect of larval density on adult demographic traits in *Ambystoma opacum*. *Ecology*, 75: 1383–1396.

Scott, W. B. & Crossman, E. J. (1973). *Freshwater Fishes of Canada*, Bulletin no. 184. Fisheries Research Board of Canada, Ottawa, Canada.

Scribner, K. T., Evans, J. E. Morreale, S. Smith, M. & Gibbons, J. (1986). Genetic divergence among populations of the yellow-bellied slider turtle separated by aquatic and terrestrial habitats. *Copeia*, 3: 691–700.

Semlitsch, R. D. (1998). Biological definition of terrestrial buffer zones for pond-breeding salamanders. *Conservation Biology*, 12: 1113–1119.

Semlitsch, R. D. & Bodie, J. R. (1998). Are small, isolated wetlands expendable? *Conservation Biology*, 12: 1129–1133.

Smock, L. A. (1994). Movements of invertebrates between stream channel and forested floodplains. *Journal North American Benthological Society*, 13; 524–531.

Taylor, B. E., Estes, R. A. Pechmann, J. H. K. & Semlitsch, R. D. (1988). Trophic relations in a temporary pond: Larval salamanders and their microinvertebrate prey. *Canadian Journal of Zoology*, 66: 2191–2198.

Vought, L. B. M., Dahl, J. Pedersen, C. L. & Lacoursiere, J. O. (1994). Nutrient retention in riparian ecotones. *Ambio*, 23: 343–349.

Wahlberg, N., Moilanen, A. & Hanski, I. (1996). Predicting the occurrence of endangered species in fragmented landscapes. *Science*, 273: 1536–1538.

Werner, E. E. & Gilliam, J. F. (1984). The ontogenetic niche shift and species interactions in size structured populations. *Annual Review of Ecology and Systematics*, 15: 393–425.

Whillans, T. H. (1982). Changes in marsh area along the Canadian shore of Lake Ontario. *Journal of Great Lakes Research*, 8: 570–577.

PART IV

Landscape change and adaptive management

Landscapes change constantly due to both natural and anthropogenic disturbances (including management practices). The varying nature of landscape structure and function increases the complexity of landscape research and management. Because landscapes are often not in an equilibrium state and there are various degrees of uncertainty, it is necessary to monitor and predict their temporal dynamics as well as their ecological consequences. Furthermore, management strategies need to be modified accordingly, because management practices suitable for previous landscape conditions may not be appropriate for new circumstances. To ensure the success of new management strategies, their potential short- and long-term consequences must be evaluated before implementation. One paradigm that encompasses these ideas is adaptive management, which is becoming increasingly popular in natural resource management but is rarely considered in the context of landscape change. Authors of the four chapters in Part IV present useful tools and approaches that link landscape change research and adaptive management.

Land use is a major driving force of landscape changes. To quantify spatial patterns of land-use changes and their impacts on land cover and species over time, Dale *et al.* (Chapter 10) developed a modified landscape-transition matrix model. This model was then applied to the Fort McCoy military base in Wisconsin to simulate the impacts of military land uses on the habitat of the endangered Karner blue butterfly. The risk maps generated from the model identify specific locations where different management actions are needed. Thus, the model provides a useful tool for land managers using an adaptive management framework.

Improving efficiency of sampling across landscapes is particularly important in monitoring landscape changes. Urban (Chapter 11) suggests that multi-staged stratified designs tend to be more efficient than simple designs (stratified or random) and that sampling designs can often be examined and adjusted beforehand by experimenting with design alternatives, using land cover maps or terrain-based indices. Furthermore, because some data are more informative about particular hypotheses than others, hypotheses should be incorporated into sampling designs using computer simulation models, decision trees, or classification trees. Model-guided designs transform landscape monitoring from passive to active and thus are a useful component of adaptive management.

Landscape changes have enormous consequences, such as alteration in wildlife habitat quantity and quality. In Chapter 12, Rutledge and Lepczyk suggest it is essential to understand the patterns and effects of landscape changes, because this kind of information is critical for adaptive management of wildlife. Using long-term information on historic and potential future landscape changes in two different watersheds in Michigan, the authors illustrate how to delineate experimental units to understand the impacts of management alternatives and landscape change scenarios. The case studies indicate that landscape change information is important for adaptive management of wildlife habitats at large scales.

Most of the lands around the world are managed to various degrees and thus pose logistical and bureaucratic challenges to conducting research. Dunning (Chapter 13) argues that it is necessary to overcome these challenges and to do landscape-scale studies in managed lands because of several major benefits to landscape ecologists. Similarly, management agencies can gain valuable information from research on their lands so that they can implement adaptive management to achieve short-term and long-term management objectives. Using examples of landscape research in intensively managed forest landscapes in the southeastern United States, Dunning demonstrates that both managers and researchers can benefit tremendously from collaboration in short- and long-term studies in both rapidly and slowly changing landscapes.

VIRGINIA H. DALE, DESMOND T. FORTES, AND TOM L. ASHWOOD

10

A landscape-transition matrix approach for land management

10.1 Introduction

Decision-makers are often unaware of the extent to which land-use changes affect biodiversity, renewable resource productivity (e.g., timber), movement of species, and the overall sustainability of ecosystems. Thus, there is a need to estimate ecological effects of land-use change. Adaptive management is a process that considers policy decisions as experimental hypotheses that are subject to testing, analysis, and mediation (Holling, 1978; Walters, 1986). The approach can be used to evaluate the impacts of management actions on natural resources and to modify management actions to protect those resources. Adaptive management emphasizes decision-making as a continuing process, not a discrete end point (Heifetz, 1994). It views management actions as experiments and accumulates knowledge to achieve continual learning (Christensen *et al.*, 1996; Stanford and Poole, 1996). Critical elements for adaptive management include (1) reviewing and synthesizing existing information, (2) defining the ecosystem based on available science, (3) identifying goals based on scientific synthesis and values of the general public, (4) developing a peer-review management system, (5) implementing management actions that meet stated goals within the parameters of acceptable risks and consequences, and (6) conducting applied research and monitoring to reduce uncertainties and evaluate management actions. Adaptive management assumes an ongoing, iterative process that can adjust to new information, changing societal goals, and changes in environmental conditions that occur over a broad scale or over a long time. Thus, adaptive management provides a useful paradigm in which to consider land-use effects on ecological systems.

The ecological impacts on which this paper focuses derive from the ecological principles for land use identified by the Ecological Society of America's Land

Use Committee (Dale *et al.*, 2000). These principles deal with species, place, landscape, disturbance, and time:

- Individual species and networks of interacting species affect the structure and functioning of ecological systems.
- Each site has a specific set of organisms and abiotic conditions that uniquely determines ecological processes.
- The presence, size, and patterns of habitat patches and abiotic conditions on the landscape affect ecological systems.
- Disturbances are ubiquitous in nature and often are an integral part of ecological systems.
- Ecological processes change with time.

Together, these ecological principles determine how land-management activities affect ecological systems.

Application of these principles requires the use of spatial data and of appropriate tools to analyze those data. Historically, the spatial data needed for such analyses have rarely been available; yet with new advances in methods to gather, store, and retrieve data, this type of information will be more widely accessible. Modeling tools have been developed as a way of relating these data to potential land-use decisions to project land-use changes on maps and consider spatial implications such as changes in edge effects or habitat fragmentation. Transition matrices are specialized mathematical models that simulate the probability of a change from one successional state or cover type to another and project changes in land cover and land use over time and space. Landscape-transition matrices offer a way to consider the ecological impacts of future land-use activities. This chapter reviews landscape-transition approaches and describes how to develop and apply those approaches to include ecological impacts in the decision-making process.

10.2 Transition matrices in the context of ecological landscape modeling

10.2.1 Background

The transition approach builds upon processes first recognized by the Russian mathematician Markov. In Markov processes, each existing state of the system has a certain probability of transitioning to a particular future state. (Caswell [1989] provides a concise overview of this approach.) In land-management applications, the state of the system refers to the condition of the land at any one time: either its successional status, its cover type, its habitat condition, or a combination of these features. The probability of being in a particular state at any one time depends upon the immediately preceding state of the process and other factors. Thus, the sequence of discrete states in time or space has fixed probabilities of transitioning from one condition to the next that depend on the existing state and environmental conditions.

The transition between a state, $S_i(t)$, at time t to its future state, $S_j(t+1)$, at time $t+1$ can be illustrated by a matrix with three states:

$$\text{Present state}\quad \begin{array}{c} \\ S_1(t) \\ S_2(t) \\ S_3(t) \end{array} \overset{\text{Future state}}{\begin{array}{ccc} S_1(t+1) & S_2(t+1) & S_3(t+1) \\ \left[\begin{array}{c} P_{1,1} \\ P_{2,1} \\ P_{3,1} \end{array}\right. & \begin{array}{c} P_{1,2} \\ P_{2,2} \\ P_{3,2} \end{array} & \left.\begin{array}{c} P_{1,3} \\ P_{2,3} \\ P_{3,3} \end{array}\right] \end{array}},$$

where $P_{i,j}$ is the probability of moving from state i to state j. Jeffers (1988) presents some of the mathematical details of this procedure.

When the Markovian approach is applied to a land area, an additional aspect must be added to the matrix that relates the state of the matrix to each location on the landscape (Debussche *et al.*, 1977). One way to map the matrix onto the land is to divide the selected landscape into cells and to categorize each cell as occurring in a certain state (e.g., occupied by a particular type of vegetation or land cover). The number of cells in each state constitutes a row vector (a matrix consisting of one row) that describes the distribution of vegetation or land-cover types for the landscape. The corresponding transition matrix consists of probabilities that determine when and whether cells of a particular state will change to another state.

For example, a hypothetical landscape may support three states (e.g., land cover in forest, scrub, and pasture) having 16 cells in state one, 22 cells in state two, and 8 cells in state three. Suppose that the probability of a state changing is given by the following transition matrix:

$$\text{Present State}\quad \begin{array}{c} \\ 1 \\ 2 \\ 3 \end{array} \overset{\text{Future state}}{\begin{array}{ccc} 1 & 2 & 3 \\ \left[\begin{array}{c} 0.2 \\ 0.3 \\ 0.4 \end{array}\right. & \begin{array}{c} 0.6 \\ 0.2 \\ 0.4 \end{array} & \left.\begin{array}{c} 0.2 \\ 0.5 \\ 0.2 \end{array}\right] \end{array}}$$

These transition probabilities might have been derived from observations of past changes. To calculate the number of cells in each state at time two, the state row vector is multiplied by the transition matrix to give:

$$[16\ 22\ 8] \times \begin{bmatrix} 0.2\ 0.6\ 0.2 \\ 0.3\ 0.2\ 0.5 \\ 0.4\ 0.4\ 0.2 \end{bmatrix} = [3.2+6.6+3.2 \quad 9.6+4.4+3.2 \quad 3.2+11+1.6]$$

$$= [13 \quad 17.2 \quad 15.8]$$

Rounding these numbers gives 13 cells in state one, 17 cells in state two, and 16 cells in state three in the second time period. The next step is determining how to spatially allocate these cells. Many rules could be used for the spatial allocation. The choice could be random so that, at any one time step, 20% of randomly selected cells in each state remain in their initial state and, similarly, the other randomly selected cells change according to the given transition probabilities. The choice of which cells to change could be determined by the current state of adjacent neighbors, as Turner (1988) describes. Alternatively, cells could change states depending on their spatial relationships to the landscape (e.g., distance from some abiotic feature, such as a river or a road) or how a particular environmental characteristic might map onto the landscape. In section 10.3.2 of this chapter, we present a method by which a land-use-impact matrix can be developed to translate the probabilities in the transition matrix to particular locations. In summary, this spatial-allocation step involves determining a rule by which the number of cells changing state is related to the spatial distribution of the cells and possibly to other features on the landscape.

When there is a probability of some cells changing state over time ($P_{i,i} < 1$), then one can consider the risk of cells changing. The spatial-allocation rules may determine a difference in the likelihood of change for some cells; and in such a case, a map identifying sites at greater risk of change can be created. Such a risk map is useful to managers who need to know which areas are likely to undergo changes so that they can plan accordingly.

Finally, the matrix increment and duration are specified to determine the time step and the length of time for the model projection. To project changes over time, the state vector is multiplied by the transition matrix (which contains the transition probabilities of each state for the given time period), and the cells are changed to a new state according to the spatial-allocation rules. The result is a change in the landscape as various cells alter state according to their transition probability, giving rise to a new state vector on each iteration.

To set up a model, extensive research and data collection are usually required for developing the transition matrix and spatial-allocation rules for the landscape under consideration. Aerial photographs or classified and registered satellite imagery of the area to be modeled are especially helpful in subdividing the landscape into cells for classification (Debussche *et al.*, 1977; Turner, 1987, 1988; Aaviksoo, 1993). Analysis of published statistics on land-cover information, rates of land-use change, topography maps, as well as field work to check that cells are classified correctly in the model are vital in obtaining valid parameters for an accurate projection (Turner, 1988; Aaviksoo, 1993). Such forms of empirical data enable development of more precise transition probabilities, state vectors, and spatial-allocation rules.

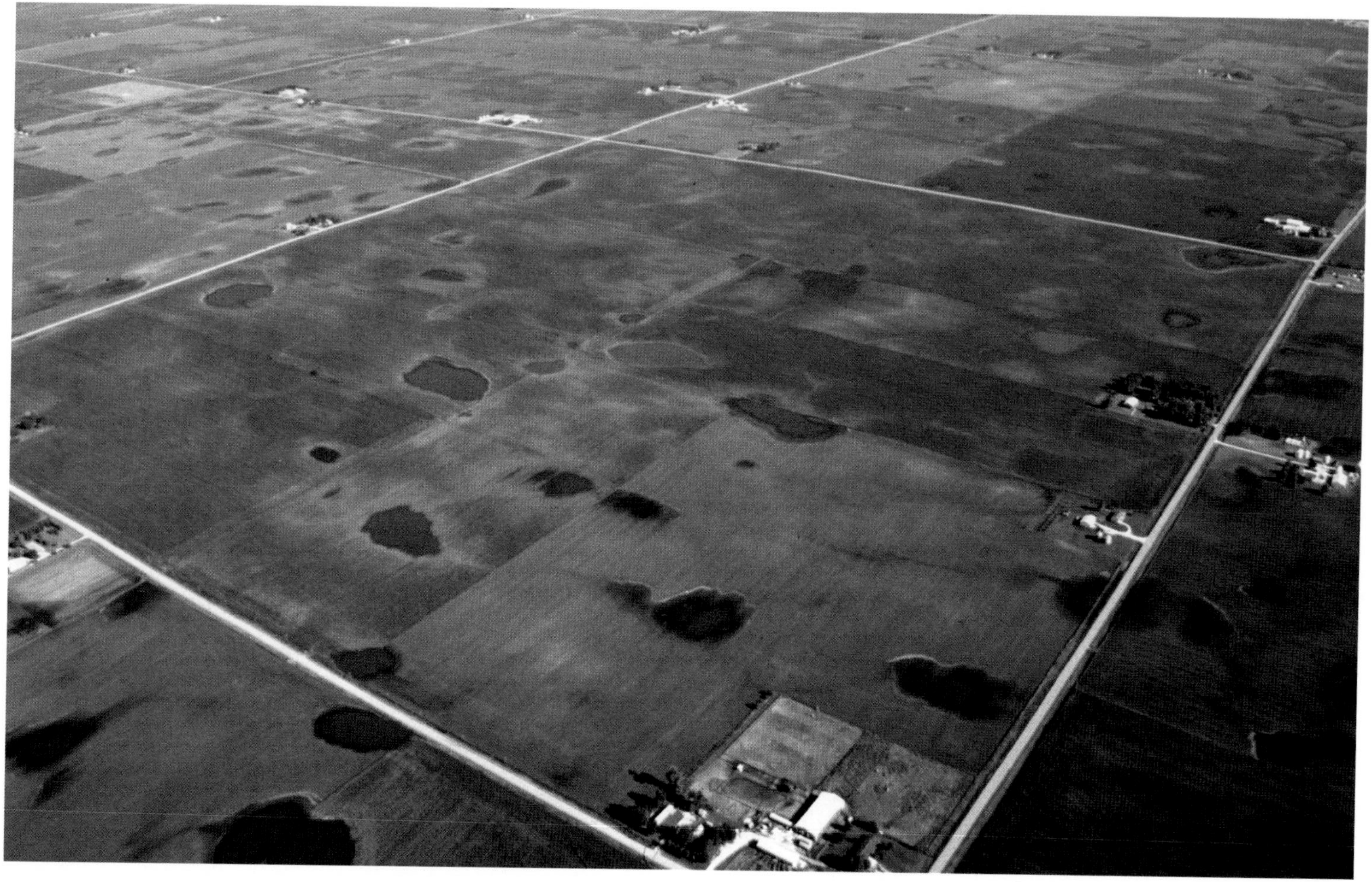

Fig. 4.2. Small-patch landscape pattern of incompletely drained hydric soils, Story County, Iowa, June 1998. (Photograph: R. Corry.)

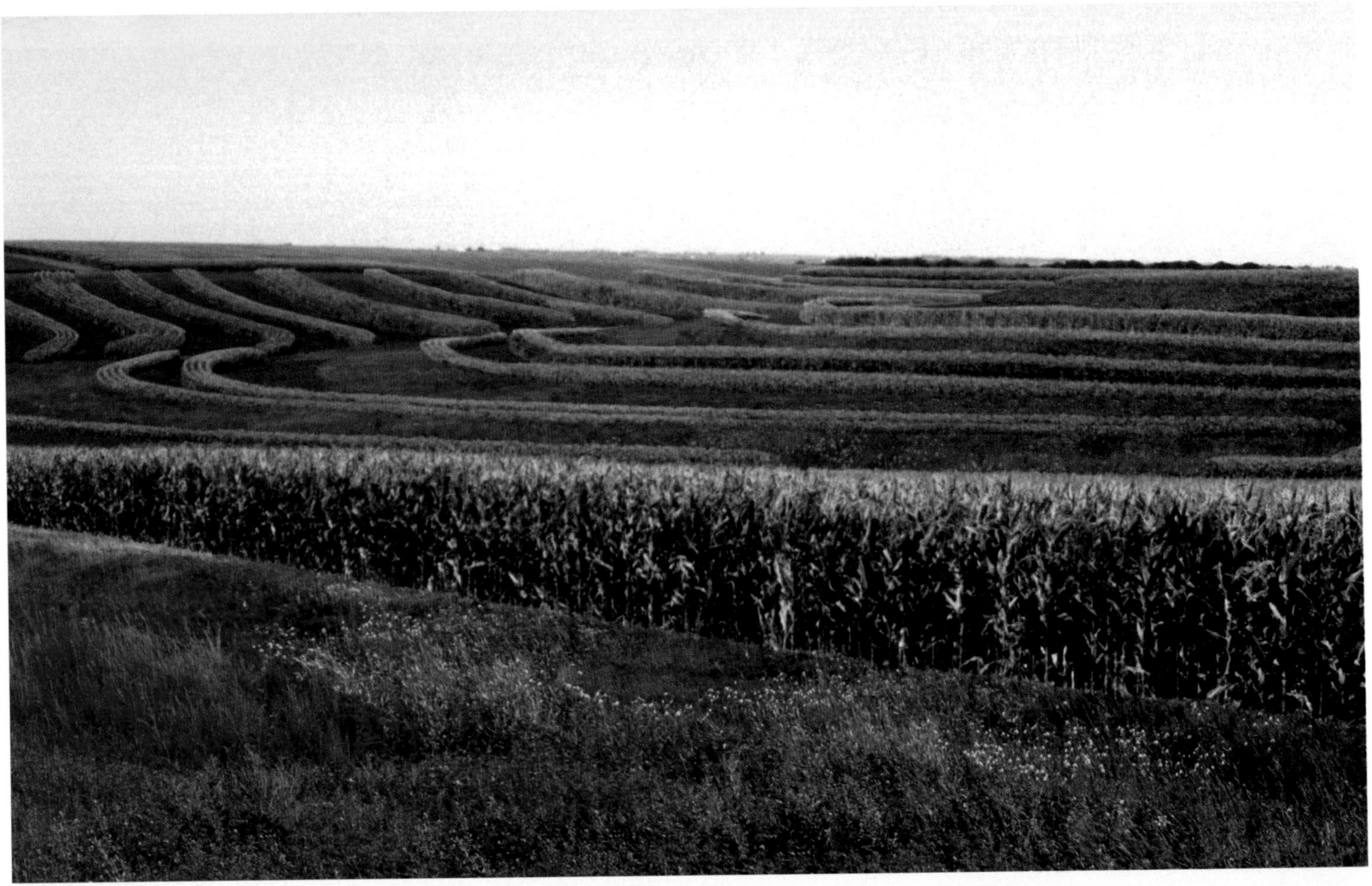

Fig. 4.3. Corn Belt landscape simulation showing corn–soybean–prairie strip intercropping to optimize native plant biodiversity and production. (Digital imaging simulation: R. Corry.)

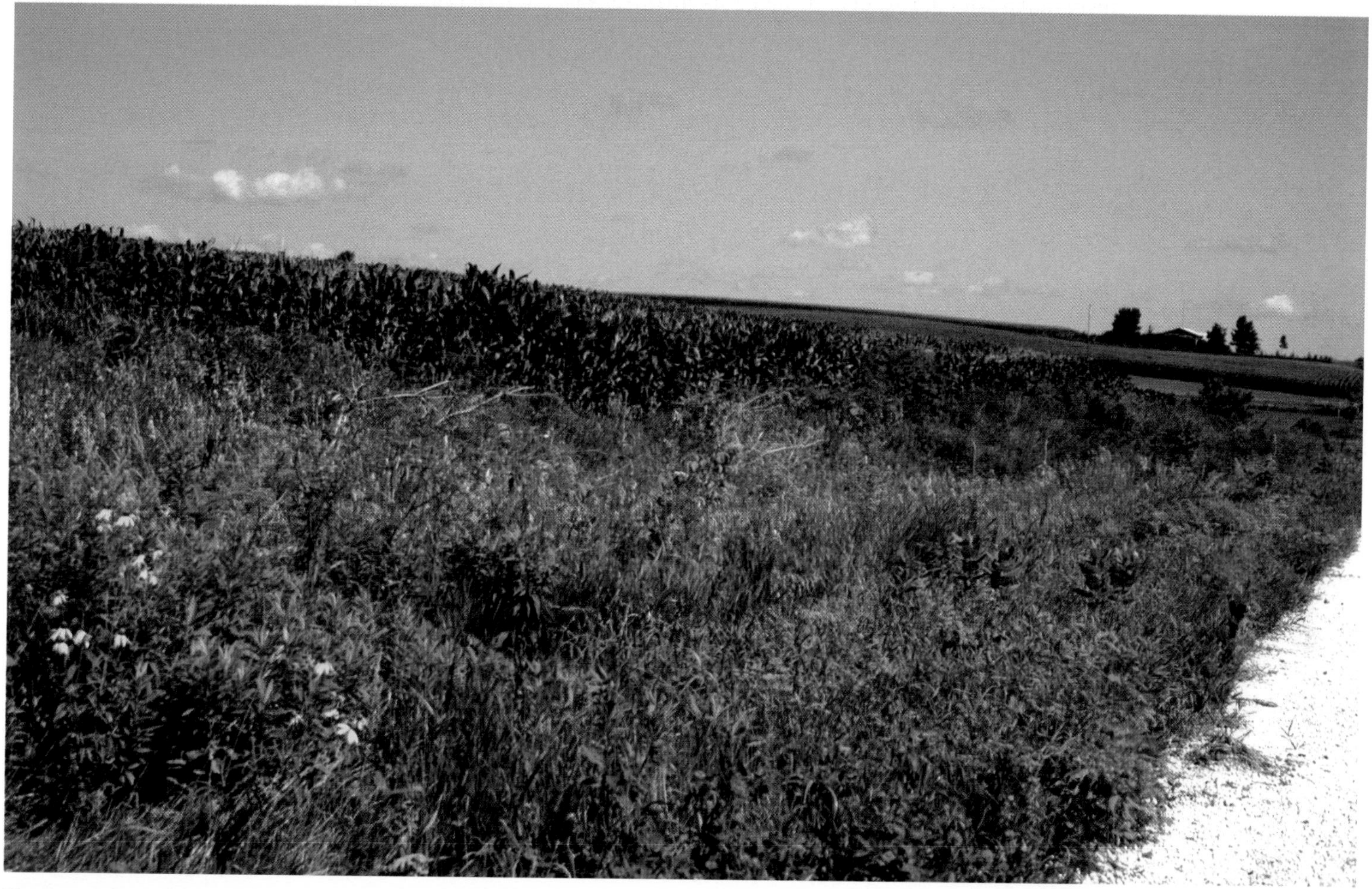

Fig. 4 .4. A Corn Belt roadside with a diversity of unmown herbaceous species; field boundaries and farmstead visible in background. (Photograph: J. Nassauer.)

Fig. 4.5. A Corn Belt remnant prairie (center; Doolittle Prairie, Story County, Iowa) and adjacent cropping patterns. (Photograph: R. Corry.)

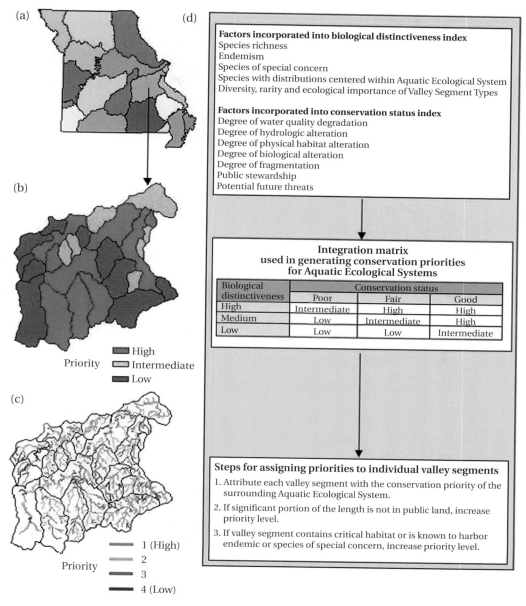

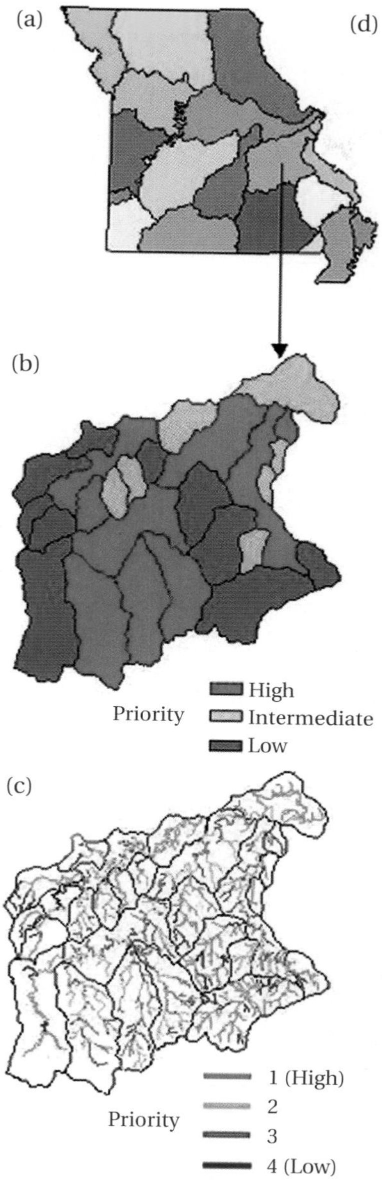

(d)

Factors incorporated into biological distinctiveness index
Species richness
Endemism
Species of special concern
Species with distributions centered within Aquatic Ecological System
Diversity, rarity and ecological importance of Valley Segment Types

Factors incorporated into conservation status index
Degree of water quality degradation
Degree of hydrologic alteration
Degree of physical habitat alteration
Degree of biological alteration
Degree of fragmentation
Public stewardship
Potential future threats

Integration matrix used in generating conservation priorities for Aquatic Ecological Systems

Biological distinctiveness	Conservation status		
	Poor	Fair	Good
High	Intermediate	High	High
Medium	Low	Intermediate	High
Low	Low	Low	Intermediate

Steps for assigning priorities to individual valley segments

1. Attribute each valley segment with the conservation priority of the surrounding Aquatic Ecological System.
2. If significant portion of the length is not in public land, increase priority level.
3. If valley segment contains critical habitat or is known to harbor endemic or species of special concern, increase priority level.

Fig. 5.3. Maps showing three levels of the classification hierarchy and the assessment process developed in the Missouri Aquatic Gap Analysis Project Pilot Project (see Table 5.1 for definitions and defining physical and biological features). (a) Map of the 18 Ecological Drainage Units (EDU) within Missouri. (b) Map showing conservation priorities for Aquatic Ecological Systems (AES) within the Ozark Plateau/Meramec River Ecological Drainage Unit. (c) Maps showing final conservation priorities at the valley-segment scale. (d) Generalized flow chart showing the factors incorporated into calculating the Biophysical Distinctiveness and Conservation Status Indices for each AES, the integration matrix used to combine these indices into a conservation priority for each AES, and the steps involved in establishing conservation priorities at the valley-segment scale.

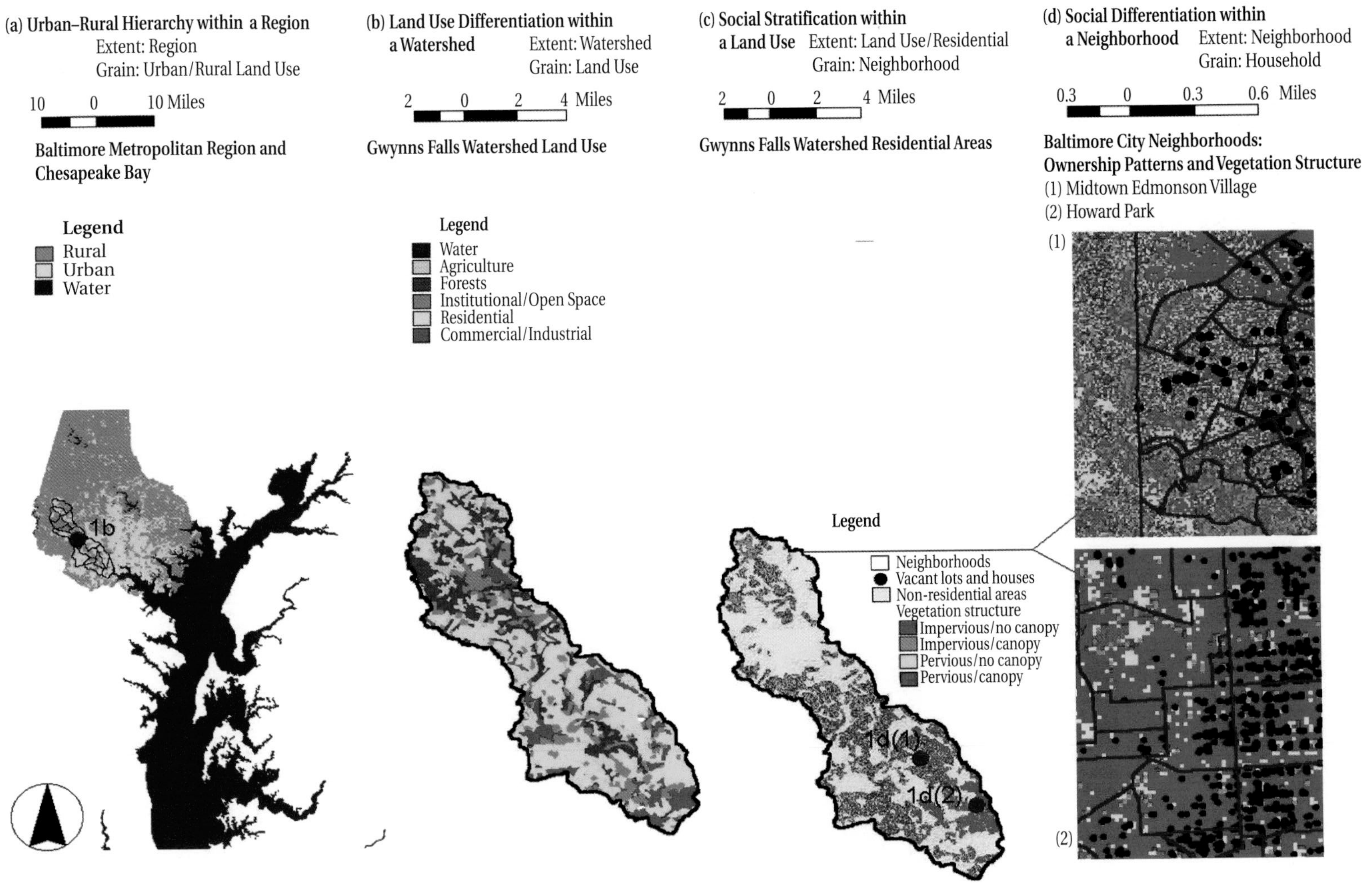

Fig. 6.1. An hierarchical approach to human ecological systems of Baltimore Metropolitan regions, Baltimore, Maryland, USA.

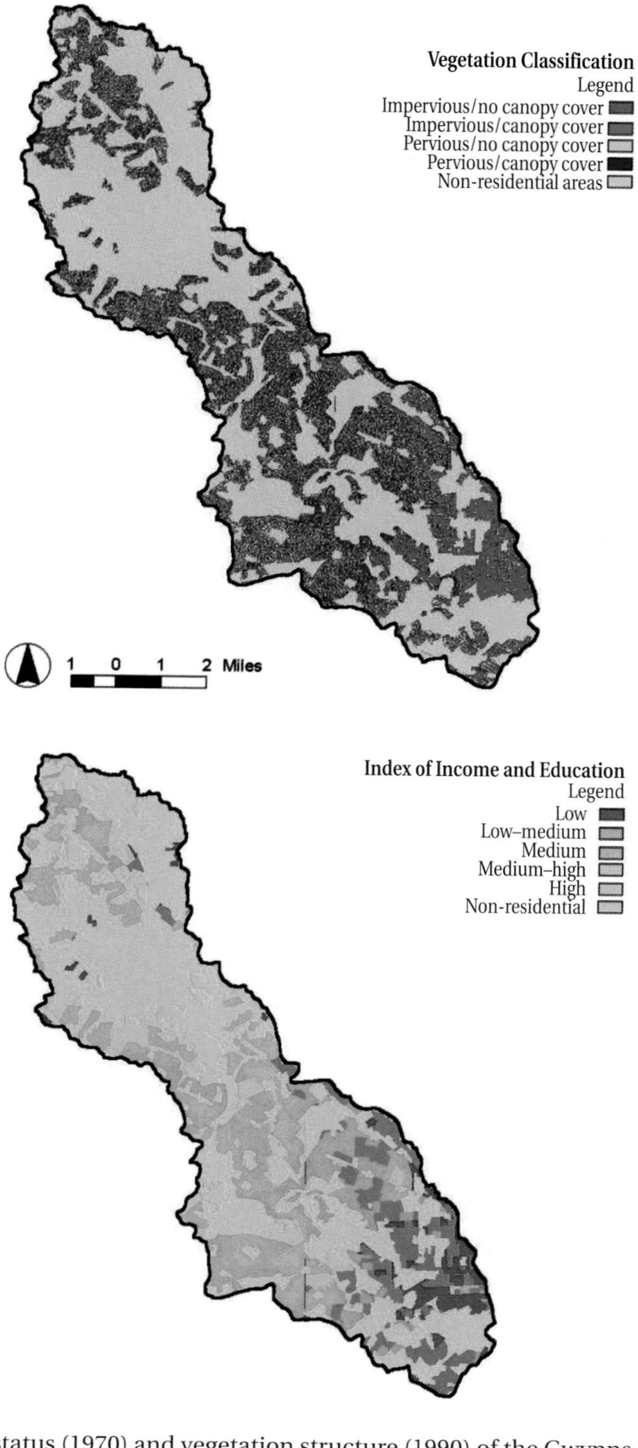

Fig. 6.2. Socioeconomic status (1970) and vegetation structure (1990) of the Gwynns Falls watershed of the Baltimore Metropolitan regions, Baltimore, Maryland, USA.

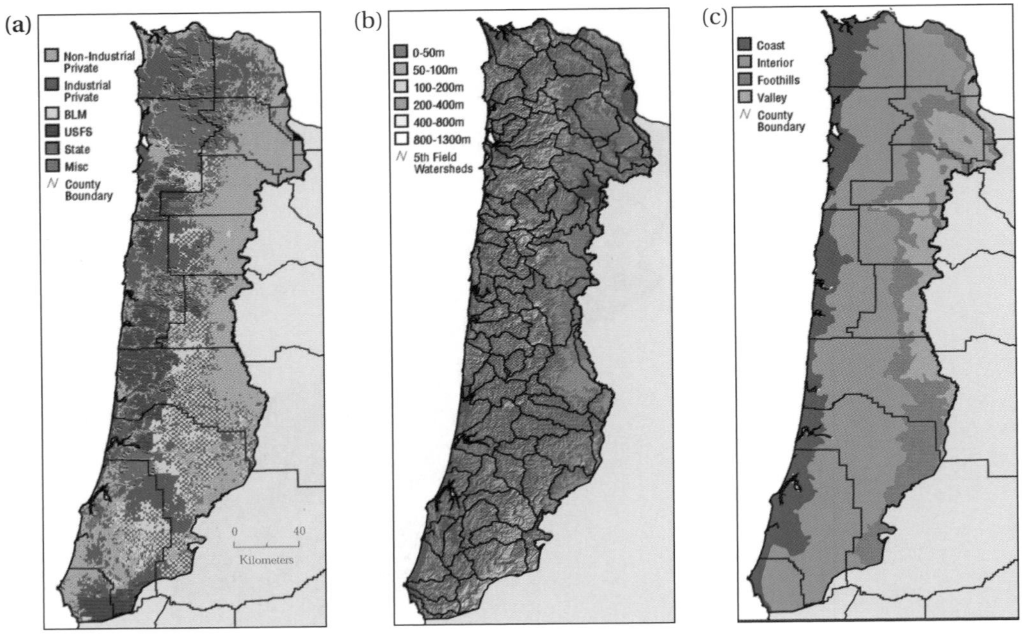

Fig. 7.1. Patterns of (a) major ownerships, (b) topography (elevation in meters), and (c) ecoregions in the Oregon Coast Range Province. Abbreviations: BLM, Bureau of Land Management; USFS, US Forest Service; Misc, miscellaneous owners. (Modified from Pater *et al.* 1998.)

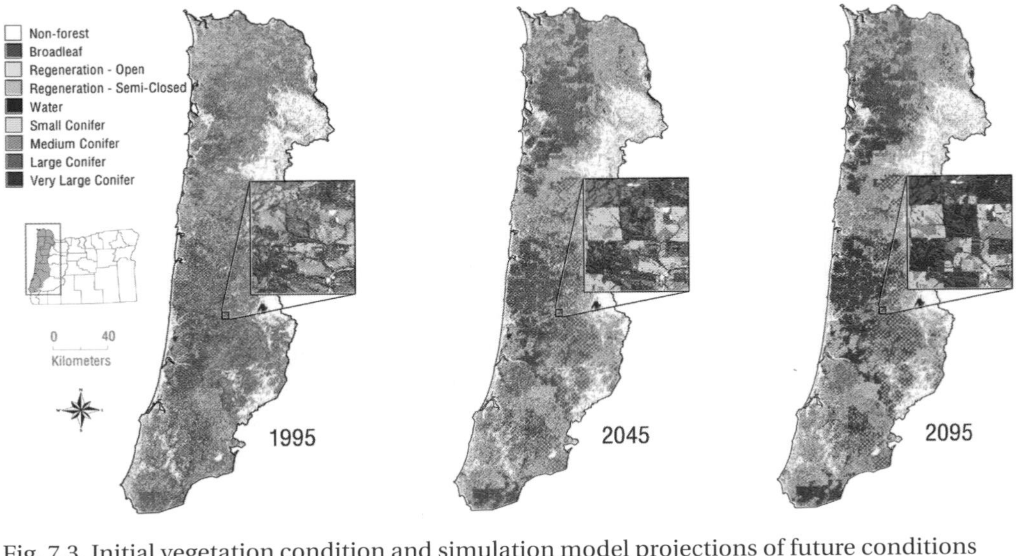

Fig. 7.3. Initial vegetation condition and simulation model projections of future conditions at 50 and 100 years into the future. Broadleaf is total vegetation cover >70% and >70% of which is broadleaf cover, Open is <40% total vegetation cover, Semi-closed is 40–70% vegetation cover, Conifer is >70% vegetation cover and at least 30% of which is conifer cover, Small is dominant and codominant trees <25 cm diameter at breast height (dbh), Medium is 25–50 cm dbh, Large is 50–75 cm dbh, and Very Large is >75 cm dbh.

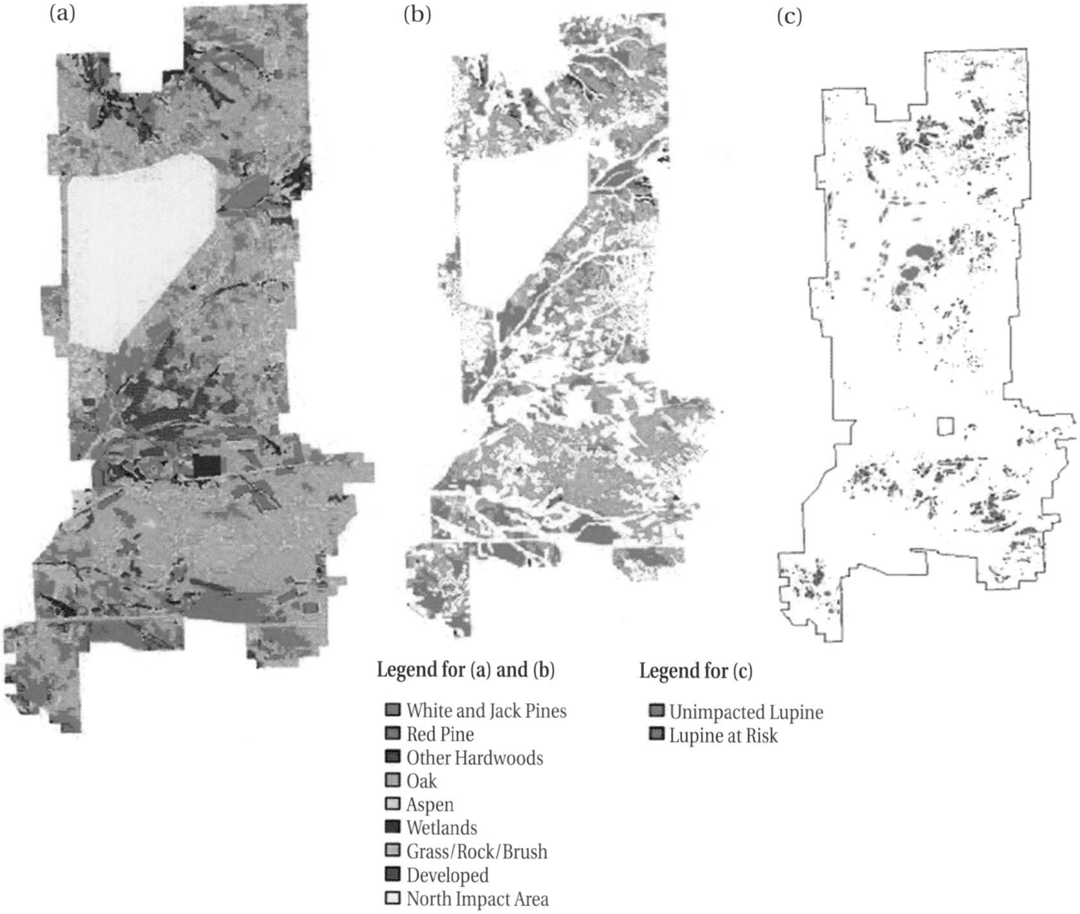

Fig. 10.2. (a) Map of cover groups at Fort McCoy and the North Impact land use. The cover layers were derived from four GIS data layers provided by personnel at Fort McCoy (D. Aslesen, personal communication to T. Ashwood, September, 1997). All data layers are in Universal Transverse Mercator (UTM) Zone 15 projection with meters as the basic unit. The forest inventory layer was digitized from the inventory map developed by the forestry staff at Fort McCoy. Mapping occurred from 1984 to 1991 with no updates since 1991. Streams were digitized from US Geological Survey 7.5 min quads. Wetlands were digitized from the Wisconsin wetlands inventory.

(b) Map of areas by cover groups that are at risk of change with tracked- and wheeled-vehicle training in maneuver areas as determined by the sites at risk of change in column 1 of Table 10.3. Areas in white are not at risk of change.

(c) Map of lupine patches at risk of change with tracked- and wheeled-vehicle training in maneuver areas as determined by the sites at risk of change in column 2 of Table 10.3. Areas in white are not at risk of change. The lupine layer was digitized from an installation-wide lupine survey conducted in 1993–4 with a partial update in 1995–6 and was provided by personnel at Fort McCoy (D. Aslesen, personal communication to T. Ashwood, September, 1997).The lines indicate the boundaries of the training area and of the installation.

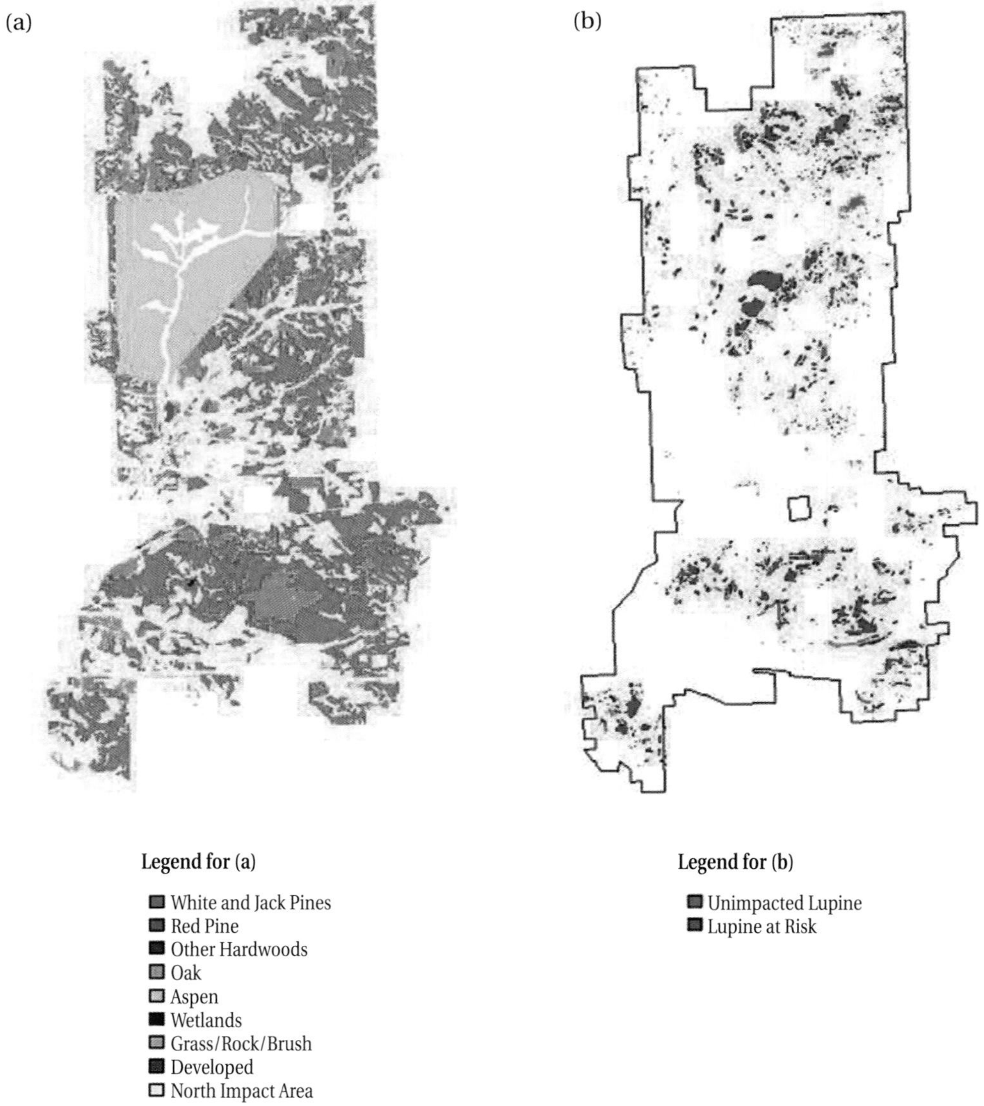

Fig. 10.3. (a) Map of the area by cover group at risk of change with prescribed burns as determined by the sites at risk of change greater than 0.01 in column 2 of Table 10.3. Areas in white are not at risk of change. The lines indicate the boundaries of the training area and of the installation.

(b) Map of lupine patches at risk of change with prescribed burns as determined by the sites at risk of change greater than 0.01 in column 2 of Table 10.3. The lupine layer was digitized from an installation-wide lupine survey conducted in 1993–4 with a partial update in 1995–6 and was provided by personnel at Fort McCoy (D. Aslesen, personal communication to T. Ashwood, September, 1997).

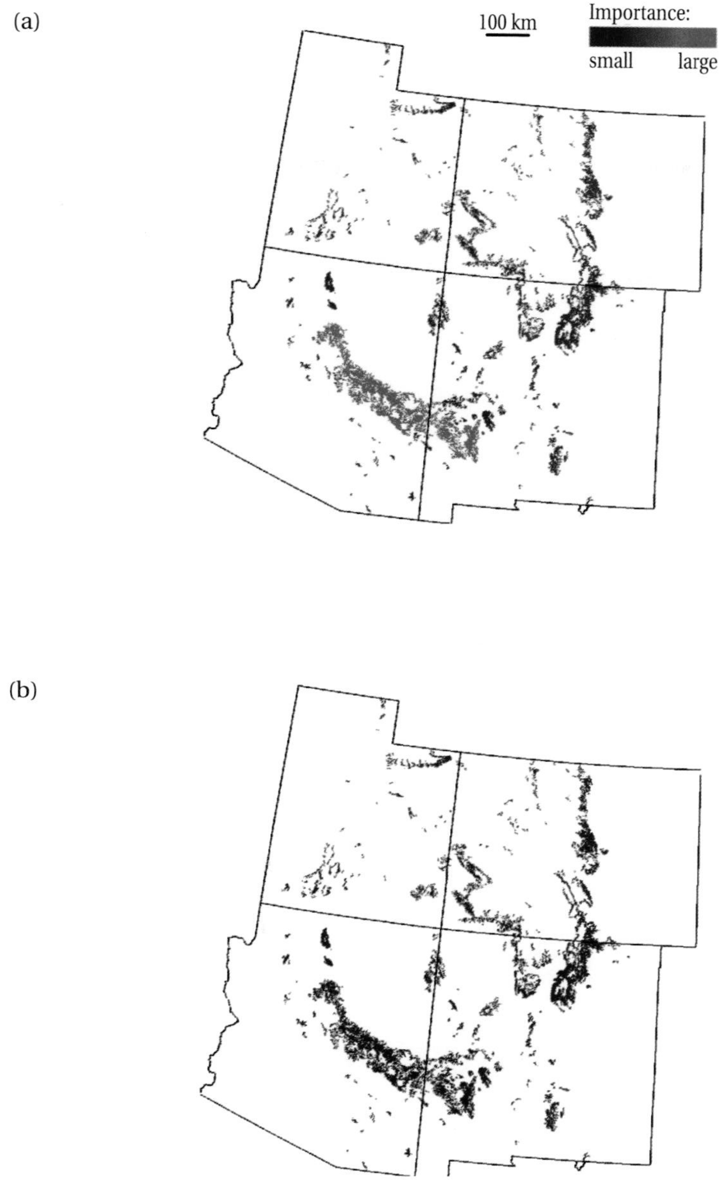

Fig. 11.4. Habitat distribution of the Mexican spotted owl (*Strix occidentalis lucida*) in the American Southwest. (a) Rank sensitivity of these patches, in terms of the impact on landscape connectivity if the patch was removed. Red patches are most sensitive; blue, least sensitive.

(b) Rank sensitivities corrected by patch area, emphasizing locational effects and highlighting stepping-stone patches. The analysis was not intended to be definitive, but rather to identify patches that would warrant further study in terms for owl dispersal and habitat use. Redrawn from Keitt *et al.* (1997).

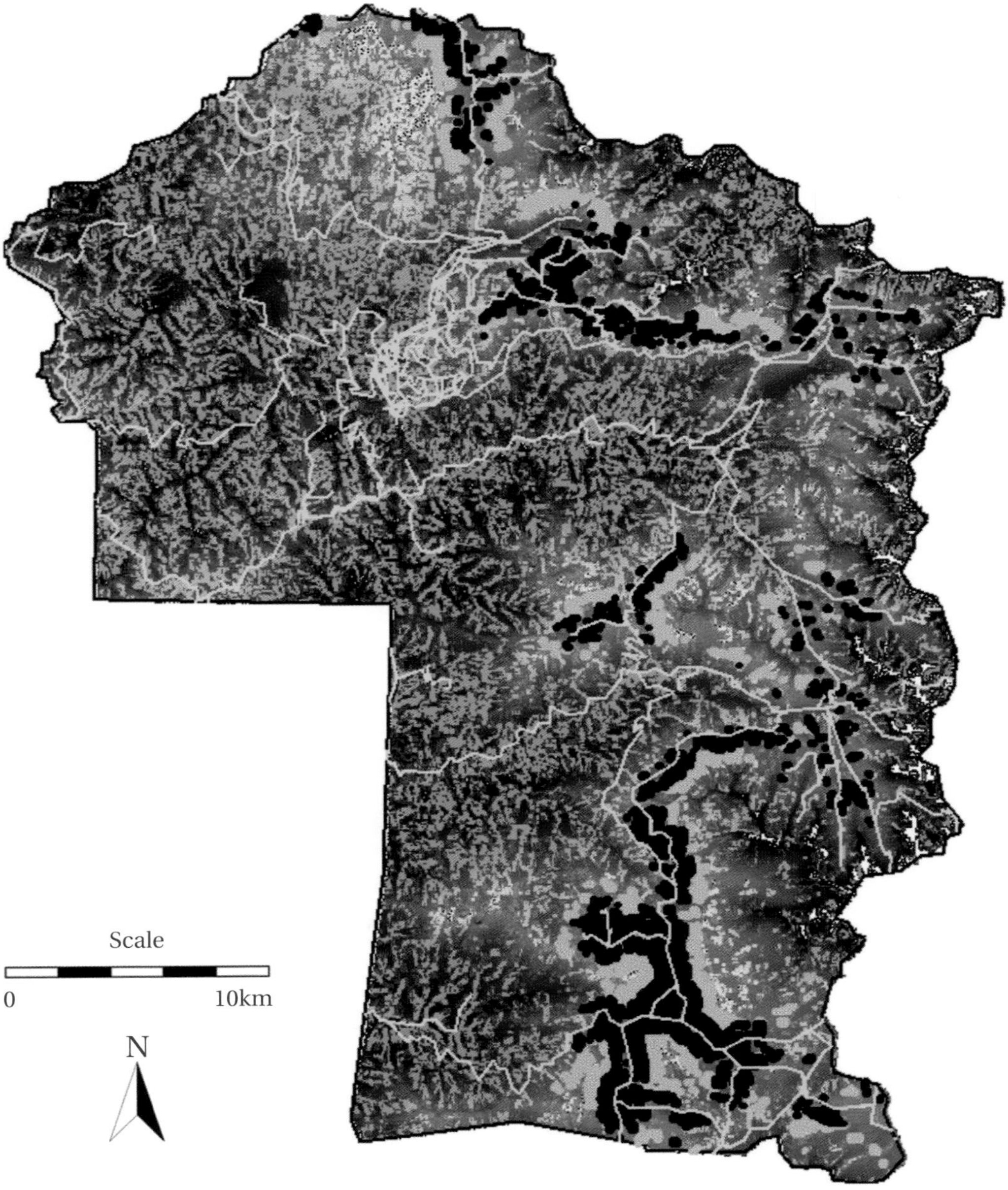

Fig. 11.5. Local sensitivity of landscapes in the Sierra Nevada to climatic variation, in terms of simulated soil moisture balance. Image of the 90 000-ha Kaweah Basin is shaded as a false-color composite in which sensitivity to variation in temperature is colored red, sensitivity to variation in precipitation is blue, and uncertainty due to variation in microtopographic effects on drainage is green. Yellow lines are roads and major trails. Gray zone (~17% of study area) is simultaneously highly sensitive and has high local variability in microtopography; black highlights those locations that are also close to roads and trails for ease of access. From Urban (2000).

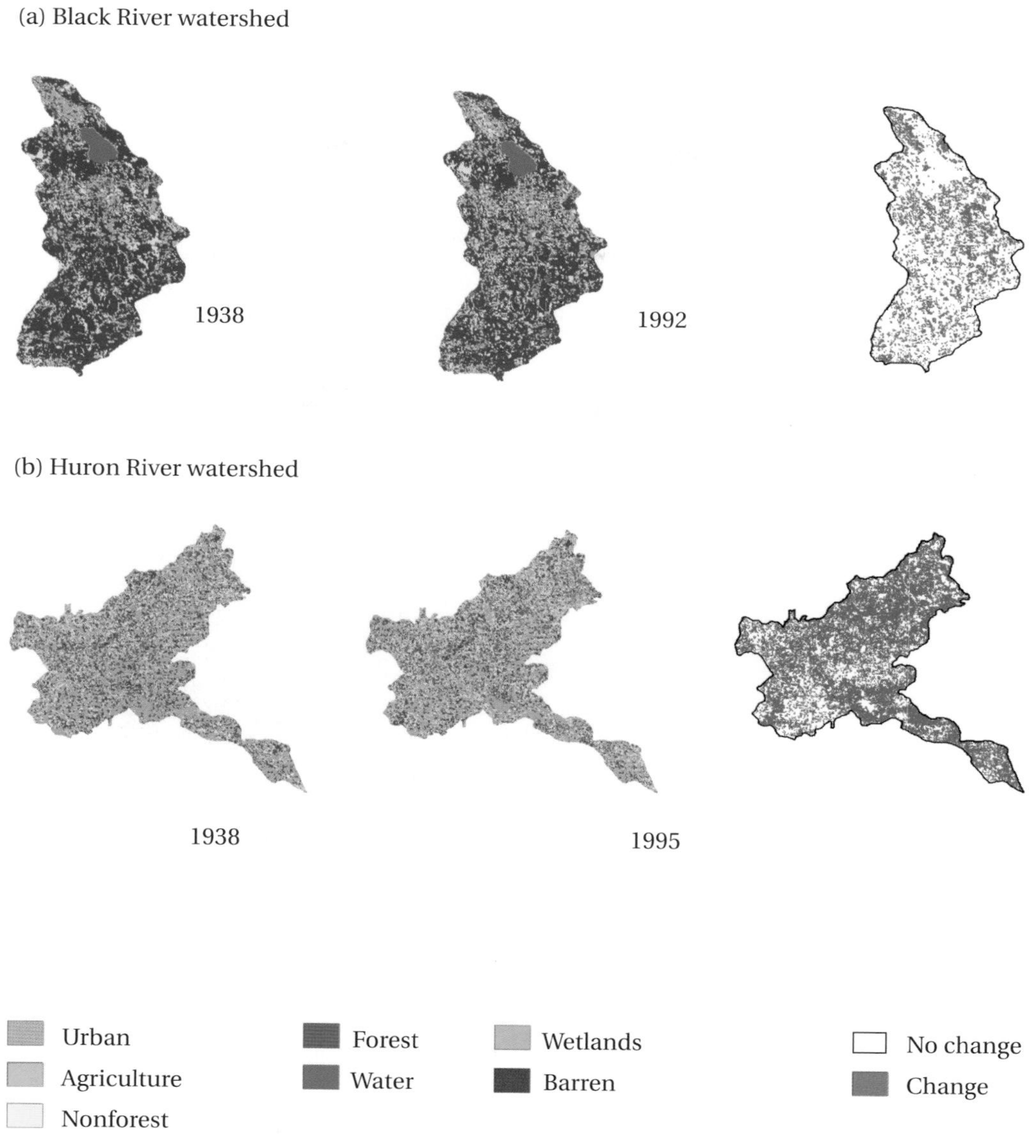

Fig. 12.4. Distribution and extent of change of land cover. (a) 1938 and 1992 for the Black River watershed; (b) 1938–40 and 1995 for the Huron River watershed.

(a)

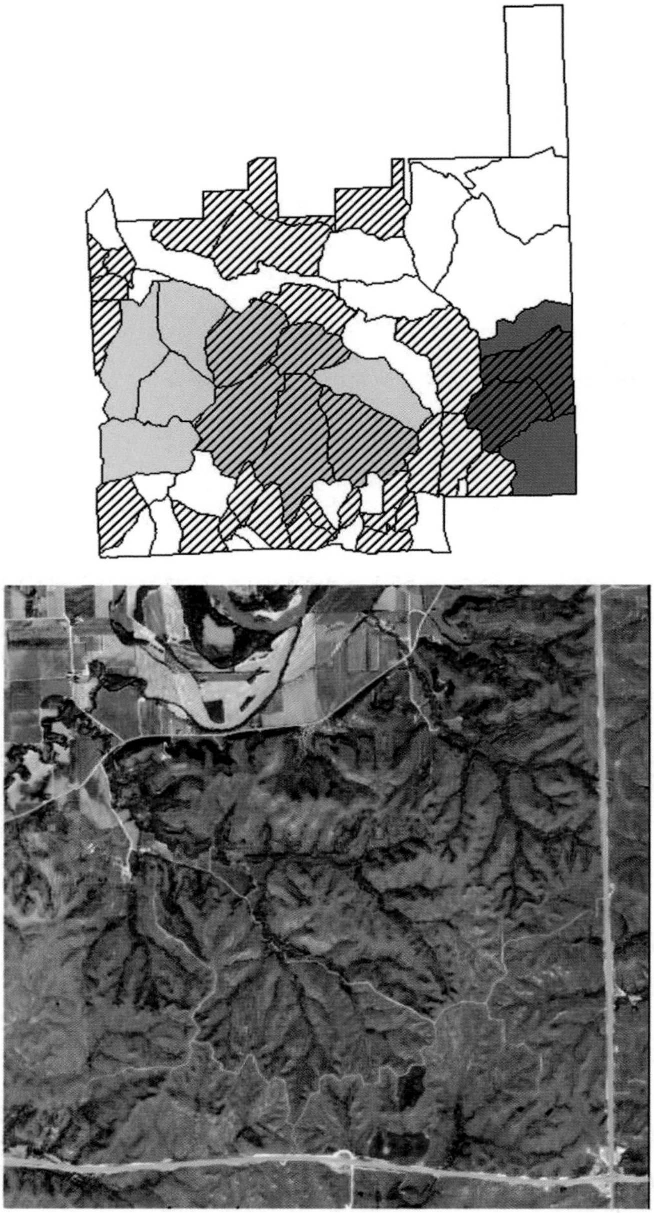

(b)

Fig. 16.2. A Landsat Thematic Mapper image of Konza Prairie Research Natural Area, September 11, 1997. In the GIS coverage (a) the 64 watershed units of Konza Prairie are outlined. The cross-hatched areas are watersheds burned in 1997, light gray areas are grazed by bison, and dark gray areas are grazed by domestic cattle.

In the image (b) note the gallery forests (bright red) defining the drainage patterns in Konza. Ungrazed burned watersheds are a brighter red indicating higher levels of net primary production. Unburned watersheds have a more blue tone due to the reflectance from the detritus layer. The Kansas River floodplain is located in the northeast corner of the image. The blue areas are non-vegetated in September (winter wheat) while the red areas are actively photosynthesizing crops (soybeans and corn). Interstate 70 is located across the bottom of the image. Note the contrasting landscape patterns between the agriculturally developed areas (rectangular) and native grassland (irregular shapes).

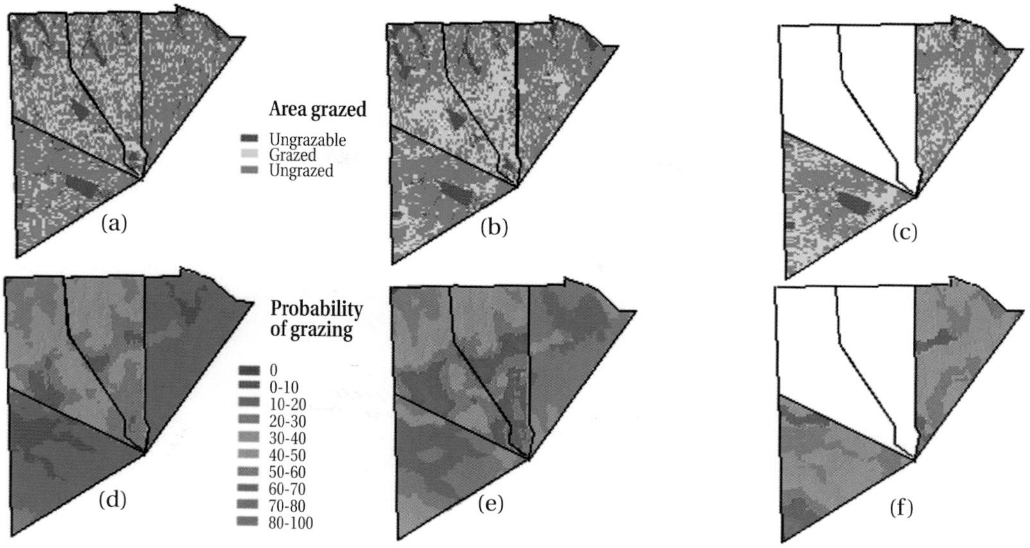

Fig. 16.4. Actual and predicted grazing distributions for three selected dates from Rannel's Ranch near Manhattan, Kansas. Each enclosure is 80 acres (approximately 32 ha) in size. (a–c) Actual distribution on May 25, July 20, and September 27, 1994, respectively; (d–f) predicted grazing distribution for the same dates.

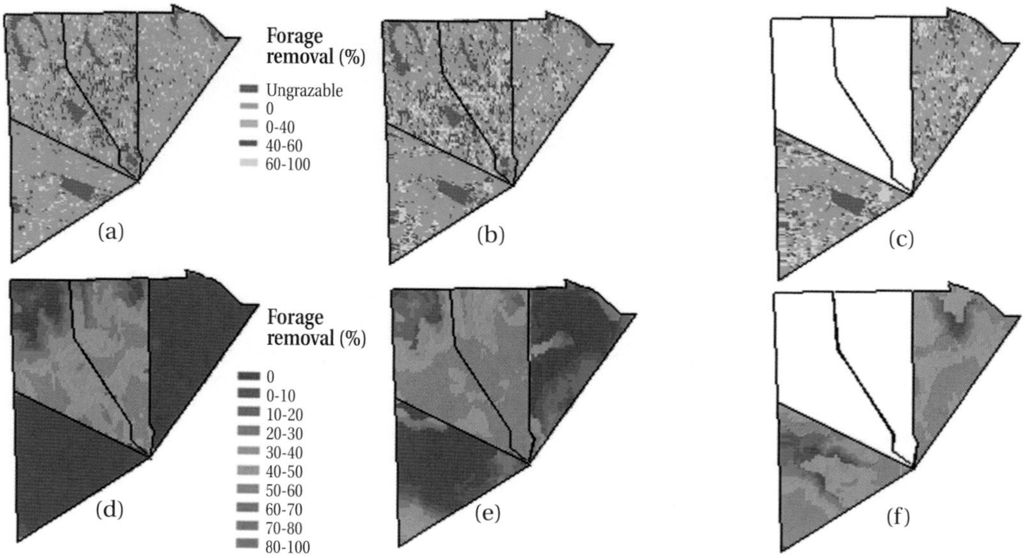

Fig. 16.5. Actual and predicted forage removals for three selected dates. (a–c) Actual removal on May 25, July 20, September 27, 1994, respectively; (d–f) predicted forage removal for the same dates.

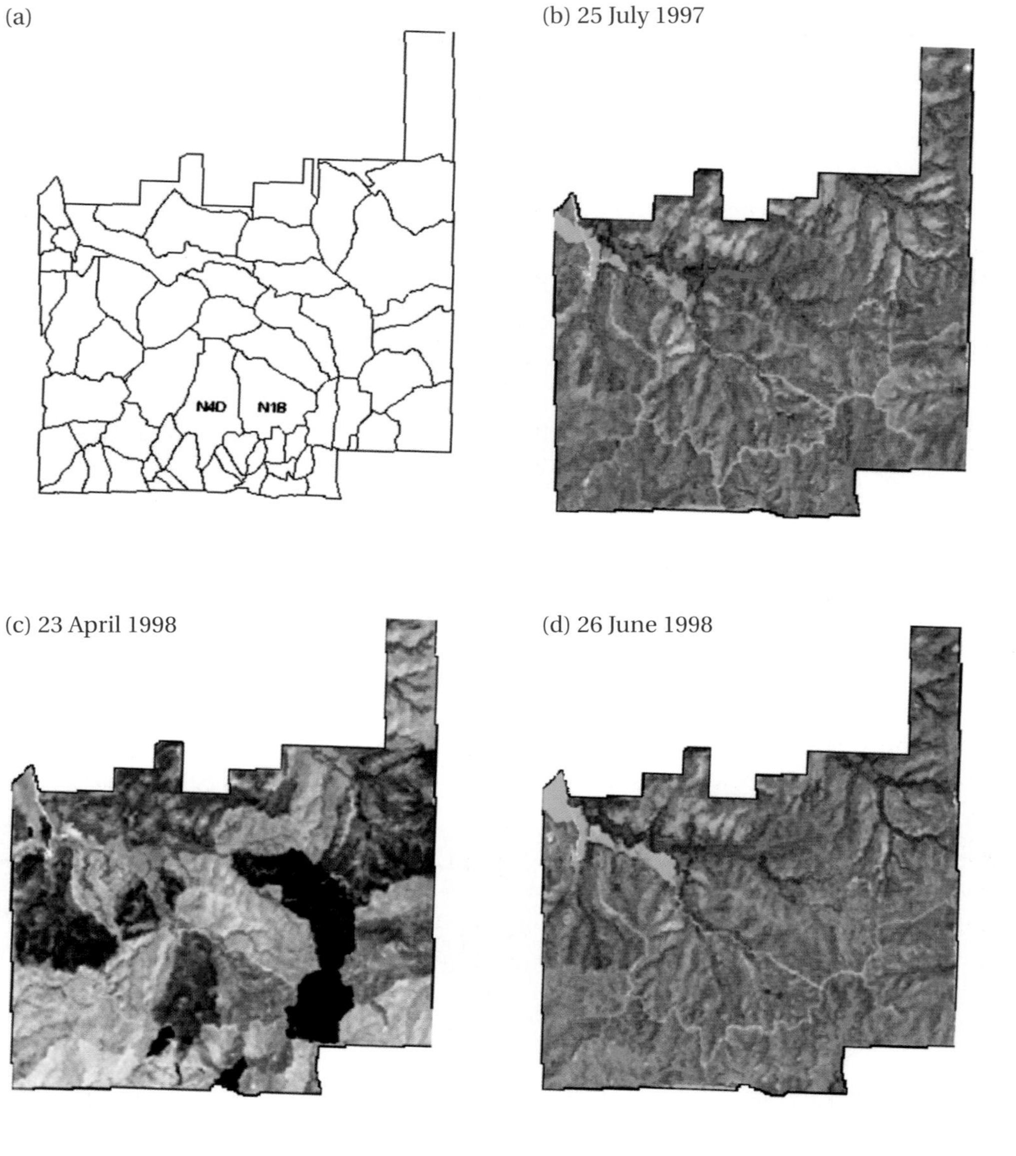

Fig. 16.6. This series of satellite images demonstrates the interaction between fire and grazing. (a) Is a GIS coverage showing the watershed boundaries on Konza Prairie.

In (b) note that watershed N1B is heavily grazed. (blue, indicating low biomass) and N4D, which had not burned for four years, is not utilized by the bison (red, indicating higher biomass) as much as N1B. In the spring of 1998

(c) N4D burned more completely while N1B burned poorly since most of the biomass has been removed through grazing. (Compare to an ungrazed burned watershed on the eastern edge of this image.)

In the summer of 1998 (d) the bison have switched their grazing to N4D (appears blue indicating lower biomass) and largely ignored N1B.

The accuracy of the matrix inputs influences the validity of the projection of future landscape changes. Changes to the system, however, that have not been experienced in the past but are possible can also be modeled to influence future conditions.

Certain assumptions are made when simulating land-use changes with transition models. The analysis is based on information about types, patterns, and changes in past land uses from some kind of hindsight (such as can be obtained from remote-sensing images [e.g., Hall *et al.*, 1991], aerial images [e.g., Kachi *et al.*, 1986; Duncan *et al.*, 1999], or historical data [e.g., Turner, 1988]). Inputs to the model are determined from previous time periods, and empirical data for those models are needed. Caution must be used when extrapolating past trends and data to new conditions (Debussche *et al.*, 1977). The overall validity of a model depends on the accuracy of its transition probabilities over periods of time of concern to the land managers and whether or not key variables are part of the model. Static transition probabilities do not change over time and should be used for short periods of time for which they provide the highest reliability. Debussche *et al.* (1977) suggest using a time interval of no more than five years, whereas Aaviksoo (1993) suggests eight years. With longer time intervals, more data collection is usually required to develop the model and the dynamic transition probabilities that can change over time and that depend on such factors as socioeconomic conditions and adjacent land-cover types. These dynamic probabilities may provide a more accurate prediction of the ongoing changes that occur over longer time intervals (Turner, 1988). Some types of simulation models project feedbacks between land-cover conditions, ecological changes, and socioeconomic and political changes (as discussed by Dale and Pearson, 1999), but these interactions have yet to be incorporated into transition models.

As with any model, transition models assume that no unknown variables will be introduced into the actual system. Models can simulate extreme situations and provide insights so that managers can decide if a change in management policy is required. As new conditions are included, the model may need to be restructured, depending on the assumptions that relate to the new variable. For this reason, some degree of uncertainty in running a model always should be expected (Usher, 1981). With this caveat in mind, management planners should be cautious when creating management schemes based on models. The models should be used as a guide in developing plans and used in conjunction with other modeling tools and site-specific information. Models should be checked for accuracy and suitability in each situation to which they are applied. The ultimate utility of models is that they enable planners to evaluate potential future conditions under various use and management scenarios.

10.2.2 Applications of transition matrices

Transition matrices have been used in ecology to model succession and land-use change, but few analyses combine the two applications (although Gibson *et al.* [1997] use different transition matrices for vegetation succession under different management regimes). The Markov approach was first used in ecology to simulate the natural succession of vegetation over time. For example, Waggoner and Stephens (1970) used an empirical approach to project the number of trees in size classes based on past trends. Their model did not take into account drought or insect outbreaks that ultimately had a great influence on the changes in forest size and species composition. Horn (1975a,b), on the other hand, developed a theory of tree-by-tree replacement probabilities. Runkle (1981) pointed out that because individual species behave in unique ways, transition-matrix approaches should be used with caution to predict equilibrium conditions. Even so, for predictive purposes, transition matrices are more accurate than geometrical or linear progressions (Usher, 1966; Debussche *et al.*, 1977). However, Usher (1981) identified seven flaws in using transition models for succession: (1) it is difficult to define the states of the model; (2) the data required are hard to collect; (3) the model includes only single independence in time and no history; (4) the transition probabilities may not, in fact, be constant; (5) spatial effects are averaged out; (6) the data must be fully representative of all species; and (7) if enough data are available to run the model, the model is often not needed. Nevertheless, Usher (1981) continued to endorse the use of transition models for prediction of vegetation change and to test concepts of succession. Shugart (1984) reviewed the development of transition models for vegetation succession and called for further extension of these models to landscapes.

A landscape-transition model can map and describe the impact of land-use activities on natural and human resources. It can project changes in landscapes or habitats and the resulting impacts on biodiversity. Land-use activities can be characterized by using a common set of parameters (magnitude, frequency, areal extent, spatial distribution, predictability) that can be applied either to specific activities or to different intensities of the same activity. This approach permits evaluation of the incremental and cumulative effects of diverse activities, such as road building, military maneuvers, grazing, timber harvests, or environmental restoration. Evaluating the risk posed to habitats and species can be expressed as a change in the abundance or spatial distribution of guilds, species, populations, or their habitat. Models that run over a decade or more should explicitly incorporate information on vegetation succession.

The landscape-transition approach is generic and, with appropriate databases, can be applied to any site. Transition matrices have been shown to be adept at modeling landscape changes caused by human disturbance (Turner, 1988; Aaviksoo, 1993). Turner (1988) points out that transition-matrix modeling can be extended to simulate such processes as dispersal of organisms, movement of water, and chemical flows between boundaries.

Turner (1988) used a transition matrix to analyze land-use changes in a piedmont county in Georgia. The data used in the study were obtained from various government land surveys. Six sample areas were selected, and five land uses were identified: urban, cropland, abandoned cropland, pasture, and forest. The landscape patterns in 1942 served as the initial conditions for the model. The change of a cell's state was determined from two factors: the transition probability, $P_{i,j}$, which was obtained empirically, and the state of the eight neighboring cells. The matrices were multiplied to simulate changes from 1942 to 1955 and from 1955 to 1980 as compared with changes documented in aerial photography for the years 1942, 1955, and 1980. Turner (1988) found close agreement between the recorded actual changes in the proportion of land-use types and the values obtained in the model. There was also much agreement in the spatial distribution of the land-use types. The study shows that accurate projections in land-cover changes can be achieved using transition matrices.

An earlier model developed by Debussche *et al.* (1977) predicted changes in vegetation types under certain management conditions. They modeled changes for 7000 ha in the French Massif Central. They mapped the 1973 land cover on a 1/25 000 scale. Aerial photographs of the same region from 1948 enabled them to develop state vectors for the years 1948 and 1973. The changes seen in vegetation were extrapolated 25 years to obtain a prediction for 1998. The analysis projected a decrease in the proportion of cultivated and rangelands because of a rural population exodus. From this observation, they went back to 1973 information and modeled a land-use strategy that would optimize utilization of resources for the rural populations. The results of this second model showed that a drastic decrease in heathland and forests would occur. The authors, therefore, suggested that actions be taken to create a balance in the land-cover types.

10.3 A protocol for developing and applying the transition approach to land management

The application of transition models to land management is not always straightforward. To facilitate its implementation, we set forth an approach for the development and application of landscape-transition matrices for particular management issues based on an understanding of land- management practices and their implications. This approach involves eight steps (Fig. 10.1).

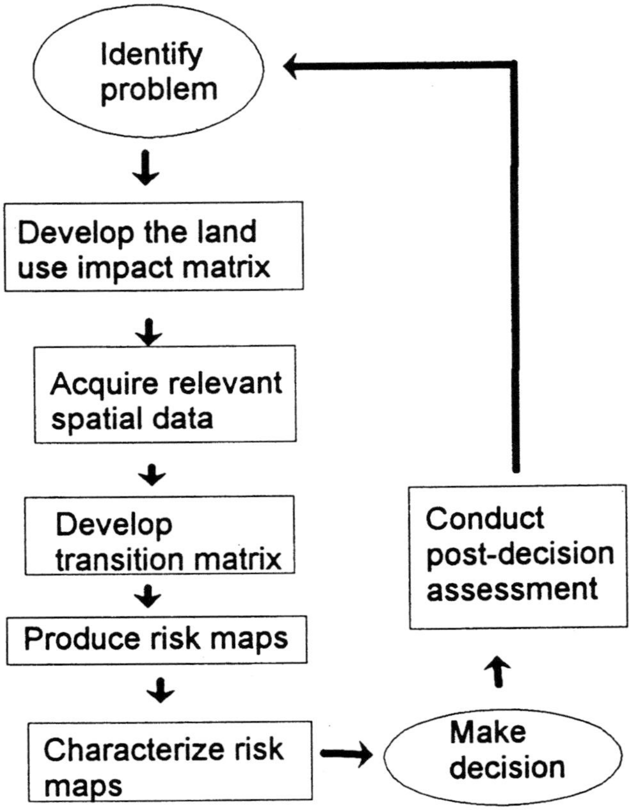

FIGURE 10.1
Approach for developing and applying landscape-transition matrix.

10.3.1 Identify the problem

The first task is to select the situation to which the approach will be applied. This choice determines the location, the issues of concern, and potential land-use activities, and requires focusing on the species or ecosystem characteristics of concern and the land-use activities that might occur. The social concerns of the local and regional setting often have a strong impact on the nature of the issues (Freudenburg, 1999). For instance, concerns often arise with the siting of an industrial facility when it is close to residential areas. Regulatory and legislative actions also dictate issues that must be addressed (Lyndon, 1999). For example, sites that support rare species or critical habitats in the United States are regulated by the Endangered Species Act (ESA) and the National Environmental Policy Act (NEPA). Environmental constraints also influence the degree to which a particular issue becomes a concern (Dale and O'Neill, 1999).

The problem analysis must be set in the appropriate landscape or regional perspective as determined by the features of the region and the issue under consideration. Sometimes, the appropriate region is a very small area; other times, it may be a large area or even a continent. Environmental conditions, such as wind patterns, can influence the effects of airborne materials from the planned facility. Also, soil and hydrologic conditions can affect runoff from the site. All of these factors must be considered in combination to identify the problem to be addressed.

The concerns at a particular location should be prioritized according to the potential land-management actions, spatial area most affected, intensity of effect, and stakeholder interests. Although many potential land-use actions could occur at a site, only a few actions are typically considered at a time. The actions for focus may center on a particular tract of land or on specific stakeholder needs. Thus, a set of potential management activities can be identified for specific consideration. These actions impact certain environmental characteristics, so the choice of activities also influences the environmental characteristics of concern (which are discussed below).

10.3.2. Develop a spatial-allocation rule using a land-use-impact matrix

As mentioned in section 10.2.1, a key step in the application of transition matrices to land management is the spatial allocation of the probability of state change. Usually, more than one type of land-management activity is considered at a time so a land-use-impact matrix can be developed to relate changes resulting from different land uses to the environmental characteristics of each cell. These characteristics can refer to any ecological conditions that broadly encompass composition, function, or structural features. Composition reflects species, ecosystem, or landscape diversity (Franklin, 1993), such as presence or absence of species or, on a landscape scale, the home range of species that requires a particular land-cover type, spatial patterns of habitat for species that exist as metapopulations, special habitat needs that relate to mating behaviors or different life stages of the organisms, or the spatial relationships of these habitats. Functional features, such as soil condition or the presence of pollinators, affect the ability of a system to grow, reproduce, and die. Structure includes the presence or absence of downed woody debris, litter on the forest floor, water-holding capacity of the soil, or other physical features that affect the composition or function of an ecological system. Impacts of past disturbances, such as the introduction of non-native species or fires instigated by lightning, should also be included when they pose management concerns (Dale *et al.*, 1998).

The land-use-impact matrix relates particular uses to environmental characteristics that are affected by those uses. Select environmental characteristics form the columns of the land-use-impact matrix. The rows of the matrix are land-use activities, such as military training and testing, forest management, prescribed fire, or land and infrastructure maintenance. The land-use-impact matrix can be depicted as:

$$\begin{array}{lccc} & & \text{Environmental characteristics} & \\ & E_1 & E_2 & E_3 \\ \text{Land-use} \quad A_1 & \multicolumn{3}{c}{\begin{bmatrix} l_{1,1} & l_{1,2} & l_{1,3} \\ l_{2,1} & l_{2,2} & l_{2,3} \end{bmatrix},} \\ \text{activities} \quad A_2 & & & \end{array}$$

where E_j represents the environmental characteristics, A_i represents the land-use activities, and $l_{i,j}$ represents the land-impact characteristics that are the elements of the matrix and ranges from no impact to a severe impact. An example of no impact is driving on existing roads, where no vegetation is harmed because none exists in the area of activity (but note that Mladenoff *et al.* [1995] document a situation where road presence disrupts wolves). An example of severe impact is the construction of a new building that involves the removal of all vegetation. Some impacts are immediate, like site preparation by bulldozers that removes most understory vegetation, whereas others are delayed. The impact on various aspects of species, ecosystems, or landscapes must also be taken into account. For example, some activities only impact understory vegetation, whereas timber harvests affect both trees and understory vegetation.

Having spatial locations associated with each environmental characteristic means that effects of the land-use activities can be identified by place. For example, management practices in longleaf pine forests can be considered. For younger stands, the selective thinning of hardwood ingrowth is more likely, while clear-cutting of older stands is more common. The land-use-impact matrix might be as follows:

$$\begin{array}{lcc} & \multicolumn{2}{r}{\text{Environmental characteristic of forest}} \\ \text{Land-use activities} & <30 \text{ yrs old} & >30 \text{ yrs old} \\ \quad \text{Selective thinning of hardwoods} & \multicolumn{2}{c}{\begin{bmatrix} 0.8 & \quad 0.1 \\ 0 & \quad 0.6 \end{bmatrix}.} \\ \quad \text{Clear-cutting} & & \end{array}$$

If the stand ages are depicted on a map, then the likelihood of these land actions can be mapped as well. Thus, land-use impacts on the environmental characteristics can provide a means to develop risk maps that identify sites likely to undergo changes to species, ecosystem, or landscape features.

Each of these land-use activities has some variability associated with it in terms of the timing, frequency, and intensity of the event. Thus, one could develop a family of curves that depict different levels of disturbance impact on ecosystem features related to intensity of each activity. Questions about the relationship between impact and intensity include: What will change the shape of the disturbance impact curve (e.g., from linear to curvilinear), and under what conditions will thresholds in impacts occur?

10.3.3 Acquire relevant spatial data

Spatial information on where specific land-use activities (A_i) are likely to occur is needed to map impacts on environmental characteristics (E_j). Useful spatial data include linear features, such as roads, rivers, or electrical transmission lines, as well as polygonal information on past land uses, soil type or texture, slope, aspect, and other factors that influence how land uses impact environmental conditions. Some of this information is generally available (such as presence of roads); other information has to be derived from independent sources. For example, vegetation-cover types often can be derived from forest inventories or satellite imagery that often are available for a site. However, mapped vegetation cover should be verified by ground-truth data to some degree. Also, it may be important to identify habitats of concern. This information can be obtained via overlays of relevant information (e.g., soils and aspect) (Mann *et al.*, 1999). Often, this step of acquiring the relevant spatial data may be quite difficult; however, with advances in remote sensing imagery, computer storage and retrieval, and transmission of data, the acquisition of such data is getting easier.

10.3.4 Develop transition matrix

The transition matrix gives the probability that one state will change to another state under the particular land use being considered. This information can be obtained from historical changes that have occurred or anticipated future changes. The transition matrix can be used in a scenario analysis to examine the consequences of hypothesized changes in states.

The states and the time frame of the transition must be specified. For example, if the states are forest types, then one would consider the potential for the states to change to be on the order of years or decades. But if the states are density of insects, then the time frame may be on the order of hours to days. Thus, the time step should be relevant to the states of the system being considered.

In land-use applications, the transition matrix can be calculated as a product of the probability of the land use occurring and the potential impact on the state. Thus for an annual time step, if there is a 5% chance of an insect outbreak in any one year and all of the trees are typically eliminated by the outbreak, then the transition probability from a forested to a non-forested state would be $0.05 \times 1.0 = 0.05$ for any one year.

10.3.5 Produce risk maps

With the transition matrix and the spatial data on the location of the environmental characteristics, a risk map can be developed for various land-use scenarios. The transition matrix combines the potential for land-use changes and their impacts but has no spatial information. The land-use-impact matrix contains the pertinent spatial information. If the location of the environmental characteristic is known, then the potential effects of each land-use activity on environmental characteristics (E_j) provide the information for specifying locations of transitions from one state to another. The key here is that the environmental features must be spatially explicit and must relate to the states of the system. For example, if the environmental characteristic under consideration is density of tree snags and the state is forest type, then the effects of land-use activities on snag density for each forest type comprise the land-use-impact matrix. The potential for each land use to occur and its effects on changes from one forest type to another form the transition matrix. Because each location has a particular forest type and each forest type has a set snag density, the maps of forest type could be used to produce maps of sites at risk of change in snag density with given land-use activities. Of course, snag density is typically associated with other features than forest type alone, and more-refined data would allow greater detail in the risk map.

Thus, resource-risk maps show locations of habitats or natural resources that are likely to change under certain land-management or use regimes and the degree of potential change. This information can be summarized as a map or video of potential changes over time and presented to land managers to illustrate graphically the resources at risk of change under specific practices. The resource-risk map can alert managers to the location and timing of particular activities or land uses that maximize or minimize impacts on the natural resources. For example, some activities could be scheduled to occur at a time when the system is less sensitive, such as avoiding the breeding season of a species of concern or times when soil moisture is high.

10.3.6 Characterize risk maps

Spatial analysis of the features of the risk maps provides a way to summarize and analyze potential changes so that managers can better use this information in decision-making. Several spatial-analysis metrics are available (O'Neill *et al.*, 1988; Li and Reynolds, 1993; Hargis *et al.*, 1998). Landscape characteristics that are helpful in the spatial analysis include patch size and distances between patches. For example, Fu *et al.* (1994) use the size, fractal dimension, and elongation index of patches to compare landscape patterns of grasslands and farmlands over time. By determining species or ecosystem requirements in spatial format (i.e., area needed for habitat), the spatial analysis can help in identifying areas that need to be targeted for management. Because the landscape characteristics often change over time, their effects on the species or systems of concern also change (Krummel and Gardner, 1987). One way to consider a risk map is to examine the landscape metrics before and after the proposed land-use activities and to use that information to determine those land-use activities that affect the environmental characteristics of concern. Alternatively, one can examine other land-use scenarios.

10.3.7 Make decision

The decision should include information from the ecological risk maps and results from the transition model run over the relevant time period as well as social, economic, and political goals for use of the land. The purpose of the risk map and transition model is to provide a way to visualize potential impacts of ecological concerns that result from the land-use decision so that these concerns can be taken into account in the decision process. Of course, other information besides ecological concerns are a part of the decision process.

10.3.8 Conduct post-decision assessment

Although this risk-based analysis allows the ramifications of a decision to be considered before the decision is made, it is also important to conduct post-decision assessment. This analysis should feed into future decisions that are made about the land. Information obtained by monitoring subsequent to the decision can be used to consider how the system has changed and could be changed by future decisions. The landscape-transition matrices discussed previously could be modified based on the new information and used to inform new decisions. The variety of tools that are available for post-decision assessment are discussed by Bergquist and Bergquist (1999).

10.4 Case study

The approach described above was applied to management concerns at Fort McCoy, a Department of Defense training installation in west central Wisconsin. Because the Fort McCoy application is largely dependent on a single species, the Karner blue butterfly (*Lycaeides melissa samuelis*), we provide some background on the selection of using this species to shape management goals.

10.4.1 The need for land management at Fort McCoy

Fort McCoy was acquired by the government in 1909 and consists of 24 300 ha, of which 8100 ha are actively used for training and maneuvers. Military facilities at the installation include ranges, training areas, an air-to-ground munitions impact area, two airborne drop zones, an airport, a tactical landing site, and a multi-purpose training range.

Aside from being of great utility for training military personnel, the land at Fort McCoy encompasses some natural areas that may be the last refuges for rare flora and fauna. Natural areas in Wisconsin's landscape consist of "the remaining scattered remnants of the plant and animal communities that formed following the melting of the last glaciers 12000 years ago and have escaped most, if not all, of the effects of civilization through the years" (*Fort McCoy Integrated Natural Resources Management Plan*, 1998). Natural areas at Fort McCoy include streams, wetlands, and oak/savanna barrens. Areas around some streams have formally been designated natural areas because they have unique habitats. Furthermore, care of the watersheds and wetlands ensures a good-quality water supply to the LaCrosse, Black, and Wisconsin river basins. Oak/savanna barrens are rare in Wisconsin and have been assigned ecological designations as natural areas at Fort McCoy. These savannas can be categorized as either low or high quality. Low-quality savannas are areas where the oak has been able to regenerate (mostly because of the lack of fire or the control of fire), and there is a denser stand of oak than was historically on the site. Typically, few of the savanna ground-layer plants are present. However, seeds from savanna plants are often in the seed bank, and when the area is harvested or burned, these will germinate. High-quality sites have had a disturbance regime (normally fire) close to the historic conditions for the site, and thus the oak component is somewhat controlled. The *Fort McCoy Integrated Natural Resources Management Plan* (1998) characterizes the savanna as having ground-layer vegetation with high diversity (more than 300 species), typical of a prairie site, with few exotics present. Only 800 ha of high-quality oak/savanna barrens remain in Wisconsin, and 120 ha are at Fort McCoy. An additional 8100 ha of low-quality oak/savanna are also present on the installation. Oak/savanna communities support the Karner blue butterfly (Fort McCoy's rarest species; Andow *et al.*, 1994). They are also excellent areas for military training, for they contain open areas necessary for the maneuverability of troops and army vehicles and provide cover for military exercises. Thus, our focus was on these oak/savanna communities and how land use could affect their quality.

The ecological characteristics of management concern at Fort McCoy fall into nine land-cover groups (Fig. 10.2a, color plate), each of which contains several cover types. Oaks are the most prevalent cover group, occurring over 10000 ha, followed by white and jack pines and grass/rock/brush areas. Red pine, wetland, aspen, and other hardwoods are less common, and none of these cover groups exceeds 1100 ha. All these cover groups are fairly well distributed around the installation. The "developed" and "impact area" cover groups are actually land-use categories considered to be sacrifice sites where intense use occurs. They contain 684 and 3112 ha, respectively.

Fort McCoy's military lands have a triple role in that they support important natural areas and rare species, they are used for military training, and they support recreation. Even though the military's prime mission is training, land stewards need to take all of these goals into account. Because military training occurs on cycles ranging from quarters up to three years, the land-management cycle is also very short. The landscape-transition approach we developed provides a means to examine how the land managers can meet Fort McCoy's military training needs and yet still ensure that the installation's natural resources are protected within the relevant time frame.

10.4.2 Applying the approach to Fort McCoy

Identify the problem

The overall problem is how to carry on the military-training regime, as well as other land-use activities, without adversely impacting the Karner blue butterfly population at Fort McCoy. Since the Karner blue butterfly was designated as an endangered species in 1992, Fort McCoy has undertaken steps to protect the butterfly and its habitat. The butterfly's habitat is characterized by the presence of wild lupine (*Lupinus perennis*). Because lupine is the sole host plant for Karner blue butterfly larvae, its presence is requisite for the butterfly. Management of land-use activities to ensure that the Karner blue butterfly is preserved, therefore, focuses on management for wild lupine as an important component of oak/savanna barrens.

Out of the many land-use activities that occur at Fort McCoy, two of the most common activities have been selected for analysis in this chapter. These two are tracked- and wheeled-vehicle training in maneuver areas and prescribed burning. Both of these activities represent significant management issues at Fort McCoy and affect the quality of the oak/savanna where wild lupine occurs.

Develop the land-use-impact matrix

Fort McCoy's land-use regime includes military training, building construction, maintenance activities, insect and vegetation controls, and forestry practices. Proper management of the KBB population requires characterization and quantification of the impact of each land-use activity on vegetation-cover groups and, specifically, on wild lupine. Military-training activities typically result in some disturbance to the land (Table 10.1). Military training with vehicles destroys individual plants, causes soil disturbance, creates favorable conditions for rapidly colonizing plant species to become established, or has no impact. In contrast to military activities, the effect of maintenance activities on vegetation is generally positive. For example, prescribed burning results in increased growth and cover of the vegetation because it provides disturbances that enable rapidly colonizing plants to invade and

Table 10.1. *Effects of land-use activities on vegetation*

			Initial impact (% of vegetation remaining)		Delayed impact (% of vegetation remaining)	
Activity	Potential effects of activity on vegetation	Areas affected at Fort McCoy	Ground layer	Shrubs and trees	Ground layer	Shrubs and trees
Tracked- and wheeled-vehicle training within maneuver areas, not including tank trails/ roads	May disturb 5 to 7.5 cm of topsoil, destroy some vegetation, and create favorable habitat for rapidly colonizing plants. Disturbance may be concentrated in specific areas or may occur only within vehicle trails. Higher densities of lupine have been found in tank tracks (Smith *et al.*, 2002). Training provides conditions needed for introduction of non-native species.	Training and maneuver areas	65–80	98–100	95–100	100
Prescribed burning	Clears land, enhances oak dominance, and sustains oak savanna, thus keeping succession in check. Increases lupine density and flowering of nectaring plants, increases seed germination and seedling establishment, and controls woody vegetation.	Occurs in oak/savanna	0–10	55–100	95–100	75–100

Sources: Larsen and Mello (1993), Wilder (1995).

establish. Other significant land-use activities that are of importance to Karner blue butterfly habitat are troop bivouacking and timber-stand improvement. Analyses of these other activities could be examined through a similar approach.

The environmental characteristic under consideration at Fort McCoy is vegetation cover. The land-use-impact matrix relates specific land-use activities at Fort McCoy to their immediate and delayed impacts on vegetation cover in two layers: plants less than and greater than 0.5 m in height. These layers loosely translate into ground cover versus cover of trees and shrubs. At Fort McCoy there is great concern about the impacts of land-use activities on vegetation, especially wild lupine and the oak/savannas in which they are found. Other landscape characteristics, however, could have been selected for the impact analysis. Table 10.1 is a partial "land-use-impact matrix" (as described under section 10.3.2) showing only impacts of tracked and wheeled vehicles and prescribed burning.

Estimates of the impact of each land-use activity on vegetation were developed both for vegetation below and above 0.5 m in height on the basis of management plans and assessments performed at Fort McCoy (Larsen and Mello, 1993; Wilder, 1995; Kerkman and Wilder, 1997; *Fort McCoy Integrated Natural Resources Management Plan*, 1998) and evaluation by the wildlife manager at the installation (T. Wilder, personal communication). These estimates consider various intensities, timing, and frequencies of the activity and are therefore presented as ranges rather than specific values. The variability in the estimates reflects the full range of intensities of the land-use activity. Intensity is a measure of effect on a per unit area basis.

Acquire relevant spatial data

Geographic information system (GIS) data were used in the analysis. GIS maps of Fort McCoy were obtained, which included layers that described forest cover, wetland cover, slope (derived from a digital elevation map), stream and lake cover, lupine cover, roads, and the impact area. To simulate the land-use activities, a land-use scenario was designed and modeled. The scenarios for the two activities included descriptions of the activities, their impacts on the land, and areas on Fort McCoy where each activity occurs. The scenarios can be described as follows.

Scenario 1: Tracked- and wheeled-vehicle training in maneuver areas Tracked-vehicle (tanks or armored personnel carriers) and wheeled-vehicle training in maneuver areas consists of the operation of these vehicles within delineated training areas at Fort McCoy (Table 10.1). Most of these training areas are made up of low- and medium-density forest (defined in Table 10.2) because

Table 10.2. *Definition of forest-density classes used at Fort McCoy*

Density class	Percentage of growing space effectively utilized by trees	Basal area
Low	10–39	20–50
Medium	40–69	51–85
High	70–100	86+

high-density forests do not allow room enough for the vehicles to move freely. Some upland grass areas are used for maneuver training. Vehicles are not able to train in areas that have a slope greater then 45%, nor are they permitted to fire weapons from areas with a slope of more then 10% (Headquarters, Department of the Army, 1992). During training, vehicles are required to avoid unnecessary damage to trees and terrain. Neutral steering of tracked vehicles, which involves locking one track and spinning the vehicle around quickly, is also unauthorized. Once in a training area, vehicles can go anywhere except within 50 m of lakes, streams, or wetlands. No tracked- or wheeled-vehicle training activity can occur in any state-designated natural areas, land rehabilitation and maintenance (LRAM) areas, the North Impact Area (NIA), or the cantonment area (where the major buildings exist).

Scenario 2: Prescribed burns Prescribed burns at Fort McCoy are carried out through a controlled burning program run by the Fort McCoy Fire Department in cooperation with the Natural Resources Management Division (NMRD) (Larsen and Mello, 1993). Prescribed burns play a large role in reducing excess fuels (the collection of which can lead to forest fires), reducing nuisance insect populations, and improving habitat for various species (Table 10.1). At Fort McCoy, prescribed burns can only be undertaken when burning will restore a site to savanna (Wilder, 1995). Prescribed burns occur on the installation at any time of the year in any cover group excluding developed/urbanized areas, wetlands, or areas within 50 m of streams. Prescribed burns are not restricted by slope and are allowed to burn up to the roads. However, prescribed burns at Fort McCoy are more prevalent in grassy areas and the understory of scrub oaks, especially because fire is an integral and natural element in the maintenance of the oak/savanna ecosystem. The purpose of prescribed fires in many of these areas is to enhance lupine and populations of plants that produce nectar used by the butterflies. In addition, prescribed fires are likely to occur with similar frequency in areas composed of jack pines and oaks of large diameter (>38 cm diameter at breast height [dbh; 137 cm above ground level]). Fires are set in these areas after harvest of the timber has taken place.

Develop transition matrix

At Fort McCoy, 99 states were found. These states were a combination of eight cover groups (defined by cover type, tree density, and tree dbh) and land use (such as campground, lake, or right of way). Data for a small sample of those 99 states are presented in Table 10.3. In that table, the probabilities of vehicular training or prescribed burns occurring in each state are given in columns 1 and 2. The probabilities are based on management plans and assessments performed at Fort McCoy (Larsen and Mello, 1993; Wilder, 1995; Kerkman and Wilder, 1997; *Fort McCoy Integrated Natural Resources Management Plan*, 1998) and evaluation by the wildlife manager at the installation (T. Wilder, personal communication). These probabilities range from zero to 1 with a value of 1 predicting a 100% chance of the activity occurring in the given state.

Calculating the probability of transitioning from one state to another involves combining the chance of the land use occurring in given cover type, dbh class, and density (from Table 10.3) with the impact that the land use would have (from Table 10.1). Table 10.4 gives the calculation for the transition matrix for oaks of all size classes and densities. As an example, we can consider oaks that are 12.8 to 27.9 cm in diameter and medium density. According to Table 10.3, there is a 1% chance of a prescribed burn impacting these forests, and, if burned, 75% to 100% of these trees will likely remain after the fire. If we use the survival rate of 75%, multiplying gives $0.01 \times 0.25 = 0.0025$ as the chance of changing to a low-density oak forest of small trees, and the chance of the forest remaining in the same state as $1 - (0.01 \times 0.25) = 0.9975$.

Produce risk map

Because these states are related directly to the map layers of cover type, tree density, and tree size, a GIS can be used to map the probability of impact at Fort McCoy. We can treat these mapped probabilities as a proportion of the map that is likely to be impacted by a particular activity and use that information to produce a map depicting sites that are at risk of a change in vegetation cover type for each activity. In situations for which these risks are dependent upon the size and density of the trees (e.g., fire), the risk map should change as successional development occurs. The risk maps for each scenario are shown in Figs. 10.2b and 10.3a (color plates).

However, because the Fort McCoy management focuses so much on lupine, it is useful to map sites where lupine occurs that are at risk to change under these land-use scenarios. To produce such a lupine-risk map, we overlaid the sites where lupine is known to occur with the map of sites at risk of change and highlighted only those lupine locations that occur in sites subject to the land use by our prior calculations (Figs. 10.2c and 10.3b, color plates). The maps are management tools, but it is the interpretation and characterization of these maps that may be most useful to natural resource managers.

Table 10.3. *Selected cover types (out of a total of 99) that have a probability of the land activity occurring according to their density and diameter at breast height (dbh, 137 cm above ground level)*

Probability of tracked- and wheeled-vehicle training in maneuver areas[a]	Probability of prescribed burns	Cover type	dbh class (cm)	Density	Cover group
1	0.01	Oak	0 to 12.7	Low	Oak
1	0.01	Oak	0 to 12.7	Medium	Oak
0	0.01	Oak	0 to 12.7	High	Oak
1	0.01	Oak	12.8 to 27.9	Low	Oak
1	0.01	Oak	12.8 to 27.9	Medium	Oak
0	0.01	Oak	12.8 to 27.9	High	Oak
1	0.2	Oak	28 to 38.1	Low	Oak
1	0.2	Oak	28 to 38.1	Medium	Oak
0	0.2	Oak	28 to 38.1	High	Oak
1	0.2	Oak	38.1+	Low	Oak
1	0.2	Oak	38.1+	Medium	Oak
1	0.2	Scrub oak	0 to 12.7	Low	Oak
0	0.2	Grass			Grass/rock/brush
0	0	Urban			Developed
0	0.01	Campground			Developed
0	0.01	Marsh/muskeg			Water/wetlands
0	0.01	Lowland grass			Water/wetlands
0	0.01	Lowland brush			Water/wetlands
0	0	Minor Lake			Water/wetlands
0	0.01	Northern hardwoods	0 to 12.7	High	Other hardwoods
0	0.01	North Impact Area			Impact area
0	0.01	Stagnant tamarack			Water/wetlands
1	0.01	Tamarack	0 to 5	Low	Water/wetlands
1	0.01	Tamarack	0 to 5	Medium	Water/wetlands
1	0.01	Tamarack	5 to 9	Medium	Water/wetlands
0	0.01	Tamarack	9 to 15	High	Water/wetlands
1	0.01	Upland brush			Grass/rock/brush
0	0.01	Rock/sand			Grass/rock/brush
0	0.01	Rock/sand			Developed

Notes:

[a] Likelihood of activity to occur: 0 = never; 1 = always possible.

Table 10.4. *The information used to calculate the transition matrix for prescribed burning for the oak cover type*

State dbh		0–12.7			12.8–27.9			28–38.1			38.2+	
	Density	L	M	H	L	M	H	L	M	H	L	M
0–12.7	L	1	0	0	0	0	0	0	0	0	0	0
	M	0.25	0.75	0	0	0	0	0	0	0	0	0
	H	0.25	0	0.75	0	0	0	0	0	0	0	0
12.8–27.9	L	0.25	0	0	0.75	0	0	0	0	0	0	0
	M	0.25	0	0	0	0.75	0	0	0	0	0	0
	H	0.25	0	0	0	0	0.75	0	0	0	0	0
28–38.1	L	0.25	0	0	0	0	0	0.75	0	0	0	0
	M	0.25	0	0	0	0	0	0	0.75	0	0	0
	H	0.25	0	0	0	0	0	0	0	0.75	0	0
38.2+	L	0.25	0	0	0	0	0	0	0	0	0.75	0
	M	0.25	0	0	0	0	0	0	0	0	0	0.75

Notes:

The diameter at breast height (dbh, 137 cm above ground level) class is given in centimeters, and the density class refers to the information in Table 10.2. According to Table 10.1, prescribed burning eventually removes 75% to 100% of the overstory trees, so the chances of changing state are assigned according to a 75% rule. In addition to these chances, it is important to consider the potential of a site being burned. From Table 10.3, there is only a 1% chance that any one site with oaks <28 cm dbh will burn; or for $i>1, P_{i,i}=1-(0.01\times0.25)=0.9975$, and $P_{i,1}=0.01\times0.25=0.0025$. For sites with oaks larger than 28 cm dbh, there is a 20% chance of a burn, i.e., for $i>1, P_{i,i}=1-(0.2\times0.25)=0.95$, and $P_{i,1}=0.2\times0.25=0.05$. L, Low; M, medium; H, high.

Characterize risk map

Scenario 1: Tracked- and wheeled-vehicle training in maneuver areas The ecological-risk map for tracked- and wheeled-vehicle training shows that the pines, oak, and grass/rock/brush cover groups have more than half of their areas at risk of change (Fig. 10.2b, color plate). These cover groups are distributed throughout the Fort McCoy area. Training would increase the number of isolated patches of these cover groups and reduce the sizes of both the largest patch and the average patch (Table 10.5). Thus, there may be secondary impacts on the species that use these cover groups as habitat may experience secondary impacts because of fragmentation.

The lupine-impact map reveals that the risks from wheeled- and tracked-vehicle training to lupine are widely distributed for lupine and are not uniformly spread across the installation (Fig. 10.2c, color plate). In particular, the North Impact Area is off limits to vehicle training and, thus, would not have any sites at risk. Overall, 56% of the lupine sites would be a possible location for tracked- and wheeled-vehicle activity, based on the map overlays. The large area of susceptible lupine sites supports the need for an active management program for sites like Fort McCoy. For example, as an ongoing management practice, some of the susceptible sites are posted for protection against training activity; this posting removes the sites from this risk category.

Scenario 2: Prescribed burns The ecological-risk map for prescribed burns shows that oaks and grass/rock/brush areas have more than 60% of their area at risk to a 20% probability of burning (Fig. 10.3a, color plate, and Table 10.5). These cover groups are distributed throughout the Fort McCoy area. Other hardwoods and other pines have less than 3% of their areas at risk.

The lupine-impact map reveals that sites at risk of change from prescribed burning are widely distributed across the installation (Fig. 10.3b, color plate). In this scenario, the change would actually provide an improved ecological condition because burning is beneficial to lupine. Most of the lupine patches occur in sites where prescribed burning is highly likely.

Make the decision and conduct post-decision analysis

At this point, a decision about where to train or burn would be made. The ecological risk map as well as other relevant conditions should be used to inform that decision. The risk map is particularly important at sites like military installations, where multiple land activities may be occurring under different parts of the organization. A common transition approach and the resulting risk map provides a means for managers to communicate about potential impacts.

A critical part of the broader adaptive-management process is to employ post-decision analysis to evaluate the ecological implications of each decision and to

Table 10.5. *Areas for cover groups before and after land-use-activity impact*

Cover group	Total area (ha)	Post-impact area (ha)	Area at risk (ha)	Percentage area at risk
Tracked- and wheeled-vehicle training in maneuver areas				
Oak (including scrub oak)	10741	4140	6034	59
Aspen	775	666	109	14
Other hardwoods	656	646	9	1
Red pine	1,086	447	639	59
White and jack pine	4047	1457	2590	64
Grass/rock/brush	3157	1017	2140	68
Wetlands	412	406	5	1
Developed	684	684	0	0
Impact area	3112	3112	0	0
Total	24670	12575	11526	47
Prescribed burning				
Oak (including scrub oak)	10174	1717	8457	83
Aspen	775	775	0	0
Other hardwoods	656	651	5	0.01
Red pine	1,086	1086	0	0
White and jack pine	4047	3921	126	3
Grass/rock/brush	3157	900	2257	68
Wetlands	412	412	0	0
Developed	684	684	0	0
Impact area	3112	372	2740	0
Total	24670	10518	13585	55

use that information in future decisions. The transition approach used here enables adaptive management to be used: monitoring information can feed into revisions of the land-use-impact matrix, and the land-use scenarios can be used to devise management actions that appropriately protect natural resources of concern or reduce the spread of exotic species. At Fort McCoy, the ready availability of mapped data and the fact that natural resources management is in the same organizational unit as range management (those who use the land for military purposes) facilitate the ability to conduct post-decision analysis.

10.5 Conclusions

10.5.1 Lessons from Fort McCoy

In addition to its use for management of natural resources, the landscape-transition approach is directly applicable to (1) planning for facility closures and realignment (e.g., identification of facility closures that provide the best conservation opportunities); (2) developing environmental-restoration and waste-management strategies; (3) supporting compliance with the Endangered Species Act, the National Historic Preservation Act, the National Environmental Policy Act, and the executive orders for floodplains and wetlands; and (4) developing integrated risk assessments that address cumulative effects.

The Fort McCoy model, which was developed at the request of the Department of Defense, is a good example of the landscape-transition approach. As far as possible, inputs to the model were obtained from empirical data sources, though in some instances these were lacking. When the empirical data were not available, estimates were substituted. In most applications, modelers should have access to all appropriate data of land-use impacts and associations and the expertise to provide for an accurate projection of land-use change and its impacts. These inputs to the transition matrix need to rely on the most recent, as well as the most reliable, data source, usually in the form of GIS maps. Often, however, no time sequence of cover maps or ground-truthed satellite imagery is readily available. Thus, for many sites the transition-matrix approach must rely on the expertise of natural resource staff and local ecologists to develop expected transitions. The modeling approach formalizes that knowledge and provides a means either to test the assumptions and implications or to use it as an explanatory factor when change-detection procedures are used to determine alterations in land-cover types over time.

In conclusion, this chapter shows transition matrices to be adept at modeling landscape changes caused by land-use activities. They provide land managers with a tool on which to base land-management decisions, as shown by the Fort McCoy model. Managers are reminded, though, that the model is to be used as a guideline when carrying out the final decision process. Other aspects of the problem must be incorporated into the process before a final plan of action is agreed upon. Transition matrices should, therefore, prove a useful tool in informing land-use decisions.

10.5.2 Use of a landscape-transition approach

As the previous example illustrates, landscape-transition matrices can be used for at least three types of activities.

(1) To develop a natural-resource-susceptibility model. Such a model can be developed to relate characteristics of species and ecosystems to land-cover patterns resulting from land-use activities, as projected by the land-cover-change model. This natural-resource model matches land-cover characteristics (e.g., frequency of land-cover types, abundance of suitable habitat, size of habitat patches, frequency of edges, and extent

of corridors) to species and ecosystems characteristics (e.g., home-range size and vegetation patterns). For example, activities that cause habitat fragmentation can be detrimental to species that require large blocks of contiguous habitat (e.g., forest-interior species). This model is probabilistic to ensure its compatibility with quantitative risk assessment. Potential effects on species and ecosystems of management decisions, alternative land-use activities, environmental restoration, or natural events can be examined. The probability of an undesired outcome (such as loss of a population of interest) is estimated by Monte Carlo runs of the models under particular scenarios and examination of the frequency distribution of outputs. The visualizations that will accompany this spatially explicit model will enable managers to see the effects of alternative activities on populations of interest.

(2) To quantify the effects of land-use activities. A matrix of characteristics can be developed that describes land-use activities in terms of magnitude, frequency, areal extent, spatial distribution, predictability, and effects on habitat quality. For example, some types of troop training cause low-intensity impacts that are dispersed throughout a site, whereas construction of an industrial facility is a high-intensity activity that occupies a limited area.

(3) To develop a land-cover-change risk model. A spatially explicit, land-cover-change model can be developed to simulate potential changes in or loss of individual cover groups in response to land-use activities. For example, in the Fort McCoy situation, we produced maps depicting areas that are at risk to wheeled- and tracked-vehicle training and to prescribed burning. Inputs to the model include the matrix of parameters describing land-use activities and gridded (digital raster) maps of site characteristics, such as present land cover, slope, aspect, and soils. The model projects the impact of land-use activities on land cover. The model provides a representation of a facet of the land-use activity (e.g., the frequency of training maneuvers) and its effect on habitat (e.g., the degree to which a forest is damaged by artillery fire). Land-use activities that are deterministic and depend on the suitability of the land (e.g., location of new runways) are easily accommodated within a probabilistic model by setting the appropriate probabilities, ranging from 0 to 1.0, and fixing specified parameters. From the model, tables and maps of potential land-cover change caused by land-use activities can be produced for a particular site. The land-cover-change projections can be developed for different scenarios of land-use activities and land-cover patterns. The summary of stochastic runs of the model can provide an estimate of the magnitude and range of potential effects.

10.5.3 Implications for adaptive management

Adaptive-management planning actions often produce models that fail to resolve key uncertainties (Walters, 1997). Walters thus suggests that experimental approaches are frequently considered too costly or risky to apply. Yet the potential for adaptive management to contribute to policy decisions is large. Designing modeling and field experiments so that they inform management decisions is cost effective.

Transition matrices can provide such a tool for bridging science and policy (Rogers, 1998). The elements of the matrix are selected from a science perspective, but the transition matrix is used for management. The manager, however, should treat the elements of the matrices as hypotheses about the scientific understanding of the system. As more information is obtained, these hypotheses often should be revised. The risk maps that come from the matrix approach should not be considered as future realities but rather as potential future conditions under specific scenarios. As a result, the manager is drawn into using the scientific method. We urge scientists involved in this process to follow Baskerville's (1997) admonishment, "to explain the relevance and potential usefulness of the science to the managers via the transition matrix approach."

10.6 Summary

A landscape perspective considers the spatial aspects of land-use changes and their impacts. Mathematical models in the form of transition matrices are able to simulate such changes and impacts over time under given rules. A review of landscape-transition models shows the type of spatial information typically used in these models, their results, and how the model can be interpreted. We have developed a modified landscape-transition-matrix model that simulates the impacts of land-use activities on land cover and relates the effects of land-cover changes to populations of species and their habitats. Inputs to the model include matrices with parameters describing different land-use activities, the effects of these activities, and maps of site characteristics, such as: present land cover, slope, aspect, and soil conditions. With this model, projections of change in land cover can be made under different scenarios of land-use activities and land-cover patterns. Based on a particular scenario of land use and management, risk maps of potential land-cover change caused by land-use activities are produced for a particular site. As an example, the model was applied to Fort McCoy, in west central Wisconsin, where there is concern about how military use of the land might affect the endangered Karner blue butterfly. This species is relatively abundant on the installation. Simulating different land-use scenarios at Fort McCoy provides a means to project the impact of these activities on Karner blue butterfly habitat and other resources at risk (as shown in Figs. 10.2c and 10.3b, color plates). This model was used to develop risk maps that can serve as effective management tools for land managers. The risk maps for two land uses (tracked- and wheeled-vehicle training in maneuver areas and prescribed burns) occurring at Fort McCoy show specific locations where a focused management plan is needed. The landscape-transition-matrix approach serves to highlight those issues related to land-use activities on species, sites, or ecosystems at risk under specific land uses. Thus, transition matrices provide a useful tool for strategic adaptive management.

Acknowledgments

Tim Wilder and Dave Aslesen from the Fort McCoy Military Reservation provided data and discussed their management approach with us. Tony King, John Hall, Jianguo Liu, Bob O'Neill, and three anonymous reviewers provided useful comments on early versions of the chapter. Mark Smith provided helpful information and guidance. Fred O'Hara edited the manuscript. The project was funded by a contract from the Conservation Program of the Strategic Environmental Research and Development Program (SERDP) with Oak Ridge National Laboratory (ORNL). ORNL is managed by UT-Battelle, LLC, for the US Department of Energy under contract DE-AC05–00OR22725. The paper is Environmental Sciences Publication Number 4891.

References

Aaviksoo, K. (1993). Changes in plant cover and land-use types (1950s to 1980s) in three mire reserves and their neighborhood in Estonia. *Landscape Ecology*, 8: 287–301.

Andow, D. A., Baker, R. J. & Lane, C. P. (1994). *Karner Blue Butterfly: A Symbol of a Vanishing Landscape*, University of Minnesota Miscellaneous Publication no. 84–1994. Minnesota Agricultural Experimental Station, University of Minnesota, St. Paul, MN.

Baskerville, G. L. (1997). Advocacy, science, policy and life in the real world. *Conservation Ecology*, 1(1) art 3, http://www.consecol.org/vol1/iss1/art 9

Bergquist, G. & Bergquist, C. (1999). Post-decision assessment. In *Tools to Aid Environmental Decision Making*, eds. V. H. Dale & M. R. English, pp. 285–312. Springer-Verlag, New York.

Caswell, H. (1989). *Matrix Population Models: Construction, Analysis, and Interpretation*, Sinauer Associates, Sunderland, MA.

Christensen, N. L., Bartuska, A. M., Brown, J. H., Carpenter, S. R., D'Antonio, C., Francis, R., Franklin, J. F., MacMahon, J. A., Noss, R. F., Parsons, D. J., Peterson, C. H., Turner, M. G. & Woodmansee, R. G. (1996). The report of the Ecological Society of America committee on the scientific basis for ecosystem management. *Ecological Applications*, 6: 665–691.

Dale, V. H. & O'Neill, R. V. (1999). Tools for assessing environmental conditions. In *Tools to Aid Environmental Decision Making*, eds. V. H. Dale & M. R. English, pp. 62–93. Springer-Verlag, New York.

Dale, V. H. & Pearson, S. M. (1999). Modeling the driving factors and ecological consequences of deforestation in the Brazilian Amazon. In *Spatial Modeling of Forest Landscape Change*, eds. D. L. Mladenoff & W. B. Baker, pp. 256–276. Cambridge University Press, Cambridge, UK.

Dale, V. H., Lugo, A. E., MacMahon, J. A. & Pickett, S. T. A. (1998). Ecosystem management in the context of large, infrequent disturbances. *Ecosystems*, 1: 546–557.

Dale, V. H., Brown, S., Haeuber, R. A., Hobbs, N. T., Huntly, N., Naiman, R. J., Riebsame, W. E., Turner, M. G. & Valone, T. J. (2000). Ecological principles and guidelines for managing the use of land. *Ecological Applications*, 10: 639–670.

Debussche, M., Godron, M., Lepart, J. & Romane, F. (1977). An account of the use of a transition matrix. *Agro-ecosystems*, 3: 81–92.

Duncan, B. W., Boyle, S., Breininger, D. R. & Schmalzer, P. A. (1999). Coupling past management practice and historical landscape change on John F. Kennedy Space Center, Florida. *Landscape Ecology*, 14: 291–309.

Fort McCoy Integrated Natural Resources Management Plan (1998). (Effective 1998–2003). Directorate of Public Works, Environmental and Resources Division, Fort McCoy, WI.

Franklin, J. F. (1993). Preserving biodiversity: Species, ecosystems, or landscapes? *Ecological Applications*, 3: 202–205.

Freudenburg, W. R. (1999). Tools for understanding the socioeconomic and political settings for environmental decision making. In *Tools to Aid Environmental Decision Making*, eds. V. H. Dale & M. R. English, pp. 94–129. Springer-Verlag, New York.

Fu, B., Gulinck, H. & Masum, M. Z. (1994). Loss erosion in relation to land-use changes in the Ganspoel Catchment, Central Belgium. *Land Degradation and Rehabilitation*, 5: 261–270.

Gibson , D. J., Ely, J. S. & Looney, P. B. (1997). A Markovian approach to modeling succession on a coastal barrier island following beach nourishment. *Journal of Coastal Research*, 13: 831–841.

Hall, F. G., Botkin, D. B., Strebel, D. E., Woods, K. D. & Goetz, S. J. (1991). Large-scale patterns of forest succession as determined by remote sensing. *Ecology*, 72: 628–640.

Hargis, C. D., Bissonette, J. A. & David, J. L. (1998). The behaviour of landscape metrics commonly used in the study of habitat fragmentation. *Landscape Ecology*, 13: 167–186.

Headquarters, Department of the Army (1992). *Terrain Analysis*, FM 5–33. Headquarters Department of the Army, Washington, D.C.

Heifetz, R. A. (1994). *Leadership without Easy Answers*. Harvard University Press, Cambridge, MA.

Holling, C. S. (1978). *Adaptive Environmental Management and Assessment*, John Wiley, New York.

Horn, H. S. (1975a). Forest succession. *Scientific American*, 232: 90–98.

Horn, H. S. (1975b). Markovian properties of forest succession. In *Ecology and Evolution of Communities*, eds. M. L. Cody & J. M. Diamond, pp. 196–211. Harvard University Press, Cambridge, MA.

Jeffers, J. N. R. (1988). *Practitioner's Handbook on the Modelling of Dynamic Change in Ecosystems*, Scientific Committee on Problems of the Environment (SCOPE) no. 34. John Wiley, New York.

Kachi, N., Yasuoka, Y., Totsuka, T. & Suzuli, K. (1986). A stochastic model for describing revegetation following forest cutting: An application of remote sensing. *Ecological Modelling*, 32: 105–117.

Kerkman, J. & Wilder, T. (1997). *Biological Assessment of Forest Management Activities on the Karner Blue Butterfly at Ft McCoy, Wisconsin*. Directorate of Public Works, Environmental and Resources Division, Fort McCoy, WI.

Krummel, J. R. & Gardner, R. H. (1987). Landscape pattern in a disturbed environment. *Oikos*, 48: 321–324.

Larsen, G. & Mello, K. (1993). *Biological Assessment of Land-Use Activities on the Karner Blue Butterfly at Fort McCoy, Wisconsin*. Directorate of Public Works, Environmental and Resources Division, Fort McCoy, WI.

Li, H. & Reynolds, J. F. (1993). A new contagion index to quantify spatial patterns of landscapes. *Landscape Ecology* 8, 155–162.

Lyndon, M. (1999). Characterizing the regulatory and judicial setting. In *Tools to Aid Environmental Decision Making*, eds. V. H. Dale & M. R. English, pp. 130–160. Springer-Verlag, New York.

Mann, L. K., King, A. W., Dale, V. H., Hargrove, W. W., Washington-Allen, R., Pounds, L. &

Ashwood, T. A. (1999). The role of soil classification in GIS modeling of habitat pattern: Threatened calcareous ecosystems. *Ecosystems*, 2: 524–538.

Mladenoff, D. J., Sickley, T. A., Haight, R. G. & Wydeven, A. P. (1995). A regional landscape analysis of favorable gray wolf habitat in the northern Great Lakes region. *Conservation Biology*, 9: 279–294.

O'Neill, R. V., Krummel, J. R., Gardner, R. H., Sugihara, G., Jackson, B., DeAngelis, D. L., Milne, B. T., Turner, M. G., Zygmnuht, B., Christensen, S. W., Dale, V. H. & Graham, R. L. (1988). Indices of landscape pattern. *Landscape Ecology*, 1: 153–162.

Rogers, K. (1998). Managing science/management partnerships: a challenge of adaptive management. *Conservation Ecology*, 2(2), http://www.consecol.org/vol2/iss2/resp1

Runkle, J. R. (1981). Gap regeneration in some old-growth forests of the eastern United States. *Ecology*, 62: 1041–1051.

Shugart, H. H. (1984). *A Theory of Forest Dynamics: The Ecological Implications of Forest Succession Models*. Springer-Verlag, New York.

Smith, M. A., Turner, M. G. & Rusch, D. H. (2002). The effect of military training activity on eastern lupine and the Karner blue butterfly at Fort McCoy, Wisconsin, USA. *Environmental Management*, 29: 102–115.

Stanford, J. A. & Poole, G. C. (1996). A protocol for ecosystem management. *Ecological Applications*, 3: 741–744.

Turner, M. G. (1987). Spatial simulation of landscape changes in Georgia: A comparison of three transition models. *Landscape Ecology*, 1: 29–36.

Turner, M. G. (1988). A spatial simulation model of land use changes in a piedmont county in Georgia. *Applied Mathematics and Computation*, 27: 39–51.

Usher, M. B. (1966). A matrix approach to the management of renewable resources with special reference to trees. *Journal of Applied Ecology*, 3: 333–367.

Usher, M. B. (1981). Modelling ecological succession, with reference to Markovian models. *Vegetatio*, 46: 11–18.

Waggoner, P. E. & Stephens, G. R. (1970). Transition probabilities for a forest. *Nature*, 225: 1160–1161.

Walters, C. J. (1986). *Adaptive Management of Renewable Resources*. Macmillan, New York.

Walters, C. (1997). Challenges in adaptive management of riparian and coastal ecosystems. *Conservation Ecology*, 1(2), art 1, http://www.consecol.org/vol1/iss2/art 1

Wilder, T. (1995). *Fort McCoy Karner Blue Butterfly Conservation Plan, Fort McCoy, Wisconsin*. Directorate of Public Works, Environmental and Resources Division, Fort McCoy, WI.

DEAN L. URBAN

11

Tactical monitoring of landscapes

11.1 Introduction

Landscapes are large by conventional definitions (Forman and Godron, 1981, 1986; Urban *et al.*, 1987; Turner, 1989) and data at that scale are dearly bought. Yet with the advent of ecosystem management (Christensen *et al.*, 1996) – which implies a larger scale of reference than prior approaches to resource management – researchers and managers are increasingly faced with pursuing sampling and monitoring programs at these larger scales. A significant component of such programs should be the establishment of long-term monitoring systems designed to detect trends in resources, prioritize management needs, and gauge the success of management activities. This goal can be especially daunting in cases where the study area is especially large, where the signal to be detected is uncertain (e.g., potential responses to climatic change), or where the objects of concern are simply difficult to locate (e.g., rare species).

Here I consider some approaches that may prove useful in designing sampling and monitoring programs for landscape management. In contrast with large-scale efforts that are coarse-grained and intended as "first approximations" (Hunsaker *et al.*, 1990), or more location- or taxon-specific methods (e.g., examples in Goldsmith, 1991), my concern here is with problems that are simultaneously fine-grained and of large extent. This is essentially a sampling problem at first, with the goal of capturing fine-grained pattern in an efficient manner. In many cases, however, even an efficient blanketing of the study area is logistically infeasible and so a second concern will be to focus sampling as powerfully as possible on a specific application or hypothesis. Two key attributes of this approach are the explicit pursuit of multi-scale designs and the integration of models as a guide to sampling. This latter aspect of the approach has much to offer in the implementation of adaptive management of natural resources, as I discuss in a closing section.

11.2 Terms and scope of discussion

The issue of sampling designs for monitoring natural resources is not new and my intent here is not to review – nor even echo – a huge and growing literature. General references (Cochran, 1997) and more application-specific texts (Goldsmith, 1991; Schreuder *et al.*, 1993) are widely available. In particular, a collection of articles spawned from a workshop by the Sustainable Biosphere Initiative provides an authoritative statement of the state of the art (Dixon *et al.*, 1998, and other articles in same special feature). As a bridge to this literature, however, some definition of terms and scope will be useful. Insofar as possible, I will try to follow the terminology of Nusser *et al.* (1998).

It is useful to distinguish multiple components of the monitoring process. *Sampling design* pertains to schemes devised for collecting measurements. This aspect has a natural correspondence to *experimental design*, the framework for statistical estimation and inference. For example, a completely random sampling design corresponds to a completely randomized design in estimating the effects; a stratified sampling design corresponds to a randomized complete block design (and see below). This distinction is important for two reasons. First, it separates the process of *acquisition* of the data from the task of *estimation* of statistical parameters for the population of inference. In general, a sample is a set of observations (cases, units, or elements) from a finite population or sampling frame. This is the scope of sampling designs. By contrast, statistical estimation typically is carried out subject to assumptions about the distribution of data (assumptions presumed of infinite populations). In this chapter I focus on the sampling problem, echoing Stow *et al.* (1998) in the opinion that if the data have a high signal-to-noise ratio and sample sizes are adequate, the analysis phase is less of a challenge.

Some elements of sampling design are especially pertinent to the illustrations I discuss in this chapter. Samples are often *stratified* over various criteria (*strata*) to achieve a balanced coverage in the sample. For example, one might stratify samples over vegetation types, topographic positions, or soil types. In landscape ecology, the stratification is often over *space*: the strata are geographic.

Monitoring programs often rely on rather complicated hybrid designs to meet multiple objectives. These designs include *multi-stage sampling* and *multi-phase sampling*. In the former, a (large) set of primary sampling units is identified and then subsequently resampled in a restricted way to generate the samples. In multi-phase sampling, the initial sample is surveyed for (typically) readily measured, coarse-resolution variables and then in a subsequent phase, some subset of these samples is revisited and a *different* set of (typically) more logistically demanding variables are measured. This second set is then related to the initial set, e.g. via regression, and thus is used to leverage additional information from the initial, coarse-resolution data set. I mention these designs because, while I do not address these explicitly in the discussion to follow, the recommendations I make are consistent with more complicated designs.

Finally, a potential source of some confusion relates to the statistical estimation of parameters from sample survey data. Classical survey statistics are *design-based estimators* in that the sampling design (or experimental design) dictates the form of the statistical estimators. For example, each sample's contribution to a parameter might be *weighted* by its probability of selection or inclusion; for many sampling designs, this probability depends on the sample's areal representation (e.g., how common that cover type is on a landscape). By contrast, auxiliary information may be used to control or calibrate these weights, leading to *model-based* or *model- assisted* estimators. In the discussion that follows, I present a different perspective on model-based sampling designs, one aimed at data collection rather than statistical estimation. I trust that this distinction will be apparent from the context of the discussion.

11.3 Sampling spatial heterogeneity: Multi-scale designs

A significant challenge to sampling over large areas is that many processes ecologists wish to capture are implicitly fine-grained but play out at large scales. For example, the process of seed dispersal takes place over distances of tens of meters but may be manifest in species distributions over larger gradients (hillslopes or landscapes; Clark *et al.*, 1999), and perhaps even at subcontinental-scale species migration (Clark *et al.*, 1998). Similarly, microtopographic effects on soil moisture gradients vary over distances of tens to hundreds of meters but are fundamental to landscape-scale patterns in plant species abundances (Halpin, 1995; Stephenson, 1998; Urban *et al.*, 2000). These patterns mandate a sampling design that can capture fine-grained details over large extent, a challenge that is not well met by simple sampling designs such as uniform, random or stratified-random designs.

The essential challenge in sampling such patterns is to collect samples such that they cover most of the study area (i.e., the sampling frame is the entire population of interest) but also to include samples that are sufficiently close together to capture the fine-grain pattern – an important consideration if geostatistical methods are to be used in analyses. For example, a uniform sampling grid provides a finite set of between-quadrat distances (i.e., x, SQRT($2x$), $2x$, SQRT($5x$), ... where x is the interval of the sampling grid) and this can degrade geostatistical analyses by constraining sample sizes within some distance classes. In the uniform case, the spacing of samples depends only on sampling

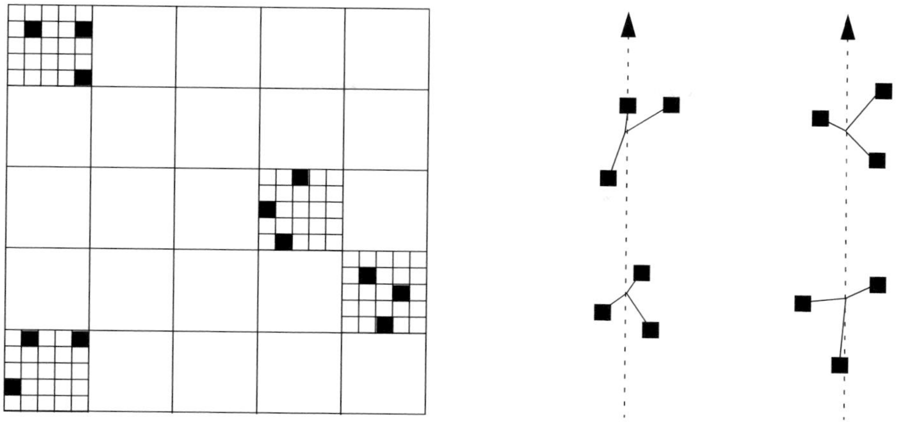

(a) (b)

FIGURE 11.1
Examples of multi-scale sampling designs. (a) Nested non-aligned blocks, in which four of the cells have been selected for sampling and each cell is subdivided by a nested grid, itself sampled with three sub-cells (filled). (b) Stratified clusters, in which four cluster centroids are stratified over the study area and three sampling points are located at random distances and azimuths from each centroid.

intensity, or the number of sample elements in the study area. Thus, for large landscapes that are sparsely sampled, the sample elements would be far apart and fine-grained patterns would be missed. Random or stratified-random sampling designs do not have as severe a drawback in terms of geostatistical analyses, but they still suffer the dependency that sampling intensity dictates the frequency of samples within short distances.

The solution to this challenge is to devise multi-scaled sampling designs to collect measurements over short distances while also covering a large study area. Two sampling designs seem especially well suited to this. *Nested non-aligned block designs* use a grid as a basic sampling template, with samples located randomly in some of the grid cells. For example, in a non-aligned block design one might specify some percentage of the grid to sample, randomly select the corresponding number of cells, and then randomly locate a quadrat within each of these cells. A *nested* nonaligned block design follows the same procedure for subsampling within the selected grid cells, by using a finer-scaled grid within each selected cell of the larger grid (Fig. 11.1a). The blocks can be nested further, as deeply as is necessary to capture the details of interest. A nested non-aligned block design is roughly equivalent to a multi-stage stratified random design (see below); nesting the blocks makes it multi-scaled and allows the samples to capture fine-grained information over large areas. The level of nesting and cell size in the grid dictates the grain of sampling.

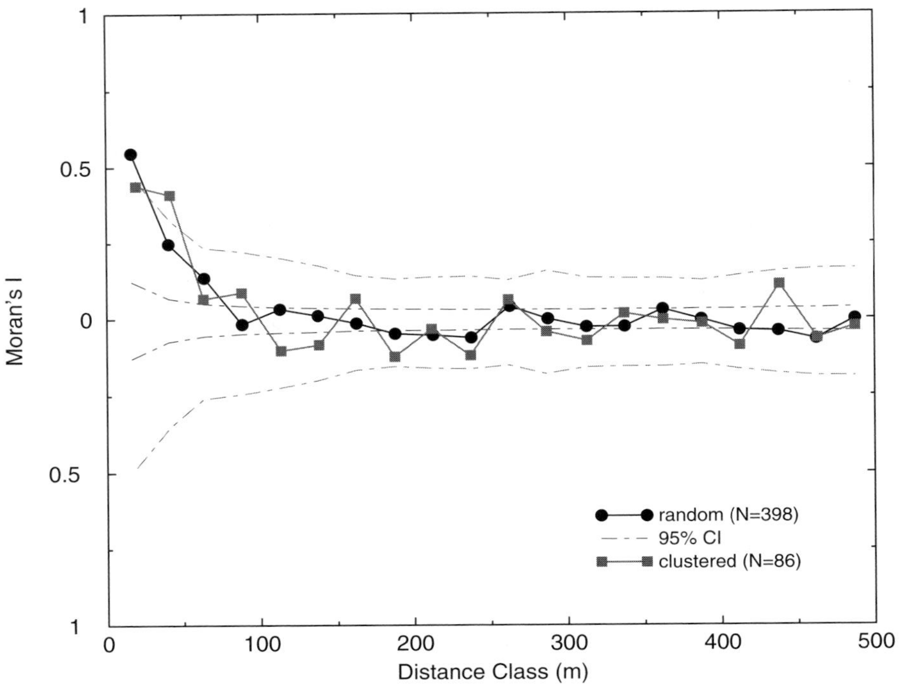

FIGURE 11.2
Examples of computer-based sampling experiments in which alternative sampling designs and intensities are compared in terms of their efficiency in reproducing a reference correlogram based on an arbitrarily large (and logistically infeasible) number of samples. Here the reference case is a correlogram of a topographic convergence index derived from a digital elevation model of a small watershed in the Sierra Nevada; the reference case was sampled using 398 random points. In comparison, the clustered design used cluster centroids arranged on a grid over the watershed, with three samples randomly located within <100 m of 29 cluster centroids (one sample fell outside the watershed boundary and was discarded). The clustered design reproduced the reference correlogram with about one-fifth the sampling intensity.

Equivalently, a multi-stage stratified random or *stratified cluster design* begins as a stratified-random design but locates multiple sample quadrats near each stratification point. A convenient method for achieving this design in the field is to lay out transects and locate cluster centers at (perhaps staggered) intervals along the transect, then locate sample units at random distances and azimuths from the cluster center (Fig. 11.1b). (This design is essentially equivalent to the multi-stage design described by Nusser *et al.* [1998], although the process for locating elements is slightly different.) The net result of a stratified cluster design and nested non-aligned blocks is the same: sets of sample elements (quadrats) with some separated by close distances yet with samples covering the entire study area. The difference in the two designs is in how they are laid out in the field; non-aligned blocks use a grid while clusters use transect lines. The choice depends largely on ease of implementation in the field.

In computer-based sampling experiments with known patterns, clustered designs often can capture the pattern (as a correlogram) using five-fold fewer samples than random samples (Fig. 11.2). Similar computer-based sampling experiments suggest that order-of-magnitude reductions in sampling intensity might be feasible for larger study areas (Urban *et al.*, 2000). To sample variables with unknown grain or pattern, a multi-scale pilot study would seem necessary to develop the most efficient possible design for actual sampling.

In designing field studies, the exercise illustrated in Fig. 11.2 can provide a useful pilot study and guide to actual sampling. For example, digital elevation models (DEMs) can provide a variety of indices that can be used as proxies for soil moisture or edaphic gradients (Moore *et al.*, 1991). DEMs (or derived secondary indices) can be sampled using a variety of designs to find a sample arrangement (number of points per cluster, cluster spacing) and intensity (number of samples) that can capture the pattern with a logistically feasible sampling effort.

11.4 Model-integrated sampling designs

Multi-scaled sampling designs are efficient when the pattern to be described is simultaneously fine-grained and of large extent. But in many cases, even a multi-scaled design is simply not supportable for logistical reasons. For example, a design to capture topographic grain in Sequoia-Kings Canyon National Park (the case considered by Urban *et al.*, 2000), might require thousands of sample points – probably too many for a single inventory, and certainly too many to consider resampling through time. In these cases, it is important to consider that all data are *not* created equal: some observations are much more informative about specific hypotheses while other data might not provide any insight at all.

In field studies over small extent, ecologists sometimes can get away with over-sampling – essentially a "shotgun" approach that collects the appropriate data along with extraneous data that are not useful for the specific application at hand. This can work for small study areas but is simply unsupportable for large-scale efforts. An alternative approach is to use a model to help discover which observations will be most useful for a specific application or research task. Here I illustrate this approach with three examples, proceeding from simple (conceptual) models to more complicated simulation models.

11.4.1 The rare herb *Fusilli puttanesca*

The first example is purely hypothetical and is used to present a logical structure for guiding sampling schemes. *Fusilli puttanesca* is a relic herb that grows in riparian meadows in the southern Appalachian foothills. Because of its showy flowers it is much prized by hikers and nature buffs, who decimate its populations near roads and trails. The research question at hand is, What limits the local abundance of this species? Is its distribution habitat-limited? Does it behave as a metapopulation (a "population of populations" in more-or-less discrete habitat patches; Harrison, 1994; Hanksi, 1998) and is it dispersal-limited? Or is human impact the chief constraint on its distribution? The key to this application is that only a few observations might be needed to shed light on these questions; the task is to isolate these observational cases. Importantly, a naive approach of simply combing the study area for the plants will be woefully inefficient and may not answer the question at hand.

First, assume that this task can be simplified by collapsing all habitat patches into binary cases: good habitat versus non-habitat, connected versus isolated in terms of population dispersal, and near versus far from trails as an index of the likelihood of disturbance by hikers. Then note that the three factors and two levels yield only eight combinations of conditions; these combinations can be represented readily in a decision tree (Fig. 11.3). From a standpoint of thoroughness, sampling each branch of the tree, with some replication, completely addresses the questions at hand. In terms of experimental design, this is a full factorial design corresponding to a balanced ANOVA model.

Sampling a decision tree is a straightforward task if it can be posed within the framework of a geographic information system (GIS). In a GIS the identification of locations that meet a number of conditions simultaneously (e.g., meet the definition of "habitat," within a threshold distance of other habitat, and farther than a threshold distance from roads or trails) is accomplished via "map algebra" (intersection), and these locations can then be subsampled using a random or stratified design (see below).

This decision-tree structure is contrived, but for a reason. This approach is consistent with a powerful statistical approach to this sort of question, that of classification and regression tree (CART) modeling (Breiman *et al.*, 1984; Moore *et al.*, 1990). A CART model is a nested regression approach in which data cases (observations) are partitioned recursively in a tree-like structure. In a typical case, the samples might be labelled occupied versus unoccupied samples for a given species, or similarly, habitat versus non-habitat, or near versus far and so on. In the case of a binary dependent variable (e.g., habitat versus non-habitat) and interval-scale predictor variables (e.g., elevation, slope, rockiness, and so

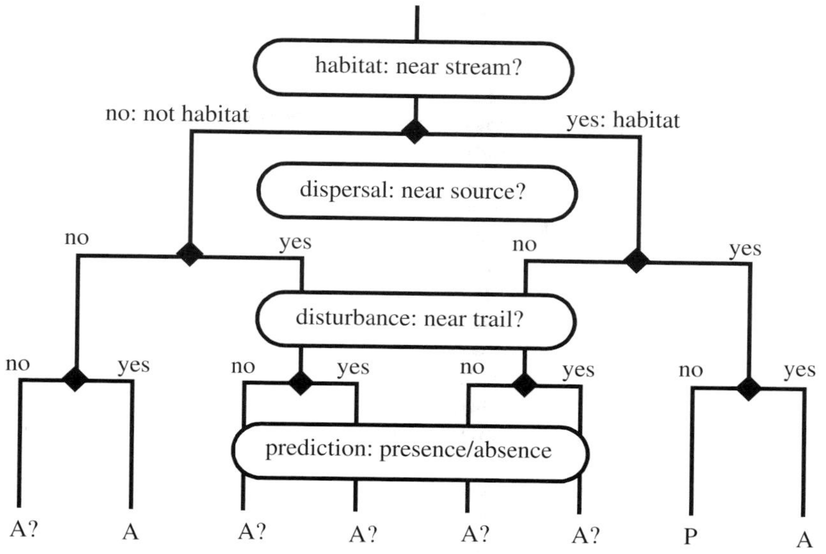

FIGURE 11.3
A decision tree highlighting the role of habitat availability, accessibility (dispersal limitation), and local disturbance (decimation by hikers) in governing the local distribution of a hypothetical species. Branches are labelled A (absent) or P (present); ? indicates an uncertain or indeterminate branch. Note that if disturbance is the primary agent of concern, only two of the branches provide data that are unconfounded by other factors. Note also that few cases seem unequivocal, depending on the strength of the three constraints.

on), the solution is equivalent to a set of nested logistic regressions that identify critical values on the independent variables that best classify the input samples. The final classification tree is comparable to the dichotomous trees used as taxonomic keys.

For my present purpose, it is especially useful that one can posit a decision tree as a guide to sampling, in effect posing a working hypothesis about the relevant factors controlling species distribution. Field data collected according to this design can then be used in CART analysis to actually estimate the model – that is, to find the actual critical values that define habitat, isolation, or disturbance probability. Of course, this approach also assumes that the first decision tree is fairly reasonable or else the sampling might miss the solution badly! Fortunately, this approach can also be self-mending in that as samples accrue, a better estimate of the overall situation (explanatory model and CART solution) can be refined.

Note that in terms of sampling efficiency, a design that represents all branches of the decision tree is thorough but not necessarily efficient. Indeed, for a complicated or multi-levelled tree, the implied sampling effort might be untenable for logistical reasons. In these cases, it is worth noting that some hypotheses can be isolated quite parsimoniously in the decision tree. For example, if the primary interest in these herbs is in hiker impact, then note that the only cases that offer any clean insight into this are those samples that are good habitat and not dispersal-limited. Samples that are isolated or poor habitat might be unoccupied for those reasons and thus can tell us nothing about disturbance. That is, only two of the branches of the tree are of immediate interest (the two farthest to the right in Fig. 11.3) and sampling effort can be adjusted accordingly. Likewise, if dispersal limitations are the primary concern then habitats close to trails or otherwise prone to disturbance are confounded and not useful for a study of dispersal. Thus, by focusing on specific hypotheses, the sample effort can be drastically reduced and focused in a tactical way. Indeed, the level of statistical control over extraneous factors might well lead to increased statistical power.

Of course, in some cases the underlying model is sufficiently complex that a simple decision tree does not provide enough leverage on the problem to be useful as a guide to sampling or monitoring. In these cases, more complicated models can be applied.

11.4.2 The Mexican spotted owl

The Mexican spotted owl (*Strix occidentalis lucida*), a sister subspecies of the more notorious northern spotted owl, occupies mixed-conifer and pine–oak forests of the American Southwest including southern Utah and Colorado, Arizona and New Mexico, and parts of northern Mexico. It was listed as federally threatened in 1993, largely under threat of habitat loss. Over parts of its range, primary habitat occurs as higher-elevation forests on mountains separated by desert (so-called "sky islands") and it is easy to envision the species acting as a classical metapopulation (Harrison, 1994; Hanski, 1998) in the sense of spatially discrete populations coupled by infrequent dispersal. The Recovery Plan mandated by the Endangered Species Act (US Department of the Interior Fish and Wildlife Service, 1995) specifically considered landscape context and connectivity in its deliberations and recommendations (Keitt *et al.*, 1995).

Keitt *et al.* (1995, 1997) devised an approach in which they attempted to identify those habitat patches that might be especially important to long-term persistence of the owl. Habitat patches might be important for two reasons. Large patches are important simply through their area alone; larger patches produce more owls and consequently have a significant impact on metapopulation recruitment. More interestingly, a patch might also be important because of its spatial location and role as a dispersal conduit or stepping-stone; these patches needn't be large yet can still have an important effect on the metapopulation via immigration and emigration.

Keitt *et al.* (1997) defined landscape connectivity in terms of average traversability, indexed as correlation length. The index is computed from raster data in which a habitat patch is a cluster of adjacent cells of "potential owl habitat" as defined by forest cover types. Correlation length depends on patch areas and shapes:

$$C_L = \sum_{i=1}^{n} A_i * R_i \tag{11.1}$$

where A_i is patch area as a proportion of total map area; R_i is the patch's radius of gyration (Stauffer, 1985), the mean Euclidean distance from each cell in the cluster to that cluster's centroid (compact clusters have smaller radii than long or irregular clusters); and there are n patches in the landscape. Correlation length is the expected distance that one might traverse the map while remaining in "habitat" and thus serves as a useful index of connectivity.

The authors performed a patch-removal sensitivity analysis in which they sequentially removed each habitat cluster and recomputed correlation length for the landscape. They then ranked the patches in terms of the magnitude of change in correlation length on patch removal; that is, the highest-ranking patch was the one whose removal resulted in the largest decrease in correlation length. Raw ranks tended to highlight the largest patches as being most important, because of the area term in the formula (eq. 11.1) (Fig. 11.4a, color plate). By dividing each patch's effect (loss of correlation length) by its area, they focused on the area-corrected importance of each patch (Fig. 11.4b, color plate). This area-relativization emphasized small patches that were located in key places for dispersal: stepping-stones.

This ranking was not intended as a definitive statement on owl population biology. Rather, the goal was to develop and illustrate a macroscopic approach that would identify key habitat patches from the perspective of landscape connectivity and metapopulation structure. For my present purpose, it is sufficient to note that these patches offer themselves as candidate study areas and monitoring locations if we wish to learn more about owl dispersal in a metapopulation context. Importantly, it should be noted that these patches (highlighted in Fig. 11.4b, color plate) tend *not* to be the places one might naturally choose as study areas when working with rare or threatened species. For logistical reasons, one would quite naturally choose locations that are prime habitat and probably large, simply because a large number of observations could be collected. The analysis of Keitt *et al.* (1997) suggests that, for spatially distributed metapopulations, the most informative locations for monitoring might not be obvious, indeed, might not even support appreciable populations.

Urban and Keitt (2001) have since extended this approach to embrace the computational framework of graph theory (Harary, 1969; Gross and Yellen, 1999). Graph theory is a well-developed body of theory concerning flux or routing in networks, broadly defined. Urban and Keitt used graph theory to index patch importance to the metapopulation in terms of recruitment flux, in the sense of Pulliam's (1988) metapopulation model, and also in terms of long-distance traversability, in the sense of Levins's (1969) original "spreading-of-risk" model of metapopulations. Patch-removal sensitivity analysis thus permits ranking habitat patches on multiple criteria in a computationally expedient framework. Again, because the approach is macroscopic, it need not provide a definitive answer about the actual importance of each habitat patch in the landscape; but the patches thus identified are certainly prime candidates for further study or monitoring.

The macroscopic approach amounts to a sensitivity analysis of an underlying explanatory model couched in metapopulation theory. The approach is macroscopic in that it relies on map analysis without actually invoking details of a metapopulation model (i.e., there is no explicit parameterization of demographic processes or dispersal). In the next example, I consider a more explicit simulation model.

11.4.3 Climatically sensitive sites in the Sierra Nevada

The mixed-conifer forests of the Sierra Nevada of California are climatically sensitive over multiple time-scales (Stephenson, 1998) and are currently the focus of an integrated research program in Sequoia-Kings Canyon and Yosemite National Parks, aimed at anticipating the possible consequences of anthropogenic global change (Stephenson and Parsons, 1993). These forests are host to a variety of species including the giant sequoia (*Sequoiadendron giganteum*), whose narrow distribution with respect to elevation (a proxy for temperature in steep mountains) suggests potentially drastic impacts of rapid climate change in a greenhouse world.

One goal of the Sierra Nevada Global Change Research Program is to identify sites that might serve as potential "early warning" sites and thus form the backbone of a monitoring program. Our approach to this has been to use a simulation model to characterize the physical template of these landscapes, and then to analyze the model to find locations that might be most sensitive to climatic change.

The Sierra has a Mediterranean climate with mild winters and very dry summers. With an increase in elevation, temperature decreases while precipitation increases; importantly, the precipitation changes from rain to snow at middle elevations, and it is the persistent snowpack that develops at middle elevations that provides growing-season soil moisture which supports the mixed-conifer zone. The soil moisture balance represents a complex interaction with temperature as it affects the partitioning of precipitation into snow versus rain, the dynamics of snowmelt in the spring, the onset and end of the growing season in terms of plant phenology, and evaporative demand during the summer. Urban *et al.* (2000) developed a simulation model that adjusts monthly temperature, radiation, and precipitation for topographic position (elevation, slope, and aspect) and that, in conjunction with soils data and plant canopy characteristics, simulates the soil water balance for these sites. Urban (2000) then performed a sensitivity analysis of the model to quantify the sensitivity of soil moisture to variation in temperature and precipitation. The sensitivity analysis was conducted across the full parametric space of the model, so that the relative sensitivity of different elevations, slopes, and aspects could be defined. Model sensitivity was then regressed on these terrain variables and these regressions were used in a GIS to map model sensitivity from parameter space into geographic space. The analysis also included a measure of uncertainty in the model. Because the model simulates a discrete point in space it could not attend the complexities of lateral hydrologic flow and consequent microtopographic effects on soil water drainage. Uncertainty due to topographic drainage was included by highlighting locations in the study area with contrasting topographic drainage indices. A false-color grid composite was generated to highlight regions of the Kaweah Basin, one of three large basins comprising Sequoia-Kings Canyon National Park, in terms of their relative sensitivity and uncertainty (Fig. 11.5, color plate).

In this figure the magenta zone is simultaneously sensitive to variation in temperature and precipitation. This zone represents roughly 17% of the basin. That is, the potential monitoring sites that seem most sensitive to climate change represent only about one-sixth of the study area – an appreciable focusing of any monitoring effort.

Urban (2000) went further, to select climatically sensitive sites that would also allow the placement of sample quadrats on contrasting topographic positions within a logisitically reasonable distance (100 m) and close to roads or major trails (500 m, a concession to the rough terrain and a humanitarian gesture to field crews!). These further restrictions reduced the target sampling domain to less than 2% of the study area: a substantial focusing of sampling effort and efficacy.

In these examples, note the trend toward increasing complexity of the "model" underlying the sampling. In the first example the model was a simple hypothesis; in the case of the spotted owl, a static analysis of an implicit model; and in this last example, a formal analysis of a dynamic simulation model. The underlying principle is the same in each case, however: by using a model as a guide to designing a sampling scheme, the scheme can be focused substantially and with greater efficiency than conventional designs.

11.5 Monitoring temporal change: Trend detection and efficiency

Note in the case of metapopulation dynamics there is a long-term commitment to monitoring implicit in the underlying model: metapopulations are defined by between-patch dispersal events that might occur only once per generation or so (Harrison, 1994; Hanski, 1998). Similarly, monitoring for the effects of anthropogenic climate change mandates an investment in monitoring that extends well beyond the scope of typical research programs. The temporal aspects of large-scale monitoring programs, however, have not received as much attention as they might warrant.

A contrived example illustrates the potential implications of ignoring spatiotemporal dynamics in long-term monitoring programs. Consider a species whose distribution is patchy and which disperses from population centers. Over time, such a population would exhibit spatial drift, as is typically seen in population models implemented as cellular automata or explicitly spatial partial differential equations. Clearly, if one were to establish a set of monitoring stations randomly (i.e., without reference to initial occupancy), then the actual stations occupied by the species would change over time. On average, one might expect the proportion of occupied stations to remain relatively constant for a stable population – a classical definition of a metapopulation. If, however, the species of interest is quite rare, then it would be completely reasonable to set up monitoring stations in locations where the species actually occurred. This would be especially likely if initial studies of the species led to site selection such that adequate sample sizes could be garnered for demographic studies. If such sites were retained for monitoring (recognizing the value of extending the initial studies), then over time the monitoring will almost certainly show a population decline as the species drifts away from the initial site. This sort of bias would seem especially awkward, to say the least, for monitoring programs aimed at rare or threatened species.

While contrived, the example is not unrealistic. For example, Sutter (1986) compared a variety of monitoring approaches for the rough-leafed loosestrife (*Lysimachia asperulaefolia*) in savanna–pocosin ecotones, a fire-maintained habitat in the southeastern coastal plain of North Carolina. Resamplings of fixed locations showed a marked population decline over as little as two years. But *Lysimachia* is rhizomatous, and in fact the population seems to be persisting quite well, even increasing: it merely moved.

Similarly, for species with fine-grained microhabitat affinities for particular successional stages, succession itself would lead to an apparent change in species abundances as monitoring sites succeed to other microhabitats and species move to find suitable sites. The "shifting mosaic" nature of vegetation (Watt, 1947; Bormann and Likens, 1979; Smith and Urban, 1988) predicts that as vegetation undergoes succession/disturbance dynamics, any species dependent on microhabitats must also ride these dynamics in space and time (Urban and Smith, 1989).

One solution to the complexities implied by spatiotemporal dynamics is to use what are called rotating-panel (Duncan and Kalton, 1987; Schreuder *et al.*, 1993) or partial resampling (Usher, 1991) designs. In this, a fixed number of sample points is established for the initial survey. At the next survey time, a percentage of the original samples is resampled (say 80%), and a set of new samples is established to fill out the sample size (here, 20% new plots). At the next survey, the procedure is repeated: some samples are discarded and some new samples are established. While it may seem costly to discard samples each time, the overall sample is in a sense refreshed by the new samples. In monitoring spatial processes, this design ensures that as populations drift the sampling can discover them. Rotating-panel designs are not much used in ecology (but see Lesser and Kalsbeek, 1997; White *et al.*, 1999), but certainly warrant further consideration.

Note that this discussion has focused on correctly detecting the trend in population dynamics through monitoring. While this is important, even crucial, to natural resource management, it begs an equally important issue of detecting the processes or constraints responsible for the observed trend. For example, is the population declining because of habitat area in itself, is habitat isolation important, or is it some other constraint or process? More in-depth goals in monitoring would seem to require sampling schemes based on model analysis, such as described above.

11.6 Opportunities in adaptive management

The issue of effective monitoring of landscapes fits neatly into a larger framework of adaptive management. Adaptive management (called "learning by doing" by Walters, 1986) is not new (Holling, 1978) but is emerging to play a central (but not uncontroversial) role in resource management (Walters and Holling, 1990; McLain and Lee, 1996; Johnson 1999a,b; Lee, 1999). Key to the concept of adaptive management are several defining elements (Lee, 1999): that management is bioregional (landscape-scale or larger), that governance and implementation are collaborative (involving stakeholders), and importantly, that managers rarely know enough about the systems they hope to manage. The framework of adaptive management is intuitive, involving an underlying model of the system which leads to a management strategy or policy, a monitoring program, and a mechanism for evaluation and reaction (Fig. 11.6). The approaches to model-based monitoring schemes described above are an attempt to strongly couple the initial stages of this

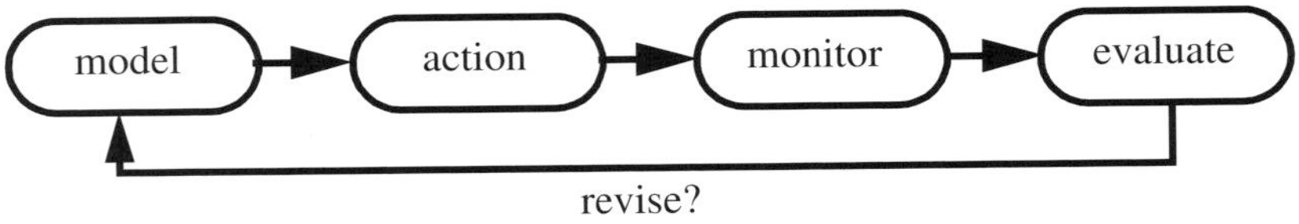

FIGURE 11.6
Schematic of the adaptive management approach. Stakeholders are involved actively in the modeling, action (management strategy or policy), and evaluation phases. Approaches to model-based monitoring schemes discussed in this paper strongly couple the first and third stages of the process.

process, by forcing the monitoring scheme to proceed directly from the underlying model.

This approach is consistent with Lee's (1999) appraisal of adaptive management on several important issues. First, the approach recognizes that a rigorous model-based approach to sampling will likely yield useful and reliable data at lowest cost and most rapidly. Second, the model analysis implicit in the decision-tree approach, and explicit in the later examples, provides a means of emphasizing the central factors identified as being important to the underlying model, while also providing a means of controlling or excluding extraneous factors. Again, data are expensive and some focus on specific factors is logically and logistically necessary. The approach using sensitivity or uncertainty analysis recognizes that "our ignorance is uneven" (Lee, 1999) and thus the most important uncertainties should be addressed rigorously and early. This is also in agreement with Johnson's (1995) advocacy of simulation models as learning tools that can be used to identify critical uncertainties for adaptive management. Finally, because model-based or experimental approaches always run some risk of "surprise" or unanticipated results, the feedback from evaluation to model revision – and by extension, to a revised monitoring scheme – provides for a flexible approach that evolves as we learn (Ringold *et al.*, 1996).

11.7 Summary

I make two points in this discussion. First, landscapes are large and often comprise patterns that are fine-grained, and so conventional sampling approaches will seldom perform as efficiently as designs geared explicitly toward capturing such patterns. Multi-staged stratified designs tend to be more efficient, capturing spatial patterns with fewer samples than simple designs (stratified or random). Importantly, sampling designs often can be tested and fine-tuned in advance by experimenting with alternative designs using digital data from a study area, such as terrain-based indices or land-cover maps. Such cyber-sampling pilot studies can lead to a substantial reduction in the sampling intensity and consequent logistical expense of sampling, while still capturing the patterns of interest. Any design, of course, should be confirmed and further modified as necessary through a pilot study in the field.

Second, I emphasize that all data are *not* created equal: some observations are more informative about particular hypotheses than others. Thus, when the goal is to provide as much leverage as possible for a particular hypothesis or working model, sampling can be focused dramatically by explicitly incorporating the model into the sampling design. This can be accomplished in a simple manner using tree-based guides (decision trees, classification trees), or more formally through the use of computer simulation models.

It should be emphasized that model-guided designs also test the model efficiently, gathering observations that would confirm or disprove the model. Thus, using a model as a guide can be useful even if the model is preliminary or inadequate, because data collected subject to the model's assumptions can only improve the model (note that the most effective way to improve a model is to force it to fail: Mankin *et al.*, 1975). Model-guided designs thus can emerge as a component of adaptive management, with the underlying model providing tests that will ultimately improve the model itself. This approach thus elevates monitoring from a rather passive role to a more active and integrative role in resource management and landscape ecology.

Acknowledgments

My work in the Sierra Nevada was sponsored largely by USGA/BRD contract No. G- 1709–1, continuing under Agreement No. 99WRAG0019, with additional support of the forest modeling activities from National Science Foundation grants DEB 9552656 and DBI 9630606. The cyber-sampling and decision-tree approaches described here were developed as laboratory exercises in my Spatial Analysis and Landscape Ecology classes, respectively, and I appreciate the student involvement that has refined these exercises over the past few semesters.

References

Bormann, F. H. and Likens, G. E. (1979). *Pattern and Process in a Forested Ecosystem*. Springer-Verlag, New York.

Breiman, L., Friedman, J. H., Olshen, R. A. & Stone, C. J. (1984). *Classification and Regression Trees*. Wadsworth and Brooks/Cole, Monterey, CA.

Christensen, N. L., Bartuska, A. N., Brown, J. H., Carpenter, S., D'Antonio, C., Francis, R., Franklin, J. F., MacMahon, J. A., Noss, R. F., Parsons, D. J., Peterson, C. H., Turner, M. G. & Woodmansee, R. G. (1996). The report of the Ecological Society of America Committee on the scientific basis for ecosystem management. *Ecological Applications*, 6: 665–691.

Clark, J. S., Fastie, C., Hurrt, G., Jackson, S. T., Johnson, C., King, G. A., Lewis, M., Lynch, J., Pacala, S., Prentice, C., Schupp, E. W., Webb, T. III and Wyckoff, P. (1998). Reid's paradox of rapid plant migration: Dispersal theory and interpretation of paleoecological records. *BioScience*, 48: 13–24.

Clark, J., Silman, M., Kern, R., Macklin, E. and HilleRisLambers, J. (1999). Seed dispersal near and far: patterns across temperate and tropical forests. *Ecology*, 80: 1475–1494.

Cochran, W. G. (1997). *Sampling Techniques*, 3rd edn. John Wiley, New York.

Dixon, M., Olsen, A. R. & Kahn, B. M. (1998). Measuring trends in ecological resources. *Ecological Applications*, 8: 225–227.

Duncan, G. J., & Kalton, G. (1987). Issues of design and analysis of surveys across time. *International Statistical Review*, 55: 97–117.

Forman, R.T.T. & Godron, M. (1981). Patches and structural components for a landscape ecology. *BioScience*, 31: 733–740.

Forman, R.T.T. & Godron, M. (1986). *Landscape Ecology*. John Wiley, New York.

Goldsmith, F. B. (ed.) (1991). *Monitoring for Conservation and Ecology*. Chapman & Hall, London.

Gross, J., & Yellen, J. (1999). *Graph Theory and its Applications*. CRC Press, Boca Raton, FL.

Halpin, P. N. (1995). A cross-scale analysis of environmental gradients and forest pattern in the giant sequoia–mixed conifer forest of the Sierra Nevada. PhD dissertation, University of Virginia, Charlottesville, VA.

Hanski, I. (1998). Metapopulation dynamics. *Nature*, 396: 41–49.

Harary, F. (1969). *Graph Theory*. Addison-Wesley, Reading, MA.

Harrison, S. (1994). Metapopulations and conservation. In *Large-scale Ecology and Conservation Biology*, eds. P. J. Edwards, N. R. Webb & R. M. May, pp. 111–128. Blackwell, Oxford, UK.

Holling, C. S. (ed.) (1978). *Adaptive Environmental Assessment and Management*. John Wiley, New York.

Hunsaker, C. T., Graham, R. L., Suter, G. W. II, O'Neill, R. V., Barnthouse, L. W. & Gardner, R. H. (1990). Assessing ecological risk on a regional scale. *Environmental Management*, 14: 325–332.

Johnson, B. L. (1995). Applying computer simulation models as learning tools in fishery management. *North American Journal of Fisheries Management*, 15: 736–747.

Johnson, B. L. (1999a). Introduction to the special feature: Adaptive management – scientifically sound, socially challenged? *Conservation Ecology*, 3(1) art 10, http://www.consecol.org/vol3/iss1/ art10.

Johnson, B. L. (1999b). The role of adaptive management as an operational approach for resource management agencies. *Conservation Ecology*, 3(2) art 8, http://www.consecol.org/vol3/iss2/art8.

Keitt, T., Franklin, A. & Urban, D. (1995). Landscape analysis and metapopulation structure. In *Recovery Plan for the Mexican Spotted Owl*, vol 2, ch. 3. US Department of the Interior Fish and Wildlife Service, Albuquerque, New Mexico.

Keitt, T. H., Urban, D. L. & Milne, B. T. (1997). Detecting critical scales in fragmented landscapes. *Conservation Ecology*, 1(1) art 4, http://www.consecol.org/vol1/iss1/art4

Lee, K. N. (1999). Appraising adaptive management. *Conservation Ecology*, 3(2) art 3, http:// www.consecol.org/vol3/iss2/art3.

Lesser, V. M. & Kalsbeek, W. D. (1997). A comparison of periodic survey designs employing multi-stage sampling. *Environmental and Ecological Statistics*, 4: 117–130.

Levins, R. (1969). Some demographic and genetic consequences of environmental heterogeneity for biological control. *Bulletin of the Entomological Society of America*, 15: 237–240.

McLain, R. J. & Lee, R. G. (1996). Adaptive management: Promises and pitfalls. *Environmental Management*, 20: 437–448.

Mankin, J. B., O'Neill, R. V., Shugart, H. H. and Rust, B. W. (1975). The importance of validation in ecosystems analysis. In *New Directions in the Analysis of Ecological Systems*, part 1, *Simulation Councils Proceedings Series*, vol. 5, ed. G. S. Innis, pp. 63–71. Simulation Councils, La Jolla, CA.

Moore, D. M., Lee, B. G. & Davey, S. M. (1991). A new method for predicting vegetation distributions using decision tree analysis in a geographic information system. *Environmental Management*, 15: 59–71.

Moore, I. D., Gryson, R. B. & Ladson, A. R.

(1990). Digital terrain modelling: a review of hydrological, geomorphological, and biological applications. *Hydrological Processes*, 5: 3–30.

Nusser, S. M., Breidt, F. J. & Fuller, W. A. (1998). Design and estimation of investigating the dynamics of natural resources. *Ecological Applications* 8: 234–245.

Pulliam, H. R. (1988). Sources, sinks, and population regulation. *American Naturalist*, 132: 652–661.

Ringold, P. L., Alegria, J., Czaplewski, R. L., Mulder, B. S., Tolle, T. & Burnett, K. (1996). Adaptive monitoring design for ecosystem management. *Ecological Applications*, 6: 745–747.

Schreuder, H. T., Gregoire, T. G. & Wood, G. B. (1993). *Sampling Methods for Multiresource Forest Inventory.* John Wiley, New York.

Smith, T. M. & Urban, D. L. (1988). Scale and resolution of forest structural pattern. *Vegetatio*, 74: 143–150.

Stauffer, D. (1985). *Introduction to Percolation Theory.* Taylor & Francis, London.

Stephenson, N. L. (1998). Actual evapotranspiration and deficit: Biologically meaningful correlates of vegetation distribution across spatial scales. *Journal of Biogeography*, 25: 855–870.

Stephenson, N. L. & Parsons, D. J. (1993). A research program for predicting the effects of climatic change on the Sierra Nevada. pp. 93–109. In *Proceedings of the 4th Conference on Research in California's National Parks.* US Department of the Interior National Park Service Transactions and Proceedings Series no. 9. eds S. D.Veirs Jr., T. J. Stohlgren & C. Schonewald-Cox, US Department of the Interior National Park Service, Washington, D.C.

Stow, C. A., Carpenter, S. R., Webster, K. E. & Frost, T. M. (1998). Long-term environmental monitoring: some perspectives from lakes. *Ecological Applications*, 8: 269–276.

Sutter, R. D. (1986). Monitoring rare plant species and natural areas: Ensuring the protection of our investment. *Natural Areas Journal*, 6: 3–5.

Turner, M. G. (1989). Landscape ecology: The effect of pattern on process. *Annual Review of Ecology and Systematics*, 20: 171–197.

Urban, D. L. (2000). Using model analysis to design monitoring programs for landscape management and impact assessment. *Ecological Applications*, 10: 1820–1832.

Urban, D. L. & Keitt, T. H. (2001). Landscape connectivity: A graph-theoretic perspective. *Ecology*, 82: 1205–1218.

Urban, D. L. & Smith, T. M. (1989). Microhabitat pattern and the structure of forest bird communities. *American Naturalist*, 133: 811–829.

Urban, D. L., O'Neill, R. V. & Shugart, H. H. (1987). Landscape ecology. *BioScience*, 37: 119– 127.

Urban, D. L., Miller, C., Halpin, P. N. & Stephenson, N. L. (2000). Forest gradient response in Sierran landscapes: The physical template. *Landscape Ecology*, 15: 603–620.

US Department of the Interior Fish and Wildlife Service (1995). *Recovery Plan for the Mexican spotted owl*, vol. 1. US Department of the Interior Fish and Wildlife Service. Albuquerque, NM.

Usher, M. B. (1991). Scientific requirements of a monitoring programme. In ed. F. B. Goldsmith, *Monitoring for conservation and ecology*, pp. 15–32. Chapman & Hall, London.

Walters, C. (1986). *Adaptive Management of Renewable Resources.* Macmillan, New York.

Walters, C., and C. S. Holling (1990). Large-scale management experiments and learning by doing. *Ecology*, 71:2060–2068.

Watt, A. S. (1947). Pattern and process in the plant community. *Journal of Ecology*, 35: 1–22.

White, G. C., Block, W. M., Ganey, J. L., Moir, W. H., Ward, J. P., Franklin, A. B., Spangle, S. L., Rinkevich, S. E., Vahle, J. R., Howe, F. P. and Dick, J. L. (1999). Science versus political reality in delisting criteria for a threatened species: the Mexican spotted owl experience. *Transactions of the North American Wildlife and Natural Resources Conference*, 64: 292–306.

12

Landscape change: Patterns, effects, and implications for adaptive management of wildlife resources

12.1 Introduction

Landscape change is one of the foremost themes underlying landscape ecology research. This theme ranges from a focus on the causes of landscape change to the effect of landscape change on ecosystems and organisms. The end result of such diverse research has been the creation of a large body of knowledge and significant advance in the scientific understanding of landscapes. However, while knowledge has advanced, scientists and resource managers have only begun to integrate the findings into natural resource management. One strategy in natural resource management that offers a strong potential for integration with landscape change is adaptive management.

Adaptive management differs from traditional resource management (Halbert, 1993) by treating management actions as experiments with testable hypotheses (Holling, 1978; Walters, 1986; Lee, 1993; Gunderson, 1999). The intent of adaptive management is to maximize the information gained and thereby reduce uncertainty about the system, especially for those areas suspected to be critical to proper system function. Moreover, adaptive management emphasizes applying new knowledge to help refine and possibly alter future actions (Holling, 1978; Walters, 1986; Lee, 1993; Gunderson, 1999). This approach can be applied to landscapes by dividing the landscapes into experimental units that meet management goals while providing information about how landscape change affects management actions.

The objectives of this chapter are two-fold: (1) to describe various patterns and causes of landscape change, and summarize its effects on wildlife; and (2) to discuss using landscape change information in adaptive management of wildlife resources. To highlight these objectives in a real world situation we will present a case study of two watersheds in Michigan's Lower Peninsula that have contrasting landscape structures and patterns of landscape change.

12.2 Patterns and causes of landscape change

12.2.1 Patterns of landscape change

Different landscapes exhibit different spatial patterns of change, including different compositions, spatial distributions, types, rates, and scales of interest. Landscape pattern depends on the number and relative proportion of patch types as well as their spatial distribution (Turner, 1989; Turner *et al.*, 1989; Forman, 1995; Hobbs, 1995). Patch distribution can range from uniform, where patches of different types are well mixed on the landscape, to clumped, where patches of the same type lie closer to one another (Forman, 1995). Landscape pattern will also depend on patch shape. Patches that follow natural gradients such as topography or nutrient flows tend to have more complex shapes than patches that follow orderly patterns such as human land ownership (Forman, 1995). These characteristics will also affect the boundaries or "edge" between patches. Edge characteristics affect the flow of nutrients and organisms among patches, which could have important implications for landscape structure (Forman and Moore, 1992; Wiens, 1992).

Patterns of landscape change depend on the types of change, the rates of change (Forman, 1995), and the scales of interest (Turner *et al.*, 1993). The types of change and their corresponding patterns can range from natural changes, such as forest succession, to anthropogenic changes, such as urbanization (Forman, 1995). Rates of change obviously vary among landscapes, but an important consideration is how fast landscapes are changing currently relative to their historic rates of change. In this case, historic typically implies "with few or no people." The scale of interest relates to the spatial extent of change relative to the extent of the landscape, the duration of change relative to the time it takes to return to stable conditions following disturbance, and the level of detail of the desired information (Turner *et al.*, 1993).

At spatial and temporal scales relevant to natural resource managers, several broad patterns are common. First, landscapes could appear relatively stable such that most areas remain in the same condition (e.g., forest, urban), and most disturbances are small in extent and short in duration. An example would be forested areas where disturbances typically create small gaps that then undergo succession. Second, landscapes could have a cyclical pattern of change, such as crop rotation in agricultural fields. Third, landscapes could exhibit moderate to broad directional changes that result in dramatically different conditions. These changes could occur via natural mechanisms, such as fire altering community composition (Turner *et al.*, 1993), or through human intervention, such as urbanization. Human-induced changes are often drastic, difficult to reverse, and usually result in a stable – albeit highly different – state.

The important thing to remember is that the patterns of change depend on the scale at which they are examined.

12.2.2 Causes of landscape change

Landscape ecologists distinguish between natural and anthropogenic disturbances as causes of landscape change (Hobbs, 1995). Natural disturbances result from physical and biological processes. Those disturbances can occur over a wide range of spatial and temporal scales, with very different implications at each scale (Holling, 1992). For example, lightning strikes are lethal at the scale of individual trees but essential at the scale of forests (Harris *et al.*, 1996).

As the name implies, anthropogenic disturbances result directly or indirectly from human activity (Liu *et al.*, 1999), such as agriculture, housing and commercial development, and silviculture (Franklin and Forman, 1987). Human-induced change not only modifies the environment directly for human benefit, but also includes resource management practices that directly affect the environment, such as wildlife management. Besides direct intervention, human-induced changes also occur indirectly (or subtly; Russell, 1993) through modification of ecological processes, such as removal of predator or keystone species that significantly affect food webs (Primack, 1993; Crooks and Soulé, 1999). New changes can also occur resulting from the interactions of natural and anthropogenic disturbances. For example, the frequency and extent of windthrow may be increased as a result of the anthropogenic related disturbance.

12.3 Effects of landscape change on wildlife

One major focus of landscape change research has been the investigation of species responses, particularly with respect to habitat loss and fragmentation (Saunders *et al.*, 1991). The viability of a species in a landscape depends on the quantity, quality, configuration, and context of suitable habitat (Pearson *et al.*, 1996; Wiens, 1996), the life-history characteristics of the species under consideration, and how that species perceives the landscape (Morrison *et al.*, 1992). While the relationship among these factors is complex, some general statements can be made based on available research.

12.3.1 Habitat quantity and metapopulations

The quantity of suitable habitat is a primary determinant of species viability on the landscape. If suitable habitat is distributed throughout the landscape in large enough quantities, then individuals could comprise a single, continuous population. As the quantity of suitable habitat declines, remaining patches become more isolated from one another. At a certain degree of fragmentation, which varies according to species and landscape conditions, populations in individual patches become separate and interact primarily via dispersal. The collection of populations is termed a metapopulation (Levins, 1969; McCullough, 1996). While individual populations may undergo rounds of extinction and recolonization (Hanski, 1994), metapopulation dynamics may be stable compared to the status of any individual population. As the amount of suitable habitat on the landscape decreases or populations become more isolated due to increased distance among suitable patches, the possibility of extinction of the overall metapopulation could increase (Hanski, 1991, 1999; Hanski and Gilpin, 1991).

12.3.2 Habitat quality

Habitat quality is a measure of the degree to which biophysical characteristics (e.g., structure, composition, function) of a given area meet the requirements of a given species. Habitat quality could affect such factors and parameters as population size, reproductive rates, survivorship, or risk of predation. At landscape scales, habitat patches are often classified as sources or sinks (Pulliam, 1988). Populations in source habitats have high enough reproduction to be self-sustaining and can contribute individuals to the overall population through dispersal. Populations in sink habitats can support reproduction but not enough to be self-sustaining.

12.3.3 Habitat configuration

Habitat configuration represents the spatial and temporal relationship of suitable patches to each other. In general, as the distance between habitat patches increases, the likelihood of exchange of individuals among those patches via dispersal decreases (Hanski, 1994, 1999). For example, Bachman's sparrow (*Aimophila aestivalis*) has the highest population size when source habitats are placed close together in the center of the landscape and can serve as sources of colonization for surrounding sink habitats. On the other hand, the lowest population sizes occur when the source habitats are placed at one corner of the landscape (Liu *et al.*, 1994).

12.3.4 Habitat context

Habitat context represents the spatial and temporal relationship of suitable habitat patches to non-suitable habitat. Intervening conditions between suitable patches are important for dispersal success (Gustafson and Gardner, 1996). For example, some species are less likely to disperse across agricultural gaps between forest patches (Grubb and Doherty, 1999), and roads often create barriers to species movements (Forman, 1995). Furthermore species may respond not only to conditions in the habitat patch but to conditions in the surrounding landscape (Titus and Mosher, 1981; Pearson, 1993; Kilgo *et al.*, 1997; Chapter 8, this book).

12.3.5 Species life history

Species life-history characteristics and perceptions of the landscape also determine the degree to which a species can adapt to landscape changes. Some species adapt easily to change by altering their foraging, reproduction, and social habits accordingly. Other species respond poorly to change, especially if they require highly specialized habitat. A well-known example in Michigan is the federally listed endangered Kirtland's warbler (*Dendroica kirtlandii*), which selects young jack pine for nesting (Probst and Weinrich, 1993). Moreover, species perceive the same landscape differently (Morrison *et al.*, 1992). For example, within a single field a butterfly might use fine-scale features such as nectar sources, a rabbit might use medium-scale features such as brush piles for cover, and a hawk might use the entire field as part of its home range. Furthermore, an organism's perception of the landscape may vary over time due to changes in breeding conditions, life stages, and climate.

Ultimately, the response of wildlife to landscape change depends on the types, spatial patterns, and rates of landscape change and the species in question. For example, some wildlife species will be able to maintain populations or even respond positively to directional changes on the landscape if rates of landscape change are low enough to allow them to adapt to the new conditions. Conversely, other species will be unable to adapt regardless of the types of change or the rate at which those changes occur. Therefore understanding landscape patterns and how they change is critical to conservation of wildlife resources.

12.3.6 Use of landscape change information for resource management

Resource management agencies and managers have increasingly acknowledged the importance of managing wildlife at the landscape scale. Accompanying this shift in scale has been the realization that the tenets of landscape ecology are very relevant for managing wildlife, as discussed in the previous section. While the importance of landscape ecology in managing wildlife has been broadly recognized, it has only begun to be put into practice.

Moreover, specifically designing and implementing management plans from a landscape perspective has only been carried out in a few instances, and primarily only on paper (e.g., Swanson and Franklin, 1992). In the case of using differing aspects of landscape change there has been no real world implementation.

12.4 Case study: Two Michigan watersheds

To illustrate different spatial patterns, types, and rates of landscape change, we present a study of two Michigan watersheds with contrasting land use and socioeconomic histories. First, we describe the study areas. Second, we show historical land-use/land-cover trends, current landscape conditions, and possible future developments. Third, we discuss factors influencing landscape changes. Fourth, we illustrate the effects of landscape change on wildlife (i.e., birds, mammals, and herpetofauna; Caughley and Sinclair, 1994). Fifth, we provide two examples to illustrate how landscape change information can be incorporated into the adaptive management of wildlife.

12.4.1 General description of study areas

Our case study focuses on the Black and Huron River watersheds located in Michigan's Lower Peninsula (LP) (Fig. 12.1). These two watersheds were chosen because they: (1) have different landscape histories, current landscape conditions, and types and rates of landscape change; and (2) represent two typical landscapes in Michigan: urban–agricultural and rural–forest.

The Black River watershed is located in the upper LP within Cheboygan, Montmorency, Otsego, and Presque Isle counties (Fig. 12.2). The present landscape of the Black River watershed is 70% forest, 14% non-forest (grassland and shrubland), 7% agriculture, 4% water, 4% wetlands, and 2% urban. Land ownership is divided almost evenly between public and private (Table 12.1). The major public landholdings include portions of the Macinaw state forest. The economy of the northern LP is based on natural resources production and tourism (Tyler and LaBelle, 1995; Warbach and Reed, 1995). Human population size and density within the townships encompassing the watershed are relatively low (Table 12.1) (US Bureau of the Census, 1992). The largest town in the watershed is Onaway with a population of 1039 persons in 1990. The watershed has no interstates or US highways and has a relatively low density of roads (Table 12.1).

The Huron River watershed is located in the southeastern LP, just west of Detroit, within Ingham, Jackson, Livingston, Monroe, Oakland, Washtenaw, and Wayne counties (Fig. 12.3). Currently, the watershed is 29% urban, 26% agricultural, 17% forest, 17% non-forest, 6% wetlands, and 5% water. Land cover in

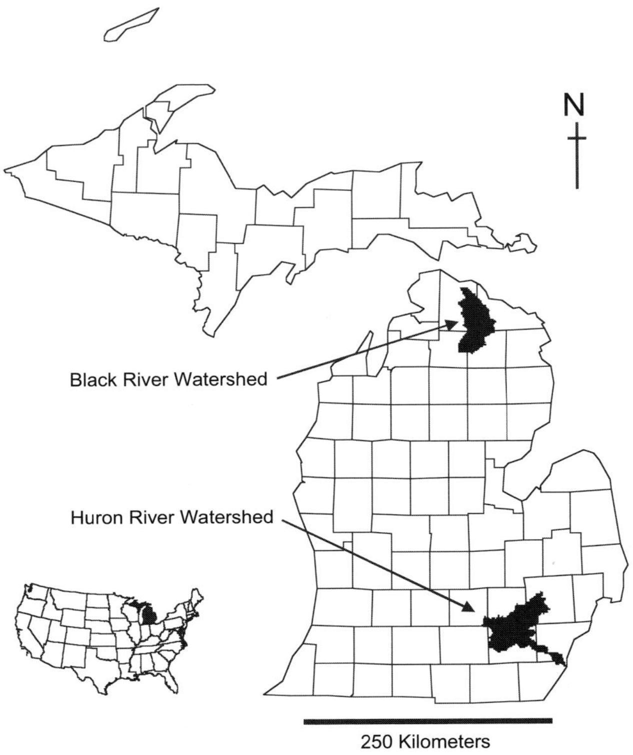

FIGURE 12.1
Location of Black and Huron River watersheds in Michigan.

the watershed is highly interspersed. The watershed has diverse physiography. The northeast contains an extensive network of lakes that form the river's headwaters. Land ownership is almost exclusively private (90%) (Table 12.1), with the major public lands being state wildlife management and recreation areas and 10 regional parks located along the Huron River. The economy of the Huron River watershed is a broad mixture of manufacturing, retail, service, and institutional uses (Tyler and LaBelle, 1995). The Huron River watershed has a much higher human population size and density than the Black River watershed and has an extensive system of highways, roads, and streets (Table 12.1).

12.4.2 Landscape change in the watersheds

To understand how landscapes in the two watersheds have changed, we developed a database of land cover for each watershed for five time periods: late

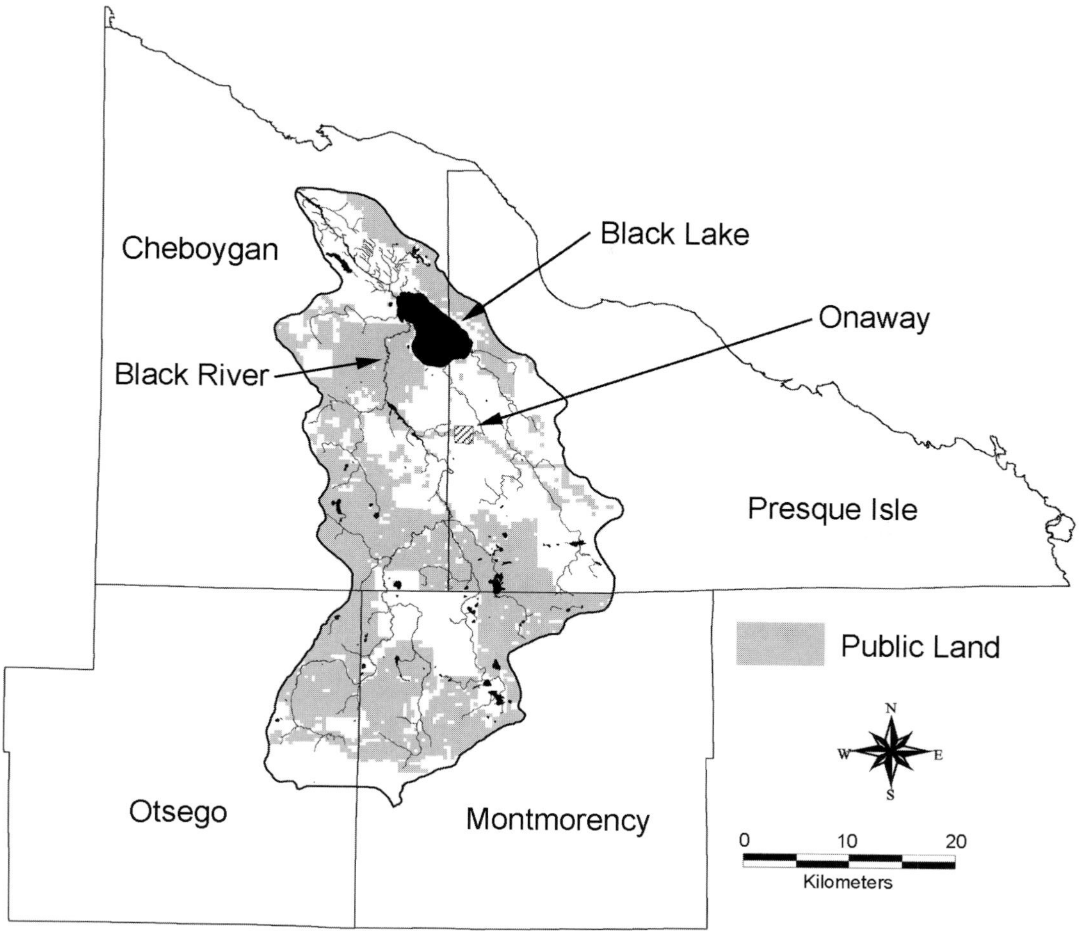

FIGURE 12.2
Location of the Black River watershed within surrounding counties.

1930s, mid-1950s, late 1960s, late 1970s, and mid-1990s (Rutledge, 2001). The Black River watershed, like most forested areas in northern Michigan, has undergone extensive changes since European settlement. The Black River watershed was predominantly forested (97%) at the time of General Land Office (GLO) surveys in the mid nineteenth century (Comer *et al.*, 1995). However, during the mid- to late nineteenth century and early 1900s, most of the forests in northern Michigan, including a majority of those in the Black River watershed, were clear-cut (McCann, 1991). By the early twentieth century, many of

Table 12.1. *Comparison of the Black and Huron River watersheds*

	Black River	Huron River
Area (ha)	155 842	235 917
Land ownership		
Private land (ha)	79 401	212 931
Public land (ha)[a]	76 441	22 986
Population of encompassing townships (1990)		
Number of persons	18 432	739 438
Density (persons/km^2)	12	313
Roads (total length in km)		
Highways: Interstates, US, State	89	750
County highways/roads	866	2920
Residential roads	60	2961

Notes:

[a] Public lands are estimates of state lands (primarily state forests) in the Black River watershed and state lands (recreation areas and wildlife management areas) and regional park land area in the Huron river watershed.

the clear-cut areas returned to forest conditions, albeit with a composition different from conditions at the time of the GLO survey, and the watershed remained mostly forested by 1992 (69.7%) (Fig. 12.4, color plate). Figure 12.5a shows the distribution of land in different cover types from the GLO survey from 1938 to 1992 for five time periods. From 1938 to 1992, land cover in the watershed remained relatively stable (Fig. 12.5a, b). Total forest cover declined slightly. Mean patch sizes for forest increased and then decreased, reflecting regeneration and renewed cutting. Mean patch sizes for other land cover remained fairly constant (Fig. 12.5b). Overall, land cover changed on 17.8% of the watershed during the 55-year period investigated (Fig. 12.4, color plate).

The Huron River watershed has a markedly different history than that of the Black River watershed. The Huron River watershed was predominantly forest (56%) and grassland (29%) at the time of the GLO survey (Comer *et al.*, 1995). By the late 1930s, agriculture was the dominant land-use practice, accounting for 55% of the total area. However, by the early 1990s, agriculture had declined to about 26% of the total landscape while urban uses increased five-fold from 5% to 29% of the landscape (Fig. 12.4, color plate, Fig. 12.5c). Forest and non-forest areas saw small increases as agricultural land went fallow. Mean patch sizes increased slightly for all land-cover types except agriculture, which decreased from 182.7 to 45.6 ha (Fig. 12.5d). Land cover changed on 45.1% of the watershed during the period from 1938 to 1992 (Fig. 12.4, color plate).

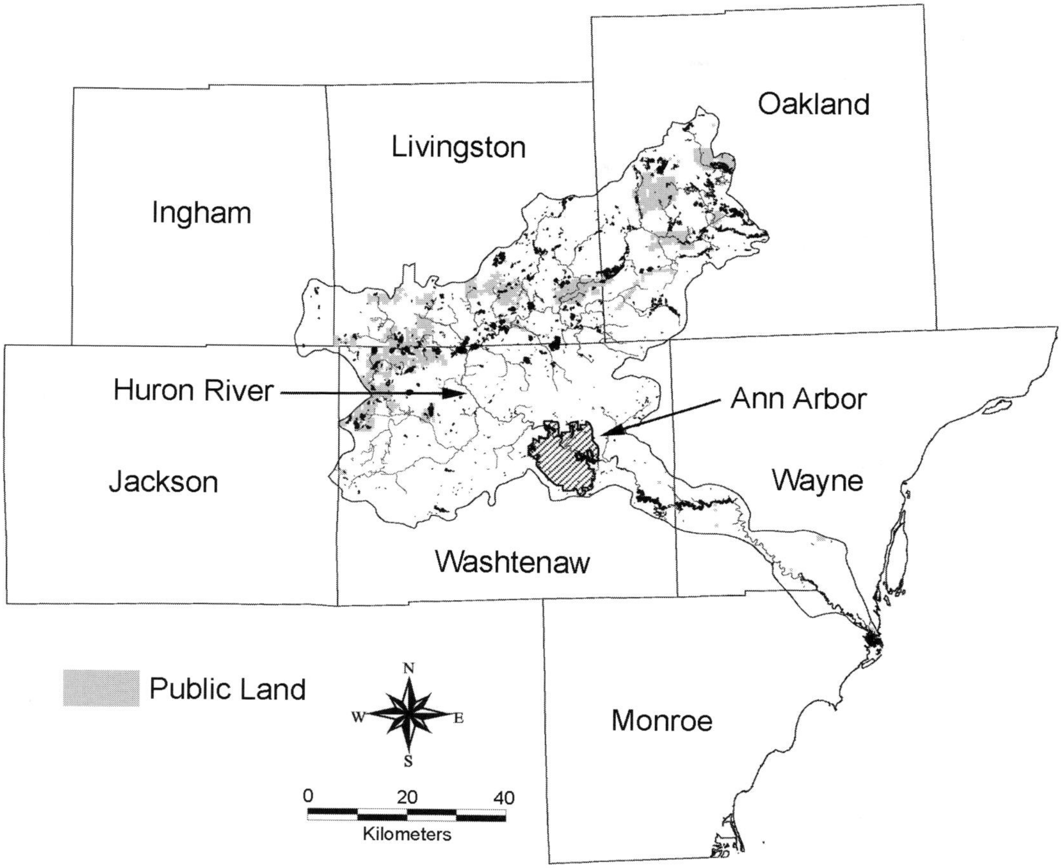

FIGURE 12.3
Location of Huron River watershed within surrounding counties.

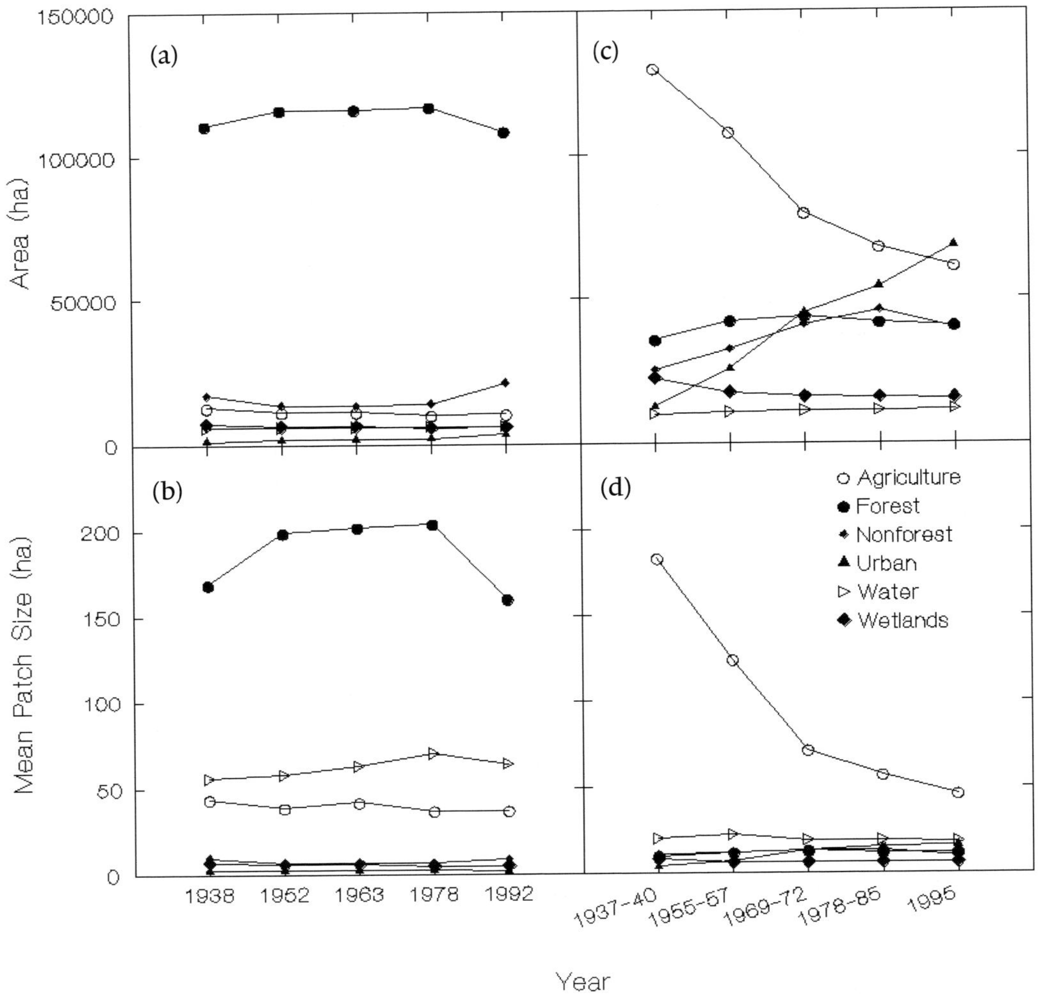

FIGURE 12.5
Total area and mean patch size for each land-cover type for the watersheds. (a) Total area for Black River watershed; (b) mean patch size for Black River watershed; (c) total area for Huron River watershed; (d) mean patch size for Huron River watershed.

12.4.3 Factors influencing landscape change

Prior to the twentieth century, the primary factor responsible for broad-scale landscape change in the Black River watershed was extensive timber harvesting of Michigan's forests, which typically meant clear-cutting. Since the early twentieth century the Black River watershed has experienced two types of landscape change: broad-scale directional changes consisting primarily of forest regeneration and fine-scale directional changes in primarily stable urban and agricultural areas. The factors influencing landscape change were (1) implementation of modern silivicultural practices on public and private lands, (2) expansion of resorts and tourism, (3) construction of vacation or retirement homes, and (4) extraction of natural gas and oil resources.

In the Huron River watershed most factors influencing landscape change are also anthropogenic. Before the twentieth century, the watershed was transformed from a forest/non-forest landscape to an agricultural landscape. However, during the twentieth century agricultural areas declined steadily as farmers discontinued operations and/or sold their land for development. Therefore the main cause of landscape change in the past 60 years was urbanization. The factors responsible for this urbanization include a large increase in the number of people moving out of urban Detroit and the development of the interstate highway system. Urbanization will likely continue as more people seek to live in areas with a more natural and/or rural character (Wycoff and Reed, 1995).

12.4.4 Effects of landscape change on wildlife in the watersheds

Based on estimates derived from accounts of species' historical ranges, the Black and Huron River watersheds historically supported 281 and 311 wildlife species, respectively. The best available information indicated that 15 species have been extirpated from the Black River watershed, and 26 species have been extirpated from the Huron River watershed. While landscape change was not responsible for all of the extirpations (e.g., passenger pigeon *Ectopistes migratorius*), it did play an important role (Baker, 1983; Winterstein *et al.*, 1995). In both watersheds the extirpations affected only birds and mammals, particularly large ranging carnivores and herbivores. During recent decades landscape change has had a notable effect on wetland-associated species through the draining and conversion of wetlands and interspersion of roads (e.g., wood turtle [*Clemmys insculpta*], Blanding's turtle [*Emydoidea blandingii*], leopard frog [*Rana pipiens*], Harding and Holman, 1990, 1999; Harding, 1997). The state of Michigan lists nearly 20% of wetland-associated species as endangered, threatened, or of special concern. Landscape change has similarly impacted forest interior birds through fragmentation and isolation of forests (Robinson *et al.*, 1995). For example, in the Huron River watershed, forest patches historically ranged from tens to hundreds of hectares in size, but today are typically 10 hectares in size or smaller. Overall the current status of most wildlife species in both watersheds is unknown beyond simple presence/absence, with the exception of certain game species (Baker, 1983; Harding and Holman, 1990, 1999; Brewer *et al.*, 1991; McPeek and Adams, 1994; Holman *et al.*, 1999).

Because the current knowledge of wildlife species on the landscape is limited, predicting the effects of future landscape change on wildlife species is difficult. Nonetheless, several general statements can be made. In the Black River watershed, the human population is expected to nearly double in the next 20 years in two of four counties that encompass the watershed (from 17957 to 34651 in Otsego County and from 8936 to 16527 in Montmorency County; Wyckoff and Reed, 1995). These increases represent the largest percentage increases of any Michigan counties. Given such a dramatic increase in the human population it is highly probable that the amount of urban land will increase, and the amount of forest land will decrease, resulting in a reduction and fragmentation of wildlife habitat. In addition, the increased human population will likely result in changes to the context of remaining habitat as those surrounding areas are adapted for human use.

In contrast to the Black River watershed, the Huron River watershed faces extreme urbanization pressure. Assuming urbanization continues, wetland-associated species, particularly some herpetofauna, will continue to decline in the watershed. Furthermore, bird species sensitive to fragmentation, such as ovenbirds (*Seiurus aurocapillus*), will likely continue to decline or be rare in the watershed. While an urbanizing effect is generally assumed to be a negative consequence for wildlife, some species will likely respond positively to the changes. For example, coyotes (*Canis latrans*) have exhibited large increases in urban–agricultural landscapes (Crooks and Soulé, 1999). Similarly, species such as opossums (*Didelphis virginiana*), raccoons (*Procyon lotor*), and gray catbirds (*Bumetella carolinensis*) that show positive affinities with human-dominated landscapes will likely increase their population sizes.

12.4.5 Delineation of experimental units for adaptive management

In utilizing an adaptive management strategy, a key step is deciding upon the experimental units needed to meet management objectives. The selection of units should be guided by the following criteria: (1) the question

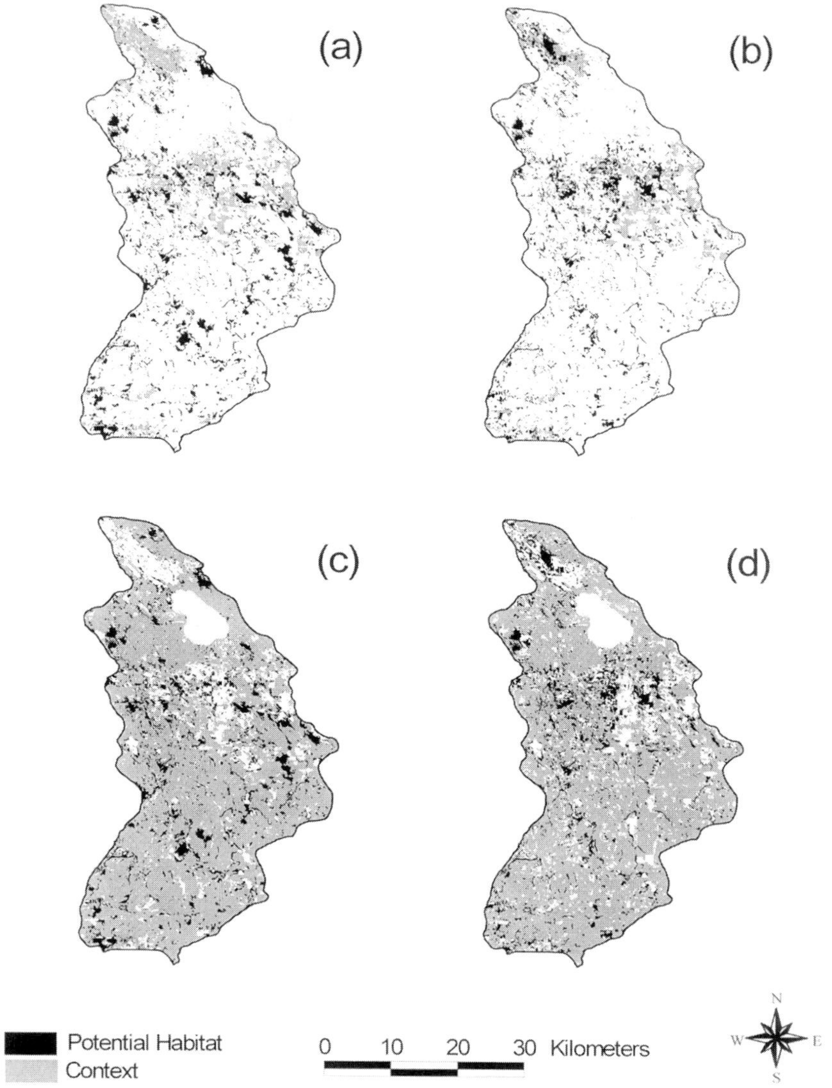

FIGURE 12.6
Location of potential habitat (black areas) for the eastern meadowlark (*Sturnella magna*) in the Black River watershed. Shaded areas indicate land-cover type that would constitute context for the experimental units in an adaptive management plan. (a) 1938 potential habitat, agricultural context; (b) 1992 potential habitat, agricultural context; (c) 1938 potential habitat, forest context; (d) 1992 potential habitat, forest context.

being asked, (2) past, present, and expected future landscape characteristics (e.g., landscape composition, types of change, rates of change), and (3) the wildlife species of interest. Following these three criteria, the delineation of experimental units can vary considerably in type and scale. For example, an experimental unit would be much larger for studying gray wolves (*Canus lupis*) than it would be for studying meadow voles (*Microtus pennsylvanicus*). Moreover, replicate units are required to reduce uncertainty and to test hypotheses related to management objectives. To illustrate these points in more detail, we present examples of management questions for two wildlife species and outline possible criteria for delineating experimental units.

The first example involves the eastern meadowlark (*Sturnella magna*) in the Black River watershed. Eastern meadowlarks prefer lush, poorly drained open areas such as hayfields, old fields, pastures, prairies, or open wetlands. Additionally, they are uncommon in predominantly forested areas (Brewer *et al.*, 1991). Eastern meadowlarks have declined in Michigan, possibly due to loss of suitable habitat such as hayfields (Brewer *et al.*, 1991). In landscapes like the Black River watershed some habitats may be available for relatively longer periods of time (e.g., wetlands) while others may only be available for relatively shorter periods of time (e.g., forest gaps and hayfields). Therefore an important need for research and management would be to quantify and manipulate the extent to which eastern meadowlarks use habitats of varying duration (e.g., permanent versus temporary) and located within different landscape contexts (e.g., mostly forested versus mostly agricultural areas).

In the Black River watershed, areas that could provide habitat for the eastern meadowlark were identified from the land-cover database (Fig. 12.6). Potential habitats were those land-cover types that may contain the abiotic and biotic resources needed by the eastern meadowlark (Morrison *et al.*, 1992; Hall *et al.*, 1997). In this example, three land-cover types could provide potential habitat: pastures, grasslands, and shrub/scrub wetlands. Although certain croplands (e.g., hayfields) could provide habitat, the land-cover database did not distinguish different crop types. Therefore cropland was not included as potential habitat, thereby yielding a conservative estimate of total potential habitat. Despite these limitations, such assumptions are necessary when dealing with broad-scale issues and coarse data resolution. Based on the land-cover database, the amount of potential habitat declined from 16 750 ha in 1938 to 15 396 ha in 1992, an 8% decrease. The number of suitable patches increased from 2044 to 2492, and mean patch size decreased from 8.19 ± 26.88 ha to 6.18 ± 14.42 ha. Many large patches of potential habitat disappeared from the landscape during the study period, especially in the central portion of the watershed (Fig. 12.6). There were also some spatial and temporal shifts in availability of potential habitat.

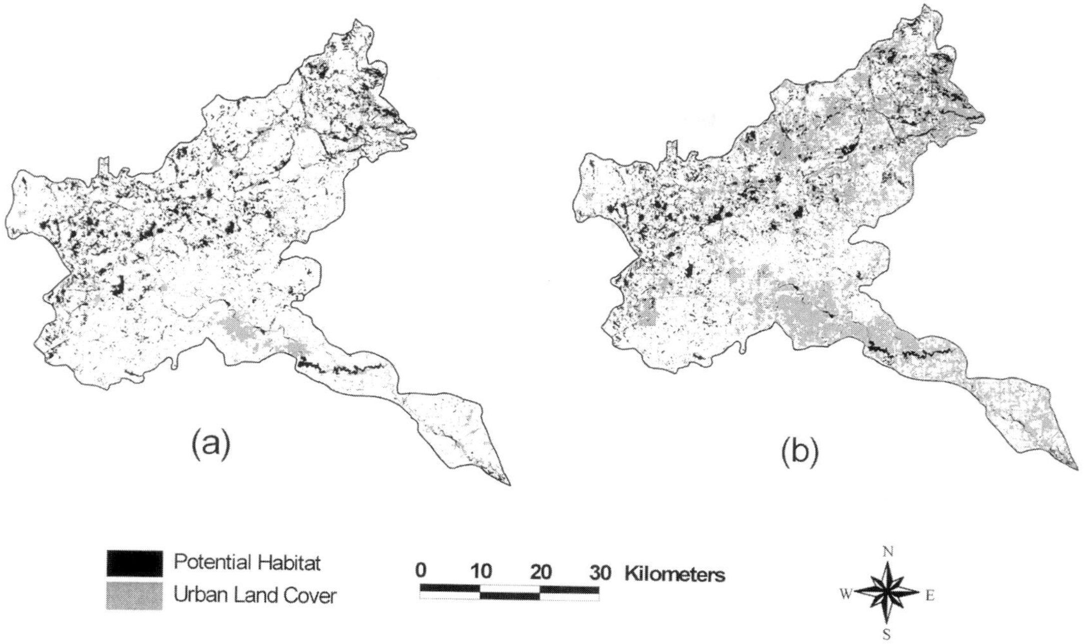

FIGURE 12.7
Location of potential habitat for the green frog (*Rana clamitans*) and urban areas in the Huron River watershed. (a) 1938–40; (b) 1995.

Using historic and existing landscape conditions in the Black River watershed, an adaptive management plan could identify areas to quantify the effects of habitat duration and landscape context on the eastern meadowlark. Experimental units would be defined by two dominant landscape contexts in the watershed: primarily forested versus primarily agricultural (Fig. 12.6). Each experimental unit would contain replicate patches of permanent and/or temporary potential habitat. Potential habitat patches could include existing patches, patches deliberately created for the management plan, or patches created through natural or anthropogenic disturbances. Surveys would be conducted to quantify the use of permanent and temporary habitat patches by eastern meadowlarks within different landscape contexts. The frequency of surveys would depend upon many factors, including the number of desired experimental units and replicate patches.

The second example involves the green frog (*Rana clamitans*) in the Huron River watershed. Adult green frogs can inhabit lakes, ponds, marshes, wooded swamps, and the banks of streams and rivers (Harding and Holman, 1999). Home range sizes are typically very small, averaging approximately 60 m^2 (Stebbins and Cohen, 1995). While adult green frogs tend to stay near water, juveniles disperse widely through woods and meadows during rainy weather (Harding and Holman, 1999). Therefore, as formerly agricultural areas become urbanized, dispersing frogs could have higher levels of mortality from such factors as increased road density and increased road traffic (Forman, 1995; Harding and Holman, 1999). If dispersal were sufficiently disrupted, green frog metapopulations might decline or eventually go extinct. Therefore an important need for research and management would be to evaluate and minimize the extent to which urbanization affects green frog dispersal and metapopulation dynamics.

In the Huron River watershed, land-cover types that could provide habitat for the green frog were identified from the land-cover database (Fig. 12.7). For the green frog, potential habitat consisted of six land-cover types: rivers, lakes, reservoirs, shrub/scrub wetlands, aquatic-bed wetlands, and emergent vegetation wetlands. Based on the land-cover database, the amount of potential habitat declined from 31 591 ha in 1938 to 26 323 ha in 1992, a 17% decrease. The number of potential habitat patches decreased from 4195 to 3947, and mean patch size decreased from 7.53 ± 18.99 ha to 6.67 ± 19.34 ha. Decreases in potential habitat area and mean patch size were due primarily to loss of wetlands in the watershed, as the number of lakes actually increased. In addition, the land cover surrounding many lakes and wetlands changed from predominantly agricultural to predominantly urban (Fig. 12.7). Therefore, the green frog experienced declines in the amount of potential habitat as well as changes in the surrounding landscape context.

Using historic and existing landscape conditions in the Huron River watershed (Fig. 12.5), an adaptive management plan could identify areas to quantify green frog dispersal and metapopulation dynamics before and after urbanization. Experimental units would consist of groups of wetlands located in areas where the amount of urban land cover is likely to increase. To make the units independent, dispersal between units should be minimized. This could be achieved by placing units at distances greater than green frogs can disperse or by placing them on opposite sides of barriers to green frog dispersal, such as limited-access highways. Furthermore, experimental units would be designated as protected and non-protected. In protected units, wetlands would be maintained and prevented from changing to other land cover types. In non-protected units, wetlands could change in quality or be converted to other land-cover types. Using techniques such as radio telemetry (Lamoureux and Madison, 1999) or genetic markers (Scribner *et al.*, 2001), dispersal could be measured as the amount of urban land-cover increases.

The information gained could then be used to develop models of green frog dispersal success before, during, and after the process of urbanization and could in turn lead to better management of the species.

12.5 Implications of landscape change studies for adaptive management

Understanding the effect of landscape change on wildlife should be an essential component of wildlife management because landscape change information can assist managers in several ways. First, the information can help managers gain insights about broad-scale factors that affect changes in wildlife habitat and populations. Second, the information can help managers understand the consequences of wildlife management practices, thereby helping to design effective and feasible management policies. Third, the information can help managers predict future landscape changes and the consequences of those changes on wildlife.

Information on landscape change needs to be coupled with information from traditional sources to enhance wildlife management. Traditional research and management provide detailed information that complements general information from landscape studies. Our examples the need to link landscape change information with species–habitat relationships to address important wildlife management issues. While our examples only considered single species, similar approaches could be used to study the effects of landscape change on multiple species and the interactions among them.

Integration of landscape change information and traditional sources of data can be best used under an adaptive management strategy. Landscape change patterns combined with knowledge of wildlife species status and life history can provide guidance for designing experimental management units that take advantage of historic, current, and possible future landscape conditions. Using what is available is especially important in areas like the Huron River watershed where direct manipulation of landscape conditions is very difficult because the majority of the land is privately owned. Furthermore, adaptive management inherently provides monitoring data that can be used to evaluate the effectiveness of wildlife management and help understand how wildlife species respond to different types, rates, and scales of landscape change.

12.6 Summary

Landscape ecology provides the theoretical and empirical foundation for studying and understanding the types, rates, scales, and causes of landscape changes and how wildlife species respond to those changes. Information on landscape changes is critically needed for adaptive management of wildlife because landscape changes result in alteration of wildlife habitat quantity, quality, and context. Adaptive management considers management alternatives as testable hypotheses and uses knowledge gained to modify future management actions. Taking advantage of available information on historic and future landscape changes, experimental management units can be delineated to determine what landscape features are important to particular wildlife species. To demonstrate these ideas, information on landscape changes was presented for two contrasting watersheds in Michigan. The Black River watershed was, and remains, predominantly forested, has a low level of population, and has an economy based on tourism and natural resources. The Huron River watershed was originally forested, underwent conversion to agriculture, and is now experiencing rapid urbanization. Examples of adaptive management plans incorporating landscape changes were illustrated using the eastern meadowlark in the Black River watershed and the green frog in the Huron River watershed. Those examples demonstrated the potential for adaptive management on varying landscapes as a means to increase the knowledge of wildlife species and their interactions with landscape patterns and processes. Ultimately, coupling landscape change information with adaptive management can help to understand, monitor, and predict wildlife habitat and population dynamics at broader spatial and temporal scales.

Acknowledgments

We are indebted to Matt Carmer, Kathy Damstra, Eric Dephouse, Jayson Egeler, Robert Goodwin, Jill Hallden, JoAnna Lessard, Doug Longpre, Josh Mohler, Risa Oram, Alison Philpotts, Brad Thompson, and Vince Videan for assisting with the database development. The Huron River Watershed Council generously provided the data for the 1992 land-cover data of the Huron River watershed. We thank Jack Ahern, Mike Jones, Hugh Possingham, and an anonymous reviewer for reviewing the chapter. The Michigan Agricultural Experimental Station, the Michigan Department of Natural Resources Division of Wildlife, the College of Agriculture and Natural Resources at Michigan State University, and the National Science Foundation provided support for this project.

References

Baker, R. H. (1983). *Michigan Mammals*. Michigan State University Press, East Lansing, MI.

Brewer, R., McPeek, G. A. & Adams, R. J. Jr. (1991). *The Atlas of Breeding Birds of Michigan*. Michigan State University Press, East Lansing, MI.

Caughley, G. & Sinclair, A. R. E. (1994). *Wildlife Ecology and Management*. Blackwell Scientific Publications, Boston, MA.

Comer, P. J., Albert, D. A., Wells, H. A., Hart, B. L., Raab, J. B., Price, D. L., Kashian, D. M., Corner, R. A. & Schuen, D. W. (1995). *Michigan's Presettlement Vegetation, as Interpreted from The General Land Office Surveys 1816-1856*. Michigan Natural Features Inventory, Lansing, MI.
Crooks, K. R. & Soulé, M. E. (1999). Mesopredator release and avifaunal extinctions in a fragmented system. *Nature*, 400: 563–566.
Forman, R. T. T. (1995). *Land Mosaics*. Cambridge University Press, Cambridge, UK.
Forman, R. T. T. & Moore, P. N. (1992). Theoretical foundations for understanding boundaries in landscape mosaics. In *Landscape Boundaries: Consequences for Biotic Diversity and Ecological Flows*, eds. A. J. Hansen & F. di Castri, pp. 236–258. Springer-Verlag, New York.
Franklin, J. F. & Forman, R. T. T. (1987). Creating landscape patterns by forest cutting: Ecological consequences and principles. *Landscape Ecology*, 1: 5–18.
Grubb, T. C. Jr. & Doherty, P. F. Jr. (1999). On home-range gap-crossing. *Auk*, 116: 618–628.
Gunderson, L. (1999). Resilience, flexibility and adaptive management: Antidotes for spurious certitude? *Conservation Ecology*, 3(1) art 7, http://www.consecol.org/vol3/iss1/art7.
Gustafson, E. J. & Gardner, R. H. (1996). The effect of landscape heterogeneity on the probability of patch colonization. *Ecology*, 77: 94–107.
Halbert, C. L. (1993). How adaptive is adaptive management? Implementing adaptive management in Washington State and British Columbia. *Reviews in Fisheries Science*, 1: 261–283.
Hall, L. S., Krausman, P. R. & Morrison, M. L. (1997). The habitat concept and a plea for standard terminology. *Wildlife Society Bulletin*, 25: 172–183.
Hanski, I. (1991). Single-species metapopulation dynamics: Concepts, models, and observations. *Biological Journal of the Linnean Society*, 42: 17–38.
Hanski, I. (1994). Patch-occupancy dynamics in fragmented landscapes. *Trends in Ecology and Evolution*, 9: 131–135.
Hanski, I. (1999). *Metapopulation Ecology*. Oxford University Press, New York.
Hanski, I. & Gilpin, M. (1991). Metapopulation dynamics: Brief history and conceptual domains. *Biological Journal of the Linnean Society*, 42: 3–16.
Harding, J. H. (1997). *Amphibians and Reptiles of the Great Lakes Region*. University of Michigan Press, Ann Arbor, MI.
Harding, J. H. & Holman, J. A. (1990). *Michigan Turtles and Lizards*, Extension Bulletin no. E-2234. Michigan State University, East Lansing, MI.
Harding, J. H. & Holman, J. A. (1999). *Michigan Frogs, Toads, and Salamanders*, Extension Bulletin no. E-2350. Michigan State University, East Lansing, MI.
Harris, L. D., Hoctor, T. S. & Gergel, S. E. (1996). Landscape processes and their significance to biodiversity conservation. In *Population Dynamics in Ecological Space and Time*, eds. O. E. Rhodes Jr., R. K. Chesser, & M. H. Smith, pp. 319–347. University of Chicago Press, Chicago, IL.
Hobbs, R. J. (1995). Landscape ecology. In *Encyclopedia of Environmental Biology*, vol. 2, pp. 417–428. Academic Press, San Diego, CA.
Holling, C. S. (ed). (1978). *Adaptive Environmental Assessment and Management*. John Wiley, New York.
Holling, C. S. (1992). Cross-scale morphology, geometry, and dynamics of ecosystems. *Ecological Monographs*, 62: 447–502.
Holman, J. A., Harding, J. H., Hensley, M. M. & Dudderar, G. R. (1999). *Michigan Snakes*, Extension Bulletin no. E-2000. Michigan State University, East Lansing, MI.
Kilgo, J. C., Sargent, R. A., Miller, K.V. & Chapman, B. R. (1997). Landscape influence on breeding bird communities in hardwood fragments in South Carolina. *Wildlife Society Bulletin*, 25: 878–885.
Lamoureux, V. S. & Madison, D.M. (1999). Overwintering habits of radio-implanted green frogs (*Rana clamitans*). *Journal of Herpetology*, 33: 430–435.
Lee, K. N. (1993). *Compass and Gyroscope: Integrating Science and Politics for the Environment*. Island Press, Washington, D.C.
Levins, R. (1969). Some demographic and genetic consequences of environmental heterogeneity for biological control. *Bulletin of the Entomological Society of America*, 15: 237–240.
Liu, J., Cubbage, F. W. & Pulliam, H. R. (1994). Ecological and economic effects of forest landscape structure and rotation length: simulation studies using ECOLECON.

Ecological Economics, 10: 349–363.

Liu, J., Ouyang, Z., Taylor, W., Groop, R., Tan, Y. & Zhang, H. (1999). A framework for evaluating effects of human factors on wildlife habitat: The case on the giant pandas. *Conservation Biology*, 13: 1360–1370.

McCann, M. T. (1991). Land, climate, and vegetation of Michigan. In *The Atlas of Breeding Birds of Michigan*, eds. R. Brewer, G. A. McPeek & R. J. Adams Jr., pp. 15–31. Michigan State University Press, East Lansing, MI.

McCullough, D. R. (ed.) (1996). *Metapopulations and Wildlife Conservation*. Island Press, Washington, D.C.

McPeek, G. A. & Adams, R. J. Jr. (eds.) (1994). *The Birds of Michigan*. Indiana University Press, Bloomington, IN.

Morrison, M. L., Marcot, B. G. & Mannan, R. W. (1992). *Wildlife–Habitat Relationships: Concepts and Applications*. University of Wisconsin Press, Madison, WI.

Pearson, S. M. (1993). The spatial extent and relative influence of landscape-level factors on wintering bird populations. *Landscape Ecology*, 8: 3–18.

Pearson, S. M., Turner, M. G., Gardner, R. H. & O'Neill, R. V. (1996). An organism-based perspective of habitat fragmentation. In *Biodiversity in Managed Landscapes: Theory and Practice*, eds. R. C. Szaro & D. W. Johnston, pp. 77–95. Oxford University Press, Oxford, UK.

Primack, R. B. (1993). *Essentials of Conservation Biology*. Sinauer Associates, Sunderland, MA.

Probst, J. R. & Weinrich, J. (1993). Relating Kirtland's warbler population to changing landscape composition and structure. *Landscape Ecology*, 8: 257–271.

Pulliam, H. R. (1988). Sources, sinks, and population regulation. *American Naturalist*, 137: 550–560.

Robinson, S. K., Thompson, F. R. III, Donovan, T. M., Whitehead, D. R. & Faaborg, J. (1995). Regional forest fragmentation and the nesting success of migratory birds. *Science*, 267: 1987–1990.

Russell, E. W. B. (1993). Discovery of the subtle. In *Humans as Components of Ecosystems*, eds. M. J. McDonnell & S. T. A. Pickett, pp. 81–90. Springer-Verlag, New York.

Rutledge, D. T. (2001). Changes in land cover and wildlife habitats in two watersheds in the lower peninsula of Michigan. PhD dissertation, Michigan State University, East Lansing, MI.

Saunders, D. A., Hobbs, R. J. & Margules, C. R. (1991). Biological consequences of ecosystem fragmentation: A review. *Conservation Biology*, 5: 18–32.

Scribner, K. T., Arntzen, J. W., Cruddace, N., Oldham, R. S. & Burke, T. (2001). Environmental correlates of toad abundance and population genetic diversity. *Biological Conservation*, 98: 201–210.

Stebbins, R. C. & Cohen, N. W. (1995). *A Natural History of Amphibians*. Princeton University Press, Princeton, NJ.

Swanson, F. J. & Franklin, J. F. (1992). New forestry principles from ecosystem analysis of Pacific Northwest forests. *Ecological Applications*, 2: 262–274.

Titus, K. & Mosher, J. A. (1981). Nest-site habitat selection by woodland hawks in the central Appalachians. *Auk*, 98: 270–281.

Turner, M. G. (1989). Landscape ecology: The effect of pattern on process. *Annual Review of Ecology and Systematics*, 20: 171–191.

Turner, M. G., O'Neill, R. V., Gardner, R. H. & Milne, B. T. (1989). Effects of changing spatial scale on the analysis of landscape pattern. *Landscape Ecology*, 3: 153–162.

Turner, M. G., Romme, W. H., Gardner, R. H., O'Neill, R. V. & Kratz, T. K. (1993). A revised concept of landscape equilibrium: Disturbance and stability on scaled landscapes. *Landscape Ecology*, 8: 213–227.

Tyler, D. R. & LaBelle, S. (1995). *Jobs and the Built Environment Working Trends*. Michigan Society of Planning Officials, Rochester, MI.

US Bureau of the Census (1992). *1990 Census of Population: Gerneral Population Characteristics–Michigan*. US Government Printing Office, Washington, D.C.

Walters, C. J. (1986). *Adaptive Management of Renewable Resources*. Macmillan, New York.

Warbach, J. D. & Reed, R. (1995). *Natural Resources and Environment Trends Working Paper*. Michigan Society of Planning Officials, Rochester, MI.

Wiens, J. A. (1992). Ecological flows across landscape boundaries: A conceptual overview. In *Landscape Boundaries: Consequences for Biotic Diversity and Ecological Flows*, eds. A. J. Hansen & F. di Castri, pp. 217–235. Springer-Verlag, New York.

Wiens, J. A. (1996). Wildlife in patchy environments: Metapopulations, mosaics, and management. In *Metapopulations and Wildlife Conservation*, ed. D. R. McCullough, pp. 53–84. Island Press, Washington, D.C.

Winterstein, S., Campa, H. III & Millenbah, K. (1995). *Status and Potential of Michigan's Natural Resources: Wildlife*, Michigan Agricultural Experimental Station Special Report no. 75. Michigan State University, East Lansing, MI.

Wycoff, M. A. & Reed, R. (1995). *Demographic Trends Working Paper*. Michigan Society of Planning Officials, Planning and Zoning Center, Inc., Lansing, MI.

JOHN B. DUNNING JR.

13

Landscape ecology in highly managed regions: The benefits of collaboration between management and researchers

13.1 Introduction

Land managers, resource biologists, and theoretical ecologists have all recognized the importance of expanding the spatial and temporal scales of their respective disciplines. Indeed, calling for a greater acknowledgement of the landscape perspective in both research and management is commonplace (Pilcher and Dunning, 2000). Actually implementing a greater reliance on landscape planning is less common. The reluctance to embrace this expansion is two-fold. First, many land managers are hesitant to embrace novel concepts and instead view research as a diversion from their primary management goals. Second, research ecologists tend to shy away from working in highly manipulated regions, preferring to study less developed or more natural regions, where the researcher is in more control of long-term changes in land treatment. The purpose of this chapter is to address this reluctance by defining how managers and researchers can both gain substantially by collaborating on research and planning, thereby expanding understanding at the landscape scale.

Land managers are increasingly called upon to manage adaptively (Walters, 1986), that is, to treat management strategies as large-scale experiments. Ideally, management practices would be conducted with a specific goal in mind regarding the kind of ecosystems that will result from the management, not just the kinds of marketable products. Scientists associated with the management agency would monitor the system to determine if these ecosystem goals were being met, and management would be modified if needed.

Landscape studies should be very relevant to adaptive management. Ecosystem attributes that could be monitored in an adaptive management framework might include landscape variables, such as the level of connectivity between habitat patches and the patterns of species diversity and habitat distributions across the entire region. If monitoring shows that these attributes are changing in unforeseen ways, managers will need access to very explicit advice on how changes across the landscape might affect organisms. For instance, if some populations occupy a patchy distribution, then metapopulation models might be important in predicting how management changes will affect the populations. For this reason, land planners implementing adaptive management need information that can be generated by landscape-level studies and analyses.

Landscape ecology as a field has been dominated by studies that were either primarily descriptive or model-driven. Examples of descriptive studies are those that seek to describe the pattern of natural or anthropogenic landscapes (Turner and Ruscher, 1988; Turner *et al.*, 1996) or that monitor the population dynamics or behavior of organisms occupying different landscapes (Pearson, 1993). Model-driven studies abound in landscape ecology, and include both simulations of landscape pattern and of population dynamics in complex landscapes (Dunning *et al.*, 1995b). What is much rarer in landscape ecology are experimental studies that directly manipulate landscape patterns or processes, and study the effects. It is precisely these experiments that would be most useful for monitoring adaptive management, because the strongest inferences about results can be generated with well-designed experiments. Thus, there have been repeated calls for landscape ecologists to become more experimental (Wiens *et al.*, 1993; Ims, 1999).

13.2 Problems with experimenting at large spatial scales

While the benefits of landscape studies are significant, the difficulties of conducting experimental studies at the landscape scale are well known. The logistics of manipulating landscape variables can be formidable, especially for species that are highly vagile. Ecologists rarely have control over large enough areas to dictate changes to habitat patches across landscapes. Assignment of treatments to create replicates and controls fitting a particular experimental design is rarely possible. In some cases, desired treatments may be legally impossible or ethically troublesome (e.g., destroying riparian habitat to reduce connectivity between patches). Ecologists who work in a particular region are well aware that no two landscapes of any size are identical, so even identifying regions that can serve as controls for landscape modifications planned in other areas can be a problem. For all these reasons, sample sizes for landscape studies in the real world tend to be tiny, rendering statistical inference difficult.

Researchers have overcome these difficulties in a number of ways. Landscapes are scaled to the organism under study. Thus, small organisms requiring small landscapes make good subjects for manipulative experiments (Wiens and Milne, 1989; Johnson *et al.*, 1992). In studies where distances within and between landscapes can be measured in centimeters or meters, treatments can be assigned randomly to experimental plots, creating replicates and controls in a formal experimental design. (Actually, even at these scales, no two plots are identical, but random assignment of treatments allows for a greater rigor in statistical treatment.)

Perhaps more commonly, some landscape researchers have adopted non-experimental techniques. By observing organism, population or community responses to landscape pattern across a wide variety of landscapes, researchers hope to discover the important factors that operate across landscape scales (McGarigal and McComb, 1995; Rosenberg *et al.*, 1999).

Hargrove and Pickering (1992) propose that landscape ecologists can do more than just observe across many landscapes. They point out that landscapes often change due to natural or human-caused actions, and that well-placed research efforts can yield a great deal by following organism response to such changes. This form of directed observations is similar to "before–after– control" experimental designs, where the research cannot fully control the treatments, but can still incorporate elements of good experimental design. Hargrove and Pickering refer to this type of research as "quasi-experiments" and propose that landscape ecology could become more experimental using this approach. Dunning *et al.* (1995a) followed this strategy by observing colonization of habitat patches created by a tornado in a timber management district. The study determined whether a bird species was dispersal-limited in the new landscape.

The problem with the quasi-experiment approach is getting the "before" data. One rarely has the foresight to know when and where a tornado is going to hit. In 1988, Bryan Watts and I selected 40 clear-cut and mature-forest study sites in the Francis Marion National Forest, South Carolina, to begin a study of habitat selection by Bachman's sparrow (*Aimophila aestivalis*) (Dunning and Watts, 1990). When Hurricane Hugo devastated the study area in fall 1989, we were nicely positioned to collect data on the distribution of the sparrows in different habitats after the hurricane, and speculate on the implications (Dunning and Watts, 1991). The response of the sparrows to the dramatic changes in the distribution of suitable and unsuitable habitat spurred us to continue studies of the bird's population dynamics in complex landscapes (Pulliam *et al.*, 1992, 1995; Dunning *et al.*, 1995a). The "experiment" was completely unreplicated and the inferences that could be drawn from the observations were limited. Still, the data collected proved useful in making before and after comparisons.

13.3 Managed landscapes as "quasi-experiments"

Working in managed landscapes has distinct advantages for the quasi-experimental approach. Unlike tornadoes or hurricanes, changes in landscape structure due to management activities are predictable. Indeed, changes are often planned years in advance, and may be specifically proposed to create landscapes of a particular design (e.g., Haddad, 1999).

Management plans take many forms. Timber-management strategies guide how many stands of trees in a forest district are likely to be harvested in a given year, and how stands will be selected for harvest, planting, and maintenance activities. In parks and other public lands, restoration and reclamation activities are designed according to multi-year plans that specify how many hectares of land will be restored, what techniques will be used, and what ecosystems are expected to result from the restoration process. On public lands used for outdoor recreation, long-term projections are made predicting the likely kinds of activities that will be conducted and the number of users likely to be conducting them. That information is then used to predict what impacts this human disturbance will have on the land.

While none of these planning documents or strategies is inviolate, and deviations in land management occur on a regular basis, the changes in landscape structure are more predictable and can easily be worked into an experimental design, unlike a natural catastrophe. If changes are predictable, one can make a priori statements on how populations should respond. Testing these predictions is a more rigorous form of experimentation than simply monitoring responses a posteriori. Managed landscapes can therefore provide a convenient framework for conducting landscape-level quasi-experiments.

There are other advantages to working in managed landscapes. First, land managers working for state or federal agencies often control access to and management of large areas of land. Cooperation with land managers gives the researcher access to large areas without having to deal with multiple owners, multiple land uses, and multiple headaches. For example, the Savannah River Institute of the US Forest Service provides management planning for the 770 km^2 Savannah River Site, South Carolina (White and Gaines, 2000). This area is large enough to treat as four to ten landscapes for passerine birds, more for less vagile organisms (Dunning *et al.*, 2000).

Second, since many managers today are highly motivated to gain further understanding of landscape-level processes (at least insofar as such processes affect the agency's priorities), managers may be willing to modify annual or short-term strategies to create landscapes to fit specific research designs. On the Savannah River Site, the local site managers created (at considerable expense) a series of small clear-cuts and corridors within a middle-aged pine forest to create a series of patches of different connectivity. This facilitated mark-and-recapture experiments with butterflies, lizards, and rodents which determined how organisms of different movement behaviors and dispersal rules were affected by corridors (Haddad, 1999; Haddad and Baum 1999).

13.4 Disadvantages of managed landscapes

In implementing a solid experimental design, a researcher wishes to have complete logistical control. This is rarely possible in managed landscapes. Changes in management strategy will reflect a variety of uses of the land including commodity production, recreational access, pollution abatement, and a host of other societal goals. Overall management policy itself changes with political change. Thus, implementing a landscape experiment that depends on long-term, consistent management actions is risky.

Even with a sympathetic land manager, research goals will have to compete with other uses of the land. A proposed research program that appears to conflict with the primary use of public land, especially in regions of commodity production, is unlikely to be accepted. Research must fit into a framework of multiple use, and this may involve some compromise in study design on the part of the researcher, even as it includes compromise in other priorities on the part of the manager.

Traditionally, land management plans have been written for five- or ten-year time frames, while strategic documents may project management objectives for longer periods. Political events can cause upheavals in policy in much shorter periods. Presidential and Congressional elections can result in the national spotlight being placed on natural resource management, for instance. Researchers may feel uneasy in setting their research program in an arena where the politics of the local Congressional delegation might dictate whether the research is likely to be completed. When political winds change, researchers may feel helpless as management shifts to accommodate the new directives.

13.5 Case study: A compromise solution of landscape research in rapidly changing landscapes

Highly managed lands can still be a suitable setting for landscape experiments, but researchers would be wise not to design their research program to be dependent on long-term consistency in management. Thus, it is useful to design quasi-experiments for managed landscapes that change rapidly. If the specific landscape pattern can be fully investigated in three to four years, then the negatives associated with working under the constraints of multiple-use management become less of a problem. Following is an example of landscape research in rapidly changing managed landscapes in the southeastern United States, to illustrate the gains that can be made.

Harvested forest stands in private or public forests in the southeast are generally replanted with monocultures of commercially valuable pine species. For several decades ending in the mid-1990s, in National Forests in the Carolinas and

Georgia, the most commonly planted species was often loblolly pine (*Pinus taeda*). Loblolly pine grows rapidly after site preparation and commercial planting. Clear-cuts (also called regeneration stands) quickly become dominated by forests of young pine trees. The loblolly pine grows more quickly than the native longleaf pine (*P. palustris*) in the southeastern coastal plain. Thus loblolly pine has been preferred by forest district managers who must meet production goals of timber board–feet per year. In the 1990s, at least some National Forest Districts were shifted to planting longleaf pine as a component of ecosystem management.

For eight years, my colleagues and I studied bird species that depend on early successional habitat in landscapes dominated by pine plantations. In such landscapes, clear-cuts often provide the only available habitat for early successional species, and each individual patch is only suitable for a few years after planting. Thus the birds existed in a landscape dominated by an unsuitable matrix (older pine forest and deciduous forest patches), where suitable habitat patches were both ephemeral and scattered widely in space. This setting proved valuable for investigating how dispersal-limited bird species maintained themselves in rapidly changing landscapes (Dunning and Watts, 1990; Pulliam *et al.*, 1992, 1995; Dunning *et al.*, 1995a, 2000; Liu *et al.*, 1995).

At the Savannah River Site, most loblolly pine stands were suitable for Bachman's sparrows one to two years after planting, and continued to be suitable for three or four years. By the time the young loblolly pines were three to four years old, the trees were 4 m tall and the individual stands no longer contained the open characteristics apparently preferred by the sparrow (Dunning and Watts, 1990). Thus a series of clear-cuts could be selected that met a particular set of landscape characteristics, and populations in those clear-cuts could be monitored for a few years. At the end, it could be demonstrated that the sites had changed enough in their suitability that what was attractive initially was no longer there. Since new habitat arose almost exclusively through the timber harvest program, it could be predicted with great accuracy where suitable habitat would be in the future. This was a great advantage when searching for successful dispersers.

These rapidly changing landscapes were used to conduct two types of studies. In the first type of study, a spatially explicit population model was constructed for the Bachman's sparrow on a portion of the Savannah River Site (Liu *et al.*, 1995). The purpose of the model was to determine how the sparrow would respond to various aspects of long-term timber and wildlife management plans. As with any model, validation of model performance was both critical to acceptance of the model as realistic, and difficult to perform. The model was used to predict distribution of sparrows across habitat types in future years, then field data were collected to test those predictions. Predicted distributions fit observed data, so confidence in the models was increased (Fig. 13.1).

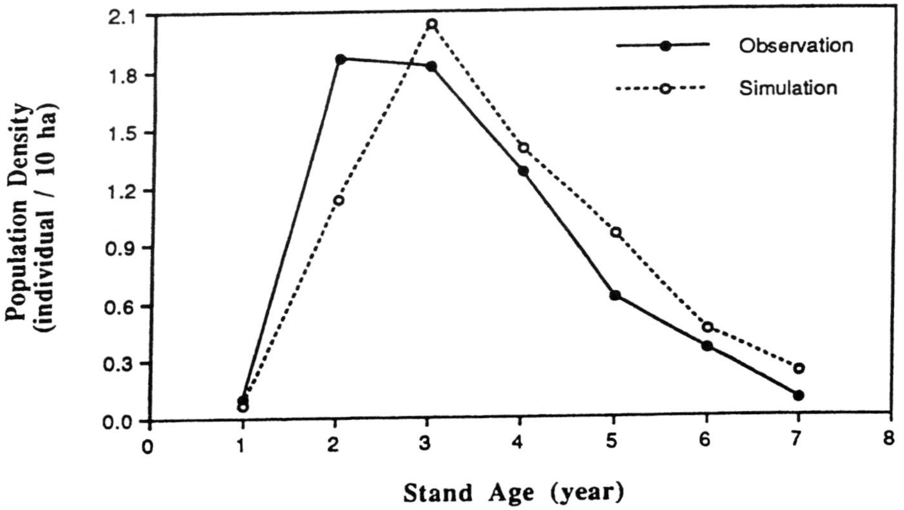

FIGURE 13.1
Observed and predicted densities of Bachman's sparrows (*Aimophila aestivalis*) in replanted forest stands one to seven years after planting at the Savannah River Site, South Carolina. Close agreement between densities predicted by a population simulation model and independently derived field data was used as validation for the model. (Reprinted from *Ecological Modelling*, volume 70, J. Liu, ECOLECON: An ECOLogical-ECONomic model for species conservation in complex forest landscapes, page 83, © 1993, with permission from Elsevier Science.)

Thus, field work provided a method of model validation that is rarely incorporated into landscape computer models.

It was important to work in a rapidly changing landscape to conduct such validation, for at least two reasons. First, the sparrows responded to new clearcuts by quickly occupying those patches that were in suitable landscapes. The speed with which the birds responded to new patches was important – researchers could not wait 10–15 years to gain validation of the model. Second, if the landscapes were not dynamic on a short time frame, then the data collected to validate the model would not have been independent of data used to parameterize the model. Data on sparrow distributions across habitat types from the first year of studies were used to initialize the model. If the landscape changed slowly (or the sparrows stayed in their initial habitat patches regardless of landscape change) then the data collected three to four years later would still reflect the initial distributions. This would not be a valid test.

In the second type of study, the rapidly changing landscapes on the Savannah River Site were used to conduct a quasi-experiment on the importance of connectivity (Dunning *et al.*, 1995a). In 1989, a tornado passed through the corner of the Savannah River Site that had been modeled. The tornado and subsequent timber salvage operations created a series of new habitat patches for early successional species. By chance, the new set of clear-cuts stretched from an area well populated with Bachman's sparrows into an area where previous searches had shown no sparrows existed. Timber salvage of the tornado-damaged areas therefore created a series of linked patches of open habitat that varied in the distances between each patch and the closest known population of sparrows.

This setting was used to test ideas of dispersal limitation. If the sparrow had difficulty dispersing, then patches close to existing populations should be colonized first. The new clear-cuts differed to some degree in site preparation and planting, and in the species of pine planted (longleaf or loblolly). But even with this variation, strong support for the dispersal-limitation hypothesis was found (Dunning *et al.*, 1995a).

The quasi-experiment was then repeated in another portion of the Savannah River Site. In this area, a series of clear-cuts were created through the normal timber harvest program. The clear-cuts stretched over a longer distance than the tornado-related patches, and the clear-cuts were not as well connected to one another. But other aspects of the tornado-alley landscape were present in the second region. The sites stretched from a region populated by the sparrow population into a region where no sparrows had been found. Results confirmed that the sparrow was also dispersal-limited in this second landscape.

The two landscapes were not replicates, and they were not described as such in analysis or discussion. However, conducting the quasi-experiment in two regions with identifiable differences allowed inferences that any single experiment would not have allowed. Most importantly, sparrows occupied all patches within the tornado-alley landscape within two years of study, while the most isolated clear-cuts in the second landscape were never occupied in the three years in which they were suitable. This demonstrated that suitable patches in unsuitable landscapes may never be colonized by a dispersal-limited organism, even a seemingly vagile one like a bird. This strongly suggested that timber policy in the Southeast may be playing a major role in the decline of Bachman's sparrow across the region (Dunning, 1993).

13.6 Implications and guidelines for adaptive management

The landscape modeling and field studies of Bachman's sparrows provided important information to the land managers of the Savannah River Site that could be used in an adaptive management framework. First, field studies indicated that the sparrow is sensitive both to the amounts of suitable habitats present in the region, and to the distribution of the habitat (Dunning and Watts, 1990; Dunning *et al.*, 1995a). Thus, land planners were alerted to the issue that their management affects wildlife through the effects of changes in the distribution of habitats across the landscape. This was true even when the species of management concern was one that was not expected to be a poor disperser (i.e., a flying bird). Landscape concerns could potentially be even stronger for species of low dispersal ability. It may be concluded that land managers should be strongly supportive of landscape studies that can feed information back to help shape adaptive management. This realization has generated support for further experiments on the impacts of corridors and stand placement (Haddad, 1999; Haddad and Baum 1999) on a variety of organisms.

Second, the simulation results (Liu, 1993) suggested that sparrow population size could be greatly increased if either (1) the period of time that clear-cuts provided suitable habitat could be increased, or (2) the age at which older stands became suitable again could be lowered. (Bachman's sparrows require dense stands of grasses and forbs, which at the start of the study were only found in extremely young pine stands [one to three years old] or in older, mature forest >100 years old [Dunning and Watts, 1990].)

Both of these were management options that had been suggested to land managers for reasons unrelated to the Bachman's sparrow. Clear-cuts could be kept in open, suitable condition for longer periods of time by planting the native longleaf pine instead of the non-native loblolly pine. Longleaf pine is more resistant to fire at early age classes, which allows fire to be used as a management tool to keep young pine stands open, providing sparrow habitat for longer periods of time. Switching from loblolly to longleaf pine had been proposed originally to emphasize the production of timber from native species.

Habitat conditions typical of the oldest mature pine stands can be created by thinning younger stands (50–60-year-old trees) to a basal area typical of older forest, removing deciduous brush and instituting prescribed burns. Mature pine stands are extremely limited on the Savannah River Site, and are critical habitat for the endangered red-cockaded woodpecker (*Picoides borealis*). Biologists associated with the woodpecker recovery program had proposed creating more habitat for the endangered woodpecker by modifying middle-aged forest to create habitat conditions similar to that found in mature forest. Results from Liu's work (Liu, 1993; Liu *et al.*, 1995) suggested this option would also benefit Bachman's sparrow.

Both of these options had been proposed to be implemented in the long-term management plan being prepared in the early 1990s. The Bachman's sparrow results indicated that an additional benefit would be gained by adoption of these management actions. Although not officially classified as threatened or endangered, the sparrow was one of the species of highest management concern for the US Forest Service in the Southeast. Managers appeared to be more willing to consider fundamental changes in their management when they received "more bang for their buck;" that is, when proposed actions would satisfy several management goals collectively.

More importantly for the purposes of this essay, the results could be easily monitored to determine if the new management practices were actually changing habitat quality. For instance, middle-aged loblolly pine stands were not used previously by the sparrow (Dunning and Watts, 1990). Surveying the middle-aged stands modified for the red-cockaded woodpecker in subsequent years showed that the sparrows did indeed colonize sites that previously were unused (Krementz and Christie, 1999; J. Dunning, personal observation). This provided an early benchmark to managers that the habitat modifications were having the desired effect.

The implications of the sparrow studies can be summarized as follows:

(1) Initial field research on the distribution and movements of species suspected of being impacted by landscape processes can yield suggestions on how important landscape patterns are in determining the overall impacts in management. In the sparrow study, such suggestions were generated within a few field seasons. This research is a worthwhile investment by management agencies.
(2) Tying modeling and field research to specific proposed changes in management strategy provides a scientifically valid research program for ecologists and also generates important information for management planning. Collaboration was extremely productive in this case.
(3) Field and modeling studies together can suggest which features of the landscape can be monitored most easily over the short term to determine if management strategies are having their desired effect. The design of effective monitoring is a neglected component of adaptive management.

13.7 Summary

There still exist logistical and bureaucratic disadvantages to conducting research on lands where the primary management objectives are not research-oriented. I argue that these disadvantages are worth overcoming, if possible, when one is conducting studies in landscape ecology. Studies benefit from working on managed lands in several ways. The large spatial areas controlled by land management agencies reduce the logistics of working in complex landscapes. Researchers can use management plans as long-term predictions of landscape change. Additionally helpful is the documented history of large-scale manipulation on managed lands. Managers should have an interest in supporting landscape-level studies. Planners in management agencies are increasingly called to manage adaptively to ensure that their short-term and long-term plans will produce healthy ecosystems. The disadvantages of conducting landscape-scale studies on highly managed lands can be mitigated to some degree by working in landscapes and habitats that respond quickly to changes in land use. There are some landscape processes that operate slowly over long periods of time. To study these processes, long-term studies will be necessary. But in cases where landscapes change quickly, short-term studies can be informative to both managers and researchers. Landscape studies of avian response to timber harvest strategies in the southeastern United States provide examples of the value of conducting landscape research in lands subject to intensive management. By working together, researchers and personnel in the land management agencies can design research that will enable planners to conduct adaptive management, and also produce innovative basic research at the landscape scale.

Acknowledgments

Research at the Savannah River Site was supported by the Biodiversity Program of the Savannah River Institute (US Forest Service), National Science Foundation, US Environmental Protection Agency, and the Savannah River Ecology Laboratory (University of Georgia).

References

Dunning, J. B. (1993). Bachman's Sparrow (*Aimophila aestivalis*). In *The Birds of North America*, no. 38, eds. A. Poole, P. Stettenheim & F. Gill. Academy of Natural Sciences, Philadelphia, PA and American Ornithologists' Union, Washington, D.C.

Dunning, J. B. & Watts, B. D. (1990). Regional differences in habitat occupancy by Bachman's Sparrows. *Auk*, 107: 463–472.

Dunning, J. B. & Watts, B. D. (1991). Habitat occupancy by Bachman's Sparrow in the Francis Marion National Forest before and after Hurricane Hugo. *Auk*, 108: 723–725.

Dunning, J. B., Borgella, R., Clements, K. & Meffe, G. K. (1995a). Patch isolation, corridor effects, and colonization by a resident sparrow in a managed pine woodland. *Conservation Biology*, 9: 542–550.

Dunning, J. B., Stewart, D. J., Danielson, B. J., Noon, B. R., Root, T. L., Lamberson, R. H. & Stevens, E. E. (1995b). Spatially explicit population models: Current forms and future uses. *Ecological Applications*, 5: 3–11.

Dunning, J. B., Danielson, B. J., Watts, B. D., Liu, J. & Krementz, D. G. (2000). Studying wildlife at local and landscape scales: Bachman's Sparrows at the Savannah River Site. In *Avian Research at the Savannah River Site: A Model for Integrating Basic Research and Long-Term Management*, eds. J. B. Dunning & J. C. Kilgo. *Studies in Avian Biology*, 21: 75–80.

Haddad, N. M. (1999). Corridor and distance effects on interpatch movements: a landscape experiment with butterflies. *Ecological Applications*, 9: 612–622.

Haddad, N. M. & Baum, K. A. (1999). An experimental test of corridor effects on butterfly densities. *Ecological Applications*, 9: 623–633.

Hargrove, W. W. & Pickering, J. (1992). Pseudoreplication: A *sine qua non* for regional ecology. *Landscape Ecology*, 6: 251–258.

Ims, R. A. (1999). Experimental landscape

ecology. In *Issues in Landscape Ecology*, eds. J. A. Wiens & M. R. Moss, pp. 45–50. International Association for Landscape Ecology, University of Guelph, Guelph, Canada.

Johnson, A. R., Milne, B. T. & Wiens, J. A. (1992). Diffusion in fractal landscapes: Simulations and experimental studies of tenebrionid beetle movements. *Ecology*, 73: 1968–1983.

Krementz, D. G. & Christie, J. S. (1999). Scrub-successional bird community dynamics in young and mature longleaf pine–wiregrass savannahs. *Journal of Wildlife Management*, 63: 803–814.

Liu, J. (1993). ECOLECON: An ECOLogical-ECONomic model for species conservation in complex forest landscapes. *Ecological Modelling*, 70: 63–87.

Liu, J., Dunning, J. B. & Pulliam, H. R. (1995). Potential effects of a forest management plan on Bachman's Sparrows (*Aimophila aestivalis*): Linking a spatially explicit model with GIS. *Conservation Biology*, 9: 62–75.

McGarigal, K. & McComb, W. C. (1995). Relationships between landscape structure and breeding birds in the Oregon Coast Range. *Ecological Monographs*, 65: 235–260.

Pearson, S. M. (1993). The spatial extent and relative influence of landscape-level factors on wintering bird populations. *Landscape Ecology*, 8: 3–17.

Pilcher, B. K. & Dunning, J. B. (2000). Rising importance of the landscape perspective: An area of collaboration between managers and researchers. In *Avian Research at the Savannah River Site: A Model for Integrating Basic Research and Long-Term Management*, eds. J. B. Dunning & J. C. Kilgo. *Studies in Avian Biology*, 21: 130–137.

Pulliam, H. R., Dunning, J. B. & Liu, J. (1992). Population dynamics in complex landscapes: A case study. *Ecological Applications*, 2: 165–177.

Pulliam, H. R., Liu, J., Dunning, J. B., Stewart, D. J. & Bishop, T. D. (1995). Modeling animal populations in changing landscapes. *Ibis*, 137: S120–S126.

Rosenberg, K.V., Lowe, J. D. & Dhondt, A. A. (1999). Effects of forest fragmentation on breeding tanagers: A continental perspective. *Conservation Biology*, 13: 568–583.

Turner, M. G. & Ruscher, C. L. (1988). Changes in landscape patterns in Georgia, USA. *Landscape Ecology*, 1: 241–251.

Turner, M. G., Wear, D. N. & Flamm, R. O. (1996). Land ownership and land-cover change in the southern Appalachian highlands and the Olympic Peninsula. *Ecological Applications*, 6: 1150–1172.

Walters, C. J. (1986). *Adaptive Management of Natural Resources*. MacMillan, New York.

White, D. L. & Gaines, K. F. (2000). The Savannah River Site: Site description, land use and management history. In *Avian Research at the Savannah River Site: A Model for Integrating Basic Research and Long-Term Management*, eds. J. B. Dunning & J. C. Kilgo. *Studies in Avian Biology*, 21: 8–17.

Wiens, J. A. & Milne, B. T. (1989). Scaling of 'landscapes' in landscape ecology, or, landscape ecology from a beetle's perspective. *Landscape Ecology*, 3: 87–96.

Wiens, J. A., Stenseth, N. C., Van Horne, B. & Ims, R. A. (1993). Ecological mechanisms and landscape ecology. *Oikos*, 66: 369–380.

PART V

Landscape integrity and integrated management

Parts II through IV of this book emphasize three separate aspects of landscape ecology (landscape structure, landscape function, and landscape change in structure and function) and their corresponding management paradigms (multi-scale management, cross-boundary management, and adaptive management). While separate aspects of landscape research and management paradigms are important, an integrated approach to study and manage landscape integrity is urgently needed. By landscape integrity, we mean overall measures of landscape health status. Although landscape integrity is a relatively unexplored subject, we believe that it can be measured by indicators, such as productivity and diversity of native species. As landscape integrity may result from the interactions between landscape structure and function, and it may vary with the dynamics of landscape structure and function, the management of landscape integrity requires an integrated approach incorporating multi-scale, cross-boundary, and adaptive management. It is essential that different types of management are balanced for different objectives and coordinated by integrating both spatial and temporal dimensions of landscapes. Integrated management considers landscape structure, function, and change simultaneously, and accounts for multiple resources at the same time. Because a landscape consists of multiple resources (e.g., forest, wildlife, land, water), considering only single resources will likely change the balance among various resources and thus result in imbalance or loss of landscape integrity. Furthermore, many resources depend on each other. For example, many wildlife species (e.g., birds) help trees in pollen transfer and seed dispersal. On the other hand, many trees provide wildlife species with food and shelter. The four chapters in Part V address various important issues related to landscape integrity and integrated management.

Multiple use and sustained yield have been important concepts for natural resource management since the 1960s, but have recently been under a variety of criticisms. In Chapter 14, Crow argues that these basic concepts do not need to be rejected, but that a landscape perspective should be incorporated to provide a guiding framework for managing natural resources in a more holistic and integrative fashion. Specifically, both temporal and spatial interactions of landscape elements should be considered, scale and context accounted for, and interrelationships among various resources better understood.

Taylor *et al.* (Chapter 15) suggest that fishery productivity is also influenced by the spatial arrangement of habitats, just as are terrestrial systems. They persuasively argue that landscape ecology is particularly useful for fisheries management to provide sustained and increasing benefits to society. Furthermore, Taylor *et al.* propose a comprehensive framework of fishery management by integrating a landscape perspective, factors outside the jurisdiction of fishery managers (e.g., impacts of land use in terrestrial systems), and expertise from multiple disciplines. The purpose of their framework is to link people, land, and water to achieve sustained production and to allow adaptability to spatial and temporal scales.

Advanced spatial technologies (remote sensing, geographic information systems, and global positioning systems) are increasingly important for studying and managing landscapes. In Chapter 16, Hoch *et al.* provide a brief introduction to these technologies and then combine them to address three major grassland management issues – spatial patterns and temporal dynamics of woody encroachment, distribution of livestock grazing and forage utilization, and productivity patterns at the landscape scale. The authors report that these technologies offer many benefits over traditional methods. They also offer important insights into use and implementation of these technologies for monitoring, analyzing, characterizing, modeling, and managing grassland landscapes.

Because nature reserves alone are not sufficient to conserve biodiversity, it is also necessary to conserve biodiversity in managed landscapes such as predominantly agricultural landscapes. However, conservation is more complicated in agricultural landscapes than in nature reserves, as conservation goals must be balanced with social and economic goals. Using a case study from the extensively fragmented agricultural landscapes of Western Australia, Hobbs and Lambeck (Chapter 17) discuss how focal species (species most at risk) can be conserved by designing spatially explicit management plans for producing agricultural products, maintaining farm profits, sustaining rural communities, and addressing hydrological imbalance.

THOMAS R. CROW

14

Putting multiple use and sustained yield into a landscape context

14.1 Introduction

When managing natural resources, foresters, wildlife biologists, and other practitioners need to consider a vast array of technical information, along with a multitude of values, opinions, and perspectives – many of which may be in conflict and therefore difficult to resolve. Ongoing discussions about ecosystem management, conserving biological diversity, adaptive management, and sustainable development reflect heightened concerns about sustaining natural resources and resolving conflicts among competing interests and demands (e.g., Walters, 1986; Rowe, 1992; Grumbine, 1997; Bunnell, 1998; Tollefson, 1998; Yaffee, 1999).

In response to these and related concerns, the Secretary-General of the United Nations established the World Commission on Environment and Development in 1983, headed by Gro Harlem Brundtland, then Prime Minister of Norway. In their landmark assessment – commonly known as the Brundtland Report – the Commission firmly connected environmental degradation with diminished economic opportunity, human health, and quality of life. In addition, they proposed long-term strategies for achieving sustainable development in a world characterized by great extremes in resource availability and utilization. They suggested multilateral approaches to transcend national sovereignties, political ideologies, and scientific disciplines so that common problems could be identified and common goals pursued.

There is increasing recognition that a more comprehensive and integrated approach is needed to resource planning and management (Boyce and Haney, 1997; Kohm and Franklin, 1997; Vogt *et al.*, 1997). In this chapter, I begin with the premise that principles and concepts from landscape ecology can contribute in a significant way to practicing integrated resource management. I explore this premise by considering the science of landscape ecology in relation to the two important management paradigms – multiple use and sustained yield – that have guided forest management in North America for the past 100 years.

14.2 Historical background

Gifford Pinchot is credited with bringing forest management to North America (Pinchot, 1987). Compared to the exploitation and destruction that occurred in North American forests during the nineteenth century, the public viewed Pinchot's message of regulating forest harvest, practicing efficient utilization, protecting forests from fire and other destructive agents, and applying science-based management as enlightened and progressive forest conservation. The fundamental tenets of forest management that are widely practiced today – namely multiple use and sustained yield – have their origins in Pinchot's admonitions.

Multiple use and sustained yield were codified into public law with the passage of the Multiple-Use Sustained-Yield Act of 1960. As a management philosophy, multiple use and sustained yield have served the national forests, and therefore the public, well. However, much has changed since their enactment and so it is worthwhile revisiting these guiding tenets to see how well they continue to serve the national interest as well as the forestry profession in this new age of conservation. In doing so, it is not my purpose to conduct a policy analysis or to survey the myriad of laws relating to public land management. Rather it is to explore the possible intersection between a widely applied management philosophy, as represented by multiple use and sustained yield, and the emerging scientific discipline of landscape ecology.

The definitions of multiple use and sustained yield that will be used in this chapter are those established by the Multiple-Use Sustained-Yield Act of 1960. As stated in the legislation (*The Principal Laws Relating to Forest Service Activities*, Agricultural Handbook no. 453, p. 156):

> Multiple use means the management of all the various renewable surface resources of the national forests so that they are utilized in the combination that will best meet the needs of the American people; making the most judicious use of the land for some or all of these resources or related services over areas large enough to provide sufficient latitude for periodic adjustments in use to conform to changing needs and conditions; that some land will be used for less than all of the resources; and harmonious and coordinated management of the various resources, each with the other, without impairment of the productivity of the land, with consideration being

> given to the relative values of the various resources, and not necessarily the combination of uses that will give the greatest dollar return or the greatest unit output.

The assumption inherent in this definition of multiple use is that many benefits and outputs, including "outdoor recreation, range, timber, watershed, and wildlife and fish," can be derived from the forest without impairing the integrity of the ecosystem.

Although the ordering of these benefits and outputs was interpreted by some at the time this legislation was crafted as having political connotations, the language in the Act did not specify a primary purpose for national forests. All statutory language, however, is subject to interpretation and the 1960 Act is no exception. Interpretations vary depending on vested interests, values, and perspectives. The public attitudes regarding forests and their resource are not static, they change with time and place. Bengston (1994) argued that a broad, deep, and enduring change in public attitudes and values has occurred in recent years, resulting in greater interest in recreational, wildlife, scenic, spiritual, and ecological values, compared to when Gifford Pinchot brought progressive forest management to North America. Many people have come to associate multiple use with management that emphasizes timber production to the detriment of other benefits and outputs, while others view the designation of an area dominated by a single use, such as a wilderness, as a violation of the multiple-use mandate.

Because of these ambiguities, Behan (1990) considered multiple use to be more a political than a scientific concept. Shands (1988) suggested that "multiple use" has become a pejorative term. He called for moving beyond the limits and negative connotations of the concept and articulating a "fresh management philosophy" that emphasizes managing for distinctive values on public lands. Compared to private lands, for example, public lands are better suited for providing long-rotation managed forests, unmanaged old-growth forests, habitat for wildlife requiring large home ranges and late-successional forests, opportunities for dispersed recreational activities, low road densities, minimum forest fragmentation, undeveloped lakes, and free flowing streams. According to Shands (1988), management for distinctive values is consistent with the interpretation of multiple use. It does not mean that every use will be provided on each unit of public land, but a wide range of uses and values will be provided on some lands (not necessarily public lands) somewhere on the broader landscape.

In addition to the problems of interpretation, there are operational problems associated with the multiple-use concept. Clearly, all multiple uses are not compatible everywhere and so conflicts are inevitable. Shands (1988) referenced a debate nearly 60 years ago between two titans of forestry – Samuel Trask Dana and G. A. Pearson – regarding the proper application of multiple use. Dana thought all uses should be given equal consideration on every parcel of land, while Pearson argued that multiple use is best applied over large areas with priority given to specific uses on local parcels. The differences between these two views reflect a difference in spatial scale – a concept that is familiar to landscape ecologists.

Likewise, sustained yield is defined by Congress in the 1960 Act as (*The Principal Laws Relating to Forest Service Activities*, Agriculture Handbook no. 453, p. 157):

> Sustained yield of the several products and services means the achievement and maintenance in perpetuity of a high-level annual or regular periodic output of the various renewable resources of the national forests without impairment of the productivity of the land.

Sustained yield has its roots in the belief that resources such as fish, wildlife, and forests can be managed for human benefit in perpetuity through scientifically based management and regulated harvest. Although sustained yield has been successfully applied at small spatial scales and over relatively short periods of time, e.g., a forest stand over one rotation, finding successful applications of sustained yield at large scales and over long time periods, e.g., at a regional level over multiple rotations, is more problematic. As a result, management of natural resources is increasingly viewed as an adaptive process in which we learn from practice, we monitor the outcomes of our management, and we adjust as we go (Walters, 1986).

14.3 Understanding landscapes

Before exploring the intersection between landscape ecology and the management concepts of multiple use and sustained yield, an understanding is needed about what constitutes a landscape. Forman and Godron (1986) recognized patches, corridors, and the matrix as the three elements that constitute all landscapes. A patch is an ecosystem differing in appearance from its surroundings. Normally, landscape ecologists define patches by their biotic composition simply because these elements are relatively easy to recognize, but patches can also be delineated from differences in their physical characteristics (Saunders *et al.*, 1998). Patches vary widely in their size, shape, distribution, density, and boundary condition, with much of this variation related to the scale at which landscape patches are viewed. Regardless of the basis for defining patches, no single spatial scale is dominant in defining patches and the patterns that they create.

Corridors are narrow strips of land that differ from the matrix on both sides (Forman and Godron, 1986). Corridors originate in the same way as patches and they often connect patches of similar composition in the landscape. In human-dominated landscapes, roads and their rights-of-way are obvious examples of landscape corridors. As with all corridors, roads can facilitate the movement of organisms, especially humans, or they can act as filters or barriers to movement. Both patches and corridors are embedded in the landscape matrix, or the dominant land cover that differs in composition from individual patches or corridors.

Although landscapes have been described as a kilometers-wide mosaic over which local ecosystems recur (Forman and Godron, 1986), there is not a consensus among ecologists about the spatial scale at which landscapes occur. There is general agreement, however, that landscapes are associations of interacting ecosystems. Further, if ecosystems are accepted as the fundamental unit comprising landscapes and if ecosystems are considered to be tangible geographic units (as opposed to a set of interactions), then we can begin to ascribe properties to landscape ecosystems.

Ecosystems are volumetric segments of the earth that are expressed through their biotic communities as well as the physical environments that support organisms (Rowe, 1961; Christensen *et al.*, 1996; Barnes *et al.*, 1998). Moreover, ecosystems may be very small, such as an ephemeral pond in a forest, or very large, the global ecosphere. Here, I consider a landscape to be a geographic unit that encompasses multiple and interacting ecosystems, and extending at spatial scales ranging from a few hectares to many square kilometers in size. It is within this range of areal extent that humans commonly perceive landscapes (Forman, 1995).

Landscapes can be described in terms of their structure and function, as well as the magnitude, direction, and rate of change. Landscape structure, as measured by the size, shape, arrangement, and composition of landscape patches, reflects variation in the physical environment as well as natural disturbances and human activities. The interaction of these factors creates pattern in the landscape (Crow *et al.*, 1999). The distribution of patch sizes, a measure of landscape structure, generally follows a negative exponential relationship with many small patches and a few large patches. When considered on an area basis, however, the few large patches can represent a large share of the total landscape area. Large patches constitute important structural elements that provide critical habitat and isolation for large-home-range vertebrates, sustain viable populations of interior species, and provide linkages across landscapes that support processes that may be similar to those provided by corridors (Forman, 1995). Within a given landscape, the composition, size, and arrangement of patches affect flows of materials and energy, the movement of organisms, and more generally, the type, quality, and quantity of outputs and benefits derived. Yet this connection between the structure of a landscape (including its composition) and the derived outputs and benefits is rarely explicitly recognized.

Human activities tend to simplify the structure of a landscape as measured by complexity of patch shape and the range of patch sizes (Mladenoff *et al.*, 1993; Reed *et al.*, 1996). Human effects on landscape pattern are neither exclusive nor independent, but are typically interactive and cumulative (Crow *et al.*, 1999). Monitoring and analysis of these interactions and their cumulative effects are needed at the scale of a few hectares to many square kilometers (Reed *et al.*, 1996).

Function is the interaction among landscape ecosystems as measured by processes such as the flow of energy, movement and persistence of organisms, and fluxes of materials. Change refers to alteration in the structure and function of the landscape with time. There can be no ecological phenomena without change (Allen and Hoekstra, 1992). Land cover is transformed by several spatial processes overlapping in order, including perforation, fragmentation, and attrition (Forman, 1995). As the term suggests, perforation is the process of creating holes in the land cover that differ in composition from the general matrix. Fragmentation occurs when a contiguous patch is divided into smaller patches. Whenever a patch decreases in size, this form of land transformation is called shrinkage. And finally, when a patch disappears from the landscape, this is considered to be attrition (Forman, 1995).

An important aspect of landscape ecology, then, is the study of the reciprocal effects of spatial patterns on ecological processes (Turner, 1989; Pickett and Cadenasso, 1995). That is, landscape ecologists study both the cause and the effect of spatial heterogeneity. Emphasis on large-scale phenomena tends to reinforce the notion that humans are an integral part of almost all landscapes. Instead of attempting to study ecological phenomena devoid of human influences, landscape ecologists embrace the human influence when studying pattern and process.

14.4 Guidelines for multiple use and sustained yield from a landscape perspective

The following principles and concepts from landscape ecology contribute in a substantive way to practicing multiple use and sustained yield forestry.

14.4.1 Considering scale

Forest managers deal with complex issues that require considering the forest at many different spatial scales. A landscape perspective supports a multi-scale perspective for multiple use and sustained yield management. Because landscapes are spatially heterogeneous, their structure, function, and change are scale-dependent. That is, the measurement of spatial pattern and heterogeneity is dependent upon the scale at which observations and measurements are made. The scale at which humans perceive boundaries and patches in the landscape may have little relevance to numerous flows or fluxes. Processes and parameters important at one scale may not be as important or predictive at another scale (Turner, 1989).

Forest managers often focus on individual stands. At this spatial scale, the manager's perspective is that of being within the forest, with the forest canopy extending above the observer. An equally valid perspective for management is that of observing the forest (and other landscape elements) from above the canopy (Crow and Gustafson, 1997a, b). The extent of the view and the amount of detail (i.e., the landscape grain) depend on the scale of observation and the technologies employed. There is no "correct scale" to view a forest; however, the landscape perspective or "view from above" greatly enhances the manager's ability to implement the concept of multiple use.

14.4.2 Managing in time and space

Since multiple use can not be practiced on every unit of land to the same degree or intensity, managers need to capitalize on the different capabilities and opportunities that various ecosystems provide. Yet a formal spatial framework is rarely presented when applying multiple-use management. When confronted with conflicting uses, resource managers tend to partition land into separate allocations to meet specific management goals. This approach works well when land is abundant and demands for its use are few, but the land base is finite and the demands for forest goods and services are many. Separate allocations result in administrative fragmentation and ultimately landscape fragmentation. This results in conflict and seemly intractable problems related to land use. The spatial framework provided by a landscape perspective facilitates a more integrated, holistic approach to resource management and conservation.

Resource managers are uncomfortable acknowledging that uncertainty is associated with the results of their actions, but in reality, there is a great deal of uncertainty due to lack of knowledge about the systems being managed and due to unanticipated events that alter outcomes. Instead of predicting a single outcome, Walters (1986) suggests defining a set of possible outcomes that are consistent with existing knowledge and historical experience, and then assigning odds or probabilities to the outcomes. Such an approach might be appropriate for estimating growth and yield of forests under management.

Researchers are not adept at predicting growth and yield over broad areas and long time periods. Most models of timber growth are based on measurements taken at small spatial scales, and in many cases, over short periods of time (Fries *et al.*, 1978; Ek *et al.*, 1988). When these predictors are applied over broad areas and long periods of time, large cumulative errors are possible. Rarely are stochastic events such as extended droughts or losses due to outbreaks of insects or pathogens incorporated into growth models. These events may be rare in the short term, but they are common over the long term.

Regardless of the uncertainties associated with estimating growth and yield, projections at the scale of a national forest are the basis for important policy decisions such as establishing annual targets for timber harvesting. Both the spatial and temporal dimensions of scale need to be incorporated into the prediction of forest growth and yield.

14.4.3 Considering context

Because landscape ecosystems do not exist in isolation, it is important to consider forest stands or management areas within their broader spatial context. Most ecosystems have permeable boundaries that allow movement of species, materials, and energy across their boundaries. Proximity affects the degree of interaction among landscape ecosystems within the matrix. The degree of interaction, as measured by movement of species, material, and energy, drops sharply with distance. The rate of decrease is somewhat less for large patches compared to small patches.

Many studies have demonstrated the importance of landscape context on ecological processes. For example, Liu and Ashton (1999) used the spatially explicit model FORMOSAIC to study the interaction between landscape context and timber harvesting on tree diversity in a tropical forest. Forests adjacent to timber harvests provide important sources of seed for regeneration and so Liu and Ashton (1999) recommended maintaining species-rich forests in close proximity to harvested areas.

Clearly the application of the multiple-use concept benefits from evaluating the spatial and temporal context in which treatments occur so that potential conflicts are minimized and so that unintended and undesirable cumulative impacts of multiple actions can be better anticipated. Regional assessments, such as those conducted in the Pacific Northwest (FEMAT, 1993), the southern Appalachian region (SAMAB, 2001), or the Lake States (Minnesota, University of, 2001) and elsewhere, provide the means for considering local decisions and subsequent actions in a much larger social, economic, and ecologic context.

14.4.4 Hierarchical organizations

Theories and concepts relating to the hierarchical organization of ecological systems have developed in a much broader arena than landscape ecology, but landscape ecologists have contributed to the thinking about levels

Table 14.1. *National hierarchy of ecological units adopted by the US Department of Agriculture Forest Service*

Planning and analysis scale	Ecological units	Purpose, objective and general use
Ecoregion		
Global	Domain	Broad applicability for modeling and sampling. Strategic planning and regional assessments. International and national planning.
Continental	Division	
Region	Province	
Subregion	Section Subsection	Strategic planning, analysis, and assessment at the statewide, multi-agency level.
Landscape	Landtype Association	Forest or area-wide planning, watershed analysis.
Land Unit	Landtype Landtype Phase	Project level management and planning.

of organization and the relationships among these levels. Comprehensive discussions about hierarchical organization are found in O'Neill *et al.* (1986) and Allen and Hoekstra (1992) as well as others. The hierarchical organization of ecological systems, with smaller systems nested within larger systems, unites the concepts of context and scale. A hierarchical perspective helps managers evaluate broader-scale influences on finer-scale conditions and processes.

The description and inventory of forest ecosystems at multiple scales is the primary objective of the Ecological Classification and Inventory Systems (EC&I) adopted by the US Department of Agriculture Forest Service (Table 14.1). This is an example of using a hierarchical approach and ecological principles for classifying landscape ecosystems based on the physical environment (climate, physiography, soil,) and vegetation across scales ranging from global to local. The selection of an appropriate scale depends on the question or issue being addressed. The Ecoregion and Subregion levels of the national hierarchy provide useful contextual information for planning and managing at a national forest or even at a forest stand level. Crow *et al.* (1999) used Sections and Subsections (Table 14.1) to consider the interaction of the physical environment and land uses by humans in creating landscape patterns in northern Wisconsin. Host *et al.* (1988) compared variation in overstory biomass in forests on different Landtype Associations (Table 14.1) in northwestern Lower Michigan. The lowest levels of the national hierarchy – Landtype Association,

Landtype, Landtype Phase (Table 14.1) – provide operational units for management on the ground. Use of the hierarchy of ecological units improves the uniformity of resource information and facilitates the sharing of resource data across administrative and jurisdictional boundaries.

14.4.5 Landscape analysis and design

Given current demands for natural resources, spatially explicit planning and management are needed at the landscape level to produce "harmonious and coordinated management of the various resources." The process of designing landscapes begins with clearly articulating the management goals, along with analyzing existing and desired landscape patterns and processes (Diaz and Bell, 1997). This information is essential for preparing a landscape design. The ultimate design, obviously, should reflect the management goals stated at the beginning of the process. Computer visualization can also help in the design phase. The aesthetic value of landscapes, for example, can be evaluated using virtual images drawn by a computer (Pukkala and Kellomäki, 1988; Caelli *et al.*, 1997).

Harvesting timber profoundly affects landscape patterns. The practices of building roads and dispersing cutting units throughout a forested landscape, for example, are major contributors to forest fragmentation. With the help of spatial models, alternative cutting techniques have been derived that greatly decrease the amount of forest fragmentation through clustering harvest units or by harvesting timber in a progressive fashion across the landscape (Franklin and Forman, 1987; Li *et al.*, 1993; Wallin *et al.*, 1994; Gustafson and Crow, 1996).

14.5 Case studies

The following case studies illustrate the previously discussed general guidelines for thinking about multiple use and sustained yield from a landscape perspective. Since resource managers are usually responsible for only a portion of a landscape, the first case study was selected because it stresses collaborative approaches across ownerships for managing landscapes. The next two case studies illustrate concepts of landscape design within a single ownership – in this case, public lands.

14.5.1 The Pinelands National Reserve

The New Jersey pine barrens are a definable physiographic feature characterized by acidic, droughty, sandy soils, and by fire-dependent ecosystems dominated by pitch pine, (*Pinus rigida*), oaks (*Quercus* sp.), and ericaceous shrubs such as *Vaccinium* and *Gaylussacia* (Forman, 1979; Good and Good, 1984). Although sparsely populated compared to most of the northeastern United States, the Pinelands are coming under increased developmental pressures from urban centers such as Philadelphia and Atlantic City. In 1976, federal legislation created the nation's first National Reserve when it became apparent that the Pinelands would not continue to exist as a functional ecological unit indefinitely without a regional plan to balance needs for increased development with conserving significant and representative Pinelands ecosystems. At least three of our four guiding tenets for landscape-level management – considering context, landscape analysis and design, and managing in time and space – have been incorporated into planning and managing the Pinelands.

State legislation implementing the federal Act provided a mechanism to guide, mitigate, and to some extent, regulate the effects of an increasing population on this regional ecosystem (Good and Good, 1984). The State of New Jersey was responsible for creating a comprehensive management plan for the Pinelands that, in turn, provided a coordinating framework for county and municipal governments when developing their local land management plans. To guide land-use planning for the Pinelands, maps depicting land capability based on flora, fauna, geology, soils, and hydrology were developed. Each land capability type has a distinct set of rules governing the types of land use allowed (Table 14.2). The combination of local plans developed within the context of a comprehensive regional plan provided a level of coordination and cooperation among various county and municipal jurisdictions that would be impossible if each political entity were acting independently. Considering biological and social factors locally as well as regionally provided managers, planners, and political leaders with valuable contextual information for making decisions.

The creation of land capability maps added a spatial element to planning land use in the Pinelands National Reserve and projecting desired future conditions added the temporal element. Opportunities for more intensive development were focused in areas categorized as Pinelands Towns, Villages, Rural Development Areas, and Regional Growth Areas (Table 14.2). The strategy was to direct new development to areas already developed, thus concentrating the effects to relatively few areas as opposed to dispersing the effects throughout the landscape. Concentrating development also increased the likelihood of keeping existing agricultural and forested lands in production as well as creating a system of reserves in which fire could be reintroduced in a limited way to the landscape. Although forest management was not intensive by modern standards, it was likely to become non-existent due to developmental pressures without comprehensive land-use planning. The maps of land capability combined with the guidelines for each category provided the basis for designing a landscape.

Table 14.2. *Land capability types identified in the comprehensive management plan and their associated land-use guidelines for the Pinelands National Reserve*

Land Capability Types	Guidelines
Preservation Area Districts	The most restricted allowable land-use category. Emphasizes the preservation of an extensive contiguous land area in its natural state while promoting compatible agricultural and recreational uses.
Forest Areas	Forested lands with less protection than Preservation Area. New development is limited to an average of one dwelling unit per 6.3 ha of privately owned, undeveloped upland.
Agricultural Production Areas	Areas where existing agricultural activities are important or where soils favor such activities. Prohibiting residential developments encourages continuance of agricultural activities.
Rural Development Areas Regional Growth Areas Pinelands Towns, Villages	More intensive and extensive development is focused in these land capability types. These areas are centered on locations that have already been extensively disrupted by development but includes some undeveloped lands in close proximity to present development.
Military and Federal Installation Areas	Federal lands. Often part of a Preservation Area District.

Source: Good and Good (1984).

Efforts to develop a comprehensive land-use plan for the New Jersey pine barrens expands upon the concept of multiple use and sustained yield as defined in federal legislation. In the case of the pine barrens, multiple use applies to the full spectrum of land uses, from urban development to high levels of protection and restoration of pineland ecosystems. Attempts to distribute varying intensities of management in time and space in the pinelands provide a useful model for public (and private) lands where increasing demands for goods and services from a finite land base are forcing planners to apply a more explicit spatial framework to land management. In the context of the Multiple-Use Sustained-Yield Act of 1960, sustained yield refers to the continuous flow of products. These outputs, however, are dependent on maintaining ecological processes that, in turn, sustain the productivity of the land. The focus, therefore, shifts from the output of goods and services demanded by people (e.g., timber, recreation, wildlife) to the inputs and processes (e.g., the soil, ecological services, biological diversity) necessary to maintain the outputs.

14.5.2 Forest planning on the Hoosier National Forest

Spatial models that combine geographic information systems (GIS) with remote sensing offer powerful tools for managing landscapes in time and space (Mladenoff and Baker, 1999). The use of one such a model, HARVEST, to evaluate several alternative management scenarios on the Hoosier National Forest in southern Indiana illustrates the utility of spatial models for analyzing and designing landscapes. The starting-points for HARVEST are a digital land-cover map derived from classifying remote sensing imagery and a digital stand map where grid-cell values reflect the age of each timber stand. The model allows control of the size and distribution of harvest units, the total area to be harvested per unit of time, and the rotation length as given by the minimum age that harvesting is allowed. HARVEST produces landscape patterns through time that have spatial attributes resulting from the initial landscape conditions and the planned management strategies by incorporating decisions typically made by resource managers (Gustafson and Crow, 1999).

The original forest plan for the Hoosier National Forest called for even-aged management using clear-cutting units averaging 15–18 ha in size and dispersed throughout the forest. Due to public opposition to this management approach, an amended plan was developed that proposed group-selection cuts that were less than 2 ha in size. In addition, reserve areas with no harvesting were identified, resulting in the concentration of timber harvesting on a smaller portion of the forest. Using these two very different management approaches as initial conditions for HARVEST, we projected changes in landscape structure on the Hoosier for eight decades. The group-selection approach resulted in a 60% reduction in harvest levels compared to the original forest plan. Despite this reduction in harvesting levels, group-selection did not result in increased forest interior (defined as >200 m from an edge) or decreased amounts of forest edge produced by timber management activities. It is not surprising that small, widely distributed harvest units result in fragmentation of the forest. In addition to the ecological argument, small and widely dispersed harvest units increase the cost of harvesting. Small harvest openings, however, are more acceptable to the public than large units and it is this visual aspect that is the determining factor for managers on the Hoosier National Forest.

Gustafson (1996) used HARVEST to simulate the clustering of harvest units in both time and space. In the simulation, the forest was partitioned into large management blocks in which harvesting was conducted in a single block for 50 years, then moved to another block for a similar time, until all blocks were eventually subjected to harvesting. The results from this simulation suggest that a strategy of blocking in time and space greatly reduced the amount of forest edge, greatly increased interior forest conditions, while maintaining an active program of timber harvesting.

In addition to evaluating changes in landscape patterns produced by alternative management scenarios, it is also possible to project changes in stand–age class distributions using models such as HARVEST, thus testing for sustainable yield on real landscapes. In simulating the effects of alternative management strategies on forest age structure on the Hoosier National Forest, Gustafson and Crow (1996) found gaps in the projected age structure of the forest that suggest a non-continuous flow of timber under more intensive harvesting given the current age structure of the forest.

14.5.3 Landscape Analysis and Design (LAD) on the Wisconsin National Forests

Using design principles presented in Diaz and Bell (1997), planners and managers on the Chequamegon and Nicolet National Forests established a network of representative ecosystems that serve as reference areas for the actively managed landscape matrix (Parker, 1997). The National Hierarchy of Ecological Units (Table 14.1) along with an inventory of ecologically significant features and an assessment of opportunities for protection, restoration, as well as traditional management provided the framework for designing the network and assuring adequate representation of the major ecosystems found on the forests.

The Landscape Analysis and Design (LAD) process had three main objectives (L. Parker, personnal communication). One was to create a representative array of high-quality reference areas to compare with landscapes under active management. A second objective was to identify areas where restoration of ecological processes is needed. The third and most important objective was to maintain biological diversity in a managed landscape. Total protection was not always the primary prescription for areas within the network. Most often, some level of manipulation such as the reintroduction of fire to the landscape and the application of innovative silvicultural techniques are necessary to restore important ecological characteristics and functions.

A logical complement to the LAD process would be to design a network of sites where intensive management for timber production is best suited on the Wisconsin National Forests. To establish a network of timber production areas, maps of ecological units based on the National Hierarchy (Table 14.1) combined with maps of existing roads could be utilized to identify highly productive ecosystems with good access. When forest productivity areas are added to the LAD network, the rudiments of a landscape design encompassing the spectrum of multiple uses – from intensive utilization to protection – begin to emerge.

14.6 Summary

Most resource management activities produce changes in landscape pattern. The effects of these changes on biological diversity, aesthetic qualities, wildlife habitat, water quality, and even the production of forest commodities are poorly understood. Furthermore, land managers and planners often ignore interactions among different elements in a landscape, but instead treat the elements as a collection of independent pieces. Concepts and principles from landscape ecology – including managing in time and space, considering scale and context, and thinking about hierarchical organization – provide a guiding framework for managing natural resources in a much more holistic and integrative fashion.

The Multiple-Use Sustained-Yield Act of 1960 provides managers with a great deal of latitude when dealing with resource management issues. The basic concepts of multiple use and sustained yield do not need to be repudiated nor does the Act necessarily need to be changed. It is a matter of interpretation in light of modern-day realities that include a larger human population now that is placing much greater demands on natural resources on a limited land base. Given these demands, multiple use requires a formal spatial and temporal framework to guide its implementation and both inputs and outputs should be considered part of sustained yield. Concepts and tools from landscape ecology offer managers the means for designing landscapes in time and space for multiple uses, benefits, and values.

References

Allen, T. F. H. & Hoekstra, T. W. (1992). *Toward a Unified Ecology.* Columbia University Press, New York.

Barnes, B. V., Zak, D. R., Denton, S. R. & Spurr, S. H. (1998). *Forest Ecology,* 4th edn. John Wiley, New York.

Behan, J. (1990). Multiresource forest management: A paradigmatic challenge to professional forestry. *Journal of Forestry*, 88: 12–18.

Bengston, D. N. (1994). Changing forest values and ecosystem management. *Society and Natural Resources*, 7: 515–533.

Boyce, M. S. & Haney, A. (eds.) (1997). *Ecosystem Management: Applications for Sustainable Forest and Wildlife Resources.* Yale University Press, New Haven, CT.

Bunnell, F. L. (1998). *Policy and Practices for Biodiversity in Managed Forests.* University of British Columbia Press, Vancouver, Canada.

Caelli, T., Peng, L. & Bunke, H. (eds.) (1997). *Spatial Computing: Issues in Vision, Multimedia and Visualization Technologies*. World Scientific, River Edge, NJ.

Christensen, N. L., Bartuska, A. M., Brown, J. H., Carpenter, S., D'Antonio, C., Francis, R., Franklin, J. F., MacMahon, J. A., Noss, R. F., Parsons, D. J., Peterson, C. H., Turner, M. G. &

Woodmansee, R. G. (1996). The report of the Ecological Society of America committee on the scientific basis for ecosystem management. *Ecological Applications*, 6: 665–691.

Crow, T. R. & Gustafson, E. J. (1997a). Concepts and methods of ecosystem management: Lessons from landscape ecology. In *Ecosystem Management: Applications for Sustainable Forest and Wildlife Management*, eds. M. Boyce & A. Haney, pp. 54–67. Yale University Press, New Haven, CT.

Crow, T. R. & Gustafson, E. J. (1997b). Ecosystem management: Managing natural resources in time and space. In *Creating a Forestry for the 21st Century*, eds. K. A. Kohm & J. F. Franklin, pp. 215–228. Island Press, Washington, D.C.

Crow, T. R., Host, G. E. & Mladenoff, D. J. (1999). Ownership and ecosystem as sources of spatial heterogeneity in a forested landscape, Wisconsin, USA. *Landscape Ecology*, 14: 449–463.

Diaz, N. M. & Bell, S. (1997). Landscape analysis and design. In *Creating A Forestry for the 21st Century*, eds. K. A. Kohm & J. F. Franklin, pp. 255–269. Island Press, Washington, D.C.

Ek, A. R., Shifley, S. R. & Burk, T. E. (1988). Forest growth modelling and prediction. *Proceedings of the IUFRO (International Union of Forestry Research Organizations) Conference*, SAF 87–12. Society of American Foresters, Washington, D.C.

FEMAT [Forest Ecosystem Management Team] (1993). *Forest ecosystem management: An Ecological, Economic, and Social Assessment*. Joint publication of the US Department of Agriculture Forest Service; Department of Commerce; National Oceanic and Atmospheric Administration and National Marine Fisheries Service; US Department of the Interior Bureau of Land Management, Fish and Wildlife Service, and National Park Service, and Environmental Protection Agency; Washington, D.C.

Forman, R. T. T. (ed.) (1979). *Pine Barrens: Ecosystem and Landscape*. Academic Press, New York.

Forman, R. T. T. (1995). *Land Mosaics: The Ecology of Landscapes and Regions*. Cambridge University Press, Cambridge, UK.

Forman, R. T. T. & Godron, M. (1986). *Landscape Ecology*. John Wiley, New York.

Franklin, J. F. & Forman, R. T. T. (1987). Creating landscape patterns by forest cutting: Ecological consequences and principles. *Landscape Ecology*, 1: 5–18.

Fries, J., Burkhart, H. E. & Max, T. A. (eds.) (1978). *Growth Models for Long-Term Forecasting of Timber Yields*. Publication no. FWS-1–78. School of Forestry and Wildlife Resources, Virginia Polytechnic Institute and State University, Blacksburg, VA.

Good, R. E. & Good, N. F. (1984). The Pinelands National Reserve: An ecosystem approach to management. *BioScience*, 34: 169–173.

Grumbine, R. E. (1997). Reflection on "what is ecosystem management?" *Conservation Biology*, 11: 41–47.

Gustafson, E. J. (1996). Expanding the scale of forest management: Allocating timber harvests in time and space. *Forest Ecology and Management*, 87: 27–39.

Gustafson, E. J. & Crow, T. R. (1996). Simulating the effects of alternative forest management strategies on landscape structure. *Journal of Environmental Management*, 46: 77–96.

Gustafson, E. J. & Crow, T. R. (1999). HARVEST: Linking timber harvesting strategies to landscape patterns. In *Spatial Modeling of Forest Landscape Change*, eds. D. J. Mladenoff & W. L. Baker, pp. 309–332. Cambridge University Press, New York.

Host, G. E., Pregitzer, K. S., Ramm, C. W., Lusch, D. P. & Cleland, D. T. (1988). Variation in overstory biomass among glacial landforms and ecological land units in northwestern Lower Michigan. *Canadian Journal of Forest Research*, 18: 659–668.

Kohm, K. A. & Franklin, J. F. (eds.) (1997). *Creating a Forestry for the 21st Century: The Science of Ecosystem Management*. Island Press, Washington, D.C.

Li, H., Franklin, J. F., Swanson, F. J. & Spies, T. A. (1993). Developing alternative forest cutting patterns: A simulation approach. *Landscape Ecology*, 8: 63–75.

Liu, J. & Ashton, P. S. (1999). Simulating effects of landsape context and timber harvest on tree species diversity. *Ecological Applications*, 9: 186–201.

Minnesota, University of (2001). http://www.ncfes.umn.edu/gla

Mladenoff, D. J. & Baker, W. L. (eds.) (1999). *Spatial Modeling of Forest Landscape Change:*

Approaches and Applications. Cambridge University Press, New York.

Mladenoff, D. J., White, M. A., Pastor, J. & Crow, T. R. (1993). Comparing spatial pattern in unaltered old-growth and disturbed forest landscapes. *Ecological Applications*, 31: 294–306.

O'Neill, R. V., DeAngelis, D. L., Waide, J. B. & Allen, T. F. H. (1986). A hierarchical concept of ecosystems. *Monographs in Population Biology*, 23: 1–272.

Parker, L. (1997). Restaging an evolutionary drama: Thinking big on the Chequamegon and Nicolet National Forests. In *Creating a Forestry for the 21st Century*, eds. K. A. Kohm & J. F. Franklin, pp. 218–219. Island Press, Washington, D.C.

Pickett, S. T. A. & Cadenasso, M. L. (1995). Landscape ecology: Spatial heterogeneity in ecological systems. *Science*, 269: 331–334.

Pinchot, G. P. (1987). *Breaking New Ground*. Island Press, Washington, D.C. (Reprinted; originally published by Harcourt, Brace, and Co., New York, 1947.)

Pukkala, T. & Kellomäki, S. (1988). Simulation as a tool in designing forest landscape. *Landscape and Urban Planning*, 16: 253–260.

Reed, R. A., Johnson-Barnard, J. & Baker, W. L. (1996). Fragmentation of a forested Rocky Mountain landscape, 1950–1993. *Biological Conservation*, 75: 267–277.

Rowe, J. S. (1961). The level-of-integration concept and ecology. *Ecology*, 42: 420–427.

Rowe, J. S. (1992). The ecosystem approach to forestland management. *Forest Chronicle*, 68: 222–224.

SAMAB [South Appalachian Man and the Biosphere Program] (2001). http://samab.org

Saunders, S. C., Chen, J., Crow, T. R. & Brosofske, K. D. (1998). Hierarchical relationships between landscape structure and temperature in a managed forest landscape. *Landscape Ecology*, 13: 381–395.

Shands, W. E. (1988). Beyond multiple use: Managing national forests for distinctive values. *American Forests*, 94: 14–15, 56–57.

Tollefson, C. (1998). *The Wealth of Forests: Markets, Regulations, and Sustainable Forestry.* University of British Columbia Press, Vancouver, Canada.

Turner, M. G. (1989). Landscape ecology: The effect of pattern on process. *Annual Review of Ecology and Systematics*, 20: 171–197.

Vogt, K. A., Gordon, J. C., Wargo, J. P., Vogt, D. J., Asbjornsen, H., Palmiotto, P. A., Clark, H. J., O'Hara, J. L., Keaton, W. S., Patel-Weynand, T. & Witten, E. (1997). *Ecosystems: Balancing Science with Management*. Springer-Verlag, New York.

Wallin, D. O., Swanson, F. J. & Marks, B. (1994). Landscape pattern response to changes in pattern generation rules: Land-use legacies in forestry. *Ecological Applications*, 4: 569–580.

Walters, C. (1986). *Adaptive Management of Renewable Resources.* Macmillan, New York.

Yaffee, S. L. (1999). Three faces of ecosystem management. *Conservation Biology*, 13: 713–725.

WILLIAM W. TAYLOR, DANIEL B. HAYES, C. PAOLA FERRERI,
KRISTINE D. LYNCH, KURT R. NEWMAN, AND EDWARD F. ROSEMAN

15

Integrating landscape ecology into fisheries management: A rationale and practical considerations

15.1 Introduction

Fisheries exist throughout the world wherever people and water meet (Nielsen, 1999). Essentially, a fishery can be defined as a complex system made up of three interacting components: habitat, the aquatic environment where an organism lives; biota, the living organisms in the aquatic ecosystem; and people, who harvest the biotic resource or who change the condition of its environment (Willis and Murphy, 1996). Throughout its history, the principal goal of fisheries management has been "to provide people with a sustained, high, and ever increasing benefit from their use of living aquatic resources" by manipulating these three components (Nielsen, 1999). Over time, the primary focus of fisheries management has shifted from providing the maximum sustainable harvest to providing a variety of different benefits that arise as a result of the interaction of people, habitats, and organisms (see Nielsen, 1999 for a brief history of fisheries management).

In the beginning, fisheries management was primarily concerned with providing food, and secondarily with providing economic benefit, for an ever-increasing human population. For this reason, fish were viewed as crops, and the efficient use of fish populations, or providing *maximum sustainable yield* (MSY), became the driving philosophy during the early twentieth century (Nielsen, 1999). To provide MSY, fishery managers focused on a single-species, single-habitat approach, using population dynamics and biological yield models to predict the maximum harvest level a fishery could sustain. However, as the human population grew, demands on fishery resources and aquatic habitats increased, and fishery scientists began to realize that maximizing the weight or number of fish harvested was not always the most appropriate goal for a fishery. Social and economic considerations also needed to be taken into account. In recreational fisheries, the size of the fish caught was frequently of equal importance to the number caught. In commercial fisheries, the idea that the cost of harvesting eventually increases more rapidly than the value of the harvest became a predominant viewpoint. MSY was also challenged from an ecological perspective; single-species management was rarely successful due to interactions between the single species and the broader fish community and ecosystem that supported the species of interest. Economic, social, and ecological concerns about MSY grew throughout the mid twentieth century, and by 1975, a new approach, *optimum sustainable yield* (OSY), became widely accepted (Roedel, 1975). The basic premise of OSY is that a unique goal, one that incorporates a wide range of considerations, not just maximizing harvest, exists for every fishery (Nielsen, 1999).

At the same time that the concept of OSY was developing, fishery managers were becoming increasingly aware that habitat had a profound impact on the production of desirable fish species. The idea that better habitat meant better fishing was incorporated into the fishery biologist's mind-set, and a great number of habitat improvement projects were started, particularly in streams and lakes. While some of these projects successfully increased fish production, many appeared to have little or no impact on fish abundance. Arguably, one of the main limitations on success (as measured by fish abundance) was that much of the additional fish production made its way into the angler's creel. As such, the choice of a measure of "success" is critical. Another limitation on habitat improvement actions was that virtually all projects focused on in-stream or in-lake habitats without sufficient consideration of the influence that land use within the watershed had on aquatic conditions. Although the concept of OSY has been generally accepted by the fisheries management community, implementation has been slow, and many management programs still focus on maximizing yields of single species (Schramm and Hubert, 1999). There seem to be at least two major reasons for this lag: (1) although the OSY paradigm recognizes the importance of habitat to successful fisheries management, it has not provided a way to integrate across different habitat types or across different spatial and temporal scales, and (2) the ability of fishery managers to implement landscape management is limited, given the limited (or lack of) jurisdiction aquatic resource managers have on the broader terrestrial and aquatic landscape and the social settings that shape valuable fishery resources.

The goal of this chapter is to demonstrate that aquatic systems possess landscape patterns and processes that affect fish production, and that activities on the terrestrial landscape can have a profound effect on water quality and fisheries management. Given that aquatic and terrestrial landscape patterns and processes are important determinants of fisheries, we propose that fisheries management should incorporate landscape concepts into its framework if management plans are to be successful. Finally, to achieve OSY, fisheries management will need to go beyond consideration of the physical, chemical, and biological attributes of the aquatic and terrestrial landscapes, to include considerations of social settings and how they interact with fisheries.

15.2 Aquatic systems are landscapes too!

Concepts of landscape ecology have been applied to terrestrial systems, but application to aquatic systems has lagged behind. Perhaps, this is due to the fact that the term "landscape" is generally used to refer to landforms that make up a region or to land surface and associated habitats (Turner and Gardner, 1991). One of the distinguishing features of landscape ecology is its focus on spatial heterogeneity and on the arrangement and connectivity among patches in the ecosystem (Pickett and Cadenasso, 1995). Using this perspective, it is easy to see how aquatic systems fit the concept of a "landscape." Aquatic systems, ranging from small streams to oceans, generally show persistent features, analogous to landforms, that contribute to a heterogeneous environment. Moreover, landscape considerations and concepts, such as spatial arrangement, patchiness, and edge effects, that are of great concern to terrestrial landscape ecologists, apply equally well to aquatic systems.

Schlosser (1991, 1995) argues that concepts of landscape ecology are applicable to stream ecology because of the repeated spatial patterns and heterogeneity found in streams. Streams show spatial heterogeneity in two dimensions: longitudinally, with trends in environmental conditions between upstream and downstream regions, and laterally, with consistent differences between stream margins and the midchannel areas (Schlosser, 1991, 1995; Rabeni, 1992). In addition to spatial heterogeneity, streams often show large changes in flow rates, resulting in variations in habitat conditions on even short temporal scales. Further, this heterogeneity can be viewed at different scales (Schlosser 1991, 1995). At small scales, pool–riffle complexes contribute to the longitudinal heterogeneity. Pools are deeper areas of the stream channel that are characterized by slower water velocity and finer sediments than riffles. Riffles are areas of shallow, fast-moving water characterized by large substrates, such as gravel and cobble. Pools and riffles develop as the stream channel cuts through the watershed and are persistent features of the channel on the time-scale of tens of years. Over longer time-scales, the location of individual pools and riffles may change, but the sequence and ratio of these habitat types usually are maintained. On a large scale, longitudinal differences between headwater streams (first to third order) and medium to large rivers (fourth to sixth order) are characterized by a decrease in channel slopes, a widening of the stream channel, increases in pool size, and increases in channel meandering. Further, the ratio of pool area to riffle area generally increases in higher-order streams.

The recurrence and persistence of features associated with this longitudinal gradient from small streams to large rivers is the basis for the *river continuum concept* (Vannote *et al.*, 1980). In brief, this concept proposes that the structure and function of biological communities in rivers follow a predictable pattern, from low- to high-order streams, due largely to the patterns in physical features occurring along the length of a stream.

Lateral heterogeneity in streams is strongly influenced by the amount of channel meandering. In small streams, lateral heterogeneity extends over short distances and generally occurs through differences between the stream margin and the midchannel. In large rivers, however, lateral heterogeneity may extend over large areas due to more complex river meandering and flooding. In these larger systems, lateral heterogeneity may extend beyond the main channel to include extensive networks of side channels and the floodplain (Junk *et al.*, 1989). The flow of water through the stream channel connects these different habitats, allowing organisms to use different habitats for different phases of their life history. Changes in flow can alter the spatial heterogeneity along both axes and the connectivity between habitat patches (Poff *et al.*, 1997) causing changes in the fish production potential of the system.

Fisheries scientists are now understanding that it is imperative to consider the heterogeneity in stream habitat and the connectivity between different types of habitat within streams to understand productivity of fish populations. Although interspersion (degree of intermixing of different habitat types) and juxtaposition (the relative location of different habitat types) of discrete habitats on the landscape have long been recognized as important determinants of wildlife population dynamics (e.g., Thomas *et al.*, 1979), their importance to fish population dynamics and production is only recently emerging (e.g., Schlosser, 1995). Several recent studies have provided evidence that the spatial arrangement of discrete habitats in riverine environments can give rise to dramatically different fish population dynamics within a particular stream reach (Grossman *et al.*, 1995; Schlosser and Angermeier, 1995). For example, Kocik and Ferreri (1998) suggest that using the concepts of interspersion and juxtaposition to define functional habitat units for juvenile Atlantic salmon (*Salmo salar*) can help to refine estimates of their abundance. Their argument hinges on the observation that the spatial location and connectivity between spawning and rearing habitat in the stream (or the interspersion and juxtaposition of these discrete habitat types) are critical to defining the production potential of a particular stream reach. Thus, fishery scientists are beginning to acknowledge that landscape concepts are important in determining fish production in stream systems.

Streams are not the only type of aquatic system that exhibit landscape characteristics. Noble *et al.* (1994) argue that spatial heterogeneity is a prominent feature of man-made reservoirs, allowing them to easily fit the definition of a landscape. Reservoirs are typically constructed by damming rivers, creating longitudinal heterogeneity characterized by predictable changes in water chemistry, basin morphology, rates of sedimentation, and productivity, moving from the headwater of reservoirs to their outflows. Because reservoirs typically flood the adjacent floodplain and tributaries, many reservoirs have a dendritic shape with many lateral branches, coves, and bays that contribute to the lateral heterogeneity of the system. Environmental conditions and the biotic community in coves and bays can be dramatically different from those of the main body of the reservoir (Noble *et al.*,1994) and may function as distinct patches. Many reservoirs and natural lakes in temperate regions vertically stratify on an annual basis, again creating repeatable patterns in environmental conditions analogous to landforms. Stratification is a predictable process that persists through much of the year, resulting in predictable patterns in species abundance and distribution on an annual basis.

Even the ocean can be considered an aquatic landscape. The persistence of features such as upwellings, downwellings, and major ocean currents makes them analogous to terrestrial landscape features such as mountain ranges, valleys, and rivers. Thus, we can define persistent features in all aquatic systems that contribute to the heterogeneity of the aquatic environment. The arrangement and connectivity between these heterogenous patches have important implications for the ecology and management of the fish fauna in these aquatic landscapes.

15.2.1 Landscape features affect fish communities: Small temperate lakes

Across large regions of the northern hemisphere, the retreat of the last glaciation left a landscape with an abundance of relatively small lakes (i.e., less than 100 hectares in size). The size of these lakes varies widely, as does their degree of isolation. Some lakes are interconnected by perennial streams, allowing fish to move readily among lakes. Many lakes however, do not have connecting streams, and are therefore isolated from other lakes. While some mechanisms exist for fish to be transported between lakes that are not hydrologically connected (e.g., predatory birds may accidentally transport living fish between water bodies), rates of exchange are generally thought to be quite low. In analogy to terrestrial systems, lakes in this region frequently occur as fragmented patches across the landscape with varying degrees of connectedness to other like patches. In addition to the degree of interconnectedness, variation in lake size and habitat conditions affect the fish community. Small lakes, for example, are more prone to the loss of species through demographic stochasticity than are large lakes. The habitat for fish in small shallow lakes may also be limiting to some fish species if the lakes are prone to winterkill (i.e., becoming anoxic during periods of heavy snow and ice cover).

In a study of 169 Finnish and Wisconsin lakes, Magnuson *et al.* (1998) illustrate how these factors interact to determine fish species richness. In their study, the investigators separated factors that influence the dynamics of fish species into two categories. First, factors such as distance to nearest lake, area of nearest lake, and stream gradient of connecting stream (if present) were classified as isolation variables that would influence the rate of immigration or exchange of fish species among lakes. A second set of variables, lake area, pH, and lake depth, was used to characterize the harshness of the lake environment and to indicate the relative likelihood of fish species extinction. Results of their study demonstrated that extinction variables tended to have greater explanatory power for species richness than isolation variables. Some of the most important extinction variables included lake area, pH, and conductivity. Among the isolation variables, the area of the nearest lake, stream gradient, and distance to nearest road were most important. These results suggest that the time to extinction after the arrival of a species tends to be less than the time between an extinction and a new arrival. Another way of looking at this is that the effects of the extinction of a well-established species may be very apparent and lasting, whereas new arrivals may not take hold, thereby resulting in a virtually undetectable extinction (Magnuson *et al.*, 1998).

The results of this study have important implications for fisheries management. One implication is that expectations for a given lake should be tempered by the size and physical conditions in a lake. For example, production by individual species in small lakes may be high, but these lakes may not consistently support diverse fish communities. On the other hand, the fish diversity and production in a large isolated lake may be relatively low because of the low rate of species recruitment. As such, fishery managers may be able to increase the production and diversity of the fish community in such lakes through stocking, which acts to break down the natural geographic isolation of remote lakes. Another insight that can be gained from this study is that human activities often tend to alter the fish species richness that would be expected in more "natural" situations by changing the balance between extinction and isolation variables. Some actions (e.g., stocking, accidental release of live bait, bilge water transport) tend to reduce isolation, while other factors (e.g., acid rain, eutrophication) often tend to make conditions harsher in lakes, thereby increasing rates of extinction. Thus, evaluations of fish community composition need to consider natural extinction and isolation factors that are derived from the landscape features of the aquatic system itself and from its setting within the broader terrestrial landscape, as well as human-induced changes in these factors.

15.2.2 Landscape features affect fish production: The Peruvian anchoveta

Another example where landscape ecology concepts are important to successful fishery management is the Peruvian anchoveta or anchovy (*Engraulis ringens*) fishery. Because of the Peru Current and an area of high pressure off the southwestern coast of South America, a strong upwelling of nutrient rich water occurs off the coasts of Chile and Peru. This upwelling creates spatial heterogeneity in the environment because primary production in this area is much higher than in the open ocean. As a result, this area has greater zooplankton and fish production than in nearby areas not supported by the upwelling (Ryther, 1969). Fish production in the Peruvian upwelling is particularly high due to the intensity of the upwelling and the ability of anchoveta to feed directly on phytoplankton and zooplankton, resulting in highly efficient transformation of primary production into fish production (Mesinas, 1994).

The presence of the upwelling, a persistent landscape feature, combined with the ability of the anchoveta to consume phytoplankton and zooplankton directly, gave rise to the largest single fishery on the planet historically. During the 1950s, the anchoveta fishery expanded greatly as the market for fishmeal and fish oil developed following the collapse of the California sardine fishery (Aguero and Zuleta, 1994). The fishery developed rapidly (Fig. 15.1), with harvest increasing steadily through 1968. The development of the fishery in such a short time was partly due to the opportunity for a lucrative fishery, but was facilitated by the proximity of the fishery to coastal port cities along the coast of Peru and Chile, which meant that fishing trips could be made in rapid succession and harvest brought directly into port for processing. With high yields and substantial economic benefits to fishers and to these nations, harvest in this fishery initially grew at an exponential rate.

Upwelling systems can be rapidly broken down by anomalous climatic conditions such as El Niño events (a climate perturbation characterized by the weakening of trade winds and the warming of the surface layers of the equatorial Pacific Ocean; McPhaden, 1993), and the impacts of resulting changes in the aquatic landscape are dramatic and have far-reaching implications for fishery management. While minor El Niño events occurred during the development of the fishery, resulting in minor declines in harvest, a series of El Niño events during the early 1970s, combined with overfishing, resulted in a dramatic decline in harvest (Fig. 15.1). In 1982–3, a particularly strong El Niño event occurred which had a devastating impact on the population of anchoveta as well as on the fishery (Aguero and Gonzalez, 1996). The combination of reduced biological productivity caused by the loss of the upwelling and the high harvest rate of anchoveta brought harvest to less than 2% of the historic high. After this decline, it took nearly a decade for the population and fishery to

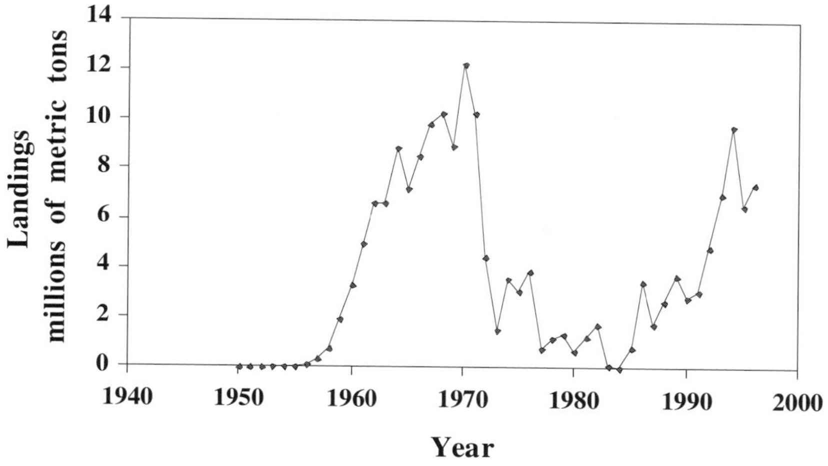

FIGURE 15.1
Annual harvest of anchoveta from Chile and Peru, 1950–96.

recover. The occurrence of another strong El Niño in 1997–8 has caused considerable concern over the amount of harvest that will be sustainable over the next several years.

Structures such as the Peruvian upwelling are persistent features of the ocean landscape. Just as terrestrial landscapes can change as a result of climatic events, upwellings can also change in response to climatic events, resulting in a change in the production capacity of the area. As a result, fishery managers must be prepared to respond (e.g., through changes in quotas) to changes in these landscape features and processes that can affect these features or the connectivity between features as they can have important implications for fish production.

15.3 Terrestrial landscapes affect the functioning of aquatic landscapes

Although fishery managers have long known that the terrestrial landscape has a strong impact on aquatic systems, their actions have often neglected this consideration. One of the tenets of landscape ecology addresses the importance of the connectivity and exchange between heterogeneous landscapes. When dealing with aquatic systems, this can easily be interpreted to highlight the importance of land-based processes and their effects on aquatic processes. Understanding the connection between activity on the land and the quantity and quality of water available to support fisheries is critical for managing productive fisheries. Management of aquatic resources needs to embrace this fact, and terrestrial resource managers need to consider consequences of terrestrial management beyond the land–water interface.

15.3.1 Activities on land affect fish communities: The Huron River watershed

The complex interaction between a stream and its watershed has long been recognized as an important factor shaping the ecology of stream fish communities (Hynes, 1970; Johnson and Gage, 1997). As a result, management of stream fish populations depends largely on management of the stream's watershed. Changes in land cover and land use within a watershed are likely to change the quantity, quality, and timing of water entering its stream which can affect the structure of stream fish communities (Poff *et al.*, 1997). To illustrate this point, we will present a case study of the Huron River, Michigan.

The Huron River watershed is located near the Detroit metropolitan area in southeastern Michigan, and is typical of a watershed that has undergone extensive urbanization. Historically, the Huron River supported a diverse fish fauna, with most species widely distributed throughout the watershed (Hay-Chmielewski *et al.*, 1995). Widespread land development and urbanization have greatly reduced the current distribution and diversity of the fish fauna (Newman *et al.*, 1999). A fish faunal survey conducted in 1938 documented 65 fish species at 90 sites across the watershed (Brown and Funk, 1945). In 1996, the survey was repeated, using the same methods, revealing that 24 species have disappeared, the distribution of 35 species has been reduced, and only 6 species showed no change or increases in their distribution since 1938 (Newman *et al.*, 1999). At the spatial scale of individual sampling sites, mean fish species richness declined significantly from 13.7 species per site in 1938 to 3.7 species per site in 1996.

Most of the losses of diversity (Fig. 15.2) or reductions in the range of many fish species coincide with those areas that have experienced the greatest increases in urban land use over time (compare Fig. 15.2 with Fig. 15.3). In 1938, agriculture was the predominant land cover (Fig. 15.4a), encompassing 131 469 hectares or 55.8% of the Huron River watershed. Forested lands comprised the next largest percentage of the watershed, covering 38 617 hectares or 16.4%, followed by non-forested cover (27 047 hectares, 11.5%), and wetlands (17 102 hectares, 7.3%). Urban cover comprised only 12 955 hectares of the Huron River drainage in 1938 or 5.5% of the watershed (Fig. 15.3a). Approximately 8576 hectares or 3.6% of the watershed was covered with water. As the watershed became increasingly urbanized between 1938 and 1996, the distribution of land use among land-cover categories changed dramatically (Table 15.1). The greatest absolute change was a reduction of more than 69 000 hectares of agricultural lands (53% loss since 1938) Fig. 15.4b). During the same

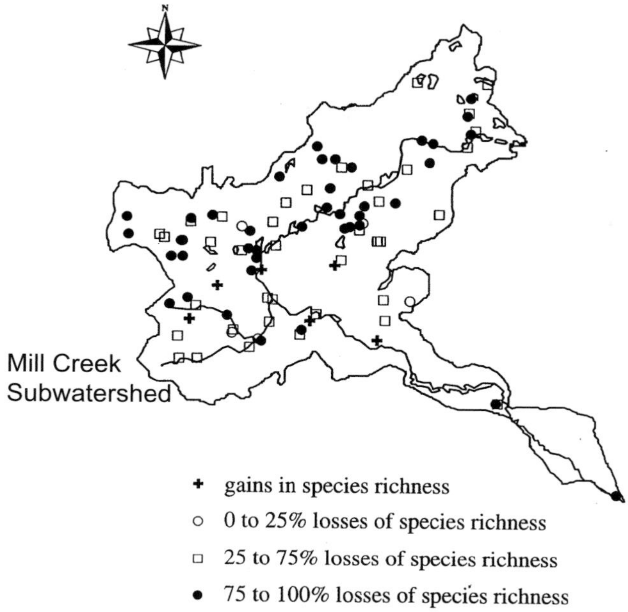

FIGURE 15.2
Percentage loss of fish species richness among sites sampled in 1938 and 1996 in the Huron River watershed.

time, urban land use increased by 51 159 hectares, nearly a four-fold increase since 1938 (Table 15.1, Fig. 15.3b). We observed the greatest concentration of increased urbanization radiating into the upper or northeastern portion and in the extreme southern arm of the watershed from the expanding Detroit metropolitan area (Fig. 15.3).

Coincident with changes in land use, numerous dams have been constructed throughout the watershed. Dam construction has been most intense, however, in the same regions of the watershed that have experienced the largest increase in urban land use. Dams are another facet of anthropogenic land-use change that potentially has a substantial impact on fish populations. Because of the overlapping patterns in land-use change and dam construction, it is difficult to separate the effects of dams from other changes in human land use in the Huron River watershed.

To gain insight as to how changes in land use within a watershed might affect the distribution and abundance of fishes, we conducted an intensive study of the mottled sculpin (*Cottus bairdi*) in the Huron River watershed. The mottled sculpin was an ideal species for our investigation because it has been documented to be sensitive to the types of habitat degradation caused by human development of the landscape (Whittier and Hughes, 1998), and it is not sought by anglers, removing the potentially confounding effects of harvest.

From 1938 to 1996, the distribution of mottled sculpin in the Huron River

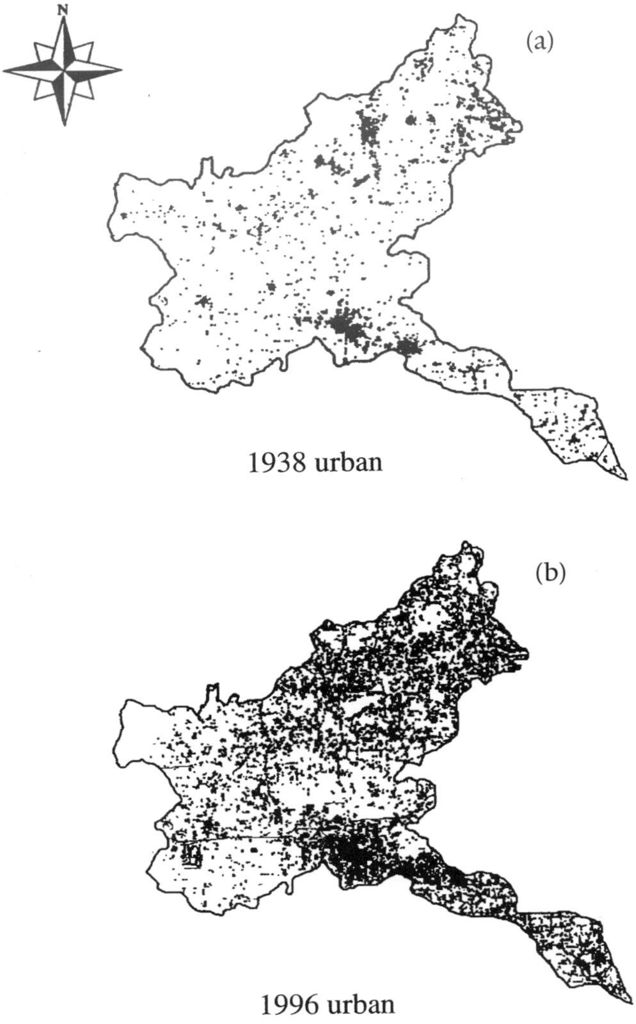

FIGURE 15.3
Change in urban land cover within the Huron River watershed between (a) 1938 and (b) 1996. Areas shaded in black are urban landcovers.

watershed was dramatically reduced. The most extensive losses occurred in areas of the watershed that have become urbanized since 1938, indicating that changes in land cover and dam construction are the primary agents of population decline for this species. However, a remnant population of mottled sculpin currently exists within the large Mill Creek sub-drainage of the Huron River watershed, where human disturbance has been minimal since 1938 and land cover remains dominated by agricultural activity (Fig. 15.4). The relative abundance and age composition of mottled sculpin among sites within the watershed where they do persist suggests strong source–sink dynamics (Pulliam, 1988; Schlosser, 1991, 1995) operating in this population. In general, sites near the core of the mottled sculpin's current distribution within the watershed

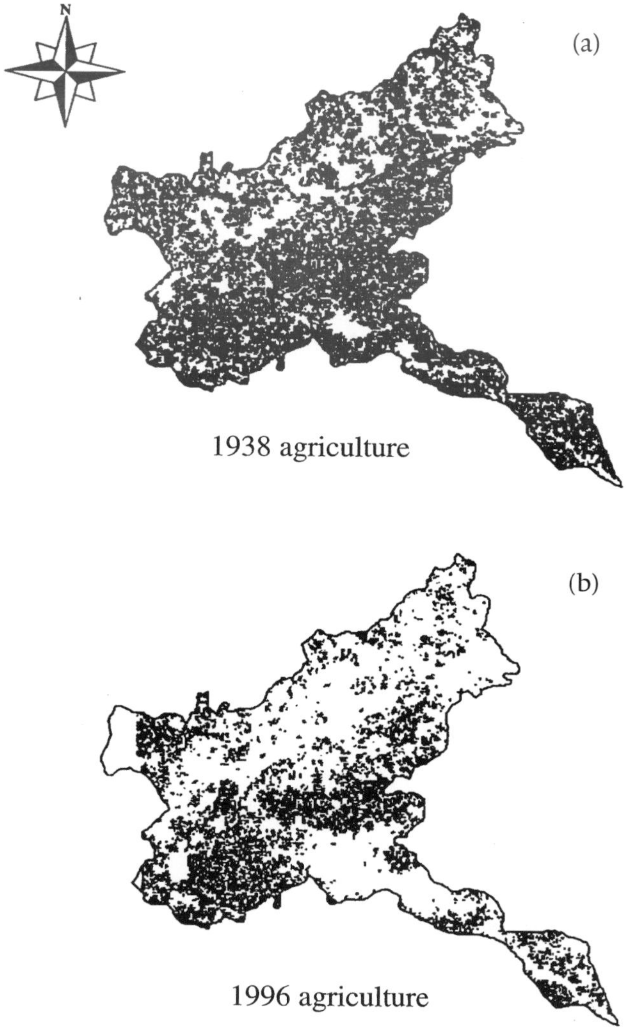

FIGURE 15.4
Change in agricultural land cover within the Huron River watershed between (a) 1938 and (b) 1996. Areas shaded in black are agricultural landcovers.

have higher abundance and more age groups present. Smaller and younger fish dominate sites near the periphery of the current distribution; it seems likely that reproduction at these sites may be insufficient to balance local mortality. Continual immigrations from sites (sources) at the core of the mottled sculpin distribution appear to support the population at peripheral sites (sinks).

The complexity of the mottled sculpin dynamics within the Huron River watershed not only requires an appreciation for the connection between terrestrial ecosystems and aquatic ecosystems, but also a landscape perspective of the population dynamics of the mottled sculpin themselves. Developers might be tempted to develop the Mill Creek drainage (the most undeveloped site within the watershed) in the future. Without a landscape perspective, it would be easy

Table 15.1. *Changes in land-cover types in the Huron River watershed, 1938–96*

Land-cover type	Hectares in 1938	Hectares in 1996	Net change
Urban/suburban	12955	64113	51159
Agriculture	131469	62094	−69375
Forested	38617	26814	−11803
Non-forested[a]	27047	42642	15595
Wetland	17102	29315	12213
Water	8576	10784	2208
Total	235765	235765	

Notes:

[a] Non-forested cover includes all herbaceous and shrub covered lands not in agricultural production.

for land managers and fishery managers to discount the importance of the Mill Creek drainage to the continued existence of the mottled sculpin throughout the Huron River watershed.

15.4 Moving towards a landscape approach: Chesapeake Bay case study

The Chesapeake Bay, located on the mid-Atlantic coast of North America, is the largest estuary in the United States. This complex system is approximately 320 km long, up to 50 km wide, and averages 6.4 m in depth. Its watershed spans 166000 km^2 and includes parts of six states (Delaware, Maryland, New York, Pennsylvania, Virginia, West Virginia) and the District of Columbia. The flora and fauna of the Chesapeake Bay region are highly diverse, with more than 2000 plants and animals having been identified (Lippson and Lippson, 1997). The Bay is renowned for its highly productive, multi-species fishery, worth in excess of $100 million annually (Miller *et al.*, 1996). The fisheries of the Chesapeake Bay highlight the importance of considering the spatial heterogeneity and connectivity of habitat patches (landscape elements), the impact terrestrial landscape management can have on efforts to manage productive fisheries, and the importance of incorporating socioeconomic concerns.

15.4.1 The Chesapeake Bay as a landscape

A significant feature of the Chesapeake Bay landscape is the spatial pattern of salinity. Unlike the ocean, where salinity levels vary little over very large areas, the waters of the Chesapeake Bay range from fresh waters at the head of the Bay, to brackish and moderately salty in the mid-Bay, to nearly full-strength seawater at the downstream end of the Bay (Lippson and Lippson, 1997). Although the salinity gradient moves up and down the Bay in response to the amount of fresh water input by tributaries, it is a persistent feature of the Bay. The wide range of salinities in the Chesapeake Bay means that it can provide suitable habitat for a wide variety of species, ranging from typical freshwater species in the upper reaches of the main channel to typical ocean species toward its mouth (Lippson and Lippson, 1997).

15.4.2 Fisheries production depends on the Chesapeake Bay landscape

The blue crab (*Callinectes sapidus*) fishery in the Chesapeake Bay is the largest single-species crab fishery worldwide in terms of annual harvest (Blue Crab Fishery Management Plan Workgroup, 1997). Of the commercial fisheries in the Bay, the blue crab has the highest value, and the recreational blue crab harvest is also important to the economy of the region. Productivity of the blue crab fishery in the Chesapeake Bay depends upon the salinity gradient present in the Chesapeake Bay. Larvae are released by mature females in high-salinity waters near the mouth of the Bay where they are transported to the continental shelf to develop for 30 – 45 days. Salinities in excess of 30 ppt are required for optimal development during this time. Postlarvae re-enter the lower Bay and settle in beds of submerged aquatic vegetation where they develop into juvenile crabs. After molting, large juveniles migrate out of the grass beds and move to lower-salinity areas in the lower tributaries and in the upper Bay. As the crabs grow, males and females segregate by habitat with large males occupying the upper reaches of tributaries and the Bay (low-salinity areas), and females remaining in the higher-salinity areas of the lower Bay and the lower reaches of tributaries. Mating occurs in mid-Bay reaches where salinity preferences of mature males and females overlap. After mating, males return to lower-salinity waters in the upper Bay, while females return to higher-salinity waters of the lower Bay where they develop an orange, external egg mass beneath their aprons. After hatching, the larvae are transported out to the continental shelf to begin the cycle once again. The blue crab has adapted to the heterogeneous environment defined by the persistent salinity gradient found in the Chesapeake Bay; during each phase of its life cycle, the blue crab uses a different portion of the Bay, depending on its salinity preference. Further, the connectivity between these areas of differing salinities is critical to the completion of the blue crab's life cycle. To manage the fishery effectively, fishery managers have had to learn to take into account how the crab moves throughout the Bay during its life cycle and how changes to the salinity gradient in the Bay might change the productivity of the fishery.

Unlike the blue crab that depends on the heterogeneous environment within the Bay, some species, such as the anadromous American shad (*Alosa sapidissima*) and the semianadromous striped bass (*Morone saxatilis*), rely on the connection provided by the Bay between the different habitats they occupy for spawning and feeding. American shad migrate from their feeding habitat in the Atlantic Ocean, through the waters of the Chesapeake Bay, to spawn in the fresh waters of the Susquehanna River. Striped bass migrate from the higher salinity waters of the lower Bay to spawn in the fresh waters of the tributaries to the upper Bay. The connection provided by the Bay between these two very different habitats for the American shad and the striped bass was the basis for two historically productive fisheries. The Maryland commercial catch of American shad often exceeded 2 million pounds (1 million kg) in the nineteenth century, making it the most important fishery of the Chesapeake Bay, and the Chesapeake Bay produced 90% of Atlantic coast striped bass. However, by the mid twentieth century, the abundance of both species had declined dramatically as a result of overfishing and habitat degradation. Major restoration efforts have focused on restoring the linkage between the spawning and feeding habitats that was disrupted as a result of dam construction and pollution. At this larger scale (including the Bay and its connecting waters), using a landscape approach has helped fishery managers to identify the importance of the connection between the two very different, and very critical, habitats for these species.

15.4.3 Activities in the watershed affect fisheries production

Although it is clear that fish production in the Bay is dependent on the landscape features and connections provided by the Bay itself, understanding the fluctuations in the fisheries of the Chesapeake Bay requires looking beyond the Bay and its tributaries to the Chesapeake Bay watershed – the physical landscape that supports the Bay, the land–water interface throughout that landscape, and the social setting of the Bay.

Since it was first settled in the seventeenth century, the Chesapeake Bay has been an important center of human population growth. As human density in the watershed increased, fishery harvest increased to meet demands and aquatic habitats began to show signs of degradation. Currently, over 15 million people live, work, and play in the Chesapeake Bay watershed using its terrestrial and aquatic resources to support many different activities (Reshetiloff, 1995; Schramm and Hubert, 1999). Some of these activities, such as the continuing growth in fishing effort, affected the Bay fisheries directly, leading to a long-term decline in yields. Other activities, such as increased agricultural activity and residential development in the watershed, led to increases in nutrient concentrations and sediments entering the Bay that led in turn to decreased fish production through habitat degradation. Increases in sediments and nutrients affected fish habitat in several ways; for example, excess sediments cause water clarity to be reduced and can silt in important spawning areas in rivers. At the same time, excess nutrients cause algal blooms that act in concert with decreased water clarity to keep light from reaching important aquatic grasses. Without sufficient light, the amount of aquatic grasses decreases, causing a decrease in the amount of food, shelter, and nursery grounds for aquatic species. In addition, excess nutrients and sediments have caused the water quality in the Bay to decline dramatically, creating areas that are hypoxic (low in dissolved oxygen) or anoxic (no dissolved oxygen) that cannot support aquatic life. Oysters and blue crabs declined in response to overharvest and habitat degradation (Reshetiloff, 1995; Schramm and Hubert, 1999).

Another activity that affected the productive capacity of the Bay was the building of dams across many of its tributaries. Dams were built to meet many different purposes such as providing hydropower, and providing water supplies for drinking or irrigation. Many of these dams impeded fish passage to historical spawning grounds, effectively severing the connection between important habitats provided by the Bay. The American shad, which had been the mainstay of the Susquehanna River fisheries, disappeared from the Susquehanna in the early twentieth century, just as four hydroelectric dams were built. And, by the early 1970s, striped bass were decreasing to dangerously low levels as a result of habitat degradation and loss of connectedness between critical habitats.

15.4.4 Developing solutions for the Chesapeake Bay fisheries

Activities in the watershed were clearly affecting the fisheries of the Chesapeake Bay in a negative fashion. However, it was not until the 1970s that agencies such as the US Environmental Protection Agency (EPA) began to realize that solutions to the problem of declining Chesapeake Bay fisheries would have to address broader issues than just the Bay and its tributaries. A major challenge to finding solutions at the level of landscapes or ecosystems was to coordinate efforts among the many governance units that had jurisdiction over some part of the Bay and its watershed (Schramm and Hubert, 1999).

The Chesapeake Bay Agreement was signed in 1987 by the EPA, District of Columbia, and the states sharing the Chesapeake Bay watershed. The agreement detailed coordinated management of the Bay, and activities within its watershed, to control point and non-point sources of pollution, manage human population growth in the watershed, restore living resources, and promote citizen participation in the restoration program. The results of this coordinated approach, which recognized the need to approach the problems of the Chesapeake Bay fisheries at a landscape level, have been very positive. As a result of the agreement, many actions have been taken to improve water quality. For example, wastewater treatment plants were installed or upgraded to include biological nutrient removal systems that led to reductions in phosphorus and nitrogen in the Bay. Changes in tillage practices were implemented on agricultural lands, and urban runoff was decreased, thereby reducing the amount of sediment that was deposited in the Bay. Improvements to fish passage have also become a priority along the Bay's tributaries, thereby improving access to habitats that were previously blocked by dams. The coordinated efforts have translated into improvements in fish habitat and production in the Bay. For example, aquatic vegetation has rebounded 70% from its lowest density in 1984 and 460 km of tributaries were reopened to passage of anadromous fishes. The striped bass population has increased dramatically, and the American shad is returning in larger numbers to the Susquehanna River (Schramm and Hubert, 1999). Without the coordinated effort of all of the jurisdictions involved and the realization that the fisheries of the Chesapeake Bay are embedded in a landscape where both terrestrial and aquatic ecosystems are important, recovery of the Chesapeake Bay fisheries would not be possible.

15.5 Incorporating landscape ecology into fishery management practices

Fishery management is often defined as the manipulation of people, aquatic populations and their habitat to achieve societal goals (Nielsen, 1999). Within this paradigm, how then does the emerging discipline of landscape ecology help fishery managers meet societal goals? Through the case studies presented in this chapter, we have tried to show how the concepts and tools of landscape ecology apply to freshwater and marine systems and how landscape processes affect the structure, function, and productivity of these systems. In closing this chapter, we discuss and speculate how landscape ecology concepts may be applied within a framework that many fishery managers operate within today.

Although fishery managers show a diversity of approaches to the task of managing fisheries, we feel that the most effective framework currently available is what has been termed the "eight steps of management" (Taylor *et al.*, 1995). In this framework, management starts with the development of a goal, proceeds through an evaluation of the resource and its limitations, follows with the development of specific objectives and management prescriptions designed to achieve the goal, and then finishes with the implementation of the management program, evaluation of the results, and maintenance of the program. Another key feature of this framework is that one can back track one or more steps if necessary. For example, if the examination of the resource's potential indicates that the goals are unattainable, then a new goal should be developed before proceeding onto developing objectives and management prescriptions.

Although the discipline of landscape ecology has much to offer to fishery managers, we feel that it does not fundamentally change the steps outlined above. A landscape perspective may be incorporated throughout much of the management process, however, and is likely to improve the effectiveness of resource managers. One of the critical points where a landscape ecology perspective enters into the management process is in the evaluation of the resource and its limitations. Throughout all of the case studies and examples we present, landscape factors clearly have an important influence on fish production. As such, managers need to take these landscape factors into account in their assessment of the suite of factors limiting production. A prime example of this need is that of the Chesapeake Bay blue crab, where an understanding of the importance of migration corridors is critical to the managers' understanding of factors limiting crab production.

Even with a clear understanding of the factors limiting fish production, fishery managers face the challenge of developing management actions to mitigate these limitations. As indicated above, the principal areas in which fishery managers act to achieve management objectives are the populations of aquatic organisms, the habitats provided within aquatic systems, and the people who use or otherwise affect the resource. For each of these areas, landscape ecology concepts and perspective are important as to the development of management prescriptions.

In the past, many of our population management actions have failed or had unanticipated consequences because we have not taken a landscape perspective. For example, early efforts at reducing the abundance of sea lamprey (*Petromyzon marinus*, an exotic parasite/predator on desirable sport and commercial fishes) in the Great Lakes effectively reduced the abundance of lamprey in individual rivers where larval lamprey reared, but were not effective at reducing their abundance in the Great Lakes as a whole. The present management effort has taken an integrated pest management approach to lamprey control, and in particular has focused on the spatial and temporal arrangement of sea lamprey source populations. Through this approach, sea lamprey abundance has been greatly reduced while minimizing the cost of the control program. We feel that this example illustrates how other programs involving the direct management of aquatic populations could benefit from a landscape approach. Fish-stocking programs, for example, could take into account the population structure of the target species by placing stocked fish where the likelihood of successful reproduction is highest. In too many cases, fishery managers have stocked fish focusing on individual lakes or sites within streams, without considering how the geographical distribution of stocked fish affects the success of the stocking program as a whole.

Another focal area for fishery managers is the aquatic habitat itself. An example of a typical management action is putting in structures, stones, or other material that serves as cover for fish. Often, however, these management actions to improve habitat are site-specific, and focus on in-stream or in-lake habitat. By focusing on the local scale habitat conditions, fishery managers often undertake "habitat improvements" in areas where there is insufficient juxtaposition and interspersion of "improved" habitat with other habitat elements that are critical to fish production. Moreover, such actions often do not take into account the underlying ecosystem or landscape processes that led to the present habitat conditions. The current evolution and future direction is to take management actions that take a landscape view whereby the location and timing of the in-stream actions take into account the surrounding landscape, including both terrestrial and upstream aquatic ecosystems. Terrestrial buffer zones where riparian vegetation is maintained is an example of where fishery managers have worked with terrestrial managers to take management actions to improve the habitat conditions for the production of desirable fish species. One limitation, however, is that many habitat limitations are the result of human activity on the terrestrial landscape and are often outside of the fishery manager's direct control. As our ability to understand the connectivity between the terrestrial and aquatic systems improves, we will improve our ability to target management actions to alter those human activities having the most impact within the watershed.

One of the hallmarks of landscape ecology is the view that people are an integral part of the ecological processes that affect system dynamics. Fishery managers have traditionally regulated fishers using methods such as seasonal closures, bag limits, and minimum size limits. When fishery management actions focus on regulating fishing activities, a landscape view may increase the effectiveness of these or similar regulations. For example, fishing seasons have historically been used to protect fish during their spawning season. While this action may be helpful, it may not be as efficient as creating a mosaic of seasonal/spatial closures that protect not only spawning fish but also important migration corridors where populations may be at substantial risk of overharvest.

15.6 Challenges to integrating landscape ecology into fishery management practices

Although it is clear that landscape concepts are indeed applicable to aquatic systems and that using these concepts can provide valuable insight into the structure and function of fish communities, fisheries management has yet to develop a way to easily integrate landscape concepts into the management of our fishery resources. The conventional natural resource management agency is typically structured along commodity group divisions. For example, the Michigan Department of Natural Resources presently contains a Fisheries Division, Wildlife Division, Forest Management Division, Parks and Recreation Division, and Land and Mineral Services Division, each responsible for different aspects of natural resource management. Although the Michigan Department of Natural Resources is developing management plans that cut across the internal divisions, its present configuration is typical of most resource management agencies. A critical problem with this arrangement is that it often leads to internal conflicts when each group tries to maximize the value of the commodities or benefits related to the resources under its jurisdiction. Because of the need to take a landscape view of resource management and to recognize the connection among different segments of the landscape, management plans can no longer be developed through the isolated efforts of segregated managers. Managers of fisheries and aquatic ecosystems must look at the landscape context in which a resource is embedded. Further, aquatic resource managers need to look beyond the water's edge as many of the threats to aquatic resources lie beyond the banks of the lake or river.

In addition to integrating landscape concepts into the management of fishery resources, we need to better understand the wide range of anthropogenic systems and processes that have frequently been acknowledged, but which have been difficult to incorporate into fishery management. Because of the substantial impact that human activities on the land can have on aquatic habitat conditions, it is becoming increasingly important to develop ways of altering people's actions that affect aquatic habitats and their productivity. This is a challenge because the economic system shapes the patterns of distribution, accumulation, investment, and incentive in a social system (Costanza *et al.*, 1991). Perhaps most importantly, resource management goals are directly and indirectly influenced by the regional economic system (Krueger and Decker, 1999). In a fishery, for example, high demand for certain species or recreational opportunities will increase the perceived value of these options, which will often result in management plans based on enhancing the desired species or experiences. Because economic goals often emphasize short-term maximization of profits and other benefits, resource managers must make sure that management goals are accompanied by an adequately long time horizon (Costanza *et al.*, 1991) that conforms to an ecological temporal scale on the order of decades. Managers also need to be able to identify the economic driving force behind management goals and be able to analyze the justifications and ecological constraints for these goals. Cost–benefit analyses of different management goals and alternatives will: (1) help determine the feasibility of certain management goals and activities, and (2) help justify the selected management alternative as being economically efficient. While government management agencies do not necessarily have to maximize profits like a private business, they do need to make the most of scarce management resources (often under severely restrictive budgets). Considering the importance of the regional economic system in resource management, a resource/ecological economist should be included in the processes of examining the resource, identifying interactions among systems, refining the goals, identifying criteria and indicators of success, and monitoring and evaluating management plans.

Political aspects of the social system also present challenges to adopting a landscape approach to management. In the United States, resource managers generally work under the Public Trust Doctrine, with responsibility for managing resources in the best interest of all citizens, current and future. This responsibility should be a fundamental consideration in determining management goals, although it is possible for other motives (financial or political) to affect goal formation. It is important to recognize, however, that many fishery resources span political boundaries, each of which may have fundamentally different cultural views on the role of resource managers and the applicability of the Public Trust Doctrine.

A final impediment to implementing true landscape management is the jungle of jurisdictions that constrain the actions that single agencies or even partnerships among agencies can take (Ferreri *et al.*, 1999). For example, even if we fully understood the impacts of changing land cover and land use on fish populations, fishery managers alone are not empowered to restrict land development. The ability to determine acceptable land-use practices and forms of development are generally widely dispersed among township planning boards (with provisions for appeals and variances on a case-by-case basis at the township level) and scattered among various state agencies (e.g., county drain commissioners can alter the drainage pattern of a watershed with a large degree of independence). In the Great Lakes basin, for example, the system of governance includes over 650 local to international jurisdictional units (Caldwell, 1994), all of which have some say in the management of land and water resources that can affect fish production and fisheries. In our Chesapeake Bay example, it took the coordination of multiple state and municipal governments, the federal government, and the support of the 15 million residents living in the Bay watershed to begin making progress towards rehabilitation of its fisheries (Schramm and Hubert, 1999).

15.7 Summary

Fisheries management generally seeks to provide sustained and increasing benefits to society from the use of aquatic living resources. Challenges to achieving this goal have become more complex through time as human population growth has placed increasing demands on natural resources to provide an ever widening array of benefits. Historically, fisheries management focused on management of single species within a particular stream reach or bay of a lake. The introduction of concepts such as watershed management and ecosystem management have caused fishery managers to become increasingly aware that managing productive fisheries requires a much broader perspective. Landscape ecology can provide the basis for this broader perspective. Just as the extent and spatial arrangement of terrestrial habitats influences the productivity of terrestrial systems, aquatic productivity is also influenced by the arrangement of habitats. Further, activities in the terrestrial landscape can have a profound effect on the aquatic landscape, and thus the habitat of aquatic organisms.

Although it has been long accepted that managing for productive habitats leads to productive fisheries, incorporating this concept into fishery management plans has only recently begun. In part, this lag is due to the fact that most fishery managers are not empowered to manipulate many of the things that affect fish habitat; decisions of land use and water use are embedded within anthropogenic systems that are generally outside of the fishery manager's jurisdiction. The challenge to fisheries management, then, is to somehow incorporate the influence of aquatic and terrestrial landscapes and the social setting into a management system that enables managers to provide benefits to society from aquatic living resources.

Our proposed fishery management framework sets forth an ambitious plan for integrating multiple landscape elements into a single, comprehensive management plan. One of the advantages of a landscape approach to understanding and managing natural resources is that this allows us to use one common management framework that incorporates expertise from multiple disciplines and perspectives throughout the landscape (as opposed to a separate ecological plan, a social plan, an economic plan, etc.). Further, a landscape approach allows us to be adaptable to various temporal and spatial scales. We acknowledge that perfect knowledge of all of these landscape elements is unattainable; nevertheless, management planners need to be as inclusive as possible. The keys to successful application of this framework lie in: (1) its adaptability to various management goals, scales, and regional landscape conditions and (2) its multi-disciplinary collaboration through the inclusion of numerous systems experts. This framework does not provide a formula or definitive answer to management issues, but provides the essential basis for creating effective management plans that link people, land, and water together in a sustainable environment.

References

Aguero, M. & Gonzalez, E. (1996). *Managing Transboundary Stocks of Small Pelagic Fish: Problems and Options*. World Bank Discussion Paper No. 329. The World Bank, Washington, D.C.

Aguero, M. & Zuleta, A. (1994). Management options for transboundary stocks: the Peruvian-Chilean pelagic fishery. In *Managing Fishery Resources*, World Bank Discussion Paper no. 217, ed. E. A. Loayza, pp. 66–78. The World Bank, Washington, D.C.

Blue Crab Fishery Management Plan Workgroup (1997). *1997 Chesapeake Bay Blue Crab Fishery Management Plan,* Chesapeake Bay Program, EPA 903–R-97–015, CBP/TRS 175/97. US EPA Program 3, Chesapeake Bay Program Office, Annapolis, MD.

Brown, C. J. D. & Funk, J. L. (1945). *A Fisheries Survey of the Huron River, its Tributaries and Impounded Waters*. Fisheries Research Report no. 1003. Michigan Department of Natural Resources, Ann Arbor, MI.

Caldwell, L. K. (1994). Disharmony in the Great Lakes basin: Institutional jurisdictions frustrate the ecosystem approach. *Alternatives*, 20: 26–32.

Costanza, R., Daly, H. E. & Bartholomew, J. A. (1991). Goals, agenda, and policy recommendations for ecological economics. In *Ecological Economics: The Science and Management of Sustainability*, ed. R. Costanza, pp. 1–20. Columbia University Press, New York.

Ferreri, C. P., Taylor, W. W. & Robertson, J. M. (1999). Great Lakes fisheries futures: Balancing the demands of a multijurisdictional resource. In *Great Lakes Fisheries Policy and Management: A Binational Perspective*, eds. W.W. Taylor & C. P. Ferreri, pp. 539–548. Michigan State University Press, East Lansing, MI.

Grossman, G. D., Hill, J. & Petty, J. T. (1995). Observations on habitat structure, population regulation, and habitat use with respect to evolutionary significant units: A landscape perspective for lotic systems. *American Fisheries Society Symposium*, 17: 381–391.

Hay-Chmielewski, E. M., Seelbach, P. W., Whelan, G. E. & Jester, D. B. Jr. (1995). *Huron River Assessment*. Fisheries Division Special Report no. 16, Michigan Department of Natural Resources, Lansing, MI.

Hynes, H. B. N. (1970). *The Ecology of Running Waters*. University of Toronto Press, Toronto, Canada.

Johnson, L. B., & Gage S. H. (1997). Landscape approaches to the analysis of aquatic ecosystems. *Freshwater Biology,* 37: 113–132.

Junk, W. J., Bayley, P. B. & Sparks, R. E. (1989). The flood pulse concept in river–floodplain systems. In *Proceedings of the International Large River Symposium*, Canadian Special Publication in Fisheries and Aquatic Sciences 106, ed. D. P. Dodge, pp. 110–127. Department of Fisheries and Oceans, Ottawa, Canada.

Kocik, J. F. & Ferreri, C. P. (1998) Juvenile production variation in salmonids: Population dynamics, habitat, and the role of spatial relationships. *Canadian Journal of Fisheries and Aquatic Sciences*, 55(Suppl. 1): 191–200.

Krueger, C. C. & Decker, D. J. (1999). The process of fisheries management. In *Inland Fisheries Management in North America,* 2nd edn, eds. C. C. Kohler & W. A. Hubert, pp. 31–60. American Fisheries Society, Bethesda, MD.

Lippson, A. J. & Lippson, R. L. (1997). *Life in the Chesapeake Bay,* 2nd edn. Johns Hopkins University Press, Baltimore, MD.

Magnuson, J. J., Tonn, W. M., Banerjee, A., Toivonen, J., Sanchez, O. & Rask, M. (1998). Isolation vs. extinction in the assembly of fishes in small northern lakes. *Ecology*, 79: 2941–2956.

McPhaden, M. J. (1993). TOGA-TAO and the 1991–93 El Niño–Southern Oscillation Event. *Oceanography*, 6: 36–44.

Mesinas, A. G. (1994). Fishery management in Peru. In *Managing Fishery Resources*, World Bank Discussion Paper no. 217, ed. E. A. Loayza, pp. 79–90. The World Bank, Washington, D.C.

Miller, T. J., Houde, E. D. & Watkins, E. J. (1996). *Chesapeake Bay Fisheries: Prospects for Multispecies Management and Sustainability*. Chesapeake Bay Program, Annapolis, MD.

Newman, K. R., Hayes, D. B. & Taylor, W. W. (1999). The effect of urbanization on fish community structure in a large Michigan watershed. In *Proceedings of the Wakefield Symposium: ecosystem considerations in Fisheries Management*, pp. 467–479. AK-SG-99–01, Alaska Sea Grant College Program, Anchorage, AK.

Nielsen, L. A. (1999). History of inland fisheries management in North America. In *Inland Fisheries Management in North America,* eds. C.C. Kohler & W.A. Hubert, pp. 3–30. American Fisheries Society, Bethesda, MD.

Noble, R. L., Jackson, J. R., Irwin, E. R., Phillips, J. M. & Churchill, J. N. (1994). Reservoirs as landscapes: Implications for fish stocking programs. *Transactions of the 59th North American Wildlife and Natural Resources Conference*, 281–288.

Pickett, S.T.A. & Cadenasso, M. L. (1995). Landscape ecology: Spatial heterogeneity in ecological systems. *Science*, 269: 331–334.

Poff, N. L., Allan, J. D., Bain, M. B., Karr, J. R., Prestegaard, K. L., Richter, R. D., Sparks, R. E. & Stromberg, J.C. (1997). The natural flow regime: A paradigm for river conservation and restoration. *BioScience*, 47: 769–783.

Pulliam, H. R. (1988). Sources, sinks, and population regulation. *American Naturalist*, 132: 652–661.

Rabeni, C. F. (1992). Habitat evaluation in a watershed context. *American Fisheries Society Symposium*, 13: 57–67.

Reshetiloff, K. (ed). (1995). *Chesapeake Bay: Introduction to an Ecosystem*. Chesapeake Bay Program, Annapolis, MD.

Roedel, P. M. (1975). A summary and critique of the symposium on optimum sustainable yield. In *Optimum Sustainable Yield as a Concept in Fisheries Management*, ed. P.M. Roedel, pp. 79–89. American Fisheries Society, Bethesda, MD.

Ryther, J. H. (1969). Photosynthesis and fish production in the sea. *Science*, 166: 72–76.

Schlosser, I. J. (1991). Stream fish ecology: A landscape perspective. *BioScience,* 41: 704–712.

Schlosser, I. J. (1995). Critical landscape attributes that influence fish population dynamics in headwater streams. *Hydrobiologia,* 303: 71–81.

Schlosser, I. J. & Angermeier, P. L. (1995). Spatial variation in demographic processes of lotic fishes: conceptual models, empirical evidence, and implications for conservation. *American Fisheries Society Symposium*, 17: 392–401.

Schramm, H. L. & Hubert, W. A. (1999). Ecosystem management. In *Inland Fisheries Management in North America,* eds. C. C. Kohler & W. A. Hubert, pp. 111–123. American Fisheries Society, Bethesda, MD.

Taylor, W. W., Ferreri, C. P., Poston, F. L. & Robertson, J. M. (1995). Educating fisheries professionals using a watershed approach to emphasize the ecosystem paradigm. *Fisheries*, 20: 6–9.

Thomas, J. W., Black, H., Scherzinger, R. J., & Petersen, R. J. (1979). Deer and elk. In *Wildlife Habitats in Managed Forests, the Blue Mountains of Oregon and Washington*, US Department of Agriculture Forest Service Agriculture Handbook no. 553, ed. J. W. Thomas, pp. 104–127. US Department of Agriculture Forest Service Pacific Northwest Forest and Range Experiment Station, Portland, OR.

Turner, M. G. & Gardner, R. H. (eds.) (1991). *Quantitative Methods in Landscape Ecology*. Springer-Verglag, New York.

Vannote, R. L., Minshall, W. G., Cummins, K. W., Sedell, J. R. & Cushing, C. E. (1980). The river continuum concept. *Canadian Journal of Fisheries and Aquatic Science*, 37: 130–137.

Whittier, T. R. & Hughes, R. M. (1998). Evaluation of fish species tolerances to environmental stressors in lakes in the northeastern United States. *North American Journal of Fisheries Management*, 18: 236–252.

Willis, D. W. & Murphy, B. R. (1996). Planning for sampling. In *Fisheries Techniques,* 2nd edn, eds. B. R. Murphy & D. W. Willis, pp. 1–16. American Fisheries Society, Bethesda, MD.

16

Applications of advanced technologies in studying and managing grassland landscape integrity

16.1 Introduction

Grasslands occupy large fractions of every continent except Antarctica (Knapp *et al.*, 1998). In the United States, the Great Plains are generally divided into three regions: short-grass steppe in the west, mixed-grass in the center, and tallgrass prairie to the east (Reichman, 1987). The tallgrass prairie once stretched from central Canada to the Texas Gulf Coast and from eastern Kansas into Indiana. While large tracts of short- and mixed-grass grasslands still exist throughout the western Great Plains, it is estimated that 95.9% of the tallgrass prairie has been lost to agriculture. Illinois, Indiana, Iowa, North Dakota, and Wisconsin have lost 99.9% of their original tallgrass prairie (Samson and Knopf, 1994). The only extensive tract of tallgrass prairie that remains is the Flint Hills region of eastern Kansas, on the western, drier edge of the tallgrass prairie (Knapp *et al.*, 1998) (Fig. 16.1).

Today, the tallgrass prairie is highly fragmented. Outside of the Flint Hills region, most prairies are remnants, often found in old cemeteries or railroad rights-of-way (Betz and Lamp, 1988). These prairies are often smaller than a hectare and usually isolated by tens of kilometers from the nearest remnant. The regional landscape of the tallgrass prairie region today is dominated by row-crop agriculture.

Grasslands provide multiple challenges to natural resource managers. Grasslands are often a complex mosaic of private, state, and federal land ownership. Land cover can consist of native or introduced (brome and fescue) species, small forests or woodlots, and agricultural crops. Land use can consist of grazing by livestock, row-cropping, and more recently residential development. Within these land uses, pastures may be stocked at different intensities and burned at different intervals or agricultural areas may be planted to different crops. Taken together, grasslands are very complex at the regional level

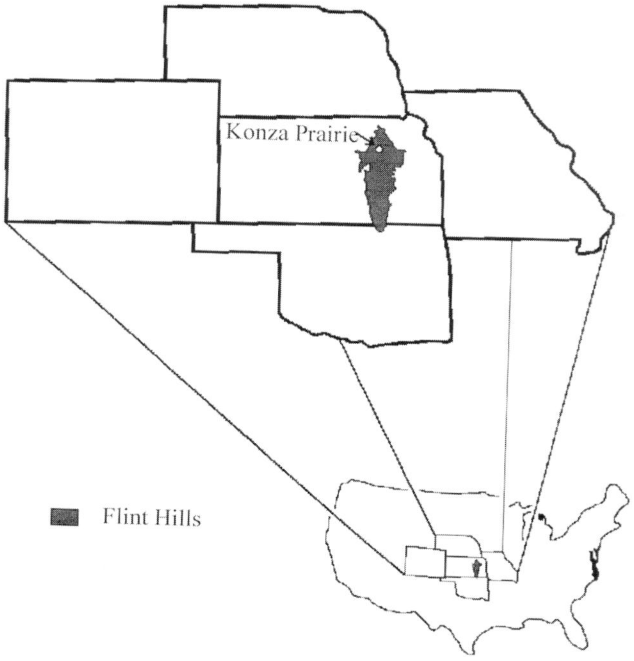

FIGURE 16.1
Location of the Flint Hills region and Konza Prairie Research Natural Area in eastern Kansas. While greater than 95% of the historic tallgrass region has been converted to agricultural use, the Flint Hills region represents the last expanse of tallgrass prairie in the United States. From Knapp and Seastedt (1998).

(Fig. 16.2, color plate) and provide multiple challenges to natural resource managers. Because of this complex mosaic of land use and land cover, remote sensing and geographic information systems (GIS) are ideal tools for studying grasslands at landscape and regional scales.

This chapter will focus on applications of remote sensing and GIS to three issues relating to grassland landscape integrity faced by land managers working in grasslands. These issues include (1) monitoring the annual aboveground net primary production (ANPP) and variability in ANPP of these ecosystems, (2) assessing the encroachment of woody species into grasslands, and (3) predicting the grazing distribution across the landscape. The monitoring of grassland productivity (Paruelo *et al.*, 1997; Tieszen *et al.*, 1997) and land cover (Belward *et al.*, 1999) is critical to both global change research and monitoring the economic sustainability of land-use practices, especially grazing. Monitoring grasslands and the ecotones, or transitional areas, between grasslands and forests or deserts may give us some of the first indicators of global climate change such as changes in temperature or precipitation patterns. These indicators may include shifts in dominance from one species or vegetation type to another, changing boundaries between grasslands and forest or desert biomes, or changes in land-use practices along these ecotones (Dale, 1997). Monitoring the encroachment of woody species into grasslands is important for the reasons mentioned above. However, woody encroachment into grasslands also reduces forage for livestock with potentially dramatic consequences for the economic sustainability of some areas (Ortmann *et al.*, 1999). It also eliminates habitat for grassland endemic species, many of which are already classified as threatened or endangered, especially birds (Knopf, 1996). By monitoring and manipulating the distribution of grazers, such as bison (*Bos bison*) and cattle (*B. taurus*), across the landscape, managers can maximize the economic returns of the livestock industry and provide guidelines for grazing management in wildlife preserves. Grazers can potentially be used as a tool to preserve and restore the ecological integrity of grassland ecosystems (Stohlgren, 2000). We will examine how tools such as satellite remote sensing, GIS, and global positioning systems (GPS) can be used to examine "old" questions and how these tools will allow us to address questions that we previously would not have been able to.

16.2 Overview of advanced technologies

Remote sensing, GIS, and GPS have emerged as the tools most often used by researchers interested in examining landscape or regional scale processes and patterns. There are several advantages in using these techniques over traditional ecological data collection methods. Traditionally, most ecological research has been conducted at the scale of 1-m^2 plots (Brown and Roughgarden, 1990). Remote sensing allows researchers to scale-up plot-level measurement and gather continuous data over large regions, even globally (Belward *et al.*, 1999). These data can be collected throughout the growing season and across years, which is costly and time-consuming using traditional field-based methods. A brief survey of the literature demonstrating the types of sensors used and regions where this technology has been applied to monitor ANPP is shown in Table 16.1. GIS is used to integrate data collected from multiple sources (e.g., remote sensing, GPS, field data) for analysis at a variety of scales. Further, GIS provides powerful analytical tools that can be used for resource inventory or to explore complex relationships among landscape features. GPS is often used in natural resource management as a surveying and mapping aid. Data collected with a GPS is easily incorporated into GIS. Used in combination, these technologies offer natural resource professionals unprecedented power in collection, processing, and analysis of spatially explicit data at landscape scales.

16.2.1 Remote sensing

By its simplest definition, remote sensing is collecting data from the earth by recording the electromagnetic radiation reflected or emitted from its

Table 16.1. *A brief survey of types of remote sensors used to monitor annual aboveground net primary production (ANPP) in grasslands. In all studies, grassland biomass was harvested in the field and these values were related to spectral characteristics of the area. The strength of the relationship is shown in the last column*

Author	Year	Location[a]	Scale	Sensor[b]	Ground methods[c]	Comparison[d]	r^2
Tucker *et al.*	1985	Sahel	Regional	AVHRR	Clip/visual assess	NDVI–I biomass	0.64–0.69
Everitt *et al.*	1986	TX, USA	1.1 ha	Aerial video	Clip	biomass–band ratios	0.58–0.88
Weiser *et al.*	1986	KS, USA	36 km^2	Radiometer	Clip	greenness/LAI/ANPP	0.59–0.97
Briggs & Nellis	1989	KS, USA	36 km^2	TM	Clip	TM1(blue)–biomass	0.79
Wylie *et al.*	1991	Niger	Regional	AVHRR	Clip/visual assess	NDVI-I–biomass	0.60–.91
Anderson *et al.*	1993	CO,USA	42 km^2	TM	Clip	NDVI–biomass	0.71–.95
Friedel *et al.*	1994	KS, USA	36 km^2	TM	Clip/LAI	greenness–LAI	0.42–0.68
Wellens	1997	Tunisia	Regional	AVHRR	Clip/point–intercept	NDVI–transpiration	0.56
Paruelo *et al.*	1997	CGR, USA	Regional	AVHRR	NRCS site description	NDVI-I–ANPP	0.89–0.93

Notes:

[a] CGR, Central Grassland Region; KS, Kansas; CO, Colorado; TX, Texas; Sahel, Senegalese Sahel. [b] AVHRR, Advanced Very High Resolution Radiometer; TM, Thematic Mapper; [c] NRCS, Natural Resource Conservation Service; LAI, Leaf Area Index. [d] NDVI, Normalized Difference Vegetation Index; NDVI-I, NDVI Integrated over growing season.

surface. These data can then be processed, manually or by computers, and interpreted. The data are useful for mapping land-cover types (Belward *et al.*, 1999), quantifying landscape patterns (Nellis and Briggs, 1989), or measuring ecological parameters such as productivity over large areas (Burke *et al.*, 1991).

Most remote sensing data are images captured from airplanes or satellites. Examples include the gray-scale photos taken each decade by the US Department of Agriculture. These are available beginning in the 1930s for some areas and are useful for examining long-term land-cover change (Nystrom-Mast *et al.*, 1997). More recently Digital Ortho Quadrangle (DOQ) images are available for much of the United States. These are high resolution (1-m^2 pixel) gray-scale images that are rectified to a common coordinate system. These images provide excellent base layers for developing GIS projects. The US Landsat program has produced images from its Multi-Spectral Scanner (MSS) platforms since the mid-1970s and Thematic Mapper (TM) platforms since the 1980s (Jensen, 1996). For large (continental) scale studies the Advanced Very High Resolution Radiometer (AVHRR) is frequently used (DeFries *et al.*, 1995). In 1999 the Landsat-7 and IKONOS sensors were successfully placed in orbit and, with their increased spatial resolution, will provide exciting new avenues of research over the coming years.

Satellites record data in discrete wavelengths, or bands, of the electromagnetic spectrum. By studying these bands individually or together, inferences can be made about the characteristics of the land surface. One of the most common indices for ANPP is the normalized difference vegetation index (NDVI). NDVI is a ratio of near-infrared (NIR) to red wavelength light. Specifically, NDVI = (NIR − red) / (NIR + red) and varies from −1.0 to +1.0 with positive values indicative of actively photosynthesizing vegetation (Box *et al.*, 1989). This scale, −1 to +1, is often converted to 8-bit data (0–255) for analysis. Grasslands are ideal for using remote sensing to monitor ANPP. In desert ecosystems, NDVI may be strongly influenced by reflectance from the soil. In forested ecosystems the NDVI–ANPP relationship can become saturated (Box *et al.*, 1989). Estimation of aboveground biomass in tallgrass prairie is facilitated by the fact that the canopies are simple in structure, with much of the aboveground biomass contributing directly to reflectance. In addition, biomass production is a cumulative process within a single season, with peak green biomass roughly equivalent to ANPP in ungrazed areas (Briggs and Knapp, 1995). In most years, peak biomass, or ANPP, in tallgrass prairie occurs in August or early September. Samples of vegetation are clipped from across the landscape to obtain a direct measure of biomass per unit area. The values are then related to reflectance values using regression models. Using these models ANPP can then be calculated across the entire landscape. For these reasons, satellite data derived from reflectance characteristics of the vegetation have proven to be valuable tools in the study of ecological processes at the landscape scale (Nellis and Briggs, 1989).

In addition to calculating ANPP, remote sensing data are often used to examine broad-scale patterns. Knapp *et al.* (1999) used texture analysis of Landsat TM imagery to demonstrate that grazing imparts greater heterogeneity with respect to standing crop. This was done by comparing grazed sites with adjacent ungrazed sites in Kansas. Remote sensing data have also been used to determine the spatial pattern of grazing intensity in Australian rangelands (Pickup and Bastin, 1997) and to assess habitat for wildlife species in western North American grasslands (Homer *et al.*, 1993). These data could be used to manage wildlife habitat, calculate livestock stocking rates, and help with economic forecasting, especially in underdeveloped regions (Li *et al.*, 1998).

Remote sensing is a useful tool but there are several cautions to using the data. Most analyses require specialized software and data acquisition can be costly. Landsat Thematic Mapper imagery currently costs anywhere from \$400 to \$2400/scene. For many analyses, such as some land-cover classification or monitoring green-up and senescence rates, multiple scenes from different points in the growing season will need to be purchased (Wolter *et al.*, 1995). Landsat images are only available every 16 days, assuming no cloud cover. Some years there may be clouds in almost every scene. Thus it may be difficult to time the date of the satellite image with the measurements taken in the field or the process being studied.

16.2.2 Geographic information systems

Geographic information systems (GISs) are computer-based packages of software and hardware used for the collection, storage, manipulation, and analysis of spatially explicit (associated with a known geographical location) data. Until the 1960s, these data were stored in the form of hardcopy maps. Analysis and integration of data stored on hardcopy maps was cumbersome. Integration of information contained on multiple maps normally required printing the maps on transparent overlays. Qualitative analysis was achieved through visual inspection of the resulting overlays. These techniques worked well for analyzing small amounts of data but became impractical when large data sets or complex questions were involved. As sufficiently powerful digital computers became available, the modern GIS was born.

The first computer-operated GISs, the Canada Geographic Information System, sponsored by the government of Canada, and the Land Use and Natural Resources Inventory of New York State, sponsored by the state of New York, were developed in the 1960s and early 1970s (Aronoff, 1993). In 1981 Environmental Systems Research Institute, Inc. (ESRI) introduced Arc/Info, a full-featured GIS still widely used today. A year later, development of the

Geographic Resources Analysis Support System (GRASS) was started by the US Army Construction Engineering Research Laboratories (CERL). GRASS is a public domain GIS still in use by government agencies and others. By the late 1980s and early 1990s, desktop GIS packages appeared with the introduction of software such as MapInfo and ArcView.

Over the past decade, development and use of GIS has continued to expand at a rapid pace. Today GIS is used in a large number of diverse applications such as municipal planning, emergency response, and natural resource management. Recognizing the potential importance of GIS technologies in scientific research in the year 2010, the National Science Foundation held a workshop in 1999 to "assess the needs for basic research in this [GIS] emerging science and technology field" (National Science Foundation, 1999). Recommendations presented by the workshop participants included that "the National Science Foundation should recognize the importance of Geographic Information Science as a coherent research field, and should focus a funding activity in this area as soon as possible." The workshop panel also identified three common barriers to current use of GIS. These were: interoperability, dimensionality and temporality, and the ease-of-use barrier. Interoperability is the ability to integrate GIS into other information technologies. Current GISs are often difficult or impossible to integrate with other research tools such as sensor processing or analysis software. Dimensionality and temporality addresses the ability of a GIS to incorporate multiple spatial dimensions and time. The ability to analyze geographic phenomena in three spatial dimensions plus time needs to be enhanced to provide better statistical and mathematical tools for GIS analysis. The ease-of-use barrier determines the extent of training required to use GIS software. Many current GIS packages are not easy to use and require extensive training. Easier-to-use software would speed the adoption of GIS technologies into research programs. Future National Science Foundation support for GIS will likely address these issues. For the natural resource professional, this means that improved technology should provide GIS that is easier to use and requires less training and integrates more easily with other software and data formats. Additionally, data will be available that are updated at appropriate intervals, produced at appropriate scales, and will include adequate documentation. GIS is used to integrate and analyze both raster (cell-based) and vector (coordinate-based) data. This is usually accomplished through a variety of overlay techniques. For a complete description of GIS methodologies and techniques, readers should consult one of the many textbooks devoted to the subject (e.g., Environmental Systems Research Institute, 1997). Once data are appropriately integrated into a GIS, a wide variety of analyses may be performed. These can range from simple calculations of area or distance to relatively complex measurements of landscape pattern (Gustafson, 1998; Riera *et al.*, 1998). For example, a manager could use GIS to easily calculate the area impacted by a wildfire or the average distance an animal must travel to reach a suitable habitat patch. At the other end of the spectrum, a manager may be interested in characterizing the pattern of a habitat type across the landscape (Fahrig, 1991). Are habitat patches clustered or dispersed? How connected are areas of habitat with one another? Is the habitat pattern determined by some other landscape feature(s)? Finally, GIS can be used to organize and process data to produce tabular data that can be analyzed using traditional statistical and/or modeling techniques. Because of the flexibility GIS offers for integrating large volumes of data from a variety of sources, its role as a tool for natural resources management continues to expand.

The level of training required to implement GIS for management decisions varies depending on the intended use. Using desktop GIS, personnel may be trained to perform simple map displays and queries in a few hours. However, development of data layers or sophisticated analyses using GIS requires extensive training to insure accurate results. Additionally, programming skills are usually required to extract the full potential of GIS. However, an increasing number of tools are available (many at no cost) that perform sophisticated analyses using "point and click" interfaces. This eliminates much of the need for programming but not the need for adequate training to assure the tools are applied appropriately.

16.2.3 Global positioning systems

Global positioning systems (GPSs) are constellations of satellites used for navigation and obtaining accurate measurement of locations on earth. As of the year 2000, there are two such constellations of satellites in operation. The Russian-owned GLONASS is similar to NAVSTAR (Navigation Satellite Timing and Ranging) which is owned by the US government and managed by the Department of Defense. This chapter will only discuss NAVSTAR and any reference to GPS refers to the NAVSTAR system. The GPS program was created by the Department of Defense in 1973 with the first satellite launched in 1978. The system became fully operational in 1995 with a constellation of 24 satellites which provide 24-hour service allowing receivers the ability to obtain information from a minimum of five satellites from any location on earth.

Positional accuracy obtained with GPS depends on the equipment used to receive the satellite data and the techniques used to correct errors. The NAVSTAR system formerly provided two types of service: Standard Positioning Service (SPS) and Precise Positioning Service (PPS). PPS provided greater accuracy (at least 22 m) but was strictly controlled by the US government and not available for civilian use. As of May 1, 2000, selective availability

(SA) was discontinued. The removal of SA increased the accuracy of SPS GPS receivers from *c.* 100 m to *c.* 10–30 m. However, with the aid of differential correction, SPS receivers can obtain positional accuracy as fine as a few centimeters. Differential correction can be performed in "real time" or through post-processing. In real-time correction, a base station receiver is positioned at a known location and broadcasts correction information to roving receivers. Roving receivers apply these corrections "on the fly" to provide nearly instantaneous display of corrected positions. Post-processing is similar except that the correction information from the base station is downloaded for computer processing at a later time rather than broadcast directly to the roving receivers. Numerous base stations are operated by both government and private entities around the globe. Many of these stations offer free downloads of correction files via the Internet. In addition, both satellite-based and radio-based real-time differential correction services are available. In the United States, the US Coast Guard and the US Army Corps of Engineers are constructing a network of radio beacons for real-time differential correction. This network is projected to provide free service for the entire continental United States by the end of 2000.

GPS is widely used in natural resource management for mapping, data collection, and navigation. Typical applications include mapping the boundaries of resource patches, recording the locations of data collection sites, or navigating to establish sampling locations for repeated sampling. Animal-borne GPS collars offer natural resource managers the potential to collect data about animal movements at higher spatial and temporal resolution per unit manpower than typically obtained using traditional radio telemetry (Cohn, 1999). GPS data are easily incorporated into a GIS where they can be integrated with other data for analysis.

16.3 Case studies: The Flint Hills of Kansas

16.3.1 Site description

The case studies presented in this chapter were conducted in the northern Flint Hills region of eastern Kansas (Fig. 16.1). The Flint Hills region is on the western edge of the tallgrass prairie ecosystem. The region is approximately 70 km wide and extends from the southern boundary of Nebraska south into northern Oklahoma. While deep organic soils characterize much of the tallgrass prairie region, the steep topography and shallow or rocky soils of this region prevented it from being converted to row-crop agriculture. The Flint Hills represents the largest remaining area (1.6 million ha) of contiguous unplowed tallgrass prairie. Areas suitable for row-crop agriculture are restricted to flat bottomlands along streams and rivers. The region is floristically diverse (>600 species of higher plants) compared with other grasslands (Great Plains Flora Association, 1986). The vegetation is dominated by warm-season (C_4) grasses, most notably big bluestem (*Andropogon gerardi*) and Indiangrass (*Sorghastrum nutans*). The variable continental climate provides enough precipitation to support woody vegetation. Historically, dominance by grasses was maintained by periodic fire and possibly chronic herbivory. These factors continue to be important influences today (Knapp *et al.*, 1998). Forests, dominated by oaks (*Quercus*), are usually restricted to the deeper soils along streams. Cattle-ranching is the dominant land use in the region today.

16.3.2 Estimating aboveground net primary production

One of the most common uses of satellite imagery is estimating ANPP (Table 16.1). Traditionally ANPP is estimated by clipping or harvesting plots of vegetation. This method is destructive, extremely time consuming, and usually done at the scale of 0.1 to 1.0 m^2 (Brown and Roughgarden, 1990). Due to the spatial variability in grasslands and the need to obtain reliable estimates of ANPP (<10% of the standard error of the mean), numerous plots often need to be measured (Briggs and Knapp, 1991). Remote sensing offers many benefits over these traditional methods including non-destructive sampling, large sample size, and continuous coverage of an area, and it can be done more quickly than traditional methods. Using the relationships between remote sensing data and ANPP, the researcher needs to clip only enough plots to develop a robust regression model relating biomass to spectral characteristics. The imagery can then be used to sample the rest of the landscape.

At Konza Prairie Biological Station (Fig. 16.2, color plate) in Kansas, an extensive database relating ground-based measures of primary production and satellite spectral reflectance measurements has been collected. Briggs *et al.* (1998) evaluated this database for the validity of using NDVI as a surrogate for direct measurements of aboveground biomass in tallgrass prairie. In the study, Landsat TM data for the years 1984 to 1991 were analyzed. NDVI was calculated for each of the scenes. The dates of the TM scenes were within two to three weeks of the time biomass was harvested to estimate ANPP. A regression model was used to describe the relationship between NDVI and ANPP using one-half of the data set (randomly selected). A significant relationship (Fig. 16.3) was found between NDVI and ANPP for the time period of 1984 to 1991 ($P < 0.001$). However, only a small amount of the variance was explained ($r^2 = 0.34$). Using this regression model for each of the years on the other half of the data set, comparisons of ANPP estimated using the regression model of NDVI with actual ANPP yielded confounding results. In four of the years (1984, 1986, 1987, and 1990), little difference (less than 10%) occurred between estimated and

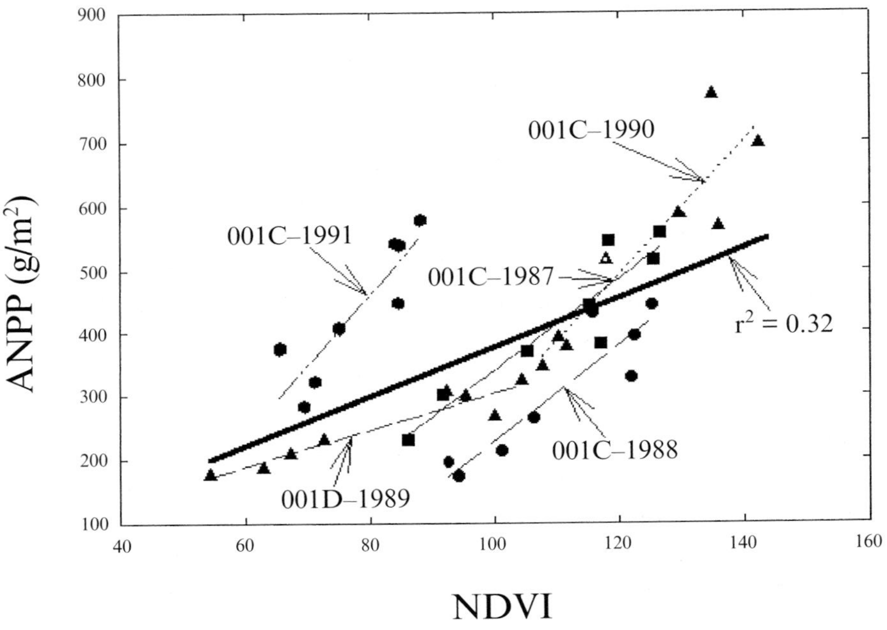

FIGURE 16.3
Relationship between normalized difference vegetation index (NDVI) derived from Landsat Thematic Mapper imagery and annual net primary production (ANPP) on annually burned watersheds on Konza Prairie over a five-year period. While the overall strength of the linear relationship was poor ($r^2 = 0.32$), relationships within years were generally strong ($r^2 > 0.80$). This suggests that separate regression models should be developed each year for accurate prediction of ANPP. Labels refer to watershed names and years. From Briggs *et al.* (1998).

measured ANPP. However, in other years, differences were as high as 49%, and overall the difference was 14.3% ± 5.65%.

Results from that analysis suggest caution when using NDVI values in tallgrass prairie as a substitute for measured ANPP across all years, especially if the relationship in one year is used to predict ANPP in another. This is also true if predictive capability is the goal of using NDVI and ANPP over a landscape that has different land-cover types. For example, we have found that, within a year, separate regression models relating reflectance and biomass on ungrazed burned and unburned areas may be necessary. The reason for this is due to the build-up of litter. Data summarized over a ten-year period show that a large amount of dead material (litter) is present (>350 g/m^2) at most sites two to five years after burning (Briggs and Knapp, 1995). This litter layer affects reflectance readings and dictates that separate relationships between remote-sensing data (i.e., NDVI) and ANPP be calculated for burned and unburned tallgrass prairie. Furthermore, a general relationship derived from data obtained over multiple years would result in less accurate ANPP estimates than could be obtained from relationships limited to a single year's observations. The benefits of this analysis are that ANPP could be sampled continuously across the entire landscape, as opposed to small plots that only sample a very small proportion of the entire landscape. Landscape-level patterns can then be analyzed across the study area (Briggs *et al.*, 1998).

Remote-sensing studies are limited in the direct measure of grassland biodiversity or species composition (Asrar *et al.*, 1986; Glenn *et al.*, 1994). However, remote sensing can be used as an exploratory tool to identify potential "hot-spots" for biodiversity in grasslands (Lauver and Whistler, 1993; O'Brien, 1999). Diversity in grasslands is most influenced by climate, fire, and grazing (Collins *et al.*, 1998). Using techniques described in this chapter, managers could monitor the influence of burning and grazing practices on landscape heterogeneity and make inferences about biodiversity. Remote sensing can be used to develop habitat models for wildlife species (Homer *et al.*, 1993), monitor grazing pressure (Pickup and Bastin, 1997), or identify land-cover change such as forestation or desertification that may be indicative of climatic changes. These tools also offer the potential for predicting the outcomes of proposed management plans before they are put into practice and testing the models after the plans have been implemented.

16.3.3 Assessing woody expansion into grasslands

Woody species are invading grasslands around the world (see Scholes and Archer, 1997). The most common reason given is the reduction, elimination, or suppression of fire from these systems (Bragg and Hulbert, 1976; Burkhardt and Tisdale, 1976; Blewett, 1986; Miller and Rose, 1995). Intensive grazing is also frequently cited, both by reducing the intensity and extent of fires and by opening the grass canopy, allowing light and water to reach woody seeds and seedlings (Madany and West, 1983; Arno and Gruell, 1986; McPherson *et al.*, 1989; Archer, 1993). Periodic drought or wet years and changing climatic factors such as warming and increased CO_2 have also been cited as possible causes (Archer *et al.*, 1995).

The increase in woody vegetation can decrease plant species diversity by >95% (Hoch, 2000). Woody invasion also decreases habitat for grassland endemic animal species, both by directly eliminating grasslands and by providing habitat for woodland species which may be able to outcompete the grassland endemic species (Knopf, 1996). In addition, woody invasion can reduce forage for livestock. For example, Hoch (2000) measured herbaceous productivity of 0.18 g/m^2 under closed canopy eastern redcedar (*Juniperus virginiana*) forests compared to 300–800 g/m^2 (Briggs and Knapp, 1995) in nearby prairie sites on the same topographic position.

A suite of studies has been conducted on or near Konza Prairie Research Natural Area looking at the increase of woody or shrubby vegetation over the past decade. Briggs and Gibson (1992) used a GIS to study the changes in abundance of several woody species and also the spatial patterns of the individual species within a watershed. The results were then related to the fire frequency (annual burning, burning every two or four years, or unburned) on each of these watersheds. All individual trees on several watersheds in Konza Prairie were identified to species, the height recorded, and the location overlaid on aerial photos. These data were digitized and incorporated into a GIS. Within the GIS a coefficient of aggregation, an index of non-randomness used with distance measurements (Goodall and West, 1979), was calculated for each species and burn treatment. On annually or biennially burned watersheds, the number of trees changed only slightly. Trees increased by 45% on a watershed burned once in a five-year period and increased by 63% on an unburned watershed. The distribution patterns were related to the life-history characteristics of the species; bird-dispersed species had a more random distribution across the landscape while wind-dispersed species had a more clumped pattern.

Knight *et al.* (1994) studied a similar question on Konza Prairie but focused on the oak forests that lined the streams in the study area. Previous research has indicated that one of the most dramatic landscape-level changes over the past 100 years was the expansion of oak-dominated gallery or riparian forests along streams. Surveys in 1859 reported only two areas of about 5 ha of continuous forests on Konza Prairie (Abrams, 1986). Although this is probably an underestimate, it is clear that forests now cover much more of the modern landscape than they did at the time of settlement. Forest expansion has occurred in two different ways. In areas that were historically forested and have higher-order streams with permanent water, the forests seem to be widening. Trees also seem to be moving up lower-order, usually seasonal streams, which would not have had a forested canopy historically. Today these younger forests are dominated by hackberry (*Celtis occidentalis*) and honey locust (*Gleditsia triacanthos*). Knight *et al.* (1994) used four sets of aerial photos between 1939 and 1985. The photos were digitized and incorporated into a GIS. Other GIS coverages such as soils, digital elevation models (DEM), and fire history were combined to examine their impact on forest expansion. In 1939, 159 ha of Konza was forested. By 1985 forests had expanded to 250 ha. By using a GIS, Knight *et al.* were able to determine that riparian forest was not being limited by the landscape. Only 10–15% of the best areas for forests to invade, alluvial–colluvial deposits along the streams, were forested. They hypothesized that other factors, such as fire history, may be controlling the expansion of forests.

Hoch and Briggs (1999) used a combination of satellite remote sensing and GIS to study the expansion of eastern redcedar across the northern section of the Flint Hills region of Kansas. A supervised classification (Jensen, 1996) of Landsat TM imagery from 1997 was used to identify closed-canopy redcedar forest. With this technique, closed-canopy redcedar forests were located in the field or on recent aerial photos. Coordinates for the forest sites were obtained with a GPS unit. Pixels in the satellite image that corresponded to these sites were identified and the spectral values of these training areas were extracted. The computer then identified all pixels across the region which were statistically similar to the training pixels. The resulting coverage was then ground truthed to determine the accuracy of the locations of the closed-canopy redcedar forests. The data were incorporated into a GIS and overlaid on a soils coverage, county boundaries, and socioeconomic data for each county. From this analysis, it was determined that redcedars prefer shallow, upland soils.

Across the seven-county region, redcedar cover was positively correlated to population growth over the last three decades ($r^2=0.81$, $n=7$, $p<0.001$). We determined that urbanization is the largest factor explaining the invasion of redcedars in the Flint Hills region. Many of the redcedar forests in this area are clearly bounded by property lines (Hoch and Briggs, 1999). As people build houses in grasslands they are hesitant to burn near their homes. They also plant trees around their home for aesthetic reasons and as windbreaks. The seeds from these trees can then be dispersed into surrounding rangeland. Under drought conditions, redcedars can ignite, almost explosively. By not controlling redcedars near houses with low intensity, periodic fires or mowing, a much greater fire danger for these homes may be created.

Integrating remote sensing and GIS has several implications for studying the expansion of woody species into grasslands. First, remote sensing can be used to identify areas where woody species are expanding across entire regions. Integrating these data into a GIS would allow resource managers to determine what soil types, elevations, aspects, land-use types, etc. are vulnerable to woody expansion and identify similar areas in the region. Management efforts could then be concentrated in these areas. Second, grazing by livestock reduces biomass and fuel loads for fires in fire-dominated grasslands. This reduced fire intensity is often cited as a cause for woody expansion. Using remote sensing to identify areas with the greatest herbaceous biomass would allow managers to identify areas that should be burned in a given year to maximize mortality of woody species.

16.3.4 Predicting grazing distribution at landscape scales

Manipulation of grazing distribution and forage utilization has been a major goal of range management (Richards and Huntsinger, 1994; Walker,

1995). Grazing distribution is the spatial pattern of grazing across a landscape. Forage utilization is "the proportion of current year's forage production that is consumed or destroyed by grazing animals" (Society for Range Management, 1989). Managers typically wish to increase uniformity of forage utilization (hereafter referred as utilization) by livestock for increased profits. Manipulation of grazing distribution and utilization is also valuable for conservationists to apply prescribed levels of grazing to meet management objectives. Development of reliable predictive models for grazing distribution and utilization would be valuable for refining the ability of managers to meet objectives or predict outcomes of proposed management schemes. Several descriptive models of grazing distribution have been previously developed (Senft *et al.*, 1983; Pinchak *et al.*, 1991; Nellis and Briggs, 1997). However, the use of these models for predictive purposes has been relatively rare (Senft *et al.*, 1983; Wade *et al.*, 1998).

We developed linked models for grazing distribution and utilization of domestic cattle (*Bos taurus*) under two grazing systems in the Flint Hills region of Kansas (Brock and Owensby, 2000). Data were collected at biweekly intervals to record the spatial distribution of grazing and utilization at 10-m resolution. Whole pasture (30 ha) distribution layers were created for each sampling date using a GIS. Additional GIS layers were incorporated to associate individual sampling points with landscape parameters. Most of these layers were derived from readily available public data. Range sites were derived from the Soil Survey Geographic Database, slope, aspect, and surface area of contiguous slope polygons were derived from 7.5-minute US Geological Survey DEMs, and weather data were obtained from the National Weather Data Library. The only data layers that were developed in-house to parameterize the models were locations of fences, water, and mineral feeding stations. Of these, fence line boundaries and water locations were easily digitized from 1:12 000 DOQ images, and mineral feeders and watering sites created after the date of DOQs were located with a GPS. All other layers were derived from data obtained from the Kansas Data Access and Support Center or the US Geological Survey.

Separate models were created to predict grazing distribution and forage utilization, with the latter model linked to the first as will be described later. Grazing was modeled using the Proc Genmod procedure in SAS (SAS Institute Inc., 1996) which performs a general linear model with a logistic link function to produce a logistic regression model for binary data. Figure 16.4 (color plate) provides a spatial representation of the observed grazing distribution and the predicted probability of grazing across pastures. Ten percent of the data were withheld from the model fitting procedure to evaluate model performance. Probability of grazing was predicted with a satisfactory degree of accuracy ($r^2 = 0.98$). A model predicting forage utilization was developed using Tobit analysis

(Tobin, 1958). Tobit analysis allowed the forage utilization model to be linked with the grazing distribution model. This method accounts for the linkage of these two parameters in nature whereby forage utilization only occurs within grazed areas (see Bailey *et al.*, 1996) for a description of mechanisms producing grazing patterns). Using Tobit analysis, the grazing data were left censored to eliminate ungrazed locations from consideration in the model fit procedure. Figure 16.5 (color plate) provides spatial representations of observed and predicted forage removal. Performance of this model was poor ($r = 0.27$).

Despite failure of the utilization model, this exercise was successful in predicting grazing distribution and also demonstrates some characteristics about ungulate grazing behavior that present challenges to landscape ecologists. The disparate performance of the two models was not unexpected. Grazing distribution and forage utilization are expressed at different spatial scales and are correlated to different parameters (Bailey *et al.*, 1996). Grazing distribution of ungulates is controlled mainly by abiotic parameters such as distance to water and slope whereas forage utilization is determined by biotic factors like forage quality and quantity. Landscape patterns of abiotic factors determining grazing distribution can generally be detected at relatively coarse spatial scales and their boundaries are readily discernible using remote sensing.

Therefore, data associated with abiotic parameters are relatively accessible to land managers and are well represented in these models. In contrast, patterns of forage quality and quantity are perceived by ungulates at spatial scales too fine for remote sensors to detect at the time of the study. Because of this, efforts to model ungulate forage utilization will require collection of extensive amounts of field data until remotely sensed data of higher spatial and spectral resolution are readily available. However, this technology changes rapidly and at the time of this writing, the IKONOS satellite sensors are operational that provide 4-m resolution multispectral data for civilian use. Despite these shortcomings, the models provide an example of how GIS, remote sensing, and statistical methods can be incorporated to produce predictive models of landscape-level phenomena that occur at hierarchical spatial scales.

The interaction between fire and grazers is well documented (Biondini *et al.*, 1999) (Fig. 16.6, color plate). Fire could potentially be used by preserve managers to control the distribution of grazers to manipulate habitat for other species. For instance, some species such as Henslow's sparrow (*Ammodramus henslowii*) prefers ungrazed, unburned prairie with heavy litter accumulation while horned lizards (*Phynosoma cornatum*) prefer heavily grazed areas. Prairie chickens (*Tympanuchus cupido*) need both grazed areas in the spring for their leks and ungrazed areas later in the spring for nesting cover. A GIS could be used to model burning programs and grazing distributions to meet management objectives for other species. Managers could run these models under a variety of management scenarios to predict the outcomes of management decisions such as manipulation of cross fences, water locations, or grazing systems. Remote sensing could be used to monitor grazing patterns and determine the effectiveness of the management plan.

Easily derived predictive models for forage utilization are also powerful tools for range resource professionals. The grazing model presented in the case study is reasonably accurate in predicting landscape-scale patterns of grazing. The model has the advantage of relying on existing or easily obtainable data. The greatest advantage of this model is its incorporation into a GIS. This could allow range professionals to take a laptop computer into the field and immediately evaluate the consequences of placing watering source and fences for forage utilization for instance. Range professionals and property owners could immediately see the predicted results of their management decisions. A manager of a nature preserve could use the same technology to minimize the impact of livestock on sensitive areas, or to encourage grazing in areas requiring increased disturbance to promote floristic diversity or specific habitat types.

16.4 Implications and guidelines for management

Incorporating advanced technologies into a natural resource management program requires careful consideration. The tools and training required to use advanced technologies can be expensive. Before investing in these technologies, managers should have a clear understanding of their objectives and how the technologies will be used to meet these objectives. Managers should also determine what data will be used for analysis and what spatial and temporal resolution is required. Finally, managers should determine whether they have appropriately trained personnel to exploit the technologies they intend to acquire.

It is difficult to provide precise guidelines for cost, level of training, personnel requirements, etc. for these types of studies. These will vary on a case-by-case basis. Software and hardware prices can be found on the Internet. Creation of in-house coverages can be expensive and time consuming but can be integrated with publicly available data from the Internet. From our experience, once base GIS coverages are developed for an area, along with coverages for a specific project, often numerous questions not originally planned can be addressed. For storage and analysis of very large GIS databases, a resource manager should consider investing in a full featured GIS (e.g., Arc/Info or GRASS) on a high-performance computer platform. Smaller databases and GIS applications concentrated on map query and display can be adequately performed in a desktop GIS (e.g., ArcView or MapInfo) on a PC.

Remote sensing and GIS continue to improve and can be applied to a much more diverse group of problems than have been described in this chapter. Additional uses of these technologies in grasslands conservation include monitoring animal movements (Cohn, 1999), developing habitat suitability models, inventorying existing wildlife habitat (Homer *et al.*, 1993), and designing migration corridors and conservation areas.

Remote sensing currently provides one of the best tools for providing baseline data for woody encroachment, grazing pressure, and grassland productivity and for monitoring landscape-level changes over the coming decades. By incorporating this information into a GIS, models that take into account soil, topography, climate, and land use can be developed. For these studies, historic satellite imagery is an underused resource as researchers can already conduct change detection studies over a 15- to 25-year period with Landsat TM and MSS imagery (Green and Sussman, 1990; Hoch, 2000). It is important to have this information as baseline data to evaluate future land-cover changes. However, we would like to emphasize that one of the lessons we have found from our long-term perspective is the danger of using one-time measurements to extrapolate to long time periods. An excellent example of this is the relationship between NDVI and ANPP, in which the relationship is not the same from year to year. This makes annual clipping of biomass a necessity.

The tools presented here allow resource managers to explore complex relationships between resources and management practices, or to extend the application of field data. Using traditional techniques such as planimetry, forest cover/woody encroachment could have been measured in all of the studies mentioned, but time allocations would have been prohibitive. However, with the combination of GIS and remote-sensing technology researchers were able to expand the scope of the studies and ask questions about the causative forces behind the process of woody expansion. They were able to relate biological processes to soil type, topography, management history, and socioeconomic data. The types of questions studied in these examples could not have been addressed, at least not in a reasonable amount of time, without the power of GIS tools. The studies also point to the tools and data available to landscape ecologists. These studies were able to incorporate manual and automated analyses of aerial photos and satellite images, spatial statistics, GPS, GIS layers created in-house, and other GIS coverages, most of which are publicly available at little or no cost over the Internet. Over the past several years many private, state, and federal agencies have developed GIS sites on the World Wide Web. Most of these sites have publicly available data that can be downloaded free of charge. A quick search of the Internet should produce a large number of these sites.

16.6 Summary

Grasslands cover large areas of every continent except Antarctica and are economically important for livestock production and agriculture. Grasslands are dominated and maintained by several types of disturbances including a variable climate, fire, and grazing and multiple types of human land use which interact to produce a complex landscape at many scales. In the United States, native grasslands have largely been replaced by row-crop agriculture, especially in the eastern tallgrass prairie. Three management issues facing grasslands today are woody encroachment, livestock grazing, and productivity. All of these issues lend themselves to analysis using remote sensing, GPS, and GIS tools. We have discussed the successful implementation of these tools for monitoring the productivity of grasslands across entire regions, demonstrated the interannual variability in productivity, and the relationships of ANPP to spectral data. Remote sensing provides an effective tool for monitoring woody encroachment into grasslands and, when combined with a GIS, can be used to characterize and model this invasion. GIS can be an effective tool for analyzing grazing patterns at multiple scales and GIS technology can be used to help managers manipulate forage utilization through predictive models. The threats to grasslands will likely increase in the coming decades. Remote sensing and GIS offer some of the best tools available for individual landowners to manage their property and for state and federal agencies to manage entire regions.

References

Abrams, M. D. (1986). Historic development of gallery forests in northeast Kansas. *Vegetatio*, 65: 29–37.

Anderson, G. L., Hanson, J. D. & Haas, R. H. (1993). Evaluating Landsat Thematic Mapper derived vegetation indices for estimating above-ground biomass on semiarid rangelands. *Remote Sensing of Environment*, 45: 165–175.

Archer, S. (1993). Vegetation dynamics in changing environments. *Rangeland Journal*, 15: 104–116.

Archer, S., Schimel, D. S. & Holland, E. A. (1995). Mechanisms of shrubland expansion: Land use, climate, or CO_2? *Climatic Change*, 29: 91–99.

Arno, S. F. & Gruell, G. E. (1986). Douglas fir encroachment into mountain grasslands in southwestern Montana. *Journal of Range Mangement*, 39: 272–276.

Aronoff, S. (1993). *Geographic Information Systems: A Management Perspective*. WDL Publications, Ottawa, Canada.

Asrar, G., Weiser, R. L., Johnson, D. E., Kanemasu, E. T. & Killeen, J. M. (1986). Distinguishing among tallgrass prairie cover types from measurements of multispectral reflectance. *Remote Sensing of Environment* 19:159–169.

Bailey, D. W., Gross, J. E., Laca, E. A., Rittenhouse, L. R., Coughenor, M. B., Swift, D. M. & Pims, P. L. (1996). Invited synthesis paper: Mechanisms that result in large herbivore grazing distribution patterns. *Journal of Range Management*, 49: 386–400.

Belward, A. S., Estes, S. E. & Klue, K. D. (1999). The IBGP-DIS global 1 km land-cover data set DISCover: A project overview. *Photogrammetric Engineering and Remote Sensing*, 65: 1013–1021.

Betz, R. F. & Lamp, H. F. (1988). Species composition of old settler silt-loam cemetery prairies. In: *Proceedings of the 11th North American Prairie Conference*, eds. T. B. Bragg & J. Stubbendieck, pp. 33–40. University of Nebraska Press, Lincoln, NE.

Biondini, M. E, Steuter, A. A. & Hamilton, R. G. (1999). Bison use of fire-managed remnant prairies. *Journal of Range Management*, 52: 454–461.

Blewett, T. J. (1986). Eastern redcedar's (*Juniperus virginiana* L.) expanded role in the prairie–forest border region. In: *Proceedings of the 9th North American Prairie Conference*, eds. G. K. Clambey & R. H. Pemble, pp. 122–125. Tricollege University, Moorhead, MN.

Box, E. O., Holden, B. N. & Kalb, V. (1989). Accuracy of the AVHRR vegetation index as a predictor of biomass, primary productivity, and net CO_2 flux. *Vegetatio*, 80: 71–89.

Bragg, T. B. & Hulbert, L. C. (1976). Woody plant invasion of unburned Kansas bluestem prairie. *Journal of Range Management*, 29: 1923.

Briggs, J. M. & Gibson, D. J. (1992). Effects of fire on tree spatial patterns in tallgrass prairie landscape. *Bulletin of the Torrey Botanical Club*, 119: 300–307.

Briggs, J. M. & Knapp, A. K. (1991). Estimating aboveground biomass production in tallgrass prairie with the harvest methods: Determining proper sample size using jackknifing and Monte Carlo simulations. *Southwestern Naturalist*, 36: 1–6.

Briggs, J. M. & Knapp, A. K. (1995). Interannual variability in primary production in tallgrass prairie: Climate, soil moisture, topographic position, and fire as determinants of aboveground biomass. *American Journal of Botany*, 82: 1024–1030.

Briggs, J. M. & Nellis, M. D. (1989). Thematic Mapper digital data for predicting aboveground tallgrass prairie biomass. In: *Proceedings of the 11th North American Prairie Conference*, eds. T. B. Bragg & J. Stubbendieck, pp. 53–56. University of Nebraska Press, Lincoln, NE.

Briggs, J. M., Nellis, M. D., Turner, C. L., Henebry, G. M. & Su, H. (1998). A landscape perspective of patterns and processes in tallgrass prairie. In: *Grassland Dynamics: Long-Term Ecological Research in Tallgrass Prairie*, eds., A. K., Knapp, J. M., Briggs, D. C. Hartnett & S. L. Collins, pp. 265–279. Oxford University Press, New York.

Brock, B. L. & Owensby, C. E. (2000). Predictive models for grazing distribution: A GIS approach. *Journal of Range Management*. 53: 39–46.

Brown, J. H. & Roughgarden, J. (1990). Ecology for a changing earth. *Bulletin of the Ecological Society of America*, 71: 173–188.

Burke, I. C., Kittel, T. G., Lauenroth, W. K., Snook, P., Yonkers, C. M. & Parton, W. J. (1991). Regional analysis of the Great Plains. *BioScience*, 41: 685–692.

Burkhardt, J. W. & Tisdale, E. W. (1976). Causes of juniper invasion in southwestern Idaho. *Ecology*, 57: 472–484.

Cohn, J. P. (1999). Tracking wildlife. *BioScience*, 49: 12.

Collins, S. L., Knapp, A. K., Briggs, J. M., Blair, J. M. & Steinauer, E. M. (1998). Modulation of diversity by grazing and mowing in native tallgrass prairie. *Science*, 280: 745–747.

Dale, V. H. (1997). The relationship between land-use change and climate change. *Ecological Applications*, 7: 753–769.

DeFries, R. S., Field, C. B., Fung, I., Justice, C. O., Matson, P. A., Matthews, E., Mooney, H. A., Potter, C. S., Prentice, K., Sellers, P. J., Townshend, J. R. G., Tucker, C. J., Ustin, S. L. & Vitousek, P. M. (1995). Mapping the land surface for global atmosphere–biosphere models: Towards continuous distribution of vegetation functional properties. *Journal of Geophysical Research – Atmospheres*, 100: 20867–20882.

Environmental Systems Research Institute, Inc. (1997). *Understanding GIS: The ARC/INFO Method*. John Wiley, New York.

Everitt, J. H., Hussey, M. A., Escobar, D. E., Nixon, P. R. & Pinkerton, B. (1986). Assessment of grassland phytomass with airborne video imagery. *Remote Sensing of Environment*, 20: 299–306.

Fahrig, L. (1991). Simulation methods for developing general landscape-level hypotheses of single-species dynamics. In *Quantitative Methods in Landscape Ecology*, eds. M. G. Turner & R. H. Gardner, pp. 417–442. Springer-Verlag, New York.

Friedel, M. A., Michaelson, J., Davis, F. W., Walker, H. & Schimel, D. S. (1994). Estimating grassland biomass and leaf area index using ground and satellite data. *International Journal of Remote Sensing*, 15: 1401–1420.

Glenn, S. M., Francis, M. L. & Butler, I. H. (1994). *Final Report: Vegetation Mapping of The Tallgrass Prairie Preserve using Landsat Thematic Mapper Imagery*. Submitted to The Nature Conservancy, TPP, Pawhuska OK and OK Natural Heritage Inventory, OK Biological Survey.

Goodall, D. W. & West, N. E. (1979). A comparison of techniques for assessing dispersion patterns. *Vegetatio*, 40: 15–27.

Great Plains Flora Association (1986). *Flora of the Great Plains*. University Press of Kansas, Lawrence, KS.

Green, G. M. & Sussman, R. W. (1990). Deforestation history of the eastern rain forests of Madagascar from satellite images. *Science*, 248: 212–215.

Gustafson, E. J. (1998). Quantifying landscape pattern: What is the state of the art? *Ecosystems*, 1: 143–156.

Hoch, G. A. (2000). Patterns and mechanisms of eastern redcedar (*Juniperus virginiana*) expansion into tallgrass prairie in the Flint Hills, Kansas. PhD dissertation, Kansas State University, Manhattan, KA.

Hoch, G. A. & Briggs, J. M. (1999). Expansion of eastern redcedar (*Juniperus virginiana*) in the northern Flint Hills, Kansas. In *Proceedings of the 15th North American Prairie Conference*, ed. J.T. Springer, pp. 9–15. University of Nebraska, Kearney, NB.

Homer, G. C., Edwards, T. C., Ramsey, R. D. & Price, K. P. (1993). Use of remote sensing in modelling sage grouse winter habitat. *Journal of Wildlife Management*, 57: 78–84.

Jensen, J. R. (1996). *Introductory Digital Image Processing: A Remote Sensing Perspective*. Prentice-Hall, Englewood Cliffs, NJ.

Knapp, A. K. & Seastedt, T. R. (1998). Introduction: Grasslands, Konza prairie, and long-term ecological research. In: *Grassland Dynamics: Long-Term Ecological Research in Tallgrass Prairie*, eds. A. K. Knapp, J. M. Briggs, D. C. Hartnett & S. L. Collins, pp. 3–18. Oxford University Press, New York.

Knapp, A. K., Briggs, J. M., Hartnett, D. C. & Collins, S. L. (eds.) (1998). *Grassland Dynamics Long-Term Ecological Research in Tallgrass Prairie*. Oxford University Press, New York.

Knapp, A. K., Blair, J. M., Briggs, J. M., Collins, S. L., Hartnett, D. C., Johnson, L. C. & Towne, E. G. (1999). The keystone role of bison in North American tallgrass prairie. *BioScience*, 49: 39–50.

Knight, C. L., Briggs, J. M. & Nellis, M. D. (1994). Expansion of gallery forest on Konza Prairie Research Natural Area, Kansas, USA. *Landscape Ecology*, 9: 117–125.

Knopf, F. L. (1996). Prairie legacies: Birds. In *Prairie Conservation*, eds. F. B. Samson & F. L. Knopf, pp. 135–148. Island Press, Washington, D.C.

Lauver, C. H. & Whistler, J. L. (1993). Hierarchical classification of Landsat TM imagery to identify natural grassland areas and rare species habitat. *Photogrammetric Engineering and Remote Sensing*, 59: 627–634.

Li, L., Liang, T. & Cheng, Q. (1998). Estimating grassland yields using remote sensing and GIS technologies in China. *New Zealand Journal of Agricultural Research*, 41: 31–38.

Madany, M. H. & West, N. E. (1983). Livestock grazing–fire regime interactions within montane forests of Zion National Park, Utah. *Ecology*, 64: 661–667.

McPherson, G. R., Wright, H. A. & Webster, D. B. (1989). Patterns of shrub invasion in semiarid Texas grasslands. *American Midland Naturalist*, 120: 391–397.

Miller, R. F. & Rose, J. A. (1995). Historic expansion of *Juniperus occidentalis* (western juniper) in southeastern Oregon. *Great Basin Naturalist*, 55: 37–45.

National Science Foundation (1999). http://www.geog.buffalo.edu/ncgia/workshopreport.html

Nellis, M. D. & Briggs, J. M. (1989). The effects of spatial scale on Konza landscape classification using textural algorithms. *Landscape Ecology*, 2: 93–100.

Nellis, M. D. & Briggs, J. M. (1997). Modeling spatial dimensions of bison preferences on the Konza Prairie landscape ecology: An overview. *Transactions of the Kansas Academy of Science* 100: 3–9.

Nystrom-Mast, J., Veblen, T. T. & Hodgson, M. E. (1997). Tree invasion within a pine/grassland ecotone: An approach with historic aerial photography and GIS modeling. *Forest Ecology and Management* 93:181–194.

O'Brien, A. (1999). Purchasing power: Why we still buy land. *The Nature Conservancy Magazine*, Nov/Dec: 12–17.

Ortmann, J., Stubbendieck, J. & Pfieffer, G. H. (1999). Projected eastern redcedar canopy expansion on a Nebraska Loess Hills site. In *Proceedings of the 16th North American Prairie Conference*, ed. J. T. Springer, pp. 88–94. University of Nebraska, Kearney, NE.

Paruelo, J. M., Epstein, H. E., Lauenroth, W. K. & Burke, I. C. (1997). ANPP estimates from NDVI for the central grassland region of the United States. *Ecology*, 78: 953–958.

Pickup, G. & Bastin, G. N. (1997). Spatial distribution of cattle in arid rangelands as detected by patterns of change on vegetation cover. *Journal of Applied Ecology*, 34: 657–667.

Pinchak, W. E., Smith, M. A., Hart, R. H. & Waggoner, J. W. Jr. (1991). Beef cattle distribution patterns on foothill range. *Journal of Range Management*, 44: 267–275.

Reichman, O. J. (1987). *Konza Prairie: A Tallgrass Natural History*. University of Kansas Press, Lawrence, KA.

Richards, R. T. & Huntsinger, L. (1994). Variation in BLM employee attitude toward environmental conditions on rangeland. *Journal of Range Management*, 47: 365–368.

Riera, J. L., Magnuson, J. L., Vande Castle, J. R. & Mackenzie, M. D. (1998). Analysis of large-scale spatial heterogeneity in vegetation indices among North American landscapes. *Ecosystems*, 1: 268–282.

Samson, F. & Knopf, F. (1994). Prairie conservation in North America. *BioScience*, 44: 418–421.

SAS Institute, Inc. (1996). *Procedures Guide*. Statistical Analysis Systems, Inc, Cary, NC.

Scholes, R. J. & Archer, S. R. (1997). Tree-grass interactions in savannas. *Annual Review of Ecology and Systematics*, 28: 517–544. (http://cnrit.tamu.edu/rlem/faculty/archer/bibliography.html for review.)

Senft, R. L., Rittenhouse, L. R. & Woodmansee, R. G. (1983). The use of regression models to predict spatial patterns of cattle behavior. *Journal of Range Management*, 36: 553–557.

Society for Range Management (The Glossary Revision Special Committee and Publications Committee) (eds.) (1989). *A Glossary of Terms Used in Range Management: A Definition of Terms Commonly Used in Range Management*. Society for Range Management, Denver, CO.

Stohlgren, W. (2000). Good cow, bad cow, a two-headed question over cattle on the range. *The Nature Conservancy Magazine*, July/Aug: 12–19.

Tieszen, L., Reed, B. C., Bliss, N. B., Wylie, B. K. & Dejong, D. D. (1997). NDVI, C3, and C4 production and distribution in Great Plains grassland land cover classes. *Ecological Applications*, 7: 59–78.

Tobin, J. (1958). Estimation of relationships for limited dependent variables. *Econometrica*, 26: 24–36.

Tucker, C. J., Vanpraet, C. L., Sharman, M. J. & Van Ittersum, G. (1985). Satellite remote sensing of total herbaceous biomass production in the Senegalese Sahel: 1980–1984. *Remote Sensing of Environment*, 17: 233–249.

Wade, T. G., Schultz, B. W., Wickham, J. D. & Bradford, D. F. (1998). Modeling the potential spatial distribution of beef cattle grazing using a geographic information system. *Journal of Arid Environments*, 38: 325–334.

Walker, J. W. (1995). Viewpoint: Grazing management and research now and in the next millenium. *Journal of Range Management*, 48: 350–357.

Weiser, R. L., Asrar, G., Miller, P. & Kanemasu, E. T. (1986). Assessing grassland biophysical characteristics from spectral measurements. *Remote Sensing of Environment*, 20: 141–152.

Wellens, J. (1997). Rangeland vegetation dynamics and moisture availability in Tunisia: An investigation using satellite and meteorological data. *Journal of Biogeography*, 24: 845–855.

Wolter, P. T., Mladenoff, D. J., Host, G. E. & Crow, T. R. (1995). Improved forest classification in the northern Lake States using multi-temporal Landsat imagery. *Photogrammetric Engineering and Remote Sensing*, 61: 1129–1143.

Wylie, B. K., Harrington, J. A., Prince, S. D. & Denda, I. (1991). Satellite and ground-based pasture production assessment in Niger: 1986–1988. *International Journal of Remote Sensing*, 12: 1281–1300.

17

An integrated approach to landscape science and management

17.1 Introduction

Science is currently at a crossroads, and some hard decisions are needed about what needs to be achieved and how to achieve it. Classical reductionist methods, while successful up to a point, cannot adequately deal with complex broad-scale environmental questions. Similarly, the fragmentation of science into many disciplines has led to a fragmentary approach to these same questions. Finally, the separation of science from other types of human endeavor has led to an isolationist view which prevents the integration of scientific information with other types of knowledge.

Set against this problem is an increasing need for methods and options for managing and planning landscapes that are in various states of disrepair. The development of such options has to take account of not only the biophysical elements and all the complexity and interrelationships between these elements, but also the social and economic contexts, and all their inherent complexities and uncertainties. Options have to take the form, not of vague guiding principles, but of recommendations that can be applied in a quantitative way in any particular situation.

Thus there is a struggle between these apparently opposing needs – the need to include as much of the complexity and context as possible in our investigations versus the need to deliver simple quantitative options for what actions to take in any given situation. In this chapter, we present an example of an approach to developing landscape management and restoration options for biodiversity conservation which can be integrated with other management goals in a production landscape.

17.2 Integrated landscape science and management: What and why?

There is an increasing need to develop management and planning options both for landscapes that are already significantly altered and in need of either improved management or restoration and for landscapes which are still relatively unaltered but which are under increasing human pressure. The ability to provide such options depends on an understanding of landscape processes and the ability to use this understanding to develop strategies which are effective in dealing with the biophysical problems and are also acceptable socially and economically and hence liable to be implemented. This means that a wide range of expertise may need to be involved in developing these strategies, including not only a variety of scientific disciplines, but also social and economic scientists, policy-makers, planners, and managers.

Recognition of the need for such an integrated approach has been limited until recently. Actually achieving it is apparently quite difficult, and the reasons for this difficulty lie in the way science has been conducted and in the structures of policy and management agencies. The prevalent trend in recent decades has been towards increasing fragmentation of scientific disciplines, with increasing specialization and narrowing of interests. In ecology, for example, which purports to be an integrative discipline, a wide range of sub-fields exists, often with relatively little communication between them (Hobbs and Saunders, 1995; Lubchenco, 1995). While continuing calls are made for increasing rather than decreasing contact between sub-fields, the opportunity for this is often lacking within existing reward and funding structures, and many scientists prefer to maintain their credibility and funding base within a relatively limited area of expertise. These problems are compounded when we try to integrate across entire disciplines. For instance, effective treatment of a landscape-scale problem may involve consideration of ecological, hydrological, and geomorphological information. This also has to involve the use of spatially explicit methodologies, increasingly using complex geographic information systems (GIS) software and remote sensing, both of which also have their own sets of disciplinary expertise. All of this then has to be set in a policy, planning, and management framework, each of which again involves different expertise and methodologies, which further intersect social and economic aspects. For a scientist interested in studying a particular aspect of a problem, this ever-widening sphere of inclusion is daunting at best, and it is hardly surprising that attempts to integrate often fail.

Even if the scientific aspects of a problem are successfully integrated, the other parts of the system often also work against the development of integrated solutions. Many current policy, planning, and management structures work to disintegrate rather than integrate, because of their sectoral focus (Gunderson *et al.*, 1995). This also feeds back into the research process, since calls for research tend to follow entrenched lines of responsibility and there may be little perceived benefit in trying to cross territorial boundaries.

Given all this, how then can effective solutions to pressing problems resulting from landscape modification be found? Clearly there is a need to overcome the difficulties of working across disciplines in an integrated way, but doing so without making every project so big that it is doomed to failure. Hence there is a need to develop methods for deciding which elements of a problem are critical, where lack of information is preventing the development of an effective solution, and what research is needed to fill this information gap. This needs to be done in the context of the broader socioeconomic picture, and also needs to present integrated options which themselves may help to hasten the necessary change in institutional structures to ensure that these options can be effectively implemented.

Elsewhere Hobbs (1997, 1999) has argued that landscape ecology is ideally placed to take up the challenge of providing the necessary integrative and inclusive approach. Here, we explore ways in which this might be achieved from the particular perspective of incorporating biodiversity conservation into an integrated planning and management process.

17.3 Case study: The Western Australian wheatbelt

17.3.1 Description of the region

The agricultural region of Western Australia covers approximately 14 million ha, and corresponds roughly with the area of winter rainfall inland from the large areas of state forests which occupy the higher rainfall and lateritic areas (Fig. 17.1). This area is characterized by a mosaic of vegetation types including woodlands, heathlands, shrublands and mallee (multi-stemmed eucalypt). The flora of the region is remarkably diverse, and the southwest corner of Australia has recently been recognized as one of the top 25 biodiversity "hotspots" for the world (Hobbs, 1992; Myers *et al.*, 2000). The area was developed for agriculture during the past 150 years, with most of the development occurring during the twentieth century. This involved the widespread clearing of the native vegetation and its replacement with annual crops and pastures. This has resulted in landscapes in which the native vegetation has been drastically reduced in amount and fragmented to various degrees. The earliest cleared areas in the central wheatbelt have as little as 2–3% of the native vegetation remaining, usually in small fragments (<100 ha), many of which are degraded to some extent by livestock grazing and weed invasion (Hobbs and Saunders, 1993; Hobbs, 1998b).

In addition to the threats to the biota arising from fragmentation, weed invasion, and introduced predators, the remaining native vegetation is under threat from hydrologic changes resulting from the widespread removal of the native perennial vegetation. Hydrological imbalance has resulted in rising water tables which bring to the surface stored salts, resulting in secondary

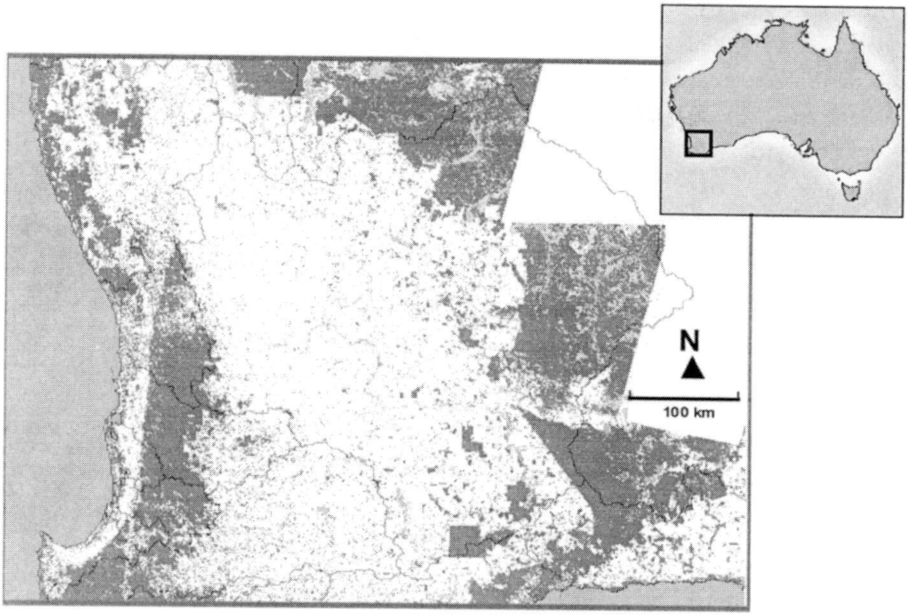

FIGURE 17.1
The agricultural area of Western Australia, indicating major catchment (watershed) boundaries, and native vegetation (shaded).

salinization. Under current estimates, 30% or more of the agricultural area is under threat from secondary salinization in the next 50 years, resulting in massive loss of both production and conservation land (George *et al.*, 1995). Landscape-scale remediation, including massive revegetation with perennials, is required if this situation is to be reversed. The opportunity arises to carry out such remediation in such a way that it has multiple benefits – for instance, revegetation to redress the hydrological imbalance can also be designed to have nature conservation benefits. It is this opportunity for integrated approaches to the multiple threats facing the region that we discuss here.

17.3.2 An integrated approach: Framework and methods

Our research group has worked in the agricultural region of southwestern Australia for over a decade, studying the fragmented landscapes which resulted from the rapid agricultural development during the last 50–100 years and trying to assist in the development of an integrated approach to the management of these landscapes (Hobbs and Saunders, 1991, 1993, 2001; Hobbs *et al.*, 1993). From early studies of the dynamics of vegetation fragments, it became clear that the dynamics of the agricultural matrix played a critical role

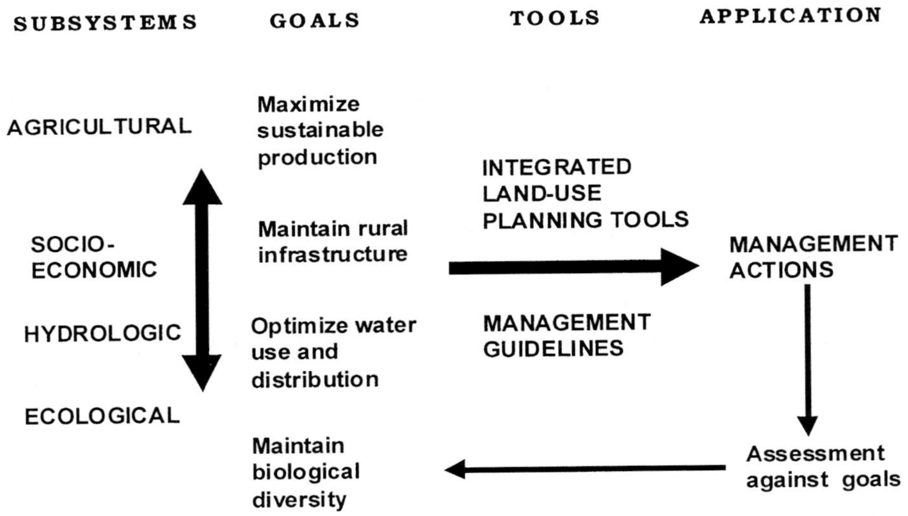

FIGURE 17.2
Conceptual model of the agricultural system in Western Australia, indicating the major sub-components of the system, examples of societal and management goals in relation to each sub-system, and the need for integrated approaches for developing options in relation to these goals.

in modifying or controlling the dynamics of the fragment itself (Hobbs, 1994). It also became apparent that the ecological system was only one component of a broader picture which encompassed the hydrological, social, and economic systems in operation in the landscape (Fig. 17.2). In developing management options for these landscapes, it is necessary to recognize the importance of these different elements, and also to recognize the variety of goals that may be relevant. This in turn needs some method for integrating these different goals, and for making any necessary trade-offs between them.

Despite the recognition of the complex and interrelated nature of the system in which we are working, our experience shows that the attempt to include all potential players and deal with all aspects of the complexity simultaneously is an immensely difficult task. Hence, our aim has been to simplify both the questions asked and the approaches to dealing with them. In this way, we hope to be able to develop a modular approach, with each module providing simple output which can be combined with that from other modules.

An integrated approach, such as that outlined in Fig. 17.2, aims to mesh biodiversity conservation options with hydrological and socioeconomic requirements. Methods for developing integrated planning and management strategies need to be spatially explicit, refer to specific areas, and require basic biophysical information together with assessments of both potential uses of individual land units and the potential levels of primary threats in each. Such methods rely on the ability to integrate different sets of land use or land allocation priorities and assign weightings to each use. Weightings can be varied on the basis of stakeholder input, and a range of options provided for future land use patterns. In our case, we have used the Land Use Planning and Information System developed by CSIRO (Ive and Cocks, 1989; Ive *et al.*, 1989; Lambeck, 1999). This allows the assessment of different sets of management options in terms of the achievement of the range of land-use goals identified. For instance, trade-offs between production outputs (and hence profits) and conservation benefits can be explored, and opportunities for synergistic solutions can be developed. For instance, revegetation strategies developed in response to hydrological requirements could be meshed with biodiversity conservation requirements (Hobbs, 1993; Saunders and Hobbs, 1995; Lambeck, 1998).

The utility of the method stems from the iterative nature of its operation, with different stakeholders being able to modify the weightings they place on different land uses and observing the impact this has on the achievement of multiple goals. It also allows for the development of innovative solutions which optimize the achievement of particular goals while minimizing the negative effects on other competing goals (e.g., conservation versus production).

While we have had some success with this approach, its utility depends on the quality of data available. Options can be developed in the absence of detailed information, but their reliability is correspondingly reduced.

17.3.3 Economic, agricultural, and hydrological modules

Since the landscape being considered is predominantly used for agricultural production, it is essential that biodiversity conservation be considered in the context of agriculture. There are three main components to be considered when setting this context, namely the agricultural production system itself (cropping systems, rotations, and so on), the socioeconomic context (farm profitability, social cohesion, and sustainability of rural communities), and the hydrology of the region. This last component is particularly important in the agricultural regions of Australia because of the problems with rising water tables and secondary salinization mentioned above in section 17.3.1.

These three components can be considered as separate modules of the overall integrated approach, and the goal is to include each as separate submodels which influence the development and implementation of management options. Information on agricultural production systems is readily available through standard farm-planning techniques, agronomic guidelines, and so on. This generally includes a good understanding of likely revenues based on various yield predictions. What is lacking, however, is detailed information on the costs and benefits of alternative agricultural systems such as integrated tree cropping, fodder shrubs, or systems which model themselves more on the native ecosystem (Lefroy *et al.*, 1999).

Information on the integrity of rural communities is harder to obtain and include, but can be based on the rate of change in rural population density, age structure, and so on, and the change in rural infrastructure such as banks, schools, and hospitals. The link between ecological integrity and social integrity is only recently beginning to be examined in a rigorous way (Price, 1995).

Finally, hydrological information can be incorporated either in the form of process models which predict water flows in different landscape elements (Clarke *et al.*, 1999), or more simply in the form of salinity risk assessments (Lambeck, 1999). Each land unit can be assigned with a level of salinity risk, and the impact of different management options on this level of risk can be assessed.

17.3.4 The ecological module: An approach to conservation management

Building the ecological component into an integrated approach proved difficult since the ecological information available was not of a type that could easily be incorporated into spatially explicit decision-making frameworks. Hence, we have attempted to clarify the "ecological" dynamics of fragmented systems and from this to develop practical methods of setting and achieving conservation goals at local and regional levels – i.e., we have examined in detail the ecological module in Fig. 17.2. To do this, we have developed the approach discussed below.

There are a number of approaches to conservation planning and management. These include:

(1) Attempts to protect single species because of their intrinsic importance.
(2) Single-species approaches using keystone or umbrella species with the intent of achieving benefits beyond the target species.
(3) Process-based approaches that aim to protect ecosystem functions on the assumption that the persistence of processes is a prerequisite for the persistence of species.
(4) Ecosystem management that attempts to bring together social, economic, and ecological issues in regional plans.

The evolution of these ideas represents a progression from single-issue problem-solving in particular locations to more complex systems perspectives that recognize the limitations of managing parts of a system without considering the interactions between system components.

Each of these approaches has merits and limitations. Single-species approaches are appropriate for endangered species but are generally of limited use when dealing with more widespread biotic decline. Ecosystem function-based approaches take into account the complexity and dynamism of the systems to be managed but fail to provide a framework for specifying the appropriate rates and pathways by which various ecosystem processes should proceed or the scale at which planning should occur.

These different approaches are all too often presented as alternatives, with new ideas substituting for old and little attempt made to incorporate existing concepts into new frameworks. We have attempted to draw together these different approaches in a framework that addresses clearly stated conservation goals and provides explicit design recommendations for land managers. This framework attempts to link species and ecosystem processes at local, landscape, and regional scales.

17.3.5 Specifying conservation goals

To argue the merits of any approach to conservation management, it is necessary to clearly articulate the goals being addressed. Arguments about methods are too often clouded by failure to clarify intentions. Approaches that may be appropriate for one particular goal will not be considered relevant by someone who is trying to achieve a different outcome.

Here we specify a conservation goal of retaining the naturally occurring biota in a given region, as part of a broader goal of ecological sustainability. Obviously the achievement of such a goal is scale-dependent – we cannot expect each manager to retain viable populations of all species in the area under his or her individual jurisdiction. Consequently we consider the above goal to be one that is to be addressed at a regional level. We therefore propose a finer-scale goal for individual land managers or for watershed management groups, which is to ensure that the land-use practices on any management unit, or in a local watershed, are not contributing to the decline of the natural diversity of the region. Implicit in this goal is a species focus: we consider that most regional conservation strategies will aim to prevent the loss of species from the region. Hence, it is necessary to ensure that the needs of the constituent species are met. In addition, ecosystem processes must continue to function if the biota is to persist and hence must proceed at rates and via pathways that are appropriate for meeting the needs of the species in the landscape. Thus, the maintenance of ecosystem function is not a goal for its own sake. Rather, functions need to be maintained for the services that they deliver to both the native species in the landscape and the human population that extracts its livelihood from the land.

17.3.6 Linking species and processes in conservation management

If our aim is to prevent the loss of species from a region, we have to ensure that the needs of all species in the landscape are met. However, it is clearly not feasible to know the requirements of all species. If species-based approaches are to have any value, we must develop solutions that are able to meet the needs of all species without considering each individually.

Umbrella and keystone species have been suggested as species whose protection will result in the protection of other species (Mills *et al.*, 1993; Paine, 1995; Simberloff, 1998). While such species undoubtedly exist, there are no clear guidelines for their identification. Most species probably act as umbrellas for some other species. While keystone species may be functionally important, their protection will not be sufficient to protect all other species in the ecosystem in which they are found.

The reason for the failure of species-based approaches to deliver operational benefits is that there has been little attempt to link these species with ecological processes in a planning context. The loss of species from any landscape is clearly attributable to the presence of some limiting or threatening processes. It is the management of these processes that is required to protect species. If we wish to retain all species that are being threatened by any given process, then the process will need to be managed at a level that will protect the most sensitive species. If species that are more sensitive to a threat are protected, then species that are less sensitive should also be protected. We therefore need to identify the species that are likely to be most sensitive to each threat and manage the threat at a level that will meet the needs of that species. Lambeck (1997) described such species as "focal species" – species towards which we primarily direct our management efforts. Where there are multiple threats, there will be multiple focal species, and where these threats affect multiple habitat types there will be a focal species for each threat in each habitat type. The result of this approach is a multi-species umbrella – a limited set of sensitive species whose requirements, if met, should meet the needs of all other less sensitive species. This approach makes the problem of species-based planning more tractable, and provides a justification for species-based studies because it can be clearly argued that the benefits extend beyond the particular species upon which attention is focused.

Any comprehensive approach to conservation management would consider all threatening processes in a landscape. However, in many instances management resources are limited and it is possible to consider only the primary threats in a landscape. In many landscapes, especially those subject to extensive alteration, the primary threats are habitat loss and habitat isolation. In such landscapes a primary aim is the assessment of the current adequacy and future requirements for habitat, including habitat type, amount and positioning.

Using the scheme devised by Lambeck (1997), species that are considered to be threatened by each of the threatening processes are grouped and ranked in terms of their sensitivity. Presence–absence surveys of vegetation remnants will indicate the distribution of the various species whose populations are considered to be limited by the amount of habitat available or by the degree of isolation of habitat patches. Analysis of the spatial attributes of the vegetation remnants in the landscape is then undertaken using GIS routines to determine the characteristics of habitat patches where species do and don't occur. This enables us to specify the minimum remnant size and the maximum interpatch distance that is required for these species to have a specified probability of occurring. It is then possible to identify all remnants that do not meet these criteria and specify the amount of habitat reconstruction required to convert a fragment that is currently inadequate to a size that is adequate. Similarly, it is possible to identify all remnants that are too isolated for the most dispersal-limited species and identify those positions in the landscape that need the construction of intermediate habitat patches or corridors in order to bring the isolated patches within reach of other suitable patches.

The focal-species planning approach has been used to determine the requirements for habitat in four watersheds in the wheatbelt of Western Australia, each covering an area of approximately 20–30 000 ha (see Wallace, 1998; Lambeck, 1999). The amount of native vegetation in these catchments ranges from approximately 3% to almost 30% cover.

Following the procedure outlined above, species that were considered at risk in each catchment were grouped according to the processes that were thought to be responsible for their vulnerability and ranked in terms of their perceived sensitivity. In all catchments, birds were identified as the species that were most area-limited. Surveys were undertaken in each catchment to determine the presence or absence of the vulnerable bird species in remnants of different sizes and different degrees of isolation.

These results were used to calculate the minimum habitat area, and the maximum interpatch distance that was required for each species to have a 60% probability of occurrence in a habitat patch. GIS routines were then used to identify all remnants that had insufficient habitat or were too isolated to meet the needs of the most demanding species. Maps were then produced which indicated the extent to which each patch needed to be expanded or connected in order to have an equivalent probability of being occupied by the species which had the greatest demand for that patch type. An example of this approach is given in Fig. 17.3.

While this approach enables us to identify the minimum patch sizes required for species to have a reasonable probability of occurrence, and to identify patches that were too isolated to be occupied, the results do not

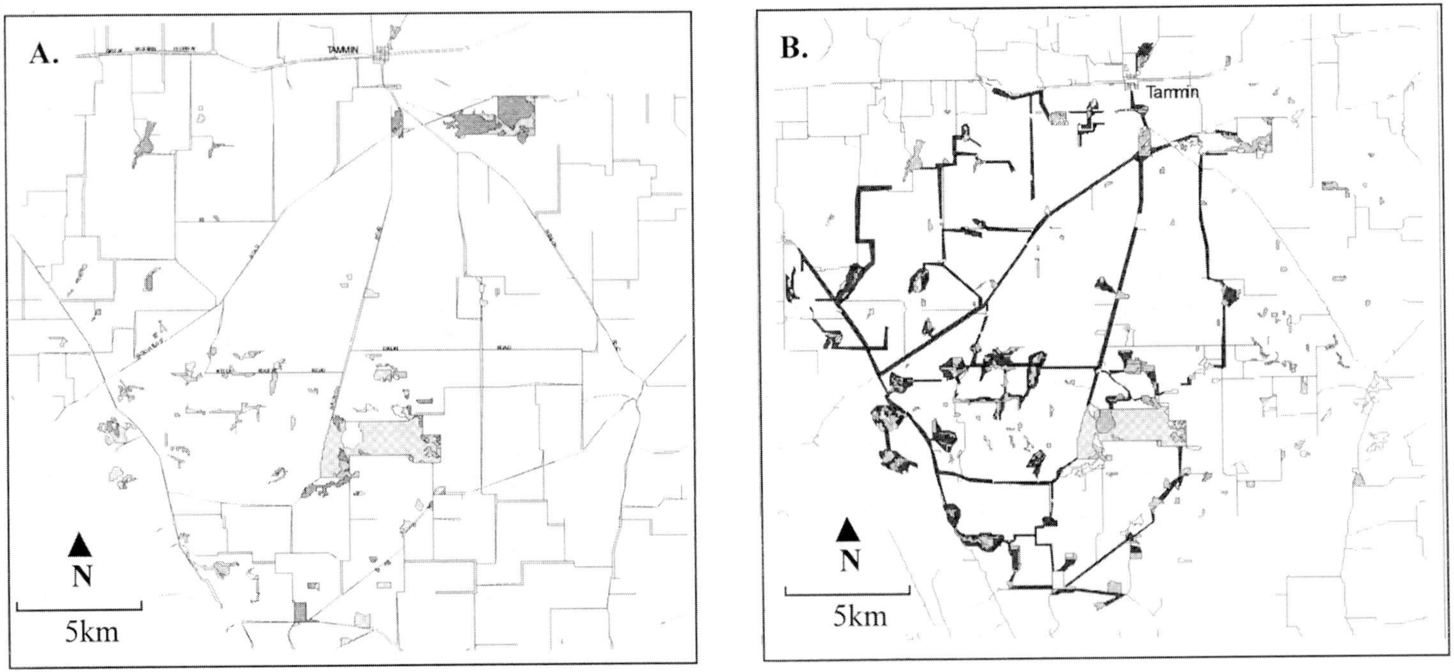

FIGURE 17.3
An example of the development of management options for a highly fragmented landscape, based on the estimated habitat and connectivity requirements of focal bird species. (A) The landscape as it currently exists in the South Tammin sub-catchment (watershed). Shaded areas are native vegetation of different types. (B) Recommendations for revegetation to enlarge existing vegetation patches and connect isolated patches. R. Lambeck, unpublished data.

ensure that populations will persist in the long term. Future work aims to explore the requirements for maintaining viable populations of the focal species and to test whether landscapes that support viable populations of focal species will also support viable populations of non-focal taxa. In the meantime, land managers are being advised to ensure that their landscapes have patches of habitat equal to or exceeding the specified size, and that these patches are separated by distances less than those specified. These patches need to be distributed from one boundary of the management area to the other and connected by high-quality strips of habitat. Such a design aims to ensure that populations of all species are linked across the area being managed. The failure of species to persist in such a landscape will not be attributable to practices in the management area, but will be due to adjoining areas failing to implement similar activities. The development of a regional management strategy based on conservation management zones, discussed below, will be used to facilitate the extension of these recommendations into adjoining watersheds. At the same time, the options developed to meet biodiversity conservation goals will be meshed with those developed in response to hydrological requirements for revegetation to combat secondary salinization in the region. Further, the economic implications of these actions can be assessed, and the findings of this analysis fed back into the process in an iterative manner.

17.3.7 From local to landscape: Cross-scale management

Conservation management can be applied at scales from individual remnants to regions. At remnant scales, management will consider the type, number, and configuration of patches within the remnant, whereas landscape management must also consider the distribution and linkage of such patches over bigger areas. Obviously the goal will vary depending on the scale being managed. The maintenance of viable populations of sparsely distributed, high-order predators is clearly not an appropriate goal for someone managing a remnant. The best that they can aim for is to provide high-quality habitat that can be used as part of a bigger activity range.

An extension of the focal-species approach described above would suggest that the minimum area over which conservation planning should be conducted to meet a goal of retaining all species is the area required to support a viable population of the species that occurs at lowest densities. Clearly this is not feasible in many locations where management boundaries are defined by watersheds or the jurisdiction of local government authorities.

If individual land managers or local groups of managers are unable to protect the biota in the area that they manage, it will be necessary to provide a regional framework that identifies the contribution that they can make to achieving that goal at a regional scale. Unfortunately, the types of action required to meet such a goal will differ from location to location as environmental conditions, patterns of land use, and the species complement vary. If the same recommendations are not appropriate for all locations, it will be necessary to identify areas that are sufficiently homogeneous that design parameters derived within the area can be legitimately extrapolated across the remainder of that area. These will be areas that are biophysically homogeneous and also have similar human land-use patterns. We term these units *conservation management zones*. These zones are identified by first partitioning the region of interest into bioregions – areas that have equivalent geomorphology and climate (Thackway and Cresswell, 1995, 1997), and then further subdividing each bioregion into areas having similar land-use patterns. The identification of landscapes with similar patterns can be achieved by using an array of landscape metrics that are available in GIS packages. Measures such as the percentage cover of vegetation, the proportion of different vegetation types, the number of patches, mean remnant size, contagion, and isolation are commonly used to characterize landscapes (O'Neill *et al.*, 1999).

By undertaking a focal-species analysis within a conservation management zone, it is possible to develop management recommendations that will be relevant for the whole of that zone. This approach enables the development of management recommendations that address strategic conservation goals in a spatially explicit manner that have application over relatively large areas. The development of conservation management zones is still in its experimental stages, and we have yet to complete the process. However, it seems possible to subdivide the Western Australian wheatbelt region into eight to ten zones within which management options will be broadly similar. If the conservation management zones can be then overlain with similar zonations based on hydrological characteristics (Clarke *et al.*, 1999), it will then be possible to develop conservation and restoration options which address the biodiversity and hydrological imperatives facing the region.

17.4 Implications for integrated science and management

The search for integrated solutions to landscape-scale problems is clearly on. A recent issue of the journal *Conservation Biology* contained several pleas for the development of an approach which is not only integrated across disciplines but also directly applicable in a management and planning framework (Babbitt, 1999; Blockstein, 1999; Clark, 1999). Is such an approach possible, and can we turn around the existing situation of disintegrating ecosystems and disintegration of the scientific and management systems used to tackle these? We are optimistic that this is possible, but not without some

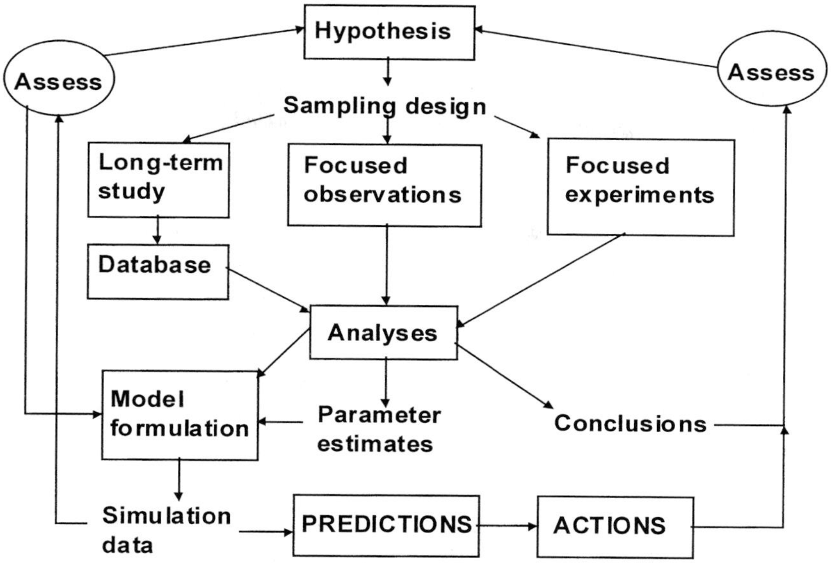

FIGURE 17.4
An approach to integrated research on landscape-scale problems, incorporating a variety of methodologies. Modified from Lavorel and Noble (1992).

fairly major changes in the way things are done. We have outlined one approach from the agricultural area of Western Australia, which we believe could have useful lessons for other parts of the world.

17.4.1 Integrated approaches to landscape science

How does one do science which is well integrated and can be linked directly to on-ground action? There are two aspects of this. One is the type of science itself, and the other is how the science interacts with the broader context. A suggested approach to these two aspects is given in Figs. 17.4 and 17.5. In Fig. 17.4, an approach is outlined which integrates a number of different methodologies. As Hobbs (1999), Wiens (1999), and others have argued, it is likely that traditional scientific methods involving statistically robust small-scale experimentation are insufficient to tackle the broad-scale problems which landscape ecology seeks to deal with. Rather, a pluralistic approach is needed which capitalizes on a variety of methods of investigation, such as straight observational studies, unreplicated management and "natural" experiments, focused small-scale experimentation, and modeling. Rather than debating the relative merits of each methodology individually, we need to recognize the strengths and weaknesses of each and combine methods into an integrated process, as suggested in Fig. 17.4.

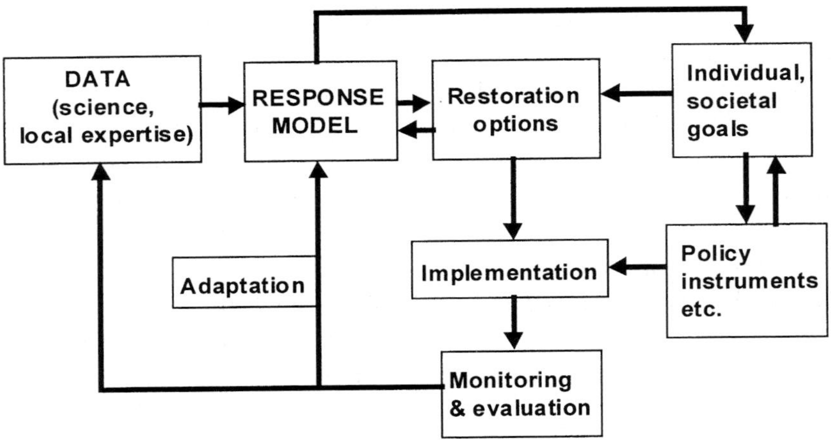

FIGURE 17.5
An adaptive management framework, in which data from both scientific investigations and local expertise are used to generate ecological response models, from which a range of management options can be derived. The options selected will depend on the goals of both individual landholders and society as a whole. Implementation of the selected options will be affected by a range of factors including the set of policy instruments (incentives, etc.) in place and broader socioeconomic issues. Implementation is accompanied by monitoring and evaluation of progress relative to the recognized goals, checked against the response models, and the management options are modified as necessary. At the same time the response models are modified as necessary in the light of new data. Modified from Hobbs and Saunders (2001).

Clearly, different elements of this process will be required during various phases of an investigation, and rates of progress in the different elements will vary greatly. However, it may frequently be necessary to continue with whatever information is available from one element, rather than waiting for more rigorous data to be gathered. It is a mistake to assume that we will ever have enough data to give a concrete answer to a particular question – there will always be unknowns in the system, and the system is, in any case, always changing. It is nevertheless important that good feedback mechanisms are in place so that further information can be fed into the process as it becomes available.

17.4.2 Linking science and management: Adaptive management

An important element in the scheme illustrated in Fig. 17.4 is the link to management action. This link is often missing in traditional scientific research (Hobbs, 1998c), but is essential if we are to bridge the gap between research and application. Figure 17.5 illustrates further how research can be carried out in a management framework. This scheme essentially illustrates the adaptive management process, as discussed by Walters and Hilborn (1978), Walters and

Holling (1990), Holling (1998), and others. This approach again emphasizes plurality and inclusivity, and indicates that use should be made of information from a variety of sources, including managers' experience and local knowledge. It also indicates that the outcomes from a scientific investigation are only one of the inputs into the development and implementation of management strategies – the social and economic context will, to a large extent, determine which options are acted upon. The results of an analysis are thus the starting-point for a negotiation among stakeholders, rather than a rigid blueprint to be stamped across the landscape. Each locality is likely to arrive at unique modifications of the generalized options arising from the analysis, and the process of reassessment and modification will continue.

17.4.3 Rules of thumb for landscape management

(1) Establish clear goals for the management to be undertaken.
(2) Consider production and conservation goals together – are there synergies that can be developed, and are trade-offs between different goals possible?
(3) Strategic conservation efforts are likely to be more effective and less costly than generalized approaches which do not have specific goals.
(4) Strategic efforts can be focused on the species with the most demanding requirements in terms of habitat, connectivity, or resources. This involves recognition of the main threats in the landscape, which in turn affect the goals that are set for particular landscapes.
(5) If landscapes with similar characteristics can be recognized and grouped, generalized management options can be established from a small number of case studies, hence reducing the need for detailed case-by-case analysis prior to action.
(6) Information on the dynamics of landscapes must be gathered from all sources possible, rather than relying on one mode of investigation.
(7) Management must be adaptive and, with effective monitoring, can both improve over time and provide greater understanding of how landscapes work.

17.4.4 Conclusions

It is worth once again emphasizing that the approaches outlined above are not easy to be fully implemented. It will not be easy to bring scientists from different disciplines and with different research emphases together. It will not be easy to convince traditional biologists with a strong belief in the importance of natural history observation that spatially explicit modelling provides useful or relevant insights. Similarly, it may be difficult to convince a GIS specialist that the results of months of painstaking field observations of a particular species are in any way relevant to his raster- or vector-based view of the world. There are simple language barriers between disciplines to be overcome, old disciplinary rivalries to be smoothed out, and the traditional empire-building academic mentality to be dealt with.

Beyond that, there is the need for scientists to interact effectively with the community at large. It has been our experience that the social interactions between researchers and the community groups with whom they work are probably more important to the success of a collaborative project than the actual conduct of the science itself. Unless the social and group-dynamic processes are right, it is likely that nothing will be achieved. Science is thus changing to a more complex process which requires a set of communication skills which are normally not part of a scientific training (Hobbs, 1998a).

These changes are happening, but slowly. They are happening out of necessity, but there is still a strong resistance amongst many scientists who either would prefer to retain the traditional approaches or are bound up in the current system which does not encourage or reward different ways of doing things. Landscape ecology can assist in developing a framework for encouraging integration and links between science and policy and management, and hence it offers real hope for the future.

17.5 Summary

In order to develop effective management strategies for landscapes in various states of repair, there is a need to mesh the different management objectives which are likely to prevail either within individual landscape elements or across multiple elements. This includes production and conservation goals, as well as broader social and economic goals. A clear statement of goals is essential to the process. We present a case study from the agricultural area of Western Australia, in which conservation goals are developed to maintain the biota remaining in the extensively fragmented agricultural landscapes. These goals are related to focal species, or those species which are most at risk from the main threats facing the region. Spatially explicit management plans are required which provide guidance on which actions are needed where in the landscape. Conservation management needs to be set in the context of management for agricultural production, maintaining farm profits, sustaining rural communities, and addressing the hydrological imbalance in the region. Although developed specifically in Western Australia, the methods outlined here could have relevance to any region where multiple management objectives have to be met and where conservation of biota occurs in a predominantly production landscape.

References

Babbitt, B. (1999). Noah's mandate and the birth of urban bioplanning. *Conservation Biology,* 13: 677–678.

Blockstein, D. E. (1999). Integrated science for ecosystem management: An achievable imperative. *Conservation Biology,* 13: 682–685.

Clark, J. R. (1999). The ecosystem approach from a practical point of view. *Conservation Biology,* 13: 679–681.

Clarke, C. J., Hobbs, R. J., Bell, R. W. & George, R. J. (1999). Incorporating geological effects in the modelling of revegetation strategies for salt affected landscapes. *Environmental Management,* 24: 99–109.

George, R. J., McFarlane, D. J. & Speed, R. J. (1995). The consequences of a changing hydrologic environment for native vegetation in south Western Australia. In *Nature Conservation 4: The Role of Networks,* eds. D. A. Saunders, J. L. Craig & E. M. Mattiske, pp. 9–22. Surrey Beatty, Chipping Norton, NSW.

Gunderson, L. H., Holling, C. S. & Light, S. S. (eds.) (1995). *Barriers and Bridges to the Renewal of Ecosystems and Institutions.* Columbia University Press, New York.

Hobbs, R. J. (ed.) (1992). *Biodiversity of Mediterranean Ecosystems in Australia.* Surrey Beatty, Chipping Norton, NSW.

Hobbs, R. J. (1993). Can revegetation assist in the conservation of biodiversity in agricultural areas? *Pacific Conservation Biology,* 1: 29–38.

Hobbs, R. J. (1994). Fragmentation in the wheatbelt of Western Australia: Landscape scale problems and solutions. In *Fragmentation in Agricultural Landscapes,* ed. J. Dover, pp. 3–20. International Association for Landscape Ecology, Garstang, UK.

Hobbs, R. J. (1997). Future landscapes and the future of landscape ecology. *Landscape and Urban Planning,* 37: 1–9.

Hobbs, R. J. (1998a). Ecologists in public. In *Ecology for Everyone: Communicating Ecology to Scientists, the Public and the Politicians,* eds. R. T. Wills & R. J. Hobbs, pp. 20–25. Surrey Beatty, Chipping Norton, NSW.

Hobbs, R. J. (1998b). Impacts of land use on biodiversity in southwestern Australia. In *Landscape Degradation in Mediterranean-Type Ecosystems,* eds. P. W. Rundel, G. Montenegro & F. Jaksic, pp. 81–106. Springer-Verlag, New York.

Hobbs, R. J. (1998c). Managing ecological systems and processes. In *Ecological Scale: Theory and Applications,* eds. D. Peterson & V. T. Parker, pp. 459–484. Columbia University Press, New York.

Hobbs, R. J. (1999). Clark Kent or Superman: Where is the phone booth for landscape ecology? In *Landscape Ecological Analysis: Issues and Applications,* eds. J. M. Klopatek & R. H. Gardner, pp. 11–23. Springer-Verlag, New York.

Hobbs, R. J. & Saunders, D. A. (1991). Reintegrating fragmented landscapes: A preliminary framework for the Western Australian wheatbelt. *Journal of Environmental Management,* 33: 161–167.

Hobbs, R. J. & Saunders, D. A. (eds.) (1993). *Reintegrating Fragmented Landscapes: Towards Sustainable Production and Conservation.* Springer-Verlag, New York.

Hobbs, R. J. & Saunders, D. A. (1995). Conversing with aliens: Do scientists communicate with each other well enough to solve complex environmental problems? In *Nature Conservation 4: The Role of Networks,* ed. D. A. Saunders, J. Craig & L. Mattiske, pp. 195–198. Surrey Beatty, Chipping Norton, NSW.

Hobbs, R. J. & Saunders, D. A. (2001). Nature conservation in agricultural landscapes: Real progress or moving deckchairs? In *Nature Conservation 5: Nature Conservation in Production Landscapes,* eds. J. Craig, N. Mitchell & D. Saunders, pp. 1–12. Surrey Beatty, Chipping Norton, NSW.

Hobbs, R. J., Saunders, D. A. & Arnold, G. W. (1993). Integrated landscape ecology: A Western Australian perspective. *Biological Conservation,* 64: 231–238.

Holling, C. S. (1998). Novelty, rigor, and diversity. *Conservation Ecology,* 2(2), art 14, http://www.consecol.org/journal/vol2/iss2/art14.

Ive, J. R. & Cocks, K. D. (1989). Incorporating multiparty preferences into land-use planning. *Environment and Planning B: Planning and Design,* 16: 99–109.

Ive, J. R., Cocks, K. D. & Parvey, C. A. (1989). Using the LUPIS land management package to select and schedule multi-site operations. *Journal of Environmental Management*, 29: 31–45.

Lambeck, R. J. (1997). Focal species: A multi-species umbrella for nature conservation. *Conservation Biology*, 11: 849–856.

Lambeck, R. J. (1998). The relationship between remnant vegetation and other land resources in dryland agricultural systems. In *Farming Action – Catchment Reaction: The Effect of Dryland Farming on the Natural Environment*, eds. J. Williams, R. A. Hook & H. L. Gascoigne, pp. 229–238. CSIRO Publishing, Collingwood, NSW.

Lambeck, R. J. (1999). *Landscape Planning for Biodiversity Conservation in Agricultural Regions.* Biodiversity Technical Paper no. 2. Department of the Environment and Heritage, Canberra, ACT.

Lavorel, S. & Noble, I. R. (1992). Ecosystem function of biodiversity: Experimentation, long-term observations and modelling. In *Biodiversity in Mediterranean Ecosystems in Australia*, ed. R. J. Hobbs, pp. 149–167. Surrey Beatty, Chipping Norton, NSW.

Lefroy, E. C., Hobbs, R. J., O'Connor, M. H. & Pate, J. S. (1999). What can agriculture learn from natural ecosystems? *Agroforestry Systems*, 45: 423–436.

Lubchenco, J. (1995). The relevance of ecology: The societal context and disciplinary implications of linkages across levels of ecological organization. In *Linking Species and Ecosystems*, eds. C. G. Jones & J. H. Lawton, pp. 297–305. Chapman & Hall, New York.

Mills, L. S., Soulé, M. E. & Doak, D. F. (1993). The keystone species concept in ecology and conservation. *BioScience*, 43: 219–224.

Myers, N., Mittermeier, R. A., Mittermeier, C. G., da Fonesca, G. A. B. & Kent, J. (2000). Biodiversity hotspots for conservation priorities. *Nature*, 403: 853–858.

O'Neill, R. V., Riitters, K. H., Wickham, J. D. & Jones, K. B. (1999). Landscape pattern metrics and regional assessment. *Ecosystem Health*, 5: 225–233.

Paine, R. T. (1995). A conversation on refining the concept of keystone species. *Conservation Biology*, 9: 962–964.

Price, P. (ed.) (1995). *Socio-Economic Aspects of Maintaining Native Vegetation on Agricultural Land*. Land and Water Research and Development Corporation, Canberra, ACT.

Saunders, D. A. & Hobbs, R. J. (1995). Habitat reconstruction: The revegetation imperative. In *Conserving Biodiversity: Threats and Solutions*, eds. R. A. Bradstock, T. D. Auld, D. A. Keith, R. T. Kingsford, D. Lunney & D. P. Silversten, pp. 104–112. Surrey Beatty, Chipping Norton, NSW.

Simberloff, D. (1998). Flagships, umbrellas, and keystones: Is single species management passé in the landscape era? *Biological Conservation*, 83: 247–257.

Thackway, R. & Cresswell, I. D. (eds.) (1995). *An Interim Biogeographic Regionalisation for Australia: A Framework for Setting Priorities in the National Reserves System Cooperative Program*. Australian Nature Conservation Agency, Canberra, ACT.

Thackway, R. & Cresswell, I. D. (1997). A bioregional framework for planning the National System of Protected Areas in Australia. *Natural Areas Journal*, 17: 241–247.

Wallace, K. J. (ed.) (1998). *Dongolocking Pilot Planning Project for Remnant Vegetation, Final Report (Phase 1)*. Department of Conservation and Land Management, Perth, WA.

Walters, C. J. & Hilborn, R. (1978). Ecological optimization and adaptive management. *Annual Review of Ecology and Systematics*, 9: 157–188.

Walters, C. J. & Holling, C. S. (1990). Large-scale management experiments and learning by doing. *Ecology*, 71: 2060–2068.

Wiens, J. A. (1999). The science and practice of landscape ecology. In *Landscape Ecological Analysis: Issues and Applications*, eds. J. M. Klopatek & R. H. Gardner, pp. 371–383. Springer-Verlag, New York.

PART VI

Syntheses and perspectives

This final section provides syntheses and perspectives regarding the interrelationships between landscape ecology and natural resource management. Although many chapters in previous sections have offered different degrees of syntheses and have touched upon various aspects of future directions, Turner *et al.* elevate the syntheses to an even higher level, while Odum and Forman provide foresight regarding the future of landscape ecology and natural resource management.

Turner *et al.* (Chapter 18) synthesize the viewpoints and findings about the spatial interrelationships among landscape elements at multiple scales and discuss the challenges in the shift toward research and management of integrated ecosystems. They then identify the causes and types of gaps between landscape ecology and natural resource management, including differences in goals, incongruities of scale, tools and methods, training and experiences of landscape ecologists and resource managers, infrastructure and data, and institutional culture. To truly integrate landscape ecology into natural resource management and use management practices as opportunities for landscape ecological research, the authors offer practical suggestions for bridging each of these gaps.

Landscape ecology traditionally has focused on scales from patches to landscapes, but Odum (Chapter 19) argues that region is a more appropriate scale for addressing many land-use and environmental problems. His argument is supported by the fact that many ecological processes occur across landscape boundaries, as demonstrated by examples in many other chapters of this book, especially those in Part III ("Landscape function and cross-boundary management"). Further, he suggests that it is necessary to have closer cooperation between academic and non-academic institutions, as well as integration between social and natural sciences at large scales.

In the Epilogue, Forman begins with his personal experiences and observations in Costa Rica, stating that landscape ecology can provide a good foundation for meshing nature and people spatially for long-term harmony and balance. He points out that this book is not only a test of a dozen emerging directions discussed in his paper 15 years ago, but that it also demonstrates how far this subject has progressed in such a short period of time. He proposes approaches to managing three major types of land and ways of putting landscape ecology principles to work on the ground. He then identifies four key frontiers in applying landscape ecology to natural resources management. Finally, he calls for more research on regional ecology and emphasizes that the ultimate objective of natural resource management is to design sustainable landscapes and to achieve sustainability.

MONICA G. TURNER, THOMAS R. CROW, JIANGUO LIU, DALE RABE,
CHARLES F. RABENI, PATRICIA A. SORANNO, WILLIAM W. TAYLOR,
KRISTIINA A. VOGT, AND JOHN A. WIENS

18

Bridging the gap between landscape ecology and natural resource management

18.1 Introduction

In every respect, the valley rules the stream. Noel Hynes (1975)

The challenges facing natural resource managers occur over entire landscapes and involve landscape components at many scales. Many resource managers are shifting their approach from managing resources such as fish, wildlife, and water separately to managing for the integrity of entire ecosystems (Christensen *et al.*, 1996). Indeed, nearly all resource management agencies in the USA have recognized that informed management decisions cannot be made exclusively at the level of habitat units or local sites. It is generally accepted that ecological patterns and processes must be considered over large areas when biodiversity and ecological function must be maintained while the goods and services desired by the public are provided. For example, forest managers must determine the patterns and timing of tree harvesting while maintaining an amount and arrangement of habitats that will sustain many species. Managers of parks and nature reserves must be attentive to actions occurring on surrounding lands outside their jurisdiction. Aquatic resource managers must broaden their perspective to encompass the terrestrial and human landscape to manage stream and lake resources effectively (Hynes, 1975, widely regarded as the father of modern stream ecology and quoted above; Naiman *et al.*, 1995). Landscape ecology also is implicit in the paradigm of ecosystem management (Grumbine, 1994; Christensen *et al.*, 1996).

Despite the acknowledged importance of a landscape perspective by both scientists and resource managers, determining how to implement management at broader scales is very much a work in progress. It is pertinent for managers to determine what is the appropriate scale of analysis when managing natural resources because a manager must investigate the trade-offs of different natural resource uses while applying an ecosystem management approach

(Chapter 6, this book). Most managers are faced with having to satisfy multiple conflicting uses of a particular management unit with different relevant scales of analysis for each resource (Romm and Washburn, 1987; Chapter 6, this book). These scale differences require a manager to determine the appropriate landscape scale of analysis where the boundaries vary with the resource being managed and the structural and functional characteristics of the landscape matrix (Maxwell *et al.*, 1999; Parry and Vogt, 1999).

The science of landscape ecology, which deals explicitly with the causes and consequences of spatial heterogeneity (Turner, 1989; Pickett and Cadenasso, 1995; Turner *et al.*, 2001), offers concepts and tools that are directly relevant to natural resource management on heterogeneneous landscapes. Applied problems clearly helped catalyze the development of landscape ecology. However, the richness of the theory, methods, and language of landscape ecology has not yet been fully integrated in resource management, despite the rapidly increasing demand from managers for knowledge, tools, and personnel trained in landscape ecology. Many landscape ecologists do not understand the needs of resource managers, and many resource managers are not familiar with developments in landscape ecology. In this chapter, we illustrate some resource management challenges that reflect the need for a landscape perspective, synthesize our viewpoints to identify gaps between landscape ecology and resource management and their causes, and offer some suggestions for bridging the gaps.

18.2 What can be gained from a landscape perspective?

In what areas of resource management may landscape ecology be particularly helpful? We highlight two general areas – aquatic resources and forest management – to provide context for our discussion of the gaps between the science of landscape ecology and its application. These examples were chosen to illustrate areas in which basic research has identified important landscape linkages that may provide a basis for management implementation. Many other examples can be found in other chapters of this book.

18.2.1 Aquatic resources

Freshwater ecosystems are integrators and centers of organization within the landscape, touching nearly all aspects of the natural environment and human culture (Naiman *et al.*, 1995; Naiman, 1996). Understanding the degree to which land uses in the uplands, and the spatial arrangement of these land uses, influence habitat and water quality in streams and lakes is a common theme underlying many studies of land–water interactions. Freshwaters are degraded by increasing inputs of silt, nutrients, and pollutants from agriculture, forest harvest, and urban development (Carpenter *et al.*, 1998). The incorporation of landscape ecology into stream management promises to contribute to the understanding of these influences. Although landscape concepts have been incorporated into stream ecosystem theory (e.g., Vannote *et al.*, 1980; Frissell *et al.*, 1986; Wiley *et al.*, 1990; Townsend, 1996), lake ecosystem theory (e.g., Kratz *et al.*, 1997; Magnuson and Kratz, 2000), and as part of watershed analyses that combine geographical information systems (GIS) and modeling (Young *et al.*, 1989; Dubayah *et al.*, 1997), they are less well integrated into real-world management. New management perspectives and approaches are necessary to restore degraded aquatic ecosystems and to maintain those that are in satisfactory condition.

Land use and water quality

The landscape mosaic is important for water quality. For example, Osborne and Wiley (1988) analyzed the nitrogen and phosphorus concentrations of streams in the Salt River Basin, Illinois, and used regression analysis to determine whether there was a relationship with land-use patterns mapped from aerial photos. Their results demonstrated that the amount of urban land cover and its distance from the stream were the most important variables in predicting nutrient concentrations in the stream water. In 33 lake watersheds in the Minneapolis–St. Paul area, Minnesota, landscape and vegetation patterns were obtained from aerial photographs and then compared with measured lake water quality (Detenbeck *et al.*, 1993). Lakes with forest-dominated watersheds tended to be less eutrophic and have lower levels of chloride and lead. In contrast, lakes with substantial agricultural land uses in their watersheds were more eutrophic. When wetlands remained intact in the watersheds, less lead was present in the lake water. Other studies have also found significant relationships between land use and concentrations of nutrients in lakes and streams (e.g., Geier *et al.*, 1994; Hunsaker and Levine, 1995; Johnes *et al.*, 1996; Soranno *et al.*, 1996; Bolstad and Swank, 1997; Johnson *et al.*, 1997; Lowrance, 1998; Bennett *et al.*, 1999).

A simple model of phosphorus transformation and transport for the Lake Mendota watershed, Wisconsin, has provided useful insights into the effects of the landscape mosaic on water quality (Soranno *et al.*, 1996). This study highlighted the importance of identifying both the spatial extent and geographic location of sources of P within the watershed. Most of the watershed did not contribute phosphorus loading to the lake, and the magnitude of input from the watershed varied based on precipitation levels. For example, the watershed contributed about 17% of loading to the lake during low-precipitation years and 50% during high-precipitation years. Riparian vegetation was also very important in attenuating phosphorus runoff. In other examples, the geomorphology of the riparian zone and the soil processes occurring adjacent to streams can have an overriding control on the nutrient retention capacity of this zone (McDowell and Wood, 1984; McDowell, 1998) and define its spatial extent (Scatena, 1990). Management actions will be most effective when they are spatially explicit with respect to the resource and consider both sources and sinks of phosphorus as well as the structural and functional characteristics of the area.

Landscape ecologists have taken particular interest in characterizing and understanding the function of patches or corridors of riparian vegetation because their functional importance is large relative to their size (Lowrance *et al.*, 1997; Naiman and Decamps, 1997; Lowrance, 1998). The spatial pattern of riparian vegetation – i.e., variation in length, width, and gaps – influences its effectiveness as a nutrient sink. Weller *et al.* (1998) developed and analyzed models predicting landscape discharge based on material release by an uphill source area, the spatial distribution of riparian buffer along a stream, and retention of material within the buffer. Again, a strong influence of the spatial characteristics of the riparian zone was demonstrated. For example, variability in riparian buffer width reduced total buffer retention and increased the width needed to meet a management goal (Weller *et al.*, 1998). Variable-width buffers were less efficient than uniform-width buffers because transport through gaps dominated discharge, especially when buffers were narrow; average buffer width was the best predictor of landscape discharge for unretentive buffers, whereas the frequency of gaps was the best predictor for narrow, retentive buffers (Weller *et al.*, 1998). The sensitivity of freshwater quality to changes in the riparian zone again underscores the need for a spatially explicit view of the watershed.

Fish habitat

Habitat for a fish may be defined as the "local physicochemical and biological features of a site that constitute the daily environment of fish" (Milner *et al.*, 1985). Although fish clearly respond to local conditions, habitat quality is influenced by activities and conditions that may occur far from the stream. Channel morphology and stability, water temperature, nutrients, dissolved oxygen, and flow variation and regime at any one site are influenced by conditions in the watershed in which the stream is embedded. These watershed influences may determine the overall habitat quality of a stream and its potential capacity to support fish (Rabeni and Sowa, 1996). Thus, fish populations and communities must be viewed in the context of the entire watershed. Intense efforts to remedy particular fisheries problems locally (i.e., within a stream reach) may be ineffective if watershed influences exert the overriding control. Managers usually do consider beyond-reach effects, but funding levels rarely permit implementation of projects at the broader scales.

Because land use within the watershed may strongly influence fish communities, there is a clear need to analyze management issues at a landscape level. In a study of fish in Wisconsin streams, the health of fish communities was negatively correlated with the amount of upstream urban development (Wang *et al.*, 1997). Fish community health was positively related to the amount of upstream forest in the watershed and negatively related to the amount of agricultural land. The response of the fish community to land-use changes was not linear: declines in the condition of the fish fauna occurred after about 20% of the watershed was urbanized. No impacts were attributed to agriculture until about 50% of the watershed was used for this purpose. Similar results obtained in other studies also demonstrate the importance of regional land use as the prime determinant of local stream conditions (e.g., Richards *et al.*, 1996; Allan and Johnson, 1997). Theoretical studies of landscape pattern have identified critical thresholds in the abundance of particular habitat that produce qualitative differences in habitat connectivity (e.g., Gardner *et al.*, 1987; Pearson *et al.*, 1996) or spatial processes that move across a landscape (e.g., Turner *et al.*, 1989). Empirical support exists for the effects of critical thresholds in habitat abundance on bird and mammal communities in terrestrial landscapes (e.g., Andren, 1994); it would be very interesting to know whether similar thresholds are widely applicable for aquatic fauna.

Land-use changes have altered the water table and runoff patterns with predictable impacts on fishes. In the tallgrass prairie biome of North America, agricultural activities have decreased water tables and increased siltation, turning small, clear-flowing perennial streams into turbid intermittent creeks (Rabeni, 1996). Altered hydraulic regimes contribute to changes in stream-channel morphology and now the typical situation is a wider, shallower, heavily eroded channel. Fishes adapted to clear water, stable substrates, and aquatic vegetation have been replaced by fishes less specialized in their feeding habits, reproductive requirements or physiological tolerances. For example, since 1850, two-thirds of the fish species in the Illinois River system have declined in abundance or been eliminated from parts of their historic range. Additionally the historical ecological ratios of species have been altered to where omnivores now predominate over the more specialized carnivores, insectivores, and herbivores (Karr *et al.*, 1985).

Land-use changes that propagate slowly and unpredictably through drainage networks are termed "complex responses" by geomorphologists (Kooi and Beaumont, 1996; Dominick and O'Neill, 1998). In larger drainage basins, many different land-use changes and natural climatic variations may take place simultaneously. Understandably, fisheries management is complicated by land-use activities that result in differential alterations of runoff and sediment yield – two important variables affecting physical habitat of fishes. For example, agricultural practices in the eighteenth and nineteenth centuries in Maryland Piedmont watersheds increased soil erosion which resulted in stream aggradation (the streambed elevated) because of excess sediment yield (Jacobson and Coleman, 1986). The recent institution of soil conservation practices and the retirement of marginal lands from cultivation in some watersheds have reduced sediment yields to the streams. Runoff continued to be higher than historical levels, however, causing the streams to incise (downcut) because of bed erosion and coarsening their beds, thus preventing historical physical habitat for fishes from being re-established.

The state of the art concerning land use–aquatic biota interactions is still primitive and limited to rather gross associations. Nevertheless, studies detecting correlations between stream biota and landscape-level activities are essential first steps in the efficient management of aquatic fauna. The next step toward management must be the elucidation of underlying mechanisms. For example, does urbanization negatively influence fishes because it results in too much water or sediment, too little water or sediment, altered water quality, all of the above, or some other factors? Understanding when the landscape mosaic is important and identifying the landscape elements critical for particular aquatic resources (and any thresholds) would contribute to more effective management of lakes and streams. These issues present a challenge to management at the watershed scale.

18.2.2 Management of forest landscapes

Understanding the dynamics and heterogeneity of natural forest landscapes has become increasingly important as management objectives for forests broaden to include maintenance of biological diversity (Spies and Turner, 1999). At the same time, multiple conflicting demands are being placed on forests by continued harvest of timber and non-timber forest products (Vogt *et al.*, 1999a,b). Forest certification developed to aid assessment of the sustainability of social and natural systems that are closely linked to natural resources (Vogt *et al.*, 1999a,b). Management has to consider the impacts of both natural and anthropogenic factors whose impacts occur at variable scales within the landscape. Natural disturbances, such as fires or storm events, create a mosaic of stand ages across forest landscapes. Forest harvesting operations also are explicitly spatial, having an immediate impact on landscape structure by creating harvested patches of varying size, shape, age, and spatial arrangements (Larson *et al.*, 1999). Understanding the interactions among the processes generating patterns in forest landscapes and the many ecological responses to these patterns and how they change through time is key to effective forest management (Franklin and Forman, 1987; Oliver *et al.*, 1999; Spies and Turner, 1999).

Forest harvesting patterns

A clear signature of forest cutting on patterns is observed in many forest landscapes (Burgess and Sharpe, 1981; Krummel *et al.*, 1987; Spies *et al.*, 1994; Turner *et al.*, 1996). Landscape ecologists have quantified many of the effects of harvesting on forest landscape structure. In the upper Midwest, for example, a harvested forest landscape had more small forest patches and fewer large patches than an unharvested landscape, and forest patches in the disturbed landscape were simpler in shape (Mladenoff *et al.*, 1993). In addition, certain types of juxtapositions between different forest community types (e.g., hemlock–lowland conifers) were present in the old-growth landscape but absent in the disturbed landscape.

Landscape ecological models have been used to explore the implications of different patterns of harvesting timber from forested landscapes (e.g., Franklin and Forman, 1987; Li *et al.*, 1993; Liu, 1993; Wallin *et al.*, 1994; Gustafson and Crow, 1996). These models typically take an area like a watershed or a national forest and simulate different sizes and arrangements of harvest areas, as well as how much time elapses until the next harvest. For example, small dispersed cuts and large aggregated cuts have been compared in terms of their effect on landscape structure. Similarly, the effects of varying the time between successive harvests – sometimes called rotation length – from 50 to 100 to 200 years have been studied. In addition to projecting the configuration of forests of different age on the landscape, the models often examine the effects of each scenario on the potential distribution of suitable habitat for wildlife populations.

Some important insights for forest management have emerged from studies using landscape models of forest harvesting. The deleterious effects of small-dispersed cutting patterns for habitat connectivity are readily apparent from simulation studies (Franklin and Forman, 1987; Li *et al.*, 1993; Wallin *et al.*, 1994; Gustafson and Crow, 1996). The small dispersed cuts such as those practiced on federal lands in the Pacific Northwest during the past 40 years created a highly modified forest landscape that contains very little forest interior. For the same total area cut, fewer but larger aggregated cuts actually can maintain greater connectivity of forest habitats. However, it is important to remember that the shift to the small dispersed cutting patterns was in part a response to negative public perceptions of large clear-cuts. Another important insight gained from these models is an estimate of the amount of time required for the patterns established by a cutting regime to be erased from the landscape.

Simulation modeling studies demonstrated that once established, the landscape pattern created by dispersed disturbances is difficult to erase unless the rate of cutting is substantially reduced or the rotation period is increased (Wallin *et al.*, 1994). To overcome the problems of dispersed disturbances, alternative cutting plans are now being considered and implemented in the Pacific Northwest (Franklin *et al.*, 1999; Halpern *et al.*, 1999)

Natural disturbance regimes

Disturbance is a major agent of pattern formation in forests and many other landscapes, and disturbance may even be required for the maintenance of ecosystem function. Results of natural disturbances range in size from small "gaps" in a forest canopy or rocky intertidal region created by the death of one or a few individuals, to larger patches created by severe windstorms, fires, and landslides occurring after hurricanes. Landscape ecologists have focused considerable effort on studying disturbance dynamics – often in forest landscapes – because disturbance is often responsible for creating and maintaining the patterns we observe (e.g., Romme, 1982; Pickett and White, 1985; Turner, 1987; Foster *et al.*, 1998). Many studies have demonstrated how intentional or unintentional shifts in the disturbance regime may dramatically alter the landscape, and these have important implications for forest management.

Baker's (1992) study of changing fire regimes in the Boundary Waters Canoe Area of northern Minnesota provides an illustration of how landscape structure varies with fire frequency. Prior to European settlement, fires were relatively large in extent and infrequent. As the upper Midwest was settled by Europeans, fire frequency increased substantially because of indiscriminate burning by early settlers, land speculators, and prospectors. A period of fire suppression followed. Settlement and fire suppression both produced substantial shifts from the pre-settlement disturbance regime and resulted in significant effects on landscape structure (Baker, 1992). Interestingly, the Boundary Waters Canoe Area was affected by a massive severe windstorm on July 4, 1999, which resulted in >100 000 ha of windthrown trees; the potential exists for large high-intensity fires to occur for several years due to this storm.

Disturbance has been increasingly recognized by ecologists as a natural process and source of heterogeneity within ecological communities, reflecting a real shift in perception from an equilibrial to non-equilibrial view of the natural world (Wiens, 1976; Pickett *et al.*, 1994). This shift clearly has significant implications for management of forest landscapes. Managing human disturbances to mimic the spatial and temporal patterns of natural disturbances and minimize deleterious effects has also been debated (e.g., Hunter, 1993; Attiwill, 1994; Delong and Tanner, 1996). Of course, meeting such an objective requires understanding the dynamics of the natural disturbance regime in a given landscape. More generally, managers must understand the consequences of naturally induced landscape heterogeneity in order to understand and manage the consequences of human-induced heterogeneity.

Managing forests from the landscape perspective is a relatively recent addition to the usual forest management approaches (Mladenoff *et al.*, 1994; Oliver *et al.*, 1999). Prior to this, the scheduling of forest harvest was based on more simplistic silvicultural rules and was done with little consideration for the consequences of harvesting regimes on spatial and temporal changes in stand structure. Integration of landscape ecological concepts and methods allows spatial dynamics and constraints to be considered (Oliver *et al.*, 1999).

18.3 Gaps between landscape ecology and natural resource management: What are they, and why are they there?

The strength and vitality of landscape ecology are due in large part to the integration of scientific insights with applications to real-world problems. Landscape ecology offers a perspective to applied questions about natural environment that complements those emerging from other levels in ecology. By linking patterns and processes, landscape ecology may provide insight into many practical problems regarding the land, how it is managed, and how it will change. This theme runs through virtually all of the textbooks and symposia proceedings in landscape ecology and is prevalent in the papers published in *Landscape Ecology*, *Landscape and Urban Planning*, and a host of other journals in a variety of disciplines. But is this expectation of real-world applications more promise and potential than practice? Is landscape ecology delivering on its stated commitment to integrate science and practice? If not (and we suggest that this potential has been only partially fulfilled), how might such an integration be fostered?

Landscape ecology has certainly fostered an increased awareness of some of the fundamental problems that confront both basic and applied ecologists. Landscape ecology tells us that homogeneity is an illusion, that scale matters, and that the effects of heterogeneity and scale will differ among organisms or ecosystems. Landscape ecology has had considerable success in bringing a variety of tools to bear on these problems, tools such as spatial modeling, remote sensing, GIS, and spatial statistics. These tools allow us to describe and analyze spatial patterns in great detail, and to explore the consequences of various forms of heterogeneity in an apparently limitless array of "What if" scenarios. As a result, we are rapidly developing a richer understanding of the first two components of landscape ecology, the effects of heterogeneity and of scale. We can realistically expect that, before very long, developments in these areas will lead to theory that actually generates useful predictions. Less progress has been made, however, in dealing with the third component of landscape ecology, the seemingly idiosyncratic nature of species and of ecosystems.

The current state of development of landscape ecology as a science bears directly on the gaps between a landscape perspective and the management of natural resources. Some of these gaps derive from the imperfect state of the science or the mismatch between the needs of managers and the current state of our basic understanding. Others relate to the current state of resource management and its ability to embrace new paradigms. Table 18.1 summarizes the major gaps between landscape ecology and natural resource management.

18.3.1 Goals

A major gap between landscape ecology and natural resource management is the difference in their goals. The main goal of landscape ecology is to understand the causes and ecological consequences of spatial heterogeneity across landscapes, whereas natural resource management aims toward maintaining or altering natural resources for societal values (e.g., timber, wildlife, fish, water quality, and biodiversity). The goal of landscape ecology is relatively easy to define and evaluate through procedures such as hypothesis testing. But how should landscape management goals be specified and success evaluated? Goal setting and evaluation are crucial for resource managers, yet the basic science of landscape ecology has not yet provided satisfactory guidance. It is more challenging to define landscape-level management goals than traditional natural resource management goals because traditional resource management emphasized the amount of product, and landscape-level goals remain difficult to translate into management schemes (Perera *et al.*, 2000). Landscape-level management goals must include the amount of product as well as the spatial patterns and ecological processes in the landscape. For example, given a certain amount of wildlife habitat, how should such habitats be arranged spatially (e.g., size, shape, and distribution of patches), and exactly what does the manager gain from such arrangements? What is the effect of alternative arrangements on aesthetics and other societal values? Note that the shift in management goals from extraction to sustainability leads directly to consideration of spatial relationships and scales, as these affect the likelihood of achieving sustainability.

18.3.2 Incongruities of scale

Issues of scale are multi-faceted and fundamental to the science and applications of landscape ecology. Scaling issues involve a coupling between the heterogeneity and spatial structuring of landscapes and the ways in which

Table 18.1. *Major gaps between landscape ecology and natural resource management and suggestions for bridging the gaps*

	Landscape ecology	Natural resource management	Means to bridge the gaps
Goals	Understand causes and ecological consequences of spatial heterogeneity	Maintain or alter natural resources for societal objectives as guided by local, state, and federal statute	Couple the goals such that both are considered important; share language
Scales	Ecologically meaningful scales	Management-oriented scales	Reconcile scales through multi-scale study and management
Tools/methods	Spatial modeling and analysis, geographic information systems, experiments	Harvest, prescribed fires, wildlife management, restoration, habitat manipulation	Apply tools in landscape ecology to evaluate management consequences; use management practices to create landscape ecological experiments; work together to develop models
Training/ experience of personnel	Training in ecology, no management experience	Out-dated or little training in ecology, rich management experience	Provide updated information for managers and offer management experience to ecologists; create opportunities for continued dialogue and education that are conducive to exchange of ideas and information
Data	Observation results, simulation results, experimental results, remote sensing data	Observation results, remote sensing data	Share data, and collaborate on obtaining data to avoid duplication of effort
Institutional culture	Publish or perish	Crisis control and problem-solving	Recognize outreach efforts of ecologists in solving real-world problems, and reward managers' participation in research endeavor for better management decisions and practices

different kinds of organisms or ecological processes respond to this heterogeneity and structure. We summarize here four incongruities of scale that are of particular importance for resource management (see also Peterson and Parker, 1998; Wiens, 1999).

One incongruity of scale is that management units are often smaller than the scale of ecological dynamics or the scale of the human ecosystem, leading to a mismatch in ecological and management scales. Watersheds, for example, are ecologically meaningful landscape units, yet their boundaries often do not match administrative boundaries – indeed, the stream or river often serves as a political boundary. Mechanisms for funding broader-scale management programs remain limited, and thus, influencing the political process becomes important. Resource management decisions within a watershed are often made by multiple independent owners or institutions. In the United States, land-use decisions – if they are made at all – are usually made at a local level (Dale *et al.*, 2000). There are regional planning commissions in some parts of the country, but they often lack the authority to influence land-use decisions. Individual changes in land use may appear to have only local significance. In total, however, the large number of local changes transforms the landscape (Turner *et al.*, 1998). Gradual but widespread change significantly impacts vegetative cover, wildlife habitat, soils, and water quality. These ecological changes also feed back to impact the human ecosystem and the type and intensity of management that will occur in a natural system (Chapter 6, this book). This can result in natural resource management occurring at the wrong scale so that sensitive indicators are not being used when making management decisions (Maxwell *et al.*, 1999).

A second important incongruity in scales relates to the scales at which data are collected and the scales at which management decisions must be made. How are the findings of research conducted at fine scales to be incorporated into management decisions made at broad scales? This is essentially a question of translating among scales; we wish to derive "scaling functions" that portray how the phenomena of interest vary with scale and whether there are sharp thresholds or non-linearities that might limit our ability to extrapolate. Although scaling functions have a long history in comparative anatomy and ecology, derivation of scaling functions in landscape ecology is more complicated because one must consider simultaneously how patterns and processes in the physical environment vary with changes in scale *and* the scale-dependency of the responses of organisms to those environmental factors. However, it also is inappropriate to assume that it is *always* necessary to scale information from the fine to broad scales to understand or manage a system. It is preferable to identify the sensitive scale and focus research on that scale (Chapter 6, this book), but identifying the "correct" scale(s) for management remains a practical challenge. In practice, managers often find their choices of scale constrained by the scales of the available data.

The third general incongruity in scales has to do with translating between ecological systems. How can we move from providing situation-specific recommendations to developing generalizations about organisms and ecosystems that will be useful to managers? This question involves whether the same principles or scaling functions can be applied to suites of species or similar types of ecosystems. Although some practical approaches to developing such generalizations have been proposed (e.g., Addicott *et al.*, 1987), we lack a generally accepted construct for achieving this.

Fourth, there is often an incongruity of scales between data in the social and the natural sciences, yet both are important for landscape management decisions (Chapter 6, this book). For example, the state of an aquatic system may be strongly influenced by human population density and development in riparian areas. Population and building data are often available for political units such as counties, towns, or census tracts, yet relating these units to water quality for individual lakes is difficult. Linking information collected at political and ecological scales was successfully used by Grove and Hohmann (1992) to assess the health of watersheds associated with the city of Baltimore (see case study in Chapter 6, this book). However, few examples are available where the information collected at the political scale was similar to the ecological scale and an analysis comprised of both scales could be used as an effective management tool. Scales should be chosen based on the patterns and processes to be characterized, with forethought given to the integration of different data sets.

18.3.3 Tools and methods

Appropriate tools and methods are essential to achieve the goals of landscape ecology and natural resource management. Numerous metrics for quantifying spatial patterns and how they change through time have emerged from landscape ecology, and these are now widely available (e.g., McGarigal and Marks, 1995). However, many potential users are not well informed about the assumptions and caveats that influence their appropriate use and interpretation (Gustafson, 1998). Spatial analyses should not become codified such that a suite of standard tools is automatically transferred from one system to the next or from one scale to another, but informed use of these methods is critical.

Models are important tools in landscape ecology, and they will continue to be powerful complements to empirical studies. It is often impossible to conduct experiments over large areas that span the range of many treatments of interest or that permit responses of the system to be followed over long periods of time. Models provide at least a partial substitute for landscape-level experiments. Most landscape models, however, have been developed as research tools rather than management tools. They are often complex, requiring information that is simply not available for most species. Only a few species, such as the northern spotted owl (*Strix occidentalis*; McKelvey *et al.*, 1993), Bachman's sparrow (*Aimophila aestivalis*; Pulliam *et al.*, 1992; Liu *et al.*, 1995), and the Cowbird (*Molothrus ater*; Gustafson and Crow, 1994; Coker and Capen, 1995; Hobson and Villard, 1998) have been sufficiently studied such that spatially explicit models can be parameterized over entire landscapes. Parameterization of the functional aspects of ecosystems over spatially heterogeneous landscapes is even more data-limited. In addition, many of the models are location-dependent and cannot easily be transported to other landscapes. For example, the spatial model used to simulate winter grazing by elk and bison in northern Yellowstone National Park (Turner *et al.*, 1994) cannot easily be run for a different landscape.

What is the relationship between the complexity of models, theories, and approaches and their actual application in management settings? Should models be relatively simple? Does increased complexity in models/theory necessarily lead to decreased likelihood of application to natural resource problems? How general can models be without sacrificing ecologically important detail? Furthermore, predictive models are not well developed. For instance, although the importance of understanding the current and past ecological effects of land use is now recognized (Turner *et al.*, 1998; Dale *et al.*, 2000), we do not have predictive models of the effects of various land-use patterns on ecological function, nor are we able to predict future land-use patterns very well.

Other tools such as spatial statistics (Turner and Gardner, 1990; Klopatek and Gardner, 1999) and geographic information systems (Johnston, 1990; Haines-Young *et al.*, 1993) have been widely used in landscape ecology to analyze spatial patterns. FRAGSTATS (McGarigal and Marks, 1995) is probably the most frequently used software for calculating landscape indices. Global positioning systems (GPS) are being used to collect georeferenced data (Farina, 1997).

Maintenance and alteration of natural resources depend on a variety of tools and methods. For example, harvest is a classic method for controlling population sizes and obtaining natural resource products such as timber (Burton *et al.*, 1999; Liu and Ashton, 1999), game (Steinert *et al.*, 1994; Lovell *et al.*, 1998), and fish (Klyashtorin, 1998). Release of wildlife is becoming a major practice to restore populations of endangered species like gray wolf (*Canis lupus*; Fritts *et al.*, 1997). Prescribed fires are a common approach to manipulating habitat for wildlife (Kwilosz and Knutson, 1999) and plants (e.g., Tveten and Fonda, 1999).

18.3.4 Training and experience

Most landscape ecologists are skillful in using tools for landscape analysis, but often lack management experience. As a result, they do not have a deep understanding of what managers need and what urgent management problems are. On the other hand, many resource managers received their technical training years or decades ago and have not had the opportunity to learn new skills that would enhance their ability to use and interpret ecological models or to measure and interpret measures of landscape pattern. In addition, computer software (e.g., modeling or analysis packages) often is not in a form that managers can use readily, or if it is, it is often ecologically simplistic. These factors inhibit application of some of the tools developed in landscape ecology to real-world management settings. In addition, there may be misconceptions about what landscape ecology actually has to offer. Even within the research community, it is often important to emphasize that landscape ecology is *not* equivalent to the quantification of spatial pattern. Quantifying pattern is a necessary component of understanding the causes and consequences of spatial heterogeneity for ecological processes – the heart of landscape ecology – but it is not an end in and of itself.

18.3.5 Technical infrastructure and data

The generation, maintenance, and interpretation of large volumes of landscape data are not trivial tasks. Such data, generated by field observation, remote sensing, manipulative experiments, and simulation modeling, must often be comprehensive across or beyond the entire management area. Availability of a common spatial data set from which stakeholders can work is necessary (but not sufficient) for landscape-level resource management. As anyone who has built a geographic database is painfully aware, data development is both expensive and time-consuming. Many management agencies are well along in their development of such spatial databases (e.g., Michigan Resource Information System developed by the Michigan Department of Natural Resources, 1978), and this is an asset to scientists and managers. However, many data owned by resource agencies and landscape ecologists are not shared and thus the potential of the data is not fully realized. In addition, effective uses of spatial data require adequate technical support and development of metadata that document the development, scales, and limits (e.g., accuracy) of the data.

18.3.6 Institutional culture

In academic settings, the major criteria for promotion and rewards are publications and grants. This academic culture often discourages the participation of faculty and graduate students in resource management activities (Carpenter, 1998) because management activities often do not result in peer-reviewed publications. In contrast, management agencies judge work performance not by the number of publications, but by whether crises are solved, problems are fixed, and legal requirements (e.g., in the United States, National Environmental Policy Act, Endangered Species Act) are met. These criteria for hiring and promotion discourage the collaboration between landscape ecologists and resource managers, impeding participation of landscape ecologists in resource management processes and involvement of resource managers in landscape-level research. Furthermore, shift within management organizations from the traditional organization of separate divisions for fisheries, wildlife, and water resources into management units based on ecosystems is not always smooth. Academic reward systems are usually biased in favor of research that is narrowly focused because it is more difficult and time-consuming to involve people from other disciplines, including personnel at management agencies.

18.4 Bridging the gap between landscape ecology and resource management

We offer the following suggestions for bridging the gaps identified in the previous section (see Table 18.1).

18.4.1 Goals

Although the goals of landscape ecology and natural resource management are different, they are not in conflict and should be coupled. Indeed, landscape ecology and natural resource management can be mutually beneficial. Perhaps more importantly, land use and its management are realities of the future, and landscape ecology must deal with these issues directly. What does landscape ecology offer to natural resource management? Landscape ecology offers a conceptual framework for understanding spatial heterogeneity and scale. Theory in landscape ecology leads to testable predictions about how patterns develop, persist, and change in the landscape, and about how ecological processes respond to these patterns. Landscape ecology also offers tools – a set of techniques to quantify and track changes in space and time. Models that permit the implications of alternative land-management scenarios to be evaluated from a natural resource perspective are also being developed by landscape ecology practitioners. Often formulated as spatially explicit simulation models, they can allow managers to visualize the effects of different options from which they must choose. For example, ECOLECON is a spatial model that links ecological and economic considerations in forest harvesting and permits resource outputs and population dynamics to be evaluated under alternative harvest scenarios (Liu, 1993; Liu *et al.*, 1995).

What does resource management offer to landscape ecology? Natural resource management provides a wide array of opportunities for further development of the theory and empirical underpinnings of landscape ecology. Landscape ecologists are typically limited in their ability to conduct manipulative experiments, yet close collaboration with natural resource managers may offer just such opportunities (Chapter 13, this book). Management actions can be viewed profitably from an experimental viewpoint, and landscape ecologists should avail themselves of the opportunities to see how well predictions hold up to actual manipulations on the land. In addition, landscape ecology is still in the process of developing a library of empirical studies that relate patterns and processes in ways that contribute to our understanding of ecological processes over broad scales of space and time. Natural resource managers have a wealth of data, often for large areas and long time periods, that may prove valuable as we continue to build our knowledge base and seek generality in the relationships we observe. Closer collaboration can yield much more robust answers to perplexing management questions.

18.4.2 Incongruities of scale

The scale issues must be explicitly addressed and discussed by landscape ecologists and resource managers. Landscape ecological research should consider the scales that are most meaningful for ecological processes and must determine how management can be scaled appropriately (e.g., by cooperation of multiple landowners and by the timing and spatial characteristics of management actions). Although management is often implemented locally (e.g., stand), the effects of management actions may extend well beyond the management sites (e.g., entire forest landscapes and adjacent areas). Thus, landscape ecological research must evaluate ecological consequences of management practices at both local and broader scales (Liu and Ashton, 1999; Liu *et al.*, 1999). Similarly, local watershed management goals and objectives can be couched in frameworks at larger spatial scales, as done in the Oregon Plan for Salmon and Watersheds (2001). As remote sensing data have become more widely available, it is now feasible to assess the ecological effects of management at broad scales.

When scaling data, special attention should be paid to the fact that information often changes with scale. When designing new monitoring schemes, the sampling should be made as congruent as possible with the scales at which decisions must be made.

18.4.3 Tools and methods

Many landscape-level models are indeed complex, and they may be site-specific. Their importance among the many tools available for landscape ecologists and resource managers mandates an improvement in training both scientists and managers in model development, implementation, and interpretation. For instance, when faced with a practical question involving land-use patterns, landscape ecologists and resource managers should seek and encourage collaborative development of models (conceptual models as well as more complex mathematical models). The role of institutions (e.g., management agencies, political institutions, and non-governmental organizations) should be considered as they affect land-use patterns, and tools should be developed to evaluate and monitor ecological and socioeconomic impacts of landscape context (beyond natural, political, and management boundaries) across landscapes.

Management methods used in natural resource management, such as harvesting techniques and patterns, provide valuable opportunities to address many fundamental landscape ecological issues like the role of disturbance in spatial patterns (Franklin and Forman, 1987) and the importance of corridors in population persistence (Haddad, 1999; Chapter 8, this book). For example, by working together with resource managers at Savannah River Site, South Carolina, Haddad (1999) created many spatial patterns that are not easily or frequently observed in natural landscapes. These patterns were essential to test a series of landscape ecological hypotheses in a more efficient and timely manner.

18.4.4 Training and experience

To shorten the time lag between landscape ecology research and applications to natural resource management, training is needed for both landscape ecologists and resource managers. Landscape ecologists should gain some management experience and understand management needs, whereas resource managers should grasp new concepts and become familiar with tools and methods in landscape ecology. The training may take different forms. Landscape ecologists may gain management experience through participating in actions led by resource managers and can offer workshops to resource managers about new concepts and approaches. For example, more than 500 people (including over 100 resource managers) attended the 1998 annual meeting of the US Regional Association of the International Association for Landscape Ecology (US-IALE) held at Michigan State University, as the theme of the meeting was "Applications of landscape ecology in natural resource management." At the meeting, a workshop entitled "Bridging the gap between landscape ecology and natural resource management" was held and resulted in this chapter. Besides scientific and technical sessions, there were several field trips to resource management areas in Michigan for the meeting attendees, and dozens of landscape ecologists took field trips led by resource managers. It is also necessary to form close communication networks and effective dialogues between landscape ecologists and natural resource managers at the local, regional, national, and international levels to foster *regular* interchange. However, new research and teaching settings that are truly interdisciplinary and go well beyond engaging good managers in a classroom setting are also urgently needed.

18.4.5 Technical infrastructure and data

Researchers and managers should work together to build and share common databases. This may require pooled resources to acquire, process, and manage data, and attention to metadata is crucial. Resource management agencies should strive toward improvements in technical infrastructure and data. For example, the Michigan Department of Natural Resources has developed a Michigan Resource Information System (MIRIS), a statewide digital archive of spatial data including base maps (e.g., political boundaries, transportation corridors) and land-cover/use maps depicting 52 categories of urban, agricultural, wooded, wetland, and other land-cover types. To facilitate the use of digital map data from MIRIS, the Center for Remote Sensing and Geographic Information System at Michigan State University specifically designed a C-Map GIS which includes comprehensive digitizing tools, an automated polygon construction module, GIS analysis functions and extensive data conversion capabilities. MIRIS data are very useful for landscape-level research, which in turn contributes to the MIRIS database (Chapter 12, this book).

Data design and sharing between landscape researchers and resource managers is increasing. For those who did share data, files were commonly exchanged using floppy diskettes and most recently CD-ROMs. Electronic technologies such as the World Wide Web (WWW) and File Transfer Protocol (FTP) are very efficient tools to facilitate data sharing among groups at different physical locations. An example of successful collaboration between resource managers and the use of WWW technology is the Colorado Natural Diversity Information Source (NDIS). NDIS supports planning by local communities by providing readily accessible information on the impacts of development on wildlife habitat (Cooperrider *et al.*, 1999; Theobald *et al.*, 2000). Through the World Wide Web (see NDIS, 2001), users can interactively specify an area to be developed in the future and assess potential impacts on wildlife. We suggest that landscape researchers and resource managers might learn from these successful applications and take full advantage of these advanced technologies.

18.4.6 Institutional culture

Institutional support is perhaps most critical to the success of bridging the gap between landscape ecology and natural resource management. In universities, where most landscape ecologists reside, recognition should be given to outreach efforts of landscape ecologists in solving real-world problems. Academic institutions, especially land-grant universities, should not be ivory towers. Besides teaching, publishing papers, and writing research grant proposals, information dissemination and outreach to the resource management community should be encouraged and rewarded. Work on resource management problems should be regarded as highly as work on basic scientific issues. In addition, scientists must be sensitive to the institutional inertia and fundamental changes being experienced within many resource management agencies at local and national levels. In management agencies, resource managers should be provided with opportunities to update their knowledge, to learn new skills, and to participate in research endeavors with landscape ecologists so that more informed management decisions can be made.

One way to strengthen the interactions between management agencies and academic institutions is to establish a close partnership, like the Partnership for Ecosystem Research and Management (PERM) between Michigan State University (MSU) and resource management agencies (Michigan State University, 2001). PERM was formally established in 1993 as a novel approach to promote active cooperation among the partners, facilitate cutting-edge natural resource research, and apply research results to resource management activities. The resource management agencies include three divisions (Fisheries Division, Forest Management Division, and Wildlife Division) of the Michigan Department of Natural Resources, the US Geological Survey, and the Great Lakes Fishery Commission. The resource management agencies provide financial support to fund more than ten tenure-track faculty positions in five different departments (Fisheries and Wildlife, Forestry, Agricultural Economics, Geography, and Sociology) at Michigan State University. These appointees are regular faculty members at the University, but each has a 20% appointment to provide outreach services (e.g., providing information and advice for resource management) to the agencies. In addition, many research projects of these faculty members and their graduate students/research associates are identified as high-priority management issues and conducted together with agency personnel. Both the agencies and Michigan State University have benefited from the arrangement.

Within academic institutions, interdisciplinary research should be encouraged and supported financially. Because interdisciplinary research projects usually take longer to complete and considerable effort to coordinate, different assessment criteria are needed. In the United States, it is encouraging that more attention is being paid to interdisciplinary projects by funding agencies such as the National Science Foundation and US Environmental Protection Agency.

Within management agencies, divisional boundaries should be bridged as well. For example, the Michigan Department of Natural Resources has historically managed Michigan's natural resources on a "divisional" basis. Each of the divisions (Wildlife, Forest Management, Fisheries, and Parks and Recreation) focused on the resources for which it was directly responsible, rarely with input or impact analyses on resources managed by other divisions. In mid-1997, the Department began a "joint venture" which brought different divisions to work together on defining goals, objectives, and infrastructure required for implementing a holistic approach to managing various natural resources across landscapes (Michigan Department of Natural Resources, 1997). If successful, the efficiency and effectiveness of resource management will be enhanced. Although it is too early to forecast the likelihood of success, it is promising to see that management agencies have been discussing these important issues and have begun to implement changes.

Clearly, both landscape ecology and natural resource management will benefit from bridging the gaps between them. To make progress, it is essential that landscape ecologists and managers communicate with one another, so that they actually ask the same questions and share the same objectives. The key areas of landscape ecology that are most likely to contribute to resource management should be identified more clearly, along with the critical issues in resource management that may benefit most from landscape ecology. Landscape ecologists must tailor their studies to the goals of management if those studies are to be directly relevant to management. By the same token, however, managers must realize that the findings that follow from landscape studies may entail implementing management at scales other than the traditional, anthropogenic scales. If resource management is to realize long-term sustainability, it must be conducted at scales most relevant to what is to be managed, rather than for whom it is to be managed.

18.5 Summary

The challenges facing natural resource managers increasingly occur over entire landscapes and involve spatial interdependencies among landscape components at many scales. Nearly all resource management agencies in the USA have recognized that informed management decisions cannot be made exclusively at the level of habitat units or local sites, and many are shifting toward management of integrated ecosystems. A landscape perspective is acknowledged as important by both scientists and resource managers, but determining how to implement management at broader scales remains challenging. Landscape ecology deals explicitly with the causes and consequences of spatial heterogeneity and offers concepts and tools that are directly relevant to natural resource management. In this chapter, we illustrated challenges in the management of aquatic resources and forests that reflect the need for a landscape perspective, synthesized our viewpoints to identify gaps between landscape ecology and resource management and their causes, and offered some suggestions for bridging the gaps.

(1) *Goals.* Landscape ecology seeks to understand the causes and consequences of spatial heterogeneity, whereas natural resource management seeks to maintain or alter resources to achieve goals set by society. These goals are not in conflict, however, and we suggest that they be better coupled so that both can be better achieved.
(2) *Incongruities of scale.* Scale issues are multi-faceted. Ecological scales and management scales are often mismatched, management decisions must often rely on data collected at disparate scales, the degree to which principles can be extrapolated to different species or ecosystems is not known, and the scales of data in the natural and social sciences often differ. The scale issues must be explicitly addressed and discussed by landscape ecologists and resource managers.
(3) *Tools and methods.* Landscape ecologists use a wide variety of tools including models, spatial statistics, and spatial pattern analyses, whereas managers actually manipulate resources and habitat. The importance of models among the many tools available for landscape ecologists and resource managers mandates an improvement in training both scientists and managers in model development, implementation, and interpretation. In turn, management actions can be profitably viewed from an experimental viewpoint, and landscape ecologists should avail themselves of the opportunities to see how well predictions hold up to actual manipulations on the land.
(4) *Training and experience.* Most landscape ecologists are scientifically and technically trained, but lack management experience. Many resource managers have not had the opportunity to learn the new models and tools of landscape ecology. To shorten the time lag between landscape ecology research and applications to natural resources management, training is

needed for both landscape ecologists and resource managers. Landscape ecologists should gain some management experience and understand management needs, whereas resource managers should grasp new concepts and become familiar with tools and methods in landscape ecology.

(5) *Technical infrastructure and data*. Spatial databases are becoming essential for both research and management, yet building and maintaining them requires considerable cost and effort. Researchers and managers should work together to build and share common databases. This may require pooled resources to acquire, process, and manage data, and attention to metadata is crucial.

(6) *Institutional culture*. The cultures within resource management agencies and academic institutions may not provide sufficient support for more collaborative efforts. Institutional support is critical to the success of bridging the gap between landscape ecology and natural resource management. Within academic institutions, interdisciplinary research should be encouraged and supported financially. Within management agencies, divisional boundaries should be bridged as well.

Both landscape ecology and natural resource management will benefit from a bridging of the gaps between them. It is essential that landscape ecologists and managers communicate with one another, so that they actually ask the same questions and share the same objectives.

Acknowledgments

This paper was developed from a panel discussion held at the annual meeting of the US Regional Association of the International Association for Landscape Ecology held at Michigan State University in March, 1998. The manuscript was improved by helpful suggestions from four anonymous reviewers. We are grateful for the funding for this workshop provided by the Michigan Department of Natural Resources, Michigan State University, the National Science Foundation, National Aeronautics and Space Administration, US Environmental Protection Agency, US Fish and Wildlife Service, US Forest Service, and US Geological Survey.

References

Addicott, J. F., Aho, J. M., Antolin, M. F., Padilla, D. K., Richardson, J. S. & Soluk, D. A. (1987). Ecological neighborhoods: Scaling environmental patterns. *Oikos*, 49: 340–346.

Allan, J. D. & Johnson, L. B. (1997). Catchment-scale analysis of aquatic ecosystems. *Freshwater Biology*, 37: 107–111.

Andren, H. (1994). Effects of habitat fragmentation on birds and mammals in landscapes with different proportions of suitable habitat. *Oikos*, 71: 355–366.

Attiwill, P. M. (1994). The disturbance of forest ecosystems: The ecological basis for conservative management. *Forest Ecology and Management*, 63: 247–300.

Baker, W. L. (1992). Effects of settlement and fire suppression on landscape structure. *Ecology*, 73: 1879–1887.

Bennett, E. M., Reed-Andersen, T., Houser, J. N., Gabriel, J. R. & Carpenter, S. R. (1999). A phosphorus budget for the Lake Mendota watershed. *Ecosystems*, 2: 69–75.

Bolstad, P. V. & Swank, W. T. (1997). Cumulative impacts of land use on water quality in a southern Appalachian watershed. *Journal of the American Water Resources Association*, 33:519–533.

Burgess, R. L. & Sharpe, D. M. (eds.) (1981). *Forest Island Dynamics in Man-Dominated Landscapes*. Springer-Verlag, New York.

Burton, P. J., Kneeshaw, D. D. & Coates, K. D. (1999). Managing forest harvesting to maintain old growth in boreal and sub-boreal forests. *Forestry Chronicle*, 75: 623–631.

Carpenter, S. R. (1998). Keystone species and academic-agency collaboration. *Conservation Ecology*, 2(1) resp 2, http://www.consecol.org/vol2/iss1/resp2.

Carpenter, S. R., Caraco, N. F., Correll, D. L., Howarth, R. W., Shipley, A. N. & Smith, V. H. (1998). Nonpoint pollution of surface waters with nitrogen and phosphorus. *Ecological Applications*, 8:559–568.

Christensen, N. L., Bartuska, A. M., Brown, J. H., Carpenter, S. R., D'Antonio, C., Francis, R., Franklin, J. F., MacMahon, J. A., Noss, R. F., Parsons, D. J., Peterson, J. H., Turner, M. G. & Woodmansee, R. G. (1996). The scientific basis for ecosystem management. *Ecological Applications*, 6: 665–691.

Coker, D. R. & Capen, D. E. (1995). Landscape-level habitat use by brown-headed cowbirds in Vermont. *Journal of Wildlife Management*, 59: 631–637.

Cooperrider, A., Garrett, L. R. & Hobbs, N. T. (1999). Data collection, management, and inventory. In: *Ecological Stewardship: A Common Reference for Ecosystem Management*, eds. N. C. Johnson, A. J. Malk, W. T. Sexton & R. Szaro, pp. 604–627. Elsevier, Oxford, UK.

Dale, V. H., Brown, S., Haeuber, R., Hobbs, N. T., Huntly, N., Naiman, R. J., Riebsame, W. E., Turner, M. G. & Valone, T. (2000). Ecological principles and guidelines for managing the use of land. *Ecological Applications*, 10: 639–670.

Delong, S. C. & Tanner, D. (1996). Managing the pattern of forest harvest: Lessons from wildfire. *Biodiversity and Conservation*, 5: 1191–1205.

Detenbeck, N. E., Johnston, C. A. & Niemi, G. J. (1993). Wetland effects on lake water quality in the Minneapolis/St. Paul metropolitan area. *Landscape Ecology*, 8: 39–61.

Dominick, D. S. & O'Neill, M. P. (1998). Effects of flow augmentation on stream channel morphology and riparian vegetation: Upper Arkansas River basin, Colorado. *Wetlands*, 18: 591–607.

Dubayah, R., Wood, E. F. & Lavallee, D. (1997). Multiscaling analysis in distributed modeling and remote sensing: An application using soil moisture. In *Scale in Remote Sensing and GIS*, eds. D. A. Quattrochi & M. F. Goodchild, pp. 93–112. Lewis Publishers, Boca Raton, FL.

Farina, A. (1997). Landscape structure and breeding bird distribution in a sub-Mediterranean agro-ecosystem. *Landscape Ecology*, 12: 365–378.

Foster, D. R., Knight, D. H. & Franklin, J. F. (1998). Landscape patterns and legacies resulting from large infrequent forest disturbances. *Ecosystems*, 1: 497–510.

Franklin, J. F. & Forman, R. T. T. (1987). Creating landscape patterns by forest cutting: Ecological consequences and principles. *Landscape Ecology*, 1: 5–18.

Franklin, J. F., Norris, L. A., Berg, D. R. & Smith, G. R. (1999). The history of DEMO: An experiment in regeneration harvest of northwestern forest ecosystems. *Northwest Science*, 73 (special Issue): 3–11.

Frissell, C. A., Liss, W. J., Warren, C. E. & Hurley, M. D. (1986). A hierarchical framework for stream habitat classification: Viewing streams in a watershed context. *Environmental Management*, 10(2):199–214.

Fritts, S. H., Bangs, E. E., Fontaine, J. A., Johnson, M. R., Phillips, M. K., Koch, E. D. & Gunson, J. R. (1997). Planning and implementing a reintroduction of wolves to Yellowstone National Park and Central Idaho. *Restoration Ecology*, 5: 7–27.

Gardner, R. H., Milne, B. T., Turner, M. G. &

O'Neill, R. V. (1987). Neutral models for the analysis of broad-scale landscape patterns. *Landscape Ecology*, 1: 19–28.

Geier, T. W., Perry, J. A. & Queen, L. (1994). Improving lake riparian source area management using surface and subsurface runoff indices. *Environmental Management*, 18: 569–586.

Grove, J. M. & Hohmann, M. (1992). GIS and social forestry. *Journal of Forestry*, 90: 10–15.

Grumbine, R. E. (1994). What is ecosystem management? *Conservation Biology*, 8: 27–38.

Gustafson, E. J. (1998). Quantifying landscape spatial pattern: What is the state of the art? *Ecosystems*, 1: 143–156.

Gustafson, E. J. & Crow, T. R. (1994). Modeling the effects of forest harvesting on landscape structure and the spatial distribution of cowbird brood parasitism. *Landscape Ecology*, 9: 237–248.

Gustafson, E. J. & Crow, T. R. (1996). Simulating the effects of alternative forest management strategies on landscape structure. *Journal of Environmental Management*, 46: 77–94.

Haddad, N. M. (1999). Corridor and distance effects on interpatch movements: A landscape experiment with butterflies. *Ecological Applications*, 9: 612–622.

Haines-Young, R., Green, D. R. & Cousins, S. H. (eds.) (1993). *Landscape Ecology and Geographic Information Systems*. Taylor & Francis, London.

Halpern, C. B., Evans, S. A., Nelson, C. R., McKenzie, D., Liguori, D. A., Hibbs, D. E. & Halaj, M. G. (1999) Response of forest vegetation to varying levels and patterns of green-tree retention: An overview of a long-term experiment. *Northwest Science*, 73 (special Issue): 27–44.

Hobson, K. A. & Villard, M. A. (1998). Forest fragmentation affects the behavioral response of American Redstarts to the threat of cowbird parasitism. *Condor*, 100: 389–394.

Hunsaker, C. T. & Levine, D. A. (1995). Hierarchical approaches to the study of water quality in rivers. *BioScience*, 45: 193–203.

Hunter, M. L. Jr. (1993). Natural fire regimes as spatial models for managing boreal forests. *Biological Conservation*, 65: 115–120.

Hynes, H. B. N. (1975). The stream and its valley. *Verhandlungen Internationale Vereinigung für theoretische und angewandte Limnologie*, 19: 1–15.

Jacobson, R. B. & Coleman, D. J. (1986). Stratigraphy and recent evolution of Maryland Piedmont flood plains. *American Journal of Science*, 286: 617–637.

Johnes, P., Moss, B. & Phillips, G. (1996). The determination of total nitrogen and total phosphorus concentrations in freshwaters from land use, stock headage and population data: Testing of a model for use in conservation and water quality management. *Freshwater Biology*, 36: 451–473.

Johnson, L. B., Richards, C., Host, G. & Arthur, J. W. (1997). Landscape influences on water chemistry in Midwestern streams. *Freshwater Biology*, 37: 193–208.

Johnston, C. A. (1990). GIS: More than just a pretty face. *Landscape Ecology*, 4: 3–4.

Karr, J. R., Toth, L. A. & Dudley, D. R. (1985). Fish communities of midwestern rivers: A history of degradation. *BioScience*, 35: 90–95.

Klopatek, J. M & Gardner, R. H. (eds.) (1999). *Landscape Ecological Analysis: Issues and Applications*. Springer-Verlag, New York.

Klyashtorin, L. B. (1998). Long-term climate change and main commercial fish production in the Atlantic and Pacific. *Fisheries Research*, 37: 115–125.

Kooi, H. & Beaumont, C. (1996). Large-scale geomorphology: Classical concepts reconciled and integrated with contemporary ideas via a surface processes model. *Journal of Geophysical Research-Solid Earth*, 101 (B2): 3361–3386.

Kratz, T. K., Webster, K. E., Bowser, C. J, Magnuson, J. J. & Benson, B. J. (1997). The influence of landscape position on lakes in northern Wisconsin. *Freshwater Biology*, 37: 209–217.

Krummel, J. R., Gardner, R. H., Sugihara, G., O'Neill, R. V. & Coleman, P. R. (1987). Landscape patterns in a disturbed environment. *Oikos*, 48: 321–324.

Kwilosz, J. R. & Knutson, R. L. (1999). Prescribed fire management of Karner blue butterfly habitat at Indiana Dunes National Lakeshore. *Natural Areas Journal*, 19: 98–108.

Larson, B. C., Vogt, D. J., Booth, M., Vogt, M. A., Palmiotto, P. A., Koteen, L. & O'Hara, J. (1999). The impacts of natural resource management practices on the ecosystem and their relationship to certification criteria. In

Forest Certification: Roots, Issues, Challenges and Benefits, eds. K. A., Vogt, B. C., Larson, D. J., Vogt, J. C., Gordon & A., Fanzeres, pp. 227–249. CRC Press, Boca Raton, FL.

Li, H., Franklin, J. F., Swanson, F. J. & Spies, T. A. (1993). Developing alternative forest cutting patterns: A simulation approach. *Landscape Ecology*, 8: 63–75.

Liu, J. (1993). ECOLECON: An ECOLogical-ECONomic model for species conservation in complex forest landscapes. *Ecological Modelling*, 70: 63–87.

Liu, J. & Ashton, P. S. (1999). Simulating effects of landscape context and timber harvest on tree species diversity. *Ecological Applications*, 9: 186–201.

Liu, J., Dunning, J. B. Jr. & Pulliam, H. R. (1995). Potential effects of a forest-management plan on Bachman's Sparrow (*Aimophila aestivalis*): Linking a spatially explicit model with GIS. *Conservation Biology*, 9: 62–75.

Liu, J., Ickes, K., Ashton, P. S., LaFrankie, J. V. & Manokaran, N. (1999). Spatial and temporal impacts of adjacent areas on the dynamics of species diversity in a primary forest. In: *Advances in Spatial Modeling of Forest Landscape Change: Approaches and Applications*, eds. D., Mladenoff & W., Baker, pp. 42–69. Cambridge University Press, Cambridge, UK.

Lovell, C. D., Leopold, B. D. & Shropshire, C. C. (1998). Trends in Mississippi predator populations, 1980–1995. *Wildlife Society Bulletin*, 26: 552–556.

Lowrance, R. (1998). Riparian forest ecosystems as filters for nonpoint-source pollution. In: *Successes, Limitations and Frontiers in Ecosystem Science*, eds. M. L. Pace & Groffman, P. M., pp. 113–141. Springer-Verlag, New York.

Lowrance, R., Altier, L. S., Newbold, J. D., Schnabel, R. R., Groffman, P. M.,Denver, J. M., Correll, D. L., Gilliam, J. W., Robinson, J. L., Brinsfield, R. B., Staver, K. W., Lucas, W. & Todd, A. H. (1997). Water quality functions of riparian forest buffer systems in the Chesapeake Bay watershed. *Environmental Management*, 21: 687–712.

Magnuson, J. J. & Kratz, T. K. (2000). Lakes in the landscape: Approaches to regional limnology. *Verhandlungen Internationale Vereinigung für theoretische und angewandte Limnologie*, 27: 74–87.

Maxwell, K., Vogt, K. A., Vogt, D. J. & Larson, B. C. (1999). Linking social and natural science spatial scale. In *Forest Certification: Roots, Issues, Challenges and Benefits*, eds. K. A., Vogt, B. C., Larson, D. J., Vogt, J. C., Gordon & A. Fanzeres, pp. 257 – 259. CRC Press, Boca Raton, FL.

McDowell, W. H. (1998). Internal nutrient fluxes in a Puerto Rican rain forest. *Journal of Tropical Ecology*, 14: 521–536.

McDowell, W. H. & Wood, T. (1984). Podzolization: Soil processes control dissolved organic carbon concentrations in stream water. *Soil Science*, 137: 23–32.

McGarigal, K. & Marks, B. J. (1995). *FRAGSTATS: Spatial Analysis Program for Quantifying Landscape Structure*, General Technical Report PNW-351, US Department of Agriculture Forest Service. Portland, OR.

McKelvey, K., Noon, B. R & Lamberson, R. H. (1993). Conservation planning for species occupying fragmented landscapes: The case of the northern spotted owl. In *Biotic Interactions and Global Change*, eds. P. M. Kareiva, J. G. Kingsolver & R. B. Huey, pp. 424–450. Sinauer Associates, Sunderland, MA.

Michigan Department of Natural Resources (1978). *Michigan Resource Information System (MIRIS)*. Lansing, MI.

Michigan Department of Natural Resources (1999). http://www.dnr.state.mi.us/pdfs/dnr/jv.pdf.

Michigan State University (2001). http://www.fw.msu.edu/orgs/perm

Milner N. J., Hemsworth, R. J. & Jones, B. E. (1985). Habitat evaluation as a fisheries management tool. *Journal of Fish Biology*, 27 (Suppl. A): 85–108.

Mladenoff, D. J., White, M. A. & Pastor, J. (1993). Comparing spatial pattern in unaltered old-growth and disturbed forest landscapes. *Ecological Applications*, 3: 294–306.

Mladenoff, D. J., White, M. A., Crow, T. R. & Pastor, J. (1994). Applying principles of landscape design and management to integrate old-growth forest enhancement and commodity use. *Conservation Biology*, 8: 752–762.

Naiman, R. J. (1996). Water, society and landscape ecology. *Landscape Ecology*, 11: 193–196.

Naiman, R. J. & Decamps, H. (1997). The ecology of interfaces: Riparian zones. *Annual Review of Ecology and Systematics*, 28: 621–658.

Naiman, R. J., Magnuson, J. J, McKnight, D. M. & Stanford, J. A. (eds.) (1995). *The Freshwater Imperative: a Research Agenda*. Island Press, Washington, D.C.

NDIS [Natural Diversity Information Source] (2001). http://ndis.nrel.colostate.edu

Oliver, C., Boydak, M., Segura, G. & Bare, B. (1999). Forest organization, management, and policy. In: *Maintaining Biodiversity in Forest Ecosystems*, ed. M. L. Hunter Jr., pp. 556–596. Cambridge University Press, New York.

Oregon Plan for Salmon and Watersheds (2001). http://oregon-plan.org/index.html

Osborne, L. L. & Wiley, M. J. (1988). Empirical relationships between land use/land cover and stream water quality in an agricultural watershed. *Journal of Environmental Management*, 26: 9–27.

Parry, B. & Vogt, K. A. (1999). Necessity of assessing the landscapes matrix within which a management unit is embedded. In: *Forest Certification: Roots, Issues, Challenges and Benefits*, eds. K. A., Vogt, B. C., Larson, D. J., Vogt, J. C. Gordon & A. Fanzeres, pp. 251–254. CRC Press, Boca Raton, FL.

Pearson, S. M., Turner, M. G., Gardner, R. H. & O'Neill, R. V. (1996). An organism-based perspective of habitat fragmentation. In: *Biodiversity in Managed Landscapes: Theory and Practice*, ed. R. C. Szaro, pp. 77–95. Oxford University Press, New York.

Perera, A. J., Euler, D. L. & Thompson, I. D. (2000). *Ecology of a Managed Terrestrial Landscape: Patterns and Processes of Forest Landscapes in Ontario*. University of British Columbia Press, Vancouver, Canada.

Peterson, D. L & Parker, V. T. (eds.) (1998). *Ecological Scale*. Columbia University Press, New York.

Pickett, S. T. A. & Cadenasso, M. L. (1995). Landscape ecology: Spatial heterogeneity in ecological systems. *Science*, 269: 331–334.

Pickett, S. T. A. & White, P. S. (eds.) (1985). *The Ecology of Natural Disturbance and Patch Dynamics*. Academic Press, New York.

Pickett, S. T. A., Kolasa, J. & Jones, C. G. (1994). *Ecological Understanding*. Academic Press, New York.

Pulliam, H. R., Dunning, J. B. & Liu, J. (1992). Population dynamics in complex landscapes: A case study. *Ecological Applications*, 2: 165–177.

Rabeni, C. F. (1996). Prairie legacies: Fish and aquatic resources. In *Prairie Conservation*, eds. F. Samson, & F. Knoph, pp. 111–124. Island Press, Washington, D.C.

Rabeni, C. F. & Sowa, S. P. (1996). Integrating biological realism into habitat restoration and conservation strategies for small streams. *Canadian Journal of Fisheries and Aquatic Sciences*, 53 (Suppl. 1): 252–259.

Richards, C., Johnson, L. B. & Host, G. E. (1996). Landscape-scale influences on stream habitats and biota. *Canadian Journal of Fisheries and Aquatic Sciences*, 53 (Suppl. 1): 295–311.

Romm, J. & Washburn, C. (1987). Public subsidy and private forestry investment. *Land Economics*, 63: 153–167.

Romme, W. H. (1982). Fire and landscape diversity in subalpine forests of Yellowstone National Park. *Ecological Monographs*, 52: 199–221.

Scatena, F. N. (1990). Watershed scale rainfall interception on two forested watershed in the Luquillo Mountains of Puerto Rico. *Journal of Hydrology*, 113: 89–102.

Soranno, P. A., Hubler, S. L., Carpenter, S. R. & Lathrop, R. C. (1996). Phosphorus loads to surface waters: A simple model to account for spatial pattern of land use. *Ecological Applications*, 6: 865–878.

Spies, T. P. & Turner, M. G. (1999). Dynamic forest mosaics. In: *Maintaining Biodiversity in Forest Ecosystems*, ed. M. L. Hunter Jr., pp. 95–160. Cambridge University Press, New York.

Spies, T. A., Ripple, W. J. & Bradshaw, G. A. (1994). Dynamics and pattern of a managed coniferous forest landscape in Oregon. *Ecological Applications*, 4: 555–568.

Steinert, S. F., Riffel, H. D. & White, G. C. (1994). Comparisons of big game harvest estimates from check station and telephone surveys. *Journal of Wildlife Management*, 58: 335–340.

Theobald, D. M., Hobbs, N. T., Bearly, T., Zack, J. & Riebsame, W. E. (2000). Including biological information in local land-use decision-making: Designing a system for conservation planning. *Landscape Ecology*, 15: 35–45.

Townsend, C. R. (1996). Concepts in river ecology: Pattern and process in the catchment hierarchy. *Archiv für Hydrobiologie* (Suppl.) 113: 3–21.

Turner, M. G. (ed.) (1987). *Landscape Heterogeneity and Disturbance*. Springer-Verlag, New York.

Turner, M. G. (1989). Landscape ecology: The effect of pattern on process. *Annual Review of Ecology and Systematics*, 20: 171–197.

Turner, M. G. & Gardner, R. H. (eds.) (1990). *Quantitative Methods in Landscape Ecology*. Springer-Verlag, New York.

Turner, M. G., Gardner, R. H., Dale, V. H. & O'Neill, R. V. (1989). Predicting the spread of disturbance across heterogeneous landscapes. *Oikos*, 55: 121–129.

Turner, M. G., Wu, Y., Romme, W. H., Wallace, L. L. & Brenkert, A. (1994). Simulating winter interactions between ungulates, vegetation and fire in northern Yellowstone Park. *Ecological Applications*, 4: 472–496.

Turner, M. G., Wear, D. N. & Flamm, R. O. (1996). Land ownership and land-cover change in the Southern Appalachian Highlands and the Olympic Peninsula. *Ecological Applications*, 6: 1150–1172.

Turner, M. G., Carpenter, S. R., Gustafson, E. J., Naiman, R. J. & Pearson, S. M (1998). Land use. In: *Status and Trends of Our Nation's Biological Resources,* Vol. 1, eds. M. J., Mac, P. A., Opler, P. Doran & C. Haecker, pp. 37–61. National Biological Service, Washington, D.C.

Turner, M. G., Gardner, R. H. & O'Neill, R. V. (2001). *Landscape Ecology in Theory and Practice: Pattern and Process*. Springer-Verlag, New York.

Tveten, R. K. & Fonda, R.W. (1999). Fire effects on prairies and oak woodlands on Fort Lewis, Washington. *Northwest Science*, 73: 145–158.

Vannote, R. L., Minshall, G. W., Cummins, K. W., Sedell, J. R. & Cushing, C. E. (1980). The river continuum concept. *Canadian Journal of Fisheries and Aquatic Sciences*, 37: 130–137.

Vogt, K. A., Larson, B. C., Vogt, D. J., Gordon, J. C. & Fanzeres, A. (eds.) (1999a). *Forest Certification: Roots, Issues, Challenges and Benefits*. CRC Press, Boca Raton, FL.

Vogt, K. A., Vogt, D. J., Fanzeres, A. & Larson, B. C. (1999b). Indicators selection criteria. In *Forest Certification: Roots, Issues, Challenges and Benefits*, eds. K. A., Vogt, B. C., Larson, D. J., Vogt, J. C., Gordon, & A. Fanzeres, pp. 177–187. CRC Press, Boca Raton, FL.

Wallin, D. O., Swanson, F. J. & Marks, B. (1994). Landscape pattern response to changes in pattern generation rules: Land-use legacies in forestry. *Ecological Applications,* 4: 569–580.

Wang, L., Lyons, J., Kanehl, P. & Gatti, R. (1997). Influences of watershed land use on habitat quality and biotic integrity in Wisconsin streams. *Fisheries*, 22: 6–12.

Weller, D. E., Jordan, T. E. & Correll, D. L. (1998). Heuristic models for material discharge from landscapes with riparian buffers. *Ecological Applications*, 8: 1156–1169.

Wiens, J. A. (1976). Population responses to patchy environments. *Annual Review of Ecology and Systematics*, 7: 81–120.

Wiens, J. A. (1999). The science and practice of landscape ecology. In: *Landscape Ecological Analysis: Issues and Applications*, eds. J. M., Klopatek & R. H. Gardner, pp. 372–383. Springer-Verlag, New York.

Wiley, M. J., Osborne, L. L & Larimore, R. W. (1990). Longitudinal structure of an agricultural prairie river system and its relationship to current stream ecosystem theory. *Canadian Journal of Fisheries and Aquatic Sciences*, 47: 373–384.

Young, R. A., Onstad, C. A., Bosch, D. D. & Anderson, W. P. (1989). AGNPS: A nonpoint source pollution model for evaluating agricultural watersheds. *Journal of Soil and Water Conservation*, 44: 168–172.

19

Landscape ecology of the future: A regional interface of ecology and socioeconomics

My theme is that when it comes to land-use research, planning, and management, there is a need to enlarge the frame of reference from the landscape to the region. Although the term "landscape" is often extended beyond the dictionary definition of "an expanse of scenery seen by the eye in one view" to include what can be distinguished in an aerial photo or satellite image, a landscape is also described by the interactions of different identifiable units (sometimes called ecotypes) on the land surface which are based upon ecological, social, and economic considerations (Turner, 1989; Turner *et al.*, 1996). In terms of an absolute spatial scale, a landscape is a large geographic expanse encompassing anywhere from ten to several thousand square kilometers (Bailey, 1996). While the landscape perspective in ecology has enlarged the scale at which research is carried out, a more appropriate scale for addressing many land-use, land-tenure, and environmental problems is the region, which is the focus of this chapter.

In the 1930s, social scientists promoted the concept of regionalism in which social indicators were used to compare different geographical and political regions. This concept considered regions to be large geographic expanses (e.g., multiple counties, or multiple states) based primarily upon political or social boundaries (Odum, 1936). My father, Howard W. Odum, and his faculty and staff at the University of North Carolina, Chapel Hill, were leaders in developing this field. His books *Southern Regions* (1936) and *American Regionalism* (Odum and Moore, 1938) were very influential in shaping the political scene of North Carolina, and the southern region of the United States as a whole. A major reason for these books' influence was that they developed 57 indexes and used them to compare different regions of the nation, thereby documenting in detail why the "South" was doing so poorly relative to other regions of the United States. During the 1930s the main problems in the South were social and economic, including poor race relations, destructive farming and agricultural practices, lack of quality industry, and substandard education. Today these basic demographic and environmental problems continue to plague the region, as is the case nationwide and worldwide. While the regional perspective may not have solved the South's problems, it is still needed as a means of detecting both social and ecological problems.

When as a student I first became acquainted with V. E. Shelford's concept of the biome, I suggested to my father that regions might be better defined by natural boundaries based upon factors such as topography, dominant vegetation, or macroclimatic conditions rather than by political boundaries. This view of a region is spatially larger than a landscape and is similar to that presented by Bailey (1996) and Forman (1995). Thus, a naturally bounded region could be defined by topography, such as the Appalachian region and the Piedmont region, or by dominant vegetation type, such as a deciduous forest region. His response to my point was that regions defined by natural boundaries could be a good idea, but that all the data on humans are tabulated by political units (e.g., counties and states). In fact, this lack of concordance between natural and anthropogenic boundaries remains a problem even today.

Today, sociologists, in general, are not pursuing regionalism. Just as with other academic disciplines, sociologists have become specialists and moved towards addressing reductionistic questions, such as urban crime by teenagers. However, it is even more apparent today than it was during the early part of the twentieth century that the environmental and social problems need to be addressed from an interdisciplinary and large-scale perspective. As a result, it is essential that social scientists return to the regional perspective and that ecologists promote a synthesis between the natural and social sciences. Only by returning to regional analyses and through cooperation between the two branches of science can any kind of realistic land use and land management plans be initiated and successfully implemented.

Integrating the natural and social sciences

Although natural science can contribute to mankind's ability to deal with environmental predicaments, it alone will not save the world from environmental degradation because the problems and solutions involve the humanities and social science areas such as anthropology, economics, demography, political science, ethology (behavior), education, and religion. Real solutions will come only with a true integration between the natural and social sciences (Wilson, 1998; Liu, 2001).

Aside from simply integrating different disciplines and scaling-up, there is an immediate need to reconstruct or extend economics to include non-market goods and services (i.e., ecosystem services; Daily, 1997). Traditional and contemporary economics values only human-made goods and services which are valuable in the market. Life-support services (air, water, soils, etc.) are considered "externalities" with no value until they become scarce (when it may be too late!). Although as early as the 1960s it was realized that non-market goods and services needed to be incorporated into economic theory (see Boulding, 1962), it has only been in recent years that these ideas have penetrated the ecological and economic literature in a serious way (Costanza, 1991; for a recent commentary, see Odum and Odum, 2000). A major point of agreement is that from now on economic development must be based on qualitative rather than quantitative growth, that is, *better* economic development instead of just *more* economic development.

How to move to a regional interface of ecology and socioeconomics

As I have tried to briefly highlight in this chapter, there is an urgent need to: (1) integrate the natural and social sciences; and (2) expand the scale of research and problem-solving from the landscape to the region. The practical question for both scientists and managers then becomes, how can such goals be achieved? In terms of integrating the sciences, researchers need to move from simply being specialists towards being members of an interdisciplinary group or team. This does not mean the loss of individual research interests, but rather it means an increased amount of cooperation and interdepartmental programs. In addition, integration will require working with both academic and non-academic organizations.

Integrating the social and natural sciences must also occur at larger scales in order to satisfactorily address land-use issues. One can see this simply by looking at how ineffective local zoning laws are, because of the ease with which short-term financial interests can null and void them. For example, the zoning problem in Georgia has become so prominent that the governor and state legislature recently passed a bill transferring local zoning decisions to a regional task force in the 13 counties surrounding Atlanta (Pedersen *et al.*, 1999). Although the scaling-up from the county to the greater Atlanta region is still defined by political boundaries, it offers a positive direction for appropriate land-tenure issues. Such is the direction that landscape ecologists, natural resource managers, and social scientists need to take.

In regards to increasing the scale of research a number of significant challenges remain. Simply defining a region can be troubling enough, let alone actually carrying out research on one. One way to move towards a regional approach would be to describe the raw data in a spatially explicit manner or on small spatial scales, thereby allowing data to be readily aggregated in different ways and different regions to be created based upon the question of interest. Another approach would be to hold workshops (e.g., the national vegetation mapping workshops held recently at the annual meetings of the Ecological Society of America) or initiate task forces (e.g., create panels at the National Academy of Sciences) aimed at developing a unified concept of a region, from both a socioeconomic and ecological perspective, and mapping their locations. Ultimately, there is no perfect definition of a region. Just as with the term landscape, the term region connotes different meanings to different people. As a result, the goal of this chapter is not to give an exact definition of a region, but rather to illustrate the need for scaling-up and integration of social and natural sciences, and how scaling-up and integration may occur.

Aside from simply defining a region more precisely, scientists and managers also need to utilize the concepts of landscape ecology at the regional scale. For instance, the conversion of landscapes into individual patches creates sharp boundaries, thereby doing away with natural gradients and ecotones (i.e., "buffers"), a tendency that Jansen (1987) has called "habitat sharpening." Creating buffers around patches has long been suggested as a means to restore or preserve the natural gradients and ecotones. However, such a suggestion falls short when it is only implemented at the patch level. In reality, many features on the landscape cross multiple patches or the entire landscape. A primary example is a river or stream, which may cross one or more landscapes, and is thus beyond the landscape scale (see chapters in Part III of this book for more information on landscape function and cross-boundary management). As a result, effective planning or legislation for stream corridor preservation must occur at the regional level. Only by expanding such landscape ecology concepts to the region can scientists and managers begin to effectively understand and manage the land and protect the environment.

Keeping the aforementioned points in mind, I would like to offer a few suggestions for landscape ecologists and natural resource managers that will help to manage natural resources more effectively.

- Seek out and interact with other academic departments, government agencies, non-governmental organizations, and private interest groups. Each stakeholder in any region has valuable knowledge that is necessary in order for any regional interface to succeed.
- Define regions not just from a biological or ecological perspective, but from social and economic ones as well. One example of accomplishing this would be to define boundaries for each of these perspectives and then consider the region of interest to be where there is the greatest amount of overlap among different component layers.
- Involve the landowners, be they private or public. The ultimate control of any piece of land comes down to the actual owners and the laws that bind them.

References

Bailey, R. G. (1996). *Ecosystem Geography*. Springer-Verlag. New York.

Boulding, K. (1962). *The Reconstruction of Economics*. Science Editions, New York.

Costanza, R. (Ed.). (1991). *Ecological Economics: The Science and Management of Sustainability*. Columbia University Press, New York.

Daily, G. C. (Ed.). (1997). *Nature's Services: Societal Dependence on Natural Ecosystems*. Island Press, Washington, D.C.

Forman, R. T. T. (1995). *Land Mosaics*. Cambridge University Press, Cambridge, UK.

Jansen, D. (1987). Habitat sharpening. *Oikos*, 48: 3–5.

Liu, J. (2001). Integrating ecology with human demography, behavior and socioeconomics: Needs and approaches. *Ecological Modelling*, 140: 1–8.

Odum, H. T. & Odum, E. P. (2000). The energetic basis for the valuation of ecosystem services. *Ecosystems*, 3: 21–23.

Odum, H. W. (1936). *Southern Regions of the United States*. University of North Carolina Press, Chapel Hill, NC.

Odum, H. W. & Moore, H. E. (1938). *American Regionalism*. Henry Holt and Company, New York.

Pedersen, D., Smith, V. E.& Adler, J. (1999). *Newsweek* July 19, p. 22.

Turner, M. G. (1989). Landscape ecology: The effect of pattern on process. *Annual Review of Ecology and Systematics*, 20: 171–197.

Turner, M. G., Wear, D. N. & Flamm, R. O. (1996). Land ownership and land-cover change in the Southern Appalachian Highlands and the Olympic Peninsula. *Ecological Applications*, 6: 1150–1172.

Wilson, E. O. (1998). *Consilience*. Knopf, New York.

20

Epilogue

Recently a landscape ecology colleague and I were consulting in Costa Rica for the President and his Minister of Natural Resources and Energy. In the Minister's tenth-floor office overlooking the stunning red roofs and palms of the capital, we studied a protected-areas map of the country. Seven large green blobs are magnets for international eco-tourism, the leading income for the national economy. I commented on the extraordinary accomplishment of having these large areas protected. The Minister mentioned that in the previous decade his country had the highest deforestation rate in the world. Then he offhandedly added: "Protected areas are really only as good as the Costa Rican economy." "What? Aren't they permanently protected? International organizations helped protect them. Doesn't the whole world visit them, and keep an eye on them?" "Maybe. But now you should go immerse yourself in one."

The single-engine Costa Rican air force plane dropped through a torrential rain to a grassy strip, and we soon reached an eco-tourist lodge in the large Tortuguero National Park and Conservation Area. Tortuguero is known for its sea turtles that leave bulldozer-like holes and tracks on the beach. The rain barely stopped for two days. At night guests enjoyed a rainforest slide show, followed by a nightlife walk with awesome reverberating howler monkeys over us. The next day we went by motorized log boat winding forever through rainforest and mangrove swamp to a village on stilts. Soccer with the local boys preceded lunch with the mayor. I asked him about a few dwellings I had seen en route, each with a clearing, some cows, chickens, and children. "Yes, some 15 000 people have moved into the area." "What? How is that possible? In a national park and conservation area?" "The people just come, cut down a hectare or two and live along the waterways." The mayor of this tiny community went on, "In fact, if the economy went bad, we'd have a hundred thousand people in here overnight. A Parque Nacional is public land. It belongs to the public. If someone has no job and can't feed his kids, he heads for a Parque

Nacional. These are the only places full of resources left – game to eat, wood to cut, flowers to sell, land to build on." Just then the Minister's earlier comment about protected areas and the economy burst into my mind, as the mayor chatted amiably amid the little buildings on stilts in a giant mangrove swamp while the endless rain poured on.

A day later we joined some civil engineers to visit Lake Arenal, the nation's largest lake and a major source of hydropower. Walking into rainforest at the southern end we learned the general layout of this working lake. I had noticed a few clearings with cows on the western slope, and inquired about them. "The state owns a protective zone 20 meters wide around the lake, so people occasionally move in on the slopes above to live for a while." "Twenty meters? Does that do much to protect the lake? Who owns the rest of the slopes?" "That's all private land." "So, could the whole landscape be transformed from rainforest to pastureland?" "Above 20 meters it could." By coincidence, just then someone discovered a three-toed sloth lazily watching us, and shortly afterward, a bizarre red fungus nearby. I continued, "Do you suppose there's any relation between biodiversity protection and the long-term energy supply for the nation?" No answer seemed forthcoming. "If for example, the rainforest of the lake's drainage basin were protected, would that also prevent the lake from filling up with sediment?"

Apparently it was time to move on to the north end of the lake, where the hydropower action is. We passed two active logging roads with channels of liquid mud heading for the lake. Some corporate logging group was mentioned. We briefly stopped by a cove, perhaps three football fields long. Two years earlier it was water, but today sediment filled the cove and a film of wet pasture plants covered the top. Finally, the north end appeared, a beehive of engineering activity. Two dredges were hard at work and earth-moving equipment transported sediment and lifted dust on shore. Twenty-four-hour dredging was required to keep the electric turbines moving efficiently to meet the nation's needs.

While watching the active movement of earth, as well as three deer feeding by a wooded patch, I pondered what I would say to the Minister. Should I say that actions in the surroundings are often more important than management within a protected area? Or, if all protected areas are multiple use, wouldn't landscape ecology emphasize spatially prioritizing uses, and then managing compatible interactions among them? The Tortuguero experience suggested that providing for nature but not people doesn't work, but Arenal suggested that the opposite doesn't work either. Therefore, is the key goal to spatially mesh nature and people for the long term?

Fifteen years ago I published a paper (Forman, 1986) precisely on the topic of this book in your hand. I couldn't find a previous paper on the subject, so the article was based on a dozen years of managing a small ecological research facility, the Hutcheson Memorial Forest Center in New Jersey, plus much thinking about landscape ecology. The dozen emerging directions in landscape ecology described in that paper are familiar today (Forman, 1995).

For the applications to natural resource management portion of the article, I focused on three questions. First, "How does one identify the sites requiring top priority protection in any landscape?" To solve this "apples and oranges" problem of comparing different types of places, each site is classified based on relative uniqueness or rarity (at three spatial scales: local, state, or national/global), and on recovery or replacement time (years, decades, or centuries). Later, this surprisingly simple and objective prioritization method was successfully used for town open-space planning (Ferguson et al., 1993; Forman, 1995).

Second, "What are the major ecological considerations in managing a natural landscape, and how do these differ in managing a remnant of a natural landscape?" Managing a whole landscape depends on: "(a) Keeping human activity inversely proportional to the sensitivity of landscape elements, (b) protecting the areas of major flows in the landscape, and (c) maintaining natural disturbance regimes. Managing a remnant of a natural landscape focuses on the same three objectives, plus two additional objectives: (d) minimizing isolation, and (e) minimizing human impacts from the surrounding matrix."

Third, "How does one evaluate a proposed alteration or change in a landscape?" Three sequential steps are valuable. "The existing site is evaluated for relative uniqueness and recovery time. The proposed alteration is evaluated for its site–matrix interactions, that is, how the site affects the surrounding landscape elements, and vice versa. Then [an] input–output model is constructed to evaluate the appropriate level of human activity, by considering direct economic gain, costs to the surroundings, and whether the site will aggrade, degrade, or remain in steady state." The article ends, "I think landscape ecology offers special promise because of the short lag period between principles and application.... Indeed it may not be unrealistic to think that we have reached a threshold in the way we view the land, and consequently that we will leave a considerably richer heritage for future generations."

The pages of this book are not only a test of those early ideas, but also clearly demonstrate how far this subject has come in a short period. Editors Jianguo Liu and William W. Taylor and 59 perceptive authors have produced an immensely valuable handbook, rife with principles and ideas. Natural resource management now has a clearer, more solid conceptual foundation, and consequently promises more solutions and successes.

But what exactly do we manage? Land is a convenient surrogate, since it combines space with any number of specific natural resources (Ludwig *et al.*,

1997). Three types of land receive emphasis in management. First, large green blobs, including many national/provincial/state parks and forests, biosphere reserves, state fish-and-game areas, wilderness areas, and large privately owned natural areas, are essentially managed as whole landscapes. Second, the loose network or group of smallish properties managed by, e.g., counties, cities, towns and non-profit organizations, represent a different management challenge. These may have a single overriding objective such as recreation or nature protection. However, often somewhat conflicting goals exist, such as providing ball fields, quiet hospital grounds, schools, nature reserves, and cycling routes, so management normally zones compatible uses on different properties. Groups of smallish properties also have a high edge-to-interior ratio, which requires additional management of edges and site–matrix interactions. Third, farmland is the other large category of managed land. Farms, however, are commonly individually owned or managed, so the agricultural landscape represents a mosaic patchwork of individual management regimes. Short-term education programs, regulations, and incentives may produce visible effects, but most management is done, day after day, by long-term farmers on the land. Land management may also be targeted for specialized uses, such as water supply, a lake or a greenway system. For all three major land-management types, the large green blob, the loose network of small patches, and the farmland patchwork, landscape ecology principles are highly useful, although solutions differ markedly.

But how would you actually put the principles to work on the ground? Suppose you became head manager of a large green blob such as a national forest, indeed one for which little useful information was available. Probably a quick survey would provide a useful background, since you could not wait for a protracted survey of all the plant and animal species, natural communities, erodible soils, wildlife movement routes, groundwater flows, surface-water characteristics, human impacts and so on. You could then begin planning with the "indispensables," the spatial patterns spawned by landscape ecology for which no known or technologically feasible alternative exists to provide the known ecological benefits (Forman, 1995; Forman and Collinge, 1995). A few large patches of natural vegetation in the landscape. Green corridors along major streams. Connectivity between the large patches. Bits of nature scattered across a less hospitable matrix. Probably more indispensables will emerge as landscape ecology continues its rapid growth.

You could certainly differentiate the outer from the inner portion of the forest, so that human activities were concentrated in the outer portion and natural resource protection concentrated in the central portion (Forman, 1989). The large natural-vegetation patches, and connectivity among them, would be concentrated in the central portion. Scattered small rare features would receive priority protection. Similarly, flux centers, where movement of animals, soil, native people, and so forth is concentrated, would also receive special management emphasis. Actual or potential linkages with other large green blobs in four directions would be identified and enhanced. Many of the longer-cutting-rotation stands would be in the inner area, and most short-rotation stands in the outer zone. Finally, places in the outer zone would be made so interesting and valuable for nature recreation – roads, loop trails, viewing platforms, wildlife plantings, aquatic exploration stations, fishing spots – that almost everyone entering your forest would stay in the outer portion and feel energized upon leaving. As head manager you chose to use landscape ecology for management solutions, but the land "decided" the locations of most of the planning and management activity.

This book also highlights an array of key knowledge gaps and research frontiers. Let me strengthen this array by pinpointing four lacunae in applying landscape ecology to natural resource management.

The pattern of natural communities in the zone immediately around a large green blob is a key landscape ecology frontier for management. For example, the bits of nature – hedgerows, ditches, woodlots, roadsides – within hundreds of meters of a large forested patch in The Netherlands affect numerous ecological attributes of the forest (Forman, 1995). Furthermore, the ability of birds both to colonize and to persist in a large patch was enhanced by the presence of many neighboring bits of nature (Harms and Opdam, 1990). I suspect that providing bits of nature near large natural-vegetation patches will become another of the indispensable patterns mentioned above. Indeed, a "neighborhood ecology" is needed (Forman, 1995). Context is often more important than content.

Second, ecological flows and movements across the landscape present another great challenge to planning and management (Harris *et al.*, 1996; Ludwig *et al.*, 1997; Forman, 1999). Thus, groundwater and stream water move horizontally across the land, and carry chemicals in solution. Sediment is transported by wind and water. Fire sweeps the land. Animals forage in their home range, disperse to a new one, and migrate seasonally. Seeds are carried by animals and wind. Providing for, rather than interrupting, these movements would be a sign of good design and management. Indeed, management budgets are lower where we do not attempt to block, or have to repair damage caused by, ecological flows across the landscape.

Third, road ecology is emerging as a key frontier for the future of natural resource management (Forman and Alexander, 1998). Often the most conspicuous feature in the landscape, roads are normally the least known ecologically. Whether criss-crossing a large green patch, a farmland patchwork, or a local loose network of protected areas, roads with vehicles affect most types of natural resources. Such ecological effects commonly extend in a band hundreds of meters wide. For example, managing a nature reserve for birds means keeping busy traffic far away. Or, managing a stream as a natural aquatic ecosystem with native fish populations means keeping road salt and bridge sediments and chemicals to a minimum. Roads tie the land together for society, but also slice nature into fragments.

Fourth, the Costa Rican management issues introduced at the outset highlighted the tight linkage between the human community of economics, social patterns, and culture, and the natural resources to be managed. By mainly focusing on the patterns and processes within an agricultural or a forested landscape, for example, landscape ecology has produced a highly useful body of theory. The natural patterns and processes are repeated in similar form throughout a landscape (Forman, 1995). Yet human systems, and even macroclimate, tend to form larger regions. Regions tend to exhibit coherence in transportation systems, town form, architecture, language, and so forth, and are often tied to a single large city. Even though a region contains highly dissimilar landscapes and natural conditions, the cultural, economic, and political commonality embodied in the word "regionalism" is quite useful for planning and management.

We should seriously explore the science of regional ecology (Forman, 1995). What are the ecological interactions between landscapes? How do patterns within a landscape vary near different adjoining landscapes? Do certain clusters of neighboring landscapes exist that may be more sustainable? Are landscape boundaries major movement routes for certain species across a region? How does location of a major city affect the ecology of a region? Do spreading suburban landscapes produce distinctive ecological effects because they are little constrained by topography? How does regional change affect the rates of landscape change, and vice versa? Meshing regional ecology with the human activities of a region could be even more significant than designing a sustainable landscape.

Finally, let us step back and visualize more broadly this linkage of landscape ecology and natural resource management. Suppose you were exploring the rooms of a limestone cavern, with an infinite variety of magnificent forms and slowly dripping water around you. The rock beneath you represents, and indeed is labeled, "landscape ecology." Looking upward, you see that the rock above each room represents a field linked to landscape ecology. For example, the top of the first room indicates forestry, and as you explore other rooms, you see biological conservation, suburban/regional planning, landscape architecture, agriculture, and even transportation. You enter the natural resource management room and look more closely. Stalagmites from below connect with stalactites from above, some intricate and thin, some massive, all impressive.

Principles from the landscape ecology foundation below flow into and strengthen the field above, and vice versa. Many short unconnected 'mites and 'tites represent emerging research frontiers. These underground symbols remain vivid in your mind as you leave the cave. Landscape ecology is emerging as a foundation, with principles spreading widely into diverse fields, all dealing with the land. Furthermore, its numerous expanding research frontiers promise much more for the future. Indeed, natural resource management may benefit the most.

The book before you is a treasure chest. Readers will be enriched. Natural resource management will be strengthened. And landscapes around us, where people care or manage, will be the primary and visible beneficiaries.

References

Ferguson, J. D., Connelly, M., Forman, R., Kellett, M., Mackenzie, C., Monahan, D., Schnitzer, S., Sprott J. and Stokey, B. 1993. *Town of Concord 1992 Open Space Plan*. Concord Natural Resources Commission, Concord, MA.

Forman, R. T. T. (1986). Emerging directions in landscape ecology and applications in natural resource management. In *Proceedings of the Conference on Science in the National Parks: The Plenary Sessions*, eds. R. Herrmann & T. Bostedt-Craig, US National Park Service and The George Wright Society, Fort Collins, CO. pp. 59–88.

Forman, R. T. T. (1989). Landscape ecology plans for managing forests. In *Proceedings of the Society of American Foresters 1988 National Convention*, pp. 131–136. Society of American Foresters, Bethesda, MD. [Reprinted 1990 in *Is Forest Fragmentation a Management Issue in the Northeast?*, pp. 27–32. General Technical Report NE-140, compilers, R. M. DeGraaf & W. M. Healey, US Department of Agriculture Forest Service, Radnor, PA.

Forman, R. T. T. (1995). *Land Mosaics: The Ecology of Landscapes and Regions*. Cambridge University Press, Cambridge, UK.

Forman, R. T. T. (1999). Horizontal processes, roads, suburbs, societal objectives, and landscape ecology. In *Landscape Ecological Analysis: Issues and Applications*. eds. J. M. Klopatek, & R. H. Gardner, pp. 35–53. Springer-Verlag, New York.

Forman, R. T. T. & Alexander, L. E. 1998. Roads and their major ecological effects. *Annual Review of Ecology and Systematics*, 29: 207–231.

Forman, R. T. T. & Collinge, S. K. (1995). The "spatial solution" to conserving biodiversity in landscapes and regions. In *Conservation of Faunal Diversity in Forested Landscapes*. eds. R. M. DeGraaf & R. I. Miller, pp. 537–568. Chapman & Hall, London.

Harms, B. & P. Opdam. (1990). Woods as habitat patches for birds: Application in landscape planning in The Netherlands. In *Changing Landscapes: An Ecological Perspective*, eds. I. S. Zonneveld & R. T. T. Forman, pp. 73–97. Springer-Verlag, New York.

Harris, L. D., Hoctor, T. S. & Gergel, S. E. 1996. Landscape processes and their significance to biodiversity conservation. In *Population Dynamics in Ecological Space and Time*, eds. O. Rhodes, Jr., R. Chesser & M. Smith, pp. 319–347. University of Chicago Press, Chicago, IL.

Ludwig, J., Tongway, D., Freudenberger, D., Noble J. & Hodgkinson, K. (eds). (1997). *Landscape Ecology: Function and Management*. CSIRO Australia, Collingwood, Victoria, Australia.

Index

Page numbers in bold refer to tables and illustrations